Three Great Sea Stories

SIMON

WALKER

Three
Great Sea Stories

Malta Convoy
Tinkerbelle
Unbroken

Collins
St James's Place
London

Three Great Sea Stories was first published 1968
Second Impression 1969
Third Impression 1971
© Wm. Collins Sons & Co. Ltd. 1968

Malta Convoy was first published 1961
© Peter Shankland & Anthony Hunter
A junior edition was first published 1965
© Peter Shankland & Anthony Hunter

Tinkerbelle was first published 1965
TINKERBELLE, Copyright © 1965, 1966 by Robert Manry

Unbroken was first published by Frederick Muller 1953
© Alistair Mars 1953
A junior edition was first published 1966
© Frederick Muller Ltd. 1966

ISBN 0 00 192327 7

*Printed in Great Britain
Collins Clear-Type Press
London and Glasgow*

THREE GREAT SEA STORIES

Contents

MALTA CONVOY
*Peter Shankland
and Anthony Hunter*

TINKERBELLE
Robert Manry

UNBROKEN
Alastair Mars

Malta Convoy

by
PETER SHANKLAND
and
ANTHONY HUNTER

TO THE MEMORY
OF ALL WHO WERE LOST
AT SEA
1939-1945

CONTENTS

CONTENTS

AUTHORS' PREFACE

THIS BOOK is meant to picture as vividly as possible the drama of a great naval action, to recreate as it happened what is now accepted as one of the most vital convoys of the war.

It is also essentially a reappraisal of the facts.

The jig-saw of grand strategy has been fitted together, leaders on both sides have opened their war diaries, and in the light of later knowledge much that was obscure in 1942 is now clear.

In telling this story we have had all viewpoints, official and unofficial, Allied and Axis, before us. A large number of men of all ranks who served in Operation Pedestal have described their experiences afresh. But when attempting to reproduce full and accurate detail of a naval action, it is inevitable that conflict of evidence should occur. In a few places we have had to use our own judgment. For instance, in the later stages of Operation Pedestal the men were so tired that their recollections of the fast changing scene of battle were often blurred or inaccurate when they came to write their official reports. In all such cases we have plotted the situation in detail, arriving at a final conclusion only from the evidence before us.

The story centres round the fortunes of the tanker *Ohio*. We chose her as our main theme because she was the last to arrive at her destination, and because, being the only tanker, she was probably the most important ship in the convoy. Her fight to Malta has an epic quality and epitomises the best war-time tradition of British seamanship. Some of the volunteers, naval officers and ratings and merchant seamen, who manned her guns and handled her towlines on the last stage of her long voyage, were American. It can now be seen that the survival of Malta, perhaps that of the free world itself, depended on the endurance of her small British crew, these volunteers who came to her assistance, and on the stoutness of this American ship's construction.

Our thanks are due to the British Admiralty, without whose close co-operation and unfailing aid this book would have been impossible. All official documents relating to the action were placed at our disposal, and the courtesy, skill and assistance received from experts in the Historical Records, Foreign Documents, Film and Photographic and other departments helped immeasurably with the many difficult research problems.

Our thanks are also due to the many survivors of the action who helped us with personal accounts, in particular to Captain Dudley Mason, G.C., of *Ohio* and his Chief Engineer Jimmy Wyld, D.S.O., Admiral Sir Harold Burrough, G.C.B., K.B.E., D.S.O., commander of the convoy close escort, who also allowed us to include two of his personal photographs, and to Sir Edward St. John Jackson, K.C.M.G., K.B.E., the deputy Governor of Malta in 1942, and many other officials and heads of departments in many services.

Much invaluable aid was also received from: Central Office of Information, *Daily Mail*, Eagle Oil Company, *Evening News*, Imperial War Museum, Ministry of Transport, Movietone News, the Royal Air Force, Sun Shipbuilding Company of U.S.A., *Sunday Dispatch*, Texas Oil Company of U.S.A., U.S. Department of Commerce, and the War Office. Grateful acknowledgment is made to Captain S. W. Roskill, R.N. and Messrs. Collins, who permitted us to reproduce the map of Operation Pedestal from *The Navy at War* 1939-45.

PETER SHANKLAND
ANTHONY HUNTER

FOREWORD

by

Admiral of the Fleet

SIR PHILIP VIAN

G.C.B., K.B.E., D.S.O.

THIS IS the story of the bravest and most fateful of all the convoys that were ever sailed to relieve Malta in the late war.

The operation was called Pedestal, and it was mounted in August 1942, at a time when the Governor of the Island was faced with capitulation in a matter of days.

Survival from a disaster whose magnitude was not easily calculable depended on the delivery in quantity of two commodities: food and fuel. Provisioning of the fortress could achieve no useful military purpose unless aircraft and warships based on the Island received the fuel necessary to enable them to continue their operations against the enemy supply line to Africa.

Pedestal began in the knowledge that the Axis powers were fully informed of the plan, and that they had made dispositions for every possible form of attack with which to destroy the convoy in its protracted passage.

The naval forces based at Alexandria usually referred to Gibraltar as the "Ladies End" of the Mediterranean, a reflection on the security from bombing of the harbour itself, and the freedom from attack by heavy surface ships almost always enjoyed by the Gibraltar-Malta convoys. The detailed description in this book of the passage of Pedestal has caused me to regard the soubriquet as wrong, for it is hard to conceive conditions demanding greater fortitude, endurance and

13

sacrifice than was undergone by the officers and men of this convoy and its escort as, in ever-diminishing numbers, way was made eastward to Malta.

As the operation drew towards its spell-binding end, the preservation of Malta from the dreaded capitulation rested on two factors. The first was intervention by Italian surface forces in the waters south of Sicily, whose attack the decimated escort could have had no chance of defeating. The second concerned a ship, the American-built tanker *Ohio*, famous, fabulous, never to be forgotten, and the centre-piece of the book. Broken-backed, near awash, without propulsion or the power of steam, could she be got into the Grand Harbour to discharge her miraculously preserved cargo of oil into the Island's empty tanks?

Success depended as much on the construction of the ship as on the continued endurance and valour of Captain Mason and his crew, and on the ability of the young officers commanding a handful of tiny warships to achieve, in face of enemy air opposition, a feat of towing which was for them unimaginable by any reasonable standard.

The reader is in fact presented with a story of greatness; great in the impact of the operation on history, great as a description of conflict at sea, and greatest as a study of sacrifice and endurance, with absolute refusal to accept defeat. By its very nature drama succeeds drama as the narrative unfolds. It would have been easy for the authors to indulge in melodrama; but this they have rightly avoided.

The fighting, point and counterpoint, which accompanied the greater part of the voyage is vividly and objectively described; while in recapturing the atmosphere both in the ships, as casualty followed casualty, and in Malta itself, which only the arrival of ships could preserve, the temptation has been resisted to introduce the writers' own emotions and opinions, for which they would have had ample justification;

for Shankland was a Lieutenant R.N.V.R. in H.M.S. *Speedy*, which played a conspicuous part in the final stages of *Ohio's* voyage, while Hunter was a Spitfire pilot. With this background, and by having been at pains to interview many of the survivors of the operation, they have produced a narrative which breathes, and is authentic.

As one reads, heroes emerge. In addition to Captain Mason of the *Ohio*, and many other merchant seamen, my heart, as a naval officer, goes out to Rear-Admiral Burrough, presented with a succession of crises, yet never wavering; and to Commander Hill of H.M.S. *Ledbury*, whose intrepidity and resource seemed to have no limit.

The authors refer to Nelson's blockade of Malta in the years 1798-1800, when Valletta—which had been seized by Bonaparte on his way to Egypt—was held for the French by the brave Vaubois. The garrison then faced a hostile population, and a British fleet which, after the victory of the Nile, was predominant in the Mediterranean.

The French found Malta costly, just as we did in World War II. They lost the only two ships of the line which managed to elude Nelson at Aboukir Bay, both when trying to run the gauntlet from Malta to the safety of their home shores. And Vaubois had to surrender, in the end, because he could not get sea-borne supplies. Even one merchant ship, fully laden, would have made all the difference at the most critical time. It is true indeed that, if history never quite repeats itself, it affords endless and fascinating parallels.

" If ever students should seek an example of the costliness in war of 'failure by a maritime power to defend its overseas bases in peace," writes Captain Roskill in *The War at Sea*, " the story of Malta's ordeal in 1942 will provide the classic case." That ordeal was matched in the ships endeavouring to supply the Island.

PROLOGUE

THE launching of a ship, be she twelve-foot dinghy, ocean-going liner or great battleship, is a solemn occasion.

At this moment the future looms nearer, unseen but not unfelt ; and pride of workmanship becomes humbled before the immensity of the challenge to mighty elements and a fate beyond man's control.

Man-the-Builder has toiled for days, months or even years to shape this new and shining tool. Now it is to be committed to the sea, to a hidden destiny ; and Man-the-Seafarer must put forth in her to test the mystery of oceans and to give her the life for which she has been cunningly made.

No one can tell if that life will be short or long, a maiden voyage wreck or years of tramping the seas to an honourable discharge in the shipbreaker's yard. Men may die for her or because of her, others may become rich or ruined through her and great issues may hang upon the seamanship of her crew or the strength of her keel.

Such a moment of veiled truth fell on the dusty shipyards at Chester, Pennsylvania, on the morning of the 20th April, 1940. A ship was about to be born and already some of the chocks had been knocked away. Her rudder was secured for the launch and a web of preventer cables had been reeved to restrain her complete escape from the land.

A wooden platform, decked in red and white canvas for the ceremony, stood like a match-box beneath the towering bows.

Nearby, groups of workmen stood gazing up at her, dressed in their best Sunday clothes for the occasion. Among them were shipwrights, riveters, carpenters, welders, steel-cutters and the host of other craftsmen whose hands and tools had helped to shape the broad hull and the intricate vitals of what was about to become one of the most modern oil tankers in the world.

An air of expectancy and the satisfaction of work well done damped down the conversation, reducing it to disjointed small talk. Unconsciously, the future possessed these men, as it was shortly to possess their handiwork. For the last time they contemplated the embodiment of a mystery—the fine artefact, assembled from disordered masses of common raw material, which had somehow become unified and beautiful in the process.

To the knowledgeable, Hull 190 was doubly beautiful. Looking at those bows where the neat white numbers of the lading gauge measured off the underwater hull, she was a skilful compromise, promising broad cargo-carrying capacity to the profit-minded merchant and the shapeliness of speed, the balance of stability, to the mariner. Above the waterline, she was both romantically and historically interesting : for the cutwater soared in the graceful outward curve of a schooner bow, which bore the now almost forgotten influence of the old

American clipper ship, carrying with it the legend of wool and grain races and the fury of Cape Horn seas.

Towering above the little men below, it seemed that she had overgrown them and was on the point of bursting out of the steel slipway gantries which confined her like a womb.

Below in the shipyard, uneasiness had replaced this mixture of satisfaction and futurity. The advertised time for the launching had come and gone, but the ceremonial platform remained empty.

Eyes began to turn towards the water and heads were shaken; for the usually placid current of the River Delaware was whipped by a rising north-easterly gale, and lumpy waves beat heavily on the tail of No. 2 Slipway.

In the main offices of the Sun Shipbuilding Company, a neat white building almost lost among the ribs of partly-built ships and the organised confusion of the shipyard, a hurried conference was in progress.

On the table lay the familiar emblems of a launch: the bouquet and the bottle of champagne; and while the men present talked of technicalities, the prospective sponsor of Hull 190, Mrs. Florence E. Rodgers, from Columbus, Ohio, stared out of the window at the wind-blown clouds.

The President of the Texas Oil Company crossed the room: " It's no good, Mother. We'll have to postpone the launch. It's too much of a risk in this wind," he said regretfully.

Mrs. Rodgers was disappointed. " What a shame. Isn't it supposed to be unlucky . . .? "

There was a second's hesitation, the realisation of
unspoken, subliminal thought, and then the ship-men
were quick to assure her and themselves. That was just
superstition . . . old-fashioned . . . after all no one
could control the weather.

Outside it seemed evident that the waters were
unwilling to receive the new ship. A full gale whistled
through the gantries and howled about the crane jibs.
The River Delaware was flecked with white, breaking
waves.

Down by Slipway No. 2, the yard manager broke the
news to the waiting men, and some of them were in
no doubt about the significance of this omen.

" No good will come of it," said one shipwright,
shaking his pipe in the air. " Better a busted stern than
a late launch. It's unlucky." Many of the men nodded
their heads.

It is doubtful whether anyone present connected this
unlucky omen with the faint rumblings from across the
Atlantic, where the " phoney war " in Europe was about
to blaze up in the German invasion of France.

No one could have guessed then that the fate of this
fine ship, built for the tanker fleet of " Texaco, "
America's largest oil company, was bound up in that
struggle, as America's own fate would be before two
years were past.

To the average American the war seemed very far
off then and would remain one of those things which
only happen elsewhere for some time to come ; but
wiser and more forward-looking men had already
measured the menace of Germany's ambitions and the

rising threat of military preparations in Japan. Indeed, their forebodings had affected the building plan of Hull 190.

Laid down on 7th September, 1939, four days after Germany had gone to war with Britain and France, the ship had been completed in the unusually short period of seven months, fifteen days.

Similarly, the approach of war had influenced her design, for unofficial conversations between military and oil chiefs had resulted in a ship of 9,263 tons, 515 feet in overall length, and capable of carrying 170,000 barrels of oil, bigger and more capacious than any tanker built before.

The Westinghouse turbine engines, which were shortly to be lowered into her, developed 9,000 shaft horse power at ninety revolutions a minute which was calculated to drive the ship along at sixteen knots, a speed never attained before by a single screw tanker.

In this, America was guarding against the possibility of war in the Pacific, where large, swift oil tankers might one day have to carry, over vast distances, the life-blood of her fleets and armies.

Her method of construction was controversial. For some years the pros and cons of riveting versus welding ships had raged on both sides of the Atlantic. Hull 190, with a bottom shell and deck of the new-fashioned welded construction, was fated to settle once and for all the reliability of this method.

A composite framing system with two longitudinally continuous bulkheads, divided the ship into twenty-one cargo tanks, and this was designed to make her literally a honeycomb of strength.

These things, and many other uncommon fitments, were dictated by a growing fear of war, and this ship, which fate seemed unwilling to receive into her natural element was, in aggregate, much more than a mere tanker made to plough the peaceful waters of the Gulf of Mexico.

The day following that scheduled for her launch was no less depressing. Unfriendly skies darkened the shipyard. A grey, continuous rain was falling, but this had damped down the wind and the waters of the Delaware, though sullen and uninviting, were calm.

The launch proceeded. Swathed in raincoats, a small party huddled together under umbrellas on the platform. Mrs. Rodgers grasped the bottle of champagne in her right hand and pronounced the words :

" I name this good ship *Ohio*. May God go with her and all who sail in her. Good luck . . ."

The bottle smashed against the bow, the launching button was pressed. For a moment there was no movement, then no more than a slight shudder. *Ohio* seemed reluctant to start upon her momentous journey.

At last she began to move slowly away from them, gathering speed on the greased slips, until she plunged with a roar of parting waters into the river.

A passing tug whistled forlornly, the shipyard siren shrilled and a thin cheer went up from the men who built her.

As she rode high and unballasted on the waters, who could have foretold the trial by fire, bomb and torpedo which was to test every plate of her in the far waters of the Mediterranean? Who could have foreseen the saga which she was to enact?

For the name *Ohio* was to be written in the roll of the world's great ships. The course of the war and the way of life in the Western world were to hang upon her strength and the courage of the men who were to sail in her.

CHAPTER ONE

LINCHPIN OF THE HINGE

*I now declare that I consider Malta as a most important
outwork of India, that will ever give us great influence in
the Levant, and indeed all the southern parts of Italy. In
this view, I hope we shall never give it up.* LORD NELSON

*The interrelation between Malta and the Desert operations
was never so plain as in 1942, and the heroic defence of the
Island in that year formed the keystone of the prolonged
struggle for the maintenance of our position in Egypt and
the Middle East.* WINSTON CHURCHILL

*Malta . . . has the lives of many thousands of German and
Italian soldiers on its conscience.* ROMMEL

I

BY AUGUST, 1942, disaster had beset Britain in all
theatres of war. Everywhere the tide had set against
her and it seemed that she was losing the struggle for
freedom.

Not that any Briton would have admitted it, far less
spoken of it, then. Life went on with a grumble or a
laugh much as it had always done, though the pinch of
hardship had already created great changes at home.

Food was short and the women queued daily, tendering

24

ration cards for a little meat, a little tea and a little sugar.

Men and women had become accustomed to living with imminent danger, and the unrelieved darkness of the black-out, the ruined gaps in many neat rows of houses, were a constant reminder of the nearness of war.

These tribulations were accepted with a certain phlegmatic adaptability which at times of crisis belies the traditional conservatism of the British. Yet at no time since the days of Dunkirk and the Battle of Britain had the situation been blacker. The Allied armed forces had taken a beating in the familiar fields of France, in the Arctic cold of Norway, in the torrid heat of the Far East and finally on the temperate shores of the blue Mediterranean.

Everywhere the coils of the Axis seemed to be strangling the life out of every effort. An unceasing expenditure of blood, will and material had shown nothing but reverses and increase of difficulties ; and even to the most optimistic it was plain that there could be no quick decision other than defeat with an alternative of long years of toil, turmoil and bereavement.

The British had been told that the air battle for Britain had been won, yet air-raid sirens still tried the nerves of the hardiest and sent the prudent to cold nights in the shelters. Searchlights probed the skies, guns crashed and night-fighters took off from their aerodromes ; but still the raiders droned on, night after night, and dropped their bombs, for no means had so far been found to stop them.

From the outbreak of war the British had looked

hopefully towards the Americans, feeling that these kinsmen of theirs would not finally desert them, and counting on their entry into the war to turn the tide of battle. Yet after the Americans had joined the Allies on 7th December, 1941, there was no interruption in the train of disaster.

Winston Churchill, the Prime Minister, confided something of the bitter disappointment felt in a dispatch to his friend the American President, Franklin D. Roosevelt, in March 1942. " When I reflect," he wrote, " how I have longed and prayed for the entry of the United States into the war, I find it difficult to realise how gravely our British affairs have deteriorated by what has happened since December 7th."

By August 1942, the British had suffered from the Japanese as badly as the Americans who, with many of their ships lying at the bottom of Pearl Harbour, could do little, it seemed, to counter the new menace.

To many it had been a severe psychological shock to discover that the little yellow man of the cartoons, with protruding teeth and a sword too big for him, had suddenly grown to the stature of a giant. He was no longer a character from a Gilbertian opera, but a determined and fanatical enemy, who had quickly proved that his weapons were newer and sharper than the quaint swords of his Samurai ancestors.

His armies had swept through the Malay Peninsula, brushing aside the British defence. His air force had sunk, within minutes, two battleships, *Repulse* and *Prince of Wales*, sent to protect Singapore, and as he closed in on that " Impregnable Fortress," the key to

British Far-Eastern possessions, the depressingly familiar tale of lack of A.A. defence, obsolete fighters, muddle and underestimation of the enemy soon began to filter back to Britain.

Armoured landing craft, marked with the Rising Sun, crossed the Singapore strait and, thirty hours later, 70,000 dazed and beaten men surrendered and passed into brutal captivity.

After the capture of Singapore, the Japanese pressed on with the speed of a forest fire. Java and Sumatra were occupied, and a heavy air-raid emphasised the threat to Australia. From invasion bases at Bangkok and Mergui in Thailand, they crossed the River Salween, intended as a major line of British defence, stormed into Rangoon, cut the lines of communication between the British Army and its Chinese allies in the Shan Hills and by the end of May 1942 stood at the gates of India.

Keeping pace with their armies, the Japanese fleet broke into the Indian Ocean, sank the carrier *Hermes*, two British cruisers and 112,312 tons of Allied shipping. Before the threat of the Japanese carriers the British Eastern Fleet, despite heavy reinforcement, was compelled to withdraw to East Africa, leaving the Japanese in undisputed control of the Indian Ocean. The invasion of Ceylon, as a prelude to the attack on India, seemed to be imminent.

The other great ally from whom so much had at first been expected had also failed to justify popular hopes. The Russian steam-roller had lumbered backwards and, with losses which boggled the imagination, the Red armies were fighting for their lives before Moscow and Stalingrad.

From the start of Hitler's invasion of their territory, the British War Cabinet had been at pains to help the Russians, but there was little they could do beyond sending the maximum amount of war material to make up for their appalling shortages of modern weapons and transport. Most of this material had to be convoyed through the Arctic Sea to Northern Russia. In these waters to fight nature was sufficiently arduous. In recurrent storms huge waves hammered the ships and left decks and upperworks dangerously top-heavy with deep coatings of ice. Gun mechanisms froze and frost-bite depleted the crews. Pack-ice forced the convoys towards the coast of Norway, a route commanded by Axis aircraft and fleet units stationed in the fjords. The British, attacked almost unceasingly, sustained frighten-ing losses both in ships and men, for no one could live long in the frozen sea.

In one convoy alone, P.Q.17, which sailed for Mur-mansk in July, twenty-three out of thirty-six ships were lost.

Coming at a time when the Battle of the Atlantic had reached its height, when Britain's lifeline of supplies from America was in serious danger of becoming disrupted, and even severed completely, such losses were almost insupportable.

In the six months preceding that fateful August of 1942, German submarines had sunk 3,250,000 tons of British and Allied shipping alone, and the U-boat packs had already begun to appear on the American east coast where a further 100,000 tons a month were being sent to the bottom.

So it seemed that, in the world struggle to maintain the supply routes upon which Britain depended, the Allies were being beaten and as yet no remedy had been found.

Then, as if to underline the fear that British command of the sea was waning, the German battle cruisers *Scharnhorst* and *Gneisenau* and the heavy cruiser *Prinz Eugen* steamed through the English Channel from Brest to Kiel, untouched except for slight damage caused by mines. That an enemy fleet could make free with Britain's own Channel without loss, for the first time since before the Spanish Armada, seemed to outrage the best traditions of a seafaring people.

At first the Mediterranean had offered the brightest prospects of a success for British arms. General Wavell had bundled the Italians out of Cyrenaica, and in the desert alone it had been possible to point to a theatre of war in which a great host of prisoners and great quantities of booty had been taken, besides vast areas of enemy territory. The scene quickly changed. A German general called Rommel, unknown then, had already begun to organise counter-measures. The Germans were also preparing to take a hand in the war in Greece where the Italian legions had made little headway against the determined resistance of a numerically inferior Greek army.

It was only when German Panzer groups were already moving through Bulgaria to attack them that the Greeks consented to accept British help, and four divisions were moved from North Africa to Greece leaving inadequate forces to maintain the desert front. When Rommel attacked with the newly-formed Afrika Korps, the British were compelled to fall back. Brilliantly exploiting the situation, the German general outflanked the opposing army and turned its withdrawal into a disorderly retreat. Only the failure to take Tobruk halted his advance on the borders of Egypt.

Meanwhile, the Greek disaster had begun. Unable to stem the German drive into Greece, and bombed relentlessly by overwhelmingly superior German air forces, the British Army was withdrawn to Crete. Nor were the British given a breathing space there. Within a month, thousands of white parachutes mushroomed in the blue sky over the island as the German airborne assault began. The garrison, ill-provided and exhausted by the Grecian campaign, was overrun by the highly trained and well armed German force. Once more the British Army had to be evacuated and of 28,000 men engaged only half escaped to Egypt.

After the attempt by the British Eighth Army to relieve Tobruk by " Operation Battle-Axe " had fizzled out in a stalemate, General Auchinleck, who had replaced Wavell, began to build up for a decisive battle in the desert. Before he could take the offensive, however, Rommel seized the initiative. After a fortnight's fierce fighting, the German armoured divisions captured a commanding ridge at Knightsbridge and, as the British fell back, Rommel turned the full force of the attack against the isolated garrison of Tobruk. Within four days the fortress had fallen, its 25,000 defenders were made prisoner and vast quantities of material were captured. Before the British could reform, Rommel again attacked. Only shortage of German supplies and a hastily constructed British defence position at El Alamein halted his advance about sixty miles short of Alexandria.

The bewildering swiftness of the German victory, the capture of Tobruk and the new threat to the Suez Canal was a staggering blow, the position threatening to bring about the loss of the Middle East and the road to India.

The situation of the Mediterranean fleet was now unenviable. They were facing a more powerful and more modern fleet, which had many alternative bases from which to operate. German and Italian bombers could dominate most of the Western Mediterranean from airfields in Sicily and Sardinia; and, with practically the whole of the north-eastern shores of Africa, and with Crete and Greece in its hands, the Axis was astride the Eastern Mediterranean as well. As Rommel's threat to Alexandria made this important British naval base insecure, steps were taken immediately after the defeat in the desert to evacuate all capital ships, leaving only a cruiser squadron and a few destroyers and minesweepers.

The British fleet at Gibraltar was already seriously reduced in strength by the demands of the Far East and it was almost suicidally dangerous to send a fleet into the Western Mediterranean at all. Yet it was vitally necessary to keep this sea route open; for almost midway between Gibraltar and Alexandria, and surrounded on all sides by the enemy, stood Malta, the one unconquered British bastion in the inner Mediterranean.

In the midst of so many disastrous losses, the reduction of this island fortress might have seemed relatively unimportant, but naval strategists believed it to be the key to the Mediterranean strategy. Admiral Sir Andrew Cunningham, following the title of Churchill's book on this troubled period of the war, called it "The Linchpin of the Hinge of Fate," and so it was to prove. It can now be seen that the fate of the Middle East and India and the whole Allied cause depended on its successful defence.

At this crucial period of the war—in August 1942, when the British had reached the nadir of their hopes —the Island was almost lost. Bombed, starved and apparently without hope of further supply, its defenders were reaching the point of capitulation.

II

More than a hundred and fifty years ago, Nelson wrote : " I now declare that I consider Malta as a most important outwork of India, that it will ever give us great influence in the Levant, and indeed all the southern parts of Italy. In this view, I hope we shall never give it up."

This was perhaps the first realisation of the Island's importance in the modern conception of global war, but as long as man has sailed the blue waters of the Mediterranean, warring races have fought for its possession, because of its wonderful harbour and because of its commanding position at the cross-roads of a sea whose shores saw the dawn of Western civilisation.

32

Through recorded history each dominant Mediterranean people held it as an entrepot of trade in peace and a citadel in war from which the approaches to three continents could be commanded. In turn it was occupied by Phœnicians, Greeks and Carthaginians. In Roman times it became a stronghold of *mare nostrum* for maintaining the peace of the Empire and with the Roman decline it passed to the land-hungry Normans, next to the Moors and then to the Spanish. Charles the Fifth of Spain gave it to the Knights of St. John, and this austere and warlike order of chivalry defended Malta for Christendom for more than 200 years. Then Napoleon took it from them on his way to Egypt.

The people of Malta, however, resented French rule and rebelled so successfully that, with the help of Nelson, they won back their Island. At their own request, they became part of the British Empire.

Thus, Malta has been a British naval base since the early nineteenth century, but did not prove to be of decisive importance until the rise of the dictatorships in the late thirties. As the warlike intentions of Hitler and Mussolini became plain, grave fears began to be felt at the British Admiralty for the safety of the Island. The army and the air force were less preoccupied with holding Malta in event of a war against the Axis, for at that time no one had envisaged the fall of France and the consequent importance the Island was to assume as an air staging point on the route to the East, once French aerodromes were denied to Britain.

Moreover, many strategists considered that, with the rise of air-power, the Island, lying within sixty miles of the Sicilian airfields, would be untenable in the event of Italy's entry into the war.

Some authorities consider that its defence was the turning point of the whole war and the crux of Hitler's overall strategic defeat. F. M. Hinsley, in his book, *Hitler's Strategy* emphasises the importance of Malta to final British success in the desert and considers that it was by failing to capture it that Hitler lost the war strategically.

Rommel, writing retrospectively, (*The Rommel Papers* edited by B. H. Liddell Hart) believed: " With Malta in our hands, the British would have had little chance of exercising any further control over convoy traffic in the Central Mediterranean . . . it has the lives of many thousands of German and Italian soldiers on its conscience."

His chief of staff, General Fritz Bayerlein wrote in *Fatal Decisions*: ". . . until the air and naval base at Malta ceased to act as a constant thorn in the flesh of our rearward communications, there was no possibility of the situation at the front improving and therefore no prospect of capturing the Nile Delta."

Finally, Churchill in *The Second World War*: " The interrelation between Malta and the desert operations was never so plain as in 1942, and the heroic defence of the Island in that year formed the keystone of the prolonged struggle for the maintenance of our position in Egypt and the Middle East."

At the beginning of the war, however, with the possible exception of Churchill, only the British Naval command considered Malta to be vital to Middle Eastern strategy.

On the German side there was one man who also understood the significance of the Island and he too was a sailor. From the start, Grand Admiral Raeder had emphasised the importance of Malta at the Nazi war councils. Fortunately for the free world, this far-seeing man seldom had the ear of Hitler, who distrusted all his naval advisers.

When the admiral visited the Fuehrer's headquarters in Berlin on the 13th February, 1942, however, he found a gratified Hitler ready to listen to his plans, for the three German cruisers had just run the gauntlet of the English Channel successfully and the German Navy was for once in firm favour with the Nazi leader.

While Hitler revelled in the discomfort which this would be causing his enemies, Raeder considered the scheme he meant to lay before him, now that he was in such a rare receptive mood. It was a plan immense in its potentialities. It envisaged not only the conquest of the Middle East, but the overthrow of India and the junction between the Italo-German and Japanese forces.

Raeder sketched out the strategic background of his vision which was to be accomplished by a giant pincer movement. The German armies, when they had beaten Russia, were to swing to the right through the Caucasus and into the Middle East. Meanwhile, Rommel, after beating the British in Egypt, would take the Suez Canal and sweep up through Syria to join them. Then, united, the Germans with their Italian allies would drive through Persia into India. With the Japanese co-ordinating their attack from the East, India, already seething with political unrest, would be impossible to defend, and the Axis would build a wall of armour from Berlin to Tokyo.

Apart from tactical gains, the success of such a movement would entail the virtual collapse of the British Empire. It would also relieve once and for all the chronic shortage of oil which was then a serious threat to the Axis war machine, for both the Caucasian and Middle Eastern oil fields would be overrun and denied to the Allies. Also, in the early stages of this huge pincer movement each of the two thrusts would be of complementary value to the other, because if the German armies succeeded in breaking through in one theatre only, they would outflank the defenders in the other theatre and hasten defeat there too.

Raeder maintained, and Hitler this time agreed, that victory in the Mediterranean theatre and to some extent in the Russian theatre as well, depended on two factors : sea power and the co-operation between naval, land and air forces. The object of Mediterranean strategy would be to co-ordinate the whole movement, with sea power ensuring supplies, supplies ensuring bases and bases ensuring sea power. It would be necessary first of all to eliminate the constant threat of British naval and air forces striking from Malta against their supply route. The capture of Malta would be the first step towards the capture of Egypt, Persia and, ultimately, India. It would also constitute an important base for the operations.

Hitler was fired by this vision. On the practical side, he saw that it fitted into the operations then in train in

Russia and North Africa. He immediately ordered that all long-range strategic considerations were to be subordinated to the plan—the " Great Plan " as he himself christened it.

III

Two major strategic events had immediately preceded the conception of the " Great Plan."

In the first place, the drive deeper into Russia had been frozen into immobility by winter, thereby releasing a large part of the Luftwaffe for other duties. In the second, the strength of the Afrika Korps had been dangerously sapped by the sea and air offensive from Malta, to such an extent that if the German attack in the desert was to continue, a counter-offensive had to be mounted against the Island.

The German reactions were a sustained air attack on Malta and then, as a prelude to the implementation of the " Great Plan," combined Italo-German preparations for the capture of the Island called " Operation Hercules."

Half-hearted moves towards the latter end had already been made by the Italians. Indeed it is surprising that they had not made greater efforts, because the Italian High Command had decided, as a result of fleet manœuvres as early as 1938, that Malta could be taken without difficulty. When Italy entered the war, lack of military preparedness on the Island would have made such an operation easy, for the defences consisted only of 172 A.A. guns. There was a complete absence of fighter defence. Moreover, there were no reserves of food, and a determined blockade could have starved out the population within a matter of weeks.

Realising their nakedness, Admiral Ford, the senior naval officer on Malta, searched the stores and found the crated parts of four old Gladiator biplanes in a warehouse and immediately had them assembled. One was irreparably damaged in the first Italian air-raid of the war, but the remaining three wrote themselves a veritable saga in the skies over the beleaguered Island. Manned by volunteers from the staff of Air Commodore F. A. M. Maynard, the air officer commanding, and christened by the Maltese *Faith*, *Hope* and *Charity*, they took off day after day against the Italian air armadas. Though obsolete, they did considerable execution against a vastly superior enemy, forced the Italians to provide fighter escorts and served as an invaluable morale-booster to the defenders until the slow build-up of fighter defence on the Island could begin.

On direct orders from Churchill, Hurricanes earmarked for home defence were flown out to Malta in successive " penny packets " until local air superiority was attained, making it possible for submarines, cruisers and bomber squadrons to follow. The attack on the Axis trans-Mediterranean supply route to North Africa then began in earnest and the sharpened sword of Malta cut deep. Like the corsairs of old, British sailors and airmen swept out from the Island by day and by night making scattered flotsam of the heavily-laden troop ships, tankers and merchantmen. In June 1941 alone, seventy-three per cent of the German-controlled shipping from Italy was sunk and this figure had risen to seventy-seven per cent by November.

Hitler had long been warned that this unhappy situation would result from neglecting the significance of Malta, but the warning had fallen on deaf ears. At that time all his febrile energies were devoted to the projected attack on Russia to an extent that he even told Admiral Raeder that " the loss of North Africa could be withstood from a military point of view." The slowing down of the Russian campaign, however, coupled with appeals from Rommel and the Italian High Command, made him change his mind and in October 1941, he announced that he intended " to transfer the centre of military operations to the Mediterranean." He then gave orders for the movement of a complete air group, Luftflotte II, which had been responsible for air operations before Moscow, to Southern Italy. Generalfeldmarschall Kesselring was sent to take command of this and Luftflotte X which was already stationed in Sicily. These formations, together with the Italian Air Force, gave Kesselring, as Commander-in-Chief Air South, the control of 2,000 first-line aircraft. His mission was defined by Hitler as, among other things, to " gain control of the air and sea between South Italy and North Africa and thus ensure safe lines of communication with Libya and Cyrenaica : in this connection the neutralisation of Malta is especially important . . ."

The Axis air attack fell on Malta with crushing violence. Despite fierce resistance offered by the defenders, airfields were blasted, the harbour laid in ruins and the scale of the offensive against Axis shipping, and even the Island's ability to defend itself, fast diminished. By February 1942, Kesselring was able to report to Goering that Axis shipping losses had been reduced from between seventy and eighty per cent to less than thirty per cent. Supplies began to flow again into Libya enabling the Afrika Korps to build up for its final thrust towards the Suez Canal.

While the air attack proceeded, Hitler, convinced of the practicability of the " Great Plan," gave in to the united pleas of Axis commanders on the spot and agreed to mount " Operation Hercules " as a combined Italo-German attack on Malta. Final top-level arrangements were made at a meeting between the two dictators at Berchtesgaden on 29th April, 1942. The Italians, represented by Mussolini, Count Ciano and the Italian Commander-in-Chief, Marshal Cavallero, were greeted at Puhl station with great cordiality by Hitler, Ribbentrop and Jodl and housed in Klessheim Castle, which was resplendent with antique furniture, hangings and carpets looted from occupied France. At the conference, Hitler harangued his listeners with long and optimistic reviews of the war, one of which lasted an hour and forty minutes. Mussolini took surreptitious glances at his wrist-watch and Jodl fell asleep. Finally, on the second day, the two parties got down to business. The date for the assault was fixed for early June and, on the German side, Hitler agreed to send two paratroop battalions, an engineer battalion and an unspecified number of German naval barges. On the Italian side, Mussolini agreed to supply the parachute divisions of two regiments, a battalion of engineers and five batteries, besides sea transports and a heavy naval escort.

The Duce also reported that for five months 10,000 Italian commandos had been exercising on the coast of Livorno, which is similar in formation to the south-east coast of Malta, using specially constructed scaling ladders by means of which they hoped to mount the 120-feet-high cliffs from their landing craft.

Broadly, the campaign plan envisaged seizure of the south-eastern edge of Malta by airborne troops as a jumping-off base for an assault on the airfields south of the town and harbour of Valletta, after a bomber blitz had softened up the defences. The main attack by naval forces and landing parties was to be mounted against strong points south of Valletta in conjunction with another paratroop attack on the harbour itself and further bombing of the coastal batteries. A diversionary attack from the sea was also to be made against the bay of Marsa Scirocco.

With these broad details settled, the conference broke up with mutual expressions of regard, and the Italian party returned home.

Training now proceeded with great energy and there seemed every chance that the operation would be successful. The forces allocated were adequate and none of the German commanders, except perhaps Goering and Hitler himself, seem to have had any misgivings about a swift victory, despite their reluctance to trust the Italians in any major venture.

There then supervened one of those strange strategic counter-marches, sudden vacillations and moments of doubt which underlie so many momentous decisions of war.

On the Italian side a defeatist attitude was evident before the Berchtesgaden meeting. Count Ciano recorded in his diary that on the eve of the meeting, Cavallero realised that the capture of Malta was " a tough nut." In May, Ciano again wrote : " Colonel Cassero (one of the operational commanders) does not share Cavallero's enthusiasm for the attack on Malta . . . Even Fourier (Italian Secretary for Air) is anxious about a landing operation . . ." Again in June : " There is . . . some hesitation about the Malta undertaking . . ." and " I am more than ever of the opinion that the undertaking will never take place."

General Carboni, who commanded an assault division, was pessimistic from the start and anticipated " a general drowning." This son of an American mother appears to have intrigued in Italian court circles against the mounting of " Hercules," for he boasted openly later that it was a letter which he had had conveyed to the Prince of Piedmont, heir to the Italian throne, which finally prejudiced the High Command against the assault.

Despite this Italian uneasiness, a word from Hitler could have launched the parachute regiments, ships and assault craft against the beleaguered island, but he hesitated. It was essentially a seaborne operation, and throughout the war, he seemed unable to come to firm decisions when planning naval action. In a confiding moment, he once admitted to Raeder : " I am a hero on land and a coward at sea."

There is, however, no doubt that any reluctance on his part must have been reinforced by his advisers as well as by the increasing coolness of the Italians themselves towards the project. According to the Italians, Rommel was entirely to blame for the Fuehrer's change of heart and this view is also accepted by Churchill. Kesselring in his memoirs declares flatly : " Hitler and the German High Command must share with the Commando Supremo the blame for that wrong decision. They were admittedly less able to appreciate the situation correctly once Rommel had got his propaganda machine working properly . . . At that period Rommel exercised an almost hypnotic influence over Hitler, who was all but incapable of appreciating the situation objectively."

One undisputed fact is that there were insufficient troops and air forces to mount simultaneously both the attack on Malta and Rommel's drive towards the Suez Canal and the Middle East. Rommel's critics say that in the elation of capturing Tobruk he imagined he would have sufficient supplies to drive straight through to Alexandria without waiting for Malta to be liquidated, and advised Hitler accordingly. That he had frequently argued for the capture of Malta is, however, attested both by his staff and by many of his dispatches, but in a radio message to the German High Command on 22nd June, 1942, he requested that Mussolini be prevailed upon to remove Italian restrictions on the movement of his troops pending " Operation Hercules."

On the 24th, a note from Hitler was handed to Mussolini which began : " Fate, Duce, has presented us with an opportunity which will not occur a second time," and asked him to support the continuance of the thrust towards Alexandria, as both Rommel and the Italian commander believed that they could annihilate the British troops with the forces at their command. On the 24th, the Commando Supremo officially postponed the attack on Malta, and on the 30th Mussolini complied with the Fuehrer's request.

Whatever " hypnotic influence " Rommel may have exerted over his leader in this fateful choice it seems reasonable to assume that Hitler's own reluctance towards the venture may have played some part. He may also have been powerfully influenced by Kesselring's own glowing account of the results achieved by the bombing of Malta, for this indicated that the Island was no longer in a condition to interfere effectively in the designs of the Axis.

Indeed the bombing of Malta had had considerable effect and there is no doubt that this and the Axis air control over the sea routes had all but succeeded in their purpose.

In August 1942, the Island, though still fighting back, was within less than a month of starvation. The defenders were in a desperate plight and it seemed impossible for the British to fight a convoy through the Mediterranean to relieve them.

CHAPTER TWO

HOLD FAST AND WE WIN

IN AN underground office of the Residency, Sir Edward
Jackson, Deputy Governor of Malta, was drafting a
report on the situation.

The sounds of battle filtered down from above,
diminished by the solid rock from which the cellar was
hewn and the blast walls which protected it from the
ground level, but the scream of straining aero engines
and the regular crump of bombs could plainly be heard.

The Deputy Governor hardly stirred, however, even
when a near explosion shook the table at which he was
writing, and precipitated a dusty rain of tiny rock
particles on the white paper before him. Months of
such experiences had hardened him, as it had hardened
most of the civil and military population of Malta, to
the fury of enemy air attack.

". . . just received information from the Secretary of
State for the Colonies that it has been decided that it
is impracticable in present conditions to send a direct
convoy to Malta from the west . . ." he wrote. ". . . the
situation of the civil population is the same as that of
any other section of the fortress in that it can hold out
if sufficient supplies are received, and cannot if they are
not. If the civil population collapses, the whole fortress
collapses . . ."

This was Sir Edward's main preoccupation. On the Governor's Council he represented the interests of the civil population, and he had also the unenviable task of announcing to the civil population the progressive cuts in their rations, and of explaining their necessity.

He paused in his writing, and his mind wandered back into history. This was a commonplace of warfare, that the strength of a fortress depended on the health and morale of the civil population. Strong walls were powerless to protect if the will within was sapped by starvation. It was obvious, and yet how different to be experiencing the diminishing supplies of a beleaguered garrison rather than reading in a history book " the defenders were starving and the castle fell."

He took up his pen again : " I say that for the following reasons," he wrote.

" (a) It is impossible to secure essential services from or even to maintain order among 270,000 people if they are not fed.

" (b) It is impracticable to quell the civil population by the use of military force, firstly because one-third of the garrison consists of Maltese troops whose families would be subjected to that force and secondly because probably opinion in England would react violently to the application of military force for such reasons to a population of whom they have come to think as they now think of the Maltese. . . ."

Yes, it was difficult for people in Britain to realise the desperate predicament they were in on this little island.

" The question, therefore, arises, how long can the civil population hold out. . . ."

The situation about which Sir Edward was writing and had been writing for some months in the same strain had resulted from another measure of neglect in peace-time which could not be rectified once the demands of war had swallowed up available material.

Guns and fighters which could have ensured the Island's supply route had not been sent in peace-time and now in war they were desperately needed elsewhere.

On this rocky mass of limestone, slightly less than 116 square miles in extent, smaller than the Isle of Wight, and the most densely populated area in Europe, the result of this neglect was more serious than on any other British possession. From the outbreak of war with Italy, the civil population of more than a quarter of a million, augmented by 18,000 troops, had been short of food.

In the past, with far smaller populations, Malta had never been self-supporting, and the agricultural trends of the past hundred years had aggravated the situation. In 1918, for instance, the Island had grown about 20,000 acres of wheat. In 1942, after strenuous efforts to return to full productivity, only 12,000 acres were cropped.

The cause of this was mainly economic. The people had drifted away from cereal production between the wars to plant vineyards. Corn could then be bought cheaply from Italy and there was always a good sale for wine. So the Island's ability to support itself had further declined. Sicily, being the nearest land, had provided much of her imports, and on the outbreak of war these had been suddenly cut off.

Moreover, the Maltese are largely a *pasta*-eating people to whom spaghetti, macaroni and bread are unvariable necessities of life ; so corn, bulky and difficult to ship, had somehow to be brought to the Island.

When the emergency arrived, the Royal Navy and Mercantile Marine stepped into the breach and convoys retained the level of Malta's supplies with varying success through 1940 and 1941. Food was rationed and often short, but no great hardship was experienced. Though difficult, the position had not become alarming.

Even at the beginning of the Kesselring blitz, one convoy of three merchant vessels got through early in January, losing only the ammunition ship *Thermopylae*. Such a situation was, however, too good to last. The year of 1942 opened with an ominous event for the safety of Malta : the fall of Benghazi on the 25th January. The airfields of Cyrenaica, which, until then had been giving fighter protection to the ships bringing food to the defenders of Malta, now harboured German bombers menacing both the Island and its best supply route.

The Axis net was closing and the enemy surrounding Malta on all sides.

Evidence of the new danger was not long in coming, for the next convoy met with disaster.

On the 12th February, the merchantmen *Clan Chattan*, *Clan Campbell* and *Rowallan Castle* sailed from Alexandria, escorted at first by the anti-aircraft cruiser *Carlisle* and eight destroyers. Some hours later Admiral Vian followed with two cruisers of the 15th Squadron and eight more destroyers.

On the following day *Clan Campbell* was narrowly

missed by a stick of bombs and so severely damaged that she had to limp in to Tobruk. On the 14th *Clan Chattan* received a direct hit and caught fire, and the same afternoon *Rowallan Castle* was disabled. Both these ships had to be sunk by our own forces and, therefore, no supplies reached Malta.

This precipitated an immediate crisis in the Island. Admiral Cunningham had already reported, on 7th February, that Malta had petrol sufficient to last only until 1st August, and that fuel oil and other essential material would scarcely be sufficient to last until the end of May.

It was also true that for the bombers and torpedo aircraft to range far out into the Mediterranean severing the life-line of Rommel's Panzer army from Italy, petrol had to be brought to their aerodromes, and, indeed, their offensive was one of the chief reasons for holding Malta at all; but it was the shortage of wheat and flour for bread which caused Sir Edward the greatest anxiety. The ability of the R.A.F. and the Fleet Air Arm to continue their offensive depended on the health and survival of the air crews, the men servicing the planes, repairing the air strips and manning the guns, and on the islanders who backed them.

Great though the contribution of the Air Arm was to both the offensive and defensive power of the Island, it was of a purely military nature. Moreover, the fighter defence was local in effect, and extended its protection only to a small part of the voyage of any convoy attempting to reach the Grand Harbour.

As Sir Edward Jackson and other leaders on the

Island realised, therefore, Malta stood or fell by the condition of the civil population and fuel oil and kerosene were as much basic needs for civilian well-being as flour.

Wood was a rare and valuable commodity. Moreover, coal, the most bulky of all fuel sources, was expensive and difficult to transport. As a result, the traditional dependence of the Maltese on kerosene for lighting, heating and cooking had been increased beyond measure by war-time conditions.

The power for nearly all public utilities was supplied by oil burning units. The bakeries, electric power for hospitals and essential industries, the water supply and sewage works all depended ultimately on oil. Without it the whole complex of community life in the Island would have broken down.

Without oil, too, the chances of a convoy arriving at Malta at all were greatly diminished. Before any ships could enter the Grand Harbour, island-based sweepers had to clear the channel and approaches of mines which were replaced nightly by Axis aircraft, submarines and E-Boats. These sweepers were mainly oil-burning ships. Then there was the necessity to refuel lighter escort units and merchantmen for the return journey to Gibraltar. The very cranes which aided the speedy unloading of goods—and the convoy now about to be described proved how vital such speed could be—derived their motive power from oil.

So it was, that as the Axis blockade tightened on Malta, oil and kerosene became, with bread, the materials upon which the fate of the Island basically rested.

The overwhelming of the February convoy and the
desperate shortages which now threatened the beleaguered
fortress alarmed the War Cabinet, and a decision was
immediately taken to sail another convoy at the earliest
possible date.

It consisted of the naval supply ship *Breconshire*,
carrying a large quantity of oil fuel, and the merchantmen
Clan Campbell, Pampas and *Talabot*.

These ships sailed from Alexandria on 20th March
and unluckily this coincided with the launching of the
all-out bombing offensive against Malta by the German
forces in Sicily and Sardinia.

Admiral Vian's escort was one of the heaviest thus
far committed, four cruisers and sixteen destroyers,
while another cruiser and a flotilla leader sailed from
Malta to join them.

Enemy air reconnaissance soon reported the convoy,
and within twelve hours Admiral Vian knew that a
major sea battle was imminent, for the British submarine
P.36 signalled early on the 21st that heavy units of the
Italian Navy were leaving Taranto.

These were the battleship *Littorio*, mounting nine
15-inch guns, *Gorizia* and *Trento*, cruisers with 8-inch
armament, and the 6-inch gun cruiser *Giovanni Delle
Bande Nere*, with ten escorting destroyers.

Despite the fact that he was heavily out-gunned, for
only one of his cruisers mounted calibres as heavy as
6-inch, the admiral was in no doubt about engaging
the enemy. The convoy sailed on towards Malta
and the cruisers steamed to intercept the Italian fleet.

The second Battle of Sirte which followed remains

the finest example of protective cruiser action. Again and again, the British ships, dodging in and out of smoke screens, turned the greatly superior enemy force away from the merchantmen. Though fourteen destroyers were damaged, the Italian fleet finally retired without accomplishing the destruction of the convoy and the British fleet set out to return to Alexandria in a rising gale.

In the meantime, however, the merchantmen, delayed by the battle, had to complete the final dash to Malta dispersed and in daylight, with a meagre escort, all ships of which were short of A.A. ammunition.

Only twenty miles from Malta, *Clan Campbell* was sighted by German bombers and sank quickly following a number of direct hits.

Breconshire, with her precious cargo of oil, got to within eight miles of the Island before she too was hit and disabled. High seas prevented the cruiser *Penelope* from towing her to the Grand Harbour and she had to be beached at Marsaxlokk. She was sunk there two days later by German bombers with only a fraction of her oil cargo salved.

Though *Pampas* and *Talabot* sailed into the harbour and the population lined the battlements to cheer them in, under 6,000 tons of their combined cargo of 26,000 tons of foodstuffs and ammunition had been unloaded when both were sunk at their moorings by German dive-bombers.

So, despite the winning of a great naval victory, the purpose of the convoy had not been achieved.

Apart from small quantities of supplies brought in

by submarines, by the fast minelayers *Welshman* and
Manxman and the pittance salved from the March convoy,
Malta had received no supplies since January.

On the 1st April, General Dobbie, the Governor,
signalled the War Office : " Our supply position has
been reassessed and may be summarised as follows :

(a) Wheat and Flour. No material cuts seem possible,
as these are staple foods. Present stocks will, with care,
last until early June.

(b) Fodder. Issues already inadequate were recently
cut ; stocks will now last until end of June.

(c) Minor foodstuffs. Meat stocks are entirely exhausted. Most other stocks will last until June.

(d) White oils. Aviation fuel till mid-August ; benzine
till mid-June; kerosene till early July.

(e) Black oils. We have only 920 tons of diesel oil
(five weeks' supply) and 2,000 tons of furnace fuel, all
of which will be needed for fuelling H.M. Ships now
in dock. The black oil position is thus becoming
precarious, and very urgent action appears necessary
to restore it.

(f) Coal. Welsh coal will last only until end of May
. . . other grades until mid-June.

(g) Ammunition. Consumption of ack-ack ammunition has greatly increased . . . and we have only one
and a half months' stock left . . ."

By 15th April, 1942, when the King's award of the
George Cross to the Island was announced, its plight
was thus desperate.

" It is obvious that the very worst must happen if we

cannot replenish our vital needs . . ." General Dobbie informed the home Government.

Two months later, when the new Governor, Viscount Gort, presented the medal at a special investiture ceremony, starvation and consequent surrender were only a matter of days away.

For civilians, rations had declined until the bread issue stood at only ten and a half ounces a day and flour and rice were unobtainable. In Britain, during the whole of the war, it was never necessary to ration bread and flour. It must also be remembered that bread and flour were the staple Maltese diet, so that the half a pound a week British meat ration, tinned meats, baked beans and other rationed goods to be had in the United Kingdom must be included with bread and flour to gain a proper comparison.

Most Maltese dishes during happier times included olive oil ; but stocks had now been completely consumed and the fat ration of lard and margarine (with the very occasional substitute of butter) amounted only to three and a half ounces a week, a little more than a third of the British issue.

Milk which was unrationed in England, where tinned milk could also be had, was unobtainable in Malta, and a strictly limited amount of powdered milk was doled out to invalids, infants under seven years of age and expectant mothers only. Cheese in the United Kingdom was issued at the rate of four ounces a week per person —in Malta only one and three-quarters of an ounce was available.

The Maltese were accustomed to drinking as much

coffee as the English drink tea, and the restriction of the
coffee issue to one and three-quarters of an ounce a week
between three people was perhaps the greatest hardship
of all, far greater than that represented by the allowance
of two ounces of tea issued to each person in England.

Most other necessities were unobtainable. There was
no sugar ration, and jam and sweets had long been things
remembered from the past. The British ration allowed
six ounces of sugar and a pound of jam a week. Potatoes
and vegetables were also in fair supply in Britain, but,
apart from an occasional issue of about one pound a head
of potatoes, the average Maltese went without; the
restricted amounts of vegetables produced locally, usually
too small to justify workable rationing, disappeared on
to the black market where they commanded very high
prices.

Apart from one hot meal issued each day in Victory
Kitchens, which began to be set up all over the Island
at the end of this period, the Maltese had no means of
augmenting this meagre supply of food except on the
black market, which, as in every other country during
war-time, flourished despite all efforts to counter it by
the authorities. Prices prevailing for unauthorised
supplies were, however, well beyond the pocket of
more than ninety per cent of the Maltese. A pound of
sugar cost a pound for instance. Apart from minute
quantities of goats' meat issued to the Victory Kitchens
in July and August 1942, there had been no legitimate
meat supplies for a year, and a pound of beef, when it
could be had at the risk of a heavy fine, cost over a
pound. Chickens fetched between one pound fifteen

shillings and five pounds, and rabbits sold easily at twenty shillings. Small quantities of fish could be obtained for about five shillings a pound, and eggs at one time reached three and six each.

Yet these reliefs from a bare diet were only for the few, and the level of rationing to which the vast majority were tied, was well below the level necessary to maintain health, particularly as it came after six months of food restrictions. And it could be reduced no further. Troops' rations had similarly been reduced to the barest minimum.

Quite apart from food, the situation was grim in the extreme. Most of those things considered as ordinary requirements of civilised life were lacking, and most of the unnecessary but sought-after amenities which contribute much to the morale of people facing difficult times had gone.

The tobacco shortage was most distressing to a large proportion of the population. Two days of the week were fixed for the issue of one packet of cigarettes or tobacco to each man between sixteen and sixty.

It was a commonplace feature of Maltese life to see up to a hundred or more people sleeping out the night on the pavement outside the tobacco shops when an issue was due the following morning. Pipe smokers soon took to a mixture of dried fig, lemon and strawberry leaves which that " mother of invention " discovered to be the best herbal substitute for tobacco.

Cinemas, owing to the shortage of oil for electric power, were rigidly curtailed, although these shows were considered important morale-boosters. When shows were given, patrons had to find their way to their seats in a pitch-dark auditorium without house lights.

All sorts of alcoholic drinks also began to disappear as soon as the Axis blockade tightened. Most of the breweries had converted to oil-burning machinery, owing to the early shortage of coal, and then had to shut down altogether because of the shortage of oil. So there was no beer.

With the disappearance of beer the run on spirits soon exhausted all stocks except those of rum. As in most purely naval ports and establishments, quantities of rum could always be found, but the demand soon forced this out of general circulation and on to the black market where it sold at two hundred per cent above the controlled price.

Most of the ordinary commodities of everyday life were now absent or in very short supply.

The women had had to give up using cosmetics because they were unobtainable even on the black market. Similarly, brushes and combs and even shoe polish could not be bought for any amount of money. Soap was rationed to about half a pound a person once a fortnight.

New clothes were a luxury few could afford, a good suit or stylish dress fetching nearly ten times their pre-war prices. It was now a question of mend and make do, with cotton at ten shillings a reel. Old clothes were patched and patched again until they held together no longer. All pretensions to smartness had gone, and indeed good clothes came to be regarded as a badge of social unworthiness and the brand of the black market racketeer. In the prevailing climate, this was less of a hardship than it would have been in higher latitudes, but the acute shortage of shoe leather on this rocky island was serious. New shoes and sandals could only be obtained at prohibitive prices ; and so, as old ones wore out, they were replaced by home-made clogs of boxwood with canvas uppers. These were usually uncomfortable and often hurt the feet intolerably.

For many years, in most parts of Malta, water had been accepted as an integral part of life, as in other civilised urban areas. A limitless supply, it seemed, could always be obtained simply by turning on a tap. That too was changed, and water was rationed to nine gallons a day for each person : less than one-third of the average British war-time consumption. With the hot, sticky Mediterranean climate in which regular baths and showers alone can make life comfortable, this was also a great hardship.

For the housewife especially, the situation had become dull, difficult and dangerous. Denied make-up, pretty clothes and most of her spare-time amusements, cooking became a burden and she often had to forage for her fuel like a primitive savage. The allotment of a quarter of a gallon of kerosene a week to each family of two, was insufficient to supply proper heating and lighting, and so camp-fire cooking could be found throughout Malta. In the country the garden became the kitchen. In the town, where few homes have gardens, it was in the street outside the front door. Open fireplaces were carved out of stone or improvised from oil drums. The women paid their daily call to the nearest bomb-ruined buildings and returned with wood and kindling to cook the dinner. Washing up was a nightmare, for the wood smoke sooted up their pots and pans, and the lack of artificial cleaners had to be made up for with sand and elbow grease. If a piece of crockery was smashed it could not be replaced, and already many families drank their meagre coffee ration out of rough-rimmed glasses made from cutting off the bottoms of bottles.

These privations would have been bad enough without the continual threat of destruction and death and the wail of sirens heralding the approach of terror. It is now a well-attested principle of war-time psychology that bombing for a time stiffens the morale and brings out a hidden fortitude and toughness in most people ; but for the women of Malta, faced with appalling difficulties in everyday life, it was becoming too heavy a trial. The constant danger to their children, to their men, many of them working in the most heavily-bombed target areas, to their homes and to everyone and everything they held dear, was slowly sapping their resistance. Nor was this surprising. The wonder of it was that they had not given in weeks before, for the Island was fast being reduced to rubble by German and Italian bombers.

By the end of May 1942, Malta had suffered 2,470 air-raids and between 1st January and 24th July there was only one raidless period of twenty-four hours. Those who remember the blitz on London in 1940 and the interminable succession of days on days when the sirens sounded and the bombs came raining down will understand just what that meant. Yet the longest number of consecutive days on which London was raided amounted to only fifty-seven, while the Maltese had suffered no less than 154 days of continual day and night bombing. The total tonnage of bombs dropped on the Island during March and April alone was twice that dropped in London during the year of its worst attacks, and, in one month, 6,000 tons of high explosive had rocked the Island's towns and villages.

Loss of civilian lives had been heavy enough to shake the fortitude of a lesser people. From the outbreak of war until December 1941, 330 had been killed and 297 seriously injured. With the coming of the Luftwaffe, the next four months was a period of death and disaster, for 820 people were killed and 915 seriously injured. Another 158 were killed and 383 injured in the following three months.

Had it not been for the nature of the rock upon which Malta is founded a far higher proportion of the population might have been wiped out and essential civil and military services completely disrupted. The natural process of erosion had formed hundreds of natural caverns below the shallow topsoil. Moreover, the construction of man-made rock shelters was made easier by the fact that the limestone is easily cut into but soon weathers to an iron-hard consistency on exposure to air.

As a result, ample underground accommodation had been constructed before the war to house oil-storage tanks, generators and workshops and to shelter a large proportion of the population during air-raids. Most of this work was inspired by Admiral Sir W. T. R. Ford, the Senior British Naval Officer, who plainly foresaw the trial by fire through which the Island was to pass. He also had thousands of picks made in the naval workshops, and with these the Maltese had been able to construct their own shelters.

Though these early precautions saved thousands of Maltese lives, no means could be found to protect their homes. As a result, 10,000 houses lay in ruins, 20,000 others had sustained serious damage and nearly 100 churches had been gutted.

For days on end, roads remained blocked with debris and were impassable, for neither the manpower nor the petrol was available to clear them.

In the bigger towns like Valletta, Senglea, Cospicua and Vittoriosa, the limited water supply suffered frequent breakdowns, some lasting for several days. The sanitary services were often interrupted for as much as a week and the telephone was more often cut off than in use.

Frequently, even the almost superhuman efforts of the Malta Water Department failed for long periods to cope with the demands for emergency fresh-water lines. Then the mobile water bowsers had to be sent out and at each stop fifty or more men, women and children would queue up with every pot, pan or ewer available, for they knew from experience that the petrol shortage would prevent another visit perhaps for many days.

A depressing desolation was everywhere to be found. No town or village was untouched, and wherever the eye rested dust and rubble disfigured the view. That dust had become a curse. In many places one waded through it ankle deep, and when the wind blew strongly it became a dirty yellow sandstorm which penetrated the cracks in the windows and swirled in under the doors. It grated on the teeth, got in the eyes and spoiled the food.

" If the civil population collapses, the whole fortress collapses . . ." Sir Edward Jackson wrote.

At every scarred street corner, behind the bar in every pub or club, spread over the still-warm ruins of homes, shops and churches, could be found gigantic pictures of Churchill with that bulldog slogan : " Hold Fast and We Win."

Through every sort of privation, difficulty and danger, through fire, ruin and death, the Maltese had held fast when none could have blamed them for loosening their hold.

Now, however, the hour approached when little more could be expected of flesh and blood. Already the long period of pitifully deficient diet had begun to manifest itself in skin and enteric diseases associated with malnutrition. Soon there would be nothing at all to eat, nothing to turn the wheels of this tiny island society. Then the white flag would fly above Malta.

CHAPTER THREE

TARGET DATE 'SURRENDER'

I

A SECRET date for Malta's capitulation had been calculated from month to month by General Dobbie, the Governor, and after him by Lord Gort, and by a committee consisting of the Deputy Governor, Sir Edward Jackson and the chiefs of the three services.

This involved no complicated evaluation of circumstances ; it depended simply on how long vital stocks of flour, fuel oil, kerosene and, to a lesser extent, petrol and anti-aircraft ammunition would last.

When these were exhausted the Island and all upon it would have to surrender.

The question of evacuating the Island, even by the troops defending it, never arose as a practical proposition because the means to do so did not exist after January 1942, and also because at no time had such plans been made.

So it was that when the fleet and the convoy of " Operation Pedestal " sailed through the Straits of Gibraltar on the 10th August, the " Target Date," as it was called, by which capitulation would have been forced on the military commands by a breakdown of food and fuel supplies, lay between 31st August and the 7th September, unless a fair proportion of the convoy's cargo could be unloaded at Malta.

Further delay in surrendering would have meant widespread death from starvation among the quarter of a million Maltese civilians, the 18,000 regular troops and the 8,000 Maltese serving with the colours on the Island.

All depended on this operation. If it had failed it would have been impossible to arrange another convoy in time; and even if a small part of " Pedestal," say only two ships, had won through, it is still doubtful whether it would have been feasible to arrange another before starvation compelled the defenders to strike the Union Jack from the staff above the Residency, where it had flown defiantly for so many difficult and dangerous months.

That Malta's plight was desperate at this time is common property, though the narrow margin by which it was saved was known only to the few immediately concerned with the Island's defence and to the leaders of the British war effort at this time. Why no evacuation had ever been considered and why no attempt to save so many seasoned troops and much valuable material had been planned is, however, something of a historical mystery.

The difficulty of holding Malta under foreseeable circumstances of Mediterranean war had been recognised since 1914. Despite the determination of the War Cabinet to hang on to the Island at any price and the efforts made to implement this determination, the stark reality of earlier forecasts must have been evident long before the beginning of 1942, when the surrender date was forecast in months, then weeks and then days.

Why then had no evacuation plan been produced? The reason probably lay in the difficulty of such an operation. The threat of the Italian fleet had been in no way diminished by British naval successes in the Mediterranean, which were offset by our heavy losses there and in other parts of the world ; and the situation was aggravated by the difficulty of assembling a big British fleet with so many commitments elsewhere. Moreover, the risk to fleet elements was probably considered too great to hazard them on what would have been essentially a negative operation ; for the Axis held command of the air over the greater part of the sea and the disasters of Greece and Crete had emphasised just how costly such operations could be without air superiority.

Psychologically this absence of plan may be another example of the positivity of thought which underlay the British direction of the war and which constituted the greatest of many qualities which the character of Churchill imparted to the British will to victory.

The British war leader's dislike for thinking in terms of defeat, even though the thought amounted only to the established military practice of providing for all eventualities, is well known.

For instance, Sir John Kennedy, the Director of Military Operations from 1940 to 1943, describes in his book *The Business of War* the storm which broke when Churchill heard of Wavell's " Worst Possible Case," a general paper on action to be taken in event of failure to check the German advance into Egypt.

The man who, providentially for Britain, believed that war was a contest of wills, flushed and lost his temper. Wavell, Kennedy and the other generals were accused of defeatism in even thinking it was possible to lose Egypt. " If they lose Egypt, blood will flow. I will have firing parties to shoot generals," he roared.

Whatever may have been the causes of this absence of plan, the situation progressively deteriorated from January, until, by the spring, any thought of an organised evacuation became impossible. By early summer, with the sinking or removal of most of the naval units from Malta, there were not sufficient ships, yachts or rowing boats in the Island to move 500 men, and the Axis sea and air blockade was such that rescue by the Navy was out of the question as a practical operation.

The Island was thus faced with fighting to the last crust and the last round.

II

After the failure of the March convoy, the Governor ordered yet another tightening of belts, and the hopes of the defenders were concentrated on the promised convoy in May.

On 18th April the Chiefs of Staff in London concluded that, in view of the general naval situation, to run a convoy to Malta would be out of the question.

This decision profoundly shocked those who were responsible for the Island's defence. They at once took stock of the larder, and Sir Edward Jackson, the Deputy Governor, calculated, from the reports which had been called for, that only seventy days' supply of wheat and flour remained.

This too was dependent upon a chance factor, for of the available stocks only thirty days of this supply was in flour. The ability to make use of wheat supplies depended upon the flour mills which were situated in the docks, the most heavily bombed military target in the Island. These had already been damaged and had recently been out of action for several days.

Calculating on the flour index, and stocks and consumption of other vital materials were roughly equivalent to this, it meant that they could not safely count on being able to hold out for more than thirty days, or at the most forty, if supplies were stretched to the final limit.

Without further supplies, in fact, they could hold out to the end of June at the longest and, if the worst happened and the flour mills were destroyed, until the end of May only.

Nor would any small convoy solve the crisis. To live, the Island required some 26,000 tons of supplies a month, which amounted to the balanced cargo of about three large ships. Experience had shown that less than a quarter of the cargo loaded in any convoy could be expected to reach the Island's underground stores. A ten-ship convoy was the greatest which could conveniently be mustered and escorted, and the extensive preparations needed for mounting so large an operation limited dispatch to a maximum of one every two months. It therefore became evident that, even upon the previous scale of effort, the Island was consuming its stocks quicker than it could be supplied. The end now seemed in sight.

General Dobbie ordered the bread ration to be cut by a quarter and appraised the War Cabinet of the results of their grim calculation.

The situation, he pointed out, had gone beyond the critical stage. " It is obvious that the very worst may happen if we cannot replenish our vital needs . . . It is a question of survival," he wrote.

When the Defence Committee met in London again on 22nd April, Churchill made it clear that he was not going to allow Malta to fall and that he was prepared to run extreme military risks to save the Island. In this he had the full support of the Admiralty.

The army, however, was less prepared to play what the Prime Minister called " paying forfeits " in India and the desert to succour Malta; and one result was that General Auchinleck, when told to mount an offensive in the desert to divert attention from the coming Malta convoys, gave the opinion that the retention of the Island was not absolutely necessary to his plans. He was therefore ordered by the Prime Minister to take the offensive.

At this critical Defence Committee meeting, the Prime Minister even discussed bringing four capital ships and three modern cruisers from the Indian Ocean to the Mediterranean via Suez to carry a convoy to the Island, with the additional hope of bringing the Italian fleet to action on the way. This plan was finally shelved, but in principle it was agreed that convoys should be fought through to Malta at the earliest possible date, and that a great degree of risk to the naval forces employed should be accepted.

The service departments, with the assistance of the Ministry of War Transport, immediately began discussing ways and means of arranging the convoys, but they were faced with a grave difficulty which had already presented itself.

The minimum speed at which a Mediterranean convoy could travel without grave danger to merchant ships and escort was sixteen knots. Many merchantmen could be found capable of this speed ; but in the available fleet of British ships, no tanker existed with more than twelve knots. Yet a tanker had to be included to supply two of the vital deficiencies from which Malta was dying ; for, although aviation spirit might be loaded in other vessels, only a tanker could carry a large enough cargo of oil and kerosene.

At an earlier meeting of the War Cabinet Committee responsible for organising the convoys, Sir Ralph Metcalfe, who was head of the Tanker Division of the Ministry of War Transport, had been present and had been asked if he knew any way of solving this problem.

Sir Ralph agreed that no fast tankers existed in the British fleet or in any of the available Allied fleets, except that of the Americans. " Why not," he asked, " try to borrow one or perhaps two of the American vessels ? " The tanker fleet belonging to the Texas Oil Company were among the fastest and finest in the world, he pointed out.

The other committee members shook their heads doubtfully. They knew that, following Winston Churchill's appeal to Roosevelt, the Americans were making sustained and generous efforts to fill the gap in British shipping needs ; but tankers, and particularly fast ones, were few even in the American fleet and urgently needed by the U.S. services to supply their forces in the Far East. Moreover, the loss of tankers, now that Germany had carried the submarine war across the Atlantic to America, had been extremely heavy.

It was unlikely, therefore, that America could afford to lend Britain any of these valuable ships, particularly for an enterprise involving the extreme danger of a Malta convoy.

However, it was agreed that Sir Ralph should try to obtain two fast tankers from America if he could.

Despite the doubts of the Defence Committee, Sir Ralph calculated that he had a fair chance of achieving his object. Some months before, he had visited America and had met most of the leading shipping people there, including chiefs of Texaco. As a result, he was aware of a tender point in the American conscience which he thought might prove a valuable psychological card to play if negotiations for the tankers proved too difficult.

A previous president of one of the biggest tanker fleets in America had been a personal friend of Goering's and had had a number of his tankers built in Germany. When America entered the war and anti-German feeling began to mount, this fact was looked upon as something of a skeleton in the cupboard. Sir Ralph calculated that a delicate suggestion that refusal to supply the tankers might be construed in Britain as evidence of German partiality among American tanker owners would produce a powerful desire in the U.S. authorities concerned to supply the tankers regardless of the cost.

He therefore cabled Sir Arthur Salter, head of the British Merchant Shipping Mission in Washington, asking him to open negotiations for the tankers and suggesting that this psychological card might be used if negotiations looked like failing.

Sir Arthur had gone to Washington in April 1941 and had already succeeded in smoothing out the difficulties of obtaining the 2,000,000 tons of American shipping earlier requested by Churchill.

Whether the psychological card was in fact played in the negotiations is not clear, but formal application for the tankers was made through the normal channels on 7th January, 1942 and Sir Arthur had talks with Harold Ickes, Minister of Commerce, Admiral Emory S. Land, the American War Shipping Administrator, and with officials of the U.S. Maritime Commission.

Reluctance on the American side to part with the tankers is expressed in a letter from H. Harris Robson, the American General Director of Shipping, sent to the chairman of the U.S. Maritime Commission on 17th January, 1942.

" *High Speed Tankers.* With reference to Sir Arthur Salter's letter of 7th January requesting that the Commission place at the disposal of the British two sixteen-knot tankers for Mediterranean service, quite a problem is involved. Through conversation with Mr. Salter's office we are informed that what the British really need are sixteen-and-a-half-knot vessels capable of keeping up with convoys of supply ships capable of such speed. The only tankers under the American flag definitely capable of sustaining sea speeds in excess of sixteen knots are the so-called National Defense tankers.

" We are told by Commander Callaghan of the Navy that these ships are urgently required by that Department. Already the Navy have taken over all of that type of vessel in existence and have signified their intention of acquiring those under construction when delivered."

Despite this and the firm stand by the U.S. Navy Department against releasing the tankers, Sir Arthur Salter's negotiations prevailed. American generosity overcame even their own urgent needs and Sir Arthur was informed late in April that the United States would make available the new 14,000 ton tanker *Kentucky* and, if a further tanker was needed, Texaco's *Ohio*.

III

While the June convoy was assembling and negotiations for the two tankers were proceeding, a change had taken place in the leadership on Malta. General Dobbie, worn down by the long strain and responsibility of governing the Island, had asked to be relieved ; and Viscount Gort, then Governor of Gibraltar, flew to Malta to take over his duties.

Gort's first action was to ensure that however many ships of the convoy might be lost on the way, those which did arrive would be unloaded in the minimum time, with the minimum loss of cargo.

His arrangements were practical and far-reaching. Specially picked members of the armed forces in the

Island were told off to reinforce the dock labourers and every available lorry or truck was commandeered. One-way traffic routes were arranged and marked with individual coloured signs, illuminated at night in such a way that they were hooded from air observation. All other traffic was banned from these routes during an unloading operation and strict traffic control organised. The lorries themselves were allocated colours, depending on the stores they carried, so that by following their corresponding colour route they would speedily arrive at the appropriate depot. A Maltese policeman travelled in each lorry to prevent pilfering.

The scheme was to come into operation immediately a cargo arrived and would continue day and night without halting until all was safely discharged.

Smoke flares were set up round the harbour so that whenever an air-raid was imminent the whole area could be obscured from the enemy bombers.

Not content with this, Gort ordered a full dress rehearsal of the scheme, which was carried out despite the expenditure of vital fuel, shortly before the convoy started.

The mid-June convoy was conceived on a massive scale, in comparison with previous attempts. If a quarter of the ships reached Malta, the Island's troubles would be over.

It was to be run in two parts. The first, from Gibraltar, consisting of six merchant ships, carrying about 43,000 tons of cargo and including the American tanker *Kentucky*, was to be escorted by Acting Captain C. C. Hardy in the anti-aircraft cruiser *Cairo*, with nine destroyers and four minesweepers. Admiral Curteis was in support in the battleship *Malaya*, with the old aircraft carriers *Eagle* and *Argus*, two cruisers and eight destroyers. This part was given the code name, " Operation Harpoon."

The second part, from Alexandria, was to be made up of no less than eleven merchant ships, with a total cargo of about 72,000 tons. Called " Operation Vigorous," the merchantmen were to be escorted by Rear-Admiral Vian with seven cruisers and twenty-eight destroyers, in addition to a number of smaller escort craft and minesweepers. He was to have no covering force of capital ships, however, because it was found impracticable to transfer further units of the Eastern Fleet to the Mediterranean. The old wireless-controlled target ship *Centurion* sailed with the convoy, mocked up to resemble a new battleship, and the planners hoped that the wide use of land-based aircraft and submarines might make up for the absence of aircraft carriers.

The convoy from Gibraltar reached the Skerki Bank, nearly two-thirds of the journey, on the evening of 14th June, with the loss of one merchantman and with the cruiser *Liverpool* disabled by a torpedo in the engine-room. This was in the face of heavy air attacks, and despite the difficulty experienced by the two slow carriers in flying off aircraft with a light following wind.

At nine-thirty p.m., Admiral Curteis's supporting force withdrew to the westward, for his capital ships could not be risked in the " Narrows " between Sicily and North Africa where they would have had no room to manœuvre, leaving only Captain Hardy's anti-aircraft cruiser *Cairo*, and the destroyers and minesweepers to care for the convoy.

Off the island of Pantelleria at first light next morning, smoke trails appeared on the northern horizon, and air reconnaissance informed Captain Hardy that a force of two Italian cruisers, supported by destroyers, was no more than fifteen miles away.

Within a few minutes salvoes were falling close to the ships of the convoy and the enemy was sighted. Without hesitation *Bedouin* (Commander B. G. Scurfield) led the fleet destroyers to the attack despite the superiority of the enemy force, while *Cairo* and smaller escorts made smoke to screen the convoy.

The British destroyers, outranged by the enemy cruisers, had to steam for some minutes under heavy fire before they could reply with their main armament of 4.7-inch and 4-inch guns.

Bedouin and *Partridge* were hit and disabled, and the Italian destroyer *Vivaldi* was put out of action with serious internal damage.

Having laid smoke, *Cairo* and four *Hunt*-class destroyers joined in, and Da Zara, the Italian admiral, uncertain of the size of the force shrouded in the smoke screen, withdrew.

So effective was the British attack that he believed " with absolute certainty " that he was engaging, besides *Cairo*, another cruiser of the *Kenya* class.

The Italian admiral's orders were not, as one might have expected, to destroy the convoy at any price, but to score an Italian victory, even a superficial one, to boost morale and offset the depressing effect of previous reverses.

Just before the battle he received a signal from Supermarina, the Italian Naval High Command, ordering him not to engage superior enemy forces. It was partly because of this signal that he believed the British force to be stronger than it actually was.

His two reconnaissance planes, launched from the cruisers just before they opened fire, gave him no news of what was happening on the other side of the smoke screen. He therefore proceeded to make a wide detour to get a clearer view of his opponents.

The convoy, now protected only by minesweepers, was meanwhile heavily bombed. Struck by a stick of three bombs, the merchantman *Chant* crumpled and sank in a few minutes, leaving only a dense column of black smoke boiling out of the sea and rising high into the blue sky.

Then the U.S. tanker, *Kentucky* was damaged by a near miss. She was taken in tow by the minesweeper *Hebe*, and making only six knots, fell astern of the convoy.

The air attacks continued with the utmost ferocity, and, an hour later, another merchantman, *Burdwan*, narrowly missed and shaken by a stick of bombs, stopped. Sooner than risk the crippled tanker falling into enemy hands, Captain Hardy ordered her to be sunk. This was a tragedy for oil-less Malta, for *Kentucky*, with a fractured main steam pipe, required only a few hours to repair the damage. *Burdwan* was also scuttled.

The Italian fleet was circling the convoy, trying to come within range of the remaining merchantmen without risking another general engagement. The damaged *Bedouin* was sunk by the Italian cruisers and topedo bombers.

Instead of six ships, the convoy now only numbered two.

Help was coming. At 14.24, two Beaufort aircraft and four naval Albacores from Malta attacked the enemy fleet. This scratch effort did no damage, but, coinciding as it did with an order from Supermarina for Da Zara to withdraw from the area unless the circumstances of the battle were particularly favourable, it seems to have made up the Italian admiral's mind for him. He immediately retired.

The damaged Italian destroyer, *Vivaldi*, reached Pantelleria, and, while *Troilus* and *Orari* were still thrusting onwards towards Malta with their precious cargoes, Da Zara with the remainder of the Italian fleet entered Naples harbour with all guns trained upwards in token of a naval victory. He had carried out Supermarina's orders to the letter.

It was dark when the convoy reached the partially-swept channel in the Malta minefield. A fleet mine-sweeper and three destroyers all struck mines, but made harbour, with the exception of the Polish *Kujawiak* which sank almost immediately. Thus, out of a convoy of six ships, only two reached port, *Troilus* and *Orari*.

Operation "Vigorous" from the eastward had meanwhile got only as far as the beginning of "Bomb Alley," the sea corridor between Crete and Cyrenaica, when one merchantman was damaged and another found

77

to be too slow to keep up. The following day (14th June) a second merchantman had to put in to Tobruk because she hadn't the speed to stay with the convoy. As darkness fell a combined air, E-boat and submarine attack accounted for one further ship sunk and another damaged, reducing the eleven merchantmen to seven. Both the cruiser *Newcastle* and the destroyer *Hasty* had also been damaged by torpedoes. The cruiser reached safety but the destroyer was too badly hit and had to be sunk later by the British forces.

Moreover, before the sun had set, an R.A.F. Maryland had spotted two Italian battleships and four cruisers leaving Taranto and steaming south to intercept what remained of the convoy.

Shortly before two a.m. on the 15th, Admiral Harwood, C.-in-C. Mediterranean, gave Admiral Vian orders to retire to Alexandria with the convoy and screen.

When dawn broke on the 15th, the Italian fleet, two of their newest battleships, *Vittorio Veneto* and *Littorio*, two heavy and two light cruisers and twelve destroyers, were still at least 200 miles to the north-west of the convoy. Admiral Harwood, therefore, ordered fleet and convoy to turn again towards Malta. But when the enemy continued to sail on a southerly course and began to approach uncomfortably close, the order to retire was again given.

Meanwhile, Malta-based Beaufort aircraft attacked the Italian battleships with torpedoes and hit and disabled the 8-inch cruiser *Trento*. Further attacks followed by American Liberators and other R.A.F. aircraft. Reports now reached Admiral Harwood that both Italian battleships had been torpedoed and he at once ordered the convoy to resume its course for Malta.

The air reports, however, soon indicated that our aircraft had lost touch with the Italian fleet, and Admiral Harwood had to decide if convoy and escort should retire or proceed.

Though the Italian fleet was now retiring, the Axis attacks from the air had reached a murderous pitch, and the cruiser *Birmingham* and the destroyer *Airdale* were both seriously damaged. Once again the cruiser limped home, but the destroyer could not be salved and was sunk by British gunfire. Shortly afterwards another merchantman had to turn back, and the Australian destroyer *Nestor* was also hit and had to be scuttled.

Vian then reported that two-thirds of his ships' ammunition had been expended and that the remainder was disappearing at a dangerously fast rate.

The Commander-in-Chief therefore ordered all ships to return to Alexandria.

On the credit side, *Trento* was sunk by the British submarine *Umbra* and the R.A.F. succeeded in scoring one bomb and one torpedo hit on the battleship *Littorio*.

Nevertheless, the Italian claims to have won a victory, though exaggerated, were substantially true. Although the loss of the cruiser *Hermione*, torpedoed returning to Alexandria, five destroyers and six merchantmen sunk and others damaged, would have been a light price to pay for the relief of Malta. It was an unfortunate fact that the two ships which did arrive were loaded with a combined cargo of little more than 15,000 tons. Thanks to the excellent arrangements made for the reception of the convoy at Malta, all supplies were unloaded, but it amounted to much less than a month's ration for the Island. The food situation remained critical and, due to the loss of *Kentucky*, the oil and kerosene shortage became desperate.

The Governor decided that it was time to take the people of Malta into his confidence. The day after the arrival of the two ships, therefore, he broadcast the following message to them.

" I must now break to you what the arrival of only two ships means to us. For some time past we have been short of supplies and further privations lie ahead of us. But let us remember that the most glorious sieges in history have always meant hardships, and without hardships there would be little glory. . . ."

Sir Edward Jackson returned to the same theme—after a conference between the Governor, his advisers and a party of food experts who had been sent to the Island— four days later, and what he had to tell the sorely tried defenders was grimmer still.

". . . greater privation than we have known hitherto lies ahead of us. We received about 15,000 tons of stores from the two ships which arrived. That is something, and certainly a help, but it is a very small part of what we had hoped for. I have come here this evening to tell you plainly what our arrangements are, and I shall tell you the worst. Our security depends, more than anything else, on the time for which our bread will last.

" So it was that when, after our disappointment over the recent convoys, we sat down to examine our position, we first calculated the time for which our bread could be made to last.

"We knew that our present ration could not be reduced and it will not be reduced. That calculation gave us a date which I shall call the Target Date, the date to aim at. Our next task was to see how we could make our other vital necessities last to the Target Date. We found that with some things we could not do so without some restriction in the ration, or without making a wider interval between the issues than we make now. And so you will understand that when a ration is reduced or a wider interval made between the dates of issue, the object is to make these things last, wherever possible, as long as bread will last.

"I cannot tell you what the Target Date is, for if the enemy came to hear of it he would learn something that he would very much like to know, but I can tell you that it is far enough off to give very ample opportunity for fresh supplies to reach us before our present stocks run out. . . ."

What the Deputy Governor had said was strictly true. The next convoy was due in mid-August and supplies would last for just about fourteen days after that. If that convoy failed, Malta was lost.

CHAPTER FOUR

REPORT AT GREENOCK . . .

On the 18th June the Commander-in-Chief of the Mediterranean fleet cabled the Prime Minister. He said that he was doubtful whether it was worth attempting to run another convoy after the disastrous failure of " Harpoon-Vigorous."

Three days later a large tanker, rolling slightly in an oily swell, steamed into the mouth of the Clyde.

Her captain, Sverre Petersen, a former Master-in-Sail from Oslo in Norway, squinted at the green hills of Scotland which he had not seen for many years.

Beside him on the bridge Chief Engineer Bush was taking a breath of fresh air. An unanswered question which had occupied the whole crew through the long voyage across the Atlantic was buzzing in his mind, but he hesitated to ask the usually uncommunicative captain about it.

" Well, we shall be there soon, Chief," said the captain, without taking his eyes off the undulating coastline.

The engineer took the plunge : " What's going to happen to us in England, Cap ? Shall we see any fun, do you think."

The captain shrugged his shoulders. He had sailed

in one war already and had been overboard in a hurricane. Whatever happened to be over the horizon at sea would be met in good time without unprofitable speculation.

" Search me," he replied. " We're ordered to the Clyde with gasoline. We're here. As far as I'm concerned the rest is rumour. I've not been told what happens after that. Best wait and see." He lifted his glasses and focused them on another tanker approaching them.

Despite the German U-boats scouring the Atlantic in search of prey and, as they approached Europe, the drone of long-range German bombers, the voyage of *Ohio* had been uneventful. In fact, from the day of her launching her whole life had been the humdrum existence of an ordinary oil tanker, plying between Port Arthur and various American ports ; except that she had once set up a speed record from Bayonne to Port Arthur covering 1,882 miles in four days, twelve hours, an average of more than seventeen knots.

Then, one day early in May 1942 a radio message had reached the captain, diverting the ship to Galveston, Texas. There was nothing unusual in that, but when he reached port orders awaited Captain Petersen which brought an involuntary whistle to his lips.

Ohio was to proceed to Britain, the first American tanker to visit what had become almost a beleaguered citadel of war. As a foretaste of what might be in store for her, two guns, a 5-inch and a 3-inch A.A, were fitted. Then she moved to Sinclair Terminal, Houston, Texas, where she loaded a full cargo of 103,576 barrels of petrol before sailing on the 25th May.

Ohio discharged her cargo at Bowling on the Clyde,

then steamed out into the tideway and anchored, awaiting orders.

Many curious eyes turned towards her as she swung easily in the current. Her long lines with the perceptible sheer were noted, the high bridge amidships and the squat funnel aft. A nice-looking ship, big for a tanker—must be fast. American? What was she doing here in ballast then? No one, least of all the puzzled American crew, seemed to know the answer.

Although *Ohio's* destiny had already been settled at the highest level between the British and American governments no word of its portent or the means by which it was to be implemented could be allowed to leak out.

There was no clue in the letter received by Captain Petersen on his arrival. This was sent by Lord Leathers, the head of the British Ministry of War Transport, bidding the master a personal welcome ". . . at your safe arrival in the Clyde with the first cargo of oil carried in a United States tanker."

A telegram received the same day by the head office of Texaco from the U.S. War Shipping Administration, therefore, created a sensation and by no means a pleasant one. It announced simply that the *Ohio* was being requisitioned " pursuant to the law."

The immediate reaction was a cabled message from Mr. T. E. Buchanan, General Manager of Texaco's Marine Department to the firm's London agent, that on no account was *Ohio* to leave her discharging port of Bowling on the Clyde.

The master was told further orders would arrive soon.

No one seemed to know what was happening; and, indeed, even the highest British and American authorities were in some doubt as to how the formalities of their concerted action should be carried out: for the circumstances were unique. Then again there was a period of doubt on the British side about using *Ohio* for the momentous operation projected, because of the unusual hazards to which so fine a ship would be subjected.

Two weeks later the decision was finally taken.

A launch sped out to the ship anchored in the Clyde and Texaco's London agent, accompanied by an official of the British Ministry of War Shipping, came over the side.

Captain Petersen received them in his cabin. " We've got some rather unpleasant news for you, Captain," the agent explained awkwardly. " You and your crew will be leaving this ship. She's to be handed over to a British crew."

" What, hand over my ship? What the blazes do you mean? " roared the captain . . . The agent and the man from the Ministry spent an unpleasant hour. The agent knew no more than the information contained in the apparently outrageous order. The man from the Ministry knew a little more, but was not allowed to explain.

" Some sort of convoy, you say? " asked the captain, by now in the last stages of exasperation. " Can't an American sail in a convoy as well as a ' Limey '? " Scores of later convoys, and indeed previous ones had proved that an American could, but the unexplained

85

orders were final. The captain had no option but to give in.

The crew was no less flabbergasted by the news and received it, understandably, with somewhat bad grace.

Such a transfer was unheard of ; the method seemed dictatorial, not to say suspect. After all, what were they supposed to be fighting against but this sort of thing ?

Next day strangers began to come aboard ; the English seamen who were to take over. Reluctantly the Americans began to pack up and the considerable amount of scramble involved did nothing to improve frayed tempers. It is surprising the amount of gear a seaman can collect on board a ship in two years and no one had enough bags. The chief mate, Ralph Kuhn, had to turn the seamen to making emergency kit-bags to hold it all.

Finally, on the 10th July, Captain Petersen handed over the ship. There was no formal ceremony and little goodwill. The American flag was run down and *Ohio* thenceforward sailed on her short trip to fame under the " Red Duster."

Overnight she was transferred from American to British registry.

For convenience in management *Ohio* was handed over on the 25th June to the British Eagle Oil and Shipping Company.

Before the transaction was completed the company was warned by the Ministry of War Transport that the tanker was required for a special convoy and that much might depend upon the quality and courage of the crew.

Accordingly a hurried search was made for the best men then available.

Soon, the telephone bell was ringing in a small suburban home at Surbiton, Surrey. Captain Mason lifted himself reluctantly from a comfortable arm-chair, yawned and said to his brother : " Don't you go, it's probably for me." Two minutes later he returned to the sitting-room.

" Something's happened," he said shortly, " but what it is and what ship, I haven't a clue. It's the usual business. Just report to the Clyde as quickly as possible and no questions."

Dudley W. Mason at thirty-nine had already held other commands. He was one of the youngest of the Eagle Oil Company's captains and had begun an apprenticeship with the company when he was seventeen years old. He had been on leave, standing by to receive the command of *Empire Norman* which was building. Now it seemed there was another change of plan, but after three years of war he was used to sudden upheavals of this sort and took them philosophically. He went upstairs to pack his bag.

At Euston Station, he met another of the Eagle's masters. He too had been ordered to the Clyde immediately without explanation.

As the train sped northwards, they speculated on the sudden summons and agreed that such a " gathering of the clans " must mean something big was in store for them.

About the same time on this Sunday afternoon, chief engineer James Wyld, another tried servant of the company, now forty years old, received a telegram at his digs in Belfast where he was supervising the installation of machinery in another tanker, *San Veronica*, at Harland and Wolff's shipyard.

The message read : " Report Greenock at once."

Next morning, he was greeted at the company's Glasgow office by the agent, Mr. W. L. Nelson.

The agent would say little about the sudden call. " I'd just like you to look at a ship, Jimmy," he said. " I think you might like her."

Together they set out in a launch and boarded *Ohio*. For more than two hours, the engineer examined the engines and auxiliary machinery, poked into dark corners and mentally assessed the complicated pattern of cylinders, pipes, pumps and boilers which make up the motive power of a modern tanker.

Then he came on deck and looked questioningly at the agent. " Well . . . ? "

" Would you like to take over the engine-room for a special job ? " asked the agent.

" Blimey, would I not ? " said Wyld enthusiastically. " She's the finest ship I've ever seen."

Wyld spent the rest of the day gloating over the machinery and savouring the compliment which was implied by sending him to so fine a ship. Most of the American crew had now gone, but the third engineer had been sporting enough to volunteer to stay behind to show the English crew the ropes. Wyld took full advantage of this chance to learn something about his new ship.

That evening Captain Mason came aboard and received a hearty greeting from Wyld. They were old friends and had sailed together in *San Arcadio*, when Mason had been second mate and Wyld third engineer. On that voyage they had spent most of their spare time playing crib together. Perhaps they would have a chance for another game or two. . . .

During the next few days the other officers and the crew began to arrive. Both Mason and Wyld saw with pleasure that they were all young, picked men of the Eagle fleet.

There was Gray, the chief officer, a quiet, fair-complexioned Scot from Leith, who had packed twelve years of seafaring into his twenty-six years of life; McKilligan, a stout, blustery western Highlander of about twenty-eight years of age, signed on as second mate; Stephen, a happy-go-lucky twenty-year-old from Dundee was to act as third mate.

In the engine-room the second, Buddle, a fine-drawn Cornishman, with delicate hands and an intelligent face, was the first to join Wyld, followed by Grinstead, the third, a burly South African, older than most of the others, a man of great experience.

Both officers and crew were delighted when chief steward Meeks joined the ship, for this imperturbable Lancashire man was one of the wits of the Eagle fleet and generally popular.

Forty-eight hours after *Ohio* had been transferred to British registry her crew was completed. The ship's company numbered seventy-seven men, an almost unprecedented number for a tanker of this size, and it included no fewer than twenty-four naval and army ratings to serve the guns.

The ship then moved to King George's Dock and

was moored under the big crane there. At once a new armament was placed aboard and fitted. This, too, was significant. Besides the 5-inch gun aft and the 3-inch gun in the bows for anti-aircraft defence, both of which had been fitted in America, a 40 mm. army Bofors quick-firing gun was bolted to a strong point just abaft the funnel and six 20 mm. naval Oerlikons were placed at suitable points round the ship. This was quite a heavy anti-aircraft armament and quite unknown in merchant ships at that period of the war. Half the Oerlikons were manned by the Maritime Regiment of the Royal Artillery and the Royal Navy and the remainder were the responsibility of the crew. Two of the guns on the bridge top were manned by apprentices who thoroughly enjoyed this unusual opportunity to run a real shooting gallery.

By this time speculation on what was to come had reached a high pitch and the most extraordinary rumours were current. No one, however, knew for certain although Captain Mason had heard a whisper that Malta was to be their destination.

The day after the guns had been fitted the captain was resting in his cabin when there was a tap on the door. A fresh-faced naval lieutenant of about twenty-five entered.

"Denys Barton, sir. I'm reporting for duty. I'm your liaison officer, I'm afraid."

Mason noted with approval the firm mouth relieved by lines of humour. Barton was obviously nervous and still standing to attention.

"For God's sake sit down, man, you're in the

Merchant Navy now," said Mason. " What do you know ? Where are we going ? "

Barton had not long returned from the Eastern Mediterranean after serving aboard an anti-aircraft cruiser. After seven of the sixty days' leave for which he was due had passed, he had received a cryptic order to report to the Admiralty and was told simply to go to Glasgow and join *Ohio*.

He shrugged his shoulders : " Search me," he said. " They never tell you anything at the Admiralty. I suppose we shall know soon enough."

As he spoke the cruiser *Nigeria* could be seen coming to anchor out in the Clyde. They were soon to know the full hazard of their mission.

CHAPTER FIVE

PEDESTAL PLANNED

AFTER THE disastrous failure of the mid-June convoy considerable doubt was expressed as to whether it was worth while attempting to supply Malta further. It was questioned if the Island could hold out on the meagre supplies rescued from " Harpoon-Vigorous " until another convoy could be organised ; and if it was possible at all for any convoy to fight through sufficient supplies to build up stocks to a point at which surrender would not be inevitable.

Running a convoy in the brilliance of a Mediterranean moonlit period was to court inevitable disaster and this limited any operations in the immediate future to the moonless period in July or August between the 10th and 16th of those months.

July was out of the question. The tanker *Ohio* could not be fitted out in time, moreover "Harpoon-Vigorous" had shown that only the most careful planning would be likely to achieve any measure of success, and this would be impossible before the July period. A much heavier escort would be needed than in June, and the requisite heavy units of the fleet which would have to take part could not be assembled in time. Could Malta hold out till August ?

The arrival of a more optimistic appraisal of the situation from Lord Gort, estimating a Target Date in September for the exhaustion of supplies, settled the matter.

Churchill and the Defence Committee were determined to try once more to save the Island fortress, and orders were immediately issued for the planning of the great Malta convoy.

The suspension of the North Russian convoys had enabled the Admiralty to draw upon the Home fleet for this operation, so for once there was no great shortage of ships. So that nothing should be lacking to ensure some success for the convoy, all resources and facilities at the Admiralty were placed at the disposal of the Flag Officer who was to command the operation.

The man to whom the responsibility of this great venture fell was a young, clean-shaven South African, Vice-Admiral Sir Neville Syfret, who had succeeded Admiral Sir James Somerville, commanding Force H, the fleet normally operating from Gibraltar in the Western Mediterranean and in the Eastern Atlantic.

Admiral Syfret was on his way home from the successful capture of Diego Suarez, the French colony on the island of Madagascar, when he received a signal to proceed at once to London.

Discussions at the Admiralty were attended also by Rear-Admiral A. L. St. G. Lyster, who was to command the carrier force and by Rear-Admiral H. M. Burrough. Admiral Burrough, who had commanded the escort of the successful September convoy to Malta in the previous year, was entrusted with the most difficult job of all, namely the close escort of the merchant vessels throughout their hazardous voyage.

The broad plan which they had been ordered to implement was to escort a fleet of fourteen merchant vessels, including the *Ohio*, from the west to Malta. The War Cabinet had considered sending another convoy through from the east, but this had finally been vetoed. As the previous June convoy had abundantly illustrated, " Bomb Alley " between Crete and the North African shore, now largely in the hands of the Germans, was suicidal. Not only did the Axis possess almost complete command of the air over this long sea corridor, but the Italian fleet could here concentrate forces superior to any which could be gathered for convoy escort at Alexandria.

The convoy from the west, then, was to be prosecuted relentlessly, with the acceptance of great danger of naval loss, and the determination of the War Cabinet to drive it through irrespective of risk can be measured by the fact that they even considered sending the whole fleet through to Malta.

This plan was finally abandoned owing to the almost certain loss of too great a proportion of heavy fleet units in the " Narrows."

The " Narrows " constituted the gravest problem and the greatest difficulty to the planning and execution of the operation. In fact, this channel between Sicily and Cape Bon, on the African shore, bedevilled the planning of all Malta convoys from the west. It is less than 100 miles wide and obstructed at the western end by the Skerki Bank, an area of shallows.

At the eastern end, the Italian occupied island of Pantelleria was a formidable fort which divided the
" Narrows " in two. Two courses only were therefore
open to the planners. The first lay south of the Skerki
Bank and round Cape Bon on the edge of French
North African territorial waters where the Italians had
hitherto laid no mines, then well south of Pantelleria
before turning east to Malta. The second involved
sailing north of the Skerki Bank and then down the
south-west coast of Sicily where Axis coastwise shipping
had prohibited the use of mines.

Either course entailed big risks, particularly to
capital ships which were unable to manœuvre in these
narrow confines ; and, owing to the ease with which
the Axis could defend such restricted waters, any fleet
of ships, large or small, could expect odds heavily
weighted against them.

The second course was the shortest but by far the most
dangerous, lying as it did within a few seconds, flying
of the Sicilian air bases. Admiral Burrough suggested
following this bold course, for it had paid him well on
the previous occasion in September, when only one
ship of the convoy had been lost. The others, however,
considered that such surprise tactics were not likely to
succeed more than once, and the first course by way
of Cape Bon was decided upon.

Against any threat by the Italian fleet to bar the
convoy's course in the Western Mediterranean the
battleships *Nelson* (wearing the flag of Admiral Syfret)
and *Rodney* were to form the principal part of the covering
force, called Force Z. These two major fleet units of the

same class were the most powerful of the older battleships in the British Navy, displacing nearly 34,000 tons each, and each armed with nine 16-inch guns, twelve 6-inch guns and heavy anti-aircraft protection. Both carried 14-inch armour plating.

The chief difference from the June convoy lay in the very heavy support given by no less than three aircraft carriers. " Harpoon-Vigorous " had shown that unless strong fighter protection could be given to the fleet heavy losses would inevitably result from the strengthened enemy squadrons stationed in Sardinia and Sicily. The old carriers used in the June convoy had, moreover, proved unsatisfactory owing to their lack of speed. In addition, therefore, to the old *Eagle*, a 22,000 ton heritage of the First World War, the force was stiffened with two of Britain's most modern carriers.

Completed in 1940, *Indomitable*, 23,000 tons, was the last word in aircraft carrier construction, and among the largest ships of her type afloat. *Victorious*, only a year older and displacing 23,000 tons, was an equally formidable unit. Both were capable of a speed over thirty knots and, with *Eagle*, these two fine vessels were able to put some seventy fighters into the air.

This carrier squadron itself represented a tactical revolution, for it was the first time that three such valuable ships had operated together.

Three cruisers, *Phoebe, Sirius* and *Charybdis*, were also to accompany Force Z. These ships belonging to the Dido class had all been completed early in the War, and carried a strong anti-aircraft armament in addition to ten 5.25-inch guns each and six 21-inch torpedo tubes.

Though lightly armoured they could call upon a speed of thirty-three knots despite their displacement of 5,450 tons.

Force Z was to be screened by fourteen destroyers of the Nineteenth flotilla commanded by Captain R. M. J. Hutton in *Laforey*. This included six modern destroyers of over 1,800 tons, each armed with six 4.7 guns and also 4-inch A.A. armament.

Close escort for the convoy was to be supplied by Force X commanded by Rear-Admiral Burrough of the Tenth cruiser squadron.

The squadron consisted of *Nigeria*, wearing Admiral Burrough's flag, and *Kenya*, both built in 1939, capable of thirty-three knots with a displacement of 8,000 tons, and a primary armament of twelve 6-inch guns and eight 4-inch A.A. guns; *Manchester*, 9,400 tons, two years older and armed with twelve 6-inch guns; and the 4,000 ton *Cairo*, an old ship reconditioned in 1939 as an anti-aircraft cruiser mounting eight 4-inch A.A. guns.

They were to be accompanied by the Sixth destroyer flotilla, commanded by Acting Captain R. Onslow in the Tribal class destroyer *Ashanti* with an armament of six 4.7-inch guns and two 4-inch A.A. guns, and ten other destroyers.

The strong force of cruisers which was thus to accompany the convoy through the " Narrows " to Malta also represented a lesson learned from the June attempt, and this time the Italian Navy would not be able to attack them with impunity after the main force had turned back.

After considerable discussion, it was decided that Force Z should return westward on reaching the Skerki Bank, the last position at which the main fleet could manœuvre safely.

This vital moment of the operation was timed for 7.15 p.m. on the 12th August when dusk would fall over the Mediterranean. This would enable Force X to pass through the most dangerous part of the Sicilian channel in darkness. For the convoy and her close escort the most dangerous time would be at dawn on the 13th, when the most favourable circumstances for an attack by the Italian fleet would exist. By then, however, long-range air cover could be expected from Malta, and this would increase as the convoy progressed to the eastward. To obtain the maximum co-operation from the Malta-based aircraft, both *Nigeria* and *Cairo* were fitted with very high frequency radio telephone, over which the escort could talk to and direct the pilots.

During the passage from the Straits of Gibraltar, which were to be passed at midnight on the 10th, the chief danger was from enemy aircraft, but it was hoped that the formidable anti-aircraft protection afforded by the combined fleet and the strong fighter escort which the carriers were capable of putting up would be sufficient to repel the fiercest enemy attacks.

Eight submarines were also to take part in the operation. Two were to patrol to the north of Sicily off Palermo and Milazzo, while the other six were given patrol lines south of Pantelleria, which they were to take up at dawn on the 13th August. As the convoy passed their patrol lines the submarines were to proceed on the surface to act as a screen. It was hoped that they might be spotted by enemy aircraft and that reports of their position would deter the Italian fleet from setting out. If the Italian fleet was sighted the submarines were allowed complete freedom of action and were ordered to attack the Italian battleships and cruisers.

Fleet, convoy and escort, when together were referred to as Force F.

At the last minute, wastage of Spitfires at Malta began to cause alarm and another operation known as " Bellows " was arranged. *Furious*, the 22,400 ton aircraft carrier, was to accompany the fleet until within about 550 miles of Malta when she would fly thirty-eight Spitfires off to join the Island's defence.

Arrangements were also made for refuelling the lighter escort ships both from tankers at sea in the Mediterranean and from Gibraltar.

Although a break-through to Malta from Alexandria was now considered too dangerous, two dummy operations were to be mounted from there in the hope of preventing the enemy from throwing the full weight of his surface and air forces against the main convoy from the west. Admiral Harwood had orders to put to sea with three cruisers, ten destroyers and three merchant ships on the 10th August, and to sail in the direction of Malta. The day after, Admiral Vian, with two cruisers, five destroyers and one merchant ship was to sail from Haifa. After joining up, the two forces were to proceed towards the west until dusk on the 11th, when they were to turn back and disperse.

The Royal Air Force at Malta, commanded by Air

Vice-Marshal Sir Keith Park, with reinforcements from the United Kingdom and from Egypt, were now able to put 136 fighters (apart from the reinforcement from " Bellows ") and thirty-eight bombers and torpedo bombers into the air in support of " Operation Pedestal." Another sixteen aircraft were available for spotting purposes. These aircraft had been allotted a number of different duties.

The torpedo-striking force was to be held to intercept the Italian fleet if it left Taranto to attack the convoy. The remaining aircraft were to combat enemy air forces from Sicily, Sardinia and Pantelleria. Their duties were first and foremost shadowing enemy fleet movements, then protecting " Pedestal ", destroying the enemy's surface fleet if it put to sea, and also bombing enemy aircraft on the ground. Liberators, based in the Middle East, were also to take part in these spoiling bombing raids.

While the orders were being made out to implement these naval plans, the Ministry of War Transport was gathering a fleet of some of the best cargo ships afloat. Three of the largest, *Empire Hope*, 12,700 tons ; *Wairangi*, 12,400 tons ; and *Waimarama*, 11,100 tons, belonged to the Shaw Savill & Albion Co., Ltd., of London. These ships had been designed for the South African run, to carry both cargo and passengers, and were all exceptionally fast. There were also two Blue Star cargo liners, *Melbourne Star*, 12,800 tons ; and *Brisbane Star*, 11,100 tons. *Dorset*, a 10,600 tonner, came from the Federal Steam Navigation Co., Ltd., and the 9,000 ton *Glenorchy* from the Glen Line Ltd., the big Scottish firm. Four others, though smaller, were among the fastest and best-equipped vessels in the British Mercantile Marine. They were *Port Chalmers*, 8,500 tons, belonging to the Port Line Ltd. ; the Union Castle mail ship *Rochester Castle*, 7,800 tons ; the Blue Funnel Line's *Deucalion*, 7,500 tons ; and the Scottish *Clan Ferguson*, 7,300 tons.

The United States contributed two of their most modern merchantmen to the convoy, besides *Ohio*. Both were leased for the occasion to the Ministry of War Transport. They were the 8,300 ton Grace Line *Santa Elisa*, and *Almeria Lykes*, 7,700 tons, belonging to Lykes Brothers Steamship Company.

Unlike *Ohio*, these ships retained their American officers and men, who were to fight valiantly beside their British allies during the course of the convoy.

Santa Elisa was a last-minute addition. After bringing military stores to Britain, she had partially loaded at Newport, Mon., for the return journey to America. On 16th June, however, the orders were countermanded suddenly and the cargo taken out of her. It was not until 24th June that she reloaded with a " Malta " cargo, arriving with this at Greenock to join " Pedestal " on 31st July.

Almeria Lykes had already been earmarked for the convoy when she arrived with army stores at Belfast. She loaded there without incident and proceeded to Greenock.

Most of the other vessels loaded at Gourock or Birkenhead and, with the Americans, they carried a grand total of 85,000 tons of cargo. With inevitable losses in view, the Ministry allocated a mixture of

Malta's vital needs to each ship with the exception of kerosene and fuel oil. The bulk of supplies loaded was flour, but each ship carried a percentage of petrol and aviation spirit in tins and also shells and other explosives.

Ohio sailed down to Dunglass in the Clyde and loaded 11,500 tons of kerosene and diesel fuel oils. She was the only ship carrying these supplies which were so vital to the survival of Malta.

Before she sailed, however, special strengthening was given to the tanker to protect her against the shock of bombs exploding in the sea close to her. In the previous convoy, *Kentucky* had had to be sunk with only a few hours' repair work needed on a steam-pipe, which had been broken by the force of such explosions. The Ministry was determined that this should not happen again, so *Ohio's* engines were mounted on rubber bearings, to reduce shock, and all steam pipes were supported with steel springs and baulks of timber.

While the merchant ships were gathering in the Clyde, the naval forces had already reached Scapa Flow. Admiral Syfret joined *Nelson* there on the 27th July and held a final conference with Flag and Commanding Officers on the 29th, at which arrangements for the operation were gone through in detail. Orders were then given for the fleet to proceed to the mouth of the Clyde to pick up the convoy.

CHAPTER SIX

WE SHALL NOT FAIL . . .

CAPTAIN Mason of *Ohio*, or *O.H.*10 as the new crew persisted in calling her, climbed the gangway of the cruiser *Nigeria* followed by Lieutenant Denys Barton, his naval liaison officer.

All leave had been stopped on that day, 2nd August, and the convoy conference they were about to attend would end all rumours and speculations. After two weeks of waiting they would be told the worst or the best of their mission.

They were shown into the aircraft hangar of the cruiser, a large bare box of steel perched high up amidships. On chairs set out on the armour-plated deck the masters, and liaison and radio officers of the convoy were shifting impatiently and whispering to one another in low voices.

As they sat down at the rear of the throng, Barton nudged his new captain (he had just been signed on in *Ohio* as a deck-hand at a wage of a shilling a month, to satisfy Board of Trade rules).

" Is it going to be South Africa, then ? " he whispered, pointing to the blackboard on which the convoy number was set out—" WS21S." The convoy prefix " WS," nicknamed " Winston's Specials," stood for the South

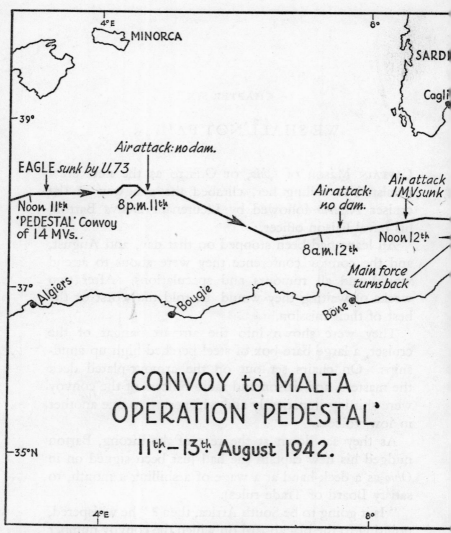

CONVOY to MALTA OPERATION 'PEDESTAL'
11th – 13th August 1942.

4°E
MINORCA
8°
SARDI
Cagli
39°
Air attack: no dam.
EAGLE *sunk by U.73*
Air attack: no dam.
Air attack 1 M.V sunk
Noon 11th
8p.m.11th
8a.m.12th
Noon 12th
'PEDESTAL' Convoy of 14 MVs.
Main force turns back
37°
Algiers
Bougie
Bone
35°N
4°E
8°

This map is reproduced from *The Navy at War, 1939-45* by Captain S. W. Roskill, R.N.

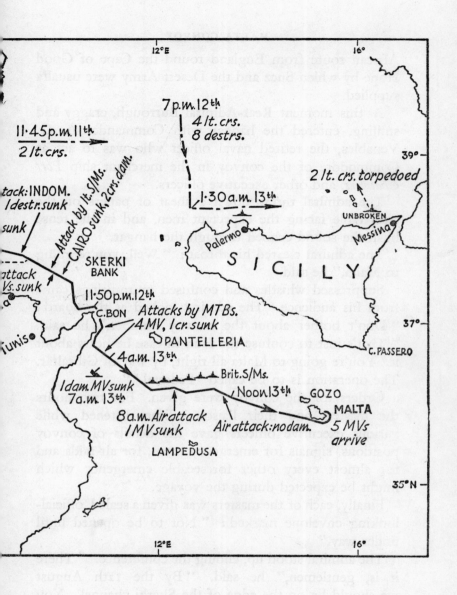

11·45 p.m. 11th
2 lt. crs.

7 p.m. 12th
4 lt. crs.
8 destrs.

2 lt. crs. torpedoed

UNBROKEN

Messina

...tack: INDOM.
1 destr. sunk

...sunk

Attack by lt. S/Ms.
CAIRO sunk, 2 crs. dam.

1·30 a.m. 13th

Palermo

S I C I L Y

...attack
...Vs. sunk

...a

SKERKI
BANK

11·50 p.m. 12th

C. BON

Attacks by MTBs.
4 MV, 1 cr. sunk

37°

...iunis

PANTELLERIA

C. PASSERO

4 a.m. 13th

Brit. S/Ms.

1 dam. MV sunk
7 a.m. 13th

Noon 13th

GOZO

MALTA

8 a.m. Air attack
1 MV sunk

Air attack: no dam.

5 MVs
arrive

LAMPEDUSA

35° N

African route from England round the Cape of Good Hope by which Suez and the Desert Army were usually supplied.

At this moment Rear-Admiral Burrough, craggy and smiling, entered the hangar with Commander A. G. Venables, the retired naval officer who was to act as Commodore of the convoy in the merchant ship *Port Chalmers*, and other executive officers.

The admiral threw down a sheaf of papers on the steel table facing the expectant men, and in the tense hush the sound echoed through the hangar.

The admiral cleared his throat : " Well, you're going to Malta," he said.

Suppressed whistles and confused murmurings came from his audience. The admiral looked at the board : " Don't bother about the convoy number," he said. " That's just to confuse the Hun in case he hears about it. You're going to Malta all right, by way of Gibraltar. The operation is to be called ' Pedestal.' "

Orders for the convoy were given. For two hours the masters and their liaison officers listened while various executive officers gave the details of convoy positions, signals for emergency turns, for air-raids and for almost every other foreseeable emergency which might be expected during the voyage.

Finally, each of the masters was given a sealed, official-looking envelope marked : " Not to be opened until under way."

The admiral stood up, ending the conference. " There it is, gentlemen," he said. " By the 12th August we should be on the edge of the Skerki channel. You know what the 12th is. That's the day grouse shooting starts and we should have plenty of birds in the Mediterranean."

The admiral raised his hand and the burst of laughter died.

" We sail to-night, so it's time you went aboard," he said. " That's the lot . . . except, good luck."

With a sharp tattoo of boots on the steel deck the seamen bustled to the door, red, sun-burned faces animated with excitement and enthusiasm. They might have been schoolboys off for the holidays rather than commanders of vital ships in what, at best, was bound to be a grim and hazardous enterprise.

Soon the waters of the Clyde were busy with the picket boats, launches and other craft taking them back to their ships.

Aboard *Ohio*, the officers had somehow contrived to be loitering near the gangway when Captain Mason and Lieutenant Barton returned.

" Well, where is it to be ? " asked the first officer as they strolled towards the bridge. Mason grinned. " Malta, I'm afraid," he said.

Two minutes later the tale was all round the ship.

At 8 p.m. that evening, two hours before dusk, the convoy sailed. Slowly and hesitantly at first, with some manœuvring, the fourteen ships, led by H.M.S. *Nigeria*, formed up. It was dark by the time they reached the open sea.

As the light grew in the east next day, a memorable sight greeted the watches on duty. On both sides of the convoy, strung out in two long lines, the grey shapes of warships heaved in the light swell of the Irish Sea. There were destroyers and cruisers, and away astern the two great " battle wagons," *Nelson* and *Rodney* followed sedately like governesses behind a school crocodile. Overhead Sunderland aircraft of R.A.F. Coastal Command weaved to and fro scanning the seas for enemy submarines.

On board *Ohio* the men were getting used to their new quarters. The comparative luxury of the American way of life afloat after the austerity of ships of their own Lines was still the subject of awed comment. The petty officers' and crew's messrooms seemed palatial. Since the British crew had also " inherited " the stores on board, the feeding too attained a peak of unaccustomed excellence. At their first meal aboard they stared in unbelieving amazement at the row of eleven varieties of sauces on the mess table.

In the second dog watch that day, all hands were called to the crew messroom over the communications system.

When they had settled themselves, Captain Mason held up a letter bearing the Admiralty crest, the " sealed orders " he had received at the end of the convoy conference.

" This letter, men, is from the First Lord of the Admiralty, Mr. A. V. Alexander," he said. " I'll read it to you."

It read : " Before you start on this operation the First Sea Lord and I are anxious that you should know how grateful the Board of Admiralty are to you for undertaking this difficult task. Malta has for some time been in great danger. It is imperative that she should be kept supplied. These are her critical months, and we cannot fail her. She has stood up to the most violent attack from the air that has ever been made ; and now she needs your help in continuing the battle. Her courage is worthy of yours.

"We know that Admiral Syfret will do all he can to complete the operation with success, and that you will stand by him according to the splendid traditions of the Merchant Navy. We wish you all Godspeed and good luck."

Without further introduction, the captain told them much of what had passed at the convoy conference the day before. Then he detailed gun and ammunition parties which had been arranged so that twenty-eight gunners from the crew would be on call at any time of the day or night.

When the orders had been given, he paused, packed up his papers and then turned again to the crew.

"You men have been specially chosen for this voyage," he said. "You probably wouldn't choose it yourself, but just remember that you are chosen men. I want no dodgers, no questions asked when an order is given. If you are called upon to do extra duties just remember this is a special voyage and one of enormous importance. I don't expect it's going to be a picnic, but just look outside and you'll see the sort of escort we've got. We're not going to have any trouble getting there— there might be a raid or two—but just remember : we're going to get there.

"I've no doubt whatsoever that you will keep up

the traditions of the Merchant Service, if the occasion demands. I have the utmost faith in you all."

Captain Mason watched them as they filed out to their various duties. He knew by the ragged cheering which had followed his talk, by the mock humorous misery, the jokes and above all the easy confidence with which his words had been received, that he had a good crew. These men would not let him down in an emergency. The naval and military gunners who had been put aboard for the trip were a tough, reliable-looking lot. The army Bofors crew, he had heard, had escaped from Dunkirk as a team and were still together.

The convoy was now steaming in fog and *Lamerton*, a destroyer, was damaged in collision and had to return to port. Later that day there was another accident. A Sunderland flying boat, appearing suddenly out of the fog, was taken as hostile and shot down into the sea where it blew up. The destroyer *Ledbury* raced to the spot and many of her crew went over the side in an effort to rescue the airmen. Only one was alive when he was brought aboard.

There were no other untoward incidents in the voyage down to Gibraltar, but day after day the ships of the convoy were kept drilling and manœuvring in preparation for the dangers to come, while the anti-aircraft gunners were long at practice.

Most of the masters and mates were accustomed to wallowing along in convoy at eight to ten knots and, at first, they felt some trepidation about carrying out complicated convolutions at sixteen knots. A day of trials, however, reassured them.

For the first time, in " Operation Pedestal " no effort had been spared to concert the movements of the merchant ships. A naval signalling staff of three had been allocated to each vessel. Previously a Watch officer had been expected to decode a string of flags while trying to avoid a destroyer racing out to depth-charge a submarine or keep clear of other ships scattered by a bombing raid. It had often proved too much for him. The merchant ships now were also able to talk to each other and to the Commodore of the convoy over a short-range radio telephone. By this means also they would receive early warning of any attack and this assurance built up considerable confidence. Usually the first thing a convoy captain knew about any unexpected happening, or an emergency, was when the death-charges started to explode, or worse, the ship was torpedoed.

By the time the convoy had drawn abreast of the coast of Spain the ships were manœuvring with speed and ease. Their efficiency drew forth the comment from Admiral Burrough that their zig-zags and emergency turns had the efficiency of a fleet unit.

In the merchantmen, the men not engaged in routine duties about the ship were busy preparing for action, for there were many minor details to be attended to.

Aboard *Ohio*, for instance, Pumpman Collins, who had been detailed as a spotter and an ammunition supply man to the Bofors emplacement, found that there was no means of hoisting ammunition up to the gun. So he constructed a hoist out of piping which looked just like an old-fashioned gibbet. He was christened " The Hangman " after that.

Before fleet and convoy entered the Straits of Gibraltar on the 10th, another operation had been planned called " Berserk." This was nothing less than a combined manœuvre of the convoy and the full fleet, under the same conditions which they might expect to meet in the Mediterranean. It began with trials for the aircraft carriers out in the Atlantic. As this was the first time as many as three carriers had operated as a squadron, it was considered that the benefits of a period working together would far outweigh any danger of the enemy being alerted by the increase in wireless telegraphy and the very high frequency telephony necessary.

Rear-Admiral Lyster sailed in *Victorious* on the 31st July with *Sirius, Argus* and four destroyers from Scapa Flow to rendezvous with *Eagle* and *Charybdis* from Gibraltar. *Indomitable* with *Phoebe* joined the squadron from Freetown. For two days the three giant capital ships raced in consort through sharp Atlantic seas manœuvring and flying off aircraft. The naval pilots were also practised in flying high and low cover patrols and in landing on the carriers in conditions of dusk and darkness. When the operation had been completed to Admiral Lyster's satisfaction the squadron turned to join Admiral Syfret's force and the convoy west of Gibraltar.

Early on the 9th the carriers with their escort were sighted by the convoy and immediately stations were taken for a final tactical practice.

First of all fleet and convoy formed up in the cruising dispositions which would be employed from Gibraltar to the " Narrows." The merchant ships sailed in four

columns, six cables—three-quarters of a mile—apart.
The anti-aircraft cruiser *Cairo* led them and *Kenya*
brought up the rear with *Nigeria* and *Manchester* flanking
the merchant ships of the two wing columns.

The battleships, *Rodney* and *Nelson* were placed on
each side of the rear ships in the convoy. Two of the
Hunt-class destroyers were stationed on either beam
to provide close anti-aircraft defence.

A destroyer screen of twenty ships was cast completely
round the convoy at a distance of about two miles with
two reserve destroyers in the rear to fill gaps caused by
destroyers leaving the screen to investigate submarine
contacts.

The four aircraft carriers (*Furious* had joined Admiral
Syfret on the 7th) operated independently inside the
screen each with an escort of one unattached destroyer.
In the event of any of them having to leave the screen
to fly off or take in aircraft two of the nearest destroyers
were ordered to augment their escort. *Victorious*, whose
fighters were mostly the slower Fulmars, was responsible
for providing low cover over the fleet. *Indomitable* and
Eagle with Hurricanes and Martlets flew a high cover
at 20,000 feet, and each carrier was responsible for
supplying its own protective air patrol. During the
Mediterranean passage these were to be maintained from
dawn to dusk.

In this order, fleet and convoy carried out emergency
turns, zig-zag patterns and other group movements
while Fleet Air Arm aircraft made practice more realistic
by carrying out dummy attacks from all quarters.

The merchantmen and Admiral Burrough's close escort

then went through the tricky operation of moving into two columns, a manœuvre which would be necessary on passing into the Skerki channel. It was carried out with complete precision. Then, with a cruiser ahead and astern of each line of merchant ships, four destroyers ahead and one astern, and three on either quarter, convoy and escort proceeded to carry out various forms of evasive action. Moving into a single line of convoy was also tried with good results.

Selected types of the aircraft used by the carriers were then flown slowly over the convoy so the gunners would have an opportunity to recognise them again even in the heat of action.

The final tests having been carried out satisfactorily, many of the smaller naval ships left for Gibraltar to refuel.

As a last reminder of the vital importance of their mission, Admiral Syfret sent the following signal to all ships : " The garrison and people of Malta, who have been defending their island so gallantly against incessant attacks by the German and Italian air forces, are in urgent need of replenishments of food and military supplies.

" These we are taking to them and I know that every officer and man in the convoy and its escort will do his utmost to ensure that they reach Malta safely.

" You may be sure that the enemy will do all in his power to prevent the convoy getting through and it will require every exertion on our part to see that he fails in his attempt. During the next few days all ships will be in the first and second degree of readiness for long periods. When you are on watch be especially vigilant and alert, and, for that reason, when you are off duty, get all the sleep you can.

" Every one of us must give of his best. Malta looks to us for help. We shall not fail them."

With these words to occupy their minds, the men of fleet and convoy set course for Gibraltar just as night fell to hide them from the prying eyes of the enemy.

The final bid to save Malta had begun.

CHAPTER SEVEN

THE AXIS PREPARES

ON THE night of 10th August, the convoy with the supporting fleet passed into the Mediterranean in three groups. As they approached the Straits of Gibraltar in the dusk a thick white fog began to form and hopes were high that this, the mightiest fleet ever to sail to Malta, might be well set upon its journey before the Axis was aware of its presence.

As the warships and the attendant merchantmen sailed blind upon a course taking them between the Rock of Gibraltar and Cape Spartel on the African coast, scores of will-of-the-wisp lights began to appear ahead, diffused into soft balls of luminescence by the fog.

Soon the British ships were passing between these lights, and it could be seen that they were Spanish fishing vessels strung out across the Straits. These boats, with their up-curving bows, each with its spluttering naptha flare at night, were a common sight in the Mediterranean. But was it by chance that on this of all occasions, when a rare fog hid the Straits from watchers on the shore, that they were conveniently placed so as not to miss any number of ships entering the Mediterranean? It was probably an unfortunate coincidence, but Admiral Syfret noted in his log that the enemy would probably be notified of his passage by their agents in Spain.

News of the convoy did in fact quickly reach Germany from across the Pyrenees. Throughout the war, a mass of information passed to and fro between Madrid and Berlin, not only through an efficient system of German agents in Spain, but even from official Spanish sources via the German Legation.

This network had been created by that enigmatic figure Admiral Canaris, head of the German Abwehr or Secret Service. The admiral had close and intimate dealings with many prominent Spaniards and visited the country frequently until 1943, when British pressure (and Allied successes) succeeded in having him barred from crossing the frontier.

Canaris knew Franco and dealt regularly with him through the dictator's brother-in-law, Suner. He was also a personal friend of his opposite number in Spain, General Vignon, and of the shipping magnate Baron de Sacrelirio.

So it had not been difficult to establish at Algeciras early in the war a special observation post manned by German Abwehr agents. This worked solely on behalf of the German Navy, observing Allied ships moving through the Straits and operating in and out of Gibraltar.

There were also other German agents near Gibraltar at the time. At Huelva, for instance, a particularly active one was known to British counter-espionage. Between them all an incredible amount of valuable naval information was gathered and transmitted to the Fatherland, particularly from Spaniards who went to work each day on the Rock, returning home at night to Spanish territory.

Despite attempts to mislead spies by dummy movements of ships, little went unnoticed.

A party of young naval officers from Gibraltar, for instance, was dining in Algeciras one night. At the table next to them, another gay gathering from the German Embassy was enjoying neutral hospitality and perhaps a more than prudent amount of Spanish champagne. As the British rose to leave, one of the Germans smiled and said in broken English: "To-morrow we see you. You sail out and you sail back, you sail out and you sail back. Then you truly sail out and don't come back. Then we go out and get you."

Since a large number of the shorter-endurance warships taking part in "Operation Pedestal" refuelled at Gibraltar, it was hardly likely that this greatly increased activity would have passed unnoticed.

In fact, enemy records show that vague information about the convoy reached Admiral Weichold, the German Naval Commander-in-Chief, Mediterranean, as early as the end of July. He had been informed by Intelligence that a "large-scale Allied operation was about to break into the Mediterranean. Large merchant ships and fleet units were being fetched from far and wide in preparation."

As early as 4th August, it was known that at least one aircraft carrier was joining the convoy as a protection against submarines and dive-bombing attacks. At about the same time, the Italian Naval High Command came to the conclusion from intercepted reports that the British were preparing an important Mediterranean operation.

This intelligence must have been partly based on the activities of the convoy and escorting fleet as it was approaching Gibraltar on 9th August, when dummy attacks were carried out on the fleet by fleet fighters followed by a fly past of all carrier-borne aircraft to help the convoy gunners to identify them during the following action. This was the first time that so many carriers had operated in company at sea and a great deal of wireless telegraphy and plain language wireless telephony resulted. That much of this would be picked up by the enemy listening stations was not lost on the Admiralty planners, but the risk was accepted and subsequent events showed that it was more than compensated for by the benefit derived by the convoy and carriers from the practice.

The first definite news of the assembling of a convoy reached the Italian Navy on the same day from an agent in Ceuta.

It seems possible however that news of the preparation of a Malta convoy had reached the enemy before the British ships had even left Britain.

The suggestion that there had been a serious leakage of information from the United Kingdom was made by Admiral of the Fleet Lord Cork and Orrery, in the House of Lords on 14th October, 1942. He said he had been told that some of the cargo loaded on the public docks had been labelled " Malta." Though a subsequent inquiry by the Ministry of War Transport seems to have been inconclusive, two naval officers taking part in the " Pedestal " convoy drew the attention of the Admiralty to loopholes in the security arrangements.

In his report of the operation, Lieutenant-Commander S. W. F. Bennets pointed out that charts of the Mediterranean were openly issued to H.M. ships before the convoy sailed from England and that the destination, Malta, had been a free topic of public house conversation.

The convoy commodore sailing in *Port Chalmers*, Commander A. G. Venables, also reported that security had in his opinion been weak. He suggested that a smaller convoy, apart from greater ease in manœuvring, would have enabled leakages of information during loading to have been suppressed. " I joined *Port Chalmers* at Liverpool," he wrote, " and was astonished to be told that the ship was bound for Malta. This information was given me by the stevedores."

To some extent it was impossible to hide the destination of a convoy from stevedores. The nature of a cargo and the way it was packed could be as revealing as a clearly-written label. Human nature being what it is, even the war-long propaganda about careless talk had failed to prevent the discussion of topics of this sort.

It seems possible, therefore, that information may have been passed to the Germans from agents in Britain, and certain that by the morning of the 11th as the convoy steamed out of the fog into an empty Mediterranean, the enemy knew that it was bound for Malta and had a good estimation of its strength.

Axis naval experts were able to predict the likely course of the convoy with considerable accuracy. They had had previous experience of a large-scale British attempt to revictual Malta in the mid-June convoy. Moreover, the sea-room in the " Narrows " restricted any break-through to the Eastern Mediterranean to one of two courses : that running close to the African shore round Cape Bon or that down the north-west coast of Sicily.

The enemy rightly guessed that the " Pedestal " convoy, about which they had had so much detailed information, would use the Cape Bon route, but their final dispositions allowed for an easy switch to the more northerly route should that have been necessary.

With ample time to concert arrangements, their plans produced the best example of Italo-German co-operation ever achieved during the war in a combined operation.

Early on the 11th August the Italian submarine *Uarsceik* sighted the fleet and reported its make-up and position, then sixty miles south of Ibiza in the Balearic Islands.

By this time the Axis submarines had already taken up their patrol lines. Eighteen Italian submarines were cruising along the expected route of the convoy between the meridian of two degrees east, roughly running through Barcelona in Spain and Algiers in North Africa, and the Sicilian " Narrows."

Eight of these were spread out in search formation north-east and north-west of Algiers covering an area which ensured that the convoy would be sighted not long after its entry into the Mediterranean.

Specific orders had been given to the three German submarines available for the operation, U.33, U.73 and U.205. They were to penetrate the destroyer screen and attempt to sink the aircraft carriers. They were strung out in a line, twenty miles apart, north and south of the expected convoy route on Meridian 2° East.

The remaining ten Italian submarines were cruising in positions between Galita Island and Cape Bon, effectively corking the bottle-neck of the "Narrows."

All submarine commanders had been carefully briefed on the approximate time and position of projected air attacks on the convoy, so that they could play their part in a combined action. Before the air strikes they had been told to show themselves on the surface at a safe distance, so that the British destroyers would be tempted to break out of the screen to attack them, thus decreasing the anti-aircraft fire-power available to meet the beginning of each air attack. During and after the air attacks, they were ordered to close in again and catch the British forces when they were still spread out providing anti-aircraft cover for the convoy.

Previous experience had shown that British supply ships frequently used French territorial waters, close to the Cape Bon peninsula, as a means of breaking through the Sicilian channel. So, to close the bottle-neck still further, the Italians laid a mine barrage between Cape Bon and Kelibia. These mines were fitted with sterilisers to destroy them after an interval, so that this stretch of French waters would not permanently be endangered, for at this time Axis policy was directed towards wooing Vichy France into closer co-operation.

The Axis naval staffs were able to calculate that by the night of the 11th-12th August, whatever might remain of the convoy would have reached the area south of Cape Bon between the island of Pantelleria and the North African coast. Here they stationed a total of nineteen Italian E-boats of Nos. 2, 15, 18 and 20 Flotillas, supported by four boats of the German 3rd Flotilla.

These light unarmoured craft, carrying only torpedoes and small calibre automatic weapons, were no match for destroyers. Moreover, the force included six new E-boats of a larger design which had only entered the service a few days before and were considered to be insufficiently worked up for battle.

The Axis planning staff knew however that the British could not commit their heavy units farther east than the " Narrows " because of the restricted sea room, as previously explained, and hoped that the combined submarine and air attack would succeed in thinning down the number of lighter escorts and scattering the convoy.

It was reasonable therefore to suppose that, under cover of darkness and making use of their high speed, the E-boats would be able to deliver a shrewd blow to the disorganised fleet, a forecast which events proved to be more than justified.

The main Axis attack against the convoy was to be delivered by the Italo-German air forces, and here, too, the concerted plans met with a higher degree of success than in any other of their combined operations.

According to Admiral Weichold, German Naval Commander in Rome, the Sicilian and Sardinian aerodromes had been packed with a total of 540 serviceable aircraft. German bombers, of the II and X Luftflotte numbered 150 with fifty fighters to support them, and there were 130 Italian bombers, ninety of them torpedo-carrying, with a fighter cover of 150 machines. The remaining sixty were presumably reconnaissance machines.

Captured Italian papers suggest numbers as high as 750, but this was probably the total for the whole Mediterranean theatre as well as unserviceable machines. According to the British Admiralty, there were eighty-five aircraft on Sicily alone on 10th August; and a further sixty-four undergoing repair.

The main strikes were carefully planned for the 12th of August when the convoy would be passing between the southern-most end of Sardinia and the approaches of Sicily, and when it would still be beyond fighter cover from Malta.

The first, shortly after 9 a.m., was to be made by twenty Junkers 88s and was timed to coincide with submarine attacks.

At midday, a big effort was to be made from the Sardinian airfields with more than seventy aircraft heavily escorted by fighters. It was to combine all known forms of air attack with the addition of an Italian secret weapon which was being used for the first time. While eighteen fighter and dive-bombers made low-level attacks, ten Savoia 79 Italian bombers were to drop " Motobomba FFs " some hundreds of yards ahead of the British force. The " Motobomba FF " was a species of circling torpedo or mobile mine attached to a parachute. When it touched the water, pressure mechanism started an electrically-operated propeller which drove the mine in wide circles.

These " Motobombas " and the low level attacks were

designed to dislocate the formation of the British force and draw their anti-aircraft fire, opening up the ships to the torpedo attack which was to follow within five minutes.

These torpedo attacks by forty-two bombers were to be launched from ahead and on either side of the convoy, so that whichever way the British ships turned to " comb " (that is turning towards the direction of the attack, to present a smaller target to the torpedoes) one group of bombers would be presented with the full length of the ships.

The next stage of the strike was to consist of shallow dive-bombing by German aircraft, after which two Italian Reggione 2001s were to attack one of the aircraft carriers with two heavy anti-personnel bombs. It was hoped that these bombers, which resembled Hurricanes, would be able to approach the carrier without being fired upon and that the anti-personnel bombs with their high fragmentation would severely damage the aircraft and men crowding the flight deck during the latter part of an action.

Another secret weapon, a glider bomb launched from a special aircraft and remotely controlled by radio, was also to have been used against another carrier, but this device developed defects and could not be employed.

The Axis plan for their final air attack on the 12th was conceived so as to make the maximum use of Mediterranean dusk conditions. Planned for 6.30, a quarter of an hour after sunset, when the convoy would be bearing towards the south-east to round Cape Bon, this main strike was to be developed from ahead, out of the darkened eastern sky. While the British gunners would be hampered by the gathering darkness in this direction, the Axis pilots would see the convoy clearly silhouetted against the sunset glow in the west. Formation leaders had orders to delay their attack until these conditions gave them the maximum advantage.

The force allotted to this was the biggest to be thrown against the convoy, numbering 100 aircraft, German Junkers 87 dive-bombers and Junkers 88 bombers and Italian Savoia 79 torpedo aircraft.

The attack was to open with dive-bombing from ahead and astern of the convoy in an attempt to scatter the ships and absorb the attention of the gunners. Meanwhile, the torpedo aircraft were to deliver an attack out of the dark side of the sky, followed by shallow dive-bombing by the main force of bombers. Heavy fighter cover was to be provided, although the Axis planners hoped that by dusk most of the fleet fighters would have landed on the British carriers. As in the midday sortie, individual attacks with anti-personnel bombs were to be made on these ships.

In theory, by dawn on 13th August, a scattered, thinned-out convoy, perforce deserted by their battleships and heavy units, would lie at the mercy of the Italian fleet. With four Italian battleships and at least two cruiser squadrons at their disposal, the Axis seemed to possess a commanding position from which no element of the convoy could escape.

The planning of this naval action, however, had to be subject to the Italian shortage of oil. This lack of oil for their ships may have been one of the minor reasons behind the abandonment of operation " Hercules." Indeed, for many months, the shortage and the German inability to make it good effectively had exercised restraint on Italian naval operations, so that it had seldom been possible for them to put to sea with their entire fleet.

In January 1942, after continued appeals from the Italians, the German Supreme Command wrote to Admiral Weichold : " Italy must realise that she is continually putting forward requirements for oil fuel which cannot be met until new sources of supply are captured."

Since then, opposing two convoys had cost the Italian fleet 15,000 tons of oil, and the German admiral had advised his superiors that their ally's oil stocks were almost exhausted.

So it was that when the Italians came to plan the attack on " Operation Pedestal " they had fuel sufficient for one battleship but only for two at a pinch. They came to the conclusion that to put out against the main British Force with two battleships would be an ineffectual gesture in the face of so powerful an enemy.

This lack of the means to sail with heavy elements created great anxiety among the Axis planners lest the British should try to run through a supporting convoy from Alexandria, and it seems that had they done so it might have met with even greater success than " Pedestal," for the Italians had no means of blocking it effectively. The oil situation was, however, not known to the British.

Under the circumstances the Italians decided to sail

with two cruiser divisions, the Third and Seventh, with the object of intercepting the convoy at dawn south of Pantelleria. Consisting of the heavy cruisers *Gorizia*, *Bolzano* and *Trieste*, armed with heavy modern 8-inch main armament, the cruisers *Montecuccoli*, *Attendolo* and *Eugenio*, mounting 6-inch guns and an escort of eleven destroyers, this fleet was in a position to achieve a notable success for they outgunned, outnumbered and had the speed to outmanoeuvre the British force, once the main fleet had turned back at the " Narrows."

As soon as the convoy was reported, the two cruiser divisions with their escorting destroyers sailed from the ports of Cagliari, Messina and Naples, with orders to rendezvous 100 miles north of Marittimo.

While the convoy was steaming on towards the " Narrows " and towards the combination of sea and air attack which had been prepared for it, Kapitanleutnant Helmut Rosenbaum, commander of the German submarine, U.73, was congratulating himself on having travelled from Spezia to his patrol position off Algiers without being spotted by British aircraft. On his previous voyage, ferrying supplies to Tobruk, his 500-ton U-Boat had been caught in shallow water by the R.A.F. Hudsons and had had its stern completely shattered by a bomb. Without wireless, leaking badly and forced to remain on the surface, he had succeeded in limping 1,200 miles back to port without being caught by the British anti-submarine patrols. After that miracle it seemed that his luck still held.

His departure had scarcely been auspicious. News of the British convoy had forced him to put to sea with a leaking exhaust cut-out, an unserviceable direction-finding aerial, leaks in the main bilge pump and periscope and a slipping clutch on the main drive of the diesel engines. Now more than half his crew were ill with enteritis and unfit, in his opinion, for the perilous duty of breaking through the convoy screen and torpedoing an aircraft carrier, one of the most heavily protected units of the fleet. If only his luck would hold . . . it was his eighth patrol and at the end of it he was due for leave and the command of a new pocket submarine flotilla in the comparatively safe waters of the Black Sea.

They were lying peacefully at a depth of a hundred feet. It was the morning of the 11th August. Suddenly a voice cut into the low humming of the dynamos : " Propeller noises approaching from the westward."

Immediately, the narrow confines of the U-Boat became a scene of feverish activity. Course was changed and tanks blown until U.73 reached periscope depth heading towards the sounds they had picked up on the hydrophone listening device.

" Up periscope." Rosenbaum, his eyes pressed firmly to a small, round window on the upper world, swept the sea for a sight of the enemy. Almost immediately he picked up the masts of a destroyer about three miles away on the starboard bow. At the same moment an aircraft carrier appeared looking like " a giant match-box floating on a pond." The commander methodically counted five destroyers and other smaller ships circling round her. The carrier was travelling at about twelve knots, zig-zagging with almost right-angled turns and varying in range from the U-boat between three and five miles.

Menacing propeller noises approached and a destroyer loomed in the periscope view. Quickly he took the U.73 down to 100 feet. Then he ordered full speed, closing the aircraft carrier on an almost parallel course, and returned to periscope depth.

The aircraft carrier was last in the starboard line of the convoy escort and he identified it as *Eagle*. There were seven destroyers between him and his prey now. A dangerous moment was approaching when he would have to dive under this screen. He took another quick look and dived. Overhead the thud of propellers could be heard and he knew that the eerie bleep-bleep of the British asdic sets would be sending out fingers of sound which could locate the submarine as they rebounded from its steel hull. The next sound was most likely to be the crash of depth-charges exploding round him, the scream of the breaking hull and the inrushing of black waters.

Somehow they escaped detection. Perhaps it was one of those density layers of cold water above him which abound in the Mediterranean and which would have shielded him from the asdic's probe. Another quick look through the periscope and he was breaking through between the third and fourth destroyer with less than 400 yards to spare on either side. Still the U.73 was undetected.

Now he was making his attack run, reading off bearings as he watched through the periscope. He held his fire while the convoy passed through the circle of sea and air which his periscope covered. Then the carrier loomed, filling all his vision. He turned slightly to port holding the great ship within the crossed wires of the sight. "Fire." With shudders and sudden air pressure in the submarine, a salvo of four torpedoes, set to run twenty feet below the surface at a range of 500 yards, were on their way.

Rosenbaum gave the order to dive deeply. As they were diving to avoid the retribution which was sure to follow, they heard four muffled explosions, then a strange cracking, creaking sound and a drawn-out rending groan.

CHAPTER EIGHT

FOR WHAT WE ARE ABOUT
TO RECEIVE

SENIOR Officer Force F to Admiralty :
H.M.S. EAGLE SUNK STOP TORPEDOED BY
SUBMARINE POSITION 038 DEGREES 05 MINUTES
NORTH 003 DEGREES 02 MINUTES EAST STOP
11/8/42 END MESSAGE

One after another, at two second intervals, great
plumes of brown water had reared up, to three times the
height of *Eagle's* mainmast, as the salvo of four torpedoes
exploded along her port side.

With clouds of black smoke wreathing behind her
she dragged quickly to a stop, and as she slowed she
listed progressively farther and farther.

Within three minutes the whole of her deck could
be seen tilted at an angle of almost forty-five degrees
and toy-like aircraft began to slide and fall from her,
splashing into the sea. The tiny figures of men could
be seen clambering, slipping and sliding down the increasing angle of her decks and now half-exposed
bottom.

The destroyers *Lookout* and *Laforey* sped towards her
at thirty-one knots in a lather of white water, and the
tug *Jaunty* bore down, her crew making ready towing
gear.

With sirens roaring, fleet and convoy turned sharply to protect themselves.

Away to the left of the sinking ship, the cruiser *Charybdis* hit back. Zig-zagging over the calm waters she dropped pattern after pattern of depth-charges, the sea boiling up behind her in great geysers of white water at half-minute intervals.

But nothing could be done to aid the stricken aircraft carrier. With slow dignity the veteran warrior of a dozen Mediterranean battles rolled gently on to her side. The crackle of exploding bulkheads and tearing metal came faintly across the blue sea and then she was gone in a swirl of debris and troubled water. She had sunk in less than eight minutes, and now the sea had a film of dark oil on it speckled with the black heads of her crew, the grey life-saving rafts and the boats from the destroyers which were picking up survivors.

Of her company of 1,160, 900 were saved including her commander, Captain L. D. Mackintosh. A patrol of four of her aircraft, in the air at the time, landed on other carriers, but twenty-five per cent of the fleet's air cover had been lost.

Northward, a distant tower of cumulus cloud marked the place where the Balearic island of Majorca lay below the horizon and a deepening of the haze southward showed that here lay the low line of the North African coast and the hostile Vichy French port of Algiers. Malta still lay 550 miles distant. The sirens boomed again and the convoy, precise as guardsmen on parade, zig-zagged ninety degrees to port, away from *Eagle's* grave.

Anxious eyes again scanned the empty sea, searching for the white ribbons of torpedo tracks or the momentary feather of a periscope. Others swept the hot, hazy sky, for the hum of shadowing enemy aircraft had been with them for five hours despite everything fighters flown from the fleet carriers *Victorious, Indomitable* and *Eagle* had done to hound the snoopers.

Up to that moment " Pedestal's " passage had been almost uneventful. At first it had seemed that complete surprise had been gained.

That morning, the fog in which they had passed through the Straits, had dispersed, the brassy sun caused the slight haze to dance and a hot east wind stippled the dark blue waters with flecks of white. The visibility was alarmingly good.

At 8.15 the corvette *Coltsfoot* had reported two torpedoes porpoising harmlessly. They had been fired by the Italian submarine *Uarsceik*, which had first reported the presence of the convoy in the Mediterranean. Fifteen minutes later, radar located the first of the snooping aircraft. Carrier-borne Hurricanes and Fulmars made five interceptions, shooting down one Junkers 88 for the loss of two of our fighters.

Admiral Syfret knew for certain that his force was discovered at 10.55 a.m. when Mussolini's Rome radio broadcast details of it to all Italian stations and units.

Then out of the sea's depth had come the salvo which had sunk *Eagle*.

The sun moved overhead, dazzling the watchers, and the convoy drove on towards Malta at fifteen knots, cutting an intricate pattern of varied zig-zags.

" For what we are about to receive . . ." murmured
a Chief Yoeman aboard the flagship, unconsciously
repeating the irreverent saying of seamen about to
stand an enemy broadside in Nelson's time.

At 2.20 p.m. the men watching the crotchets of light
on the radar screen saw them suddenly lengthen in a
compact group on the southward side of their graticules.
In every ship the warning was broadcast : " Enemy
aircraft approaching from the starboard beam."

Gun mountings swung in unison as the barrels of
the anti-aircraft batteries groped skywards. The gunners
adjusted their tin helmets and waited tensely, fingering
the triggers. Perhaps this was " it."

Presently the thin drone of engines could be heard.
They seemed directly overhead. With a rending crack,
the primary anti-aircraft armament of *Nelson* and *Rodney*
opened up, firing a controlled barrage. Again and again
the guns' flashes sparkled even in the bright daylight
and the crackle of the reports smote the onlookers with
physical force.

Overhead, stars of black shell-burst dotted the sky
very high up. Except those serving the heaviest armament the gunners held their fire, for no aircraft
was visible. Evidently, the enemy was carrying out
a photographic reconnaissance. Then the battleships
fell silent and the bumbling drone drew away northwards.

Later that afternoon Admiral Syfret received the
welcome signal that " Operation Bellows " had succeeded.
Thirty-six Spitfires had landed in Malta.

The flying off of these aircraft from *Furious* had been

interrupted by the sinking of *Eagle*. Then the remainder of the Spitfires had been launched. One, which developed engine trouble, landed on *Indomitable*.

Furious then stood back to Gibraltar with her escort and success remained with her. *Wolverine*, one of her screen of destroyers, rammed and sank the Italian submarine *Dagabur* on the way.

The afternoon waned away and the blue of the waters deepened. The sun approached the sea, a red ball in a haze of violet and gold. It was almost too late for an air attack.

Vice-Admiral Commanding North Atlantic to
Senior Officer, Force F:

INTERCEPTED ENEMY WIRELESS TRAFFIC
INDICATES THAT AIRCRAFT MAY ATTACK CONVOY
AT DUSK MESSAGE ENDS

Admiral Syfret ordered the fleet to take up action stations again and the destroyers fanned away from the convoy. Then radar detected the new raid approaching.

The carriers, only two of them now, belched smoke and turned into the wind, racing away from the convoy at full speed to fly off their protecting aircraft. The gnat-like formations of fighters formed up and climbed away, glinting in the setting sun.

Then the leading destroyer on the port side of the convoy was firing with everything she had got. Cruisers, then the battleships, joined in with an inferno of shock and sound.

The convoy could see them coming now—thirty-six little cruciform shapes, Junkers 88s and Heinkel 111s with torpedoes, diving from 5,000 feet out of the blackness of approaching night. Tracers streaked. Red, green and gold, they made an umbrella of light in the dusk, picked out with the tinsel of scores of bursting shells.

Above the roar of the gunnery, the whine of aero engines rose to a tortured scream. The aircraft grew bigger and began to pull out of their dives.

A half-heard cheer sounded. A Junkers 88 came spinning down to port with both wings on fire. It had been hit by the tug *Jaunty*. Another Junkers, streaming black smoke, flattened as the automatic pull-out came into action, and crashed belly first in a flurry of spray.

Columns of sea shot into the air as the bombs landed with the heavy drumming of underwater explosions. Aircraft howled overhead, jinking and turning, followed by the turning, spitting barrels of the guns.

As the torpedo bombers turned away short of the convoy, the water creamed with torpedo tracks and the warning roar of the sirens added to the din as the warships heeled over in emergency turns followed by the convoy.

The last of the enemy aircraft skimmed overhead, living miraculously in a hail of crossfire, till a red glow lit the fuselage, and then it spun away in the gathering darkness flaming like a misdirected rocket.

Suddenly the guns stopped. The silence was almost painful. It was night now. Somehow fleet and convoy had escaped damage. The gunners removed their tin hats, blew out their cheeks and wiped the sweat from their eyes. Then they moved, stretching stiffly. The fight was over for the present.

It was a blessedly peaceful night. The hot decks cooled and while the off-duty men of fleet and convoy slept, Beaufighters and Liberators of the R.A.F. from Malta bombed and straffed the enemy aircraft at their aerodromes.

As a turquoise glow began to appear in the east, radar warned that the enemy snooping aircraft were about again and the admiral ordered the guns to a first degree of readiness.

The day began with a victory for the Fleet Air Arm.

As the convoy moved into defensive positions again and as the men snatched a hasty breakfast at action stations, a squadron of twelve fighters took off from the carrier's decks, the sun touching their wings with golden fire as they turned.

At five-past nine, the deep drone of twin-engined enemy bombers could be heard. Soon after they came into view, flying very high in close formation. The British fighters were there too, up sun of the enemy, and were diving now in line astern weaving through the enemy's ranks. The high whine of engines was followed by the distant crackle of machine-guns.

Lieutenant R. H. P. Carver, flying a Hurricane of 885 Squadron, drove into the enemy formation and attacked a Junkers 88 from astern firing burst after burst into it. It turned and dived away with its port engine smoking. The lieutenant turned his attention to another 88 and carried out a stern attack, then diving, turning and climbing he attacked it again and again from the beam. It turned over and crashed into the sea.

The other fighters, too, were attacking the formation. Two more Junkers 88s came spinning down, while another turned back towards Italy, one engine smoking. Already the enemy had begun to break up, so that when the bombs fell they were widely scattered and fell harmlessly into the sea.

Not long after the fighters were landing on the carriers again, the pilots jubilant because they had destroyed eight enemy aircraft for certain and probably three others.

Other convoy hunters were early astir. Fifteen minutes after the aircraft had been driven off *Fury*, on the starboard wing of the convoy, confirmed by asdic contact the presence of an enemy submarine. *Fury* and *Laforey* attacked, dropping pattern after pattern of depth-charges.

Two hours passed, punctuated by spasmodic firing from the screen ships as snooping aircraft ventured too near and by the occasional depth-charging of submarine contacts by the destroyers.

Then, at 11.35 a.m., the German U.205 made a determined attempt to break through the destroyer screen and attack the merchantmen.

Destroyer *Pathfinder*, steaming on the port bow of the convoy, reported the contact first and, assisted by *Zetland*, went in to the attack. Down the side of the convoy they hunted the submarine, forcing her to dive deeply, jinking desperately this way and that to avoid the underwater explosions.

Thus far no casualties had been suffered except *Eagle*, and as Admiral Burrough forecast, the shooting season had opened well; but while these attacks were being countered another was developing. At noon, another air-raid was reported coming in from ahead of the convoy. The distant smoke of falling aircraft was seen, then the destroyer *Ashanti* sighted the enemy hotly engaged by fleet fighters.

This was the major effort from the Sardinian airfields, but the first wave of ten Italian torpedo bombers, harried by the fighters, and daunted by the terrific barrage put up by the fleet, which included *Rodney's* 16-inch armament used for the first time against aircraft, failed to press home their attack.

Ahead of the convoy black canisters on parachutes could be seen falling. Some of them appeared to be exploding in the water. An officer in *Nelson* made a note in the action diary on the first use of an Italian secret weapon. "Black canisters dropped. Probably circling torpedoes."

To avoid them fleet and convoy heeled in a ninety degree emergency turn, faultlessly carried out despite dive-bombing and machine-gunning from eight fighter-bombers.

As they turned, forty-one torpedo-bombers could be seen diving in from the port bow followed by another twenty-one on the starboard. The emergency turn had exposed the full length of the ships in the fleet and convoy to at least one group of bombers.

Up came the barrage again, black and crackling in the path of the torpedo-bombers, and another emergency turn was begun. The shooting was fast and accurate and it defeated this attack too. The Italian bombers turned away dropping their torpedoes 8000 yards short, well out of range of the convoy.

Only the screen destroyers on either side were in any danger, particularly those on the port side, and they were twisting and turning as the torpedoes passed close down their sides.

Then, with the scream of dive-brakes, twenty black German Junkers 87s fell upon the British ships. Bombs whistled down and towering columns of water sprang up beside *Nelson*. The battleship rocked as they exploded not far from her keel, and *Rodney* and the cruiser *Cairo* were also narrowly missed. This time the gunners failed to protect the convoy completely.

M. V. Deucalion to Senior Officer F Force :
NEAR MISSED BY BOMBS STOP PLATES BUCKLED
UNDER STRAIN STOP NUMBER ONE HOLD HALF
FILLED WITH WATER STOP NUMBER TWO HOLD
COMPLETELY FLOODED MESSAGE ENDS

Deucalion, leading the port wing column of the convoy, rolled almost on her beam-ends as three bombs exploded alongside sending cascades of water crashing down on her foredeck. Destroyer *Bramham* sped to the merchantman's assistance. Slowly the injured ship slipped astern of the convoy, the crew working to shore up straining bulkheads, with the destroyer standing by. Then she began to steam slowly towards the African coast.

As the last of the dive-bombers was retreating, two aircraft approached Rear-Admiral Lyster's flagship,

Victorious, and no one fired on them because they looked like Hurricanes. In the admiral's own words it seemed as though they were going to land on the carrier. Then they opened their throttles and two bombs dropped. The two pilots of these Italian Reggione fighter-bombers were less fortunate than their daring warranted, for the one bomb which hit the carrier's flight-deck amidships broke up without exploding.

The gunners now had time to wipe their blackened faces again. Aboard the cruiser *Nigeria* the ship's cat came out of a hiding-place behind the main armament and fed her three kittens in the hot sun.

Fighters had destroyed nine of the enemy aircraft and the ships had shot down two, but there was no rest for the destroyers of the screen, at least ; for the following two hours brought innumerable reports of submarine sightings and asdic contacts. In a brief exchange of signals Rear-Admiral Burrough suggested dropping a depth-charge every half-hour on either side of the convoy to " discourage " the hovering U-boats, and Admiral Syfret at once made this suggestion an order.

Another message came in later that afternoon. *Bramham* reported that the fight to save *Deucalion* had failed. After two further air attacks, an aerial torpedo had hit the merchant vessel amidships and she had caught fire and blown up.

At 4.16 p.m., *Pathfinder's* brilliant team of asdic operators again reported a submarine working into an attacking position ahead of the convoy. The destroyer dashed in to counter it and two close patterns of depth-charges thundered down, apparently without result.

Twenty minutes later, the badly-shaken Italian submarine *Cobalto* bobbed suddenly to the surface close to the destroyer *Ithuriel*. With forward armament quick-firing, the destroyer bore down on the submarine and her sharp bows crunched into it behind the conning tower.

A boarding party leapt on to the outer casing of the submarine to seize her crew and papers, but before they could enter the conning tower she had already begun to sink. The boarding party just had time to pull away before she submerged for the last time. Three Italian officers, one of them the captain, and thirty-eight enemy ratings were captured. Meanwhile both *Tartar* and *Lookout* had sighted running torpedoes and carried out attacks, hounding two more U-boats until they were driven away to a safe distance. *Ithuriel*, with crushed bows, limped back to Gibraltar.

So it was that, until the fleet and convoy reached to within twenty miles of the Skerki channel, the combined enemy attacks were beaten. The destroyer screen, thanks to the unwavering skill of radar and asdic operators, had looked deep into the sea, so that swift counter-attacks had kept the U-boats at a safe distance. Despite well co-ordinated air attacks, the gunners of fleet and convoy had put up a terrific barrage, described by all who saw it as the greatest and most lethal ever experienced in the war at sea ; and this, aided by the determined onslaught of the fighter pilots, had either resulted in wild and inaccurate bombing or had pre-vented the enemy aircraft from approaching to within effective range.

For a full day, however, the British seamen had endured continual attack from sea and air in the blistering Mediterranean sun. The Axis forces were constantly being thrown into the battle in fresh relays : there was no respite for the defenders, no opportunity to relax or sleep. Even when the attacks were not pressed home, even when they didn't materialise, Axis aircraft were continually threatening, hovering and circling round the convoy and were being picked up by radar. Consequently, the crews had to be always ready to repel an attack. With a few seconds warning, or with none at all, the dive-bombers might come screaming down at them out of the sun, and then only rapid manœuvre and instantaneous barrage could save the ships from destruction. Whether by accident or design, the Axis tactics were wearing down the physical resistance of the defenders.

The gunners were half choked with cordite fumes, their senses dulled with the drumming of the barrage. The pilots of the Hurricanes and Fulmars were almost asleep in their cockpits. Deep down in the ships, the asdic and radar operators knuckled their tired, red-rimmed eyes and steeled their ears to the crash of more close bombs clanging on the hulls.

At 6.30 p.m., when the fleet altered course to steer for the Skerki channel, it was evident that the enemy were building up for another great air attack. This was to come from the strongly held enemy airfields of Sicily, now dangerously close, and it was to consist of more than 100 bombers, strongly escorted by fighters.

For nearly an hour the enemy aircraft had been

reported by radar and reconnaissance aircraft about twenty-five miles away from the convoy. Here they had been assembling, evidently to co-ordinate their attack.

Five minutes later thirteen Savoia torpedo bombers were seen diving in from ahead. Once again they were met by fierce barrage and once again they were compelled to drop their torpedoes 3,000 yards outside the screen.

Almost at the same moment, dive-bomber after dive-bomber screamed down upon the convoy from both astern and ahead.

In the pandemonium of bomb bursts, flying water and the roar of guns, the convoy began to turn to port to avoid more circling torpedoes. As they did so more torpedo-bombers could be seen attacking from the unprotected flank.

The exact sequence of the next few minutes is lost. With a brilliant flash, a torpedo hit the stern of the destroyer *Foresight*, lifting it almost out of the water, and she slewed to a stop, stern, rudder and screws all blown off. *Tartar* raced to her aid and, as both ships were rocked violently by bombs exploding nearby, a tow-line was passed. Both crews fought desperately to save her, but she was settling fast and, as she was without motive power, she had to be sunk later by her own forces as the fleet returned.

Indomitable to Senior Officer F Force :

SHIP HIT BY TWO OR THREE BOMBS DAMAGED BY

NEAR MISSES STOP PETROL FIRES ON FLIGHT DECK
MESSAGE ENDS

Though bombs were dropping among the merchantmen of the convoy and many were narrowly missed,
the main enemy attack was being concentrated upon the
carriers.

At two second intervals, forty black Stuka bombers,
their wing sirens screaming, peeled off from high above
the fleet and dived at *Indomitable*. Columns of water shot
into the air obscuring the carrier from the convoy.
Then there was a great orange flash and billows of black
smoke. Through it all the spark of the guns could be seen
firing back continually.

As the curtain of water fell again, huge fires were
burning fore and aft on the flight deck, but the guns
were still firing.

The carrier turned down-wind to the westward to
minimise the fanning of the flames. The cruiser,
Charybdis and her destroyers swept round after the
carrier to form a protective screen against other attacks.

Though blazing petrol was swilling over the decks
and cascading over the stern and beam in a fiery rain,
Lookout ran alongside and men could be seen passing
hoses on to the carrier's flight deck. Fire parties on the
carrier had also been organised and as she disappeared
astern of the convoy the fires were dying. This attack
was carried out by the cream of Kesselring's Luftwaffe.
Captain Frend of *Phoebe*, astern of *Indomitable,* reported
that the enemy aircraft had dived through the thickest
of barrages to press home the attack. They had scored

146

a notable success. Had it not been for the twenty-two British fighters, all that could be mustered to repel the attack, casualties would probably have been much heavier. Though outnumbered by enemy fighters by two to one, the Hurricanes, Martlets and Fulmars had destroyed seven of the enemy. Two more had been shot down by the ships.

Admiral Syfret now had to make a vital decision. The capital ships with their escort could not be risked in the " Narrows." Two hours previously he had sig-nalled that Force Z, with the carriers, would turn back to Gibraltar at 7.15 p.m. leaving the convoy and its escort to proceed Maltawards. Now it was 7 p.m. and the " Narrows " were less than an hour's steaming away. Should he proceed farther with the convoy until night had removed the danger of air attacks, as Admiral Curteis had done in the June convoy, or should he retire at once, shielding the damaged carrier, the speed of which had been considerably reduced ?

If he turned to the westward at once, the convoy would have to steam for two hours in daylight and twilight without the protection of the main fleet. Admiral Burrough had previously pointed out that these two hours were the most dangerous of all and the time at which the most successful air attacks were likely to be made. Admiral Burrough had also asked for some fighter protection at this period. This was now impossible. With the damage to *Indomitable* and the loss of *Eagle*, only about one-third of the fleet's protection remained. Moreover, the carriers had made a maximum effort in fighting off the last raid. In order to clear her

decks *Victorious* had had to send off a patrol of four
Fulmars which had been earmarked for the escort of
Force X. These now had to be refuelled and rearmed and
it would be impracticable to fly them off later to escort
the convoy.

The admiral also had to consider the safety of the
heavy units of the fleet under his command. He had
already received warning to expect that a large force of
enemy submarines would be waiting in the " Narrows."
With no room to manœuvre, the battleships would be
sitting targets there for the enemy torpedoes. Moreover,
the strength of the recent attack gave him cause to
hope that the enemy had expended, at least for the
moment, most of their force, and it seemed unlikely
that they could mount another large raid before night
covered the convoy.

Perhaps the hardest decision Admiral Syfret had to
take was whether or not to reinforce the convoy with
more cruisers. In the mid-June convoy, inadequate
cruiser strength with the escort, after the fleet had turned
back, had contributed to the loss of all but two of the
merchantmen. Signals already received from the R.A.F.
indicated that the Italian fleet might be at sea, although
this report was not yet confirmed, and it was possible
that early next morning Admiral Burrough's force
would be beset not only by the enemy bombers but
by a superior force of enemy ships as well. At the same
time the admiral had to consider the safety of his own
fleet and, in particular, *Indomitable*, now crippled and
making not much more than thirteen knots. If he had to
escort the carrier back to Gibraltar at slow speed, he

would need every cruiser he had to supply anti-aircraft cover.

The admiral weighed all these considerations, then made his decision. At 7 p.m., fifteen minutes before he had previously intended to leave Force X, he signalled a heartfelt " God Speed " to Admiral Burrough, and orders were given to Force Z to retire to the westward.

The battleships gathered speed, then, heeling over, turned towards Gibraltar while their screen of cruisers and destroyers closed in upon them, and they were soon disappearing into the sunset.

The convoy, shaken but intact except for *Deucalion*, plodded stubbornly towards Malta and the oncoming night.

CHAPTER NINE

DISASTER IN THE NARROWS

AXUM to CSC
SALVO SIX TORPEDOES FIRED AT CONVOY
POSITION 037 DEGREES 40 MINUTES NORTH 010
DEGREES 05 MINUTES EAST AT 1956 HOURS STOP
TWO CRUISERS AND ONE MERCHANT SHIP
BELIEVED SUNK END MESSAGE

Kenya to Admiralty:
FORCE X POSITION AT 2030 37 DEGREES 40
MINUTES NORTH 10 DEGREES 06 MINUTES EAST
STOP NIGERIA AND CAIRO TORPEDOED STOP
CONVOY PROCEEDING MALTA STOP VICE-ADMIRAL
MALTA PLEASE ARRANGE FIGHTER DIRECTION
END MESSAGE

Captain Mason, tin hat tilted backwards, peered into
the dusk from *Ohio's* bridge. He turned to the naval
liaison officer, Lieutenant Denys Barton.

" I think there are some more Jerry aircraft coming.
Listen," he said. The crew of *Ohio* already felt that
their ship, clearly recognisable as a tanker, with the
funnel so far aft, had been singled out as a target by the
German aircraft.

So far, however, they had received no more than a
wetting from near misses. The cargo upon which the
future of Malta depended was intact.

The convoy was now entering the "Narrows," and the merchant ships had slowed down to form from four into two lines.

Mason and Barton, and on the right wing of the bridge First Officer Gray and Stephen the Third, could see the cruisers moving up to their stations ahead of the convoy and destroyers forming screen in front of the cruisers.

"It's getting dark," said Mason. "I shouldn't be surprised if . . ."

A bright flash lit up the flagship *Nigeria*. Flames and smoke billowed from below the port side of her bridge. Then the force of an explosion slapped into their faces. The damaged ship slewed to starboard and began to list farther and farther until it seemed she must capsize. There was another flash and a huge geyser of water spread up at the stern of *Cairo* just ahead of them. Huge chunks of iron plate were hurled into the air.

"Hold on to your hats," shouted Stephen. "If there's another torpedo in that salvo, we've . . ."

A roar, almost soundless in its immensity, knocked them all flat on the deck. Pieces of hot metal and deluges of water rained down round them.

Instinctively Mason crawled towards the chartroom and collided at the door with Stephen.

"What's happened?" he gasped.

Fire above them was making a new daylight. Mason jumped to his feet. "We've hit a mine or something. Come on." All four officers ran towards the bridge ladder and hesitated. Behind them, from the amidships section, a huge pillar of flame leapt high into the air above mast height, sighing and howling.

Captain Mason turned and scanned the sea ahead quickly. He saw that the convoy, disorganised by the stricken cruisers which were charging across its route, was scattering in all directions. *Ohio*, too, seemed to be out of control. He grabbed the engine-room telegraph : " Shut down and come up," he ordered. " Get the deck water lines on. We're on fire."

This was probably the end. Once hit and on fire a tanker stood little chance.

As Mason slid down the bridge ladder, a flight of hostile aircraft screamed by at almost deck level and bombs thundered into the water. Another close one. A boat was being launched aft, but the guns were still firing. The gunners seemed to be ignoring the flames altogether. Other men were running towards the boats. Two were already in one. The flames seemed to die a little. Perhaps they could save her yet, but would the men rally ?

" Come out of that boat, Ginger," the captain shouted. " You're not getting among those Algerian women yet."

The men in the boat turned, looked at him for a moment, then made fast the falls. Mason realised that there would be no panic. He could hear them laughing.

" Come on. Let's get that fire out," he ordered and seized a fire-extinguisher. They streamed along the twisted cat-walks shielding their faces from the heat with their free arms.

The heat was intense, but twenty men were already fighting the fire at close quarters. The guns went on firing. Another stick of bombs crashed into the sea, sending water cascading all over the deck.

"They'll put the fire out if they're not careful," somebody panted.

Lighted kerosene was bubbling up from the fractured tanks. Little gouts of flame spattered the deck to a distance of thirty yards from the blaze.

The chief steward, Meeks, was beating them out with his cap methodically. "Like swatting flies," he said later. He had been one of the first on the scene, and had found his second steward, a green first-voyager whom he had had to chivvy remorselessly during the journey, standing virtually on top of the seat of the explosion. The boy was covered in fuel oil and dazed but miraculously preserved. "I suppose you're going to blame me for this as well," he wailed.

"Of course I shall," Meeks replied, "so you'd better come and help put it out."

The flames dipped lower and then blazed up again. There were cries for more extinguishers. The men made another charge on the wall of heat.

Meanwhile, in *Nigeria* all the lights had gone out. The steering gear had jammed, causing her to circle out of control, and throughout the ship the roar of water pouring in to her could be plainly heard.

The men began to clamber on deck ready to abandon ship. They found Admiral Burrough leaning calmly over the side of the bridge in the negligent attitude of a peace-time yachtsman on the Solent.

"Don't worry, she'll hold," said the admiral casually. "Let's have a cigarette."

That settled it; the men ran to emergency stations. Under the orders of Captain Paton gallons of water were swiftly pumped into the starboard tanks and the heavy list was soon reduced to a gentle tilt. Other parties manned the emergency steering equipment and the cruiser was brought under control again.

The admiral unhurriedly transferred his flag to the destroyer *Ashanti*, and the damaged flagship was able to proceed at fourteen knots back towards Gibraltar.

Before he left *Nigeria*, Admiral Burrough shouted a last message to the ship's company : " I hate leaving you like this, but my job is to go on and get that convoy to Malta. And I'm going to do it whatever happens." The men wanted to go on. " We'll all see it through," they shouted. The admiral shook his head. " No," he said, " your job is to stop here and get your own ship safely home." They cheered him as he went over the side.

Cairo, however, was in a desperate situation, sinking fast, and it was plain that she could not outlast the night. Orders were given to take off her crew and sink her with gunfire.

On *Ohio* the fire was under control. A hail from the port side distracted Captain Mason's attention from the blaze. He saw that the destroyer *Ashanti*, now the flagship, was gliding alongside. Admiral Burrough leaned over the bridge.

" Are you all right ? " he called.

Mason wiped the sweat from his eyes. " Fine, thanks. We can attend to this."

" Oh, good show. I'll have to be off now. Rather busy, you know," said Burrough, and the destroyer raced away again.

The captain went back to the job in hand. The amidship pump-room door had been blown open by the explosion, and regardless of flying spatters of burning paraffin he and Pumpman Collins peered in.

" More extinguishers here," the captain shouted. There was a rush of feet and the flames, fought from another quarter, began to die still further. Pumpman Collins paused for breath and glanced over at a merchant ship passing close to port (she was probably the American *Almeria Lykes*).

He nudged the Bofors gun-layer : " Look at that." A mine had caught on the cab of the bridge and was swinging gently on its parachute lines. A man was calmly sawing away at the silk strands with his clasp knife.

" If *that* mine goes up it'll blow his ruddy tin hat off," said Collins. The two men looked at each other and roared with laughter. The mine fell with a splash into the water and the man, leaning out over the side, watched it float astern. The fire in the pump-room was now almost out.

Mason shouted : " Keep at it, men," and after a quick look round returned to the bridge, ducking as another flight of Junkers 88s roared over, their bombs cascading the foredeck with water.

On the bridge he called the engine-room : " How long before we can get under way ? " he asked.

Chief Engineer Jimmy Wyld had been watching the steam-gauge in the engine-room when the torpedo had struck. In the darkness he had struggled on deck to help fight the flames and then, returning to the engine-room, found that Higgins, the electrician, had restored the electric circuit.

Having made an examination of the engines, he was able to tell the captain : " We've a fairly clean bill of health here. The fires were blown out but we'll have the engines going within half an hour. How's the ship ? "

Mason's voice crackled back : " Seaworthy, I think. You'd better come up and we'll have a proper look."

On the bridge, the second officer pointed towards the binnacle. " Gyro's gone, sir." Gray, the chief officer, added : " Steering gear, too ; we'll have to use the emergency gear." Wyld joined the group.

" How are the phone lines ? " he asked.

"We've still got one line to the after steering position," Gray volunteered.

The captain nodded. " We'll have to steer from aft. You take over there, Gray. I'll con her from here by phone." Then, as an after-thought, " Thank God for an American ship. Plenty of telephone lines."

Gray hurried aft. Together the captain and the chief engineer surveyed the damage. A hole, twenty-four feet by twenty-seven feet, had been torn in the port side of the amidships pump-room. The blast had also blown another smaller hole in the starboard side and the compartment was flooded. There were jagged tears in the bulkheads and kerosene was bubbling from adjoining tanks, seeping in a film out through the holes in the hull. The deck had been broken open, so that one could look down between the tongues of torn plates right into the vitals of the ship. From beam to beam the deck was buckled but the ship still held together.

Wyld grunted : " That's welding. Rivets would never have stood it."

The captain nodded and said : " Let's hope she goes on holding. Take it slowly when you open up or she'll break her back." Wyld went below to start the engines.

A new problem awaited Mason on the bridge. The gyro compass was broken and the magnetic compass seemed to have been blasted off its bearings. In the darkness, and unsure of their position, there seemed no way of steering a course to Malta.

As soon as *Nigeria* had been torpedoed, Captain A. S. Russell of *Kenya*, not knowing what had happened to Admiral Burrough, took over command of the convoy. He immediately made two emergency alterations of course to starboard by siren, followed by a general signal for increase of speed.

Some of the ships obeyed the orders and some did not. Before many minutes passed the merchantmen were in a heterogeneous mess, " all scrummed up," as one liaison officer described it, and despite *Kenya's* efforts to lead them back into the original course, all formation was lost.

Three destroyers, *Bicester*, *Wilton* and *Derwent*, were

escorting *Nigeria* back to Gibraltar; and many of the remaining ten destroyers were standing by damaged ships and out of touch with *Kenya*.

In this scattered and disorganised condition, screen and convoy were in no shape to resist the heavy air attack which now fell upon them.

At 8.35 p.m., just after the sun had gone down, twenty German Junkers 88s came roaring in for a mast-high bombing attack.

The convoy fought back as best it could. Aboard the American *Almeria Lykes*, they made some good shooting and two of the enemy planes, caught in the merchantman's vicious barrage, crashed into the sea.

As the first attack waned, they changed the barrel of their Bofors gun. The other had been worn smooth by the continual firing.

One twenty-year-old American seaman, chewing gum imperturbably behind the bridge-wing Oerlikon, shouted to another crew man: " Get a bucket of water, bud, this barrel's melting and there's more of the devils coming."

Twenty aircraft were diving in with torpedoes. This time with the convoy straggling over some miles of the Mediterranean, there could be no concerted emergency turn, no controlled barrage.

From astern of them, Admiral Burrough ordered his flagship *Ashanti* and the destroyer *Penn*, which had been rounding up stragglers, to make smoke in the rear of the merchantmen to prevent their silhouettes from showing up in the dusk glow to the west, but it was too late.

One torpedo blew a great hole in the bows of *Brisbane Star* and the merchantman, out of control, careered across the path of the convoy.

To avoid being rammed, *Empire Hope* stopped her engines, and, while in this position, three dive-bombers delivered an attack on her. The second stick obtained a direct hit on hatch No. 4 and the three other bombs dropped close. The cased aviation petrol caught fire at once and within a moment she was burning fiercely. With blazing petrol spreading swiftly over the sea, the crew abandoned ship. From *Brisbane Star* they could hear the screams of badly-burnt men as the boats pulled away.

The bombers delivered attack after attack. The water round the ships boiled and seethed with exploding bombs. Then, with a crash which could be heard plainly on the Tunisian coast, *Clan Ferguson*, hit by a stick of bombs, blew up. An orange mushroom of flame, black smoke and flying debris gushed from her amidships. Within a few minutes nothing was left but a great blazing pyre of petrol on the surface of the sea. The Italian submarine *Alagi* later picked up fifty-three of the surviving members of her crew.

The convoy was now scattered over an area of twenty miles, lit eerily by the two flaming patches which were all that remained of *Empire Hope* and *Clan Ferguson*.

Force X had lost the protection of two of its cruisers, *Nigeria* and *Cairo*, and of the fourteen merchantmen eleven only remained, and two of them, *Ohio* and *Brisbane Star*, lay astern, stopped and seriously damaged.

Of the screen, Admiral Burrough now had only the

two cruisers, *Kenya* and *Manchester*, and ten destroyers.

It was at this critical juncture, with the convoy scattered and hard hit that the admiral received a signal informing him that the Italian fleet was at sea. Definite sighting reports from the R.A.F. at Malta informed him that three heavy and three light cruisers with a destroyer screen were making south.

It meant that at dawn he was likely to have to fight an action, outnumbered and outgunned, somewhere in the neighbourhood of Pantelleria with the enemy airfields only fifteen miles away.

CHAPTER TEN

E-BOATS ATTACK

I

As Admiral Burrough made his way at full speed towards the van of the scattered convoy, he knew that the situation was critical.

When Admiral Syfret, returning to Gibraltar, had learned of the loss of *Cairo* and the damage to *Nigeria*, he had immediately sent back the cruiser *Charybdis*, escorted by two destroyers, to join Force X and Admiral Burrough had received a signal to the effect that they would reach him just before dawn.

The Italian force, however, which he might expect to meet early next day, still greatly outnumbered and outgunned the ships he could bring to bear.

Moreover, they were now approaching the narrowest part of the Tunisian channel where both U-boats and E-boats would be lying in wait for them. What was more, the convoy had broken up and it would be next to impossible to gather it together during darkness.

Even among the warships themselves, muddle and uncertainty was rife. As the position stood at 9 p.m. on 12th August, Captain Russell in *Kenya*, not knowing where Admiral Burrough was, had signalled Force X that he had taken command.

When the admiral heard this, he called for full speed so as to reach the van of the convoy without delay. As *Ashanti* hurried through the dark, they had a very narrow shave. As the last of the torpedo-bombers carried out an attack, *Ashanti's* captain saw a torpedo approaching his starboard bow, and, travelling at full speed, he ordered a maximum turn to starboard. *Ashanti* heeled over sharply, shuddering as she turned. For a tense moment it seemed that they must be hit, then the torpedo passed swiftly down the starboard side missing only by two feet.

As Admiral Burrough reached the head of the convoy, a brilliant flash followed by a loud report told him that more trouble had beset the convoy. This time it was not so serious as it might have been.

Lying in wait in the narrowest part of the Tunisian channel, the Italian submarine *Alagi*, had fired four torpedoes at *Kenya*. At the moment the salvo was discharged, *Kenya's* lookout spotted the submarine on the surface, and a turn was made at full helm towards her. One torpedo hit the forefoot, blowing off the stem from the waterline downwards. Due to the quick turn, the other torpedoes, which would probably have sunk her, passed, one under the bridge and two close to the stern.

After stopping for a moment to examine the damage, it was found that the cruiser could still proceed with a fair turn of speed, so she rejoined *Manchester* at the head of the convoy. Shortly afterwards Admiral Burrough took over effective command of the convoy again, or that part of it which still remained in sight, consisting of only three of the merchantmen.

Meanwhile the damaged *Brisbane Star* had been plodding on alone following a course round Cape Bon given her by Admiral Burrough.

Suddenly the shape of a warship loomed out of the night. They were about to signal her when she was recognised as an Italian, a cruiser, they thought. In fact it was a large Italian destroyer, *Malocello*, laying mines, but she did not attack the merchant ship for fear of giving her position away as she was laying mines in French territorial waters.

Later, while close in to the shore, Captain Riley had an amusing exchange of messages with the hostile Vichy French signals station in the Gulf of Hammamet.

Hammamet signalled them first : " You should hoist your signal letters."

Brisbane Star : " Please excuse me."

Hammamet : " You should anchor."

Brisbane Star : " My anchors are fouled. I cannot anchor."

Hammamet : " You appear to be dragging your bow and stern anchors."

Brisbane Star : " I have no stern anchors."

Hammamet : " You should anchor immediately."

Brisbane Star : " I cannot anchor. My anchors are fouled."

Hammamet : " Do you require a salvage or rescue ? "

Brisbane Star : " No."

Hammamet : " It is not safe to go too fast."

Brisbane Star then steamed off at her maximum five knots.

II

On board *Ohio*, steam had been raised and by 8.45 p.m. they were ready to get under way once more. After discussion with Lieutenant Barton, Mason decided that it would be best to steer for the coast and then to stop while making a more thorough examination of the damage. They also decided that it would probably be impracticable to rejoin the convoy and therefore determined to keep as long as possible in French territorial waters and then proceed independently to Malta.

The problem was how this was to be accomplished without any serviceable compasses. In the darkness on the starboard side lay the African coast. To port were minefields.

Mason and Barton did some quick navigational reckoning and fixed upon a star which they hoped would give them a rough course towards the Cani rocks. Captain Mason rang for slow speed and *Ohio* began to move again. Despite the damage the crew of the tanker had succeeded in improvising a workable means of steering during the hour since the torpedo had struck.

The steering gear in the wheelhouse was not working, but the rudder could be moved by operating the valve on the steering engine at the after end of the poop. From this position no one could see ahead nor could the operator tell how far to move the rudder because the funnel and the deck-house stood in the way. Gray and Stephen were therefore sent to the poop to operate the steering engine, keeping in touch with the bridge by the one remaining telephone line.

From the bridge, Mason, Barton and McKilligan passed back directions to the poop checking the turns made by the ship on an electrically operated rudder indicator which was still working. Barton, at the telephone, would tell the chief officer, for instance to " put some port rudder on." Barton then watched the rudder indicator and the swing of the bows, judging when to put some opposite rudder on to stop the ship swinging too far. This elaborate method seldom worked accurately and the ship proceeded on her way in a series of none too gentle curves, but with practice they were soon making good a fairly constant course.

Thus the direction of the ship was controlled from two isolated islands connected only by a single telephone line.

On the " after island " when the initial difficulties of steering had been ironed out, Gray remembered that he had a full gallon jar of rum down in his quarters. The jar was fetched and a large tot served out to all hands on the poop. It seemed to help a lot.

Whether *Ohio* would have survived the navigational dangers of the night with these makeshift methods, and whether she would have lasted the next day, alone and a tempting target for the enemy airmen, it is impossible to say, though it seems doubtful. Help was, however, close at hand. About an hour and a half after they got under way again the profile of a *Hunt*-class destroyer loomed up out of the night and a British voice hailed them.

" You must steer 120° if you want to catch up with the convoy," it said. " Or do you want a tow ? "

Mason went to the wing of the bridge : " No, thank you, we're under our own steam, but we haven't got a compass. Can you lead us to the convoy ? "

The destroyer was *Ledbury* (Lieutenant-Commander Roger Hill) which had been sent to round up stragglers.

Hill soon had a stern light rigged. Slowly he began to lead *Ohio* along the course previously taken by the remainder of the convoy.

The sea ahead was still lit by flaming petrol from two stricken merchantmen. On the bridge of *Ohio*, Mason suddenly realised that they must pass almost through one of the patches of flames. He seized the loud-hailer : " For God's sake keep clear of that. We're oozing paraffin," he shouted, and the destroyer sheered sharply to port.

Ohio steamed on following the shielded blue light in *Ledbury's* stern. They were now inside the minefields of the " Narrows," and the gleam of Cape Bon lighthouse stood abeam and began to slide astern. Slowly the tanker's speed began to increase, first to ten knots then to twelve, finally she was making a good sixteen knots, though she had to carry a continuous five degrees of starboard helm because of the great rent in her port side.

Mason made frequent examinations of the shattered deck. The ship creaked and groaned and the scraping of jagged metal could be heard somewhere down in the hold as the increased speed put greater strain upon the damaged section. The ship still held together, however. The buckling across the deck had not visibly increased, so they carried on and hoped for the best.

There was now time for a roll-call to be held and it showed that four men were missing, and No. 5 boat was trailing from the falls. It seemed that, when the fire broke out, two gunners and a galley-boy attempted to launch the boat and it had capsized. Assistant Steward Morton, serving one of the guns, had also disappeared.

It was thought that he had been washed overboard by the cascades of water from near misses.

It was very quiet now. Most of the crew were asleep. Only the suspicion of a breeze rustled the surface of the dark Mediterranean.

At 2 a.m., a star of brilliant light blazed in the darkness ahead.

Lieutenant Barton gripped the captain's arm. " The convoy's catching it again," he said.

More parachute flares lit up and hung brilliantly in the sky. Then the crash of heavy firing began.

" I expect it's E-boats," said Barton. " Let's hope it isn't the whole Eytie fleet. It strikes me we're better off out here after all."

III

Just before midnight the head of the convoy had reached Cape Bon and turned south on a course close to the Tunisian coast.

The British ships were now in the narrowest part

of the channel with a hostile shore on one side and a minefield on the other.

The three TSD destroyers led the van, streaming paravanes to sweep any mines which might have been laid in the channel.

This precaution was soon fully justified for *Ashanti*, *Kenya* and *Manchester*, who were following with the only two merchant ships remaining in visual touch, *Melbourne Star* and *Wairangi* all sighted loose mines bobbing in the sea close to them.

Two passed down the side of the *Ashanti*, so near that the lookouts were able to see their horns, which if touched would detonate them.

It was very quiet now, the darkest hour of the night. The only sounds to be heard were the dull beat of engines and the rustle of water at the bows. The lookouts strained their eyes trying to pierce the darkness ahead.

On *Ashanti's* bridge the telephone buzzer sounded :

" Radar plots bearing Red 5. Looks like small boats," said a voice.

" Fire with everything you've got, on the radar plot," the captain ordered.

Simultaneously, the whirr of a starter and the roar of a high-speed engine could be heard out to port. A star-shell fired by *Kenya* burst high in the air, flooding the sea with a dim, milky light.

" E-boats to port," came half a dozen voices. The guns of all the British warships opened up together, tearing the calm sea into a lather around the dim forms of the E-boats.

These two MTBs, the first of four flotillas numbering

nineteen boats which were waiting to receive the convoy between Cape Bon and Pantelleria, were both under way now. They dashed in to deliver their attacks, then, turning at high speed, began to lay smoke-screens to shield themselves from the withering fire. The British ships turned towards them to comb torpedo tracks.

The guns stopped firing, the E-boats were out of range. Five minutes later radar detected two more boats to starboard and the British engaged with a full broadside.

The enemy was temporarily driven off without loss to the convoy.

A running fight now developed with E-boats on both sides of the convoy. Fast motor-boats would come tearing in, fire their torpedoes, then retreat again behind smoke. Each time they were greeted with heavy fire and neither side scored any success.

At 1.20 a.m., when the battle was reaching its height and the regular gleam of the Kelibia light could be seen abeam, two E-boats, MS.16 and MS.22 of the Italian second flotilla, pressed home a courageous attack upon *Manchester*, coming to within fifty yards of the cruiser before discharging their torpedoes.

Manchester went to full speed, turning hard to starboard and firing with both forward turrets, when there was a terrific explosion under the forward 4-inch gun deck as one of the torpedoes struck. With her steering locked the cruiser careered in a wide circle out of control, disappearing into the night.

Both engine-rooms were flooded and the after boiler-room damaged. All lights went out and the power was cut off. *Manchester* was now stopped and helpless and preparations were made for abandoning ship. The destroyer, *Pathfinder* came alongside and took off 158 ratings and five injured men.

Meanwhile the E-boats had found the straggling remnant of the convoy which was following not far behind the warships.

Parted from the convoy, the master and lookouts on the bridge of the American *Santa Elisa* were peering into the darkness. Suddenly Captain Thompson saw the dark shape of an E-boat appear almost alongside the ship.

" See that damn killer," he shouted to Cadet Midshipman Francis Dales. " Get him."

Dales opened fire with the bridge Oerlikon. The sea creamed astern of the E-boat as she opened her throttle and then her guns began to spit back at the merchantman.

Dales's loader fell dead beside him but the cadet went on firing. The E-boat sprayed the bridge and smoke stack with bullets, and the captain and the naval liaison officer had to throw themselves to the deck to avoid being hit. Two more gunners were killed at their posts.

As Dales exhausted his ammunition, he saw that his adversary was on fire. In the same instant, he spotted another E-boat dashing in from starboard. He reached for more ammunition, saw the E-Boat fire a torpedo and then turn away in the darkness.

There was a terrific explosion as the torpedo struck the starboard side of *Santa Elisa's* No. 1 hold. Simultaneously, the petrol stacked everywhere went up with a roar and a blaze of flame. Dales saw men blown over the side by the force of it. Others were casting themselves into the sea.

As he ran with the captain to launch the boats, fire was engulfing the whole ship.

They managed to launch three of the boats and picked up as many survivors as they could find in the dark. Two hours later they were rescued by *Penn*.

Almeria Lykes had no chance to defend herself. She was following in the wake of two British destroyers when a torpedo fired by an unseen E-boat exploded on the port side of No. 1 hold and split the ship right across the deck in line with the forepeak bulkhead. The ship began to sink by the head and the engines failed. She was then abandoned.

A little later, the British ships *Wairangi* and *Glenorchy* were torpedoed. Both caught fire shortly after the crews had escaped. Most of these men and those from the *Almeria Lykes* were picked up by *Somali* and taken to Gibraltar.

It was now about 3.30 a.m., and at the head of the convoy the warships were fighting off another E-boat attack. As they were doing so they saw *Rochester Castle*, which had just regained contact with them, torpedoed out to starboard. Though heavily damaged forward, she succeeded in getting under way again shortly afterwards and soon worked up to a speed of thirteen knots.

Admiral Burrough had had no news of *Manchester* since she had been torpedoed. Accordingly, when *Charybdis* joined with *Somali* and *Eskimo* at 4.30 a.m., he despatched the two destroyers to search for the cruiser. The disastrous engagement with the E-boats had lasted until dawn. Altogether, eight Italian E-boats (Mas 552, 553, 554, 556, 557 and 564 and MS 26, and 31) and two German (S.30 and S.36) had delivered fifteen attacks and although several had been damaged none were lost.

Now the admiral had only the cruisers, *Charybdis* and *Kenya* (which had a damaged bow), and a force of seven destroyers, to meet the Italian fleet.

As the sun rose, he fully expected to see the smoke of the enemy ships smudging the northern horizon and within a short time to feel the full weight of their salvoes to which, with his depleted force, he would have small chance of replying effectively.

The convoy would never reach Malta and the most he could do would be to inflict as much damage as possible before superior weight of metal pounded his cruisers and destroyers into blazing hulks.

CHAPTER ELEVEN

R.A.F. BLUFF THE ITALIANS

DAWN came slowly. First a tinge of eggshell-coloured light appeared in the east, changing to rose.

Aboard the flagship *Ashanti*, Admiral Burrough could see the barrels of the forward guns. Then the wires of the radio aerial were visible. Day was approaching.

The admiral was grey and drawn with sleeplessness. He knew that the testing time of his life was probably at hand. Soon he might have to order 2,000 men to action with the Italian fleet and most of them would die. He would almost certainly die with them.

Worse still, his mission would end in failure. After the warships had made their fruitless, suicidal attack, and after they had been beaten into blazing wrecks, the Italians would sail in and finish off the remaining merchantmen of the convoy at leisure. Malta would starve, another bastion of the British Empire would fall to the Axis and he knew what that might mean— at the best victory longer delayed, at the worst defeat.

Other officers on the bridge were already scanning the northern horizon where the Italian fleet was due to appear. He would wait a little. It was too dark yet.

He paced slowly down to the wing of the bridge. The flecks in the sea were becoming visible. He turned and raised his glasses unhurriedly to the north.

For a full ten minutes, he scanned the skyline. There were no smudges of hostile smoke, no long grey shapes or even the blobs of warships' top-hamper showing above the arc of the sea in the growing light. His hopes rose buoyantly in a gust of relief. Somehow the Italians had failed to rendezvous with their kill.

A combination of many factors had saved the convoy and its escort from destruction at this stage of the operation. Chief among them was a psychological attitude which was to dog the Italian Navy throughout the war. From the start of hostilities, a general order of the Italian High Command sapped the will to attack and placed even the most determined admiral in an intolerable position.

This order, issued in September 1940, completely renounced the initiative. It read:

" Naval actions occur for one of two reasons : first, an encounter between two enemy squadrons, one of which seeks to prevent the other from fulfilling its mission ; second, determined search by one squadron for the enemy fleet with the purpose of destroying it. The first situation may develop unexpectedly : in such a case the Italian Navy, if it has a chance of success, will fight with extreme resolution. The second alternative is not open to us because we are the weaker. To conceive of a battle as an end in itself is an absurdity not worth discussing."

Since the destruction of the enemy might be considered the only way of gaining complete control of the sea, the Italian Supermarina's overall naval plan, if it had one, was faulty from its basis.

Added to this, the destruction of Italian ships at Taranto by the British fleet torpedo aircraft had made the Italian naval command highly nervous of putting to sea with heavy elements unless they received strong air protection. As the Italian fleet steamed at speed towards the convoy which they might confidently have expected to destroy, a top-ranking conference was taking place between the Axis commanders in Rome. The Italian naval staff, with the British attack on Taranto still in mind and also intelligence that a torpedo strike against their fleet was being planned at Malta, demanded air cover for their ships. They specified that they could not steam south of Pantelleria into waters covered by aircraft from Malta unless they were given this protection.

Such fighter cover would have to be provided by the Germans as the Italians had insufficient suitable long-range fighters. Field-Marshal Kesselring, as Commander-in-Chief Air South, was therefore asked to make sufficient German fighters available.

All ranks of the German Air Force were already filled with indignation against the Italian Navy over their conduct during the previous mid-June convoy. They held that their own good work on this occasion had been denied a fully successful outcome by what they considered to be a pusillanimous withdrawal by the Italian fleet when the complete destruction of convoy and escort had been within their power.

Moreover, Kesselring and his subordinates had, in the opinion of their own Admiral Weichold, " a bigoted view of air results which had a bad effect on operational decisions."

The German air commander refused point blank to grant the Italians' request, giving as his reason the need to protect his own bombers during the operation. An acrimonious argument ensued, with both sides firmly digging in their toes. Despite efforts by the Italian Commander-in-Chief, Cavallero, to compose their differences, the row reached a deadlock at which it was evident that the fighters would have to be used either for the fleet or the bombers, and could not be divided between the two.

Vital minutes ticked by, but the deadlock remained. Finally, in desperation, Cavallero proposed that Mussolini be asked to give a casting vote. After much more argument this course was adopted and the Italian Commander-in-Chief telephoned the Duce.

This enforced role of umpire in an explosive situation placed Mussolini in a quandary. He did not like to come out in blatant opposition to Kesselring for fear of offending Hitler or of appearing to favour Italian interests unduly ; yet politically he would have welcomed a successful action by the Italian fleet. Finally, he gave in to the Germans and air cover was denied the Italian ships.

The two Italian cruiser divisions pressed on, however, towards their dawn interception with the convoy. Meanwhile, the R.A.F. at Malta had taken a hand.

Air reconnaissance had detected enemy fleet movement as early as the evening of 11th August when the Italian Seventh Cruiser Division, comprising *Eugenio, Montecuccoli* and *Attendolo*, escorted by eleven destroyers, were sighted leaving Cagliari Harbour in Sardinia by Beaufighters returning from airfield raids. The following morning R.A.F. pilots had seen the Fifth Division, *Gorizia* and *Bolzano* leave Messina. Later they were observed joining forces with *Trieste* which had come from the north.

When a Baltimore aircraft reported the rendezvous of the two divisions fifty miles north-west of Ustica at 7 p.m. it was plain that an attack on the convoy was planned and that it was likely to begin at dawn.

The R.A.F. were in some difficulty. Air Vice-Marshal Sir Keith Park had been promised the use of a force of Middle East Liberators. These were not available and he had insufficient aircraft to mount an effective strike against the Italian fleet.

He therefore decided upon a stratagem. In the absence of proper means of attack perhaps the enemy could be frightened into turning back.

Wellington " O for Orange " was dispatched at last light to take up the search and located the cruisers still steaming south. The pilot was then ordered to drop flares over the fleet. Wellington " Z for Zebra " was also ordered to illuminate and attack with bombs. When this had been carried out " Zebra's " pilot was told to send a signal in plain language directing imaginary aircraft to the scene.

This seemed to be partially successful, for the signal was picked up by the enemy and by 2.30 a.m. the cruisers had altered course towards the north-east.

To speed the parting guest, Park then sent another plain language message : " Report result of your attack and latest enemy position for Liberators—most immediate."

Then again, at 3.45 a.m., Wellington " Y for Yorker " was ordered in plain language : " Contact cruisers— illuminate and attack."

All these plain language messages were picked up by the Italians, as was intended, and probably reinforced the decision by Supermarina to recall the cruisers. At the same time, fortune, in the guise of the Italo-German row over air cover, was the principal reason for abandoning what must have been a decisive attack. Almost within striking distance of the convoy, they turned back.

The story of this ill-judged fleet manœuvre did not end there. The British had another rude shock in store for the Italians.

When " Pedestal " passed through the Straits of Gibraltar, the submarine *Unbroken*, captained by Lieutenant Alastair Mars, was ordered to patrol two miles north of Cape Milazzo lighthouse which lay eighteen miles west of Messina naval base. After being repeatedly hunted and depth-charged by the enemy in this uncomfortable spot, Lieutenant Mars decided to vary the instructions he had been given. After a careful appraisal of the situation he came to the conclusion that a position half-way between the islands of Panaria and Salina was the best point at which to intercept any cruisers using the port of Messina. He turned a " blind eye " to the fact that if he had miscalculated he was in for trouble, for the new position was thirty miles away from his ordered patrol line.

Early on the 12th he received a signal from Vice-

Admiral, Malta : " Enemy cruisers coming your way."

Since " your way " meant his proper position thirty miles away to the south, Mars was now faced with a difficult decision. Should he steam south to his official patrol line which he could not reach before the cruisers passed it, or should he remain where his own judgment told him the course of the cruisers was likely to lie ? Trying not to think about courts-martial, he stayed where he was.

At breakfast time, hydrophone echoes of heavy ships were heard approaching from the west.

Mars swung the periscope, and in the dawn light saw three or four cruisers in line ahead coming straight for him. He manœuvred for attack. He dived under the destroyer screen, missing one of the vessels by a hair's breadth, and then, with an 8-inch cruiser as target, fired three torpedoes.

As they spiralled down into deep waters to avoid the counter-attack, the men of *Unbroken* heard two loud explosions.

The heavy cruiser, *Bolzano*, was seriously damaged and played no further part in the war. The light cruiser, *Attendolo*, had her bows blown off and was many months repairing at Messina.

Two hundred miles to the south-westward, the sun shone over the convoy.

Five merchant ships, *Melbourne Star*, *Waimarama*, *Rochester Castle*, *Port Chalmers* and *Dorset*, had now been rounded up. *Brisbane Star* had reported that she was still making thirteen knots astern of them.

Then, as the sun rose higher and friendly Beaufighters

and long-range Spitfires from Malta flew in to protect them, *Ledbury*, followed by *Ohio*, hove in sight.

" I knew we could rely on *Ledbury*," Admiral Burrough signalled.

Then the battered tanker, " sailing like a yacht " despite the great rent in her port side, took station once again astern of the line of convoy.

The admiral's worries were by no means over. To begin with, he doubted whether the air cover which had been promised to his force from Malta during that day could be used efficiently. The only two very high frequency radio sets which had been supplied to the convoy for directing the fighter cover were aboard *Nigeria* and *Cairo*, the one damaged and out of action, the other sunk.

The lack of any air force intervention during the previous dusk air attack was evidently due to the fact that both these sets were immobilised when the two cruisers were struck by the enemy.

In fact, six Beaufighters of 248 Squadron had arrived on patrol over the convoy at about the time the cruisers were torpedoed. Receiving no fighter directions, this flight repeatedly dived from 5,000 feet in an attempt to find out what was going on. On each occasion they were fired on by their own ships.

Finally, they had returned to base without being able to assist the convoy in any way.

To prevent this happening again, Admiral Burrough's flag lieutenant worked through the night trying to improvise a suitable set.

With the help of the signals officer, Flags had finished his home-made set by the time the first Beaufighters appeared on the scene shortly after dawn and an air plotting board had been set up. Malta had been asked to arrange for the Beaufighters to work on a high frequency of 5,570 kilocycles which was the best they had been able to improvise.

For more than an hour he stood on the bridge of *Ashanti* shouting the call sign " Bacon-Apples " into the microphone or listening intently for some answering call. Sometimes his face would light up with expectation, only to be quickly followed by a look of disappointment. Suddenly his face wreathed in smiles and he began a conversation in code which was quite unintelligible to the admiral or anyone else on the bridge. At frequent intervals he glanced at the Beaufighters in the sky, then down again at the plot, for he was trying to give the aircraft a course to steer to intercept the enemy snoopers which had already appeared. Unfortunately the Beaufighters did not seem to understand. They went cruising on without any apparent effort to obey his instructions. After more guarded conversation in code, the flag lieutenant's face wrinkled in despair and he flung down the microphone with an oath. He had just discovered that he was not talking to a Beaufighter at all but to the cruiser *Charybdis*.

After this noble effort, wireless contact had to be abandoned, and so it was that when the full force of the enemy's Sicilian air fleet fell upon Force X, they were without any means of fighter direction.

CHAPTER TWELVE

A 'SITTING DUCK'

Ohio's gunners squinted into the rising sun, waiting for the attack which they knew might materialise at any moment.

Enemy spotting planes had followed them since first light until a flight of Beaufighters arrived from Malta to chase them away.

To the north-west and now slipping behind them, the two rounded hills on the Island of Pantelleria, fifteen miles away, could be clearly seen. Malta was still over 170 miles distant and, owing to the hard-fought night battles the convoy was not yet within effective range of the majority of the fighters from the island.

As Mason received a signal to prepare for action against an incoming raid the drone of the approaching planes could be heard. Then he saw three Italian Savoia aircraft flying low down the side of the convoy, well out of range.

A shout from Pumpman Collins, at lookout on the poop, brought Bofors and Oerlikon barrels swinging quickly towards the stern as five Junkers 88s dived at the tanker. Accurate bursts of fire split the formation into jinking units and the bombs began to fall. Gray could see the whole black length of them as they left the aircraft and they gradually turned over, looking like footballs. Every second seemed an hour of time in a world of slow-motion. He flattened himself on the deck, but the bombs crashed into the sea harmlessly, well over to port.

Other aircraft were diving from the starboard beam, and Gunner Laburn calmly changed the barrel of the Bofors gun as he turned towards the new attack, directing a withering and accurate fire on the new danger. Once again the formation scattered, and *Ohio*, now the chief target of the bombers, had escaped unhurt.

This first attack of the day at 8 a.m. was being made by twelve Junkers 88s, diving from 6,000 feet.

Two of them swept down on the *Waimarama* 200 yards in front of *Ohio*. They came through the heavy barrage which spotted the sky with black, white and golden puffs. A stick straddled the merchant ship, scoring direct hits aft and forward. The 100 octane aviation spirit stowed in the bridge deck took fire. She blew up with a roar, disappearing in a sheet of flame and clouds of billowing smoke, rising higher and higher with more violent explosions as the cargo of shells and other combustibles ignited. The second attacking enemy plane disintegrated in the heart of the flame.

Melbourne Star was following close astern of *Waimarama*. Her master, Captain MacFarlane, and other members of the crew took cover as the ship was showered with huge pieces of debris. A steel plate, five feet long, fell on board. The base of a ventilator, half an inch thick and two and a half feet high partly demolished one of the machine-gun posts, and a piece of angle-iron at the same moment narrowly missed one of their cadets. A 6-inch shell fell on the roof of the captain's day cabin.

Ahead of the *Melbourne Star*, which carried the same dangerous cargo as the stricken ship, the sea was a mass of fire, spreading every moment wider and wider to engulf them. Captain MacFarlane put the helm hard a-port, but the approaching furnace of heat drove him from the monkey island down to the bridge. Blinded by smoke and flame he shouted to the men to go forward for he expected the ship to blow up at any moment.

Flames all round them now were leaping mast high and the heat was terrific. The air became dryer and harder to breath every minute as the oxygen was burned out of it. The paint on the ship's sides took fire, and the bottoms of the lifeboats were reduced to charcoal. For what seemed hours, but could only have been a matter of seconds, the ship ploughed through the holocaust, then she was clear and the blaze receded astern.

As the men resumed their stations it was found that thirty-six men were missing. Thinking that the forward end of the ship had been struck, and expecting her to blow up, they had jumped over the side.

Ohio, with a damaged steering gear and gaping kerosene tanks was also making straight for the flames. Mason was shouting : " Hard a-port ! For God's sake, hard a-port ! " down the telephone to the first officer on the after-deck. Stephen, on the poop, saw the flames leap up ahead and thought they had been hit. He rushed to the ship's side and then shouted to Gray to port the helm.

At first the tanker did not answer. Flames loomed directly in her path, and the officers on the bridge waited tensely, measuring distances. At last she swung to port and just pulled clear.

The destroyer *Ledbury* now came racing from the screen. It seemed impossible that any man in the *Waimarama* could have lived through the explosion, and, indeed, eighty of the crew of 107 had perished ; but as the destroyer approached the edge of the flaming petrol men could be seen struggling in the water and the shrieks of others inside the pool of flame could be heard. Despite the danger to his own ship, Lieutenant-Commander Roger Hill of *Ledbury* steamed on and ordered boats to be launched.

The courage of the men in the water was amazing. Though the rapidly spreading film of blazing petrol threatened to engulf them at any moment, they were singing and encouraging one another. As *Ledbury* passed some of them, the captain spoke to them through the loud-hailer explaining that he must get those nearest the flames first.

"That's all right, sir," and "Yes, get them first," they shouted back, and went on singing. It was impossible to lay the ship's whaler, in charge of Gunner Musham, close enough to the flames : but men could be seen beyond in islands of unfired sea. Roger Hill immediately decided to take the destroyer in, and ordered rescue nets to be rigged along the ship's sides.

Slowly *Ledbury* edged in to the blaze, and to Admiral Burrough away in the convoy it seemed that she plunged straight in. The ship was given up for lost.

Petty Officer Cook went over the side again and again on a line to pick up men in the water.

Ledbury went astern and edged out again. Four times she plunged into the blazing sea in an attempt to get at men who still seemed to be alive.

One man could be seen, badly burnt, on a raft well within the circle of flame. *Ledbury* went in yet again, and this time she was enveloped from stem to stern in fire. She swung the wrong way and missed the raft. She circled round and re-entered the flames. Officers-Servant Reginald Sida volunteered to go over the fo'c'sle and take a line to the man on the burning raft. As he dived overboard he knew that the ship might have had to retreat leaving him at any moment. He reached the raft, carefully placed a life-saving belt round the injured man and then both were pulled to safety.

No other survivors being visible in the flames, *Ledbury* backed out again and began picking up survivors beyond the petrol patches.

The destroyer had passed one of them a number of times. On each occasion he bobbed up in the water and knuckled his forehead shouting " Don't forget the diver, sir ! " He was picked up, and turned out to be Bosun J. Cook who had jumped overboard from *Melbourne Star*.

The senior surviving officer of *Waimarama*, Radio Officer Jackson, had an extraordinary tale to tell. He was crossing to the starboard side of the bridge to bear a hand with the guns when the bombs struck, two aft, one abaft the bridge and one forward.

A great wall of flame leapt up in front of him. He turned, but could not see the gun mounting he had just left no more than two yards away. There were flames all round him.

Instinctively he ducked into the bridge deck-house and ran down the ladder gaining the boat deck through a hole where the door had been. He clambered over a pile of debris with difficulty as the ship was listing sharply to starboard and saw about twenty men struggling in the water. The ship was sinking rapidly, and, apart from the corner on which he stood, completely enveloped in flames. The sea, too, was blazing all around except for the patch where the men were swimming. Shielding his eyes from the fire, he ran to the side and jumped overboard.

He could not swim, he was swallowing water and everything began to go black. In a sort of haze, he saw that the ship had swung round and the bows appeared to be falling down on top of him.

Somehow, he managed to struggle away, and when he looked round the ship had disappeared.

He lay on his back for a few minutes trying to decide what to do. The flames and black smoke were closing in on him. At that moment he saw Cadet Treves swimming towards him. The cadet, without any attempt to save himself from the oncoming wall of fire, helped Jackson to keep afloat until they came to a piece of wood which the non-swimmer could cling to.

Jackson, holding tight to the piece of wood, began to propel himself away from the burning petrol by kicking his feet, but to his horror the flames began to catch up with him. The heat was terrific and he decided that when the fire reached him he would undo his life jacket and slip under. It was not to be. A fluke in the wind turned the blazing petrol aside and for two hours he floated until picked up by *Ledbury*.

Cadet Treves, whose action had saved Jackson's life, was also picked up.

Away to the south-east, the convoy steamed on towards Malta, and under his care Admiral Burrough could number now only the merchant ships *Ohio*, *Port Chalmers*, *Melbourne Star*, *Dorset* and *Rochester Castle*, formed up in two columns.

Although the roundelled wings of Malta Spitfires and Beaufighters could be seen high above in the brassy sky, the admiral knew that the enemy had not yet developed the full power of his air attack from the nearby Sicilian airfields. The severest test was at hand.

On the bridge of *Ohio*, Captain Mason and Lieutenant Barton scanned the skies until their eyes ached. They knew that it was " any time now."

The R/T crackled : " Stand by for dive-bombing attack." Ahead, tiny dots in the sky could be seen, circling. The alarm bells rang and the gun crews swung their guns restlessly, waiting for the strike.

It came at 9.25 a.m., the most determined attack they had yet encountered, from more than sixty black Stuka dive-bombers escorted by Italian fighters, and *Ohio* was the main target.

One after another the dive-bombers peeled off and came down. As the menacing " W " shapes of the wings got bigger and bigger, the howl of the engines and panic-provoking sirens reached a crescendo. The bombs thundered down, spraying *Ohio* with great gouts of water tossed from the sea, and the aircraft raced by at mast height, machine guns chattering as they jinked this way and that to avoid the heavy counter fire.

They seemed to come from every quarter, and Mason and Barton on the bridge now ducked instinctively only at the last minute when the danger seemed most acute.

One exceptionally near miss sent an avalanche of water over the foredeck. The ship shuddered violently. A few minutes later the captain received a report that the plates had buckled and that the forward oil tank had filled with water.

The 6-inch gun at the bows twisted in its mounting and was put out of action.

At the after-end of the ship, Pumpman Collins, who was serving the guns endlessly with his home-made ammunition hoist, saw his friend Ginger Leach walking calmly aft, scorning to duck as successive waves of Stukas flashed by.

"Ruddy murder, ain't it?" Ginger said laconically.

Every gun of the *Ohio* blazed away continually. Barrels grew red hot and had to be changed, but the protective barrage hardly slackened.

On the bridge, the Bofors gun had been in action for nearly half an hour. Gunner Billings, peering over the sights with red-rimmed eyes, saw a Junkers 87 snaking into the attack, lower and coming closer than his companions had dared. He pressed the trigger again. The shells were hitting the black fuselage, bits were dropping off. "Got her," Billings shouted, still pressing the trigger. '

The plane crashed straight into *Ohio's* starboard side forward of the bridge and exploded. Half a wing slammed into the upper-work of the bridge and a rain of aircraft parts showered her from stem to stern. The bomb, which Billings had unconcernedly watched as it left the aircraft, fortunately failed to explode.

The men on the bridge got off their knees, looked at one another and laughed as if it had been a big joke.

Steward Meeks, quite unperturbed, appeared at the top of the bridge ladder with a kettle of coffee and sandwiches.

" Hot work, sir," he commented, handing the captain a pint mug. Mason suddenly realised that this was the second time the chief steward had appeared with food and drink since the action had begun.

On the poop, Stephen was diving under the same water tank every time an attack developed. Each time he thought : " If that tank shifts, I'll be crushed," but he continued to take shelter under it. The attack was dulling the men's minds. They were getting " bomb happy." They laughed inanely when near missed, but the guns kept on firing and firing accurately, the ammunition continued to come up from the magazines, *Ohio* steamed on towards Malta.

Their luck couldn't last. The guns turned to meet twenty Junkers 88s diving in from ahead, dropping parachute mines, torpedoes and circling torpedoes. The ship turned slowly to comb torpedoes. Then came the bombs. Two sticks of them burst down either side of *Ohio*. The ship lifted and went on lifting, until her bottom was out of the water. Cascades of spray and bomb splinters lashed the deck. Then she fell back with a teeth-shaking crash.

Down in the engine-room, it seemed to the chief, Jimmy Wyld, as if the ship had suddenly become airborne. This was a totally new experience. Automatically his hand went to shut off steam, but the special differential gearing had slowed the propeller automatically. It occurred to him that in another ship a screw racing so far out of the water would have shaken the engines out of her.

Mechanically he checked over the engine-room. Nothing was damaged, but it couldn't last. Every few minutes the nearby concussion of bombs clanged on the ship's sides like giant hammers. Sooner or later one would find its mark, but somehow this self-evident conclusion did not seem to worry him at all.

A gigantic crash to starboard sent *Ohio* reeling to port. The engine-room lights went out and they were in darkness. There were simultaneous shouts for torches, but before the groping engineers could find them, Electrician Higgins had felt his way to the master switches which had been thrown out by the violence of the explosion and turned the lights on again.

This time the ship had not escaped damage. The boiler fires had blown out and it was a race against time to restore them before the steam dropped too low to work the fuel pumps.

With practised co-operation the engineers went to work. Fuel starter torches were lighted to refire the furnaces. The complicated routine of restarting the engine went forward smoothly, and within twenty minutes *Ohio* was steaming at sixteen knots.

Then another salvo of bombs shook every plate in the ship. Once more the engine-room lights went out and the engines slowed, shivered and stopped.

When Higgins succeeded in switching on emergency lighting he found that the main switch had been torn off the bulkhead. More serious still, the electric fuel pumps had been broken by the concussion.

The bridge telephone rang and Captain Mason's voice asked : " Anything serious, Chief ? "

" Looks bad, sir," Wyld replied. " Pumps have gone. We'll get her going again somehow."

" Good luck," Mason answered. " We'll try to keep 'em off up here."

The engineers went to work trying to forget the hollow crashes of bombs falling close by and the stark fact that at any moment the sea might invade the dimly lit trap of the engine-room.

The floor plates were removed, and Wyld and Buddle, the second engineer, crawled through the bilges to the valves which would connect up the steam fuel pumps to replace the broken electrical system.

Meanwhile the junior engineer, Harry Sless, the only Jew anyone could remember in a ship's engine-room, took on one of the most dangerous jobs, wriggling his way over the boiler casing looking for fractures and checking for oil in the water.

The steam auxiliary system was connected to the pumping mechanism. Wyld and Buddle emerged from the bilges covered with oil and slime. The critical moment had arrived. Was there still steam to pump oil into the fires ? Wyld watched the gauges and gave the order. Grinstead, the third engineer, thrust the flaming starter torch into the cooling darkness of No. 1 furnace. With a hollow " woof " the vapourised oil under low pressure exploded, blowing out the sides of No. 1 boiler and filling the engine-room with black smoke.

In the murky half light, they tried again. This time the other boiler fired properly, and life began to come back to the engines. Wyld, watching the revolution counter, saw the indicator climb slowly to five, ten, fifteen and then waver at twenty. The bridge telephone shrilled.

" She's making alternate black and white smoke," came Mason's voice. " No more than four knots at the moment."

" Ay, oil in the water somewhere," Wyld replied.

" We're losing vacuum in the condenser," Buddle shouted.

Wyld relayed the information to the captain.

At that moment the engines stopped.

" It's all over, lad, I'm afraid. In five minutes we won't have steam to steer her. Sorry." Wyld turned away from the controls and went to close the engine sea cocks.

Ohio lost way slowly and came to a stop, rolling slightly in the small beam swell. A pair of Stukas screamed down, wavered in the face of the determined fire and dropped their bombs short. The ship was now a " sitting duck," and an easy target.

Malta, with her life in the balance, and *Ohio* with her vital cargo, seemed very far apart.

CHAPTER THIRTEEN

OHIO ABANDONED

PARRYING every form of air attack, Admiral Burrough in *Ashanti* led the convoy on towards Malta. *Ohio* was immobilised far astern and S.S. *Dorset* straddled by a stick of bombs, lay similarly crippled while her engineers struggled manfully in the forlorn hope of repairing extensive blast damage and pumping out the flooded engine-room.

The admiral's protective screen of warships had been further reduced. *Ledbury* was picking up *Waimarama* survivors in the blazing sea, and destroyers *Penn* and *Bramham* had been sent to assist *Ohio* and *Dorset*. The destroyers *Eskimo* and *Somali* were miles away looking for *Manchester* survivors.

So, to protect the remaining merchantmen, *Port Chalmers*, *Melbourne Star* and *Rochester Castle*, strung out in line astern, he now had only *Ashanti*, the cruisers *Kenya* and *Charybdis*, and the destroyers *Intrepid*, *Icarus*, *Fury* and *Pathfinder*.

The earlier Stuka attacks had been partly frustrated by the fierce " Umbrella " barrage, but, lacking an outer screen, Admiral Burrough grimly calculated that if the enemy attacked with torpedo bombers there would be small means of keeping them at a safe distance.

The first torpedo strike came at 10.50 a.m., when twelve Italian bombers were sighted flying in low on the port beam. The cruisers immediately engaged them with their heavy armament, but the enemy airmen pressed home their attack. At the same moment another higher flying group of aircraft released parachute mines and circling torpedoes.

Sirens boomed and the ships heeled into a sharp emergency turn. The mines and circling torpedoes fell all round the ships, but none were hit. The torpedo attack was partly foiled by the quick turn and heavy barrage, but *Port Chalmers* had an almost miraculous escape. One torpedo passed right under her. Then her master, Captain H. G. B. Pinkney, noticed heavy vibration on the wire of the starboard paravane. Paravanes are submerged floats towed from the bows of a ship by wires which stream out at an angle and protect the ship's sides from mines; when *Port Chalmers's* crew had almost wound in their paravane wire, they found that the float had caught an unexploded torpedo.

With this lethal " fish " firmly hooked to the ship, the master sent a frantic signal to *Ashanti* : " What shall we do with this ? "

His predicament was a dangerous one. To let go the paravane might immediately explode the torpedo close to the ship's side. Similarly, the torpedo might also explode if he went ahead to veer the paravane away from the ship.

Admiral Burrough, who could now plainly see the fouled torpedo, ordered him to stop the ship, let her slowly gather sternway, and then cut the paravane adrift when it was as far away as the wire would take it.

Slowly *Port Chalmers* went astern until the paravane and its deadly companion lay about a hundred yards ahead. As the wire was cut there was a gigantic explosion, but a swift examination showed that there had been no damage and the convoy sailed on.

As another dive-bombing attack was being beaten off, a column of water shot up close to *Kenya's* bows. The cruiser slowed to ten knots and signalled the flagship that her forward engine-room was on fire. After twenty minutes of anxiety, however, the fire was put out and *Kenya* was steaming with the convoy again at sixteen knots.

Despite considerable difficulties, the Malta-based long-range Spitfires and Beaufighters were giving fleet and convoy some protection, but the Axis formations were coming out from Sicily at low level and could not easily be picked up by radar. The intercepting planes, without communication with the ships, were frequently unable to engage their opponents before the attacks developed. Four enemy planes, however, were shot down and seen to fall into the sea. Admiral Burrough also noticed that a number of formations broke up and turned for home without making an attack.

The close-range Spitfires, now reinforced by the thirty-six flown in from the carrier *Furious* in " Operation Bellows," were still unable to reach the convoy, but they carried out sweeps towards Sicily and succeeded in intercepting some of the attacking aircraft.

In addition, a Wellington bomber circled the stricken

Ohio in case the Italians should hazard a daylight E-boat attack.

Another friend of *Ohio* was also about to come to her aid. *Ledbury* had finished picking up survivors from *Waimarama* and had increased to full speed to join the convoy thirty miles ahead. She sent a signal to Admiral Burrough :

INTERROGATIVE STOP REJOIN OR GO HOME

When the signal rating handed Commander Roger Hill the admiral's reply, he found that the code groups of the message had been received corruptly. He was apparently ordered to proceed to the Orkney and Shetland Islands ! The captain and his number one, Lieutenant Anthony Hollins, considered the signal. It was plainly intended as an order to return to Gibraltar, but they might be forgiven for not interpreting it correctly. Ahead of them lay *Ohio*, the ship they had led back to the convoy the previous night, and consequently both men had a proprietary feeling about her. Now she was alone, evidently in trouble, and exposed to the full force of the air attack. Plainly it was *Ledbury's* duty to go to the assistance of the tanker. So, as a great seaman had done before him, Roger Hill turned a blind eye to the signal and set course for *Ohio*.

As she approached the tanker was making less than two knots and great gouts of alternate black and white smoke were pouring from her funnel.

The destroyer ranged alongside and Hill shouted an offer of a tow to Captain Mason. At that moment, the engines finally expired with a great puff of black smoke.

197

Ohio presented a sad sight. She was low in the water, there was a great rent in her port side and daylight could be seen streaming in from the starboard. Paint was scorched and blackened where the fire had taken a hold and her deck upper-works and smoke stack were so peppered with machine-gun bullets and splinters that they looked like colanders.

The fuselage of the broken German bomber lay on the forepeak and one of the wings straddled the side of the bridge. Aircraft parts, shell and bomb splinters were strewn on her decks, so that it was difficult to walk without stepping on them.

The men were bleary and red-eyed and almost asleep at their posts, but when a Junkers 88 came out of the sun towards them, the gun barrels swung swiftly on to the target and the stiff defensive fire caused the pilot to drop his stick of bombs short of the destroyer and tanker. Battered, battle-scarred and disabled she might be and the men dazed and tired, but *Ohio* could still hit back.

At this critical moment in Malta's destiny, *Ledbury* stood by the crippled tanker as successive waves of enemy bombers dived in to finish off so valuable a prize. The addition of her guns probably tipped the scales between victory and defeat, for in each case the enemy was beaten off. Then the destroyer *Penn* arrived with orders to take over the protection of *Ohio* and, if possible, tow her to Malta. The alternative was to take off her crew and scuttle her, for at all costs so valuable a cargo had to be denied to the enemy.

As the captains of the two destroyers were concerting arrangements for the tow, *Ledbury* intercepted a signal from Vice-Admiral Leatham in Malta, suggesting that she should be sent to look for the missing cruiser *Manchester*, for at this stage he did not know that she had sunk.

Regretfully, Roger Hill set course for Cape Bon. He did not know it then but he was soon to see *Ohio* again.

As *Ledbury* sped away westwards towards the African coast, where *Manchester* had last been seen, Lieutenant Commander J. H. Swain, R.N., edged *Penn* alongside the battered *Ohio*.

" I'm going to try to tow you out of this, Captain," shouted Commander Swain. " Can you take a 10-inch manilla ? "

Captain Mason waved assent and despatched a party forward under the second officer, McKilligan. It took them nearly twenty minutes to clear away part of the cockpit of the crashed German aircraft and other debris from the bits to which they meant to attach the towing line.

When all was ready Mason signalled the destroyer. *Penn* ranged slowly alongside, then a rating on the stern flung a heaving line. Quickly they began to haul in the tow. The heavy manilla rope came over the side, and as it did so a German bomber came howling out of the sun. The men flung themselves to the deck as two near-misses deluged the fo'c'sle with water. The brisk return fire, however, drove off the raider, and the men began once more to heave in the rope.

At last the tow was secured with four turns round the bitts, and the captain signalled *Penn* that all was now ready. Slowly, the destroyer began to go ahead. The rope tightened, shedding a fine spray as the strands bit. With a jerk the destroyer stopped as the full weight of *Ohio* came upon her, then, ordering further revolutions she forged ahead again and *Ohio* began to move. The hull gathered way, and as it did so the great rent in her side began to turn her inexorably to port. Without motive power it was impossible to operate the steering gear to counteract this movement. *Penn* was straining on the tow at almost full revolutions. The bitts creaked and the rope stood straight and hard as an iron bar. Still *Ohio* turned until the destroyer was towing at an angle of ninety degrees.

The tanker came almost to a stop and her head began to pay off slowly in the direction of Malta. *Penn* tried again, but *Ohio* still turned away to port.

They were making no progress at all, in fact with the easterly wind they were drifting backwards.

Mason seized the loud-hailer : " It's no good," he shouted. " The only way is either to tow from alongside or with one ahead and another ship astern."

" Where's the other ship coming from ? " came back the reply. " Let's have another try."

On board *Ohio* the engineers, blackened, oil-stained and weary, came out on deck. They could do nothing now until a full inspection of the boilers could be made, and for that the casings would have to be allowed to cool. Even then, although they refused to entertain the idea, there was nothing that they could do, nothing, that is, without hours of time and spare parts, which lay many miles away.

All were in the last stages of exhaustion after their

fight to keep *Ohio* moving, but all of them immediately volunteered to help serve the guns. Unfortunately, at this stage, many of the Oerlikons were temporarily out of action. The sudden cooling of barrels and mechanism by continual deluges of water from close bombs had caused all manner of minor stoppages and other damage. Many of them were already red with rust.

Grinstead, the third engineer, was almost all in. Down in the engine-room he had performed prodigies of strength and dexterity. Now he was to experience the full shock of air attack on deck. Wiping the grease from his face with an oily rag he asked Collins at the ammunition hoist : " Where's the best place, Jumbo ? "

" Where they ain't gonna drop," said Collins. Then with sudden urgency : " That's here. Quick. Get down." The pumpman pulled Grinstead down beside him. As he did so a huge gout of water drenched them both. In eighteen inches of water, Grinstead was struggling to get up and retrieve his tin hat which had been washed off. Collins, wise from bitter experience, held on to him tightly. An eighteen inch bomb splinter crashed down just in front of them—just where Grinstead would have been had he gone for the tin hat.

As the attack developed, *Penn* went to full speed to part the tow. At the end of the line she was a " sitting duck " and, moreover, in a poor position to protect the tanker. The manilla snapped, frayed ends snaking back viciously, and the destroyer turned hard to port with all her guns blazing.

Another bomber came screaming down towards the *Ohio* from the starboard beam. The lower bridge

Oerlikon opened up and the first few rounds were close. Then the gunner found the range and the aircraft disappeared with a crack into flying smoke and splinters. But in the split second before death had come to the German airmen the bomb-aimer had released his cargo. A bomb hit *Ohio* just under the water amidships, where the torpedo had already rent the side.

As water and splinters crashed down on the deck, Captain Mason could see the ship bend to port.

" I reckon that's broken her back," he shouted grimly to Barton. Wearily he got up from the deck and made his way down to make an inspection.

The plates had opened farther. Now there was more water in the amidships section and it looked as though the adjoining tank was being flooded. The captain thought it was only a matter of time now. He straightened up and looked around him. The men were practically asleep. They had plainly reached that stage of exhaustion at which even the greatest danger could only call forth a slow, sluggish movement. Many were already nodding at their posts.

Gray, the first officer, still stood by the immobilised steering engine, leaning his head, cushioned upon folded arms, against the steel plates of the deck-house. He had been on duty for more than thirty hours, first on the bridge, then conning the ship from astern since she had been torpedoed the day before.

The protecting destroyer, *Penn*, nosed her way almost alongside, and the captain cupped his hands : " There's nothing we can do at the moment, I'm afraid," he shouted ; " We'll have to wait for dark. Why don't you

abandon ship for the present, and come aboard here?
You're just risking your lives to no good. You can go
back to-night."

" I don't think she'll last that long," Mason shouted
back. " She's broken her back by the look of it. We'll
come aboard if you don't mind."

He looked round the battered decks. So this was what
they had fought for all this time—to leave the ship,
their mission unaccomplished. He hated the idea, but
the destroyer captain was right. He gave the order to
abandon ship.

With easy skill, *Penn* manœuvred alongside, until the
two ships were nearly touching. The crew of *Ohio*
mustered their last reserves of strength to jump on to
the destroyer's deck. When all had gone, Captain Mason
bid what he thought was likely to be a last farewell
to his ship, and followed them.

He looked mechanically at his watch as he did so.
It was still only 2 p.m.

Aboard *Penn* the decks were already crowded with
survivors from other merchant ships. The men of *Ohio*
sought out empty corners and dropped into immediate
slumber. Many of them could not be woken when the
stewards of the destroyer came round with tea.

The tanker now stood alone, deserted. She was low
in the water, and as *Penn* circled her slowly there was
not one man who thought she would survive.

Meanwhile, *Ledbury* was racing westwards at speed
in search of *Manchester*. So far, no word had been received
from the destroyers *Eskimo* and *Somali*, which had
left five hours previously to look for her. These

two ships had picked up part of the crew of the American merchantman *Almiera Lykes* and *Wairangi* before continuing with their search. Though abandoned, both of these merchantmen were still afloat, but the commanding officer of *Eskimo* did not sink them as he thought he might have an opportunity later of salvaging them. Close in to the Tunisian shore, *Eskimo* and *Somali* had found some of *Manchester's* company on rafts and lifeboats, and they then learned for the first time that the cruiser had been scuttled upon the orders of her captain. Other survivors could be seen on the beach being marched away by French soldiers to internment. While these rescue operations were proceeding, an Italian plane circled and, instead of attacking the destroyers, dropped a raft near some swimmers. A German Junkers 88, which followed it, was not so gentlemanly. It machine-gunned both ships.

Having picked up all the men they could find, the two destroyers set course for Gibraltar, and it was then that they found among the survivors the four missing men from *Ohio*. According to them, they had launched a lifeboat as soon as the torpedo had struck, but in the process the lifeboat had capsized, throwing them into the water. Later they had been picked up by *Manchester*, only to have to take to the boats once again.

All this was unknown to the captain of *Ledbury*, for he had received neither the signal reporting the sinking of the *Manchester* nor that detailing the picking up of her survivors. For some time, the signal staff in the destroyer had been showing signs of serious deterioration of efficiency in receiving and decoding messages. The reason was clear. They were desperately tired. As with the crew of *Ohio*, and, indeed, with the crew of every ship in the fleet, the men in *Ledbury* were reaching the limit of their endurance. A number of them were also suffering from painfully swollen ankles.

Commander Roger Hill realised that the fatigue of his ship's company had reached a dangerous point. He sought for a means of reviving them, and realised that some surprise, some sudden success, that would wake them up again was needed. A few minutes later the opportunity occurred.

Two three-engined Italian torpedo-bombers came in suddenly on the port beam. With only a split second to weigh the consequences, Commander Hill rang the cease-fire bells for the heavy 4-inch guns. He calculated that if they held their fire the Italians might come close enough for accurate shooting by the Oerlikons and light armament before releasing their torpedoes. On came the bombers. Their markings were plainly visible now. The number one, Lieutenant Anthony Hollins, stared at the captain as if he was mad. The captain ordered " Hard a-port," and, as he did so all the guns opened up together. Flames burst from the port engines of one of the aircraft. Then fire began to stream from the other. The crew cheered as both plunged into the sea.

The captain's ruse had succeeded, but it nearly ended in disaster. Torpedoes, launched by both aircraft, were running towards them, and one almost scraped down the side of the ship ; but the crew were awake now. Tiredness seemed to have fallen from them.

" I think we might splice the mainbrace. Don't you, Number One ? " said the captain with a grin. The signal for splicing the mainbrace was solemnly hoisted, and the coxswain and supply petty officer got up the rum. This completed the cure for the time being.

As *Ledbury* pressed on, two columns of smoke appeared on the horizon. They altered course towards them, but as they approached they saw that it was blazing oil and petrol marking the graves of two merchant ships sunk early that morning. Soon after they sighted the Tunisian coast through the thick heat haze. They had made an almost perfect landfall, off the village of Hammamet.

They could not, of course, find any sign of *Manchester*. *Ledbury* cruised slowly down the coast, searching, and when she was off Ras-mahmur, the Vichy signal station at Neboel started calling up in morse : " VHM—VHA." *Ledbury* made no reply. They had already hauled down their ensign as a precautionary measure. Farther down the coast at Hammamet the signal station there ran up a series of international flags, reading : " Show your signal letters." The captain immediately ordered the hoisting of an Italian group consisting of the flag : " I " and three other flags tied in knots so as to be unreadable. This seemed to satisfy the Frenchman, for he broke out a large French " N " sign and there was no more communication.

Preparations were then made to bury the body of one of the men picked out of the burning sea during the morning. It had been sewn up in canvas, but there was difficulty about finding something to weight it down.

The chief engineer refused point-blank to supply fire-bricks, which were usually used, for he was already short of them. Despite protests from the gunner's mate, an armour-piercing shell was used instead.

The body was buried with full military honours, a firing-party and a white ensign draped over the canvas-shrouded corpse, and Lieutenant Hollins read the funeral service.

For more than two hours *Ledbury* steamed up and down the coast searching, but could find nothing. Then they received a signal from R.A.F. Reconnaissance that an Italian cruiser and two destroyers had been sighted off Zembra not much more than thirty miles to the north-ward of the destroyer. It was clearly time to go. The captain rang down for twenty-four knots and set course back to the eastward. He was determined to return to the assistance of *Ohio* if she still remained afloat.

Meanwhile, the leading ships of the convoy and their escort had experienced their last air attack. At 12.30 p.m. they came under the protection of the close range Spitfires from Malta. With more than a score of British planes patrolling, the Axis decided to call it a day.

Two hours later, the Malta force of minesweepers, commanded by Commander Jerome in *Speedy*, joined Admiral Burrough and took over responsibility for the convoy. *Rye* was detached to assist *Ohio*.

At 4 p.m. Admiral Burrough with Force X withdrew to the westward.

Preceded by minesweepers searching the channel, three battle-scarred ships, *Port Chalmers*, *Rochester Castle* and *Melbourne Star* whose sides were burned and blistered by the flames from *Waimarama* approached Valletta. They passed into the Grand Harbour at 6.18 p.m. to the cheers of the inhabitants lining the medieval ramparts.

Now, Malta had the food to sustain the siege, but, unknown to the jubilant Maltese, the position was as desperate as ever. Without *Ohio's* cargo of oil and paraffin, the Island could not survive, and that cargo was still seventy miles away in an abandoned and apparently sinking ship.

CHAPTER FOURTEEN

TOO LATE TO SAVE *OHIO*?

Rye to Vice-Admiral Malta :
JOINED PENN WITH MLS. 121 AND 168 STANDING
BY OHIO POSITION 36 DEGREES 00 MINUTES
NORTH 12 DEGREES 59 MINUTES EAST 13/8 AT
1740 HOURS STOP TOW WILL BE ATTEMPTED
MESSAGE ENDS

On board H.M.S. *Penn*, Chief Officer Stephen shook two of the sleeping members of the tanker's crew : " Captain wants volunteers to go on board the ship again," he said, as they looked up sleepily.

Captain Mason, standing nearby, stiffened : " Volunteers be damned," he shouted. " We've still got a crew, haven't we ? "

He sprang on to a water tank and cupped his hands. " *Ohio, Ohio*—wakey wakey ! "

Along the main deck of the destroyer the sleepers were stirring now. They turned over and shook themselves, then slowly sat up like tired animals. As Mason shouted again they looked towards him.

" Listen, men. The ship is still afloat. If you look out there you'll see there's a minesweeper joined us. The Navy's going to tow us. It's our duty to be back there and take that tow in. Shake it up now. We'll be alongside in a minute, and I want everyone aboard."

209

Slowly, the men got up, staggering a little with tiredness. Then they looked around them. Out on the starboard quarter lay *Ohio*, low in the water but still intact, still floating. Circling slowly round her were the two launches 121 and 168 and the fleet minesweeper *Rye* from Malta. Aboard the minesweeper men were already preparing the towing gear.

Penn came slowly alongside the battered tanker. Captain Mason was the first to jump aboard, and he was followed by the whole crew.

Without a word the engineers disappeared down the engine-room companionway. The gunners settled down behind their guns, cocked the mechanism and examined the magazines. The deck-hands were told off for various duties.

When they had abandoned the ship four hours before, they had been at the end of their tether. They could scarcely have fought the ship a moment longer. Now, after resting aboard the destroyer, a new spirit had surged up in them. Their bodies were tired but the will to resist had returned.

Chief Officer Gray had led a party forward and was preparing to receive the tow.

Down below, in the pitch dark, groping round the intricate mass of machinery with the aid of torches, the chief engineer, Jimmy Wyld, aided by Murray, the fourth, and Junior Engineer Sless was checking valves and closing those which had been left open during the hurried abandonment of the ship.

At the after-end of the steering flat the second and third engineers, Buddle and Grinstead, were superintending the rigging of emergency steering gear, while Stephen, the third officer, stood by with four men at the one remaining telephone which connected with the bridge, waiting to operate it.

Meanwhile, Pumpman Collins and the storekeeper, " Ginger " Leach, had been told off for a tough job.

In the darkness of the engine-room, feeling every foot of the way to make sure the gratings were still in position below their feet, they tried to locate two sets of chain blocks which had to be used on the relieving gear for the emergency steering. In this part of the engine-room behind the boilers there was a strong smell of ammonia, which happened to be Collins's pet aversion. However, the search went on, both men holding their noses, and the blocks were finally located between two water tanks. Laboriously they dragged them to the steerage flat and, feeling rather pleased with themselves, for doing a job which would normally have occupied five or six men, they reported to the chief officer. Gray, however, was unimpressed :

" Where have you been ? Stop to have a cup of tea ? " he asked.

Out in the Mediterranean sunlight *Penn's* tow had been made fast to *Ohio*. The destroyer went ahead, but once more the gaping hole in the tanker's side made her turn sharply to port. *Penn* slacked the tow. Then her captain hailed Mason : " You'll have to get that rudder working," he shouted over the loud hailer, " we can't tow her like this."

Mason phoned Stephen : " For heaven's sake get that

rudder cast off," he shouted, " or we'll never get to Malta."

In the steering flat, engineers and deck-hands were struggling to rig the hand steering gear. The chains connecting the rudder to the now useless emergency steering engine were cast off. Cables were then attached to the chains and reeved through the relieving tackles. It was a heavy job yet somehow they managed to finish it in half an hour.

With the deck-hands manning the cables, Stephen phoned the bridge.

" All ready, sir. We've set the rudder to give her about five or six degrees to starboard. You can try now to tow."

Captain Mason signalled *Penn*, and slowly the towing wire took the strain. The tanker began to forge forward again. The destroyer increased speed and now *Ohio* was going forward at five or six knots, with only a slight tendency to turn to port.

This speed, however, could not be maintained. A fluke of wind here or a fluke of tide there would begin to send the tanker into a turn and the destroyer at the end of her tow veering to starboard with her stern would be dragged inwards by the deadweight of the tanker.

Captain Mason phoned the steering flat : " We're still swinging. Do you think you could steer her with the tackles ? "

The reply was a sharp and impolite negative. The tackles were too heavy.

Penn and *Rye* then had a short conference. A new

plan was devised. *Rye* passed 300 fathoms of her sweep wire to the destroyer, who made it fast amidships. Both naval vessels went ahead again, *Rye* acting as a stabilising factor for the destroyer. *Ohio* was soon towing again at between four and five knots, and the tendency to swing had been overcome.

Air activity had been unusually absent while these towing operations were going on, but shortly after 6.30 the ominous drone of engines could be heard and the gunners peered anxiously through the haze awaiting the inevitable attack. Mason ordered the engineers on deck as a safety precaution.

Unfortunately, the strike developed from astern. Four Junkers 88s came in at low level and the two towing naval vessels had difficulty in bringing their guns to bear. One bomb landed close astern of *Ohio*, immobilising the rudder. As Mason ducked he saw that another would hit the ship.

It crashed through the fore-end of the boat deck, exploding on the boiler tops, forcing the engine-room staff out on deck. As they tumbled out of the engine-room companionway, coughing and choking, it could be seen that they were blinded with asbestos lagging off the top of the boiler. Their faces, clothes and hands were smothered with blue powder.

Simultaneously, an engine-room ventilator fell on to the Bofors gun.

The gun-crew picked themselves up and began burrowing frantically at the debris.

" There's a man under here," someone shouted, and other members of the crew ran to help them.

Finally they dragged out the body of Gunner Brown, the gun trainer. He was still alive, but plainly critically injured internally.

Mason made another examination of the ship. The bomb had had a delayed action. It had pierced two decks and then blown most of the engine-room to pieces. Had he not just given orders to Wyld and his men to come on deck, many of them would have been killed. The rudder was now useless, and the tow had been cast off by the destroyer. Even a superficial examination of the rent amidships showed that the gap had widened and that *Ohio* had almost certainly broken her back. Two more air attacks were made and bombs fell close to both *Penn* and *Rye*. Cascades of water crashed aboard the fore-deck of *Ohio* as a stick narrowly missed her.

Once more Mason gave the order to abandon ship and the two motor launches, anticipating this, were already alongside.

Despite a continuous air attack the crew left the ship in an orderly fashion. First, the injured gunner was lowered slowly over the side on a stretcher, then, one by one, the crew left.

The chief engineer went to his own quarters and grabbed a bag. On deck he found the captain with the ship's papers. " I suppose this is the finish ? " said Wyld.

" I'm afraid so. Anyhow, we'll have to get off her for the present."

Wyld went over the side, and Mason had a last look round to make sure that no one was left behind. As he reached the rail again, he hesitated.

"Hurry up," said the commander of the motor launch. "I want to get away from here. It doesn't look too healthy."

"I think I'm going to stop," Mason replied.

"Don't be a damn fool. You can't do any good there. She'll be sinking any moment," said the ML captain. Mason knew he was right. There was little chance that *Ohio* would outlast the night. He threw his case over the side into the launch and quickly followed it.

Night, bringing the blessed relief from air attack, was now falling, but astern of *Ohio* and her little group of protectors, the merchantman *Dorset* had ended her brave struggle to reach Malta. Hit by three more bombs, she settled down slowly by the head. Not many minutes after her crew had abandoned her, she sank. *Dorset's* escort, the destroyer *Bramham*, picked up the survivors, and then joined the fight to save *Ohio*.

There now came a parting of the ways for *Ohio's* crew. Chief Engineer Wyld, Chief Officer Gray, and Third Mate Stephen, with some thirty of the crew, had gone aboard Launch 168. They took it in turn to smoke thirteen cigarettes contributed by Pumpman Collins, the only ones remaining amongst them, then all dropped off into a dreamless sleep. When they awoke they were in Malta. The launch had developed an engine defect and had been ordered to return to the Island. Ashore they settled down to what seemed the greatest feed of their life—tinned herrings, dry bread and tea. They were safe, yet every man felt vaguely cheated. Collins expressed it like this : "Don't know what you chaps think, but I wish we could have stood by the old girl

215

to the end," he said. The others nodded and murmured agreement.

Meanwhile, the other launch had put the critically injured gunner and Captain Mason aboard *Penn*. The tanker's master was immediately called for a conference with Lieutenant-Commander Swain, captain of *Penn*.

" Do you think she'll last ? " he asked, as Mason reached the bridge.

Mason shook his head : " Difficult to say, sir," he replied. " The engine-room and after end are flooding but the forward end is holding its buoyancy. She'll have to break her back if that goes on. Still, we've got to get some of that oil to Malta if we can."

Lieutenant-Commander Swain nodded : " We'll do everything we can. But you'd better get some sleep, Captain. You look all in."

" I suppose you're right," said Mason, with a grin. " We've had a fairly busy day, you know."

While Mason at last found sleep in a corner of the wardroom, the captains of *Penn* and *Rye* had a parley. A new plan was made. A small party from *Penn*, under the leadership of Lieutenant George Marten, the executive officer, went aboard the tanker. *Rye* took the towing position ahead, securing the chain cable previously slipped by *Penn*. *Penn* made fast astern of the tanker, acting as rear tug to keep *Ohio* from swinging. Meanwhile, *Bramham* circled the group, watching for submarines.

Slowly they worked up speed and not long after midnight had reached four and a half knots. At one o'clock, however, *Rye* decided to attempt a further increase of speed. It was too much. The tanker took charge and careered to port, out of control. Before the tow-lines could be cast off, both had snapped.

Lieutenant-Commander Swain was now in a quandary. In the pitch dark a renewal of the tow would be difficult, moreover, the method they had been using plainly would not work. While some new means of getting the tanker moving were being sought, *Bramham* signalled the suggestion that attempts should be made to move the tanker by towing alongside. This scheme was immediately adopted and Swain began the delicate manoeuvre of laying *Penn* alongside the damaged tanker in the dark.

With engines scarcely turning over, the destroyer glided up to the tanker. As the two ships came together, the jagged rent in the derelict's side grated ominously on *Penn's* plates despite the fenders over her sides.

The ships were made fast and Swain rang down for slow ahead. The grinding and grating increased, but *Ohio* remained stationary. The destroyer tried full speed, but it soon became apparent that the tanker was too heavy to be moved by a single destroyer. Moreover, the alarming noises from between the two ships threatened serious damage if this method was continued. Commander Swain rang *Penn's* engines to stop.

Since the destroyer had gone alongside *Ohio* a steady stream of men had been passing between the two ships. Despite their own ordeal, the American survivors from *Santa Elisa* could not resist a souvenir hunt. Pieces of crashed aircraft, shell splinters, bullets and mangled pieces of metal from *Ohio's* own wounds were all quickly snapped up. Many of *Penn's* crew were also busy. Some items in the magnificent stores aboard the American tanker were rare aboard His Majesty's ships at that time. Also the tanker had a well-stocked N.A.A.F.I. No one believed *Ohio* would last the night and there seemed to be no harm in " liberating " such valuable supplies from the hungry sea. When Captain Mason awoke next morning he saw his own typewriter installed on *Penn's* wardroom table.

Finally, Commander Swain decided that further attempts at towing in the darkness were hopeless. *Penn* cast off, and once more the tanker was alone. Low in the water, her engine-room flooded and groaning now with every movement of the Mediterranean as the sinking after-part placed more and more strain on the torpedo damage, the end seemed near. Malta was still more than sixty miles away.

To the westward, Admiral Burrough's Force X was rounding Cape Bon at twenty-one knots on their voyage back to Gibraltar. Meanwhile, *Ledbury*, returning from her search for *Manchester*, was steaming at full speed to the aid of *Ohio*. As darkness began to tinge with the pink of dawn, they had arrived at the estimated position of the tanker, but could find no sign of her. A little later Commander Hill sighted gunfire ahead. It was *Ohio's* escort beating off the first snoopers of the day.

As *Ledbury* approached in the gaining daylight, her crew sighted *Ohio*. She was lying deep in the water now, down by the stern; the line of the deck seemed to be decidedly bent.

Hill turned to Hollins, his number one : " It looks as though we're too late," he said.

CHAPTER FIFTEEN

THE LONG TOW

Penn to Senior Officer Minesweepers :
14/8/42 0755 POSITION 36 DEGREES 2 MINUTES
NORTH 013 DEGREES 10 MINUTES EAST RYE
BRAMHAM AND MLS IN COMPANY STOP OHIO
DEEPLY DAMAGED WITHOUT STEERING WILL NOT
TOW STOP RYE TRYING AGAIN AND WILL
CONTINUE TO TRY MESSAGE ENDS

While the little fleet of ships surrounding *Ohio* were preparing to make further attempts to tow after a night of failure, Captain Mason stood on an oil drum on the low stern of *Penn*. A few of *Ohio's* crew, who had awakened, stood round him. On a grating rigged by one of the entry ports lay a tighty-sewn bundle of canvas. It contained the body of Gunner Brown, now ready for burial at sea. He had died during the night.

Mason took off his steel helmet and the men standing round him followed suit. Unhurriedly, he began reading the burial service. Some of *Penn's* ratings, paying out a steel hawser, paused in their work, took off their tin hats and also stood silent with their heads bowed.

" We therefore commit his body to the deep."

Bosun Thacker of *Ohio* tipped the grating. The swathed body slipped into the sea. A swirl of water, a few bubbles, and it was gone.

". . . according to the mighty working, whereby He is able to subdue all things to Himself." Mason put on his tin hat, got down from the oil drum and looked over the side. It seemed an age since the ventilator had fallen, years and years since they had passed Gibraltar. Now the dawn of another day was breaking, and there was work to do. He shook the tiredness off him and went to report to the captain of *Penn*.

During the night Commander Swain had tried once more to tow the tanker with her own 10-inch manilla, but this too, had failed.

As Mason reached the bridge, the commander had just received a message from *Ledbury* : " May we help ? " Commander Swain turned to his Chief Yeoman : " Send ' For goodness' sake, yes, we need it ' to *Ledbury*," he said. Then, turning to Mason : " Well, Captain, we're going to have another try. We've got more ships now. But I don't like the looks of your tanker."

Mason gazed at *Ohio*, carefully measuring levels. " I doubt if she's got much more than three or four foot freeboard," he said. " But tankers are funny things. This one's really tough. She might stay afloat."

The two men watched as *Rye* passed the end of her 300 fathoms of sweep wire to the small naval party aboard the tanker. Meanwhile, *Ledbury* was making fast astern of her so that when the tow began they would have more control over the tendency of the derelict to sheer.

Once more *Rye* got the tanker moving, and *Ledbury*, going astern, tried to keep her straight ; but she pulled too hard and both tows parted.

On *Penn's* bridge Captain Mason commented : " If they try that too often they'll pull the ship in half. She's only hanging on amidships with about half her keel."

Ledbury cautiously approached the port side of *Ohio* and made fast alongside. She immediately put aboard a small party of men under the gunner, Charles Musham, and the men busied themselves on the tanker's fo'c'sle, passing down a big towing hawser to *Ledbury*. The most active man amongst them was Cook, the bosun of *Melbourne Star*. Despite his dreadful experiences in the blazing grave of *Waimarama*, and nearly two hours in the sea waiting to be picked up, the bosun was back on duty, a mine of energy and practical seamanship.

Other survivors of the merchantmen were also anxious to bear a hand, amongst them the American third officer of *Santa Elisa*, Frederick Larsen. He went to Commander Hill and asked if he could take a party aboard *Ohio* to repair and man one of the anti-aircraft guns. *Ledbury's* captain gladly accepted the offer. Many of his own crew had had no sleep for three days and it was as much as they could do to cope with the problems aboard the destroyer.

Larsen, with Cadet Dale and three of the British gunners from *Santa Elisa* then boarded the tanker and at once set to work clearing the debris of the ventilator from the Bofors gun, and within half an hour they were ready to meet the next air attack which, to judge by the activity of snooping aircraft, could be expected at any time.

None of these men, in spite of their previous

experiences, seemed to worry about the fact that *Ohio* now had no lifeboats, was sinking and would be a certain target for every enemy attacker.

Ledbury, her tow secured, now sheered off, and, despite the fact that she was only alongside about five minutes, unofficial boarding parties "acquired" one large typewriter, a number of telephones of which the destroyer had much need, two Oerlikon cannons and twelve magazines, besides a variety of smaller articles including a fine megaphone with S.S. *Ohio* stamped on it.

Meanwhile, *Rye* had again begun to tow *Ohio* with *Ledbury* acting as stern tug. With less pull from *Ledbury*, a fair speed was maintained, but, once again, steering proved impossible. The shattered tanker was pointing more often in any direction except towards Malta.

Clearly, a stabilising factor was needed, and Commander Swain edged *Penn* into the starboard side of *Ohio*, and made fast alongside her.

As soon as this manœuvre had been completed, two more parties went aboard the stricken tanker. One was led by *Penn's* engineer officer, Lieutenant-Commander John Sweall, R.N., who had orders to try to improve *Ohio's* buoyancy.

The other consisted of Captain Mason who, with Commander Swain's permission, went to examine his ship with eight members of *Ohio's* crew.

Mason began by sounding all the tanks and he found the picture better than might have been expected. Empty tanks and holds were still intact and dry, though kerosene was still overflowing from the port tanks where the lids had been buckled by torpedo explosion. Evidently, the chief doubt was whether the keel plate could hold *Ohio* together or not. With the forward part of the tanker buoyant and the stern sinking, an intolerable strain had been placed on the amidships section, rent as it was, right across and almost down to the bottom.

Meanwhile, Commander Sweall had examined the tanker's compressed air system to see if it could be used to increase the buoyancy of the tanks which were not leaking or which could be sealed. So great had been the battering that the tanker had received during days of attack, that scarcely a foot of compressed air-line was undamaged, and it was plainly out of the question to attempt to use it. He, therefore, sent to the destroyer for portable pumps, and these were brought aboard and set to work pumping the water out of the engine-room.

Mason and Sweall had a hasty conference.

" The ship is pretty sound except for the amidships section," said Mason. " But unless we can check the flooding aft she's bound to break her back. Do you think you can hold the water with your pumps ? "

Commander Sweall shook his head : " It's difficult to say. If there's no further damage she might hold up." He did a quick calculation : " As far as I can see she's still making about six inches an hour in the engine-room, and we're now doing the best we can."

Commander Swain passed the master's report to Commander Jerome in *Speedy* who was now the senior officer. He had returned with the fleet minesweepers

Speedy, Hebe and *Hythe* to help with the tow and to form
a protective screen.

Aboard *Ohio*, Gunner Musham, organising the manning of the guns, was swearing quietly under his breath :
" Some devil has pinched all the Oerlikon gun
sights," he muttered.

Nevertheless, he placed himself behind one of the
sightless Oerlikons and saw with satisfaction that
ammunition parties were at the ready.

Behind the Bofors gun, the American, Larsen,
hummed gently to himself : " Sister Anne, Sister Anne,
can you see anyone coming ? "

Then, as *Ledbury* was stopped, the wire hawser she had
made fast to the stern of the tanker hung down in a
great bight between the two ships. It was found to be
resting on her starboard propeller, threatening to become
foul of it as soon as she got under way. After a short
flap, the danger was averted. *Ledbury* went ahead slowly
on her port propeller and the hawser was eased out of
harm's way.

Rye and *Bramham* slowly got under way again with
Ledbury acting as a rudder. Gradually working up speed,
they soon had the tanker crabbing through the water
at more than six knots. The tendency to sheer had been
overcome, and success at last seemed to be within their
grasp.

Now, however, when hopes had risen high, and when
it seemed that the vital cargo could at last be brought
to Malta, the drone of many bombers' engines filled the
air. It was plain that the Axis were making another
attempt to finish off the tanker. At 10.45 the first wave

of dive-bombers could be seen coming in to attack. The dark shapes of six Junkers 88s came streaking over the water towards *Ohio*. All the guns opened up together. Gunner Musham, without sights to his guns, sprayed the oncoming formation hose-pipe fashion. The leading aircraft began to stream black smoke, broke formation, and dived into the sea at nearly 300 miles an hour, sending up a great column of spray. The other aircraft, daunted by the thick, accurate barrage, dropped their bombs and turned aside too early. Only one oil bomb crashed close to the bows of *Ohio*, showering her prow with black burning liquid.

Three more echelons of German planes could now be seen approaching, but help was at hand. Sixteen Spitfires of 249 and 229 Squadron from Malta, despite lack of R/T direction, and with no warning from radar of the impending attack, had sighted the enemy. Diving in from 6,000 feet, they attacked the Junkers 88s from ahead. The first enemy formation wavered and broke. Half the Spitfires pressed on to attack the two following flights while the other half turned sharply and got in among the disorganised German aircraft. Two black bombers fell out of the air flaming. The second flight of Junkers also broke as the Spitfires flashed through them. Dog-fights had now developed all over the sky, but part of the third German formation pressed on towards the ships. One section of Spitfires broke away from the general engagement and pursued it. It was a question of whether the bombers could reach the tanker before they were overtaken by the Spitfires. The British planes closed in, their guns firing. Three of the German aircraft began to jink, their bombing fatally interrupted. A single Junkers 88 held its course, and a 1,000 pound bomb came hurtling down towards *Ohio*.

It landed directly in the wake of the tanker, and she was flung violently forward, parting *Rye's* tow. The stern plates buckled, and the dark waters gushed in through a great hole.

Meanwhile, the only other straggler from the convoy left afloat, the battered *Brisbane Star*, was sailing proudly towards the Grand Harbour under her own steam, protected from above by a strong escort of Beaufighters and Spitfires.

Since his exchange with the signal station at Hammamet, her master, Captain Riley, had passed safely through many vicissitudes.

No attempt had been made to stop him as he sailed on down the Gulf of Hammamet until after several hours' steaming the lookout sighted a U-boat out to sea. There followed a game of hide-and-seek among the tricky shallows which border this part of the Tunisian coast. The situation was a strange one, for the U-boat dared not attack her in French territorial waters. He had been specifically warned not to do this by the Axis High Command. At the same time, Captain Riley knew that it was only a matter of time before he would be stopped by the French authorities. Yet he dare not cut out into the open sea and set course for Malta. The U-boat would at once have torpedoed him. The English captain therefore continued to hug the shore while the U-boat cruised slowly along, parallel with him and just outside territorial waters.

At first it seemed as though luck was with the merchantman. There had been no further air attack and now the sun was low in the sky and soon, hidden by darkness, she would stand a good chance of being able to evade the U-boat.

At five o'clock, however, the lookouts reported a small vessel putting out from Monastir Bay. As she approached, she broke out the French Tricolour, and Captain Riley realised that this was a French patrol boat and that the game was probably up. The French Ensign was followed by a signal to " Heave to." Captain Riley altered course away from the patrol boat and called for an Aldis signalling lamp. He proceeded to flash a series of messages which were far too fast to be decipherable. The patrol vessel once again hoisted the signal to " Heave to." Captain Riley once again flashed a series of indecipherable dots and dashes. As the sun sank lower the tragi-comedy proceeded. Every time the Frenchman signalled, Captain Riley turned his ship away and sent back an unintelligible signal. Finally, long before it got dark, the Frenchman's patience was exhausted and the warning shot fired across *Brisbane Star's* bows came unpleasantly close. The captain had no option but to heave to.

Two French officers then boarded the merchantman. Both saluted the captain punctiliously and he, with courtesy equal to their own, bowed them into the captain's cabin.

Now that all else had failed, this tall, good-looking Irishman meant to try the effect of blarney as a last resort.

The Frenchman came straight to the point : " I regret,

Monsieur, that you will have to follow us to port. You and the crew must be interned," he said.

"But surely, Captain," said Riley, with a charming smile, "you realise that that is impossible for me." He rummaged in a locker and brought out a bottle of whisky. "I regret, my friends, that I cannot offer you wine. It is not easy to get, now your charming country is inaccessible to us. Perhaps the wine of Scotland would please you ? "

The conversation proceeded pleasantly. Half an hour later the two Frenchmen returned on deck with the captain, laughing and chatting gaily. An injured crew member of *Brisbane Star* was put in the boat to be taken to hospital. Both French officers shook hands enthusiastically, wishing the captain "Bon Voyage." Then, in the gathering night, the Frenchmen sailed back to port while *Brisbane Star* proceeded on her voyage.

Now that the French had been pacified, Captain Riley set himself to outwit the U-boat. With brilliant navigation, he twisted and turned amongst the inshore shoals until he rightly judged that he had thrown his would-be attacker off the scent; then, mustering no more than eight knots, *Brisbane Star* headed out to sea and on towards Malta.

Next day she was escorted into Grand Harbour, down by the head with her forward holds badly flooded but still preserving most of her cargo intact.

All the surviving ships had now reached Malta safely, except *Ohio* and her devoted protectors.

Force X, retiring to the west, weathered a series of dive-bombing attacks, but these appeared to be desultory as though the Axis forces were tiring at last. Making twenty-five knots they rejoined Admiral Syfret's force at dusk on the 14th and returned to Gibraltar.

Yet, Malta's fate still depended upon *Ohio*. Unless her cargo could be saved, all the effort and loss of " Operation Pedestal " had been in vain.

CHAPTER SIXTEEN

PROUD TO HAVE MET YOU

Ohio was sinking slowly not much more than forty-five miles west of Malta, which she had been sent to save. As if to prove how much lower in the water she had become, one of the gunners walked aft, leant over the side and drew a bucket of water to cool off one of the gun barrels before changing it. The ship had little more than two feet of freeboard left.

From her decks came the steady beat of portable pumps struggling to check the water in the engine-room, but when Captain Mason and Commander Sweall peered down the companionway, the marks they had made an hour earlier at water level were no longer visible. Slowly but inexorably they were losing the battle to maintain the tanker's buoyancy.

The danger from the air was receding and a whole circus of Malta Spitfires now weaved and circled above the little convoy of ships ; but, grouped as they were about the unmanœuvrable 30,000 tons of deadweight represented by the derelict tanker, all were sitting targets for the first U-boat which could approach unobserved. Moreover, even if the tanker stayed afloat, night would come before they reached safety. It was unlikely that the Axis would miss the opportunity then of attacking so valuable a target with the E-boats which had already struck at the convoy in darkness off the Tunisian coast with such devastating results.

Nevertheless, these seemed minor details in the race for time which faced Commander Jerome if he was to save *Ohio* and relieve Malta. The tanker's life at sea was clearly to be measured in hours—no one knew how few. It was with the certainty that she must sink, perhaps at any minute, that he began to reorganise the tow, dislocated by the Axis air attack.

In this attempt to get the tanker moving again, a less tangible barrier loomed like a spectre denying them final passage to Malta. When all depended on the speed of their action, the men of the little rescue fleet were rapidly running down, like engines progressively starved of fuel. To most of them sleep had now become as a distant view of Paradise. For days they had conquered sleep or given way to it only in small, disturbed snatches, and now the demands of their tired bodies, shaken by the drumming of the barrage, drenched with sea water, and worn by the incessant call to action, could scarcely be resisted. Fingers fumbled, co-ordination was lost and judgment failed. Determination and grit began to dissolve into the wavering motifs of a dream.

Ledbury, still secured to *Ohio* by a heavy wire, had been pulled round by the yawing tanker and had ended up alongside *Penn*, facing the wrong way. *Rye* was ordered to tow from ahead, and came alongside to take *Ledbury's* end of the wire. Lieutenant Hollins, driving himself and his tired men, had the tow quickly passed, but aboard *Rye*, too, lack of sleep and strain were beginning

231

to overcome seamanship. Someone made fast the wire with a slippery hitch and, as soon as the destroyer went ahead and the strain came on, the cable snaked through the towing bitts and splashed into the water. Soon it was hanging straight down from *Ohio's* bows into the depths. There was no question of hauling it aboard the tanker. Without power for the winches it would have taken 100 fresh men to carry out such a heavy job. There was nothing to do but slip it, as the trailing end would have collected any moored mines in the vicinity, as soon as the derelict was got under way again.

Commander Jerome, who with the crew of *Speedy* was less troubled with the deadening effects of tiredness, for they had only recently sailed from Malta, saw that any further complicated patterns for towing the tanker were likely to degenerate into a series of frustrating errors. Somehow an easier method of moving her had to be found.

After a quick analysis of possible means, he decided that despite the danger of damage from the sharp metal edges of *Ohio's* torpedo hole, they would have to try to tow the tanker with a destroyer made fast on either side. This would tend to offset the drag and also act as something of a " splint " for the broken and dangerously strained amidships section of the derelict. *Bramham* was immediately ordered to make fast to port while *Penn* remained coupled to the starboard side.

As the *Bramham* moved in, her number one, Lieutenant the Marquess of Milford Haven, O.B.E., R.N., was working marvels with the sleep-soggy men. Additional fenders to guard the destroyer's sides were speedily improvised and steel wires made ready, so that the destroyer was secured to the tanker within a few minutes of going alongside, and all was ready for another attempt to tow.

Slowly the destroyers began to get under way. White water creamed behind their sterns. The cables creaked, slipped and bit on the bollards. The amidships section of *Ohio* groaned and the working of the damaged plates could be heard harshly grating. Yet the tanker began to move and to gather speed.

As she did so, Mason anxiously gazed into the torpedo rent in the pump-room. They had reached five knots and the " old girl " was still holding together. As the speed increased a little more, a rending, tearing sound began to murmur through the bones of the ship. He could feel and hear that she would not stand much more.

He hailed *Penn's* captain : " I don't think she'll take any more speed, sir. Can you keep it at that ? " he shouted. Commander Swain nodded and gave an order to his number one.

The speed was held at five knots, a steady five knots now in the direction of Malta, but in the engine-room of the battered tanker water swirled over the marks scratched on the walls of the companionway and the gentle swell of the calm Mediterranean now washed over the deck amidships.

Just past midday, when hopes were beginning to rise again, one of *Bramham's* wires parted with a crack. The destroyer sprang away from the tanker's side and with *Penn* manœuvring desperately with her engines to keep the derelict straight, the tow came to a sudden stop.

The men of *Bramham* looked woodenly at the parted tow. It seemed impossible to go through the effort of making fast again. Milford Haven fought down tiredness. In an instant he was down among the men again, lending a hand himself, joking, encouraging. Like sleepwalkers the ratings responded to his driving spirit, the broken wire was cast off and a new one run out, the fenders were manned, and once more *Bramham* glided alongside the tanker. Somehow they made fast again, slower this time, for the naval party aboard *Ohio* were also heavy with sleep and even that giant of energy, *Melbourne Star's* bosun, moved wearily with reluctant limbs ; but the job was done somehow, and within half an hour *Ohio* was once more moving through the water at five knots.

The men were finally beginning to give way to the imperative need for rest. Gunners slumped behind their guns staring glassily at nothing, though they remained at their posts they were asleep. It was doubtful whether they could have awakened in time to fight off another air attack. All about the ships men lay, sat or leaned in awkward, unnatural attitudes, either asleep or on the edge of sleep. If the tow parted once more, it seemed doubtful if enough men could be found fit to secure it again. Helmsmen clung to the wheels for support and the captains and officers were blinking sleep away in desperate efforts to concentrate.

The afternoon wore on, and then through the haze ahead the tired eyes of the lookouts sighted a dim blue blotch of land, the high cliffs of Dingli—Malta.

The men gathered themselves for another effort, for

here along the south-west coast of the Island the enemy submarines would probably be waiting. *Ledbury* and *Speedy* began circling *Ohio* and her three lined consorts. Every twenty minutes *Ledbury* dropped a depth charge hoping to scare any lurking submarine away or at least to discourage it from surfacing and taking sights on so perfect a target.

After several of these warning explosions had detonated, a new danger presented itself. Shock waves from the depth charges were shaking *Ohio*. Captain Mason and Commander Sweall, now almost constantly watching the damaged pump-room saw that the rent was gradually opening. Then one of the underwater disturbances was followed directly by a loud and ominous crack. Mason quickly informed *Penn's* captain and a message was flashed on the signalling lamp to *Ledbury* : " Stop depth charging. The shock is sinking the tanker." This was greeted by groans from the more wakeful. After all that effort and within sight of their goal, surely they were not going to lose *Ohio* now ?

The light was waning slowly. As the towing destroyers forged on, the coastline of Malta became plainer and they were approaching Filfla, the tiny rocky islet five miles to the south-west of the Island. Here it was necessary to alter course to port to make the entrance to the swept channel in the minefields off Delimara Point. This was a tricky operation as it placed a heavy strain on the towing wires. There was also considerable anxiety over imparting any lateral strain to *Ohio*. The two halves of the tanker on either side of the torpedo gash amidships were held together by only a few plates.

At a given signal, *Penn* increased speed slightly while *Bramham* slowed. For nearly a minute the wires held and the derelict tanker began to turn to port. Then a slight swell rocked the ships and with loud reports the towing wires parted.

Once more the officers succeeded in rousing the men and the now laborious business of making fast was begun all over again. At this stage, an old paddle-wheeler naval tug named *Robert* was sighted approaching from Malta.

In her was the King's Harbour Master who took charge of the tow. The tug was secured to *Ohio* and, as she went ahead, the tanker began to swing to port dragging her as easily as if she had been a cork. It soon became evident that unless her crew could slip the tow she would collide with *Penn*. A party struggled hard to unshackle the pin which held the hawser, but whether, as her captain maintained later, there was too much strain on to do so or whether her crew had omitted to grease the pin as some suspected, her stern drove relentlessly into *Penn*, holing the destroyer in the wardroom, fortunately above the waterline. For some minutes the air was blue with the comments of *Penn's* captain.

After this episode, in which precious time was wasted, *Robert* was sent back to Malta and the destroyers ranged up again on either side of the tanker. By sheer force of spirit, the nightmare of making fast was accomplished and *Ohio*, embraced on either side, began to move onwards, while the minesweepers searched the channel ahead.

At Malta, anxiety for *Ohio* and for her cargo, upon which the survival of the Island rested as if on a sharp knife edge, had reached a high pitch. Coastal defences had been alerted, lookout stations and the radar-room scanned the seas with desperate urgency for signs of enemy activity. In the combined operations room, chiefs of staff waited tensely for news, as the tanker and her escorts crawled round the darkening extremity of the Island. Night was succeeding the dusk when a radar plot of a submarine was confirmed following the slowly-moving derelict on the surface.

Colonel C. J. White of the Royal Artillery ordered his men to go into action with the coastal batteries. Searchlights began to finger the calm waters and men strained their eyes to pick out the tiny silhouette of the submarine, while Commander Jerome, informed of the danger by wireless, ordered all guns to readiness.

Suddenly a strong beam of light found and held the tanker and her two consorts in dazzling brilliance. Readily seen for miles and her defenders blinded by the searchlight, the tanker was a sitting target for the submarine.

"For God's sake don't show me up," Jerome signalled. Lights winked desperately from the destoyers warning the soldiers to turn off the light. Then the searchlight went out. In the little fleet, the men waited tensely for their night sight to return, conscious that at any moment an unseen torpedo might rip into one of the ships. For the damage had been done and if the enemy submarine was anywhere in the vicinity she must have sighted them.

Meanwhile, *Hebe* sighted something and opened fire. The shell passed over one of the coastal batteries and the gunners, taking the minesweepers for an enemy, were about to open fire too. Fortunately, their central control stopped them in time. The coastal defences which had unknowingly jeopardised the whole rescue operation, were soon to remove the danger, however. Higher up the coast, another searchlight picked out the U-boat speeding towards the convoy on the surface. Immediately, the 9.2-inch coastal guns opened up and shots were observed falling round the shadowy conning tower. The submarine hurriedly submerged and was not seen again.

Then a new danger, greater than the other, materialised. Once again, radar men scanning the seas on the north side of the Island, picked up a number of small fast-moving plots. There could be only one interpretation of these " blips " on the radar screens. A flotilla of E-boats was steaming down the north-east coast of Malta to intercept the tanker as she came up the east coast of the Island to make Valletta. The rescue fleet and all shore stations were once again alerted.

Colonel White had, however, already worked out a plan to counter just such a situation. As the enemy approached the coast they were greeted by a heavy barrage from the coastal batteries firing on the radar plots. Then, ahead of them, the beam of a strong searchlight was exposed in the path they would have to take to close *Ohio* and her protectors. If they steamed into the beam, they would be subjected to accurate visual fire from the coastal batteries and if they succeeded in

passing through it they would still be a silhouetted
target for the British MLs which were now in line abreast
ahead of the tanker and destroyers preparing to meet the
attack.

The E-boats held their course. Aboard *Ohio* and her
consorts, the men could hear the firing which came
perceptibly closer as new coastal batteries opened up to
engage the approaching enemy ships. The tired naval
gunners again stood by for action. The radar scanners
watched the two groups of ships and the diminishing
distance between them. Would the enemy risk a bold
dash across the wide beam of the fighting light? It
was a tense moment, because no one could be certain
that the full force of an attack could be successfully
countered. Once the E-boats got among the little fleet,
hampered as it was with the unmanœuvrable derelict,
and in darkness, some of the enemy ships would no
doubt be able to carry out an attack on the tanker. In
her precarious state of buoyancy, even the distant
concussion of an exploding torpedo might be sufficient
to send her to the bottom.

The plot of the E-boats crept slowly towards the area
of water which the scanners knew was illuminated.
Suddenly, the little blobs of light faded. The E-boats
were turning. Then, as they brightened again, it could
be seen that they were travelling in the opposite direction. Faced with the certainty of accurate fire from the
coastal batteries as he passed through the brightly-lit
corridor of sea, the E-boat flotilla commander decided
not to take the risk and gave the order to retire. The
defenders were able to breathe again.

Ohio and her escorts now approached a difficult corner in the swept channel where it rounded Zonkar Point and made a sharp turn to the north-west. With only a matter of a few cables-length separating him from mine-fields on either side, Commander Jerome knew that there would be considerable danger here to both the tanker and her towing destroyers.

When half the turn had been made, the tanker began to take charge. Despite the efforts of *Penn* and *Bramham*, she swung slowly but inexorably towards the mine-field and the destroyers were forced to halt progress altogether. They then lay stopped, the bows of the tanker pointing towards the side of the channel. All three ships were slowly drifting towards the minefield.

An emergency signal was made for *Ledbury* to take them in tow ahead and attempt to draw them away from the disaster which now lay not more than fifty yards distant. The destroyer went alongside and passed her faithful 6-inch manilla to *Ohio*. Then began half an hour's struggle to edge the tanker away from the minefield. As *Ledbury* towed, the two MLs assisted by pushing against her bows and keeping her going in the right direction. As they grated down *Ledbury's* side, agonising cries from the destroyer's sick bay echoed across the water adding horror to the anxiety of the situation. The badly burned survivors of *Waimarama* were now suffering from secondary shock and the noises on the ship's hull had awakened them. They kept screaming and shouting that the ship was being blown up.

A grey light began to appear in the east and the longed-for dawn was at hand. But light brought with it the danger of renewed air attacks, and an overcast sky which began to be visible seemed ideal for sneak raiders. The gunners, rested now despite the alarms of the night, anxiously peered at the breaks in the cloud, fingering their triggers.

At 6 a.m., with *Ohio* still hovering on the edge of the minefield, the situation was eased by the arrival of the Malta tugs. With the destroyers still linked on either side of the tanker, two of these sturdy little ships made fast ahead and astern and the tanker was soon proceeding up the channel to the Grand Harbour entrance.

There a fabulous welcome awaited them. On the ramparts above the wreck-strewn harbour, on the Baracca, at St. Angelo and Senglea, great crowds of Maltese men and women waved and cheered and a brass band on the end of the mole was giving a spirited rendering of *Rule Britannia*.

Captain Mason, however, standing at the salute on the battered bridge of *Ohio*, could spare no moment's thought for the pride of bringing his wounded ship to port. The tanker's main deck was now freely washed by the sea. The tortured plates amidships creaked and groaned alarmingly with every movement, and the captain knew that at any moment, the epic fight of *Ohio* might end with the tanker at the bottom of the Grand Harbour.

As the destroyers cast off, *Penn's* captain called across to Mason. "Just got this message from Admiral Burrough, with Force X," he said. "It reads: 'To *Ohio* stop I'm proud to have met you message ends.' That goes for us too."

Mason smiled wanly: "We're here thanks to you

chaps. But it isn't over yet. This poor old hooker hasn't got many minutes now. I hope to God she lasts long enough."

The tugs dragged the derelict slowly towards the quays. There, waiting, was the tanker's chief engineer, Jimmy Wyld, Gray, the first officer, and the other crew members who had been brought to Malta in the damaged ML. Wyld had spent several hours with the Dockyard Superintendent, Rear Admiral Mackenzie, discussing the difficult technical problem of discharging the tanker. All was prepared to reap the priceless harvest of oil and kerosene without a moment's delay.

Now, as Wyld watched *Ohio's* slow approach, he realised how close might be the time margin for discharging the tanker, bereft of all her power pumping equipment.

" Look at that freeboard," he said to Gray. " I can't think how she stays afloat. We'll have to get a move on."

Slowly *Ohio* drew in alongside *Plumleaf,* an auxiliary tanker lying bombed and sunk by the quayside, her upperworks showing. A hundred willing pairs of hands helped to make her fast. At the same time another fleet auxiliary, *Boxall,* secured on the seaward side.

Wyld boarded the tanker and wrung Mason's hand warmly : " Good show, lad. You've made it."

Now that the moment for action was passed, a great wave of tiredness surged over the captain. Now he had to sleep.

" See to her, Jimmy," he mumbled. " I must get ashore." Like a man in a dream he stumbled towards the ship's side followed by the other members of the crew who had brought the tanker in.

Pipes were now hauled aboard and, superintended by Wyld, emergency salvage pumps began to discharge the kerosene. At the same time *Boxall* began to pump the 10,000 tons of fuel oil into her own tanks.

As the tanker's holds were pumped out and the forward end of the ship lightened, it became plain that she would soon break her back, for the waterlogged afterend continued to sink. There was a hurried conference of experts, for a real danger still existed that they might lose the remainder of the oil. If the ship broke in half, the lighter half might easily capsize. They decided to flood the tanks with sea water as the oil was removed. In this way the oil floated on top and could easily be removed by the pumps as the water flowed in and acted as ballast.

As the oil flowed out, *Ohio* sank lower and lower in the water. The last gallon left her and simultaneously her keel settled gently on the bottom. She had found rest at last.

On the bridge, which with the poop now alone remained above water, Buddle, the second engineer, saw a Maltese stevedore idly scraping the oxidisation away in flakes from the twisted rail. Suddenly, an unreasoning anger took possession of him.

" Leave it alone," he roared. " Don't you think the poor old cow's suffered enough ?"

EPILOGUE

ONE fine September morning, four years later, early risers on the quays of the Grand Harbour, Malta, were treated to an unusual spectacle. Two busy posses of tugs were passing through the harbour entrance making for the calm blue sea beyond.

They carried with them two strange, rust-streaked boxes of metal ; and, from the larger of the two, with its bridge-work still intact and its graceful schooner bow, some of the watchers might have inferred that the remnant of a war-damaged tanker was being taken to sea in two halves.

At this date, the 19th September, 1946, with the war over more than a year and more than two since the Island had seen any enemy action, it is unlikely that her name would have meant very much to them.

Someone with a retentive memory might have hazarded : " Wasn't that the tanker that brought the oil in ? You remember . . . when we had almost had it in August 1942."

Another might have replied : " Well, perhaps it is. What were we saying before that . . . ? "

The war was over. No one likes to remember times of starvation, death and danger. And then so much had happened. The invasion of Italy, the surrender of the Italian fleet at Valletta, the invasion of the Continent, the fall of Hitler, V.E. Day. Then the eclipse of the Rising Sun, the atom bomb and V.J. Day—the war's end.

The day they cheered *Ohio* into that same harbour was so long ago and so was the award of the George Cross to Captain Dudley Mason. Few now remembered the epic of " Operation Pedestal," the many awards for heroism which followed it—and the casualty list. Who can blame them? That was their yesterday and their to-morrow held the problems of peace not those of war.

The ship which had saved Malta and perhaps the free world, had herself become a familiar part of the harbour scenery, and familiarity had soon shorn her of her heroic trappings. Not long after her precious cargo had been discharged, she had been hauled away and had later broken in half at her moorings.

Some efforts were made at repair. The bulkheads of the two halves were shored and sealed watertight ; but it had proved impossible to provide the skilled techniques for joining the ship together locally, and the expense of towing the two halves to Gibraltar or Alexandria was too great to justify.

For a time the dismembered ship was used as a store. Then, towards the end of the war, she was fitted out to house Yugoslav troops. Now, even these services were no longer required in peace-time and the hulks had become a nuisance in the busy waterway.

The two halves of *Ohio* passed through the harbour entrance and what remained of this ship of destiny felt once more the surge of the open sea.

Steering north-eastward over the tail of St. George's

Shoals, over the site of the old minefield, the tugs headed for deep water, towards the lithe shape of a destroyer, shining in peace-time paint and waiting for them.

Ten miles from Malta they cast off the tow and the two halves of *Ohio* were alone again on the deep, heaving gently in the swell.

Aboard the destroyer, the number one rubbed his hands with satisfaction and remarked to the captain : " This will make a useful shoot, sir. The men can do with it." By this time, there were men aboard who had not seen a shot fired in anger, and any suitable opportunity for gunnery practice was welcome to the first lieutenant.

" Load armour piercing," the gunnery officer ordered. " Fire."

A forward gun spat flame and smoke and the report echoed across the sea.

" Over," remarked the gunnery officer conversationally and began to bracket. Soon the guns were registering on the two halves of the tanker, and the rear portion, weakened by the battering it had received from Axis airmen long before, soon disappeared from sight.

Shell after shell pumped into the buoyant forepart of the tanker. " Can't think why she won't sink," said number one. " Must have been a tough old ship. In some convoy or other, wasn't she ? "

The bridgework had been blasted away, the foremast had fallen, and now the shored-up amidships section, where the torpedo had struck, caved in. Slowly the forward half also sank and the graceful bows reared up like a finger pointing to heaven. Then she was gone, and seventy-five fathoms below the blue water of the Mediterranean the rippled sands received the brave bones of *Ohio*.

" Cease fire," the captain ordered. " Carry on, Number One."

There were no fine words for this great ship, no flowers, no wreaths bobbing on the water. Only the laurel of fame not soon to die.

Tinkerbelle

by
ROBERT MANRY

FOR VIRGINIA, ROBIN AND DOUGLAS

Contents

I

EVEN with shortened canvas *Tinkerbelle* rushed headlong through the darkness at about seven knots, her top speed. Her spray-soaked sails strained against their fastenings as the relentless wind probed for some point of weakness that could be forced to give way. Every now and then a foaming wave cap slammed into her starboard side, sending up a geyser of spume and sloshing rivers of salt water back along her deck, half filling her self-bailing cockpit. Under each blow of the waves she lurched like a wounded doe, dipping to leeward with a tense, stomach-churning heave. She told me through her tiller, by the way she wanted to point closer to the wind, that she was unhappy. But I forced her to go on, full tilt.

I wrapped the mainsheet once around the tiller and held both in my left hand. Then, struggling to keep *Tinkerbelle* on course with this hand, I shined a flashlight into the cabin with my right hand and peered through the tiny porthole in the drop panel of the battened-down hatch. I'd hung a wristwatch inside where it was relatively dry. From the Greenwich mean time indicated by the watch, I calculated it was roughly 2 a.m. at our meridian of longitude; 2 a.m. *Tinkerbelle* time. Oh, God, another two and a half hours to sunrise! I'd be frozen stiff by then. Not to mention blown silly or drowned.

My teeth chattered even though I had on four layers of clothing. I wore padded thermal long johns next to my skin, cotton underwear over these, then a woollen shirt and woollen trousers and, on top of everything, a yellow rubberized anti-exposure suit. And still I shivered.

My socks, canvas shoes, feet and the lower halves of my trousers and legs were soaked despite the waterproof outer suit. Rivulets from my sodden hair trickled across my face and down my neck, stabbing icily at my back, making me wince. My hands were puckered and swollen from prolonged saturation. They hurt, especially the tips of the fingers and thumbs, which made untying knots and adjusting the sheets painful tasks. Salt-water sores on my buttocks turned the necessity of sitting into pure misery.

The cabin barometer was an enigma. I wasn't sure what its strange behaviour presaged. During the day it had fallen gradually. Then, between sunset and about 11 p.m., it had held steady. But since eleven it had zipped upward again at an alarming rate. I suspected it meant we'd soon encounter even stronger winds than those we were already battling.

The wind, whistling out of the south at twenty-five knots, the most that *Tinkerbelle* could stand up to under reefed main, built up menacing seas that threatened to bowl her over on her beam ends. She had to be swerved around periodically to meet the biggest of the cross-waves almost head-on or she'd have got into serious trouble.

Yet we kept moving, despite our vulnerability, because I wanted to make up for the seven or eight hours we'd spent hove to in a hard blow during the day. It would take forever to reach England if we had to spend that many hours out of every twenty-four lying to a sea anchor. We were already several days behind schedule. So on we raced, taxing our endurance to the limit, reeling off a fraction less than two nautical miles every fifteen minutes.

Except for glimpses at ocean, sails and sky, I kept my eyes fastened on the orange glow of the compass, shifting the tiller to right and left as required to keep the index line opposite the mark for 105°, our eastward course, printed on the swaying card. We bucketed along, our position at that hour being approximately 40° 43′ N and 60° 50′ W, which meant we were some two hundred and ninety nautical miles south of Canada's Cape Breton Island and four hundred and eighty miles east of Long Island.

Tinkerbelle

It was Monday, June 14th, and we were fourteen days out from Falmouth, Massachusetts, on the first leg of a transatlantic voyage I had dreamed of most of my life and carefully planned for more than a year.

'England, here we come!' I yelled at the stars.

2

THAT was one of the moments I remember best during a voyage that had had its practical beginning about seven years before. As a sub-editor on the copy desk of a morning newspaper, the *Plain Dealer* of Cleveland, Ohio, I had a chance at about ten-forty every working night to peek at the ads. the regular subscribers didn't see until they got out of bed the next morning. It was a benefit I hadn't even considered when I applied for the job, but during the summer of 1958 I availed myself of it with considerable appreciation because my wife Virginia and I had decided that at long last our heads were far enough above water, financially, to permit us to buy a small sailing boat.

Every night when first-edition copies of the paper were brought up from the presses to the second-floor city room, I took advantage of the first lull in the night's work to turn to the want ads. listed under 'Boats—Marine Supplies' to see what I could find. Most of the ads. concerned motorboats; only a few sailing boats were offered for sale and none of these seemed suited to us. We needed a boat large enough to accommodate both of us, our daughter, Robin, and our son, Douglas, and yet small enough to keep at home in suburban Willowick, in the garage we hoped to have before long. This would enable us to avoid mooring fees which, at that stage of our fortunes, would have bankrupted us. But it also meant that the boat had to be a centreboard craft that could be rolled on and off a conventional boat trailer with ease. A boat with a keel was out of the question as it would be much too difficult to haul on a trailer.

Finally, after weeks of looking, I found a promising ad. in the paper of August 2nd. It said: 'SAILING BOAT, 13½-ft. Old Town, needs some repair, cheap. EN 1-7298.'

Getting the edge on the *P.D.*'s three hundred thousand-plus paying readers, I dialled that telephone number at once and made arrangements to see the boat early the next day. It turned out to be a most memorable occasion.

The owner was a fine old gentleman of Greek descent who met me with a twinkle in his eyes. From the way he spoke, I could tell the boat had played the same unifying role in his family that Virginia and I hoped it would play in ours. He and his wife had brought up their daughter on sailing very much as we hoped to bring up our youngsters, for, in addition to all the other reasons we had for wanting a boat, we listed the part it could have in shaping our children's personalities.

But my first glimpse of the boat gave me quite a shock. It looked so lonely and forlorn turned bottom up in the owner's back yard, its bow and stern resting on rough crates. What struck me like a blow, however, was the sight of two enormous splits in the hull, one on each side at about waterline level. They were about five feet long and up to a quarter of an inch wide. I couldn't imagine what had caused them and I didn't ask for fear of embarrassing the owner; he was such a nice old man. Anyway, all I needed to know was whether they could be repaired.

Sensing that I wanted to examine the boat thoroughly, the elderly gentleman left us alone. He had said the boat was thirty years old, and she showed her age in her multilayered and multi-coloured coatings of paint, which was peeling in spots. But the planking, except for the two splits, appeared healthy and strong.

I lay on my back, pushed my head and shoulders under the boat and, as soon as my eyes grew accustomed to the gloom, studied every nook and cranny of her interior. I discovered the 'needs some repair' of the ad. was an understatement. Nearly two dozen of the boat's steam-bent ribs were broken and half a dozen others were infected with dry rot, which had also decayed chunks of the mast step and a portion of the centreboard casing. The canvas deck was badly worn and needed replacement, and the sails, as I discovered later, were too mildewed and threadbare to use. Everything else, though, was basically sound.

For about forty-five minutes I lay there under the boat. After I'd examined her insides completely and had decided her split planks were mendable, I drifted into day-dreaming about our plans for her, fixing her up, the place she'd occupy in our family and how she'd fare with us and we with her. Finally I got down to the business of listing all the pros and cons, weighing her cost, a hundred and sixty dollars, and the expense of repairing her and buying new sails, which I estimated would come to around three hundred dollars, against the cost and the possibility of buying a boat in better condition. I decided that, dilapidated as she was, she was the boat for us. So I paid a deposit and told the owner I'd be back soon to pick her up.

On August 4th (Virginia has the date underlined in her diary) the whole family bundled into our car and, with a rented trailer hitched on behind, we drove off to take possession of our boat. The owner and his friendly wife and daughter came out to greet us on our arrival. We chatted for a few minutes, completed our transaction, and then everyone pitched in to turn the boat right side up and winch it on to the trailer. Virginia told me later that, as we drove slowly down the driveway, she noticed tears glistening in the old man's eyes as he and his wife kissed their hands and patted the boat with affectionate gestures of farewell. We were sorry to be taking away an object that had meant so much to them, but were happy to know that, despite its run-down state, the boat had been loved. Unquestionably, it had provided this pleasant family with many happy experiences, and we felt certain it would do the same for us.

Earlier in the day Robin and Douglas had broadcast the news to their friends that we were going to get a boat, so nearly all the children of the neighbourhood were waiting for us on our return home. They paraded along shouting to one another as we proudly towed our new acquisition up our drive, and, from that moment on, the boat seemed to be surrounded by children. I suspect the neighbourhood mothers often told their offspring to 'go up and watch what Mr. Manry's doing' just to get them out from underfoot for a while. Anyway, they seemed to congregate around the boat whenever I was working on it, which was practically every day between 9.30 a.m. and 4 p.m., when I had to stop to have dinner and then leave for my job on the *P.D.* copy desk.

Sometimes I was able to pull off a stunt like Tom Sawyer's the day he had to whitewash his Aunt Polly's fence, except that I was taking paint off, not putting it on. I'd scrape away as though the task were sheer ecstasy and pretty soon one of the young observers would ask if he could share my fun; and I'd say yes and give him a scraper or some sandpaper. And then another would ask, and then another. Once I had four junior boat renovators working at the same time. Usually they didn't get a great deal accomplished; the paint-removal project was too arduous. But we all had a good time.

I used every minute I could take from the demands of my job, family and home to work on the boat, for steady progress had to be made if it was to be ready in time for the 1959 sailing season, which opened in May. In fact, I spent so much time working on the boat I'm sure Virginia and the children often wondered whether we had taken possession of it or it had taken possession of us. I must say, though, that they bore up remarkably well under the strains created by the occasional conflicts between its needs and ours. Like the time I had to soak the new ash ribs in the bathtub for five days to make them pliable enough to bend into place.

But the grim days of having to take sponge baths or none came to an end as the new ribs were installed and bolted down to the planking. A new mast step was put in next, and the decayed portion of the centreboard casing was cut out and replaced with fresh wood. Then those cruel, ugly splits in the sides were repaired with plywood strips, waterproof glue and fibreglass.

During all this time we had to be careful to keep the boat dry. Whenever I wasn't working on it, we kept it covered with tarpaulins and old plastic tablecloths. And, of course, this made that fall seem like the rainiest one we'd ever had.

One night Virginia was ready for bed when I telephoned from the *Plain Dealer*, as I always did at about 10.00 p.m., during my supper hour.

'Is it raining?' I asked. (It was impossible to tell from the *P.D.* city room, which had no windows.)

'Yes.'

'Better make sure the boat isn't getting wet.'

'O.K.'

So my wonderful wife put on a raincoat over her pyjamas and rubber boots on over her bedroom slippers and went out into the cold, blustery, wet night to make sure the boat—this nautical object that was being treated with the deference we might have shown a third child—was not suffering from the dampness.

One of the tarpaulins was flapping wildly, threatening to come adrift; so Virginia took hold of a car tyre we used to weigh the tarpaulins down and heaved it into position. It was an easy operation. She'd done it scores of times before. The only trouble was that this time the tyre was full of ice-cold rain water.

Virginia gasped and sputtered, drenched to the skin in spite of the rain gear she wore, and nearly frozen. It was a moment of crisis for me and for the boat, although at the time I remained tranquilly oblivious at my *P.D.* post miles away, with nothing more serious on my mind than the split infinitives and faulty syntax in a reporter's news copy. I didn't hear of it until the next day at breakfast.

We passed through such troubled waters as these on several occasions. However, a rising tide of good humour always saw us through, as the boat gradually changed in appearance from an abandoned hulk to a craft that might conceivably return someday to the element for which it was designed.

Our growing plans for the boat were rather unconventional. In fact our intentions went far beyond simply restoring it to a seaworthy condition. We wanted it to take us on cruises, which meant that it had to have sleeping accommodation for all four of us within the meagre space provided by its 13½-foot length and

5¼-foot beam. Seldom has so much been expected of so small a boat. And yet these expectations were, in a manner of speaking, realized.

The mid-section of the hull was converted into a tiny cabin separated from the cockpit by a watertight bulkhead and covered with a roof that could be partly opened, to permit entry and use of the folding-down seats at its rear, or removed entirely. Virginia and I could sleep on air mattresses, in sleeping-bags, in this area; one on each side of the centreboard casing, with our feet extending into the bow.

Next, I built a removable panel that could be fitted over the foot well to convert the cockpit into a flat space where Robin and Douglas could put their air mattresses and sleeping-bags. Since this cockpit sleeping area was elevated eight or ten inches above the floor where Virginia and I would sleep, it gave our accommodation plan a split-level effect that was certainly in tune with the times, from the point of view of domestic if not of naval architecture.

Naturally we had to consider the weather. It wouldn't be very pleasant on our yacht in a rainstorm; the joint between the two sections of the cabin roof wasn't absolutely rainproof, despite the use of weather stripping, and would have let water drip below, maddeningly. Besides which, the cockpit double-bunk layout was entirely open to the elements. These difficulties were overcome through the fabrication of a tent we could sling over the boom and snap to fasteners installed on either side of the boat just below the rubbing strake. The tent enclosed both cabin and cockpit, giving us all the headroom we needed, as well as privacy and shelter for cruising.

At last, in early May, after more than nine months of toil, our tiny yacht was ready. Then came the unforgettable day when we brought home our own trailer, pulled the boat on to it for the first time and, just for practice, pitched the tent to see how it would look. It looked great, at least it did to us. I think it would be accurate to say the boat was unique; and the entire rig, assembled with the tent up, had the extraordinary appearance of an amphibious Conestoga wagon. Robin and Douglas and their friends had a wonderful time playing in it. And Virginia and I began to feel like pioneers on the threshold of exciting explorations that would add an entirely new dimension to our lives. We could hardly wait to get started.

Mother's Day, Sunday, May 10th, was only a day or two away and I thought what a treat it would be for Virginia if we launched our boat and went for our first sail on this special day. So that's what we did; only it didn't work out quite the way I'd hoped it would.

We took the boat to Cleveland's Gordon Park on Lake Erie and used the public launching ramps there to get it into the water. That much was easy. But then the complications set in. First it began to rain and, for half an hour or so, Virginia and the children huddled uncomfortably in semi-reclining positions in the minute cabin trying to keep relatively dry. There wasn't room for me in there too, so I stayed outside tending the mooring lines and getting soaked.

When the rain finally stopped, the wind began to blow with alarming force. Frankly, it scared me. Even as a novice I realized it would be dangerous to be out on Lake Erie in such a stiff and gusty breeze. But we'd come to sail and sail we would. At least, one of us would—me.

I felt like Captain Bligh when I told my family I'd decided to go out alone, but there were no significant protests. All three got out of the boat and into our car and sat there, protected from the wind, eating the picnic lunch Virginia had prepared, as the boat and I left the shore.

As we headed into the maelstrom of winds and waves the words of Tennyson's 'Crossing the Bar' came to me:

> *Sunset and Evening star,*
> *And one clear call for me!*
> *And may there be no moaning of the bar,*
> *When I put out to sea.*

It wasn't the time of sunset, and there was no evening star in sight, but I could hear that 'clear call for me' and a frightful moaning that filled me with dread. Fortunately, the moaning was of the wind in the rigging, not of the bar. That was a relief.

I didn't dare to venture far into the lake; in fact, I stayed within the protecting arm of a nearby breakwater. Even so, it was one of the most breath-taking sails of my life. The boat whizzed along so fast that I had to come about every twenty seconds or so to stay within the breakwater's shelter, which I was determined to do. Violent puffs of wind made the craft heel over so far and so fast that I repeatedly let go of the main sheet in alarm, whereupon it would run through the boom block as far as the knot in its end.

In less than fifteen minutes I'd had my fill of sailing under those conditions and returned to the quay. We soon had the boat back on the trailer and were on our way home.

'It was kinda gusty,' I told Virginia.

'Kind of gusty!' she exclaimed. 'I was sure you were going to upset. And the waves were so big we couldn't even see you when you were down between them! All we could see was the tip of the sail!'

'Yeah. I guess it must have looked pretty exciting from the shore. And it sure wasn't much of an outing for you. All you had to do was sit in the car and watch your husband sail.'

'You mean watch him nearly drown!'

When we got home, the neighbours hurried out to greet us as though we had all returned from the grave. However, I couldn't afford to hang around wallowing in the delightful role of a latter-day Lazarus; I had to eat a quick lunch and rush off to work at the *P.D.* Virginia, left with the duty of hanging up the sails to dry, spent most of the evening in deep reflection, pondering the meaning of Mother's Day.

Undaunted, we set forth again a few days later for another attempt at sailing. It was a bright, sunny afternoon and for me a day off from work, which meant we wouldn't have to hurry home as we had before. We had an opportunity to sail and sail; until dark, if we wanted to, or even later than that. I'd never been sailing in the moonlight and wondered how it would be. Marvellous, I guessed.

This time we decided to launch the boat at Wildwood Park,

nearer our home. We got it off the trailer and into the water again without any trouble, stepped the mast, then, with what seemed to us an exceedingly seaman-like flourish, hoisted the sails and headed for the narrow channel leading from the harbour into the lake. We were propelled by a wind that had had its teeth pulled, a gentle breeze that couldn't have hurt a fly. It was comforting to know that, whatever else might happen, we had nothing to fear from Aeolus, god of the winds.

But, alas, that 'else' began happening almost at once. The boat seemed to have a will of its own. Refusing to respond to my excited pushes and pulls on the tiller, it moved with unwavering aim on a course destined to pile us up on the huge blocks of stone that formed one of the harbour's walls. I had a nightmare vision of losing my dear wife and children in a grotesque in-harbour shipwreck and of spending the rest of my days racked by remorse, imprisoned for improper operation of a sailing vessel. I believe I was as close to skidding into utter panic as I have ever been, and the children didn't help to calm my nerves. Both of them yelled in terror, 'We're going to hit the rocks! We're going to turn over!'

Fortunately, I retained enough of a grip on myself to get out the oars. I gave one to Virginia, and together we fended the boat off the rocks. Then it came to me—I hadn't lowered the centre-board!

In a matter of seconds we had the board down and immediately almost everything subsided into normality. I say almost everything, because, even though the wind caught our sails and wafted us peacefully out into the lake, even though the boat was now fully under control, Douglas, then not quite five, was far from gleeful.

'Take me back to the shore!' he yelled at the top of his lungs. 'Take me back! Take me back!'

Virginia and I held a hurried conference. We agreed that he was truly frightened and that if we wanted him to grow up enjoying boats and sailing, it would be prudent to respect his wishes and return to shore, to await a more auspicious time to start him off as a sailor. So, without sailing in the moonlight, or even much sailing in the daylight, we returned to the quay and set off for home.

For a while Virginia and I saw our hopes of family unity built on a foundation of happy sailing experiences slipping into oblivion. But we persevered. Recalling the rider's dictum to remount at once after a bad fall, we soon cast off from home again, this time on an overnight voyage of discovery to Pymatuning Lake, an attractive reservoir sixty miles east of Willowick. This was to be our shakedown camping cruise.

When we got to the camp grounds, our fellow campers found us, or rather our boat, a trifle startling. In fact, it was plain they had never seen anything like it in their lives. A woman at a neighbouring camp site watched spellbound as I prepared our yacht for the night. When I hoisted the tent over the boom and started to fasten it down, Virginia overheard her exclaim to her husband, 'George, look! He's building a house on that boat!'

I must confess that we were secretly both amused and pleased by the apparent consternation our craft caused among the more conservatively equipped campers who saw it. We loved the dropped jaws and surprised looks it produced. And we were pleased with ourselves, in a way, for our refusal in this one respect at least to follow in the crowd's footsteps like sheep. We enjoyed daring to be different.

Also, on later trips, we found our boat-tent paid unexpected dividends, for we were allowed to sleep in it offshore at crowded camps where all the onshore sites were occupied.

As we settled down for the night at Pymatuning Lake, Virginia, unknown to the rest of us, began what was undoubtedly the supreme test of her life, an excruciating ordeal of physical endurance. This night of torture was imposed by a regulation government-issue sleeping-bag, otherwise known as a mummy sack. The children and I fell asleep in our sacks almost at once. It wasn't until morning that we learned that Virginia had spent most of the night tugging, turning, twisting and thumping—struggling to find a comfortable position in the shroud that encased her. To top it off, she nearly froze—and in silence. She allowed the rest of us to go on sleeping undisturbed as she played martyr, suffering without a word of complaint, Even at dawn, when we awoke, she continued to be brave. The nearest she came to releasing the inner pressures that threatened to explode was to say, 'I take my hat off to the American soldier. Any man who can go out and fight after spending the night in one of these woollen booby traps has my undying admiration.'

A surge of admiration flowed through me, too, at that moment, but it wasn't for the American soldier.

After breakfast we provided our fellow campers and yachtsmen with a spectacle that was no doubt, to them, hugely entertaining. It happened as we were launching our boat. I was busily engaged in sliding the boat off the trailer into the water when Virginia, at the wheel of the car, mistook something I said for the signal that the boat was launched and the trailer could be hauled away. She took off prematurely with a forward jerk that sent the boat careening into the water with a mighty splash and me following after, legs and arms whirling like windmills. By the time she heeded my shouts of distress and looked around, I was on my hands and knees in the lake and the boat—with Robin, our beloved firstborn, on board—was skimming off beyond reach.

I swam out and towed the boat back to shore; getting soaked, but saving our daughter. Meanwhile, Virginia remarked to a camper standing near her that perhaps, in view of the havoc she'd wrought, she had better start driving and never come back. And he said he reckoned that might be a good idea.

Robin and Douglas thought the whole episode was the best fun they'd ever had. In fact, it was then they decided that sailing was a great sport, after all, and began to enjoy it thoroughly. Virginia and I were a little slower about savouring the humour of the situation, but as soon as we got under way, spanking along before a fresh breeze, we were able to laugh at ourselves. We could imagine how energetically tongues were wagging back at the camp about the performance of that nutty family with the boat that converted into a tent, or the tent that converted into a boat, or whatever it was.

During the months that the drive of our home had had the

appearance of a boatyard, and the weeks since then, our craft had been nameless. It had been known simply as 'the boat' or as 'our boat' or (when its seemingly excessive consumption of time and or money piqued other members of the family) as 'Daddy's boat'. Now, however, the time had come to give it a name and we put our heads together to choose one we all liked.

It was Doug's love of pirates that led, indirectly, to the name we chose for our boat. He knew more about Blackbeard, Captain Kidd, Long John Silver, Henry Morgan, Captain Hook and other freebooters of the Spanish Main than other boys his age knew about baseball heroes. He and his friends were constantly playing pirate on the boat, making imaginary foes walk the plank and sailing off to hidden islands to bury chests full of treasure. And whenever we went sailing on Lake Erie or Lake Pymatuning, we always had to fly the Jolly Roger from the masthead, as befitted a buccaneer's sloop.

This got us to thinking about Captain Hook, and that led to Peter Pan and Tinker Bell, who, at one point in J. M. Barrie's story, was poisoned by Hook and brought to the brink of death. The only thing that could save her was for the children of the world to affirm their belief in fairies, which they did. So, believing in our boat fully as much as these children believed in fairies, we decided to name her after Tinker Bell. In addition to the connotations of the fairy tale, it reflected the fact that I was forever tinkering with her. However, we changed the spelling to Tinkerbelle, since the boat certainly was an enchanting belle, although, like all things feminine, it could on occasion be exasperating.

Tinkerbelle, now definitely a 'she' rather than an 'it', exhibited her exasperating side on our next cruise, an expedition to Erie, Pennsylvania, a lakeshore city about ninety miles east of our home. We launched her in the bay formed by the curving arm of Presque Isle Peninsula and planned to sail through the channel into Lake Erie and on to a beach where we could go swimming. It was a sunny day and the lapping waves and glistening sails made us feel vigorously alive. We looked forward to an exceptionally enjoyable afternoon.

All went well until we got to the channel and then the breeze dropped to less than a whisper. We stopped moving. *Tinkerbelle* just sat there motionless as motorboat after motorboat passed by. When an excursion boat out for a tour of the peninsula came along, we were admired, photographed and waved to. And then, an hour later, when the excursion boat returned, we were admired, photographed and waved to again; but this time, since we hadn't moved ahead more than a few feet, we also became the butt of some snide remarks, such as: 'Get a horse'. 'Why don't you use a motor?' and 'Maybe you'd better swim for it'. Even the fishermen on the banks of the channel chimed in with caustic comments.

We had prided ourselves that, in the great tradition of the sea, ours was a happy ship. But it didn't require 20/20 vision to see that the first mate was going into a manœuvre that even in non-nautical circles was known as 'coming to the end of one's tether'. So, finally, when one of those beastly motorboats offered us a tow, I accepted.

The return trip, after our swim, was just as slow, maybe slower. It took us more than twice as long to sail the four miles from the beach back to the quay as it had taken to drive the ninety miles from Willowick to Erie. Without a doubt, Virginia and the children earned their Ph.D.s in patience that day. I guess I'd already picked one up somewhere but nevertheless I resolved that we'd get a little outboard motor as soon as possible.

In June and July we did a lot of day sailing on Lake Erie and went on several more overnight trips to other, smaller bodies of water. Then, in August, we brought the summer to a climax with a seven-day camping cruise through Michigan.

Virginia and the kids look back on this as our non-stop vacation race through Michigan because we didn't spend more than one night at each place we visited. Nevertheless, the trip became a high spot of our lives. Some of our most vivid memories are of lovely Higgins Lake, where, for the first time, we slept aboard *Tinkerbelle* while she was water-borne; of the gigantic Mackinac Bridge connecting the state's upper and lower peninsulas; of

Manistique, a former logging town which still has a friendly frontier atmosphere; of Indian Lake in the heart of the Hiawatha country, where we imagined ourselves camping 'by the shore of Gitche Gumee'; of Traverse City, where we nestled in a grove of sweet-scented pines, and of Ludington State Park, where we again spent a night afloat, snug and dry in our boat-tent despite the driving rain of a thunderstorm.

During the summers of 1960 and 1961 we continued our day sailing on Lake Erie and occasional overnight trips elsewhere, but our three-week vacation each summer was devoted to camping and sailing in the delightfully remote wilds of Algonquin Provincial Park in Canada's Ontario Province. The fun we had living on an island in the park's Lake Opeongo has left indelible impressions on our minds, and the sailing experiences we had there were equally joyful.

It was an enchanting blue-sky day on Lake Opeongo that we came to the realization, suddenly, that *Tinkerbelle* had crept deeply into our lives and hearts. She wasn't a boat any more; she was a friend. She was helping us to grow, individually and as a family, by bringing us, together, into confrontation with basic forces of nature and fundamental situations in living. She was giving us a foundation on which to make wise decisions about what was important in life and what wasn't. She was providing experiences through which we were acquiring self-reliance, appreciation for the outdoors, respect for others, instincts of mutual aid and co-operation and all the other qualities, skills and attitudes that contribute toward the development of mature personalities. She was teaching us how to endure what couldn't be cured. And she was helping us to avoid some of the pitfalls that abound in today's urbanized environment.

Don't assume for a second that the children were the only beneficiaries, or even the principal ones. Virginia and I gained enormously, too, in our understanding of our children, of ourselves and of each other, and in innumerable other ways. We didn't always act with flawless wisdom and love, we were far too imperfect for that; but we seemed to be moving in the right direction. Anyway, I hoped we were.

Tinkerbelle

And we owed a debt of gratitude to our boat. She was accomplishing for us what we had originally hoped she would accomplish, and more. This does not imply that these things might not have been achieved equally well, or even better, in some other way, by some other family. It simply means that for us the key to fulfilment was our beloved *Tinkerbelle*.

3

Our proficiency as sailors gradually increased. As we gained in experience, we also gained in skill and we became better and better acquainted with our boat, her good points and her shortcomings.

We found that her beaminess and flattish bottom gave her considerable initial stability, making her stiff, up to a point, so that she preferred to sail fairly upright rather than heeled far over to one side. If she did heel over farther than was comfortable for her, she developed a strong weather helm that called for a firm hand on the tiller to make her behave herself and stay on course. This, over a long haul, could be exhausting. However, by taking a reef in the mains'l, or by easing off on the sheet to allow more of the wind to spill out of it, I usually restored the helm to normal balance.

The bright side of this pattern was that if an unexpected puff of wind struck *Tinkerbelle* it forced her bow to windward as she heeled over, thus lessening the danger of capsizing. Instead of going 'bottoms up', she tended to swerve around into the wind and stop 'in irons'. I liked this for I saw it as a valuable safety factor.

Another thing we discovered was that she was lamentably slow in light breezes; so slow, in fact, that we joked about the way it took a hurricane to make her get up and go. Actually, we did some of our most enjoyable sailing when small-craft warnings were out and the wind was blowing so hard that few other sailing boats ventured out on the lake. But in light winds, *Tinkerbelle* simply wallowed in the water like a decoy duck while racing boats of comparable size moved along as effortlessly as swans. It was embarrassing to be left behind, but this facet of *Tinkerbelle*'s personality also had its advantageous side. The squat sail plan that made her slow in light winds gave her extra stability in hard blows. She could stand up to strong winds better than the racing craft.

As we became more familiar with *Tinkerbelle* and her idiosyncrasies, I kept thinking of ways to make her more seaworthy. Most sailors, I'm sure, study their boats with an eye to improving them in one way or another, and I was no different except that the changes I proposed to make in our boat were a trifle drastic and some of them, perhaps, of questionable value. Nevertheless, in the late spring of 1962, I began to rebuild *Tinkerbelle* nearer to my heart's desire; to make her as able a vessel as I possibly could, without spoiling her portability by trailer.

About eighteen months before this we had acquired a garage so I took over the whole place as my boat-rebuilding shop, and for the time being, relegated our car to the drive. Virginia, who invariably anthropomorphizes the family car, thought this was scandalous. To her it was disrespectful, if not downright cruel, not to mention immoral, to leave the poor thing outside, exposed to the ravages of wind and rain. I had somewhat the same feelings, only they were directed towards the boat, not the car. An automobile, to me, was simply a mass-produced contraption of metal, glass and rubber, stinking of petrol and oil, that couldn't possibly have feelings, much less a soul. But a sailing boat ... That was different. A sailing boat could feel joy and pain, hope and despair; it could be co-operative or cantankerous, well-mannered or insulting, a lady or a floozie. And every sailing boat had an individuality that set it apart from all others, even those of the same class. It also, most assuredly, had a soul.

If anyone deserved to inhabit the garage, I told Virginia, it was our boat. I reminded her that before we got the garage our car had endured the rigours of more than one winter out of doors; and I recalled the trouble we'd had keeping the boat covered with tarpaulins. I think the memory of the tarpaulins was what turned the tables in *Tinkerbelle*'s favour, for it was right after I'd mentioned them that Virginia agreed to let her have the garage to herself.

So, for the second time since she had become ours, the boat underwent something like a nautical metamorphosis. I was adequately skilful with woodworking tools, having taken a manual-training course in high school, and had acquired from my reading a sufficient understanding of the principles of boat-design to plan and execute the metamorphosis with confidence. It required a full year of spare-time labour to complete the transformation, but when it was done *Tinkerbelle* was a proper little yacht, with a cabin, cockpit, running lights, compass and other gear usually found only on much larger vessels.

Instead of her original centreboard, she now had a dagger-board-keel that could be moved up and down by winch in the slot of a watertight housing that passed through the keel timber and extended upward through the cabin roof. When the dagger-board-keel was retracted, *Tinkerbelle* could be moved on to a trailer without difficulty, and when it was lowered it provided the same lateral resistance the centreboard had supplied, plus a dividend of increased stability, for it was made of iron plate and weighed a little more than a hundred pounds.

The cabin roof's height above the deck was proportionately much greater in *Tinkerbelle* than it was in larger boats and this detracted somewhat from her appearance, but there were three good reasons for making this dimension as ample as practicable: to give plenty of headroom in the cabin; to house (in the through-cabin slot) as deep a daggerboard-keel as possible, and thus (when the daggerboard-keel was down) lower the hull's centre of gravity to the maximum—to provide, in effect, additional free-board—thus raising the hull's centre of buoyancy.

The second and third factors, taken together, reduced the chance of capsize and also mightily improved the prospect of righting the boat if she should happen to be overturned.

Abaft the self-bailing cockpit was a storage compartment, accessible through a small hatch at the stern and separated from the rest of the boat by a watertight bulkhead. By bolting down the storage compartment and cabin hatches, the hull now could be sealed shut, giving it many of the storm-weathering properties of, say, a corked bottle. This, it seemed to me, was approaching the ultimate in seaworthiness.

I also made a new mast, eight inches taller than the original, so that the boom would be high enough to clear the cabin top, and hinged in a tabernacle to permit easy raising and lowering. The hull's lapstrake planking was coated with white fibreglass, and the cabin top, cockpit foot well and deck were coated with red fibreglass, the deck also being treated with an anti-skid preparation.

When all the work was done, *Tinkerbelle* looked like a brand-new boat. Her white hull, red deck and cabin top and varnished mast, cockpit seats and cabin sides gleamed in the sunshine. To me at least she was a thing of beauty and there was no disputing the fact that no other boat like her existed anywhere in the world.

We decided she should be christened, to give her a decent start in her reincarnation, but we didn't particularly favour the customary bottle of champagne smashed against the bow. We were afraid the blow might mar her lustrous finish and anyway the symbolism of champagne was entirely out of keeping with both our financial circumstances and our drinking habits. So we settled on a ritual that diverged slightly from standard protocol, and of course Virginia did the honours.

'I christen thee *Tinkerbelle*,' she intoned gravely as, watched intently by the rest of us, she ceremoniously sprinkled the stem of our lovely craft with soda pop. It was a scene of breathtaking pageantry.

Naturally, now that the boat was ready to take to the water again, I wanted to try her out to see if she measured up to my expectations. There were sceptics in the neighbourhood who silently pitied Virginia for being tied to a husband gone berserk and who needed to be shown that the remodelled boat was not the feckless creation of a deranged mind. These doubters were mostly men, of course. The women, none of them sailors or even the wives of sailors, had no doubts whatever that I was balmy; anyone interested in boats was bound to be. They were beyond being shown the error of their belief. With the men, however, I had hopes. They were willing to grant that a fellow male who fooled around with boats could be sane. It was only what I'd done to the boat that made them doubt my sanity.

'That old tub will never take him anywhere,' one man told his wife. Another said, 'It'll never go to windward; cabin makes too much resistance. Makes it top-heavy, too.'

A third fellow came over one afternoon while I was away on some family errand, and with Virginia's permission, studied the boat for about fifteen minutes to see exactly what I was up to. Later his wife revealed his private opinion: 'He's making a mess of that boat. The tabernacle will never stand up; too much strain on it. And that daggerboard thing he's got!'

So there was a lot hinging on the outcome of the new *Tinkerbelle*'s trial runs. Fortunately, nothing untoward happened. The boat and I, and all who sailed with us, came back safely every time, and at least it showed that, if I was a nut, I was a passably competent one, or else exceedingly lucky. In any case, no more unflattering comments came my way via the housewives' grapevine.

I think what did more than anything else to restore my reputation was my first singlehanded cruise, a seventy-mile sail from Fairport, a city east of Willowick, to Erie. By surviving that voyage on Lake Erie I did more than I could have done in any other way to bring myself back from beyond the pale, to convince my friends and neighbours that I actually did know enough about boats and sailing to indulge my passion safely.

It pleased me to find that *Tinkerbelle*'s behaviour had been changed scarcely at all, except for the better, by the alterations she had undergone. The cabin's windage did keep her from sailing quite as close to the wind as she had before, but the difference was so slight, only a degree or two, that it didn't distress me. Anyway, she had never been a good pointer. The best she had been able to do was sail within fifty or fifty-five degrees of the wind, whereas most modern boats could sail within forty-five degrees of it.

The loss in windward ability was more than compensated for by the added stability imparted by the below-hull weight of the daggerboard-keel, the all-weather comfort of the cabin and, when the two hatches were closed, the watertight integrity of the hull. This last point, especially, made me confident of the boat's ability to weather fairly severe sailing conditions. In fact, on the voyage to Erie, she took a beating off Presque Isle Peninsula as winds of thirty to thirty-five miles an hour built up steep, six-foot waves; but she bore up under the pummelling in fine style. I began to feel she was fit to embark on much longer voyages.

The next winter, in January or February, 1964, a friend who owned a 25-foot cruising sloop proposed that we sail it across the Atlantic Ocean together to England. I guess he said it half in jest, not knowing that such a voyage had been a dream of mine for nearly three decades and that I would latch on to the idea with enthusiasm and tenacity. We had long discussions about the problems of ocean cruising, both of us having read widely on the subject, and began making plans and assembling the necessary equipment. Virginia, Robin and Douglas knew of the proposed voyage, of course, and approved. So I was jubilant. I have seldom been happier than I was during those days when the prospect of achieving my long-held ambition seemed within easy reach. I went about my work at the *Plain Dealer* in a sort of ecstatic trance.

After more than a month of planning I wrote, on March 18th, to the newspaper's executive editor, requesting a leave of absence in the summer of 1965 to make the voyage. When he wrote back granting the request, my joy knew no bounds. I felt the major obstacle in our path had been surmounted. In an all but uncontrollable surge of elation I told my friends of our plan to cross the Atlantic under sail; and, despite my fears, I was pleased to find they received the news fairly calmly. Most of them made it clear they thought the voyage would be hazardous, but very few of them thought we had lost our minds, and two or three even admitted they wished they could accompany us.

I was on Cloud 9 for about six weeks. Then came a crushing blow. The prospective skipper backed out of the venture, persuaded by his wife, father and business associates that it was ill advised; not that it was too risky, but that it would require too much time. I was heartbroken; inconsolably wretched. It was like dropping from paradise to purgatory at the flip of a switch.

The instant descent left me stunned. But, of course, groggy as I was, life had to go on. Somehow I continued to perform my duties as husband, father and journalist, but it was a desperately trying period of my life.

As I regained my psychological balance, however, the thought struck me: Why not make the voyage in *Tinkerbelle*? And the more I mulled over the idea, the less fantastic it appeared. After all, voyages had been made in small boats before. There was the 19-foot-long *Pacific* that Bernard Gilboy sailed from California almost to Australia in 1882–83. There was the 18-foot *Elaine* in which Fred Rebell, using a homemade sextant, sailed from Australia to California in 1931–33. There was the 19-foot *Mermaid* sailed by Kenichi Horie from Japan to California in 1962. There was the 16-foot *Little Western* that Frederick Norman and George P. Thomas sailed from Massachusetts to England in 1880 and, the following year, sailed back to Nova Scotia. There was the 15-foot *Sea Serpent* that Si Lawlor sailed non-stop from Massachusetts to England in 1891. And there was the 14½-foot *Sapolio* that William Andrews sailed, in 1892 (the four-hundredth anniversary of Columbus's famous voyage), from New Jersey to Palos, Spain (Columbus's port of embarkation), with a stop at the Azores.

Other unusual Atlantic crossings had been made by the 18-foot rowing boat *Richard K. Fox* (1897), the 15-foot pneumatic raft *L'Hérétique* (1952) and the 17-foot folding kayak *Liberia III* (1956).

All these voyages were remarkable. But there was another, even more remarkable, voyage that made me feel *Tinkerbelle* should be able to sail across the Atlantic. This was the voyage of *Half Safe*, an 18-foot amphibious jeep that Ben Carlin and his wife took from Halifax to West Africa, via the Azores, in 1950–51. If a get up such as Carlin's aquatic vehicle could traverse the broad ocean, *Tinkerbelle* could do it, too; I was convinced of that.

So, without telling anyone except my wife and children of this change in plans, I began making preparations.

4

SAILORS have seldom been envied by confirmed landlubbers and, until recent times, with good reason. Their lives were hard and usually short.

Boswell reported in 1759 that Samuel Johnson said: 'No man will be a sailor who has contrivance enough to get himself into a jail; for being in a ship is being in jail with the chance of being drowned. ... A man in a jail has more room, better food, and commonly better company.' Conditions under which seamen existed at that time were so atrocious that press gangs often had to be employed to fill out the crews of naval ships; and once a man was pressed into service he did not escape, except through death.

About a hundred years later Ralph Waldo Emerson echoed Johnson's opinion. Writing of a voyage he took to England in 1847, he said, 'The wonder is always new that any sane man can be a sailor.' He was referring to the sailor's 'life of risks, incessant abuse and the worst pay', for conditions at sea hadn't improved greatly in a century.

Nowadays, of course, few people talk this way about life at sea, either in the merchant marine or in the navy. The impressment, harsh discipline, bad food, outbreaks of scurvy and brutalizing environment of the old days are gone. Yet, while life aboard a commercial freighter or naval battleship is no longer regarded with horror, a rather large segment of the landbound population (at least in the United States) now looks askance at a new breed of sailors—those who go down to the sea in small pleasure boats. With Emerson, this group wonders how any sane man can do such a thing.

Tinkerbelle

The reason for the attitude today is, I suppose, compounded of a fear of deep water and the widespread thumb-rule judgment that a vessel's safeness depends on its size—the bigger the safer.

Although I hadn't conducted any private opinion polls, I had learned enough in the course of everyday living to have a fairly good idea of the reaction I would get if I let it be known that I planned to sail across the Atlantic in little *Tinkerbelle*. I could plainly see the raised eyebrows and hear the expressions of alarm such a confession would produce among my *Plain Dealer* associates and Willowick neighbours. I wouldn't have minded if that had been all, for these things couldn't have hurt me or my family. What did worry me, though, was the possibility that some well-intentioned person who knew nothing about boats or the ocean, but who had an unreasoning fear of both, would go to work on Virginia and try to convince her that, for my own good, she should refuse to give the voyage her blessing. I'm sure Virginia would have withstood such pressures admirably, but at the same time they would have made her life a great deal more difficult, psychologically, than it needed to be, and I didn't want that.

So I engaged in a deception for which I hope the good Lord and my friends will forgive me. I let everyone continue thinking I expected to cross the ocean with another man, in his 25-foot boat, and whenever anyone inquired about our plans I answered as if a voyage in the larger boat were still in prospect. Actually, almost all the planning I did for the voyage in *Tinkerbelle* was the same as it would have been for a voyage in the bigger craft (except that the provisions were reduced by half), so the amount of fabricating I had to do was minimal. It consisted mainly of simply allowing a false impression to remain uncorrected.

I started my studying and planning with the determination that if at any time prior to embarkation I encountered a difficulty of such magnitude that it presented a serious threat to success, I would call off the voyage. I was resolved not to let foolish pride sweep me into a bad situation or, being in one, make me continue in it to the bitter end. For my family's sake as well as my own I refused to be concerned about loss of face, for I considered it far better to be a live coward than a dead hero.

What I had to do first of all, it seemed to me, was to determine as precisely as I could the nature and full extent of the hazards to be expected on a transatlantic voyage, and then, once this was done, come to a levelheaded decision as to whether or not they were surmountable. If they weren't, I'd simply have to go back to being a copy-desk Walter Mitty, at least until another, more propitious opportunity for oceanic adventure came along.

The weather was the first major hazard to be reckoned with. I knew from reading about other voyages and from studying the marvellously informative pilot charts of the North Atlantic issued by the U.S. Naval Oceanographic Office that the summer months were best, but I lacked more precise information. I wrote to the U.S. Weather Bureau in Washington and the summaries it sent me, while still not so detailed as I had hoped for, were most encouraging. They contained sentences such as these: 'The weather of June is usually very pleasant over the North Atlantic. . . . The wind speeds average force 3 to 4 over most of the ocean. . . . Gales are infrequent. . . . Weather conditions are relatively settled during July with the buildup of the Azores high. . . . Wind speeds average 10 knots or less, 40 to 60 per cent of the time. . . .'

Then I ordered, from the Naval Oceanographic Office, an *Oceanographic Atlas of the North Atlantic Ocean* and a book entitled *Wind Waves at Sea* and these gave me all the information I was looking for, as precisely as was feasible. I learned that the highest wave ever reliably reported was a monster a hundred and twelve feet high observed from the U.S.S. *Ramapo* in the North Pacific in February, 1933, and that the highest waves seen in the North Atlantic were sixty-footers, also observed in the winter. The *Atlas* yielded the prediction that on a transatlantic voyage lasting through June, July and August I would have approximately two days of waves twelve feet high or higher, about four days of eight- to twelve-foot waves, about nine days of five- to eight-foot waves, and smaller waves the rest of the time. It also forecast roughly four days with winds of twenty-eight knots or stronger, eighteen days of seventeen- to twenty-seven-knot winds, nineteen days of eleven- to sixteen-knot winds and weaker winds on the remaining days, with nine or ten days of calm.

Tinkerbelle had already taken six-foot waves and about thirty-knot winds on Lake Erie without having to heave to, and I was confident that, hove to, she could survive conditions that were far more severe. I realized, of course, that the Oceanographic Office statistics were averages that wouldn't necessarily hold true for a given summer; there was always a chance one of those infrequent storms would strike. Red tracks on the pilot charts showed that storms had crossed my proposed transatlantic course in the summers of 1952, '54, '55, '56, '59 and '60, so the probability seemed to be much greater than fifty-fifty that I would take either a head-on or a glancing blow from a storm. Still, I was confident my little boat would acquit herself well, especially since I planned to make her unsinkable. I won't say I believed she could live through a hurricane, but I did believe she could take a terrific amount of punishment.

Many small-boat voyagers have stated in their books that size has little or no bearing on a boat's seaworthiness and, visualizing conditions at sea in a storm, I was inclined to believe they were right. A small boat, first of all, is a great deal stronger, pound for pound, than a big ship. Secondly, a small boat, being light and buoyant, will recoil before the waves and tend to ride over them, whereas a big ship will offer immense resistance. The predicament of a big ship in a storm is that of an almost irresistible force meeting an almost immovable object; something is likely to give, and fairly often it is the rivets or plates in the big ship's hull. That is why big ships are sometimes battered and broken, even sunk, by storms that do no more than cause a few hours' inconvenience to properly handled small boats.

So far so good. But what about the differences between my boat and other sailing boats less than, say, twenty-five feet in length? Would *Tinkerbelle* equal them in ability to weather a storm?

It seemed to me that the Achilles' heel of the usual ocean-going yacht was its keel, a thick slab of iron or lead that, in some boats, weighed more than a ton. The purpose of this weight was to keep the boat sailing right side up, a most worthy objective. But what if the boat sprang a bad leak or through some other misfortune filled with water? It would sink to the bottom like a lead casket. As I saw it, the prime function of a boat was to float, and, preferably, to go on floating no matter what calamities befell it. For even if its sails were torn, its rudder lost, its mast broken, even if it capsized or had its planking ruptured, those aboard it would have a fighting chance to stay alive as long as it continued to float. So, to insure that *Tinkerbelle* would remain afloat (with me and all my supplies and equipment on board), I filled the spaces between her deck beams with polyethylene-foam flotation material and, in addition, made five or six thick planks of the material to be packed inside the hull with my supplies. Of course the boat and all my gear had to be weighed to make certain the total weight didn't exceed the buoyancy factor of the flotation material, but when all this was accomplished, I had a vessel that was virtually unsinkable. And that contributed to my peace of mind.

I came to the conclusion that the dangers posed by the winds and the waves had been successfully neutralized; this meant that the biggest single obstacle to the voyage had been hurdled.

Then it occurred to me that next in importance to the assurance of staying afloat was the assurance of being able to call for help in case of need, so I bought a surplus Air Force 'Victory Girl' distress-signal transmitter, a neat little waterproof gadget that, on being cranked, automatically sent out SOS signals on two frequencies. One of these, 500 kilocycles, the marine distress call frequency, had a range of a little more than a hundred miles; the other, 8,364 kilocycles, the aircraft distress channel, had a range of about fifteen hundred miles, which was far enough to reach shore from the middle of the ocean.

Taken together, the guarantee of staying afloat and the guarantee of being able to summon aid seemed to me to eliminate or reduce most of the risks of the voyage. A lot of things could still go wrong, but the likelihood of their being fatal was now slight. Consequently, from this point on, my preparations went full steam ahead.

The next biggest problem, the danger of being run down by a big ship while I was asleep, was disposed of much more easily. I would, in so far as was possible, stay away from the regular shipping lanes, all of which were clearly marked on the pilot charts. Where it was impossible to stay clear of these lanes, while crossing them near New York and at the entrance to the English Channel, I would stay awake, with the aid of pills if necessary, until I was safely into the untravelled sea beyond.

O.K. Next problem.

What about navigation? It was obvious that simply by sailing east I was bound to fetch up, sooner or later, somewhere on the western coast of Europe; but I hoped I could be a little more accurate about my landfall than that. I wanted to sail to England. It would be mortifying if, instead of landing there, I landed in France or Spain or Portugal or Ireland. It was essential that I learn the rudiments of celestial navigation, a subject whose very name filled me with dread, for as a mathematician I was a great tennis player. Calculus, spherical geometry and related areas of mental torture were distinctly not my forte. I was the sort of guy who, in college, had had to take high-school algebra.

But as it turned out navigation wasn't the bugbear I had thought it was. Some wonderful, anonymous men had taken all the pain out of it by producing a book of logarithm tables called *H.O. 214*, which reduced all the required calculations to simple addition and subtraction. And add and subtract I could, just.

So, armed with George W. Mixter's *Primer of Navigation*, Carl D. Lane and John Montgomery's *Navigation the Easy Way*, *H.O. 214*, the *Nautical Almanac*, charts on which I could pinpoint the position of our home and a surplus Air Force sextant, I set out to teach myself how to guide a boat from one port to another across the trackless, roadless, signpostless sea. And I did it on our home's front porch.

My sextant could be used either with the natural horizon or with an artificial bubble horizon. In my practice sessions I used the bubble, and the check I had on the accuracy of my calculations was the known latitude and longitude of our house. If my sun lines came close to this position, I knew my sextant sights and figuring were reasonably accurate. They didn't come close at the beginning, though. If I remember correctly, my first sight put me somewhere in the middle of Hudson Bay, Canada, hundreds of miles to the north. That was a mite alarming. If I couldn't do better than that, I might as well throw away the sextant and rely on a ouija board. But I improved in time. In the end my position lines usually came within nine or ten miles of being right on the nose and, from my reading, I gathered that that was pretty good going with a bubble sextant.

Of course, it remained to be seen whether I could do as well from the cockpit of a little boat on the bounding main, but I had the feeling I could. So I decided another difficulty had been overcome.

Next I bought a short-wave radio with which to get the time signals that were essential for navigation and to maintain some sort of contact, through news programmes, with what was happening in the world ashore while I was alone at sea. I also hoped that musical and entertainment programmes would help me while away some of the hours I'd have to spend at the tiller.

I had an idea sharks wouldn't bother *Tinkerbelle* or me, as long as I stayed out of the water (and I planned, in any case, to take along chemical shark repellent), but I was a little concerned about what whales might do. I knew of several lone voyagers whose boats had been damaged by whales and also of two instances of real-life Moby Dicks having sent large whaling vessels to the bottom. In November, 1820, the Nantucket whaler *Essex* was attacked by a whale in the Pacific and sunk, thus providing a model for the climax of Melville's novel. And in August, 1851, while the novel was at the printer's, the *Ann Alexander* of New Bedford was done in by a whale, also in the Pacific. I didn't enjoy contemplating what might happen if an enraged whale were to assault my miniature sloop, yet I couldn't decide what I might do to guard against such a catastrophe. The best plan I could devise was to blast away on the compressed-gas foghorn I expected to carry with me and to put my faith in the theory that an animal won't bother you if you don't bother it.

One danger at a time, I tried to think of every conceivable

misfortune that could beset us and to contrive a way of taking the sting out of it. What if lightning struck? I put a lightning rod at *Tinkerbelle*'s masthead and grounded it through the shrouds to a hefty copper plate on her bottom. What if a wave washed me overboard? I rigged a lifeline to prevent my being separated from the boat. What if the rudder broke or was somehow lost? I built a spare rudder and, in addition, bought spare gudgeons and pintles. What if the hull were damaged or the mast broken? I assembled a complete tool kit and a supply of wood of various types and sizes with which to make repairs. What if the boat capsized? I bought an inflatable life raft and figured out a way of using it, with a line running from it to the sunken masthead, to right the boat. What about my health? I had a complete medical checkup (in fact, I had two) and passed without any ifs or buts. What if my water supply was spoiled or lost? I bought a solar still for converting sea water into fresh water. What if my food supply didn't last? I acquired an extensive fishing outfit. What if my SOS transmitter failed? I collected flares, signalling mirrors and dye markers. What if something forced me to abandon *Tinker-belle* and take to the life raft, how would I stay alive? I studied survival techniques perfected by the Navy and put together a complete survival kit, including emergency food and water. What if I were becalmed in the path of a ship? I took along a radar reflector to make my presence known to ships equipped with radar and also took along oars with which to row out of the way. (I decided against taking our little 1.7-horse-power outboard motor, or any other outboard. I couldn't have carried enough fuel to make it worth while.) What if the sails were badly torn? I got together a sail repair kit and spare sails; in fact, I bought a red nylon mains'l to make the boat as visible as I could. What if a shroud parted, the stem plate gave way or something else broke? I bought replacements for every piece of equipment that was under strain. What if I became ill or suffered a serious injury? I put together a complete kit of medical supplies, including anti-biotics, disinfectants and pain killers, with the help of a Cleveland physician and pharmacist.

What about appendicitis? I knew that this malady had almost

brought William A. Robinson to grief while he was cruising among the Galapagos Islands off the coast of Ecuador and I certainly didn't want to go through the same ordeal. However, I felt the chance that my appendix would act up was so remote that I didn't need to have it taken out in advance. If it did act up, I hoped to be able to keep the infection under control with antibiotics until I reached help.

And so it went on.

In the summer of 1964, before the planning had gone very far, Douglas, then ten, and I took a cruise on Lake Erie that was the longest voyage yet for *Tinkerbelle*. We sailed in easy stages from Cleveland's Wildwood Park to Thunder Bay, Ontario (seven miles west of Buffalo), covering more than two hundred miles. This was a trial voyage in preparation for the assault on the Atlantic, and it made me more confident than ever of *Tinkerbelle*'s capability. In a thunderstorm one day she ran up against stiff, squally winds and the biggest waves she had yet encountered, white-crested rollers six to eight feet high. The spirited way in which she rode the waves made me more optimistic than ever about the Atlantic venture, especially when I remembered having read somewhere that Howard Blackburn of Gloucester, Massachusetts, a former Grand Banks fisherman who had lost the fingers of both hands through frostbite and yet had twice taken small boats across the Atlantic, believed the sailing he had once experienced on Lake Erie was more dangerous than anything he had met on the ocean.

I began in January, 1965, to gather food supplies from widely separated sources: dehydrated meat bars from Chicago; components of Army C rations from Council Bluffs, Iowa, St. James, Minnesota, and Dawson, Georgia; canned white bread and fruitcakes from Nashville, Tennessee, and cereal bars, dehydrated eggs and a number of other items from Newton, Massachusetts. Most of the food was purchased at neighbourhood grocery stores, however, and all of it was acquired with an eye to easy preparation of meals. I didn't want to spend much time cooking, so practically all the food was precooked. It needed only to be warmed, or, if I was hard pressed, it could be eaten cold. I had a little canned-heat stove in gimbals, a frying pan, a saucepan and a knife, fork and spoon with which to prepare and eat my victuals. And, naturally, I had a can opener; in fact, several of them.

A few weeks later, when I broke the news of my proposed voyage to my mother, one of her great fears was that I would forget to take a can opener and would find myself out on the ocean with plenty of food but no with way of breaking into the cans to get at it. She was relieved to hear I was taking precautions to avoid this catastrophe.

Acting on the principle that it is unwise to put all one's eggs in one basket, I decided to carry twenty-eight gallons of water divided among forty half-gallon plastic bottles, three one-gallon plastic bottles and one five-gallon plastic container. By doing this I hoped to prevent any mass loss or spoilage and to facilitate keeping track of my water consumption. And, by refilling emptied bottles with sea water, I hoped to maintain most of the boat's inside ballast. According to the usual allowance of half a gallon a day I had enough water to last fifty-six days. However, this was supplemented by numerous cans of fruit juice and carbonated drinks, plus a supply of canned water in my survival kit, so I felt it was adequate. Besides, I knew from experience that my consumption of water would be far less than half a gallon a day. And if I did run short, I could use the solar still to make more, or catch rain water in a sail.

I expected the voyage to take about sixty days, but guessed that it might possibly take as long as seventy-five days so, to be on the safe side, collected enough provisions to last a minimum of ninety days. Other west-to-east crossings of the Atlantic had taken between twenty-two and a hundred and twenty-three days, which indicated to me that my estimate of the trip's duration was reasonably realistic.

One point about my food supply worried me. How would I protect all those cans from the corrosive action of sea water? The contents of any cans that rusted through would spoil very quickly so that, if worst came to worst, I might be reduced to living on fish and plankton, a prospect that didn't appeal to me in the least. So I packed my food supplies into heavy plastic bags sealed shut with a hot iron, two bags containing the food required for one day. Each week's supply of food was then packaged in a larger plastic bag, which, in turn, was put into a protective canvas bag. I had eight of these large bags of food, enough for two months at sea, with enough additional food in the form of emergency rations to last more than another month. As all these preparations neared completion, I began to feel confident that, no matter what my other misfortunes might be, I would at least have plenty to eat.

My provisions included two canned plum puddings Virginia had got me, with hard sauce to go with them, and my plan was to eat one of these when I reached the halfway point of the voyage and the other when I reached England. These little celebrations, I thought, would give me something special to look forward to.

As spring arrived, my preparations moved ahead more quickly, I wanted extra insurance coverage during the voyage so that if by some unlucky stroke of fate I lost my life Virginia and the children would be protected. I wanted to be sure of funds for the children's education and Virginia's future.

In applying for this insurance I naturally revealed my real intention of sailing in *Tinkerbelle*, and I was distressed to find that Lloyd's, which reputedly stood ready to insure anything, wouldn't insure me. That gave me a bad jolt, for it made me feel I wouldn't secure coverage anywhere. But then two other companies, apparently impressed by my knowledge of previous voyages, extensive preparations and the emphasis I put on safety factors, decided to risk money on me. Each of them insured me for twenty-five thousand dollars at a premium of two hundred and fifty dollars; so, in effect, they were betting a hundred to one that I'd make it. That encouraged me greatly, for it meant that if I was lost at sea Virginia would receive fifty thousand dollars over and above the insurance we already had, and it also meant that a couple of hardheaded business organizations had enough faith in me to regard my voyage as something more than a harebrained stunt.

By this time my close relatives had been told of my planned

expedition in *Tinkerbelle* (all of them being sworn to secrecy) and, on the whole, they took the news calmly. My father and father-in-law were no longer living, but I believe they would have given me their blessing. Virginia's mother accepted the project with good grace, and my own mother wrote, 'Of course, your letter made me catch my breath; I am sure you can understand. But I can understand the urge within you to do this thing, and this will be your adventure of a lifetime!' Later I learned that her greatest fear was that the loneliness of the ocean would drive me insane, a possibility that, I confess, hadn't even occurred to me.

One of my sisters, Dorothy Dole, was also concerned about the loneliness, but believed I would be able to endure it without ill effects. In a letter to my mother, my other sister, Louise, said: '. . . at first I couldn't take it [the planned voyage] in, it seemed incredible, and then I became very excited about it. I can't say that I really understand it; it's something I think we'd all like to do in the abstract, but when it gets to actuality, most of us draw back. The main thing I feel is that it is wonderful to see someone carry out his dream—so few of us get or take the chance. And Robert is a dreamer. . . .' I'm not sure the characterization of dreamer was meant entirely as a compliment, but I was pleased to hear that Louise believed in the pursuit of dreams.

My brother, John, and Virginia's brother, John, also gave their full support, each of them having yearned at one point in their lives to take a voyage such as I was planning. They offered many good ideas for making the trip safer and more comfortable and even assisted in more tangible ways. One bought me some excellent waterproof bags in which to store books and film, and the other presented me with a wondrous little contrivance—a hand warmer.

My colleagues on the *Plain Dealer*, still believing I was going with someone else in a boat nearly twice the length and several times the weight of *Tinkerbelle*, offered all their good wishes as well as innumerable helpful or humorous suggestions. During our supper hour from nine-fifteen to ten-fifteen every night we frequently gathered in the paper's cafeteria and discussed the voyage. I remember one night someone brought up the possibility of our meeting icebergs. And then someone else, recalling the *Titanic* disaster, suggested that we'd better take along a record player and a recording of 'Nearer My God to Thee' to play if the occasion arose.

Ted Mellow, the *P.D.*'s news editor, secretly solicited contributions from my companions on the copy desk and used the money to buy a bottle of brandy to be taken on the voyage 'strictly for medicinal purposes'. The bottle was presented to me in a ceremony that left me deeply moved—partly because I thought Robert Havel, chief of the copy desk, had called us together to chastise us for lousy headlines we'd been writing, or for some other dereliction. It was indeed a pleasant surprise to receive liquor instead.

Then, in what seemed to be scarcely enough time to turn around, it was May 1st and I was up to my neck in last-minute preparations. I had already gathered all the necessary charts, pilot books, light lists and so on, but I still had to get a passport and a smallpox vaccination, fill out a voyage plan and check-off list and have a signed disclaimer statement certified for the Coast Guard, fit a bilge pump to *Tinkerbelle* and do a number of other chores. Every minute away from my job was spent attending to these details.

The plan was for my mother to come from her home in Warner, New Hampshire, on Saturday, May 15th, to be with us for a week before my departure. She would remain to care for Robin and Douglas, whose school holidays were still two weeks away, while Virginia and I and Virginia's brother set out on Sunday, May 23rd (the day my leave of absence from the *Plain Dealer* began) to drive with *Tinkerbelle* to Falmouth, Massachusetts. After two or three days of exploring about Cape Cod and launching and loading the boat, John and Virginia were to return with the boat's trailer to Willowick. (Before setting sail I wanted to be sure Virginia reached home safely.) Then, on June 1st, *Tinkerbelle* and I would begin our transatlantic adventure.

My mother arrived on schedule on May 15th, at the beginning of what I'm sure was one of the most hectic weeks of her life; but she endured it with good cheer and before we knew what had happened we began what was to be my last day of newspapering for some time to come.

That morning, in anticipation of the coming weeks at sea, I had the local barber give me a close-cropped haircut. I hadn't worn my hair in that style since my Army days and the reaction to it was mixed. Virginia didn't like it because, she said, it reminded her of the haircut a condemned man receives before he is strapped into the electric chair. And John Hilton, an Englishman who had joined the *Plain Dealer* copy desk six or eight months before, didn't like it either.

'They'll never let you into England with that haircut,' he said.

When it was time to leave work that night, I was touched by the sincerity of my colleagues' genuine concern as they wished me a pleasant voyage. Yet how much more concern there would have been if they had known I was about to set sail in a 13½-foot boat rather than a 25-footer.

When I went to bed that night, on the eve of departure for Falmouth, I felt that I'd probably done the right thing after all to keep the true nature of my voyage a secret.

5

WE arose early the next morning, Sunday, May 23rd, and after a hurried breakfast started loading my supplies into our little station wagon. This job took much longer than expected, and we weren't ready to leave until after 3 p.m.

The goodbyes were relatively painless. We kissed and hugged with assurance that we weren't doing it for the last time. My mother and the two children understood what I aimed to do and were confident I would survive, although they may have had some doubts about whether I would get all the way across the ocean. It may seem odd, but the goodbye I was most concerned about at the time was my goodbye to Chrissy, our five-year-old German sheep-dog. After all, I was able to explain to my mother and the children why I was leaving and how long I'd be away, but I couldn't explain to Chrissy that I'd be back in three months. Nevertheless, I tried to be reassuring by speaking affectionately and rubbing noses with her and scratching her neck the way she loved me to. And anyway, maybe she wouldn't miss me so much, for now, instead of having to sleep at the foot of my bed, she'd get the whole bed to herself. Come to think of it, after three months of such indulgence she might be sorry to see me return. No matter; she was my special girl and I loved her.

Then I bade farewell to Fred, our cat, and to Puff, Douglas's iguana, and climbed into the driver's seat beside Virginia and her brother. The car's springs sagged with the weight of the provisions and of *Tinkerbelle* hitched on behind, but all we could do was hope the strain wouldn't be too much for them. So, with waves to mother, the children and the gathering neighbours, we struggled off.

We arrived in Falmouth safely the next day at about 7.30 p.m., put up at a very comfortable motel about a quarter of a mile from Vineyard Sound, and before we went to bed that night, drove down to the shore and looked out over the water which, in a few more days, *Tinkerbelle* and I would traverse. I'm not sure what the others felt, but I tingled with an intense sensation of awe.

The next day we devoted to sightseeing, and in Chatham I bought Virginia a little silver dolphin for her charm bracelet. 'A lucky dolphin,' I called it.

What made Chatham especially interesting to me was the fact that in 1877 Thomas Crapo and his wife had sailed from there in the 19½-foot *New Bedford*, bound for England. They arrived at Newlyn, near Penzance, Cornwall, fifty-one days later, after a truly remarkable voyage.

We went on, next, to a lovely sandy beach where we ate a fine picnic lunch as we looked out over the blue Atlantic, which, that day, was in a warm, contented mood. And then we visited Provincetown and saw some of the fascinating characters of that famous art colony. We also fed a huge flock of sea gulls from the end of a long pier where the fishing boats tied up.

The following day, Wednesday, May 26th, we drove *Tinkerbelle* over to Falmouth's Inner Harbour and, at a marina operated by Bill Litzkow, a big, friendly man, *Tinkerbelle* was hoisted from her trailer and lowered into the salt water. It was her first taste of the sea and she took to it as though she'd been tasting it all her life.

But there was a lot to be done. I paddled her over to a nearby quay and went to work raising her mast and bending on her sails while Virginia and John filled all the plastic containers with water and brought them over to be stowed away under her cockpit. Then I packed in the eight big bags of food and the Victory Girl, sextant, radio, blankets, charts, spare batteries, flotation planks and all the rest of my equipment. There were an awful lot of things to go into that little boat, but somehow I found a spot

49

for everything. When the loading was completed, *Tinkerbelle* was sitting lower in the water than she'd ever done before. She had only eight or nine inches of freeboard instead of the usual twelve or more.

The lack of freeboard didn't worry me. I believed the weight would give her increased stability. And I kept thinking of something Ben Carlin had written in *Half Safe*. He had said freeboard was like a chin stuck out to be hit. To me, that made a lot of sense.

While the loading was under way, Bill Litzkow's eyes must have bulged at the sight of all the material we were putting aboard.

'Where's he going?' he asked Virginia and John in a confidential tone. 'England?'

My two fellow conspirators were taken aback, for no one else suspected our secret.

'How'd you guess?' said John, with a mysterious grin.

Then he and Virginia swore Bill to silence, and Bill promised he wouldn't breathe a word to anyone. He kept his word, too. He didn't even mention it to me in the five days I remained at his quay preparing for departure. I found out later that after I'd gone he telephoned Virginia and finally got her permission to break his silence. Bill was a man you could trust.

Another man you could trust was Virginia's brother, John Place, a rewrite expert on the Pittsburgh *Press*. He was using a week of his vacation to help Virginia and me, and, although he considered my voyage extremely newsworthy, he didn't even tip off his own newspaper until I was safely out of reach at sea. That was rare trustworthiness.

Late that afternoon we did some more shopping. Virginia bought me a fine sweater and a book about sea birds to help me identify the birds I saw on the Atlantic (I already had two other books I hoped to read along the way: Margaret Mitchell's *Gone With the Wind* and John Le Carré's *The Spy Who Came In From the Cold*), and John got me a harmonica and some books of music to help pass the time if and when I was becalmed. In the evening we had a delicious farewell dinner at a restaurant overlooking the harbour. I think we all felt a little self-conscious, not knowing quite what to say, but we enjoyed ourselves, anyway.

The next morning John and Virginia began their journey back to Willowick with *Tinkerbelle's* trailer.

There is an old superstition of the sea that if you wave a ship out of sight you'll never see it again. John and Virginia wouldn't be there to wave me out of sight when I set sail, but I was there to wave them out of sight as they set off for Willowick; and I brought them a heap of misfortune. Not even the lucky dolphin I'd given Virginia could forestall it. On the New York Thruway, near Oneida, right at a tollgate, the car gave up the ghost and refused to budge. Virginia told me about it later over the telephone.

They'd had the car towed to a garage, where they learned that the engine was beyond repair. So Virginia wired our bank for some money and they got the new engine and finally, after dark on May 29th, a day late, they arrived back in Willowick.

For the next two days I occupied myself aboard *Tinkerbelle* moving my stores into what I hoped would be the most convenient arrangement and lashing them down so firmly that they wouldn't shift even if the boat was turned over. I also did some last-minute varnishing and worked out a way to carry the oars on either side of the cockpit with their blades extending out beyond the stern of the boat. I wanted them where I could get at them easily, for I might have to put them to use at a moment's notice.

Once all my gear was packed away as I wanted it, I swung the boat to check the compass. It's a good thing I did, for I found a substantial error on the east-west heading. However, once it was discovered, it was easily corrected and I had the satisfaction of knowing that I could then rely on the instrument.

The night of Monday, May 31st, my last night ashore for some time, I had supper at a little restaurant on the city's main street and, while I was eating, reviewed the circumstances that had led me to select Falmouth as my port of departure. Actually, the first thing I'd done was to choose the port I wanted to arrive at in England. I'd thought the best one would be Penzance, for it was near the tip of England that stretched out toward the United States like a hand offered to a friend. But the *Sailing Directions* mentioned various difficulties and dangers connected with entering Penzance, or Newlyn, the adjacent harbour where the Crapos had landed, so I decided to go on to Falmouth, which seemed to have an excellent harbour, although there was one sentence in the *Sailing Directions* that made me a bit nervous: 'Falmouth experiences a remarkably high number of strong winds and gales.'

I'd just have to hope no gale was blowing when I arrived on the scene. Anyway, I decided to end my voyage at Falmouth, in Cornwall, and it remained only to decide where to start it.

I thought I'd best embark at a port from which I could sail southeastward handily to get across the shipping lanes out of New York City as soon as possible. Next to the approach to England, I expected this first part of the voyage to be the most dangerous because of the heavy shipping. I decided that some harbour on the southern shore of Cape Cod would do very nicely as a starting point and then I discovered a Falmouth there, too. So that settled it. I'd sail from Falmouth, U.S.A., a former shipbuilding centre and whaling port, to Falmouth, England, a famous maritime town and resort.

About 9 p.m. I telephoned Willowick and said goodbye to mother, Robin, Douglas and Virginia, all of whom were still confident of my success. As I left the telephone booth and walked slowly back to *Tinkerbelle*, I was seized by an intense realization of my great good fortune in having a mother and family like mine. How many mothers, sons, daughters and wives were there who would let their son, father or husband do what I was doing? Probably very few. I'd seen too many men whose lives were hemmed in by strict adherence to the conventional demands of a business or profession or marriage; too many whose lives were made pallid by the fear of being different, of being criticized, of failing to meet all their responsibilities (as *others* saw them). I knew these fears well because I had cringed before them myself. The pressure to conform that pervades our society has a basically useful function, I suppose, but I wonder if it isn't too intense, too rigid, or perhaps misdirected, so that it stifles the freedom that leads to happiness and, incidentally, to an intellectually richer environment for everyone.

I was positive no one in the world had as wonderful a wife as mine. Virginia's quiet faith was an extraordinary compliment and a gift such as few men receive in their lives from anyone. She could have insisted that I behave as other 'rational' men did and give up any notion of taking this 'crazy' voyage. But she didn't. She knew I was stepping to the music of a different drummer and she granted me the boon of self-realization by allowing me to keep pace with the music I heard. I was poor in dollars and cents, but rich in love. I hoped I would prove worthy.

On the way back to the boat I mailed some letters. One was to the *Plain Dealer*'s executive editor and others were to friends on the copy desk, and they all revealed the truth about my voyage: that instead of going with someone else in his 25-foot boat, as I had originally expected to, I was going alone in my own *Tinkerbelle*. I hoped that no one at the *P.D.* would think too harshly of me for my deception.

There were also letters for Virginia and close relatives who already knew the facts.

When I got to the quay, *Tinkerbelle* somehow seemed to be in an expectant mood, as though she knew what was ahead. She was certainly as ready, as prepared, as any boat her size could be. There was just one thing missing. I hadn't been able to find the chemical shark repellent anywhere and when I'd mentioned it to Virginia on the phone she had informed me the repellent had accidentally been left at home.

'You'll just have to make friends with a dolphin and have him keep the sharks away,' Virginia had said.

I said, yes, I guessed that was what I'd have to do. It didn't worry me because I understood the repellent wasn't especially effective. I'd read a report by a 'shark research panel' of navy and civilian scientists that said the trouble with most shark repellents was that those that worked at all were as likely to attract sharks as to shoo them off. So maybe I was better off without the chemical shark chasers.

Tinkerbelle

Soon I was in *Tinkerbelle*'s cabin, curled up under a blanket. Tomorrow would be a long, hard day of sailing, in fact, I might have to continue sailing for two or three days and nights without sleep to get safely across the shipping lanes. I told myself I'd better get all the rest I could that night, for it was the last one I'd spend in the safety of a harbour for many days to come.

6

A TREMOR ran through *Tinkerbelle* as she bumped gently against
the quay. Lying doubled up in her tiny darkened cabin, I felt the
tremor and it sent a sympathetic tingle of anticipation down my
spine.

I shifted to the most comfortable position I could find in that
cramped space and tried to sleep. It was difficult. I was keyed up.
I couldn't help listening to the mingled sounds of the sea and the
land that came through the night air.

Across the small harbour a burst of 'quack-quacks' marked the
spot where I knew a family of semi-tame ducks was bedded down.
I knew, too, that an elderly duck couple spent each night under
a cruiser stored on a wooden cradle scarcely a dozen paces from
where *Tinkerbelle* lay, and I waited for their reply. Finally it came,
a single no-nonsense 'quack'. And then I heard the singing of
distant truck tyres rolling fast over concrete, and then the splash
of a fish jumping and the slap, slap of the ripples it stirred up
striking *Tinkerbelle*'s hull, and then the wail of a police siren (or
was it an ambulance?), and then the muffled hum of an outboard
motor, the bang of a door slamming shut, the cat-like meow of a
sea gull, a woman's voice far away calling in the darkness, the
beep of a car horn, the crunch, crunch of footsteps on gravel, and
then the throbbing rumble of the returning Martha's Vineyard
ferry, which, for several minutes drowned out every other sound.

It was a clear night. Through the open hatch I could see a
patch of bright stars. It was a bit on the cool side, too, and I
pulled the blanket around me more tightly, trying to seal in my
body's warmth.

Tinkerbelle

When the wake of the ferry reached *Tinkerbelle*, it jostled her against the quay. I could feel another tremor each time her rub rail bumped the pilings. It seemed as though she were quivering with excitement.

It won't be long now, old girl, I thought.

Both of us were tugging at our moorings, anxious to be off. *Tinkerbelle*'s mooring lines were strong, of three-eighths-inch Dacron; mine were made of invisible stuff, the social conventions, habits, thought patterns and bonds of affection that held me to the life on shore. But in their own way mine were as strong as hers, maybe stronger.

Nevertheless, in the morning we would cast off the lines, sever our links to the familiar land and begin a new life, an ocean voyage under sail. Soon after daybreak the voyage would begin, an age-old *élan vital*, the wind, expelling us from the comfort of the harbour and the sound beyond, pushing us forth into the vast outer world of the North Atlantic Ocean, bound for England, 3,200 miles away.

I watched a pattern of light reflected from the outer water as it shimmered and danced on the cabin ceiling, little more than a foot above my face. It cast a hypnotic spell, and soon I was drifting back mentally to the eternal questions of time and space, cause and effect, questions that had fascinated me since my teens. Only now, as I lay sprawled in *Tinkerbelle*'s diminutive cabin, on the brink of a long, lonely voyage, they seemed more poignant than ever.

A great many thoughts sailed through my mind that night.

I remember I nearly had to pinch myself, literally, to make myself realize it was really *me* in that cabin, ready to begin a voyage that had been a dream of mine since high-school days in India, where I had been born and raised by American missionary parents, the eldest of four children. It seemed incredible that a dream so old was on the point of becoming a fact.

Most of the thoughts that flowed from this wonderment sprang from questions that began with 'How?' or 'Why?' The most basic one of all was: Why was I there? That is, why was a middle-aged, married, sober, sedentary and presumably sane copy editor of the *Plain Dealer* now, on the night of May 31st, 1965, lying in the cabin of a 13½-foot sailing boat in the harbour of Falmouth, Massachusetts, intent on departing the next day on a voyage to Falmouth, England? What interplay of events, thoughts, feelings, desires and other causes had brought it about?

The causes began, I suppose, at Woodstock School in Landour, a town situated 7,000 feet above sea level on the first range of the Himalayan Mountains, about as far as one could be from the ocean and still be in India. To an assembly one Thursday in the early summer of 1935 came a handsome German of about twenty-six to tell of a voyage he and some friends had made from Sweden to the island of Tierra del Fuego at the southern tip of South America. They had rented a fair-sized sailing vessel for the week-end and then had kept it for the six months or so it took to complete their voyage. The young German showed movies that included some spectacular shots of mid-ocean storms and skiing on the snow-covered slopes of a Fuego mountain.

I was enthralled by the adventures of the voyage. Vicariously, I had never enjoyed anything so much in my life, and inevitably, although from afar, I fell in love with boats and the ocean. I became a sort of landlocked Dante pining for a seaborne Beatrice.

It was a love seldom gratified for I wasn't able to acquire a boat of my own until August, 1958, when I bought the craft that became *Tinkerbelle*, but from that day on I read every book I could find about voyages in small boats. The first one was William A. Robinson's tale of sailing around the world in his lovely *Svaap*. Then came Harry Pidgeon's story of circling the earth in *Islander*, which he had built himself. Dwight Long's book about his circumnavigation in *Idle Hour*, and Captain John C. Voss's report on his voyage in the converted Canadian Indian dugout, *Tilikum*.

By the time I got to Captain Joshua Slocum's classic account of his pioneering singlehanded voyage round the world in the *Spray*, I had made up my mind that if I ever got the chance I, too, would sail around the globe or, at least, make a long voyage in a boat under thirty feet in length. And so a dream was born.

The dream never died although there was seldom any noticeable evidence that it was alive. Whole years went by without my so much as mentioning boats to anyone, as I graduated from Woodstock; attended Lingnan University in Canton, China, for a semester; visited Japan (where one afternoon I did my only pre-*Tinkerbelle* ocean sailing); earned a degree at Antioch College; served with the 66th Infantry Division in France, Germany and Austria during and after World War II; worked as a reporter on newspapers in Washington Court House, Ohio, and Pittsburgh and Erie, Pennsylvania; married the former Virginia Place of Pittsburgh; acquired a daughter and a son and, in 1953, joined the *Plain Dealer* copy desk.

During all these events the dream of ocean voyaging remained in the back of my mind like an incubating microbe waiting for the right moment to flare up as a full-blown disease. Every so often, after reading some particularly gripping tale, I became afflicted with virulent sailing fever. Books about adventurous voyages periodically raised my temperature alarmingly, making it an enormous struggle to continue on course through college and into a journalistic career. But somehow I always managed to get a grip on myself and wrestle the fever back down to normal before it was too late; that is, I managed it every time but the last time, which was why I finally found myself in *Tinkerbelle* in the harbour at Falmouth, Massachusetts.

The first actual sailing I did was on the Jumna River at Allahabad, India, where my father taught philosophy at Ewing College and where my brother, two sisters and I spent our winter vacations from school. That first sailing experience became a landmark in my life. I'll never forget it.

A couple of young American instructors at Ewing College had bought an Indian rowing boat, a craft about sixteen feet long made of galvanized sheet metal stretched over a heavy wooden frame, and had converted it into a sailing boat. They had equipped it with a sheet-iron centreboard, a mast and boom of bamboo, galvanized solid-wire shrouds, and a mains'l and jib of light canvas. I'm sure it was the only boat of its kind anywhere on the Jumna or, for that matter, on the Ganges either, except possibly at Calcutta on the sea coast.

Tinkerbelle

My brother and I obtained permission to use this little sloop soon after its completion. As we bent on the sails, a crowd of Indians gathered on the shore and on a nearby bridge, and every Indian boatman in the area turned our way to see the fun. I feel certain that very few of these spectators had ever seen a fore-and-aft rigged sailing boat, since all the Indian vessels that plied the Jumna and Ganges had square sails that could be used only when the wind blew from astern. The Indian boats also lacked centre-boards, which undoubtedly made our craft seem that much stranger to the massing crowd.

I don't know what went through John's head as we prepared to sail, but I do know that I had feelings that must have paralleled those of the Wright brothers as they took to the air at Kitty Hawk, North Carolina, and of Edison as he gave the electric light bulb to the world. We were pioneering a great step forward in sailing technique and, by demonstrating it for all the Indians ashore and afloat to see, passing it on to them as a priceless gift. After centuries of abysmal ignorance, they would at last learn how to sail with the wind abeam; even how to sail upwind by tacking from side to side. My pleasure and pride at being able to bestow this great blessing on the Indians was only made more intense by the sceptical expressions of some of the watchers who seemed to be saying to themselves, 'It'll never work.'

We'll show 'em, I thought. We'll show 'em it works and that we know how to make it work. It didn't matter to me that neither John nor I had sailed a boat before, fore-and-aft rigged or not. Our only asset was some reading I'd done. But that was enough for me. The reputation of all Americans, if not all westerners was at stake.

Despite my cockiness we started out rather timidly, John stationed near the mast to handle the jib sheets while I sat in the stern controlling the mainsheet and tiller. It was pure beginners' luck that we weren't immediately caught in irons, bow to windward, and blown ashore stern first. Surprisingly, we got under way with reasonable dispatch and as we picked up speed I could sense a wave of amazement sweeping through the crowd. You see, I said to myself, we aren't being pushed sidewise as you expected; we're moving ahead just fine, and at a pretty good clip. And look! We can even go a little bit into the wind! You never saw one of your flat-bottomed barges doing that!

Everything went well, considering it was our very first attempt at sailing, and as we glided back and forth under the bridge and from one side of the river to the other, we rapidly gained self-assurance. We discovered that sailing was a delightful, exhilarating sport, and that we were pretty good at it; no, very good at it. Our confidence soared.

'Let's put on a real show for 'em,' I said.

We adjusted the sails for maximum draw on a beam reach until the boat, heeling excitingly, knifed through the water at top speed. Wow! What a frolic! We knew our audience had never before seen wind power move a boat so fast and the thought made us, or at least me, delirious with the heady pleasure that accompanies unrestrained showing off.

And then *it* happened.

The centreboard and rudder caught on a sand bar and spun the boat into a jibe. The boom lashed around like a giant club. I ducked just in time. John didn't.

My brother took the full force of that flailing boom on the side of his head and it nearly knocked him out double, both unconscious and overboard. He could easily have been killed. I was lucky; only my pride was hurt, although that grievously. My face turned as red as John's turned white.

We limped back to the boat landing, disembarked and slunk away. To the everlasting credit of the dozens of Indians who witnessed our comeuppance, not one made a gloating remark or in any way called attention to our embarrassment. And I'm still grateful.

As the wounds to skull and pride healed, we discerned a lesson in our mishap. It was that the Indians' boats were perfectly adapted to navigation conditions on the Jumna and Ganges. Centreboards and fore-and-aft-rigs were out of place there. Tradition and centuries of experience, we had to admit, should not be scorned or tossed overboard lightly.

After that whack on the head my brother's main recreational

interest turned from boating to mountain climbing. I guess he decided in the quietness of his own mind that it was much better to risk being clobbered by falling rocks at high altitude than by whiplashing booms at water level. It was a good decision, for he has developed into an accomplished mountaineer.

My own enthusiasm for boats and sailing not only survived the catastrophe on the Jumna, but increased in the months and years that followed. However, it is conceivable that if that swishing spar had struck me instead of John I might never have followed the trail that eventually led to *Tinkerbelle* and to the Atlantic. John might then have taken to the ocean while I scaled lofty peaks in India and western Canada. Psychologists agree, I think, that bumps on the head (or the lack of them) can have a profound influence on one's life. They call it the pleasure-pain principle.

In the period between that initiation on the Jumna (it was in 1936) and my purchase of the boat that developed into *Tinkerbelle* in 1958, I went sailing no more than five times. But this was sufficient to magnify my love of sailing into something resembling a passion, which, in turn, made it inevitable that as soon as we as a family could afford it, I would buy a boat.

In the early spring of 1964, my dream came into fortuitous conjunction with the opportunity to make it come true. It was, like my first sail and the day I got married, another great moment in my life. I recalled some lines by Thoreau: 'If you have built castles in the air, your work need not be lost; that is where they should be. Now put the foundations under them.' So I began in earnest to put the foundations under my air castle.

The main factor, naturally, was my love of the type of sailing that goes under the heading of cruising, as distinct from racing. Sailing, for me, has been a way of achieving both companionship with my family out of doors and much-needed solitude away from jangling telephones, car exhaust fumes, too-eager salesmen and other unpleasant details of civilization. This love, this need, fundamentally is a feeling in my bones, a pulsating in my viscera so personal it cannot be adequately explained. (I'm not trying to be mystical or mysterious. That's just the way it is.) Nevertheless, I'll try my best to account for it.

As every human does, I have expended a large part of my life searching, often blindly and sometimes painfully, for Truth. (But maybe searching isn't the right word because quite often the whole game's been reversed and Truth has found me, notwithstanding my kicking and screaming and panic-stricken efforts to avoid it.) The result has been that through the years I have collected a few miscellaneous chips from the Mother Lode; at least, I hope I have. These, as far as human conduct is concerned, include the golden rule, Thomas A. Edison's axiom 'Everything comes to him who hustles while he waits'; Socrates' adage 'The beginning of knowledge is the awareness of ignorance'; and the Anglican Archbishop Richard Whately's postulate 'A man will never change his mind if he have no mind to change'. But in all my days on this earth I have come across no more than a handful of chips that, assayed for their Truth content, came anywhere near equalling the pure, unvarnished verity of what Water Rat said solemnly to Mole in Kenneth Grahame's delightful story *The Wind in the Willows*.

'Believe me, my young friend,' said Water Rat, 'there is nothing—absolutely nothing—half so much worth doing as simply messing about in boats.'

Of course, I'm being half facetious. But also half serious. Water Rat's statement, for me, comes very close to being the revealed Word, the supreme Truth.

I find immense pleasure in the gurgle and splash of a boat propelled by a direct force of nature, the snapping of canvas and the humming of rigging in a fresh breeze, the rattle of ropes running through blocks, the crying of gulls, the lift and heave of a buoyant hull, the pressure of wind against my body, the sting of flying spray, the sight of billowing sails and the swirling foam of the wake. To me, nothing made by man is more beautiful than a sailing boat under way in fine weather, and to be *on* that sailing boat is to be as close to heaven as I expect to get. It is unalloyed happiness.

It is sheer delight to whisk myself off on a 'small planet', as

Tinkerbelle

Joseph Conrad once described a boat, and, for a few hours or days, escape from the troubles and tensions of life ashore. Difficulties and stresses fall into perspective while you are sailing, for in sailing you are dealing with elemental forces of wind and water that have been here for aeons and are likely to remain long after we mortals are gone; forces that can be gentle and yet, stirred to fury, are so powerful they make all else shrink into insignificance. Sailing also helps to keep a man aware of his lowly place in the universe, especially if that sailing involves celestial navigation and its concerns with the sun and stars, for there is nothing to equal the astringent effect on one's ego of a long, thoughtful look into outer space. There is a challenge, too, in sailing; a summons to learn how to master wind and water and how to master yourself when you are in a crisis, balancing on the edge of panic.

My life on shore, especially in India, conditioned me to enjoy sailing, I think, because a sailor must be somewhat fatalistic, as the Hindus are. He must be prepared to accept whatever comes, from flat calms to hurricanes; and he must, like the Hindus, train himself to enjoy the conditions he gets if he doesn't get the conditions he enjoys. From the Indians, too, I absorbed the patience that serves a sailor well, and an appreciation of the fact that there is a great deal more to life—and to a voyage—than mere movement from one place to another.

Sailing has also been a handy escape valve for the psychological pressures that tend to build up on the newspaper copy desk where I have laboured for the last thirteen years correcting, in so far as I could, the facts, the spelling, grammar and style of reporters' stories, weeding out possible libels and double meanings, and writing headlines. These pressures go with the job as certainly as paint-spattered hands go with a career in art. They are a product of recurring press deadlines, sedentary work, occasional friction between divergent personalities and the ever-present conscious-ness that regardless of how knowledgeable one may be one's reservoir of information is never entirely adequate; that the only perfect copy-desk man would be one who knew all there was to know about everything. The pressures may at times build up to considerable intensity, but putting my hand on the tiller of a sailing boat releases them as surely and almost as swiftly as touching an earthed wire frees my body of static electricity.

A fondness for large bodies of water, particularly bodies of salt water, is a last major factor in my love of sailing. The clean, saline tang of sea air is a powerful attraction. So is the awe inspired by the ocean's (any ocean's) enormous breadth and depth, by the ghostly presence of all the famous and infamous ships and men and women it has carried through the centuries, and by the mysteries hidden beneath its sometimes placid, sometimes stormy surface. Perhaps there is an inherited something in the protoplasm of my body cells that feels an agreeable kinship with the sea, where life on earth began and where it existed for such a long time before it took to the land. At any rate, the sounds of the sea, especially of breakers pounding on a beach, have a strangely soothing effect that I crave only slightly less than an addict does drugs.

Aside from my love of sailing, I looked forward to a small-boat voyage because of an inexplicable notion I had that a voyage was a kind of microcosm of life, a life within a life, if you will, with a birth (beginning), youth, maturity, old age and death (end), and that it was possible for a sailor to express himself in this miniature life—with his technique, responses to changing conditions and endurance—somewhat as an artist expresses himself with paint and canvas. It seemed to me, too, that in this abbreviated life a sailor had an opportunity to compensate for the blemishes, failures and disasters of his life ashore.

This was a curious idea. Where it came from I don't know. It may have arisen from an awareness of behaviour I was ashamed of, of unlovely shortcomings in my life ashore, linked with a hope that in the compressed life of a sea cruise I could, perhaps, redeem myself. I had to concede that my voyage would benefit few persons other than myself, except in so far as it might, momentarily, lift some who heard of it out of the routine of their own lives, but it did give me a segment of existence that, God willing, I might fashion into something nearer to a work of art than my life on land had been. This idea gratified me strangely although I knew perfectly well that at sea, alone, I would of necessity be an unsocial being.

So I was there in Falmouth Harbour, ready to begin a transatlantic voyage in a midget sloop, because I loved sailing, I loved the sea, I had long wanted to make an ocean voyage and I had finally got the chance to make one. Contemplating all this, I decided I knew and understood the 'Why?' of the voyage, except for two final points: Why was I making the voyage alone? And why was I making it in such a small boat?

Actually, these questions were easily answered. I was sailing in *Tinkerbelle* because she was the boat I happened to have and I was confident she was equal to the task. And I was sailing alone because I felt *Tinkerbelle* was too small to carry the supplies for more than one person. If there was anything I was absolutely certain of, it was that I was *not* there to commit suicide or perform a stunt or set a record or advertise a product. No one had given me financial assistance and I wasn't sponsored by anyone, not even by the *Plain Dealer*, my own newspaper. Nor was I actuated by the expectation of vast monetary gain, although I did dare to hope that I might, by writing articles or a book, recoup the cost of the voyage and, if I was lucky, make enough more to help my children through college without going deeply into debt.

Most people, I think, understand the urges that prompted me to take the voyage; at least, most of those I've spoken to about it, now that it is over, have been satisfied with my brief explanation of why I did it. Occasionally, though, a person will ask me 'Why did you do it?' with an inflection that makes the query sound as if the person were asking 'Why do you play Russian roulette?' The crux of it, of course, is the implied dangerousness of a voyage like *Tinkerbelle*'s and the inference that it is a bad policy, if not morally wrong, to do anything, ever, that is the least bit dangerous.

It seems to me there are two sides to the danger coin, two reasons for questions like this. One is that the values of comfort and safety are being overemphasized in our society to the detriment of other, perhaps more important, values for which it may be worth enduring a little discomfort, even danger. The other is that persons who are shorebound, who have had no opportunity to learn about boats and the sea, tend to exaggerate the dangers of a small-boat voyage.

Essentially, I believe, it is a question of familiarity, of what one is used to. The same man who quakes at the idea of sailing across an ocean will, paradoxically, drive a car from coast to coast with hardly a thought about the annual toll of deaths on United States highways. He doesn't dwell on the hazards of driving because they are so familiar. If he were equally familiar with the hazards of the sea, I am sure he would accept them with equal equanimity. I accepted them with a fair degree of composure, not because I am more courageous (or more foolish) than the average person but because I took the trouble to familiarize myself with them and prepare ways of coping with them. I admit that luck played a part in the success of the voyage, but not so big a part as might be imagined. I feel that intensive and extensive planning reduced this element to an absolute minimum. I planned with utmost care, first, because I am a husband and father with responsibilities toward those who love me and depend on me, and, second, because I feel it is the height of thoughtlessness to voluntarily get oneself into a predicament necessitating a call for help that may endanger the lives of others.

The moral questions evoked by my voyage caused me grave concern. Did I have the right to endanger my life, even slightly, and consequently jeopardize the future of my family? And did I have the right to separate myself from all human society and, for two or more months, occupy myself solely with doing something I had longed to do for years, but which would be of little value to others; in other words, did I have the right to surrender unconditionally to hedonism? With much soul-searching I answered these questions in the affirmative, although I am willing to concede I may have been wrong in doing so.

Although I'm convinced the riskiness of the voyage was far less than many people believe, I still must confess it was this riskiness that made the voyage seem adventurous, exciting—a wonderfully far cry from the immobility, tedium and sometimes harrowing predictability of copy-desk existence.

Tinkerbelle

I remember thinking that night about the uncertainties ahead, about what might be waiting for *Tinkerbelle* and me out in the open ocean. I wondered whether this watery world would be kind to us. Or would it tax us beyond endurance, cut our voyage short, perhaps even destroy us? The more I thought about it, the more I realized I really didn't want to know the answers to those questions. Not in advance; not for certain. For it was the uncertainties, the surprises, the risks that added up to the challenge that made life—and a voyage—interesting and worth while. Without them the sources of hope would dry up and life would indeed wither into a monotonous meander from womb to tomb.

But lying there in *Tinkerbelle* on the eve of departure, I was mindful of the extent of my preparations and it gave me a feeling of assurance. I didn't have the sensations of a man about to step off a cliff, as I had expected to have. My mood was one of calm inner confidence. And yet, remembering my Jumna introduction to sailing, I was only too aware that confidence is often that quiet faith, that euphoria, that pervades your being just before you fall flat on your face. So I held my feelings in bounds, well on this side of bravado.

Sleep was a long time coming that night. Being on the verge of a dream cruise was too exciting. The sounds of the harbour and surrounding area fell too insistently on my ears. Even though I couldn't feel it inside the cabin, I knew a gentle breeze had sprung up because the ripples it roused made clicking sounds as they hit the crevices in *Tinkerbelle*'s lapstrake hull. The air currents also, now and then, made the halyards bang against her mast—clack, clack, clack, clack.

I heard a dog bark a couple of times somewhere off the port beam and then the garbled sound of boys' voices—teenagers', I guessed—too far off to decipher. But soon the voices drew closer and I could make out a word here and there. It seemed that the boys had been fishing down near the harbour's mouth and were now, at about midnight, on their way home. I couldn't decide how many there were; probably no more than three.

When they came to the spot where *Tinkerbelle* was tied up, one of the boys said, 'Hey! Look at that!'

Tinkerbelle

Footsteps plunked out on the quay. There was a brief pause, and then *Tinkerbelle* heeled over as someone stepped on to the cabin top.

'Whatcha doin'?' one of the youths said.

'Just wanna look in her,' the boarder replied.

I heard him kneel. Then his silhouetted head, upside down, moved into the open hatchway from above. I could feel his eyes trying to pierce the darkness.

I was sure he didn't have the least suspicion that anyone was in the cabin. If I spoke or moved, he might be so startled he'd fall overboard. I didn't want that. So I froze, and tried not to breathe.

He was breathing so heavily himself I needn't have worried about his hearing me. He stayed there for what seemed like a couple of minutes. I wondered if he could make out my face or the outlines of my body under the dark-grey blanket. He gave no indication that he could.

Finally the head withdrew and *Tinkerbelle* rocked silently when the boy stepped back on to the quay.

'Gee!' he said. 'Never saw a boat that small with a cabin on it. You s'pose someone goes cruisin' in it?'

'Nah,' came the answer. 'It's much too small.'

7

THE alarm clock jarred me awake. It was already 9 a.m., broad daylight, and the sun was beating on the deck and cabin roof. Soon the interior of the boat would be an oven. It was time to get moving.

I washed, had breakfast, attended to a few last-minute chores and said a quiet goodbye to Bill Litzkow at the marina. Then, at about ten-thirty, I hoisted *Tinkerbelle*'s red mains'l and white genoa and she and I set forth on our great adventure.

It was a beautiful day. The sky was dark blue overhead, shading to lighter blue near the earth and sea; it was pleasantly warm, and a gentle breeze caressed *Tinkerbelle*'s sails. There was just one little flaw in the otherwise perfect picture: the breeze was from the southwest, which meant we had to tack out of the harbour. But that was a small price to pay for a blue sky and warm sunshine. Fortune was smiling on us.

We skimmed from one side of the harbour to the other, dodging between handsome moored craft, and with each jog we drew closer to the exit into Vineyard Sound, about half a mile away. As we moved along, I saw on our portside a sleek boat owned by Joseph P. Kennedy, former United States ambassador to the country to which we were headed, and off to starboard the fine restaurant where Virginia, her brother and I had had our farewell dinner a few nights before. In a few more minutes we slipped through the rock-lined channel into the sound.

From here it would have been possible to follow the course Crapo had taken in the *New Bedford* exactly eighty-eight years and one day before, and sail directly eastward to Chatham and then on out into the open ocean. But Crapo's account of the voyage mentioned his having run aground several times near Chatham, and the *United States Coast Pilot* for the area contained frightening notations such as: 'The channel is used only by small local craft with a smooth sea; strangers should not attempt it. . . .The wreck of the steamer *Port Hunter* is on the south-western side of Hedge Fence. . . . Because of the numerous shoals, strong tidal currents, thick fog at certain seasons . . . the navigator must use more than ordinary care when in these waters.' Consequently, I decided not to follow Crapo's example.

Another possibility was to sail more or less southward and pass through Muskeget Channel, between Nantucket and Martha's Vineyard islands, to the sea. Here again the *Coast Pilot* dissuaded me. One ominous sentence said, 'Although this channel is partly buoyed, strangers should never attempt it, as tidal currents with velocities of two to five knots at strength make navigation dangerous.'

We couldn't sail directly east or south, safely. There was just one other possibility and, fortunately, the *Coast Pilot* had no scary remarks about that. We could continue tacking and go southwestward around the western coast of Martha's Vineyard and thus reach the open ocean approximately at the point where the meridian of 71° W longitude intersected with the parallel of 41° 22' N latitude. So that's what we did.

We beat down Vineyard Sound, passing Nobska Point and, beyond it, Woods Hole, in the early afternoon. I was intrigued by a peninsula on the chart called Penzance, which bore about the same geographical relationship to Falmouth, Massachusetts, that Penzance, England, bore to Falmouth, England.

We had the sound to ourselves all afternoon except for one small trawler that hurried by in the opposite direction as we approached the Elizabeth Islands, hilly and partly wooded mounds of sand rising from low shoreside bluffs off to starboard. These islands have fascinating names: Nonamesset, Uncatena, Naushon, Pasque, Weepecket, Nashawena, Penikese and Cuttyhunk, most of them Indian.

I wondered if Cuttyhunk had been named by Bartholomew Gosnold, the English adventurer and explorer who landed there in 1602. It was he who had named Cape Cod and Martha's Vineyard, the latter for his daughter and the grapevines he found, so it seemed possible that Cuttyhunk was his idea, too.

It was pleasant, easy sailing, with a breeze of ten or twelve knots, just enough to keep *Tinkerbelle* moving along contentedly without any fretting or straining. After a long starboard tack across the sound we came about off Martha's Vineyard's Cape Higgon in the late afternoon and headed toward Nashawena. Along the way *Tinkerbelle* rose and fell to the first big swells coming in from the open sea, and showers of spray shot up from her bow, drenching her foredeck.

'Here we go,' I said.

I don't believe I had any strong feelings of trepidation. It just seemed that we were out for an enjoyable sail. I knew that many rough, uncomfortable days probably lay ahead, but I felt sure my preparations had been adequate and, more important, I had tremendous faith in my companion, my friend, *Tinkerbelle*. She was the main reason for my serenity.

A voyage made by a solitary person is sometimes called a singlehanded voyage or a solo voyage, but neither of these terms gives proper credit to the most important factor in any voyage: the boat. Far from being a solo, a one-man voyage is a kind of maritime duet in which the boat plays the melody and its skipper plays the harmonic counterpoint. The performances of the boat and the skipper are both important, but if it comes to making a choice between the two the decision must be in favour of the boat. I had read about dories from fishing vessels on the Grand Banks occasionally breaking loose with no one on board, drifting all the way across the Atlantic and being found weeks later on the coast of Ireland or England. But I had never heard of a man accomplishing that feat without a boat.

And there was the famous case of the *Columbine*, a 50-foot sailing vessel used in the Shetland Islands toward the end of the nineteenth century for trade between the port of Grutness and Lerwick, about twenty miles away. One January day this ship, carrying its skipper, crew of two and a partly paralysed woman passenger, was bound for Lerwick when the mainsheet broke and the heavy boom began swinging back and forth dangerously as the vessel rolled from side to side. The skipper and the mate tried to retrieve the end of the parted line but a violent lurch threw them into the sea. The mate managed to get back on board, however, and he and the other member of the crew, without pausing to consider the consequences, put out in the ship's dinghy to rescue the skipper. They never found him. And they never got back to the *Columbine*. They did manage to get ashore, however, and sound the alarm.

The invalid passenger, Betty Mouat, had expected a voyage of less than three hours; instead, she got one that lasted more than eight days. And all that time she remained below, unable, because of her paralysed condition, to get on deck. The *Columbine* sailed herself all the way across the treacherous North Sea, finally running aground on the island of Lepsoe, north of Alesund, Norway. Betty Mouat was rescued.

So, remembering the incredible voyage of the *Columbine*, I had no illusions about the relative contributions of *Tinkerbelle* and myself toward making our cruise a success. *Tinkerbelle*'s part would be the greater, by far. I was just there more or less for the ride and to keep her pointed in the right direction.

Near Nashawena we went over on to the starboard tack again and soon were due west of Gay Head, the westernmost point of Martha's Vineyard. I could clearly see the headland's cliffs, topped by a lighthouse, reddened by rays of the magnified sun that was now setting far astern beyond the Elizabeth Islands. 'Red sky at night, sailor's delight.' If that old jingle was right, we'd have good weather for the next day. We could use it. We needed it in order to get as far away from shore as possible, as quickly as possible, because, contrary to what many non-seafarers believed, the most dangerous thing about the sea was not the sea but the land. As long as a vessel was in the open sea, with plenty of room around her, she could manage quite well. But if she was unfortunate enough to be blown against the land, perhaps on a rocky coast, she would be smashed like an eggshell. We had to get far enough from land to prevent that from happening to us.

Tinkerbelle

The day was dying in a blaze of glory in the west as we slipped gently out of the womb of Vineyard Sound into the open ocean. Our voyage was born. It was a thrilling moment for me. How long had it been since I'd heard that German adventurer speak at Woodstock, creating my vision of an ocean voyage? Twenty-nine years and eleven months, to be exact. That was a long time to cherish an ambition. But think how few of the ambitions of youth are achieved by anyone. One of the tragedies of life is the way teen-age boys and girls have to abandon their dreams, one by one, as they grow to adulthood and are forced to cope with the harsh realities of existence. I was fortunate beyond measure.

As we sloshed and splashed out into the dark of the night and the immense space of the ocean, I was swept by a feeling of elation derived partly from the satisfaction of crossing the threshold of a longed-for adventure and partly from an eerie sensation that I was sailing along in the afterglow of history, in the wake of splendid, momentous, exciting events.

These same Cape Cod waters, it was said, had been plied by Vikings about the year 1000, and by French and Spanish fishermen in the fourteen-hundreds. Historians believed John Cabot, an Italian sea captain employed by England, probably sailed along the Massachusetts coast in 1498 and, after him, Giovanni da Verrazano, an Italian navigator and pirate, who entered what is now New York Harbour and discovered the Hudson River in 1524. Then came Gosnold, and then another Englishman, Henry Hudson, who was employed by the Dutch and who, in 1609, sailed his ship, the *Half Moon*, up the river that bears his name.

Still another Englishman, Captain John Smith, arrived on the scene in 1614, explored the Massachusetts coast and drew maps of it that seamen used for many years thereafter.

The waters we were passing through had been alive with whalers, packets, down-easters, schooners, and those beautiful trim greyhounds of the sea, the clippers, in the eighteen-hundreds. But then came steam power to drive these lovely sailing craft out of ocean commerce. Praise be the Lord, though, sails had not been banished altogether from twentieth-century America. They lived on, mostly in pleasure boats of varying types and sizes, and I hoped they would continue to do so. I tried to picture a world without tall masts raking the sky, without gracefully curving, wind-filled sails, and what I saw was dismal.

Behind us now, on the other side of the Elizabeth Islands, was Buzzards Bay, where the doughty Joshua Slocum had taken his first trial run in the *Spray* before proceeding to Boston to begin his historic globe-girdling voyage. The waves of Buzzards Bay had also been parted by the 20-foot *Nova Espero* as Stanley Smith and Charles Violet neared the end of their voyage from London to New York, and by the famous 96-foot *Yankee* in which Irving and Electa Johnson had cruised the world with amateur crews. And New York, a short sail to the south-west, had been the terminus of one of the most nearly flawless small-boat voyages on record, the classic cruise from England of Patrick Ellam and Colin Mudie in the 19½-foot *Sopranino*. There, too, had ended fine voyages of the Frenchman Alain Gerbault in the 39-foot *Firecrest* and the Englishman Edward Allcard in the 34-foot *Temptress*. In fact, that part of the ocean had been criss-crossed by the tracks of innumerable small sailing boats, some of them participants in recent single-handed transatlantic races.

In the midst of these musings I felt a pang of hunger and realized I hadn't eaten anything since breakfast. I reached into the cabin, got myself a meat bar and munched on it as we continued on our way. I didn't want to stop to warm up some food because we had to keep moving offshore as quickly as we could and also across the shipping lanes leading eastward out of New York. I knew I wouldn't be able to sleep safely until we were well south of these lanes.

As we sailed southeastward on a course of 157°, we had the wind just a few degrees forward of the starboard beam, so we were able to make good time. *Tinkerbelle* frisked along like an energetic colt and gave me my first clear view of the pyrotechnic display put on at night by phosphorescent plankton and other minute oceanic creatures. I watched bewitched, for it was a spectacular show. The water ruffled by the boat's passage glittered and shone with a starry fire. *Tinkerbelle* appeared to be floating on a magic carpet of Fourth of July sparklers more brilliant than any I'd ever seen, and trailing behind her was a luminescent wake resembling the burning tail of a comet.

Spray at the bow occasionally tossed on to the foredeck tiny jewels of light that winked for a few seconds and then went out, only to be replaced by other blinking gleams. An examination by flashlight of the spot where a kernel of radiance was last seen sometimes revealed a microscopic blob resembling a fish and sometimes a fibrous mass that looked like a tuft of matted wool from someone's sweater. How such unlikely organisms could produce bright glints of light was a mystery that would some day be unravelled. Perhaps the phenomenon had already been explained without my having learned of it. That didn't make it any less wondrous.

It was a dark night and it rapidly grew darker as a curtain of clouds moved across the sky, screening off the stars' light; but I didn't mind, for the darkness made the phosphorescent sorcery of the sea appear even brighter, more enchanting. Although I couldn't see it, I knew from the chart that we were passing, off to port, the small island of No Mans Land. The breeze was holding up well and we were stepping along smartly. Soon the last lighted navigation aids disappeared from view and we were alone in darkness relieved only by the warm glow of the compass light and the fireworks in the water. It was eerie. And it was beautiful.

We must have been well to the southeast of No Mans Land when I looked at my watch. It was 2 a.m. The new day, the second of our voyage, was already two hours old. It was Wednesday, June 2nd, my birthday, and I was forty-seven, ten years older than *Tinkerbelle*, who was no spring chicken. According to the statistics, I was headed down the sunset trail, past the milestones of middle age, but somehow I didn't feel ancient enough to be on that particular trail just yet. Life was supposed to begin at forty. If that was true, *Tinkerbelle* was beginning her life early and I was seven years late getting across the starting line. No matter. Better late than never.

We kept moving all night and through the morning of what

turned out to be a cloudy day. No land was in sight. I ate a cold breakfast so I wouldn't have to stop to prepare anything but shortly after noon the wind died and we came to a halt anyway. The ocean was a grey sheet of glass. I'd never seen it so placid, so flat, so motionless. It had an otherworldly quality.

Since we couldn't move, and since I was tired, having had no sleep for more than twenty-four hours, it seemed an appropriate time to get some rest. So, leaving the red mains'l up to render *Tinkerbelle* visible to any ships that might approach, I stretched out in the cockpit as best I could for forty winks. It wasn't a particularly comfortable place for a nap, but I was fearful of sleeping in the cabin. I thought I might sleep too soundly there and fail to awake promptly if a breeze sprang up.

I slept longer and more soundly than I wished. It was about 2.30 p.m. when I awoke and found to my dismay that we still had no breeze and, worse, that we were surrounded by dense fog. We couldn't move, and I couldn't see beyond a few feet. Nor could the red mains'l now warn passing ships of our presence. A ship could run us down without even knowing it. I hoisted the radar reflector to warn at least radar-equipped vessels of our presence, and I got out the oars to be ready to row for my life if a vessel should slice out of the fog directly toward us. I also got out the compressed-gas foghorn and sounded it from time to time. There were no answers. In fact, there were no sounds at all, except those we made ourselves. And the fog seemed to intensify these, reflecting them back to us. It was spooky.

In an hour or two a very light breeze came along and I put away the oars. We had just enough wind power to maintain steerage way. That was a slight improvement. And every now and then it rained for a few minutes, clearing the fog a little. That helped, too. But as soon as it stopped raining, the fog returned, becoming as thick as before. It gave me a closed-in feeling that must have been related to claustrophobia. I was decidedly uneasy, for we were obviously in a ticklish situation, and when I began to hear ships passing by it didn't help to calm my nerves.

I was surprised at the intensity and variety of the sounds produced by these passing ships, and by the speed at which they travelled invisibly through the fog. And most surprisingly of all, few of them blew their foghorns—at least, not regularly. Some of them throbbed by so close I could hear their bow waves breaking and, if they were travelling light, their propellers chopping the water. Several times I expected to see one come charging out of the fog on top of me, but I never even saw the dim outline of one; not just then, anyway. I'll never forget one of those ships, however. It passed by with music from a radio or phonograph, amplified through a loudspeaker, blaring out across the sea. That music was as effective as any foghorn. It was so loud it seemed entirely possible that even the people ashore on Martha's Vineyard, thirty-five or forty miles away, could hear it.

According to my dead reckoning, we were down approximately to the latitude of the Nantucket Shoals Lightship and about thirty miles west of it. This put us very close to the shipping lanes between New York and Europe, which was undoubtedly why I heard so many vessels going by. We were in an area where numerous shipping disasters had occurred and I hoped that we wouldn't be added to the list of casualties.

Somewhere in these waters, in January, 1909, the White Star liner *Republic* had been rammed and sunk by the Italian ship *Florida*. However, all but six of the *Republic*'s passengers had been saved by a CQD (this was before SOS came into use) sent out by the doomed vessel's wireless operator, Jack Binns. It was the first time radio had ever been used in a sea rescue.

Also nearby was the final resting place of the Italian luxury liner *Andrea Doria*, which, on July 25th, 1956, had sunk with the loss of fifty-one lives after colliding with the Swedish ship *Stockholm*. I wondered if the ghost of the Genoese admiral after whom the *Andrea Doria* had been named was keeping watch over his sunken namesake. He had been a great sea captain; as great as that other son of Genoa, Columbus, some said. He was credited with making it safe for seamen to sail against the wind. In the early sixteen-hundreds hardly anyone dared to do so because whoever did risked being burnt alive as a wizard. Seafarers almost always waited for a favourable wind from astern before leaving port, but Admiral Andrea Doria flouted this prejudice. He tacked against the wind whenever he chose and his enormous prestige preserved him from the wrath of the superstitious.

The admiral, who lived to be ninety-four, must have been a grand old sea-dog. If his spirit was in the vicinity, I hoped some of his strong character would brush off on to me. I wouldn't need much of his talent for going against the wind, though, because on a course for England the prevailing winds were westerlies. We wouldn't have to do much tacking.

Just then a mammoth black apparition with steel masts, funnel and hull slid out of the fog off our port quarter and, apparently seeing *Tinkerbelle*'s red mains'l, let go with a tooth-rattling blast on its steam horn that made me jump with such involuntary vigour I nearly fell overboard. What did a single blast on a ship's horn mean? And what was the appropriate reply? I wasn't sure and there was no time to look it up in my book. I thought I recalled, though, that the signal for a sailing vessel becalmed in fog was three blasts on the horn, so that's what I sounded. We weren't totally becalmed, of course, but we were so close to it that I thought we might as well ignore the difference and, anyway, at that particular moment I couldn't think of any other signal more suited to our circumstances. Luckily, it worked out all right; at least the ship, on a course to pass a comfortable distance astern of us, stayed on that course and didn't head straight for us. A minute or two later, when it had disappeared back into the mist and my heartbeats had slowed to their normal pace, I got out my book and found that the signal I'd given was for 'wind abaft the beam'. I really hadn't made a liar out of myself, though, because the wind (what little we had) *was* abaft the beam. However, it was plain to see that I needed to review the rules for horn signalling in fog.

The skipper of that-freighter, the only ship I saw all that day, probably shook his head and said, 'Why the heck do amateurs have to clutter up the ocean?'

Shortly after nightfall the breeze picked up and we began moving again at a more satisfying pace. At about 2 a.m. it rained very hard, dispersing the fog. Off to port I saw bright lights which

I took to be ships, and one especially bright point of illumination, which, since it was stationary, I decided must be a large buoy serving to guide ships toward New York. *Tinkerbelle* and I passed several miles to the south of it and, soon afterwards, were overtaken by a violent thunderstorm. The flashes of lightning and crashes of thunder made me thankful for the lightning rod at the masthead, although I earnestly hoped it wouldn't be put to use.

The noisy commotion in the sky passed quickly, fortunately, but then the wind freshened and, almost before I could get the sails down, it was blowing at what seemed to me to be gale force, forty or forty-five miles an hour, and, again, raining very hard.

We were in for it. I crawled to the foredeck, holding firmly on to the bounding boat while I put out the sea anchor as speedily as I could.

Our sea anchor was an army-type canvas bucket. It was streamed from the bow on a hundred and fifty feet of half-inch nylon line, with a polyethylene float attached to it by another, much lighter line to keep it from sinking farther than fifteen feet below the surface. Its function was to act as a brake, and to hold the bow facing into the wind and the waves as the boat, its sails doused, drifted slowly sternward. This was the safest way for a small boat, especially a boat with *Tinkerbelle*'s underwater shape, to weather a storm.

Although I'm ashamed to admit it, I must state that this was the first time I'd ever had *Tinkerbelle* tethered to a sea anchor, so I was afraid she wouldn't respond as I hoped she would, by facing into the wind and waves. In less than a minute it became apparent that my fears were well founded; she didn't face the waves, she turned her side to them. That position meant calamity, for she could be bowled over by a breaker. What should I do? I didn't know for sure; all I knew was that, whatever it was, it had to be done soon.

The rudder! It extended deep into the water; it must be the cause of the trouble, I thought. So I took it off and stowed it securely in the daggerboard-keel slot. That was the right thing to do, for *Tinkerbelle* immediately swung around and faced the waves. Her motion became less frantic, easier, smoother. She began to look after herself, enabling me to think about something besides the basic necessity of keeping her upright.

Since the wind was blowing from the northwest, we were drifting slowly toward the southeast, the same direction in which we had been sailing. That was providential, for we were moving farther into the open sea, away from the land and its dangers.

Lights appeared astern and drew closer and closer as *Tinkerbelle* drifted. Were they buoys, or were they ships, or were they something else? I couldn't be sure because the pelting rain obscured my vision, but I thought most probably they were small ships. In any case, one fact was clear: it would be wise to avoid contact with them. So I got out an oar, put it into the rowlock I'd fixed at the stern for just such an occasion as this and, by rowing one way or the other, controlled the direction of our drift sufficiently to prevent collision with the lighted objects. I never did find out what they were, but in an hour or so we were safely through them with nothing but blessedly black ocean beyond. And to make the situation even better, the rain stopped. Glory be! Now I really could relax a little.

Sitting towards the rear of the cockpit and looking forward into the wind, I saw staggered ribbons of phosphorescent wave crests bearing down on us. The entire sea, from the port beam all the way round to the starboard beam, was filled with graceful undulating, luminous forms. It was a spectacularly beautiful sight. It would have been a most enjoyable one, too, if it hadn't been for the danger; for as I assessed our predicament that night, as *Tinkerbelle* and I rode out our first full-fledged storm, any one of those waves could have been lethal if it had broken at exactly the wrong moment and had caught *Tinkerbelle* in exactly the wrong position.

Yes, every wave was a potential disaster, but I was relieved to discover that, in the midst of those acres and acres of crashing, thundering breakers, very, very few waves broke at precisely the moment when we were in their path. The great majority broke either before or after they reached us. And they came in cycles. We would ride up and down average-sized waves for several minutes and then along would come a group of four or six much larger waves. Then we'd have another few minutes of average-sized fellows, and then another batch of whoppers. It continued like that, on and on.

And *Tinkerbelle* always seemed to be ready for those few waves (maybe one every ten minutes or so) that broke at the wrong moment and slapped against her. She met them like a trouper, head-on, and rode over them with a jounce that gave me the impression of being in the saddle of a bronco.

Measuring the waves as well as I could against *Tinkerbelle*'s eighteen-foot mast, I estimated the biggest ones we met were ten or twelve feet high, from trough to crest. These were not monsters, as waves go, but they were definitely bigger than any waves either of us had experienced before at such close quarters. At the beginning of the storm they were especially ominous because they seemed to be steeper then than they were later on. As the wind continued, it seemed as though the waves grew bigger and, at the same time, more rounded, somewhat as if new, sharply pointed mountain peaks were, in an hour or two, ground down by the erosive forces of geological ages and at the same time elevated to new heights by diastrophic movement of the earth's crust.

At long last the sky began to fill with light and at about the same time the sea grew less tempestuous. It appeared that *Tinkerbelle* and I were going to get through our first big oceanic crisis without mishap. Well, not exactly without mishap because when I looked up I found that sometime during the night the radar reflector had been shaken loose from the masthead and was gone forever. I could have kicked myself for not securing it more firmly, and for not bringing along a spare. All right, so it was gone. We'd just have to do the best we could without it.

During the half-light between night and day I had a moment of fright when a small vessel, probably a trawler, passed too closely astern for comfort, apparently without any knowledge of our presence. No one appeared on the deck of the ship, which remained on an unswerving southwestward course and was soon out of sight over the horizon. *Tinkerbelle* and I once more had the ocean to ourselves.

My little boat rode the waves as gracefully as a gull: up, over and down, up, over and down, up, over and down. I was pleased beyond words, as proud of her as I could be. I patted her cockpit coaming and told her, 'Good going!'

8

By mid-morning the wind had fallen off sufficiently to resume sailing safely, so I pulled in the sea anchor, rehung the rudder at the stern and ran the sails aloft. It felt good to be moving forward again, able to steer, instead of drifting stern first with scant manoeuvrability.

During the brief storm we had drifted steadily, though slowly, southeastward. I was sure my dead reckoning was highly inaccurate, for any one of half a dozen good reasons, but I wasn't especially worried about it because there was nothing but open sea for hundreds and hundreds of miles to the southeast or east. Even to the northeast we had three hundred or more miles of ocean between us and the coast of Nova Scotia and that graveyard of ships, Sable Island. So why worry? As long as we moved on a course between, say, 45° (NE) and 135° (SE), we could keep on going for days, maybe even weeks, without any danger of running against the land. We really didn't have to know *exactly* where we were for quite a few days yet.

I had a hunch, though, that we were many miles to the south of the shipping lanes; in fact, I believed we were some miles south of the parallel of 40° N latitude, which was roughly ten miles to the south of the more southerly of the two main shipping lanes between New York and the English Channel. I didn't want to go any farther south than this because it would add extra miles to our voyage. My plan was to sail more or less directly eastward until we reached the meridian of 40° W. This would take us to the south of most of the foggy Grand Banks area and what the pilot chart called the mean maximum iceberg limit. Then, at 40° W, we would sail northeastward parallel to, but well away from, the great circle shipping track between the Panama Canal and Bishop Rock in the Scilly Isles, at the entrance to the English Channel.

If the voyage became too difficult, so filled with hardships that I couldn't go on, I would make for Flores, in the Azores, and either rest for a few days before continuing or end my trip there. I had a chart of the island to use in case that became necessary.

In my mind's eye I pictured the voyage as a tremendous countdown in degrees of longitude from 71° W, the meridian at which we had entered the open ocean near Martha's Vineyard, to 5° W, the approximate meridian of Falmouth, England, our destination. I viewed this countdown as a series of ten-degree steps, except for the first one, which was eleven degrees (71° W to 60° W), and the last one, which was only five degrees (10° W to 5° W). I thought it would be useful, psychologically, if I divided my main objective of a transatlantic voyage into this series of lesser goals. The first of these to aim for, then, was the meridian of 60° W; and after that would come 50° W, 40° W, 30° W and so on.

After we reached 40° W longitude, we would also begin a single, ten-degree countup in latitude, from 40° N, my anticipated latitude at that time, to 50° N, the approximate latitude of Falmouth. In fact, I thought we had better begin a short countup immediately because, according to my hunch, we were some miles to the south of 40° N latitude. Consequently, when we started sailing, it was on a course of 50°; that is, just a little eastward of true northeast.

By this time I had gone without sleep for more than forty-eight hours, except for the nap I'd had in the cockpit the second day out, and although I'd been taking stay-awake pills to keep myself alert, my body's desperate need for rest (ashore it had been used to a full eight hours' sleep every night) was becoming acute, unmistakable. Or rather, it should have been unmistakable. Actually, I didn't recognize the symptoms immediately because the pills I was taking contained a chemical mood elevator that made me feel great even though I was on the borderline of exhaustion. The symptoms were so unexpectedly fantastic, so far removed from any previous experience, that I didn't realize their import until many days later, after I'd encountered them once or twice more. Lack of sleep may not have been the sole cause; the pills themselves could have been partly to blame. But, whatever the cause, I floated off in the early afternoon into a realm of wild fantasy, a strange world of mixed illusion and reality such as I had never known before. I lived through an hours-long hallucination.

It provided an interesting subject for contemplation, after it was all over, but while it was occurring it was most vexatious, decidedly unpleasant. It made me waste a whole afternoon sailing hither and yon about the ocean. And the incident was so unusual, so completely different from any earlier happening in my life, that I have great difficulty in describing it satisfactorily, especially for anyone who has not had a similar experience. I suppose, in a sense, I went off the deep end, out of my mind, into a Never Land, where real things and dream things existed side by side without distinction; where reality and imagination merged, leaving no hint of which was which. I have attributed what took place to lack of sleep and stay-awake pills, but anxiety and, even more likely, loneliness, as my mother had feared, may have contributed to it, too. Like a person in a hypnotic trance, I simply began seeing and hearing things that weren't really there.

I became aware, gradually, that I was not alone; someone, a man, was on *Tinkerbelle* with me. This man had no face that I can recall; nor can I remember what he wore, although his clothing seemed to be appropriate for sailing. He was a quiet man with very little to say, and he was friendly. At first I reciprocated with equal friendliness, but later on his presence became inexpressibly annoying, intolerable.

It developed that he was on *Tinkerbelle* as a seagoing hitch-hiker and I was taking him to his home, which was on a small island somewhere in our vicinity. (Of course, there really was no island in that part of the Atlantic.) But we had a terrible time finding the place. We sailed this way, and that way, and around, and back, and north, and south, and east, and west, trying to catch sight of a scrap of treeless land with a couple of houses on it.

Sometime during the afternoon I recalled the storm *Tinkerbelle* and I had been through the night before and, fearful that we might be hit by a southeast wind that would batter us toward a lee shore,

I decided I should try out the storm sails I'd made of heavy canvas to see if they would enable us to beat away from such a hazard. However, my phantom companion thought I should take him to his home before I spent any time experimenting with the storm sails, and we got into a slight hassle about it. My arguments prevailed, though, for at sea the skipper's word is law. I tried out the storm sails.

I replaced the white genoa with a minute jib and the red main with a small trysail. The heavy-weather suit of canvas seemed to fit the boat all right, but beyond that the tryout was a flop; there simply wasn't enough wind to move the boat with such small sails. The only adequate tryout would be in a storm.

So I reset the original sails and we continued our island hunt, to the great satisfaction of the hitch-hiker. In fact, preposterous as it seems, my airy chum took over the tiller and I became the passenger. Such is the remarkable stuff of hallucinations. On we sailed. We never seemed to talk out loud; that is, we seldom actually moved our lips, but we did converse in a miraculous, soundless way. I kept pressing my shipmate for descriptions of the island and for clues to the course to be sailed to reach it, all the while straining my eyes to spot a bit of sand or rock.

My companion then admitted that the island would be hard to find because it rose only a few feet above the level of the sea and was mostly rocky, the rocks being a blue that blended almost perfectly with the colour of the sea—camouflage *par excellence*. Several times I thought I'd spotted the island and cried out to the phantom to steer in that direction, but when we drew close it became evident that what I'd seen was merely rock-like wave forms. It was discouraging and irritating. This bloke I had on board was wasting my time on a wild-goose chase. I grew more and more peevish, more and more impatiently eager to find his blasted rock pile and put him on it so that I could continue on my way. I had started out as a good Samaritan, but now I was entirely disenchanted with that role.

I guess he sensed my rising exasperation because he kept saying, 'It won't be much longer. Just be patient, we'll soon be there.'

By early evening I was in a frenzy. I'm reluctant to own up to it because of what it may indicate about my character, but I was ready to run amok and toss my unwanted guest into the sea. Then I could resume my own hunt, for England. But at that very moment, in the nick of time, he yelled, 'There it is! There it is!' And, sure enough, there it was. I saw it too.

It was a solid patch no bigger than a city block, and if it was composed of anything besides sea-blue rocks I couldn't see what it was. No sand was visible anywhere, and no vegetation of any sort. There was nothing but rock, rock, rock. Even the two small houses at the centre of the island were made of the same type of rock, which made it hard to distinguish between them and their surroundings. About the only way you could tell they were houses was by the windows and doors.

Some people came out of one of them and waved to us and we waved back. The hitch-hiker (I never learned his name, unfortunately) wanted to sail right up to the shore, but I was determined not to risk *Tinkerbelle*'s life on such foolishness. Why, she'd be battered into splinters! So, to be on the safe side, I took over the steering again.

We sailed around the island looking for a place to land, but there was no suitable place. Good Lord! Now what? Was I going to have to put up with this guy even longer? I'd had about all the delays I could take. I was on the point of telling him to swim for it or else when, through the magic that exists only in fantasies, he was suddenly ashore with his family, grinning and waving me on my way. I waved back happily, delighted to be rid of him at last, and without wasting another minute I resumed my original course of 50°. The daylight was waning fast and I wanted to get as far away from that island as I could before turning in for some badly needed sleep.

Except for the two-and-a-half-hour nap, I had now gone without sleep for about fifty-five hours and I was drooping dangerously. I couldn't keep my eyes open. I'd force them open and they'd stay open for a time, but inevitably the eyelids would grow heavy and slowly close. I'd go on sailing with closed eyes for a little while and then a wave would jolt *Tinkerbelle* and I'd start to keel over, all but dead to the world. I'd catch myself just in time to avoid cracking my skull on the deck or rolling overboard. Several times, in my somnambulistic state, I put *Tinkerbelle* into an accidental jibe that sent the boom zinging around with a murderous slash. The spar itself hit me only once, painfully. But another time it drew the mainsheet across the bridge of my nose, giving me a bad rope burn that took many days to heal.

It was perilous to continue while so near the edge of complete exhaustion; I still had enough of my wits about me to realize that I simply had to have some rest; my whole being cried out for it. So, finally, somehow, I put out the sea anchor, struck the sails, unshipped the rudder and crawled into the cabin. Luckily, the sea was fairly calm, making it safe to risk sleeping in the cabin; but even if it hadn't been calm I think I would have slept there that night. I had to.

I lay down on top of my supplies on the starboard side, pulled the blanket over me and dropped into unconsciousness as if I'd been dealt a knockout blow.

9

WHEN I awoke, the sun was shining brightly, dotting the undulating cobalt of the ocean to the east with diamond flashes of intense light, and *Tinkerbelle* was tugging good-naturedly at her bucket anchor, nosing into a docile, westerly breeze. Happiness, that morning, was a body replete with rest—a body gorged, crammed, satiated with sleep—and I was happy. It was great to be alive.

I cooked a breakfast of hot cereal and coffee, and, as I ate, ruminated on the events of the previous day. That seafaring hitch-hiker, where had he come from and where had he gone? Was he part of a daydream? Or something else? Or was my mind coming unglued? It seemed possible that I *had* dreamed the encounter. In any case, it would do no good to worry overmuch about it. I knew that truck drivers who took pep pills to stay awake sometimes 'saw' things, and even Slocum had been visited by an apparition—the pilot of Columbus's *Pinta*, so he, the shade, had said. Slocum had ascribed the visitation to cramps caused by eating Azores plums and white cheese. I hadn't had any cramps, so I had to look elsewhere for a cause. The hallucination, I theorized, must have been induced by lack of sleep and the pills.

Neither *Tinkerbelle* nor I had suffered a serious mishap, we were both in good shape, but the weirdness of the experience left me feeling uneasy—half fearful, half embarrassed. The whole affair seemed so unnatural, so preposterous. I was so sensitive about it that I refrained from mentioning it in my log. Not until much later, after I'd had other, similar experiences, did I write anything about the illusory events of that afternoon.

After breakfast I washed my saucepan, cup, fork and spoon in the sea and tidied up the cabin. Then I heated some water and shaved for the first time since leaving Falmouth; that is, I shaved all but my upper lip, for, in response to Virginia's urgings, I had decided to grow a moustache. I hoped that by the time I reached England it would be a luxuriant, sea-doggish growth. I'd never had a satisfactory moustache, although once before I'd tried to raise one. The in-between days, when the bristles were ample enough to make your lip look dirty and yet too puny to keep your friends from inquiring (if only with their eyes) why you hadn't shaved, were slightly discomfiting. But now I had a chance to escape all that; I would be out of sight for enough days. I could simply turn up on the other side of the ocean with a mature set of handle-bars.

A gentle breeze of about ten miles an hour blew steadily from the west, so I rigged *Tinkerbelle* to steer herself. I had tested the self-steering arrangement on Lake Erie and it had worked well. It consisted of twin genoas winged out on either side of the forestay (the oars having been adapted to serve as whisker poles for that purpose), with sheets running back from the clew of each sail, through blocks on either side of the cockpit, to the tiller. The sails were adjusted to slant slightly forward from the forestay. Then, if *Tinkerbelle* veered a little to port, the portside genny caught more wind and the starboardside genny spilled more, which, in turn, caused a pull on the port sheet and an easing up on the starboard sheet. That put the tiller over to port, making the boat return to her proper course before the wind. And, of course, it worked the same way, but in reverse, if she veered to starboard. As a matter of fact, by adjusting the sheets, the boat could be made to steer herself on a course that was a few degrees to port or starboard of the exactly-before-the-wind course. (However, I was never able to get the boat to steer herself on a reach or when the wind was forward of the beam.)

Tinkerbelle tobogganed along amiably, steering herself skilfully and, seemingly, without effort. She was a good girl. I delighted in her obedient behaviour and in my freedom from the tiller. I could do anything I wished now without impeding our steady eastward progress. To be sailing without any effort whatever, without having to be concerned with steering, that was undiluted ecstasy!

But I couldn't spend all day glorying in ecstatic idleness; there were other things to be done. I brought on deck clothes and blankets dampened by the humid sea air and spread them in the sun to dry. Then I took a sextant shot at the sun in an effort to get a clue to our position, but something went wrong with the shot or the figuring, for I wound up with a sun line that was too fantastic to be believed. At noon I tried again, this time for a latitude shot, but again something went wrong. The latitude I got was 45° N, which couldn't possibly have been right unless *Tinkerbelle* had flown three hundred miles or more during the night while I was asleep. She was a marvellous boat, no doubt about that, but a three-hundred-mile flight did seem a trifle beyond her capacities. Oh, well, tomorrow I'd try once more to pinpoint our position.

About five-thirty that evening a trawler hove into view and, seeing *Tinkerbelle*, churned over to within a few yards of us, its diesels clattering noisily. It was the *Major J. Casey*, American or Canadian, I couldn't tell which. I cupped my hands and shouted to two fellows at the rail, asking if they'd give me my position, but I guess they couldn't hear me above the strident din of their vessel. I needed a megaphone to focus and project my voice. Boris Petroff of the *Plain Dealer*'s library staff had urged me to take one along despite the valuable space it would consume. 'It's a vital piece of equipment,' he had said, and now this inability to make myself heard tended to confirm his opinion.

I could understand the men on the trawler, however.

'Where you bound?' one of them yelled.

'England,' I hollered back with all my lung power.

They didn't even flick an eyelid, so I imagine they either didn't hear me or thought I was having a little joke. Anyway, they swerved right after that and sped off to the southeast. In a few minutes I was alone again. Not really alone, though; I had *Tinkerbelle* with me, and she was good company.

As darkness fell, the wind grew stronger and I had to discontinue the self-steering. (It turned out that I never used the twin genoas for self-steering again, as one of the pair was an old canvas sail that tore to shreds in a hard blow a few days later. The surviving genoa was a Dacron sail I had made myself. I should have made two of them.) I returned to my post at the tiller and we went on under a single genny at four or five knots until nearly midnight. Then I 'parked' *Tinkerbelle* to the sea anchor, secured the anchor light between the mast and starboard shroud and turned in for some sleep.

After breakfast the next day, Saturday, June 5th, I experimented with different sea-anchor setups to determine which worked best. One rig I tested had the regular Danforth anchor and the canvas bucket drogue linked in tandem at the end of the hundred-and-fifty-foot nylon anchor line. I studied the boat's behaviour for about an hour, eventually deciding this arrangement wasn't a success, for instead of sloping off from the bow, the line hung straight down and didn't keep the boat headed squarely into the waves. Several times she nearly turned broadside. When I started to pull the line up to test another setup, I found that either the Danforth was a lot heavier than I had thought or it had snagged a fish or some other heavy object. It was hard work getting it on board. I finally hauled it up, though, and when the bucket broke the surface I got a terrific shock; it was filled with sand! No wonder it had been heavy. There was only one possible explanation: we were in a shoal area where the sea was no more than a hundred and fifty feet deep and possibly a good deal shallower than that.

This threw my dead reckoning for a loop since, according to it, we were supposed to be in water that was more than a mile deep. How could I have gone so far wrong? I couldn't answer that question, but in view of the circumstances it seemed reasonable to conclude that the time had come to obtain a better indication of where we were.

Just before the sun reached its zenith, I got out the sextant and, summoning forth my best efforts, took as accurate a noon latitude sight as I could, using the natural horizon rather than the bubble. When I worked out the sight, I got another shock; the figures said our latitude was 41° 2′ N, about sixty miles north of my dead-reckoning latitude. I got out the chart and deduced from this latitude figure and the shallowness of the water that we were probably at the southernmost edge of Cultivator Shoal, some ninety miles east of Nantucket Island. That made our longitude roughly 68° 32' W, not nearly so far eastward as I had imagined.

This blunt exposure of my shortcomings as a navigator left me shaken. Had I, in attempting an Atlantic crossing, bitten off more than I could chew? Was I likely to sail into, say, Brest, France, thinking it was Falmouth, England, or do something else equally ridiculous? I earnestly hoped not. But if the navigational clumsiness that had just been laid bare continued, it seemed possible that I would. Of course, there were important lessons to be learned from this chastening experience, the principal one being not to put much faith in dead reckoning (the boat's speed over the bottom and the influence of currents were too difficult to assess), but that didn't make me feel any better. Here I'd thought we were south of the shipping lanes and, actually, we were still thirty miles or so north of them.

I re-examined the chart, reread the *Coast Pilot* and sent my mind ranging back over the days since we had left Vineyard Sound, trying to find clues to how our actual course had varied from my dead reckoning. What about those bright lights I'd seen in the early morning darkness on the third day out? I had supposed they were on a buoy, but now I had doubts. Soon I found a paragraph in the *Coast Pilot* that appeared to solve the mystery. It said, 'A Texas tower with lights and a fog signal surmounted by radar and radio towers, is in 41° N and 69° 30' W, near the southwest side of Fishing Rip. The entire structure is floodlighted at night.'

So that's what had made that 'buoy' seem so bright; it had been floodlighted.

Fishing Rip was a shallow area at the southern end of Nantucket Shoals, southeast of Nantucket Island, and the Texas tower on it was about twenty-five miles from the island. What *Tinkerbelle* and I had done, then, was to sail between the tower and the Nantucket Shoals Lightship, which was roughly twenty-seven miles due south of it. When the storm hit us, right after we passed the tower, we had drifted fifteen or twenty miles southeastward, and the next day, while I was in the grip of that hallucination, we had cruised around aimlessly, getting nowhere. Then, after those sublime hours of sleep, we had steered the 50° course that brought us to the southern tip of Cultivator Shoal, where the bucket startled me by scooping up sand from the bottom. Now I had an inkling of where we were.

Late in the day, after more sea anchor experiments, I tethered *Tinkerbelle* to what seemed to be the most efficient rig, the canvas bucket used by itself with a float and line attached to keep it from sinking more than fifteen feet below the surface, and took a short nap in the cockpit. Afterward, I fixed myself a tasty dinner of curried beef, potatoes and peas, lit the hand warmer John Place had given me, for it grew uncomfortably chilly when the sun dropped below the horizon, and set off on a south-eastward course of 150°. I was determined to get to the south of the shipping lanes before heading directly eastward.

We sailed all night at a delightful wave-slapping pace and shortly after dawn arrived smack-dab in the middle of the lanes. There were seven or eight ships in sight, some headed east, others west; and as one left, another would appear to take its place. Two identical black-hulled trawlers came up over the sharp rim of the horizon and one of them picked up its skirts and hurried over to examine *Tinkerbelle*. As it drew near, I heard music blaring from a loudspeaker. So that's what had passed by invisibly but far from soundlessly in the fog on the second day of our voyage—a trawler. When it got closer, I saw that it was Russian, as was its sister ship. And its music reverberated just as deafeningly as had that of the phantom ship in the fog. It was wonderful classical music, mind you; there was nothing wrong with it except that it was so loud it made the atmosphere quake.

Russians must be avid photographers because when the trawler drew to within fifty yards or so every member of the crew seemed to be on deck with a camera pointed at *Tinkerbelle* and me. Shutters clicked at a great rate. It reminded me of the time Virginia, Robin, Douglas and I had been becalmed in the channel to Presque Isle Bay. This time, however, I decided to join the fun:

I got out my own cameras, a 35-mm. still camera and a 16 mm. movie job, and clicked right back.

'*Tovarish!*' I yelled, using up with that one word fifty per cent of my linguistic resources in conversational Russian. And even that was a failure, apparently, for I got no response. The Soviet fishermen smiled in a friendly way, though, and when I waved they waved back. Then they raced away.

It was a perfect sun-drenched day, with a cloudless turquoise sky and a lustrous blue sea. The waves were just large enough to make things interesting and the wind strong enough to keep us moving along briskly. To all appearances we could have been on a pleasant Sunday afternoon sail on Lake Pymatuning; as a matter of fact, it *was* Sunday—Sunday, June 6th. I told myself that if most of the days ahead were as pleasant as this, our trip would be a breeze, or, as the English say, a piece of cake.

About midday I hove *Tinkerbelle* to under sail and prepared a meal of dehydrated scrambled eggs and bacon, with coffee, and ate it out in the cockpit where I could watch the steady stream of ships going by to north and south. We seemed to be on the blue-water centre strip of a multi-lane oceanic turnpike. Trawlers, freighters and liners passed in processions that were exciting to see.

After I'd finished off my meal with some canned pears, we got under way again, still headed southeastward, and in the early afternoon met another Russian trawler, this one white and much larger than the black trawlers I'd seen in the morning. It was slowly hauling what must have been a huge net through the water. No doubt the fishing was good, for the trawlers were on the edge of Georges Bank, a fishing ground that some authorities have rated next to the Grand Banks.

Tinkerbelle and I cut across the big ship's bow, about two hundred yards ahead of it, and continued towards the southeast. By the middle of the afternoon every ship was out of sight; we were alone again. Moving so rapidly from an ocean teeming with ships to an ocean without any ships in sight made the aloneness claw into my mind, creating a keen awareness of my, I hoped, temporary separation from fellow humans. It was an intense feeling, but not an especially unpleasant one. Who has not yearned with all his heart to leave the 'rat race' and get away from it all for a while? I was a privileged character; I was actually doing what so many people longed to do. No more rat race for me for at least a couple of months.

During the afternoon I took another nap in the cockpit; then, when we started moving again, it was on a due-east course of 90°. That night I wrote in the log:

'I saw a school of about eight whales after I resumed sailing after my nap. They were too far away for pictures, though. I've also seen a lot of gulfweed. And quite a few birds, which always seem to be too far away to photograph.

I still don't know exactly where I am although I presume (from my dead reckoning) I'm near 40° N and 68° W. I'll take some sextant sights tomorrow and try to pinpoint it.

I haven't seen a ship since leaving the lanes. The ocean is a vast empty expanse. I'm beginning to find out what real loneliness is.

My nose is a bit sunburned and the backs of my hands are getting raw from being wet so much and chafing against my cuffs. But my biggest problem is my bumteratum, which is getting awfully sore from the dampness and constant jostling. I'm sitting on the life preserver cushion now and that helps, but tomorrow I'll have to render some first aid.

Otherwise I'm in good shape. Have been eating and drinking less than I allowed for.

But the cabin is a shambles. Everything is piled helter-skelter. The trouble is, when I want something it's usually under an assortment of other things and I have to get everything else out of the way to get at it. And it goes on and on like that. When I've eaten some of the food and drunk some of the water there will be more room and, I hope, less mess.

The barometer has been holding steady at 30.8. I hope that means several days of good weather.

Everything on board is now damp as can be, even these pages.

At dusk we got into a tide rip, probably a tributary of the

Gulf Stream. Some dolphins, the first I'd seen, had been following us, but they left us at the tide rip, unfortunately.

I hove to with the sea anchor at 11 p.m. (Eastern Standard Time) and got about six hours' sleep.'

My log notations for the next day, June 7th, were:

'Had a nice big breakfast of hot cereal (cereal bars crumbled into water and heated), hot coffee, fruit, etc.

Then got moving. It was a glorious day of sailing: blue sky, sunshine, wind and waves just right. *Tinkerbelle* just scooted along.

Best of all, I finally got some good sun sights and established our position—40° 4' N and 67° 31' W. This is not as far along as I had hoped to be at this time, but I had a couple of bad days there at the start and maybe I can make up for them now.

I'm a little north of my planned route, too, but that may be an advantage.

Sighted quite a few whales—all far off.

Also sighted a ship to the north, which made me fearful that I was too near the shipping lanes, so I turned south for a couple of hours. Then hove to to sleep.'

I remember that night well. I was worried because it was fogging up and I no longer had a radar reflector with which to warn ships away. That made it difficult to rest. I lay awake in the cabin for a long time, fretting, but in the end I dropped off to sleep. What helped was that I was warm. It was the first night I'd been warm since putting to sea, probably because we had moved out of the cold coastwise currents from the north into the warmth of the Gulf Stream.

That night I didn't shiver and shake as I had on all the previous nights. I was cosy in the cabin. It was a welcome change and a very pleasant way to end my first week on the ocean.

IO

In the morning of the eighth day, as I lay asleep, a sound insinuated itself into my unconscious mind and tugged me towards wakefulness. It had the tone and timbre of a chorus of shouts—men's shouts. But that was absurd. Men's choruses simply didn't go about the Atlantic shouting. I must have dreamed it. I squirmed into a new position under my blanket and began to drift back into sleep. Then suddenly I was exploded into wide-eyed consciousness by:

'Ahyouuuuuuuuuuuga! Ahyouuuuuuuuuuuuga!'

That was no dream! Such a dreadful, ear-busting noise could mean only one thing: my time on earth was up. And when I identified the accompanying roar as that of diesels I was sure of it. Without a doubt a big ship was bearing down on *Tinkerbelle* and noticing her at the last minute, too late to swerve aside, it had sounded its klaxon in a desperate bid to save the life of whoever was aboard her. Any second now there would be a grinding crash as the ship ploughed us under. My one chance of survival was to abandon *Tinkerbelle* at once and swim for it. If I moved fast enough, I might get out of the ship's path in time.

When I realized what I had to do and that my life depended on it, I sprang into action. I must have been hitting Mach 3 as I threw open the cabin hatch and flew out on deck ready to dive overboard.

Fortunately I was moving just slowly enough to have half a second to notice that, really, there was no ship headed towards us, and pull myself to a halt before plunging over the side. We were not about to be run down, but what I saw nearly made my eyes pop out of their sockets. Lying alongside *Tinkerbelle*, so close I could almost have jumped aboard her, was an enormous submarine. And on its bridge, staring at me, were three or four men, no doubt the chorus I'd heard.

I felt foolish. To be scared out of my wits was bad enough, but to be scared thus in front of an audience was too embarrassing to bear. I tried to salvage my pride by deftly changing my expression of panic into an expression of nonchalant greeting, which, I hoped, would convey the impression that, far from being hurried by fright, I was accustomed to shooting out of the cabin like that every morning, and equally used to meeting submarines on the high seas. It's a shame my performance wasn't caught on film, for it may have been worthy of an Academy Award. Or it may have served a useful purpose, later, as a medical-school exhibit on the muscular contortions a human face can achieve. Despite my histrionics, however, I had a suspicion the men on the sub weren't the least bit deceived, and I learned afterwards the suspicion was well founded.

What should I say? What should I do? I was racking my brain for answers to those questions, and trying to decide what the sub might want or do, when one of the men on the bridge (I heard subsequently it was the captain) called out, 'Do you need any help?'

So that was it. They thought I was in some sort of trouble. I felt a great load slide off my shoulders, for I had begun to have wild notions such as maybe war had been declared since I'd left shore, or maybe the Coast Guard had sent the sub out to stop me from making what it considered a foolhardy voyage. Actually, it had only stumbled on to me, thought I was in distress and wanted to help. That was all.

I appreciated the offer of assistance immensely, but in my startled condition I could think of nothing I needed. So I shouted back, 'No, thanks!'

Whereupon we lapsed into numbed silence, for the men on the submarine were undoubtedly as astonished by the sight of *Tinkerbelle* and me as I was at seeing them. We couldn't think of anything to say. We just stood there looking blankly, unbelievingly, at one another as we slowly drifted farther and farther apart. Soon we were so far apart we couldn't have made ourselves heard, even if we'd wanted to, over the shuddering clangour of the sub's engines. (I had no idea submarines, even non-nuclear subs like this one, made so much noise while running on the surface.) As the sub's stern passed by, I saw markings which told me it was an American craft, the *Tench*, named after a Eurasian fish noted for its ability to survive out of water. Finally its propellers began turning and in a very short time it slid out of sight over the horizon.

When I had recovered my composure, I berated myself for two serious omissions: one of courtesy, the other of seamanship. I felt I should have invited the sub's skipper over for a gam and a cup of coffee, and I should have asked him for a position report against which to check the accuracy of my navigation. I managed to get along without the position report, but my failure in courtesy was not so easily overlooked. After my voyage was completed, I wrote a letter of apology to the *Tench*'s skipper, Lieutenant Commander James A. Bacon, and he replied, kindly, with his impression of our meeting.

'At 0800 on 7 June,' he wrote, '*Tench* departed New London for sea.... On arriving at Nantucket Lightship in the early evening of the 7th fog and numerous fishing vessels impeded our progress. As a result I spent the night in the conn or on the bridge.

First light found *Tench* some 150 miles east-south-east of the lightship with the fog clearing. As the sun rose we broke out of the fog and the lookouts [one of them was Yeoman Robert R. Rentschler, a fellow Cleveland suburbanite] spotted a very small mast on the horizon some distance to the south of our track.

At first I thought the mast belonged to one of the trawlers we had been playing tag with all night, but as we approached it became apparent that it belonged to a small sailing boat. At this point I altered course to pass close aboard in order to hail the boat.

When the small size of the boat became obvious, I thought it probably had been blown out to sea and no one would be aboard. Until this time no one had been seen in the boat and now I decided to stop alongside and examine it in detail. As we approached within a few hundred yards, it could be seen that the boat was riding to a sea anchor and was provided with oars and other gear lying in the after section—the forward area being decked over and having a small cabin.

I stopped *Tench* with *Tinkerbelle* about 10 yards abeam of the bridge, and we continued our examination. Although no one had been sighted on board, it now was apparent that someone could very well be in the cabin. Mustering all the lung power of the bridge watch and using a megaphone, we hailed the *Tinkerbelle* but to no avail. It became obvious after a few minutes that if there was in fact someone on board another means would have to be found to rouse them.

The solution to the problem was readily available. I reached over and gave a long blast on the ship's whistle, and there you were, leaping out of the small cabin as if you thought you were about to be run down by the *Queen Mary* or some equally large ship. I must now admit that I found your reaction somewhat amusing.

We exchanged greetings as you have already stated. After you gave a negative response to my offer of assistance, I was at a loss for words. Since I had been delayed during the night and there was a good chance I was going to be late arriving at my assigned station . . . I proceeded on at best speed. I came to the conclusion that you were where you wanted to be and little could be gained by *Tench* remaining in your vicinity. I entered your position (39° 46' N, 66° 27' W) and the name of your boat in the ship's log in case the Coast Guard should start looking for you.

I thought at the time that you most probably were a sailing enthusiast on vacation and sailing to Halifax from Boston or some place in the Cape area. I am sincerely glad that I did not know what your true destination was. I am sure that if I had known what you were attempting, I would have had a guilty conscience on leaving you there.'

I, too, am glad Lieutenant Commander Bacon was spared the pain of a guilty conscience. There really was no reason for him to have had one, even if he had known where I was bound, because, as he said in his letter, I was where I 'wanted to be'; no one had dropped me off there against my will. And, since I was there of my own choice, I had won the right to experience whatever that entailed, good or bad. So far it had been mostly very good and I was optimistic about the future.

I have just one bone to pick with Captain Bacon: he called that noise he made with his submarine a 'whistle'. How euphemistic can you get? I've called it a klaxon sound, but even that falls pitifully short of being an adequate description. There simply is no word for the sound the *Tench* produced, a sound that seemed to be a nerve-jangling synthesis of the wailing of banshees, the booming of thunder and the screeching of all the demons of hell.

Tinkerbelle spent the hours of darkness after our meeting with the *Tench* riding big waves to her sea anchor while I tried as best I could to rest in her cockpit. It was a chilly, wet, miserable, dragged-out night. I was still too afraid of a capsize to seek shelter in the cabin when the waves were ominously large, so I had to bear the discomforts of the cockpit. It wasn't easy to sleep in that exposed, perpetually joggling place.

The next morning (Wednesday, June 9th) the wind continued to blow at twenty-five or thirty knots and my bleary eyes got their first good look at the waves that, until then, had been partly hidden by the mantle of night. Some of them must have been seventeen- or eighteen-footers, the biggest waves we'd yet encountered. I watched them in awe and was mightily pleased and relieved to see how gracefully *Tinkerbelle* climbed to the summit of each one in turn, glissaded into the valley beyond and then climbed the next peak, on and on. My little craft performed her nautical functions with all the agility and stamina of a ballet dancer. I was delighted with her and praised her to the skies.

The threatening waves were not to be trifled with; I was sure of that. It was better to be wary of them than wrecked by them. It was equally true, though, that every minute we stayed tied to the sea anchor meant another minute added to the duration of our voyage, and a lot of those extra minutes could add up to one or more of several different crises that ought to be avoided, if possible. Consequently, I was eager to be moving.

Still, the waves held me transfixed with fright. I tried to envisage what it would be like to brave them under sail and the only pictures that came into my mind were of disasters. Did Si Lawlor in his little *Sea Serpent* and William Andrews in his collapsible *Sapolio* sail through waves like these? That they might have done so seemed unbelievable, utterly fantastic. Yet Lawlor got across the ocean in only forty-five days, an astounding accomplishment for a boat only fifteen feet long. Andrews, in a boat half a foot shorter and with a greater distance to go, took eighty-four days, but he couldn't have achieved even that mark if he had spent much time hitched to a sea anchor.

I wrestled with fear through the whole morning as I studied the waves. Finally, in the early afternoon, the conviction grew that we should get under way. 'After all,' I wrote in the log, 'the whitecaps are small even though the waves are big.' So, marshalling all my courage, I decided to put up one of the small jibs and proceed tentatively under it alone. If conditions proved to be too hazardous, I'd get the sail down again immediately and go back to the sea anchor.

I steeled my nerves and we started moving eastward once more. I was sure that, even under just the one small jib, we would take off like a jet-driven aquaplane. But I was wrong. We barely crawled. I had to hoist the mains'l, too, to get *Tinkerbelle* to move at a satisfactory pace. (However, I'm happy to be able to add that as the voyage progressed my ability to size up sailing conditions improved.)

I tried to get some pictures of Mother Carey's chickens (storm petrels) the next afternoon, June 10th, but they moved so fast it was extremely difficult. They were fascinating to watch, though, because of their odd habit of walking on the water. I'd never seen these birds before, although I had crossed the Atlantic several times previously on ocean liners.

The book Virginia had given me said they were Wilson's storm petrels, migrants from the Antarctic and the commonest members of the storm petrel family. Mother Carey, it said, was a corruption of Mater Cara, an appellation of the Blessed Virgin Mary, and storm petrel was derived from Saint Peter, who also walked on the water, according to the Bible, until his lack of faith brought on a ducking. The Maoris of New Zealand had a poetic term for the birds, *takahi kare moana*, which meant 'dancing on the waters'. I thought that was a particularly apt description.

Wilson's bird was a little smaller than a robin, brownish-grey and black, with a white spot at the base of its tail. Sometimes it seemed to hop along on the water, sometimes it used its feet like skis and sometimes it simply walked. Two or three times I was amused by a bird that just stood on the water flapping its wings, as though it were trying to pull its feet out of hardening cement.

Not once did I see Wilson's storm petrels *in* the water, floating and resting like other water birds. They were always flying, beating their wings without let up, moving erratically like butterflies and usually very close to the water's surface. They must be tireless creatures, or else embarrassed to have anyone see them inactive. The bird book said they occasionally alighted on the water, but I never saw one do so, although I watched them intermittently all the way across the ocean.

One other variety of bird accompanied me almost all the way to England, the greater shearwater, a brown-and-white bird about twenty inches long, with a wingspread of more than two feet. I also saw, occasionally, pretty black-and-white terns and, of course, gulls.

The greater shearwater was a lovely bird to watch in flight, it rode the wind so elegantly. It, unlike the storm petrel, was frequently to be seen bobbing on the water, resting or feeding. However, it never accepted the titbits I offered.

One day I came upon an oceanic melodrama, a tragedy of the sea in which the innocent victims were little fishes, probably herring, and the villains were giant tuna and ravenous shearwaters. The poor herring found themselves in a terrible fix: if they stayed in the water the tuna got them, and if they jumped out of the water in their frantic efforts to escape the tuna followed right on their tails; besides which, in the air or near the surface, the shearwaters got them. They were trapped between two devils and the deep blue sea: doomed, no matter what they did.

I watched this battle for survival with horror-stricken fascination. The greedy tuna and shearwaters gorged themselves on the hapless herring. But as *Tinkerbelle* and I drew within twenty yards or so all the shearwaters in the area, alarmed at the sight of us, took to their wings. All except one, that is. This particular bird cut loose with a great squawking and flapping of wings, but, try as it would, it couldn't get airborne. At first I thought the squawks and the inability to fly meant it had been injured—by a tuna, perhaps—and was in distress, so I headed towards it with the intention of seeing if I could render first aid. However, in a very short time it became clear that the bird was simply swearing away in bird language for having eaten so piggishly that it was now too heavy to take off. And, believe me, that bird knew how to swear. I am no prig and yet I was shocked! And so were the tuna, for, as the air turned blue, they left.

As we bore down on the bird, its cursing and wingbeats became more frenzied. Finally, goaded by fear into making one last, do-or-die, superbird effort, it flogged itself into the air like an overloaded cargo plane and lumbered away. I don't know bird language, so I can't say for sure what it said as it fought for altitude, but the tone and inflection sounded like 'Geehookers! That was a close one!'

Shortly after sunset I noticed the barometer was down a tenth of an inch. That wasn't much of a drop, but sure enough it began to blow hard and I had to stream the sea anchor again.

'Wow! What a night!' I wrote in the log the next morning (June 11th), 'I hope I don't have to go through any more like that, but I probably will. It was cold, too, as the wind had shifted from west to north.'

The wind relaxed a little at about 12.30 p.m., however, and then the sun came out for the first time in three days and we had a gloriously sunny, warm afternoon of sailing. I hove to contentedly in the moonlight at about ten that night and, just before going below to sleep, saw a big liner rumble westward a few miles north of us, its portholes agleam and its decks bathed in soft light.

The next morning, I awoke at about sunrise after a full seven hours of warm, relaxed sleep, and lay there in the cabin luxuriating in the pleasure of being rocked gently by the waves. Sounds of water had enchanted and soothed me all my life: the roar of a fast-flowing stream in a valley of the Himalayas; the patter of monsoon rain on the tin roof of our home in Landour; the crash and hiss of breakers hitting the beach at Ventnor, New Jersey, where our family had thrice vacationed; the slap and gurgle of Lake Erie fresh-water waves around the breakwater at Wildwood Park harbour, and now the happy laughter of Atlantic salt-water billows as they toyed playfully with *Tinkerbelle*.

It was Saturday, June 12th, and one of those 'God's-in-His-heaven-all's-right-with-the-world' mornings that come along every once in a while to give you a taste of how wonderful life can be. And then, just as I was beginning to slip into utter harmony with the delights of the environment, I became conscious of a subtle something. I heard nothing whatever that could be termed alien or out of place and yet, gradually, imperceptibly, I was infused with an eerie feeling that *Tinkerbelle* and I were not alone, that we had company. It was an uncanny sensation, as if I were on the receiving end of a telepathic message.

I opened the hatch and went topside. Good Lord! There was another vessel!

This one was much larger than the *Tench*. It towered above us, its tremendous bow jutting higher than *Tinkerbelle*'s masthead. It was a Canadian naval vessel and to me, then only twenty-five yards away, it seemed large enough to be a battleship. However, I found out later it was a destroyer escort, H.M.C.S. *Columbia*, a beautiful light-grey ship with a well-cared-for look about it.

At the *Columbia*'s rail, when I emerged from the cabin, was an officer in a smart white uniform. He had an electronic megaphone in his hands and, when he saw me, he used it to project his voice across the water between us.

'Good morning,' he said cheerily.

His friendly tone and casual manner seemed to imply that the sole mission assigned to the *Columbia* by Royal Canadian

Tinkerbelle

Navy Headquarters was to conduct a genteel wake-up service for singlehanded Atlantic yachtsmen.

'Hi!' I yelled back, attempting to sound just as casual and cheery as the naval person at the rail above me.

'Are you all right?' he asked.

'Everything's A.O.K. here!' I shouted.

Then I remembered what I had neglected to ask the captain of the *Tench* and added, 'But I'd appreciate it if you'd give me a line on my position.'

'Will do.'

As we waited for the *Columbia*'s navigator to work out the position, the officer asked me where I had come from and where I was bound and what my craft's name was. I yelled back the replies and asked him if he would report *Tinkerbelle* and me to the Coast Guard in Boston and he said he would. Then the position report came. We were at 40° 17′ N and 63° 7′ W. That was great news! It showed that my navigation was reasonably accurate, for the position I had calculated was less than six miles from that given by the *Columbia*'s navigator.

It was a tremendous relief to find out that my sun shots and calculations hadn't gone haywire; that, apparently, I had got the hang of it and could now rely on my sextant and arithmetic to take *Tinkerbelle* and me where we wanted to go. I grew confident that we would actually land at Falmouth, England, and not unexpectedly at some other port.

'Smooth sailing to you,' called the *Columbia*'s blithe officer. And I yelled back, 'Thanks! Same to you!'

Then the big ship quietly pulled away stern first, turned northward and moved off with an air of majesty, its red-and-white ensign fluttering in the breeze. For the first time since we'd met, I looked about the ocean. There were three other warships in sight and off to the west aeroplanes were streaking through the sky. I must be mixed up in some naval manœuvres, I said to myself. It turned out I was right, but at that moment I didn't know how right.

Later I learned that *Columbia*, commanded by Commander P. R. Hinton, was participating in Exercise Polestar as a member of the NATO Matchmaker Squadron, which was composed of four ships, one each from Great Britain, Holland, the United States and Canada. I must have seen all four.

'On the morning of 12 June at 0615,' Commander A. C. McMillin of the Royal Canadian Navy wrote to me, '*Columbia* was patrolling her station when ordered to investigate a small radar contact. This contact turned out to be the *Tinkerbelle*, and at first sight it appeared to be derelict, as there was no sign of life. As *Columbia* came alongside *Tinkerbelle* you appeared and spoke to Sub-Lt. E. J. Kelly, who was the officer-of-the-watch at the time.'

I learned, too, that Exercise Polestar was an anti-submarine exercise in which units of the United States and Canadian Navies and the NATO squadron were divided into teams and pitted against each other. In fact, the *Tench* was a participant, but on the side opposite the *Columbia*, as the 'enemy'.

Meeting both 'friend' and 'foe' in a naval exercise was a thrilling experience, one I shall remember always. But I feel mortified about the way *Tinkerbelle* and I blundered like bumpkins into those war games and diverted two vessels, for some minutes, from their assigned duties. Here and now I want to thank the officers and men of the *Tench* and *Columbia* for their solicitous concern for our safety and, humbly, beg the Navies of Great Britain, Holland, the United States and Canada to pardon our intrusion.

The next night, following our encounter with H.M.C.S. *Columbia*, we had another beautiful, easygoing sail in the moonlight until 11.45 p.m., when I turned in.

On Sunday, June 13th, I awoke to find a stiff breeze blowing so I kept *Tinkerbelle* tethered to the bucket drogue and utilized the time that gave me away from the tiller to rearrange the stowage of my supplies. I was getting more and more fed up with having to root through everything I had to find what I wanted. I also took the opportunity to write some letters, to Virginia and others, which I hoped a passing ship might eventually pick up and mail for me when it reached port. We were hove to for seven or eight hours altogether, not counting the night hours when I was sleeping. It was a pleasant time on the whole for the waves were not quite big enough to scare me out of the comfort of the cabin, but I was impatient and fretful because we weren't moving eastward. In fact, we were falling behind on the schedule I'd set and if we didn't get cracking soon it would take more than three months to reach England instead of the two months I had estimated.

Fortunately, the wind abated a little at about one in the afternoon. I hauled in the sea anchor, put a tuck in the mains'l and then *Tinkerbelle* spread her red-and-white wings. We took off at top speed.

II

ALL through the night of June 13th and into the next day *Tinkerbelle* raced along before the strongest wind we had yet encountered. It was exhilarating, and it was exhausting, for the sea grew heavier every hour. Waves slammed into our starboard side without warning, and it was all I could do to handle the sheet and the tiller and stay on course. But I was determined to hang on, tired, sore and scared though I was, in order to make up for lost time; and so we kept driving on through the day and into the cold night.

It was no time for exuberance; we were perched too precariously on the thin line between maximum speed and minimum safety. To remain on that perch demanded senses tuned to their greatest receptivity. It called for unwavering alertness; instant detection of the slightest change in conditions and swift, appropriate responses. A moment's inattention could be disastrous.

I knew all this well, but it didn't help. The wind pulled a diabolical trick. It increased in force so stealthily I failed to perceive it until whammo! a puff caught the mains'l at the same time a wave struck the stern and *Tinkerbelle* spun around a full eighty degrees, paying no attention whatever to my frantic yank on her tiller. She wound up stopped dead in her tracks, facing into the wind, her sails flogging ineffectually with snapping sounds like firecrackers going off that meant the fabric might soon be ripped to shreds.

Fortunately, she started drifting backward almost at once and the rudder drew her stern round so that she went over on to the port tack and the flogging stopped. The sails were saved. I kept the genoa jib sheeted to the weather side and fastened the tiller and mainsheet on the lee or starboard side to heave her to. A reduction of the sail area was overdue.

A few minutes later the big red mains'l was down and lashed to the boom and we were continuing on our way under the genny alone. Even so, we sped along almost as fast as before, for the wind in those few minutes had increased markedly. It had also veered toward the west.

By the time the first lightening of the eastern horizon signalled the approach of daybreak and the longed-for blessing of the sun's warmth, the wind had moved all the way round to the west and now blew from directly astern. For a while the sea was confused. Then the waves, by degrees, adjusted to the changed direction of the wind. They grew higher and steeper as they bore in from behind, rank on rank, flinging us forward in spasms of breakneck speed. Clutched in a welter of sizzling foam, we surfed giddily down the forward slope of a breaking wave, paused for a moment in the trough as the wave raced ahead and then, when the next one grabbed us, repeated the manoeuvre. And so it went, on and on. It was exciting. It was also dangerous.

The chief hazard was that we might broach; that is, slew around broadside to the waves. A breaker striking *Tinkerbelle* in that position could knock her down, even roll her over and over. It might dismast her or inflict other dire injuries. It was a catastrophe to be resolutely avoided.

So, favouring discretion over sailing valour, I decided the time had come to put out the sea anchor again. I hated to end our eastward gallop, but consoled myself with the knowledge that even while riding to the sea anchor we would continue moving eastward, drifting at less than a knot, perhaps, but still that was better than drifting toward the west or even the north or south.

As soon as I got the bucket anchor out, the rudder off and the genny down, the strain on my nerves eased up and I could almost relax. *Tinkerbelle* seemed to appreciate the change, too. For a little while her motion was less violent; water sluiced across her deck less often. But the waves continued to grow. I could see them clearly in the brightening daylight. They were huge. They resembled rows of snow-capped mountains marching towards us.

Tinkerbelle

The mountains themselves weren't especially terrifying, or even their snow-capped tops. What really made my hair stand on end was the sight of one of those snowy tops curving forward and falling, carumpf! sending an avalanche of tons of frothing, hissing water cascading into the valley. What if one of those avalanches rammed into *Tinkerbelle* broadside? Oh, brother . . . !

I was tired. So far I'd gone more than twenty-three hours without sleep and goodness only knew how much longer I'd have to go. The skin of my face felt stretched taut. It burned from the protracted buffeting of wind and spray. I was shocked to discover my eyelids were beginning to droop and my head to nod. I even had some trouble focusing my eyes.

This is no good, I said to myself. I've got to snap out of it.

Quickly, I opened the cabin hatch, leaned inside, rummaged in my medical kit until I found a stay-awake pill, downed it with a swallow or two of fresh water and closed the hatch again. I moved fast, for I didn't relish the prospect of maybe having *Tinkerbelle* flipped over while the hatch was open.

The pill took effect swiftly. In a minute or two I was bright-eyed and bushy-tailed, the need for sleep seemingly vanished. That was better, much better.

I thought how wonderful it would be to crawl into the cabin and at least get out of the reach of the wind, but I didn't have the courage or the faith in *Tinkerbelle* to do it. I feared she might be capsized, trapping me inside her, and I imagined that that wouldn't be much fun. So I remained outside in the pitching, bounding, rolling, yawing, dipping, swaying, reeling, swivelling, gyrating cockpit, exposed to the merciless clawing of what by then was either a full gale or the next thing to it.

Hanging on to avoid being tossed overboard by my little craft's furious bucking, I offered up prayers to God, and Neptune, and Poseidon, and all the sprites who might be induced to lend a hand in my hour of need. And then, just to be sure I hadn't overlooked a bet, I prayed 'To whom it may concern'.

I hunched down behind the cabin to escape the worst of the wind and flying spindrift, but every ten minutes or so I popped up to take a quick look around the horizon to see if there were any ships about. It would have been a splendid time, while we were riding to the sea anchor, helpless, unable to manœuvre, for a big freighter to come along and run us down. We made a dandy target with that hundred and fifty feet of line stretched out from the bow. A picture flitted into my mind of *Tinkerbelle* and me being chopped into little pieces by the slashing cleaver-like propellers of an Atlantic juggernaut.

From the tops of the waves I could see four or five miles, maybe farther. A reddish glow in the east foretold the imminent appearance of the sun. How I yearned for its heat! It would make life worth living again. Banks of orange-looking clouds hugged the northwest quadrant of the horizon, making it seem as if there must be land there, although of course there wasn't. The sky had already turned from black to grey to white and now was turning from white to pale blue. Except for the northwest sector, close to the sea, it was almost clear. Only a few small billowy clouds dotted its vastness.

With the arm I didn't need for holding on, I beat my chest and rubbed my legs in a frantic effort to generate warmth. I wriggled my toes and, as well as I could under the circumstances, made my legs pedal an imaginary bicycle. The exercise and the friction helped. It produced a mild internal glow that dulled the icy sting of the wind. It also gave me something to do, which, for the moment at least, relieved the mounting apprehension aroused by the incessant crashing of breaking waves and raving of the wind.

In another twenty minutes or so, at about 4.30 a.m., the sun bobbed up and so did my spirits. The red-gold rays burnished the varnished mahogany of *Tinkerbelle*'s cabin and sent waves of radiant relief deep into my chilled hide. The sight of my own shadow made life appear ever so much brighter and, somehow, this deep blue ocean of the day didn't seem nearly as threatening as the inky black one of the night had seemed.

What happened soon afterwards happened so fast and, believe it or not, so unexpectedly, that I still don't have a clear picture of it in my mind. I remember I was revelling in the growing warmth of the sun and in the improved prospects for the day when a wall of hissing, foaming water fell on *Tinkerbelle* from abeam, inundating her, knocking her down flat and battering me into the ocean with a backward somersault. One moment I was sitting upright in the cockpit, relatively high and dry, and the next I was upside down in the water, headed in the direction of Davy Jones's locker.

I flailed my arms and legs, fighting to gain the surface. I wasn't exactly frightened; it had all taken place too fast for that. But the horrible thought of sharks passed through my mind and I was gripped by the awesome feeling of being suspended over an abyss as I recalled that not long before I had figured out from the chart that the sea was about three miles deep at that spot. No use trying to touch bottom and push myself up to the surface.

I struggled harder as pressure began to build up in my lungs and behind my eyeballs. I hoped I could get my head above water in time to avoid taking that first fatal underwater breath that would fill my lungs and, no doubt, finish me off.

My lungs were at the bursting point when, at last, my head broke out of the water and I gasped for air. I expected to find *Tinkerbelle* floating bottom up, her mast submerged and pointed straight at the ocean floor, but she had righted herself and was riding the waves again like a gull. We were no more than eight or ten feet apart.

I reached down, caught hold of the lifeline around my waist and hauled myself back to my loyal friend. Then, gripping the grab rail on her cabin top, I tried to pull myself on board. I couldn't do it; the weight of my wet clothes made the task too great for my limited strength. Nevertheless, I tried again. Still no go, so I rested a moment.

There must be an easier way, I thought, as the boat and I rose and fell to the waves in unison. Of course, I could have taken off my clothes, put them on board, and then climbed aboard after them, but I hoped there was a quicker way. And then it came to me: hold the grab rail with one hand while floating close to the surface, get a leg hooked over the rub rail and on to the deck, and then pull up. I was given extra impetus by the mental image of a vicious, snaggle-toothed shark possibly lurking nearby and preparing to take pounds of flesh out of my quivering body, so, on the next try, I made it.

Puffing heavily, I flopped into the cockpit and lay there clutching the handhold above the compass as my breathing slowly returned to normal. The situation, to state the case mildly, could have been a lot worse. I had been given a bad scare and was soaked through, but nothing really calamitous had happened. *Tinkerbelle* was still right side up and clear of water, and neither she nor I had suffered so much as a scratch. And, best of all, I now had evidence of exactly how stable she was. That one piece of empirically gained knowledge transformed the whole harrowing experience into a blessing in disguise. There would be no more torturous nights in the cockpit; from now on I would sleep in comfort in the cabin, even in the foulest weather, with the assurance that my boat would remain upright. No longer did I need to fear being trapped there by a capsize. This discovery made the remainder of the voyage immensely more enjoyable than it would otherwise have been.

The steepness and dangerous size of the breaking waves remained undiminished, however, so I had to remain alert. There was no telling when we might be bowled over a second time. Although sopping wet, I was reasonably comfortable because my rubberized suit kept out the wind and the rising sun was beginning to produce the warmth I had longed for all night. It was a beautiful day, in fact, with white, cottony clouds flecking the inverted bowl of the sky, and white, foaming wave crests flecking the undulating, deeper indigo platter of the sea. If it hadn't been for the force of the wind and the size of those waves it would have been a perfect day for sailing.

12

WITH *Tinkerbelle* doing her stuff, I bore up well under the waves' onslaught, but I began to have troubles of another sort, for by this time, about 10 a.m. *Tinkerbelle* time, I had gone without sleep for nearly thirty hours. As it had done the day I picked up that 'hitch-hiker', my mind began to play strange tricks on me.

During the next hour or so, as closely as I can recall, my being was gradually permeated with the inexplicable feeling that *Tinkerbelle* and I were accompanied by other people in other boats, none of them identified specifically, and that we were there to search for a small quay and community known as Ada's Landing. I didn't know why the other sailors had to find the place, but I had a clear understanding of why I had to do so: I was to meet Robin and help her overcome some sort of serious trouble she was in. I didn't know exactly what her problem was; all I knew was that it was extremely serious and that a solution was essential for her future happiness.

I took in the sea anchor and, sailing under genny alone, began to hunt for the landing. We sailed and sailed and sailed; and now, looking back on it, I realize the sailing I did that day, through those giant waves, must have been remarkable, even fantastic. Or maybe the magnitude of the waves was itself a part of the hallucination.

Eventually we got to a part of the ocean called the Place of the Sea Mountains, an aptly named spot, for the waves there were as lofty as snow-capped Alpine peaks; so enormous, in fact, that I realized, even in my hallucinational state, that for safety's sake *Tinkerbelle* should be returned to her sea anchor. So I streamed the bucket again and we resumed our roller-coaster ride, slowly drifting eastward, stern first.

As we climbed and slid over those aqueous peaks, the notion seeped slowly into my mind that we were in a kingdom of the sea ruled by a crusty old Scotsman named MacGregor, a man with scraggly white sideburns, plaid tam-o'-shanter, knobby knees showing below his kilt and an even more knobby cane in his hand. And for some unknown reason he was determined to do me in.

Of course, I wasn't going to let him knock me off if I could avoid it, but he *did* seem to have a rather unfair advantage in the form of a demonic choir of evil-faced, surplice-clad cut-throats. This horrendous assemblage of gravel-voiced killers had the miraculous power of controlling the size of the waves by the loudness of their singing. They were singing their lungs out, goaded on to ever-increasing volume by vociferous tongue-lashings administered by MacGregor. Louder and louder they sang, and bigger and bigger grew the waves. It seemed as though my hours, maybe my minutes, were numbered.

During all this (and it went on for several hours) I had strange visions of MacGregor and his choir in the sky that appeared very much like the double exposures one sometimes sees in a cinema or on television, where two or more images are super-imposed on the same background. And as the minutes passed, old MacGregor grew increasingly enraged by his choir's inability to sing loud enough to put an end to me. He raved and stormed all over the heavens, threatening his dealers an *a-capella* death with horrible punishments if I survived their vocalizing. Mean-while, I waxed more and more confident that, with *Tinkerbelle's* help, I would be able to hold my own. Perhaps I even became over-confident because, even though the waves had not dimin-ished in size, I felt I had to go on and find Robin. I was sure she was in desperate need of my help.

So I drew in the drogue again, set the genny and, with that single sail, started to swoosh up and down and around the wave mountains as if I were crossing the Rockies by bobsled. I did some of the fanciest sailing of my life, swishing around the edges of those huge waves, dodging the breaking crests, and sometimes planing down their forward slopes at breakneck speed.

But I never seemed to get anywhere, much less to Ada's Landing. And neither did the people in the other boats accompanying me. We all seemed to be trapped in a maze, unable to find the way out. That's what the trouble was: the Place of the Sea Mountains was a maze-like ocean realm, set entirely apart from the regular ocean we had been on the day before. We had to get out of it before we could get to Ada's Landing.

Eventually, after hours of struggling to find our way out, *Tinkerbelle* and I came upon a little elfin character who looked like a cross between a leprechaun and Gunga Din.

'How can we get out of this place?' I asked him in a tone of intense urgency.

He stood there on the water studying me for a long time in an impish way that I couldn't fathom. Then he scratched his bald head, threw out his arms, palms up, in a gesture of sad amazement, and said:

'Sir, the trouble is you have been sailing clockwise. If you want to get out of here you must sail counterclockwise.'

And with that he was gone.

I put *Tinkerbelle* about and started moving on a counterclockwise course. It seemed to be the correct manœuvre, for soon we came to a place where the sea descended in a gigantic staircase leading off to the eastern horizon. The whole world seemed to be tilted and yet, marvel of marvels, none of the water in the sea ran down the staircase and off the edge of the horizon.

Tinkerbelle and I now did some even fancier sailing than we had done already; we went down that mammoth staircase lickety-split. What we were actually doing, I guess, was to surf-ride the waves, which, through some sort of perceptual distortion induced by the hallucination, appeared to be great downward steps in the sea. The thrills of the downhill runs were electrifying, far more stirring than any I'd had before in all my life. They warned of danger, but I was in no condition to heed them.

We charged down wave after wave as if we were on a toboggan and then along came a wave we couldn't handle. It flung us forward so fast we broached and over we went. I found myself in the ocean a second time. I wasn't knocked as far from *Tinkerbelle* this time, though, because I had kept a firm grip on the tiller. I was back on board in a jiffy.

Two more times that afternoon *Tinkerbelle* broached and I was knocked into the sea by waves slamming into us from abeam. I held firmly to some part of the boat each time and got back aboard quickly, but the repetitious way in which I was being dumped overboard was as exasperating as my boat's self-righting accomplishments were gratifying.

Late in the afternoon we got to the bottom of the wave-formed staircase and again met the Gunga Din pixy. He told me Ada's Landing was off to starboard, not much farther, and so I turned and headed in the direction he indicated. In a few minutes I began to 'see' bits of land ahead that I took to be the landing, but they always disappeared before I got right up to them. It was most perplexing, and equally infuriating.

I came to the conclusion—reluctantly, because he seemed a nice fellow—that Gunga Din was having prankish fun at my expense and that I had better not rely further on anything he said. I'd simply have to do the best I could on my own. I felt that I was bound to get out of the Place of the Sea Mountains, sooner or later, but I was assailed by painful shafts of doubt about whether I would be able to reach Robin and help her. The search for Ada's Landing began to seem futile.

My misgivings and anguish increased with each passing minute. My very soul was on the rack, tormented between the desperate ardour of my desire to help my daughter and the accumulating suspicions that I would not be able to do so, that I would fail her at this time when she needed me more than she ever had before. It was agony.

At about sunset *Tinkerbelle* and I (alone now, for our sailing companions had vanished) came to what seemed to be the brow of a long, easy slope off to port; and at the bottom of it was the 'regular' ocean. This was the way out of the Sea Mountains. We'd found it at last.

Tinkerbelle, still sailing under genny alone, all but flew down that ocean hill and rushed happily out into the normal, unjinxed, unbewitched sea. Oh, what a relief it was to be in it again! The face of our predicament was transformed from a frown into a smile, as though we had moved with one leap from hell to heaven. Goodbye, MacGregor! Goodbye, you sinful singers!

I had a queer feeling that Ada's Landing was nearby and that maybe we'd find it after all. But I needed sleep; every cell in my body cried out for it. So I decided to rest and go on to the landing in the morning, hoping that Robin would be able to wait that much longer. I put out the bucket drogue, took down the genny, hoisted the anchor light in the rigging, unshipped the rudder, changed into dry clothes (those I had on were still wet from my duckings) and climbed into the cabin, closing the hatch (all but a crack left open for air) after me. It was good to pull that blanket over me and close my eyes!

I now had no qualms whatever about sleeping in the cabin. In any case, the sea had settled down considerably; it wasn't making nearly as much fuss as it had during the daylight hours. Conditions seemed ideal for sleeping, but just before I dropped off, the boat jiggled violently in a way that, I felt, couldn't possibly have been caused by wave action. I stilled my breathing and strained my ears for some clue to what was going on outside. I thought I heard someone, or rather, two people, holding on to the boat and whispering. And then the boat jiggled again in that peculiar way. It was clear what was happening. Two jokers had swum out from the landing and were jostling the boat to annoy me, to keep me from getting the sleep I needed and to see how far they could go before I flew into a rage.

I tried to control my temper, but it steadily became more and more difficult. When I heard my tormentors pulling themselves around the boat, hand over hand, and, in low voices, planning more trickery, I could hardly contain myself. Then they jiggled *Tinkerbelle* again.

'Cut that out!' I yelled in as threatening a tone as I could produce.

Quiet reigned for two or three minutes and then I heard more whispering. Soon the boat began to rock. Those damnable swimmers were hanging on to the rub rails, one on each side, and seesawing the hull with fiendish delight. I could stand their impudent maliciousness no longer. Adrenalin gushed into my veins, making me hot with anger, and I stormed out of the cabin ready to beat my harassers to a pulp.

'Dammit! You bastards are going to get it now!' I roared.

But nobody was there.

13

In the morning (Tuesday, June 15th), after more than ten hours of sleep, I awoke to find *Tinkerbelle* again riding mountainous waves. But I wasn't worried; I knew she'd stay upright. All day the wind blew hard, too hard to do any sailing; so I remained within the shelter of the cabin, going out on deck only occasionally to see if any ships were in sight.

It was a huge relief to be myself again, to realize that Robin really wasn't in any difficulty, that all my fears about her had been part of a nightmarish hallucination. Robin wasn't in trouble, there was no Ada's Landing, no Place of the Sea Mountains, no MacGregor, no sinister choir, no Gunga Din, no staircase or hill in the ocean and no aquatic pranksters. O.K., granted. But what about those duckings? Were they hallucinatory, too? Had I or hadn't I been washed overboard four times?

The clothing I'd worn the previous day was tucked away in a corner of the cabin and it was still sopping. It couldn't possibly have got that wet unless I had actually been *in* the sea at least once. And if I'd been in the sea once, and knew it was for real, then the other times must have been real, too. Besides, the flashlight I'd had tied to a line in the cockpit was now gone. The knot must have come loose, allowing it to slip away when it, too, had been washed overboard. Yes, I really had been knocked into the sea four times. No doubt about it. (Fortunately, I had a spare flashlight, as well as a marvellous signalling spotlight a friend had presented to me as a bon-voyage gift.)

Describing the previous day in the log, I understated the case somewhat when I wrote, 'This was one of the most unusual days of my life'. Then, after telling about everything I'd 'seen' and 'done', I summed it up with, 'This was a weird experience. It must have been at least partly hallucination, but part of it must have been real because I *know* I was sailing around, was swept overboard four times, and used up a whole day. I must have just slipped a cog.

I must say that I have had the most uncanny feeling of having someone with me most of the time. It's not always the same person. Sometimes it's Virginia, sometimes Doug, sometimes Robin and sometimes John (John Manry, my brother). I'll have to get a psychologist to explain all this.'

Perhaps this feeling of having members of the family with me was a technique my mind had of coping with loneliness, for I did at times feel extremely lonely. However, I didn't miss human companionship in a general way, probably because I am inclined to be an introspective, self-contained sort of person, lacking strong inclinations towards gregariousness. I missed my family and close, personal friends intensely, but as for mankind in the abstract, no. I got along without human company (considered simply as human company) very well. And, after all, I knew from the very beginning that I wasn't going to be alone for more than three months.

Besides feeling that I had members of my family with me, I sometimes heard voices in the wake. This was in the first part of the trip before any weeds or barnacles had attached themselves to the hull, and *Tinkerbelle* could sail quite fast, leaving a bubbling wake behind her. To me, sometimes, the bubbles sounded as if someone were talking down there under the water and once I imagined that someone under the boat was calling for help and I even went so far as to look down over the stern to see who it was. I didn't see anyone.

To help face the loneliness I kept one of my watches set to Eastern Standard Time, the time of Willowick and Cleveland, so that I could visualize what might be happening at home. At 7 a.m. (E.S.T.) Doug would be getting out of bed, I knew, for he was the earliest riser in the family. As soon as he was dressed (if it happened to be Saturday), he would go out to the living-room to watch the cartoons on television; otherwise he'd have a hasty breakfast and depart for school.

Robin spent the time between getting out of bed and leaving for school fixing her hair and making sure she was dressed to suit herself. And Virginia would have to keep urging her on so that she wouldn't keep her friend, Jean Perkey, waiting. Then the two girls would go on to school together.

After the children had left, if I was at home, Virginia would spoil me outrageously by serving me coffee in bed and then she would sit beside me and we'd have the most wonderful conversations. How I missed those talks and cups of coffee. The talks I had now were rather one-sided and the instant coffee I made for myself wasn't nearly as delicious as the coffee Virginia brewed.

All day long I had only to look at the Eastern Standard Time to picture what was probably happening at home at that moment. It made the family seem much nearer than it might have seemed otherwise. I hoped that at the end of the month Virginia wouldn't have trouble paying the bills, a chore that previously had been in my province.

Wednesday, June 16th, dawned with *Tinkerbelle* bobbing gently on a smoothed-out sea. I ate a hasty breakfast and we got going as quickly as possible. It turned out to be a fine, sunny day, the highlight of it being that, finally, after sixteen days at sea, we crossed the meridian of 60° W, completing the first step in the giant countdown to England.

It was a wonderful feeling to have passed this first oceanic milestone, but it required very little arithmetic to see that if we continued to move at the rate we'd established in the first two weeks we'd require about eighty-seven more days to reach England, making the duration of the voyage more than a hundred days. And I was provisioned for only ninety days. It looked as though I might have to go on reduced rations.

I wasn't really worried, however, because I was consuming my provisions more slowly than I'd thought I would, and I was confident we'd move faster as I grew better acquainted with the ocean and with *Tinkerbelle*'s performance in relation to it. During these first two weeks I had been sailing cautiously, feeling my way, getting my sea legs.

About noon the next day *Tinkerbelle* almost slammed into a shark that was lallygagging at the surface with its dorsal fin sticking out of the water; I think it must have been sleeping. It was eight or nine feet long, not very big as sharks go.

In mid-afternoon we had our first serious mishap: the rudder broke.

The fibreglass covering of the rudder had cracked near the stock where the tiller fitted on to it, and water had seeped through the crack to the three-quarter-inch plywood underneath, causing it to soften. Finally, the enormous strain set up by the opposing pressures of water on the rudder and my pull on the tiller caused the stock to snap. I thanked my lucky stars that I'd brought along a spare. In less than five minutes it was in place and we were moving again.

We were becalmed for about four hours on June 18th and again for most of the morning of the next day. Shortly after noon, however, a breeze sprang up and, as it veered from the north all the way around to the south, it increased in force. *Tinkerbelle* was soon zipping along, headed due east.

'About midafternoon,' the log says, 'we were racing along at a great rate on the starboard tack when a large tanker popped into view over my right shoulder, no more than 25 yards away. It had sneaked up on me without making a sound and gave me quite a start. I must make it a practice from now on to scan all around the horizon from time to time to prevent this sort of thing.'

The tanker was the S.S. *Otto N. Miller* of Monrovia. The crew at the rail waved and cheered as it sped past, and I waved back as well as I could while holding the tiller and mainsheet in my hands. The ship seemed to be going at terrific speed and the huge waves it sent out from its bow and stern gave us an exciting bouncing around. It didn't even slow down as it passed and was soon out of sight.

Captain Orlando Rolla, skipper of the *Miller*, told me later of his experiences that day. His ship had left St. John, New Brunswick, Canada, the previous day and was bound for Bandar Mashur, Iran, via the Suez Canal.

'In the afternoon of June 19,' he wrote, 'Chief Officer Salvino Gallinaro was on watch. We had showers all round us and our radar was working.

Mr Gallinaro advised me that a little object, not well defined, was showing on the radar screen. It was about 60° on our port bow and some three-quarters of a mile away. The horizon was clear of showers in that direction and, with binoculars, we saw a small red sail.

We immediately headed the ship in that direction to investigate. We steered as close as possible so that no particulars about the sailing boat would escape our attention. In fact, we passed so close I was able to see clearly the number marked on the bow of your boat and I saw you sitting at the tiller, looking as if you were sailing on a small lake rather than the Atlantic Ocean.

I told the U.S. Coast Guard of our meeting, giving it the number and description of your boat, and advising it that no assistance was required.

The night following our meeting we had a moderate sea and often our thoughts ran to you, alone in the open ocean.'

I'll have to agree that Captain Rolla's ship passed close to *Tinkerbelle*, so close the shock nearly made me jump out of my skin. But, as I noted in the log, it taught me an important lesson: keep scanning the whole horizon so that you'll know when a ship is approaching. It was very kind of the captain to report me to the Coast Guard and to think of me that night. Conditions probably weren't as bad as he imagined them, though.

'Towards dusk,' my log says, 'the wind grew too strong for the genoa so I stopped to take it in and put out the sea anchor. Just then a cloudburst hit. It rained so hard I could hardly see 10 feet away. But I managed to get bounding *Tinkerbelle* bedded down without mishap.

I stayed in the cockpit for a long time watching her take the huge waves. She did very well, but I'll have to improve the jigger sail at her stern. [I had rigged this to help keep her pointed steadily into the waves.]

I was fearful of getting into the cabin and going to sleep because of the brush with the *Miller*, but *Tinkerbelle*'s anchor light seemed perfectly visible, so finally I did go inside where it was quiet and dry and got some sleep.'

At dusk the very next day (Sunday, June 20th) we met another ship, the S.S. *Exilona*, a 9,598-ton freighter commanded by Captain Helgi Loftsson. We had been through some squalls earlier in the day, but now the wind was light, although huge swells were running. Dark, threatening clouds partly covered the sky and caught orange-red rays from the setting sun. It was a scene El Greco might have painted if he had painted sea-scapes.

The *Exilona*, when I first saw her, was to the north of us, headed west, and I thought she would go on by, but then she saw us and came lumbering over, rolling and pitching through the swells. As she drew near, Captain Loftsson stopped her engines, but even without her propellers turning she moved so fast, blown by the wind, that *Tinkerbelle* could barely keep pace with her. I shouted to men at the stern rail and they relayed what I said to Captain Loftsson on the bridge by telephone, and then, in turn, passed his questions and answers back to me.

I learned the ship was on its way from Beirut to Boston, and told the captain I was bound for England and needed no assist-ance. I added that I'd appreciate a position check and would like to give him some letters to be mailed when he reached port. He gave me the position figures promptly and they showed that my own were reasonably accurate, but transferring the letters wasn't so easily done as I was afraid to get closer than about a hundred feet to the *Exilona*'s stern because of the danger of having my craft slammed against her and smashed. A husky seaman tried twice to span the distance between us with a line, but failed. It was hopeless.

The captain said he'd report me to the Coast Guard so that it could keep track of my progress, and I yelled back, 'Thanks!' I found out later the message he sent was:

'Latitude 40.57 north; longitude 58.04 west. Passed sailing boat OH-77013-AR, 14-foot [How he came so close to estimating

Tinkerbelle's length correctly I can't imagine] lapstrake sailing boat with red mainsail and white jib.

One person aboard bound for Falmouth, England, from Falmouth, Massachusetts. Nineteen days at sea. Requested notify U.S. Coast Guard, Boston, that all is O.K. Required no assistance.'

After I thanked Captain Loftsson, we bade each other good-bye and I exchanged waves with the seamen at the *Exilona*'s stern. Then we turned back to our original courses and went our separate ways as darkness closed in. A little while later a wonderful, steady breeze sprang up and *Tinkerbelle*, with a reef in her mains'l, gambolled over the waves as if she were a spirited fawn out for a romp in the woods. It was glorious sailing and I wished that Virginia and the children could have enjoyed it with me. It was so pleasant, in fact, I took a stay-awake pill and went on all night.

Three more days of good sailing followed. On the third night, Wednesday, June 23rd, the ocean was as calm as a millpond. Hardly a ripple disturbed its glassy surface as *Tinkerbelle* ghosted along noiselessly on a shimmering cushion of phosphorescence. I lay on my back in the cockpit with my legs extending into the cabin, my head propped up on a cushion, the tiller in my right hand, steering by the stars that bejewelled the black velvet sky. What an enchanting out-of-this-world night that was, with the sparkling diamonds in the water seemingly competing in brilliance with the diamonds in the heavens.

It was so calm I hove to for sleep without streaming the sea anchor, by simply hauling the jib to windward and tying the tiller to leeward. I slept like a baby and, in the morning, had the pleasure of beginning a new day without having to go through the arduous task of hauling in the bucket.

We had been at sea more than three weeks now and I had a daily routine more or less established. I usually awoke at about 4 a.m., *Tinkerbelle* time, shortly before the sun popped up from below the eastern horizon, and I began the day in sheer luxury. I treated myself to a delightful experience that, at home, was reserved for mornings when I was indisposed or had done something extraordinary to merit extra-solicitous indulgence: I had breakfast in bed.

As a matter of fact, I also had dinner in bed, for *Tinkerbelle*'s cabin was too small to permit my dining within it in any other way. Of course, my use of the word 'bed' is a slight exaggeration. It wasn't *really* a bed; it was a couple of bags full of clothing on which I sat and a rolled-up blanket to my right against which I leaned and rested my head.

Tinkerbelle's interior was too crowded with gear to allow me to stretch out at full length, so I had to experiment with other positions for sleeping. I tried out several, but the one that worked out best was this semi-sitting-up position in which I planted my stern on the bags of clothing and leaned to starboard against the blanket. Then, to have breakfast in bed, all I had to do was to straighten up and my food and canned-heat stove were within easy reach.

Breakfast usually consisted of hot cereal with raisins, canned fruit of some sort and coffee. Sometimes I had scrambled dehydrated eggs and dehydrated bacon or, about once a week, a dehydrated Spanish omelette. The first time I prepared an omelette, it wound up with a taste and texture resembling shoe leather, but, happily, I became more adept at omelette cookery later on.

After breakfast I washed my utensils in the ocean and brushed my teeth; and every other week I shaved my face, all except my moustache, which, by the third week, was beginning to look quite respectable. And once a week, if the weather was favourable, I took a sponge bath in the cockpit with sea water, afterward giving myself a rinse with fresh water. Water for shaving and bathing was warmed on the stove.

When breakfast and these chores were completed, I prepared to get under way. I took the anchor light out of the rigging. I removed the rudder from the daggerboard-keel-slot where it had been stowed for the night and secured it in the cockpit, ready to be hung at the stern when I was ready. I also took down the improvised stern jigger sail, which helped to keep the boat headed squarely into the waves. Then I crawled to the foredeck and hauled in the sea anchor, stowing the line in the daggerboard-keel slot and lashing the bucket and float firmly in place aft of the mast. The next steps were to put the rudder on and, finally, to hoist the sails. We were then ready to go. In good weather the whole rigmarole took about twenty minutes, but if the sea was rough, forcing me to hold on tight to keep from being pitched overboard, it sometimes took twice that long.

When I got back to the tiller and we started moving, we kept it up until the sun (if not hidden by clouds) was at least ten degrees above the horizon. Then I hove to for the morning sun shot by backing the jib and lashing the tiller down.

Most navigators, I believe, take a series of sextant sights and strike an average, but since I had to stop the boat every time I used the sextant, I tried for the best possible single shot I was capable of and relied on that. For accuracy's sake I always used the natural horizon, except once or twice at night when I used the bubble to get our latitude from Polaris. After I had gained some experience, I found that I could usually tell whether a given sextant sight was a good one.

When the sight had been worked out and the position line recorded on a plotting sheet, we resumed sailing and kept it up until just before noon. Then we stopped for the noon latitude sight, which usually took me twenty or thirty minutes, longer than was required for the morning or evening sights. By bringing forward the morning north-south position line, in accordance with the estimated distance and the course we had sailed, until it intersected the noon east-west position line, I got a fairly good idea of where we were at noon.

After the noon sight we again set sail and I ate a snack as we sloshed along. I'd have biscuits, or a meat bar, or a candy bar, or a concoction of dried fruit and nuts called pemmican. And I'd top it off with fruit juice or a carbonated drink. (Ben Carlin had written that he developed a craving for carbonated beverages while at sea so I brought along a good supply and was glad to have it.)

When the sun was far down in the western sky, but not yet closer than ten degrees to the horizon, we stopped for the evening sextant shot, which gave me another north-south position line on the plotting sheet. Then, by drawing a line from our noon position, according to the course we had travelled, to intersect the afternoon sun line, I established our position with sufficient accuracy for my needs. This type of position finding is called a running fix. It is not as precise as a regular fix in which position lines taken from two or more celestial bodies, in quick succession, establish the location of the vessel; but it nevertheless served us well, for we were not moving very fast, our average daily run being about forty miles.

Following the evening navigational exercise, I had dinner (in bed, usually; although I occasionally 'lived it up' and ate outdoors, in the cockpit). The menus had a great variety of entrées: beef slices and potatoes, turkey loaf, shrimp, tuna and noodles, stuffed cabbage, stuffed peppers, spaghetti and meat balls, corned-beef hash, chicken and noodles, ham loaf and others. Dessert was usually fruit or a candy bar, but once a week I treated myself to a tiny fruitcake. The beverage was coffee, most often, with an occasional switch to an orange drink or cocoa. Sometimes I added beef or chicken bouillon, and I always added a vitamin pill and an ascorbic acid, anti-scurvy tablet.

Dinner over, I washed the saucepan or frying pan and silverware in the ocean and got under way again. Usually I sailed until well after darkness had fallen, stopping for sleep between 9 p.m. and midnight, *Tinkerbelle* time; but once in a while, as I've already reported, I continued all night. The all-night sailing came, generally, when I was trying to get across shipping lanes quickly and safely, or was battling an adverse current.

The procedure for parking *Tinkerbelle* for the night was the same as the procedure for getting her under way in the morning, except that it was done more or less in reverse. I hove her to under sail, put out the sea anchor, lowered and secured the sails, unshipped the rudder and stowed it in the daggerboard-keel-slot, raised the jigger sail at the stern and hung the anchor light in the rigging. If it was a pleasant night, I sometimes stayed in the cockpit for a few minutes, facing sternward with my back resting against the cabin, enjoying the sights and sounds of the night-time ocean. At other times I played the harmonica or listened to the radio, most frequently to programmes of the Voice of America, the Armed Forces Radio and Television Service and the British Broadcasting Corporation. Then I descended into the cabin, closed the hatch after me (except for the crack left open for ventilation), got into 'bed', pulled a blanket over me and went to sleep. I'll have to confess that I didn't observe such amenities as wearing pyjamas and sleeping between sheets. I went primitive, to a certain extent, and slept in the clothes I'd been wearing all day—many times even when they were wet.

Usually I was so tired I had no trouble whatever getting to sleep; the sea rocked me as though I were in a cradle. (Luckily I have never been bothered by seasickness.) In rough weather, though, waves sometimes broke over the boat sending streams of water gushing through the ventilation crack left open in the hatch. This was annoying because it soaked the blanket, though it didn't seem to reduce its warmth.

Tinkerbelle's cabin was a marvellous refuge, now that I had learned it wouldn't, couldn't become a trap. I couldn't imagine how Dr. Alain Bombard, Dr. Hannes Lindemann, and George Harvo and Frank Samuelson had achieved their crossings in cabinless craft. They weren't ever able to get out of the wind's clutches, away from its buffeting and shrieking, as I was. How they stood the hardships of constant exposure to the elements is more than I can comprehend. In *Tinkerbelle*'s cabin I was able to shut myself away from the occasionally harrowing difficulties of the sea world of waves and winds and enter a world of cosy comfort and order, where there was a place for everything and everything (I hoped) was in its place. The snugness and enveloping protection of the cabin touched latent atavistic inclinations within me that had no doubt been passed on from long-gone ancestors who lived in caves. The cabin was a little world unto itself, safe and compact. There I could fall asleep to the music of the sea, the chuckling, giggling and laughing of wavelets strumming the laps in the boat's clinker-built hull. There I could wait out storms with ease, passing the time with reading, eating, letter writing, napping, navigation figuring, radio listening and harmonica playing. There, too, I could raise my braying voice to top volume and burst into song without fear of annoying a soul, except maybe the birds or fish.

I loved the smell of the cabin. It was an exotic compound of the odours of paint, caulking material, a tarry aroma that came from I know not where, damp blankets and mould, the whole business being delicately seasoned with a faint scent from whatever type of food had been accidentally spilled into the bilge at the last meal.

June 25th (Friday) was a fine sailing day; so good, in fact, that I decided to keep going all night in an effort to catch up on our schedule. Sometime after midnight an amazing thing happened; at least, it was amazing to me. I wrote about it in the log, thus:

'We were sailing along at a good clip with the usual phosphorescent phenomena [you see, by this time I was getting rather blasé] when all of a sudden a big patch of ocean the size of a baseball field lit up as though it were illuminated by underwater floodlights. And there was *Tinkerbelle* sailing on a sea of light. It was one of the most spectacular sights I've ever seen.'

This was a unique experience for me. I had never seen anything remotely like it before, although I had once read a little about similar occurrences. I certainly can't explain it.

It was a beautiful sight, but it made me so nervous I failed to appreciate it properly at the time. The thought darted into my mind that maybe a whale was under the boat, stirring up the ocean's luminescence, and that it might at any moment rise under the boat and smash it. I hung on, waiting for the fatal blow, but it never came; and in a minute or so I sailed out of the floodlit tract, awestruck and mystified.

Having sailed all night with the aid of pills, I should have suspected that something of a hallucinatory nature might occur the next day (Saturday, June 26th), but I didn't. My guard was down and I drifted right into another fantastic experience.

This one began at about sunset. I believed I was sailing in an inlet, close to the shore, and that I heard two apish men on a small wharf talking in conspiratorial tones.

'One shot between the eyes is all it'll take,' one of the men said.

'But how'll I know it's him?' the other asked.

'You can find his boat without no trouble 'cause he always puts out that there anchor light.'

Oh, oh! A couple of killers were obviously out to get me. I had to move far away from there, quickly. I sailed for my life, taking all sorts of devious routes in order to escape from the assassins. I even sailed into fog and stealthily circled back, hoping to lose them.

Sometime after darkness fell, I grew conscious of having Douglas and an elderly man on board *Tinkerbelle* with me. They were in the cabin, the man supposedly taking care of my son.

A little later we approached an island and somehow I knew that if we got on to the island we'd be caught and killed, so I steered *Tinkerbelle* away from it. But no matter what I did, she seemed determined to put us ashore and wreck herself in the process, for the coast was a mass of jagged rocks against which the waves hammered with sickening thunder. My boat simply went berserk. She became gallingly cantankerous, impossible to control. Nothing I did diverted her from drifting towards those terrible breakers. She would come about and then get into irons, come about and get into irons, over and over. She absolutely refused to obey me and to sail as she should. It was maddening, and I grew very angry. I shouted at *Tinkerbelle* and scolded her unmercifully. It was the first time I had said a harsh word to her. (I hope I'll never do it again.)

I don't know how it happened, but finally, by some means, I swerved *Tinkerbelle* away from her compulsive determination to kill us and herself. We broke away from the island's threatening rocks and headed out to sea.

Then, gradually, the feeling crept over me that the man in the cabin with Douglas was not a friend at all. He was really one of the assassins, bent on disposing of us both. As Doug's father it was up to me to save him from the clutches of the masquerading murderer.

The only tactical plan I could think of was to move slyly, silently to the cabin entrance holding the signalling spotlight at the ready, and then to turn it on in the killer's eyes. The blinding light and the surprise of the attack might enable me to get his gun away and save Doug. I'd seen men do things like that in the movies, so maybe I could, too.

I moved forward to the cabin hatch like a panther about to spring. I picked up the spotlight without a sound and then, zip! I switched it on and thrust it inside.

No one was there.

Undoubtedly it seems peculiar, but the revelation that I was in the grip of another hallucination jarred me considerably. I realized, as I should have done long before, that I needed rest. So I put out the bucket drogue and prepared *Tinkerbelle* to look after herself while I was asleep. I was just about to secure the anchor light in the rigging when I recalled what one of the assassins had said, 'You can find his boat without no trouble 'cause he always puts out that there anchor light.'

'O.K.,' I said to myself. 'I'll fool those lousy hoods.'

I outsmarted them with devilish cunning: I didn't put out the anchor light.

14

From the log:

'Monday, June 28—It's blowing up a bit this morning. I can't get going yet, anyway, because I've two chores to do. I've got to get the spare battery for the anchor light and fix up an aerial for the radio so I can get the WWV time signal. I couldn't hear it at all last night. If I'm left without the time signal I'll be in a bad spot; won't be able to tell my longitude.

After monumental rooting around, while being tossed about in the boat, I found the battery. I also have an aerial rigged as the topping lift and I got the 9 a.m. (Eastern Standard Time) time signal from WWV. I think I'll just wait here another hour for the noon sight and then I'll get going.'

Sometime during the day we completed another ten-degree step in the big countdown toward Falmouth: We moved to the east at 50° W longitude.

Again from the log:

'Wednesday, June 30—The last day of June and I'm only about one-third of the way. I don't think the rest of the trip will take two months, but I think it will take me until Aug. 15, all right.

I was becalmed for a couple of hours. Lay out on deck and snoozed a bit. When I looked around again the ocean seemed full of dolphins, in widely separated groups. I wonder how those far in the rear kept from getting lost.

Later in the afternoon *Tinkerbelle* was visited by some very colourful fish, three or four feet long, with dark iridescent blue bodies, two forward fins of lighter blue, and bright yellow tails. They cruised back and forth under the boat as I was having supper and wouldn't take any of the juicy morsels I offered them. [I learned later they were probably dorado.]

Sailing in the dark, later, I was "pursued" by a couple of thunderstorms. Lightning flashes lit up the entire sky, although they were too far off for me to hear the thunder.

Finally, at about 1.30 a.m. (*Tinkerbelle* time), I decided to bed down and, wouldn't you know it, that's when the first ship I've seen in days appeared. Fortunately it passed well to the south.'

The next day (July 1st) I got my first good shots at the sun in four days and discovered that we were about ninety miles south of where we should have been. There are places in the Atlantic where the Gulf Stream meanders, even doubles back on itself, and I think we must have run into one of these places. The current, then, began taking us south at the same time that we ran into cloudy weather, which prevented my taking sun sights that would have revealed what was happening to us. As soon as I found out, I headed *Tinkerbelle* northeastward and we sailed hard to regain the latitude we had lost.

On Friday, July 2nd, we went right through the centre of what I took to be a cyclone, or rather, it passed by us. The wind was coming from the southeast and, as the centre of the low passed over, it shifted a hundred and eighty degrees very quickly, in no more than five or six minutes, to the northwest. And it rained very hard, both before and after the shift.

'Saw what I can only describe as a giant sea worm,' I wrote later in the log. 'It was about the same colour as an ordinary garden worm, but about 10 feet long and fatter in proportion to its length than an ordinary worm.'

We got back up to the latitude we should have been at on Sunday, July 4th, and the next day I awoke at about 5 a.m., *Tinkerbelle* time, had a good breakfast and got under way.

The sun was peeking through clouds and it looked as though the day could go either way; cloudy and dreary or sunny and cheery. It went sunny, at least for most of the day. And I went cheery. The breeze was perfect, ten to thirteen knots, just the right force. And it was out of the south, which made it easy for me to steer our course of 67°. We made good time. The fine weather, the blue beauty of the sea and the easy, smooth rolling of the swells put me into a wonderfully happy frame of mind.

'The only thing that could make this day more perfect,' I said to myself, 'would be for a ship to come along and pick up my mail.'

About twenty minutes later I took my eyes off the compass and looked round the horizon and there, over my right shoulder, steaming towards me like the answer to a prayer, was a ship. It turned out to be the 12,640-ton cargo vessel, S.S. *Steel Vendor*, bound from India and Ceylon to New York.

Its master, Captain Kenneth N. Greenlaw, manœuvred the big ship very well, making it easy for me to bring *Tinkerbelle* in close, to within fifty feet of its starboard beam. The day was so calm, and the 492-foot *Steel Vendor* and the 13½-foot *Tinkerbelle* were so close to each other that Captain Greenlaw and I had no difficulty making ourselves understood. He wanted to know if I was lost and I assured him I wasn't, but that I'd appreciate a check on my navigation. So he gave me our position: 40° 53′ N and 47° 2′ W.

'Do you need any provisions?' he asked.

I assured him I had all the provisions I needed, and yet he looked sceptical, as though he just couldn't believe it. He seemed to be a big man, and he had a friendly face and a warm manner about him.

He readily agreed to take my mail aboard and soon a seaman heaved a line to *Tinkerbelle*. I had a bundle of ten letters all ready in a waterproof plastic bag and attached it quickly to the end of the line. Then the man hauled away. The letters were aboard the ship in a jiffy, on their way to my family and friends ashore.

'Thanks!' I yelled, waving to the captain and all the crew. 'Have a nice trip.'

'You have a nice trip!' the captain shouted back.

We all waved again, slowly drew apart and then turned stern to stern and resumed our separate courses. In a few minutes I was alone again on the restless sea.

Three days later, at one in the afternoon, we were becalmed

at the centre of a flat disc of blue. I used the time to bathe, dry blankets and clothing, write in the log and play the harmonica. *Tinkerbelle* had a small forest of gooseneck barnacles clinging to her bottom by then, for she had been at sea more than five weeks, so I also reached down as far as I could all around her and pulled off as many as possible. I think my efforts enabled her to sail a little more jauntily for several days afterward.

It remained calm until long after dark, the lengthiest period of calm we had yet encountered; but when I awoke in the morning a nice breeze was agitating the surface of the ocean. We started moving eastward again. Although it was rainy and dismal, we had good sailing all that day and the next.

'Looks as if it's going to be another dull, cloudy day, and the wind seems a bit strong for comfort,' I wrote in the log shortly after awaking on Sunday, July 11th.

This was an important day to me because sometime during the next ten hours (if the sailing was good) I expected to pass the meridian of 40° W, the next step in the longitudinal countdown to England. Passing this meridian would put me very close to the halfway point in the voyage, which, for my purposes, I decided was the meridian of 37° W. Since the winds were mostly westerlies, 40° W also was what I considered to be the point of no return; that is, the point from which it would be as easy, or easier, to sail on to England as to return to the United States, although, in case of trouble, the Azores still offered the closest haven. So I was hoping to have a good, long day of swift sailing.

'During the night the wind shifted from west to northwest,' I continued in the log. 'The shift has made it considerably cooler, but now we'll be able to reach rather than run. I just hope the wind doesn't get so strong we have to quit and put out the sea anchor.

Well, now, up and at it.'

The wind *was* strong and the waves seemed huge (some of them, I thought, were twenty-footers, the biggest yet), but I kept *Tinkerbelle* boiling along under genny only.

Conditions continued like this, teetering on the verge of being too obstreperous to handle, until just after twelve o'clock. Then, dramatically, the sky cleared and we were presented with a lovely sunny afternoon.

My spirits were beginning to soar when, crrraaack! the rudder snapped, rendering *Tinkerbelle* unsteerable.

It took me a few minutes to collect my wits and formulate a plan of action to deal with this crisis, but eventually I got organized and started to repair the original rudder, the one that had broken first, as it seemed to be the more reparable of the two. While I was pulling myself together, a breaking wave crest caught *Tinkerbelle* beam on and knocked her down, plopping me into the ocean for the fifth time. The boat righted herself at once, good girl that she was, and I scrambled back on to her very quickly, for by that time I had amassed considerable boarding experience (I knew exactly what to do to get back on her with the least effort and loss of time) and I immediately threw out the drogue so that the knockdown wouldn't be repeated.

It was desolating to have such a fine day and not be able to sail, but the cruel fact had to be faced—and dealt with. I gathered together my tools and with pieces of oak, brass bolts, fibreglass and waterproof glue, went to work on the rudder in the relative comfort of the cabin.

Late in the afternoon I took a sun shot. It indicated we were only three or four miles away from 40° W longitude, but the news cheered me scarcely at all. I wasn't in despair, for I knew I could fix the rudder. I was as confident as ever that we'd reach England safely. But the enforced halt for repairs and the slowness of our progress made me melancholy. I missed Virginia and Robin and Douglas, and I didn't want to be delayed and cause them unnecessary concern.

'*Tinkerbelle* and I will make it all right,' I wrote in the log, 'but I hate to be so far behind schedule because I think V. and the kids may worry.'

By nightfall I had stewed myself into a state of severe depression. For a few frantic moments I even considered swinging southeastward, once the rudder was serviceable again, and making for Flores, in the Azores. But after dinner that evening, as I was writing of the day's events, I spotted the tip of a piece of paper sticking out from between the pages of the spiral-bound note-book that served as my log. I pulled it out. It was a leaf from a little notebook that only Virginia could have put there. It said, in part:

'Charles A. Lindbergh, flying the Atlantic alone, came to the point where he could go no farther. He was exhausted. His hands were so tired they refused to obey his mind. Then he said he made this simple prayer: "God give me strength." From that moment on he declares that he sensed a third part of himself. It was "an element of spirit", which took control of both mind and body, "guarding them as a wise father guards his children".'

Finding this message at that moment of utter dejection was a bit of a miracle, for I desperately needed something or someone to snap me out of it. Despite my having been reared by missionaries, I have never been able to get on intimate terms with God (not that I wouldn't like to), so I cannot attribute its appearance on the scene to divine intervention. Nevertheless, it satisfied a keenly felt psychological hunger. The content of the message was helpful, of itself, but what did most to lift my sagging spirits, I think, was the realization of the loving devotion that led Virginia to slip the message into my log. That gave me strength and lifted my mood. Before long I was back on an even keel.

The ocean was calm the next day (July 12th), so calm we couldn't have moved even if the rudder hadn't been broken. That was O.K. with me, for it meant we weren't missing out on a favourable breeze.

I finished the repairs and all that remained was to wait over-night for the waterproof glue to harden. We'd be able to sail in the morning. I felt like my old self, and that evening I took a sextant shot at the sun that made me feel even better. It showed that while I'd been working on the rudder the Gulf Stream had carried us eastward past the meridian of 40° W longitude. We had completed another giant stride towards our journey's end and had passed the point of no return.

15

On Tuesday, July 13th, after nearly two days of drifting to the sea anchor while working on the rudder, we started sailing again and it soon became evident the repair job would hold up. The rudder was now as strong as iron; I expected no further trouble from it.

That day and the next the weather was cloudy. Then came July 15th, a wonderful, sunny day, and my sextant sights revealed we had passed 37° W, the halfway mark. That evening I celebrated the occasion by eating, with delicious hard-sauce topping, the plum pudding I had brought along for that specific purpose. I felt we were getting somewhere at last. It would be a downhill run the rest of the way.

But there was a tinge of sadness in this fact, too, for it meant the voyage was now middle-aged, moving closer and closer to old age and, after that, 'death'. I didn't think I'd want it to go on forever, yet, whether I did nor not, its end, no matter how happy or how longed for, would be accompanied by sharp twinges of pain, an undercurrent of profound regret. For then the voyage —and all it meant to me in happiness—would have moved from anticipation through realization into the past, where events, once lodged, existed only in the limbo of memory and could not (no matter how hard we tried) be relived. I consoled myself with the thought that there would be other challenges to face, other dreams to fulfil, even though none in the future could compare with this one.

When darkness descended on us, a fairly gentle southwest breeze was blowing, so I decided to wing out the small twin jibs for self-steering and let *Tinkerbelle* continue moving eastward, taking care of herself while I slept. The small jibs didn't perform quite as well as the twin gennies had, since their smaller area meant less force exerted on the tiller and less responsiveness to changing conditions. They allowed the boat to weave from side to side somewhat, but nevertheless kept her headed in a generally eastward direction. I managed to get six hours of sleep. However, the possibility that the wind might increase dangerously while I slept made me so nervous I never again tried the self-steering stunt. I didn't even try it during the day, when I was awake, because the twin jibs were so small they couldn't keep *Tinkerbelle* moving at her best.

Between noon, Saturday, July 17th, and noon the next day, *Tinkerbelle* made her best day's run of the entire voyage: eighty-seven miles. To achieve that mark I had kept her going all night, but it was worth it, for it made the step from 40° W to 30° W the briefest of the whole countdown: only nine days. In comparison, the first step, from 71° W to 60° W, had taken sixteen days; the second step, to 50° W, had taken twelve days, and the third step, to 40° W, had taken thirteen days. (The next two ten-degree steps in the countdown were to take, in succession, eleven days and twelve days; and the last step, a five-degree hop, was to take five days.) By July 18th, too, we had moved along more than four degrees in the ten-degree countup from 40° N to 50° N.

Three days later, in the early afternoon of Wednesday, July 21st, we were becalmed for several hours. I lowered the sails, secured the boom in the boom crutch and sat in the cockpit, leaning back against the aft end of the cabin, resting and thinking. The ocean in a dead calm must be the quietest place on earth. Not a sound was to be heard except that of my own breathing. There were no birds to be seen or heard, and no chuckling of ripples against the lapstrakes of the hull, for there were no ripples. The ocean was flat and round like a gigantic blue coin, and it was as silent as a motionless penny. The scene was eerie and yet so peaceful, so soothing, so soul-refreshing. I revelled in it. It seemed almost as though I had achieved the blessings of the Buddhist's nirvana, the Moslem's paradise and the Christian's heaven without having gone through the qualifying preliminary travail. I was fortunate indeed.

At about five o'clock a westerly breeze started to blow, and the sea's surface stirred as if it were a counterpane on the bed of a sleeping giant. I didn't feel the breeze right away; I heard it first, or rather, I heard the breaking wavelets it caused. When the little breakers approached to within half a mile (or maybe it was closer than that), they sounded—amid that vast stillness—like lions roaring. My ears made them seem frightening, but my eyes told me they weren't worth worrying about.

Soon the breeze reached us and with it the midget breakers. The usual sounds of the sea resumed; the chuckling, gurgling, sloshing, hissing, bubbling that had grown so familiar in the weeks since we had slipped out of Vineyard Sound. I hoisted the sails and we got under way again.

Observed from the high deck of a liner, the sea had seemed rather drab and monotonous; nothing but unbroken stretches of water and sky divided by the horizon. But on board *Tinkerbelle*, down close to the water, the sea became immensely more interesting; first, because of the seemingly infinite variety of wind, wave and sky combinations and, second, because down low it was easy to see things in and on the water that could seldom be seen by anyone from a fast-moving ship.

The waves, of course, were formed by the wind; and their size depended on the force of the wind, the length of time it had been blowing in a given direction and the distance it had travelled over the sea during that time. A moderate westerly wind blowing for, say, four hours over a hundred miles of ocean might start six-foot waves marching eastward. This, for *Tinkerbelle,* meant a relatively uncomplicated run before the wind; enlivened, perhaps, by some surfboarding down the forward slopes of the waves. Good enough. But now imagine the wind backing forty-five degrees into the southwest and starting other waves marching northeastward. This sort of change occurred frequently and kept things from getting dull, since the two different sets of waves periodically got into step, reinforcing one another and producing waves considerably bigger than those that came before or after. That was why, so often, bigger-than-average waves came in definite cycles, with smaller waves in between. Then, gradually, as the original waves lost their energy and subsided into swells, the newer waves grew and, if the wind continued blowing from the same direction long enough, erased all traces of the earlier waves.

But this was just the beginning of the possible variations. Sometimes eastward-moving waves met platoons of northward-moving cross-waves or even northwestward-moving waves. Sometimes a gentle northwesterly breeze pushed *Tinkerbelle* north-eastward while the waves, marching out of the southeast, moved directly against the breeze. Sometimes the swells moved in one direction, the waves in another and the wind in still another. And once, unforgettably, *Tinkerbelle* was becalmed in the midst of rows of steep swells moving south while other equally steep swells moved north. As these opposing ranks of swells met, they shot up into sharp peaks that made our presence among them interesting, to say the least.

On another occasion *Tinkerbelle* was ghosting along before a very light westerly breeze, against big swells coming towards her from the east. Each swell was so big that it pushed a great mass of air in front of it, creating a breeze in opposition to the light westerly. And that produced a maddening afternoon of sailing for me. *Tinkerbelle*'s mains'l was swung out to starboard to catch the light westerly, but when a swell came along, the breeze it made backwinded the sail and sent the boom flying towards my head. As the swell moved astern, the gentle westerly took hold of the mains'l and pushed the boom back out to starboard. And then, of course, along came another swell with another counter-breeze to shoot the boom at my head again. It went on like that for four or five hours, during which I got a number of nasty knocks on the noggin.

There was no need to worry about *Tinkerbelle*'s relationship to the waves as long as there were no breaking crests. As the waves grew, they broke, first, in a gentle, sliding manner which allowed the foam of the crests to remain on the rear slopes of the waves; but then, as they grew bigger still, they broke with a definite curling forward which made the crests fall and thunder down the front surfaces of the waves. When the waves began to break in this forward-curling way, *Tinkerbelle* had to watch her step. And when the breakers got too big to sail among safely—usually when the wind was blowing at thirty-five knots or more—she had to be tethered to her bucket drogue to keep her headed straight toward them, so as to take them bow on.

The waves we encountered always seemed to be perfectly straightforward creations of the wind. Even the complicated patterns of waves, cross-waves and counter-cross-waves were born of the wind, and the steps in their genesis usually could be deduced from observation of their behaviour. We never, that I know of, encountered 'freak' or tidal waves one hears about occasionally, which are caused by undersea earthquakes or similar disturbances; but we did meet, fairly frequently, a peculiar type of wave that differed markedly from its fellows in deportment. We'd be moving along at a brisk pace, minding our own business (I, paying no attention whatever to the waves which were approaching, say, from the starboard quarter), when all of a sudden a chunk of frothing wave top the size of four basketballs would break off from a whitecap and come charging diagonally across the established path of the waves and give *Tinkerbelle* an impudent swat on her behind as though chastising her for some sort of misconduct. Or maybe they were love pats; I never did really decide which. Anyway, *Tinkerbelle* got a lot of them.

Besides the variations produced by winds and waves, the expressions of the sea's face were constantly being altered by changes in the sky. When the sky was an inverted bowl of translucent blue, unblemished by a single cloud, the sea, too, was a brilliant blue; deep, rich, so saturated with azure pigmentation it seemed as though *Tinkerbelle*'s white hull would be stained. At the other extreme, when the sky was blotted out by grey clouds, the sea also was grey, gloomy, foreboding. There were numberless variations between these extremes, of course, and the clouds themselves—cumulus, stratus, cumulo-nimbus, alto-cumulus and cirrus, varying in shape, extent and degrees of darkness—added a whole new set of possible combinations to keep the sea environment from becoming dull. No two days were exactly the same.

Sometimes cumulus clouds lay in banks right on the surface of the ocean, making it look as if they marked a nearby shoreline. At other times they spaced themselves in tiny clumps that made the sky look as if it were polka-dotted with cotton balls. And at still other times they grouped themselves in huge, miles-long canopies that took hours to pass by. I remember one of these gigantic canopies that passed overhead. *Tinkerbelle* and I had been sailing under it all day and then, shortly before sunset, I looked back and there was its end a few miles astern, with clear, blue sky beyond. It was delightful to watch the sharp, trailing edge of that cloud blanket pass over us and move on ahead, leaving us under a cobalt dome with golden sunlight cavorting on a pathway to the west. It was like coming out of a cave into the daylight.

Objects I saw in and on the sea also helped to keep the trip from becoming tedious. I saw whale, dolphin, dorado, sharks, tuna, storm petrels, shearwaters, terns, flying fish, gulfweed, and a sea worm, which I have already mentioned. In addition, I saw odd, translucent things drifting through the water, just below the surface, some of them rectangular, like shoe boxes, but about half that size. Each one of these had a bright orange patch on one side that, I guessed, could luminesce. And I saw countless Portuguese men-of-war.

I began seeing the Portuguese men-of-war as soon as we got into the Gulf Stream and kept on seeing them almost all the way across the ocean, although the nearer we got to England the smaller and scarcer they became. They were most numerous in the area between 40° W and 20° W. While in this part of the ocean, I amused myself one afternoon by counting those I met; I spotted thirty in half an hour. Since I saw one a minute in the narrow strip of sea through which we were travelling, the total number must have been fantastically large, probably well into the millions.

The Portuguese man-of-war is a strange-looking creature (some experts say it is three creatures) with a transparent elongated balloon float, surmounted by a sail-like crest, showing above water; and with long, evil-looking tentacles dangling below it, sometimes to a depth of three or more feet. The floats of a few I saw were almost colourless, but most of them were pale blue, and some of these blue ones had violet-tinted sails. They were pretty but, as I found out, painful.

I awoke one morning to find a Portuguese man-of-war entangled in a jib sheet that had been trailing in the water through the night. When I pulled the sheet on board, some of the man-of-war's tentacles clung to it, without my knowledge, and I touched them. They caused a pain very much like a bee sting and soon red welts appeared on my fingers. I had read that anyone heavily stung by a man-of-war would be lucky to survive and, after having suffered one small sting, I could well believe it. I henceforth made sure trailing sheets were free of tentacles before I handled them.

Once we were moving slowly before a gentle breeze and I noticed that many of the Portuguese men-of-war we passed had small fish, five or six inches long, hovering under them and that some of these fish left the men-of-war and took up new positions under *Tinkerbelle*. Before the day was out, my craft had a troop of more than a dozen fish accompanying her. I suppose they felt *Tinkerbelle*'s red bottom would scare off bigger fish that might otherwise be tempted to gobble them up. I was glad to let *Tinkerbelle* watch over them as long as the breeze was gentle and we couldn't go any faster, but the next day the wind picked up and we had to leave the little fish behind. I imagine they found other men-of-war with which to hobnob.

Besides living things, there were interesting inanimate objects to see in mid-ocean. An empty fifty-gallon oil drum sped by one day before a strong southeasterly wind. I also saw drifting mooring buoys, gasoline cans, glass fish-net floats, and planks, beams and tree trunks of varying sizes, all heavily encrusted with gooseneck barnacles. I came across pieces of orange-red fish net, too, the same sort of net I saw later on trawlers in England. But the most surprising non-living thing I bumped into was an electric light bulb. It was bobbing through the waves, buoyant as you please, untroubled by the breakers and seemingly capable

of continuing indefinitely. Only the Lord knew how long it had
been afloat and how many storms it had survived, but I'll wager
it had been through more than one.

Well, I thought, that ought to prove something about the
strength and safety of small boats too.

While I was still becalmed on July 21st, I saw three ships, two
of them at the same time. It was the first time I'd had more than
one ship in sight since June 6th when I had seen the Russian
trawlers. 'Made the spot seem like Times Square,' I wrote in the
log.

One of the ships came up over the eastern horizon headed
straight for us, moving at full speed on an unwavering course.
I was beginning to think it didn't see us and that I had better
dive into the water and swim for my life when it finally swerved
off to port and passed with no more than twenty-five yards'
clearance. It had a hammer and sickle emblem on its funnel, so it
was Russian; and on the stern was its name, *Neptun*. There
wasn't a single person to be seen on deck, but just after it passed,
someone, possibly the captain, came out on the port wing of the
bridge and studied us through binoculars. I'd have given more
than a penny for his thoughts. Then the ship disappeared over
the western horizon as speedily as it had approached from the
east.

That night I was sailing along happily when suddenly I saw
a phosphorescent streak in the water headed directly toward
Tinkerbelle. Startled out of my wits, I thought, Lummy! We're
being torpedoed! But almost at once, of course, I realized that
was ridiculous. Nevertheless, I half shut my eyes and held my
breath, bracing myself for the impact of whatever it was against
the boat. But none came. A few seconds later I heard a peculiar
popping and the sound of air being expelled. That gave the show
away. The torpedo was a dolphin.

Several other times, later on, I saw these luminous streaks in
the water and they never failed to excite me. Dolphin visited us
frequently, both day and night, but they never stayed with us
for long. I think their longest visit lasted all of thirty seconds.
Tinkerbelle was just too slow to be interesting to dolphin, so

they'd swim circles around her for a few seconds and then off they'd race about their own high-speed affairs.

The wind was so strong all day Thursday, July 22nd, that I kept the boat hitched to the sea anchor while I remained snug inside the cabin. I relaxed, did a few maintenance jobs and listened to the radio. In addition to the BBC and the other stations I've already mentioned, I began to get a station in Lisbon, Portugal, regularly, and a delightful place in Holland that called itself 'The Happy Station'.

On Friday (July 23rd) the wind was still blowing hard and I was sure many of the waves were twenty-footers, equal to the largest waves we had met, but we started sailing anyway because I was determined to reach Falmouth, if I possibly could, by August 15th. It was wet going; I was soaked from the waist down, in spite of the anti-exposure suit I wore, but nothing untoward happened. There were no knockdowns or other crises.

The weather was cloudy, with scattered rain squalls to contend with, but nothing more serious than that. I remember I felt extremely pleased with *Tinkerbelle* and with myself when we managed to manœuvre between two squalls, thus avoiding the rain they were dropping on to the sea.

The twenty-fourth was a beautiful, sunny day, with fluffy white clouds in the sky and a breeze of just the right strength. Then on the twenty-fifth the weather about-faced, as it did so often during the voyage. Here's what I put into the log:

'Overslept just a bit this morning. Didn't hear the alarm. It's now 6 a.m. *Tinkerbelle* time.

The wind and waves seem O.K. for sailing, but it's a dismal, cloudy day. (Barometer's up, though.) The weather sure has pulled a switch.'

Just before sunset the sky cleared and that evening I logged this:

'Soon after it cleared, the wind died out for a bit, then shifted to the west for about an hour, still very light. Then it shifted to southwest, closer to south than west, and picked up in force. The sky stayed clear most of the night and it was very pleasant sailing.

The wind was just right, strong enough to move us at a good rate, but not so strong as to make me nervous. I spent almost all night listening to the BBC. I heard a fine discussion on acting by Noel Coward, a moving essay (with sound effects) on the seasons in Britain, news, music and commentaries.'

During the first half of the voyage I hadn't used the radio for much besides getting the time signals since I didn't want to exhaust the batteries too swiftly (although I carried three sets of spare batteries). But in the second half of the trip, when I found the batteries were holding up extremely well, I spent many hours listening. The sound of voices helped to soften the aches of loneliness that occasionally wrenched my inner being.

July 26th (Monday) was a cloudy, gloomy day and at about 2 p.m. the wind grew so strong we had to heave to. The next day started out even worse, for in addition to being cloudy the wind shifted to northeast, exactly the direction in which I wanted to go. We'd have to beat against it. I wrote:

'The day began cold, cloudy and miserable. I'm afraid I was quite depressed. It got very foggy later on.

I forced myself to pull in the sea anchor and get going.

And then, about 9 or 10 a.m. (T.T.), a remarkable thing happened. All the fog and clouds disappeared. And *Tinkerbelle* and I had a day of restful, easy sailing under a blue sky and on a blue ocean.

Took the opportunity to dry clothes and towels. My spirits rose again to normal and above.'

This type of mood change occurred about half a dozen times during the journey. Cloudy and adverse weather, or other setbacks, would get me into a state of melancholy and then, just as my spirits hit bottom, along would come a magnificent, sunny day of fine sailing that made me the happiest, luckiest man alive.

July 28th (Wednesday) was memorable for three events. I described the first of these in the log like this:

'This has been quite a day. Started sailing with just the jib because the following waves were pretty big and the wind quite strong. But I didn't get much speed with just the jib, so I decided to add the reefed mains'l. That was a mistake, under the conditions. We started surfing down the forward slopes of the bigger waves and then, while doing this, we broached and I got knocked overboard for the sixth time.

That wasn't so bad. I climbed back on board very quickly. But when I went over I was holding the tiller and the "axle" part of the rudder fitting was badly bent. [I held fast to the tiller because I wasn't wearing a lifeline and didn't want to risk being separated from *Tinkerbelle*.] Luckily, though, I had brought along a spare "axle" and I put it into place without the loss of much time.'

The second memorable incident occurred immediately after the rudder had been repaired, before we got under way again. I'm embarrassed to admit it, but in the interests of making this an absolutely true account of *Tinkerbelle*'s voyage I'd better do so. The painful fact is that while I was moving about the deck, preparing to resume sailing, I lost my balance and simply fell overboard with a great splash. I came to the surface, furious at myself for being so clumsy, but by then, of course, it was too late.

The third big event of the day was recorded thus in the log: 'I was breezing along between 23° W and 22° W in the late afternoon and happened to look back and there was a big freighter hot on my heels. It was the S.S. *Bischofstor* of Bremen.

I waved as it passed and got a lot of waves back. Someone inquired if I was all right and I assured him I was.'

The ship didn't stop, as I was in no need of assistance, and soon was out of sight. I was thankful that it hadn't passed by any earlier, for it might then have witnessed my ignominious fall into the sea. My clothes were still sopping when it went by. An hour or so later, when I stopped for dinner and the evening sun shot, I got into relatively dry clothes.

Some weeks after the voyage was completed, I got the *Bischofstor*'s side of the story of our meeting in a letter from Lothar Steinhoff, third mate of the 8,487-ton vessel. He wrote:

'We had been at sea for 11 days, coming from Tampa, Florida, and bound for Rotterdam with 11,000 tons of phosphate. For the crew and passengers of the ship the 28th of July, 1965, will ever be unforgettable. The sky was overcast and poor visibility made navigation very difficult. According to our log-book, the sea was smooth; we noted veering westerly winds of Force 2. A sharp lookout was necessary because of the misty weather.

At about 1800 G.M.T. [Greenwich Mean Time] the visibility became better. At 1830 G.M.T. a very small object was sighted on our portside. It looked like a buoy. Our true course was 75° and the estimated position 47° 14′ N, 22° 37′ W.

Capt. [Wilhelm] Beck altered course to approach as near as possible. Some minutes later at about 1840 G.M.T. we were surprised to make out a small red sail, which we thought must belong to a lifeboat; so we got ready to save shipwrecked persons. But then we noticed it wasn't a lifeboat, but a very small sailing boat, with what was probably a one-man crew. It was certainly a memorable occasion for us.

Capt. Beck asked the lonely man if he needed help. With gestures he indicated to us that all was well. So we continued our voyage, and at 1913 G.M.T. we notified Portishead Radio [in England] of the sighting.'

Tinkerbelle was about seven hundred and fifty miles off Land's End, the westernmost tip of England, when she met the *Bischof-stor*. Two-thirds of her voyage was behind her. Before much longer it would be over.

The next day, July 29th, we met another ship. This is how its master, Captain Olav Viken, described the meeting in a letter to me:

'Our meeting was at 47° 30′ N, 22° 00′ W.

When I saw your boat I thought it must be a lifeboat, so we changed our course about 90° to see if assistance was needed. When we found out that you needed no help I wired Rogaland Radio about our meeting and it said it would ask other ships in the area to keep an eye open for you. That was our duty.

We were on a voyage from Liverpool to Hamilton, Bermuda, and Nassau, in the Great Bahamas, with a general cargo.'

Captain Viken's ship was the 9,350-ton M.S. *Vardal* of Haugesund, Norway. It passed *Tinkerbelle* to starboard, going southwest. I thought it had disappeared over the horizon, but a little later I looked around and there it was steaming directly towards us. It had finally spotted us and had doubled back on its course to make sure everything was all right. Captain Viken certainly lived up to the very best traditions of the sea in going to all that trouble to make sure I was O.K. I appreciated what he did, and what Captain Beck of the *Bischofstor* did, more than I can say, for it meant loss of valuable time for both of them.

Two days later I wrote in the log:

'Seems like every time my morale sags sharply and I begin to feel I've "had it" a good day comes along to put me on my feet again. Today [Saturday, July 31st] was such a day.'

We had a marvellous sail and, to make this last day of our second month at sea even better, we passed to the east of the meridian of 20° W, completing another stride in the countdown to England. Falmouth was only fifteen degrees away.

I had hoped to continue sailing all that night, but at about 1 a.m., Sunday, August 1st, a thunderstorm hit us. I streamed the drogue and, buttoning *Tinkerbelle* up tight, got into the cabin out of the blustery, wet weather. All that day and through the night we remained parked to the drogue. It was comfortable enough inside, away from the wind and rain, but it was nerve-racking to have to stay put when I wanted so much to be moving and end our long voyage. And the whitecaps that slapped the boat every now and then didn't add to my peace of mind.

To help pass the time I decided to launch a bottle with a note inside, just for the fun of seeing if anyone found it. I wrote this message:

'To the finder: This bottle is being released in the Atlantic Ocean at about 48° 30' N, 19° 10' W on Aug. 1, 1965.

If you will send this message with your name and address—with information on where you found the bottle and when—to Robert Manry, 31003 Royalview Drive, Willowick, Ohio, U.S.A.—he will send you $5 to compensate you for the trouble. Thank you.'

I put the message in an empty plastic bottle that had contained part of my supply of drinking water, screwed on the cap and tossed it into the ocean. It floated so high in the water that the northwest wind got a good grip on it and blew it rapidly into the southeast. It was soon out of sight.

Two months later, after completing the voyage, I was back at my home in Willowick and had forgotten all about the message and bottle, when a letter came from Francisco Maria Baleizao, a resident of a suburban town near Lisbon, Portugal. The letter, in difficult English, said:

'Dear Sir: I find your message on 25th September at three o'clock p.m. in Praia Grande Beach, Sintra, Portugal. I wait, then you send me $5 to compensate. Thank you.'

My message, tattered now, apparently from the beating it had received as the bottle in which it travelled rolled over and over on its way to Portugal, was enclosed with Mr. Baleizao's letter. I was surprised and delighted to receive both. The five dollars I had promised and a ten-dollar bonus were on their way to him in short order, and in a subsequent letter, written in Portuguese, he told me a little about himself.

'I was born in a picturesque village of Baixo Alentejo called Moura, on March 27, 1925,' he wrote. 'I resided there until the age of twenty, but because of the poverty of the area I moved into the surroundings of Lisbon, where I have been for the last twenty years. I am a mason by profession. I am married and my wife's name is Gracindo Pechoso Baleizao. I like all sports, but like bicycle racing best. However, I practice none of them. My parents lived in the Hawaiian Islands close to seven years.'

I was pleased that my message was found, but especially pleased that it was found by a man who apparently could use the token reward I offered. I was happy, too, that it was found by a Portuguese because some of the world's greatest seamen have come from Portugal: Prince Henry the Navigator, the stern bachelor who, although he never sailed himself, founded Europe's first school of navigation and sponsored numerous voyages of discovery; Bartholomew Diaz, discoverer of the Cape of Good Hope; Vasco da Gama, who, following on Diaz's heels, reached the riches of India, and, naturally, Ferdinand Magellan, whose fleet was the first to circle the globe.

In the evening of Friday, August 6th, six days after releasing the bottled note, I wrote in the log:

'This was a nice sailing day—sunny, with fluffy clouds. I can hardly believe I'm getting all this good weather. It's quite a switch. Hope it continues.

We're about halfway to 14° W (it's now 6 p.m. T.T.). I've just finished a huge supper of curried turkey and peas. I'll go on sailing until it starts getting dark. Then I'll size things up and decide whether to stop for sleep or go on all night. This good weather should be used to the fullest.

I hadn't seen a ship for days and, of course, thought I was miles from the shipping lanes, which I was. But about 5 p.m. I began hearing a sound that I at first thought was a plane. Then I looked around and saw it was a ship, almost on top of me. It was Italian, the *Sirio* of Palermo.

It went by awfully close and fast. I was afraid the bow and stern waves might tip us over, but we rode them all right. The crew at the rail gave us a hearty cheer and, as usual, snapped our picture.

I continued all night. Saw about five more ships. They're getting thick.'

Later I heard from Livio de Manzolini, master of the M.S. *Sirio,* which was bound for London from Vera Cruz, Mexico. He wrote, in part:

'At 1630 hours [on August 6th] we met your boat in latitude 49° 12′ N and longitude 14° 16′ W.

You didn't notice our vessel approaching, but when we got close you turned around and saw us. And when we drew abreast of you, you waved to us as if an encounter such as ours was perfectly normal.

When I saw that you didn't need help, I continued my course supposing that you were one of those men who are compelled to cross the Atlantic Ocean alone. . . . I telegraphed the English Coast Guard your position.'

My thanks to Captain Manzolini for reporting my position and for his kind concern.

On Sunday, August 8th, two days after our meeting with the *Sirio,* we met another ship, the 556-foot, 18,000-ton tanker *Belgulf Glory,* of Antwerp, probably the largest ship we spoke to on the whole voyage. And the meeting was one of the most memorable.

Tinkerbelle

The big ship, skippered by Captain Emile J. A. Sart, was on its way from Port Arthur, Texas, to London, when it overtook *Tinkerbelle* at 12.30 G.M.T. at 49° 30′ N and 12° 45′ W, about three hundred miles west of the English coast. Captain Sart, an extremely friendly man with a wonderfully jovial face, stopped his vessel and hailed me through an electronic megaphone.

'Are you American?' he asked.

'Yes.'

'What is your name?'

'My name is Robert Manry, M-A-N-R-Y. I've come from Massachusetts.'

'Where are you bound?'

'Falmouth, England.'

The captain said he had heard on a BBC news programme the day before that planes of the Royal Air Force had been searching for me, but I couldn't believe that was true because, according to the voyage plan I had filed with both the American and the English Coast Guards, I wouldn't be considered overdue until after August 15th. So I'm sorry to say I disagreed with the good captain.

'I don't think they're looking for me,' I said. 'They may be looking for another man who left Florida in a twelve-foot boat a week before I left Massachusetts. He was headed for Ireland.'

I was referring to Captain William Verity, master of the diminutive *Nonoalca* (a Mayan word meaning 'mute ones' or 'those who don't speak our tongue'), who had hoped his voyage would help to prove that Irish monks came to North and South America in the fifth and sixth centuries. I found out later that Captain Verity had been plagued by bad luck and had had to abandon his projected cruise, at least for the time being.

'Do you need any provisions?' Captain Sart called across the ten yards of water between us.

'No, I really don't need anything,' I shouted back. But I could see he already had the food there on deck and might be disappointed if I refused to take it, so I added, 'But I sure could use some fresh fruit.'

The food was sealed in plastic bags and these were then secured in a larger canvas bag, which, in turn, was tied into a life jacket to keep it afloat. One end of a heaving line was thrown to me and the other end was tied to the food parcel, which was then lowered into the ocean. I soon had it aboard and was inspecting its contents. Captain Sart had given me a banquet, the entrée of which was still hot from the oven: a whole roast chicken and potato croquettes (Poulet Rôti and Pommes Croquettes from the ship's officers' Sunday menu). The bag also contained a huge loaf of freshly baked bread, apples, plums, lemons, a pound of Dutch butter, a huge slab of chocolate with nuts in it, two cans of a soft drink and two bottles of beer.

I had to eat the chicken and the potato right away because there was no refrigeration on *Tinkerbelle*. And what a meal it was! I was more stuffed than the turkey at our family's last Thanksgiving dinner. It was extremely generous of the captain to give me all that food, I appreciated it immensely, but I couldn't help worrying that maybe one of the *Belgulf Glory*'s officers didn't get enough to eat at dinner that day because of the captain's kindness to me. I sincerely hope not.

Even with its engines stopped, the tanker moved too fast for *Tinkerbelle* and soon was beyond shouting range. So it circled around and moved by again, and, after that, two more times; and each time it passed we got in a little more conversation. Captain Sart was extremely considerate.

'Is everything all right?' he asked again as his ship passed by the fourth time. 'Do you need anything more?'

'No, I'm fine. Thank you very much,' I said. 'Thanks for the marvellous banquet.'

The *Belgulf Glory*, chivalrous ship that it was, dipped its flag in salute as it returned to its eastward course, and then it gave *Tinkerbelle* and me a salute of three blasts on its deep steam whistle. I had no flag flying with which to return the dip, unfortunately, but I was able to return the big ship's whistle blasts with my small gas-operated foghorn. I let loose three gas screams that made the hair on my head vibrate but which, to those on the *Belgulf Glory*, must have sounded like the peeps of a baby chicken.

The hefty tanker churned off towards the English Channel and I followed after it as fast as *Tinkerbelle* would go. We took the course Captain Sart had given to reach Bishop Rock: 85°. I had one hand firmly on the tiller and the other on the chicken dinner. It was an unforgettable experience.

The captain later sent me a Christmas card and his best wishes. He said he was spending a brief holiday leave with his wife and two children at their home in Belgium; it was only the fourth Christmas he had been able to enjoy with them in the last thirty years.

Events began to move swiftly after the meeting with Captain Sart and the *Belgulf Glory*. About 5 p.m. (T.T.) that same day, an R.A.F. Shackleton bomber found us (aided, no doubt, by a position report radioed by the *Belgulf Glory* to Lloyd's of London). It was flying quite low, under a layer of dark clouds, when the pilot spotted *Tinkerbelle*'s red sail and headed straight for us. It roared by overhead, circled and then roared by twice more, and each time I waved. On the next pass it came toward us very low, so low I thought it might clip off the tip of *Tinkerbelle*'s mast; but it didn't, luckily. Instead it dropped two bright orange cylindrical canisters tied together with a buoyant line.

I sailed over and pulled the canisters aboard. They contained a wonderful supply of fruit, apples and bananas, and a very friendly message from Wing Commander R. A. Carson of the 42nd Squadron of the R.A.F. based at St. Mawgan, Cornwall, not far from Falmouth, our destination. The message said:

'Welcome to British waters! You are "big news" and we shall be bringing gentlemen of the press to see you tomorrow, 9th Aug.—at approx. noon. Your present position is: 4845N 1220W. Good luck.'

It was great to be welcomed so warmly to British waters by the R.A.F. Commander Carson's greeting was a wonderfully gracious gesture; but the thought of being 'big news' and meeting gentlemen of the press gave me more than a moment of trepidation. As I tried to cope with that, the big four-engined plane zoomed towards us again and I gave it the hands-clasped-over-the-head salute as it swept by so close I could make out every detail of its construction. (Those R.A.F. chaps are great fliers.)

That night after dinner, as I sat in *Tinkerbelle*'s cabin listening to a Voice of America news broadcast in French, the plot thickened dramatically. I was taken aback when I heard the announcer say something about Robert Manry, *navigateur solitaire*, and then some stuff that went too fast for me, with my high-school French, to comprehend. But the newscast was repeated in English a few minutes later, and that *really* bowled me over. It told practically all there was to tell about me and *Tinkerbelle* and our voyage. I couldn't imagine where the Voice of America had got all that information, or why it was interested in the first place. Somebody on shore must be doing a lot of talking, I decided, and the circumstantial evidence seemed to point to Virginia. But I knew she wouldn't be talking unless she was being asked questions; so it seemed probable that the V.O.A. had heard of the voyage and had questioned Virginia about it. However the V.O.A. wouldn't have heard about it unless the *Plain Dealer* had run a story on it that the Associated Press had picked up and put on its wires. The *P.D.* was apparently more interested in the voyage than I had thought it was. And the reports from the V.O.A. and the R.A.F. seemed to indicate that other papers, beside the *P.D.*, were interested.

I hove to about midnight for some sleep and got up early the next morning, ate a quick breakfast and got moving again. The wind was just a few degrees south of due east, which made it impossible to steer directly toward Bishop Rock, on a course of 85°. The best we could do was about 57°, which meant we were moving northward of the direct course. So, at about 11 a.m. (T.T.), I went over on to the port tack to regain our southing.

Not long afterwards I saw a trawler approaching from the south on a course that would bring us within hailing distance and I wondered what nationality it was and whether it would stop to exchange a few words. When it got closer, it became apparent that it was steering to meet us rather than just to pass by. It turned out to be English, the *Roseland* of Penzance, the port west of Falmouth and not far from Land's End, and standing at the rail was a man in a handsome turtle-neck sweater whose face looked vaguely familiar. And behind him stood another man who was operating what I took to be a motion-picture camera.

Gradually it dawned on me where I'd seen the face of the man in the sweater before; it was on the screen of our television receiver at home. Now I knew it; he was a TV newsman. I had heard his broadcasts hundreds of times, but at the moment I couldn't remember his name. And I couldn't imagine what he was doing there; surely he hadn't travelled all the way from Cleveland to see *me*. Undoubtedly he was there for some other reason and happened to bump into me by chance. But, incredibly, he said he really was looking for me and no one else.

That made our meeting what might be termed 'an occasion'. All my instincts told me that now was the time for me to say something genuinely profound, something that would ricochet endlessly down the corridors of history, something with the adroitness, depth and impact of, say, 'Dr. Livingstone, I presume.' But all I could think of was, 'Haven't I seen you somewhere before?'

The man finally had to tell me his name, but he took my mental lapse with good grace. He was Bill Jorgensen of Cleveland's Scripps-Howard Station WEWS, and the cameraman with him was Walter Glendenning. They had been cruising about on the *Roseland* for about thirty-five hours, looking for me. The spot where we met was roughly two hundred and seventy miles from Land's End.

As soon as I realized whom I was talking with, a question of newspaper ethics arose in my mind. Could I in good conscience report details of my trip to these men from WEWS, a competitor of my employer, the *Plain Dealer*? Well, I reasoned, the WEWS men are apparently very interested in the voyage, so interested they have gone to enormous lengths and expense to find me, so I think I should tell them whatever they want to know. I felt this way especially when I recalled that the *Plain Dealer* and national magazines I had queried before my departure (all of them at that time believing, because of what I had told them, that

I was going on the voyage with another man in a 25-foot boat) had expressed only mild interest in printing stories about the venture. I'll have to acknowledge, frankly, that I didn't think *Tinkerbelle*'s smaller size would make much difference in the interest shown by the *P.D.* or other newspapers or the magazines. It's painful for me to have to admit it now, because my experience should have developed a keener insight into what makes news, but I failed to assess properly the news value of my own story. And this failure probably was the greatest miscalculation of the entire expedition. I'm afraid it brands me as somewhat less than perfect as a newsman.

So I spoke freely with Jorgensen; in fact, we talked steadily for three and a half hours while Glendenning took both movies and still pictures. It was good to see a familiar face, at last. That made it seem as though I was actually approaching the end of the voyage. And Captain Victor Watling, skipper of the *Roseland*, and his crew were most kind to me. They gave me some delicious apples and some wonderful, fresh hot coffee, the best I'd had since leaving Massachusetts. The captain also gave me a position report and a tide table that proved invaluable as *Tinkerbelle* and I approached the coast of England.

During our conversation Jorgensen showed me a copy of the Falmouth *Packet* dated August 6th, and right there on the front page was a story that nearly floored me. It said:

'A hero's welcome awaits 47-year-old American newspaperman Robert Manry, when he sails his tiny boat *Tinkerbelle* into Falmouth Harbour, a few days from now, at the end of his epic single-handed Atlantic crossing from Falmouth, Massachusetts.

For nearly 70 days, since he set sail on June 1, Bob Manry has braved the elements, mastering loneliness and enduring as-yet-untold discomforts, because of the cramped conditions aboard *Tinkerbelle*, to make his dream of an Atlantic crossing come true.

Yesterday newspaper reporters and cameramen from the United States flew into Falmouth to join those of the British press and international news agencies already in town ready to record the scenes as Manry completes his 3,200-mile crossing at Custom House Quay.'

Tinkerbelle

There was more to the story and there were even two pictures: a drawing of me and a photograph of *Tinkerbelle* that could only have been taken from the deck of one of the ships we met along the way. How the Falmouth *Packet* happened to have either or both was more than a little puzzling.

A 'hero's welcome!' What on earth was building up there in Falmouth? All I could say to Jorgensen after reading the first three paragraphs of the story was 'My goodness! Boy, oh, Boy!'

Finally we talked ourselves out and it was time to go our separate ways. Jorgensen and Glendenning, who had been my guests aboard *Tinkerbelle*, scrambled back on to the *Roseland*, which then headed back towards Penzance. The breeze was very light, so *Tinkerbelle* and I were soon left far behind.

A few minutes before the *Roseland* departed, the R.A.F. returned, as it had said it would, presumably with the 'gentlemen of the press'. This time there were two Shackletons and a third, twin-engine civilian plane that flew very fast and low, passing over us again and again, while the four-engine bombers circled on a broad radius. After the civilian plane had flown over about eight times, it sped away and one of the Shackletons came in low, just above masthead height. Then it wheeled and came back, this time dropping two brightly coloured canisters, like those that had been dropped the day before. The R.A.F. fliers must have been using their fancy bombsight for dropping the canisters because they wound up in the water no more than ten yards away and directly in front of us. *Tinkerbelle* didn't have to change course a single degree to enable me to pick them up. The drop and pickup went like clockwork.

The first canister contained a bunch of English newspapers, no doubt so that I could catch up on the news I had missed while out at sea. I was glad to have them. Then I opened the second canister. It had another huge supply of fruit inside—oranges this time. The way things were going, I'd reach England with more food than I'd had at the start of the voyage. The gifts from the R.A.F., added to what Captain Sart of the *Belgulf Glory* and Captain Watling of the *Roseland* had given me, nearly filled the cabin. It had never been so crammed.

Also in the second canister were three notes. The first one said:

'Your position this time: 50° 12′ N, 12° 17′ W—with the compliments and best wishes of No. 42 Squadron, Royal Air Force—Coastal Command—St. Mawgan, Cornwall.'

It sure was nice of those R.A.F. fellows to keep track of my position for me; made me feel pretty secure. I knew I wouldn't get into trouble with them there, shepherding me along.

The second note was a blockbuster. When I read it, the recoil nearly knocked me out of the boat. It said:

'Bob—we're waiting for you in Falmouth with Virginia and your children. Dangerous to sail in at night. This harbour is jammed with traffic. . . .

You will see our boat somewhere out of Falmouth. Virginia and the children will be aboard with us. . . .

Keep sailing. Good luck, God bless you, and we'll see you soon.'

The note was signed by Bill Ashbolt, George Barmann and Russ Kane, three men from the *Plain Dealer*.

The news that Virginia and the children were in Falmouth was a real bombshell. I was simply overjoyed, almost delirious with happiness. And oh, how I wanted to get into the harbour quickly and meet my family. It had been a long time since we had been together—a long, long time.

It turned out that the third note was from Virginia herself. She wrote:

'Dearest Robert—Just think, in a very few days I'll be seeing you.

The *Plain Dealer* has sent us all over and we've been here since last Friday.

We've been living in luxury like royalty, but we surely do wish you were here. You will be soon.

Lots of love. We'll be in a boat to meet you. Virginia.'

This was so much more wonderful than anything I had dared hope for that I was struck numb. It was just too much to comprehend all at once. I had to take it in little doses to keep from becoming dangerously intoxicated with joy. Virginia and Robin and Douglas were in Falmouth. They were actually there now, at this very moment, waiting for me. Soon we'd all be there together, reunited. It was marvellous, terrific, super—colossal.

And how generous it was of the *Plain Dealer* to arrange it.

Thoughts raced through my mind. That guy Jorgensen! He certainly was a sharp newsman, talking with me for more than three hours and not letting me know that the *P.D.* had three men in Falmouth to cover my arrival or that my family was waiting for me there. Not that I blamed him for keeping mum. In his place I'd have done the same thing because if he'd told me the *P.D.* men and my family were in Falmouth I might not have spilled the whole story of the voyage to him.

He was just being a remarkably enterprising reporter.

William A. Ashbolt, one of the *Plain Dealer* men, was the newspaper's director of news photography; George J. Barmann was a veteran of the paper and one of its ace writers, and Russell W. Kane was an assistant to the publisher and the *P.D.*'s promotion director.

All three men were good friends of mine and I was delighted to know that I would soon be seeing them again—and on the eastern side of the great Western Ocean, as Europeans often called the Atlantic. There was just one little point that worried me: the fact that Russ Kane was the *P.D.*'s promotion director. Did that mean my voyage was going to be turned into a promotional gimmick for the paper? I hoped earnestly, ardently, that was not so; for I had dreamed of the voyage for too long and it meant too much to me to have it spoiled at the end by being transformed into a commercial enterprise. If that's what Russ intended to do, I would oppose him with every resource at my command. But first I'd have to wait and see what he actually *did* intend to do.

16

THE fact that Virginia and Robin and Douglas had got to Falmouth ahead of me, were there now, made it hard to wait to see them and hear all about everything that had happened on shore since May 31st, when I had telephoned home from the Falmouth on Cape Cod to bid them and my mother goodbye. In some ways it seemed like years since then; in other ways it seemed like hours.

Naturally, I didn't hear about the things that had befallen members of my family until after I got to England and was reunited with them. However, this seems to be the appropriate place to tell that part of the story, so I shall do so. What follows is quoted from Virginia's diary, with my comments set off by brackets.

'*Tuesday, June 1*—Today Robert left. He called last night to say goodbye. Next time I hear his voice he will be calling me from Falmouth, England, to say he made it.

Wednesday, June 2—We got up at 6.30 because Nana [my mother, Mrs. James C. Manry] had to catch an early bus home. It was pouring and the freeway was bumper to bumper. Then the bus was half an hour late.

David Losh [one of Robin's classmates] brought a harness for Puff [Douglas's iguana] to wear. While he was telling me about it the phone rang. It was George Barmann of the *Plain Dealer*. Seems they had received Robert's letter telling them he was going alone and they wanted to know the details. George was so excited he had to call back a couple of times for more facts.

Tinkerbelle

Ray Matjasic [a *P.D.* photographer] came and took pictures of us toasting Robert in milk. The kids didn't like all the fuss, but they co-operated. On the 7 o'clock news Bud Dancey told about Robert.

Thursday, June 3—At 7.30 a.m. the *Press* called and asked to use the story. A girl from the *News-Herald* came to interview me.

The phone rang and it was Bill Litzkow of the Falmouth marina [from which I had embarked]. He sounded so concerned and wondered if I had heard from Robert. I said no, and he asked if he could tell anyone now. Bless his heart.

A few more minutes and the phone rang again. It was John Hough of the Falmouth *Enterprise*. He promised to pass on any word he might come by.

Monday, June 7—Just a week ago tonight I said *bon voyage* to my own dear Robert. He's never far away from my thoughts. Just sort of counterpoint to everything I say and do.

Tomorrow is Douglas's birthday. Not much of a celebration without his Dad, but I'll try to make it a nice one.

Robin said today: "People speak about Dad as though he were dead." Won't they be surprised when he turns up 75 days from now, tanned, lean and fit.

The astronauts are back down. I wish Robert were across. I imagine he has begun to miss his nice bed, lumps and all.

I can't seem to accomplish much. Lonesome, I guess.

Friday, June 11—I've been working in the back yard all day. It's 9.30 and I've just crawled out of the tub and now I'm going to rest.

I discovered some little rose bushes sprouting round under the trees. I've weeded around them and I hope they'll grow. I cut the grass and I felt like the Neighbour in Edna St. Vincent Millay's poem: I left "the clover standing, And the Queen Anne's lace!"

Funny the things I remember about Robert and me. While I was mowing around the lovely pink clover I remembered a field near a motel where we had stopped during a vacation trip. We were walking Chris [our German sheep-dog] and the smell of clover brought the whole scene back so clearly. Made me kind of sad.

I cleaned his darkroom yesterday, too, and that brought him near.

Sunday, June 13—Mother and John [Virginia's mother and brother] came today. Mother will stay with me for as long as she can take us. Poor Chris got a walk finally. She pestered John so he took her for a nice long one.

Sunday, June 20—At about 10.15 p.m. the *Plain Dealer* called to tell me the Coast Guard received word from a Canadian freighter [the *Exilona*] that Robert was 500 miles out and needed no assistance. It was wonderful to hear he is all right. He's not making much time, 19 days out, but he will eventually, I'm sure. Perhaps I'll even get a letter next time. I'm glad Mother and John were here when the word came; they are so anxious. Mother is not too fond of boats, but she is being very brave about Robert. Of course, she has confidence in him and that means a lot.

Monday, June 21—Fred [the family cat] seems to like her name even though she is a girl. She got out around 11.15 tonight and we had quite a time rounding her up.

Wednesday, June 23—I couldn't sleep last night. All sorts of visions racing through my head. I do wish we had enough in the bank to take us all to England to meet Robert. That's been my dream for years, to visit England and see all I've read about.

Seems Robert had gone 585 miles instead of 500.

Thursday, June 24—George called to tell me he had been to New York to talk to the captain of the freighter. The captain thinks at his present rate of speed, it will take Robert 91 days to reach England.

Friday, June 25—A quiet day. It's good to have one now and then. Since the excitement began I've had trouble sleeping. I know Robert will be all right, but when the captain said 91 days it conjured up all sorts of pictures. If it took Crapo 51 days, Robert should surely make it in less than 91.

I hope he won't be too annoyed with all the publicity.

Tinkerbelle

I'm planning to go to Pittsburgh for the Fourth of July. I hate being away from home for so long. Chris seems sad to me.

Thursday, July 1—If Robert were on schedule he'd be pretty close to eating his plum pudding. I wish he were halfway there.

Poor Robert, I feel sorry for him, but then he may be enjoying it. [I was, most of the time.]

Paid all our bills today and we're all set for another month, at least.

Sunday, July 4—People are beginning to ask me if we are going to England to meet Robert. They're even talking about having a parade in his honour! I can't imagine him sitting on the back of a car waving. When I asked Robin if she would like to go to England to meet him she said that if she went the kids would think she was stuck-up. I can't imagine why.

Monday, July 5—We're going to Pittsburgh tomorrow. John is coming for me. Douglas is disappointed. He wanted to take his vacation on a bus; says now it won't seem like one. Wish I could take him to England. Robin says she still wouldn't want to go to England because of the kids' attitude.

Wednesday, July 7—John is trying to figure out a way to get me to Cornwall. He keeps giving me guidebooks to read, the rascal. One of them, *Rambles in Cornwall*, calls Falmouth "The Happy Harbour". I surely wish I could be there to meet Robert. Maybe if I wish hard enough I can.

Friday, July 9—We heard from Robert again tonight. Jo Talladino [one of our neighbours] called [to Pittsburgh] to tell me someone had called when she was in our house feeding the menagerie. She said a Mr. Larrick from the Isthmian Lines steamship company telephoned to tell me that the *Steel Vendor* had picked up 10 letters from Robert and that he was about 1,000 miles east of Boston. All was well aboard and he expects to make England about August 15.

Last night before I went to sleep I looked at the full moon and thought that Robert was watching the same moon. I wished on it and said a little prayer that we'd hear from him. My prayer was answered.

Tinkerbelle

Monday, July 12—Today began with a bang. Three letters from Robert for me and two for the children. Then began a struggle between the newspapers as to who should print them. Of course, the *Plain Dealer* is his paper and they deserved first chance.

The family scolded me for permitting even the *Plain Dealer* to use them. As they said, "Dad won't like it a bit." [They were right; I didn't like it.] I hope they don't use the entire letter, parts of it are personal. [They used the whole thing.] I should have typed out a passage and made them settle for that.

Robin was interviewed for the second time. She sounded as though she had been doing it all her life.

Everything is fine with Robert except he is lonesome. Says no more solo sails for him. Also, he's losing weight. Good.

Tuesday, July 13—A very exciting thing happened today. A Mr. Davis from the London *Daily Express* called from New York asking for a story about Robert. I told him how we envied his seeing England and we would have to be content just to hear about it, and how he had orders to stop at Liverpool to pick up just any old piece of soil that the Beatles might have stepped on once.

The battery in the car is dead again and the kids had a grand time pushing the car up and down driveways to Perkeys' [neighbours] for a booster for the battery.

I'm collecting the rocks the neighbours dig up in their yards when they have swimming pools put in. I want to make a rock garden. Can't seem to do much else about it, though. Lonesome, I guess.

Wednesday, July 14—Victor Davis of the *Daily Express* called to tell me his paper carried the story. He's sending me a copy.

I called the insurance company about extending Robert's special policies, in case he does take 90 days. Also the lawyer about my will.

I blew myself to *Mary Poppins* tonight. I needed to get away from the house and get my mind off things. *Goldfinger* is coming on July 28, at last. Now Douglas can stop worrying about missing it. He is counting the days.

Tinkerbelle

Thursday, July 15—The editor of the Falmouth *Enterprise* tells me Falmouth, Cornwall, is planning a royal reception for Robert.

Friday, July 16—Today started out badly. The washer hose broke and I had a regular geyser of steaming water shooting all over the ceiling and then on to the washing. What a mess. The place was like a Turkish bath. I got a new hose and installed it all by myself. Robert would be so proud of bumbling me.

About 4.30 Ray Matjasic called to ask if I could hurry down to see a movie of Robert taken by the *Steel Vendor*'s cook. Douglas went with me. Robert was all in the shadow, but he looked so dear and familiar, waving just as we used to see him doing on Lake Erie.

Next week Phil Porter [the *P.D.*'s executive editor] and Russ Kane want to talk to me about a possible trip to Falmouth!

Julian Wilson, the Associated Press photographer, said: "He doesn't belong just to us now, he belongs to the world," and he formed a huge circle with his arms. Imagine, my husband! I'm glad he belongs to me, too.

John Metcalfe said: "You have to watch these quiet ones. They're the ones to stir things up," or words to that effect.

It's hard for us to realize how famous he has become. One thing is sure. Life can't ever be the same for Robert. With a taste of adventure, he's bound to want more; and so will we.

Monday, July 19—Today was hectic. I'd rather have them that way, though; I don't miss Robert so much then.

This morning I took Chris to the veterinarian's for a blood sample. Just as they thought, she has a serious infection and must have her uterus removed.

Doug and I went to town for some school clothes for him, and some to wear to England. We're going there, it seems.

This evening we got the television picture tube fixed: $33. Tomorrow I have to have my tooth fixed. More money. Chris's operation will be at least $50, plus the additionals. The bank account sure is disappearing fast.

Tonight Mother called to tell me she has my birth certificate (needed to get a passport). I also splurged and bought two pairs of shoes, on sale, and a handbag and stockings for my visit to the *P.D.* tomorrow.

Tuesday, July 20—Hectic is no word for today. Fantabulous about fills it. I got in early at the *P.D.*, had a cup of tea and a cookie, talked to Mary Hirschfeld, who writes the "Mary Hears . . ." column, and then met Russ Kane, Phil Porter and Russ Reeves, day managing editor.

Well, Robert is to receive his pay for the entire six weeks he's been gone, praise be! They are talking about paying our way over, the whole family, and Russ Kane is even talking about returning *Tinkerbelle* by air freight.

Wednesday, July 21—I finally got a little cleaning done. John is going to Miami for a few days and Mother will come here while he's gone.

I can't find Robin's birth certificate. I know we have one, but I can't find it. I sent for both hers and mine.

We finally got to see *Goldfinger*. At a drive-in. James Bond is quite a fellow. Doug was in ecstasy!

Wonder what Robert is doing now. Sleeping, I guess. Must not think past the present. It's too thrilling.

Thursday, July 22—More phone calls. Phil Porter called to tell me a cheque for six weeks' pay will be here soon, with another one each week until Robert comes home. We surely can use it.

Friday, July 23—Big day today. At about 8.15 a.m. Chris had her operation. Dr. [James F.] Robertson performed it. He saved her life once before, too.

It's 90 degrees. I went with Douglas for a dip in Perkeys' pool.

Chris came through her operation all right. I'm exhausted. Hope I can sleep.

Saturday, July 24—I brought Chris home today. The doctor said she came through very well. It was 99 degrees today, not a breath of air stirring. I wish I could be out on the sea with Robert. I'll bet it isn't this hot there. A letter from Sheila Beveridge in Newcastle, England, says they think Robert will make it the third week in August. They do a lot of sailing, so they may be right.

Monday, July 26—I couldn't sleep and finally took a pill.

I'm sort of boiling under a tight lid most of the time. When things get too bad I sit down at the piano and play some hymns and any other simple music I can figure out.

I have to shop for Robin's birthday present tomorrow.

Thursday, July 29—We heard from Robert again today. A West German ship [the *Bischofstor*] sighted his red sail and reported to Lloyd's of London. He was 1,000 miles from Land's End.

I got our passports today. Lucky Mother was along because my birth certificate wasn't right. It hadn't been recorded until I was 25. Mother had to sign a statement and swear that I was born.

Friday, July 30—Mother and I took Chris to have her stitches removed. She had taken all but one out herself.

Saturday, July 31—The AP in Rotterdam is going to talk to the captain of the West German ship to see whether he was able to talk to Robert.

Phyllis Verity wrote saying her husband has called off his voyage to Ireland in his 12-foot boat. The weather is too bad. He's had a terrible time.

Sunday, August 1—I dreamed Robert came home last night. He needed more film. Came in on a train. He looked nice and brown and had lost some weight. I don't remember whether he had a moustache. He told me he was 641 miles from England. [That was pretty close. I was actually about 650 miles from England.] We talked awhile and then he said he had to get back to *Tinkerbelle* and finish sailing to England.

When I read this morning's paper, I saw that the Coast Guard in Boston says he was probably 635 miles from England when he met the German ship. Maybe Robert and I are still in tune with 2,500 miles of water between us. Or ESP, maybe???

Monday, August 2—Boy, has this been a day! Falmouth, England, cabled that they sighted a boat with two men in it and they think it is Robert's. I said it couldn't be, unless he had picked up a hitch-hiker, but everyone is all shook up. That boat is blue, too, and ours is red. Oh, well.

The R.A.F. will be going out to look for him at dawn and George [Barmann] will call London at noon to hear the results. I can't imagine he has picked up so many miles in such a little while.

Russ Kane is off on vacation in North Carolina and they can't find him. He didn't expect to be leaving for a couple of weeks.

My passport hasn't come yet and the wires have been burning between here and Washington. The phone rang almost constantly from 4 until 8 today. Washing, dry cleaning, shopping, house cleaning, all in one big jumble because of Robert's arriving early —if he is!

Tuesday, August 3—Holy cow, what a day! First it looked as though we might not go until Thursday and Mother and John went home. Then I sort of went to pieces for the first time. Just nerves. One minute we're going, then we aren't, and still no passport.

About 4 p.m. Ted Princiotto [the *Plain Dealer*'s city editor] called to tell me to begin packing. We're leaving at 6.30 a.m. tomorrow. They say Robert is practically there.

My ear has a callous from talking on the phone so much. I called Beverly Banci [one of Virginia's very good friends] to come over because I was in such a state. She took charge and soon things began to even out a little.

During all of this the assistant superintendent of the Willowick post office, Mr. [Charles] Rittenhouse, appeared at the door holding my passport. He had had every available person looking for it. I was talking to Ted Princiotto for the umpty-leventh time when it came, and I gladly put Mr. Rittenhouse on the line.

In the midst of this chaos the dumb iron stopped working, and me with scores of things to iron. Lee Orpse [another neighbour] brought her iron over and while she was here told me that Frank is hard at work planning a reception to greet Robert on his return!

Tinkerbelle

Jean [Perkey] and Will [Hughes], friends of Robin's, were here to help Robin pack. They will take care of Chris and Fred. David Losh came for Puff yesterday.

Russ [Kane] has been located and will join our little band in Washington. Surely broke up his family's vacation. I'll be so glad to see Robert.

Poor Chris. She knows something is up and we can't explain that soon her beloved Daddy will be back. I do wish we could communicate better with animals.

I really must stop, but to paraphrase Eliza Doolittle, "I could just write all night", and I very nearly have. It's 2 o'clock, and I have to be up and going in three hours. Such fun. I do wish Robert were here, but he soon will be. I miss him so at times like this. He is so levelheaded and plans seem to go more smoothly for him. I've never had to plan even a vacation without him and here I am trying to organize our departure for England. At least the *Plain Dealer* is handling all the important decisions and thinking.

Wednesday, August 4—I haven't written a line in here until today. Everything has moved so fast I haven't begun to catch my breath.

We left Cleveland at 8.55 a.m. Mike Roberts, a reporter from the *Plain Dealer*, came for us and drove us to the airport. Jean and Willie came to see us off at the house, and to clean up the mess we left.

We flew to Washington and, since we were to be there a few hours, we got a room at the Willard. It was huge, almost as big as our whole house.

We drove to Baltimore by taxi and then to Philadelphia where we left for London. I don't know why the change in plans, unless it was for secrecy. I'm being guarded like I was an atomic secret.

It's a strange feeling to leave at dusk and see the sun set and a bit later see the sun rise from the same side. They say it's because of the earth's curvature.

Russ was still wearing his fishing clothes, those being all he had. He had a plaid shirt, tan levis and suède sheepskin-lined hushpuppies. Hardly the outfit in which to arrive in London, but he had no other and no time to buy any.

He and Bill Ashcroft spent almost the whole trip trying to fix a second-hand movie camera they had bought in Washington, and whose footage indicator wouldn't work. They never knew how much film there was left. Bill took some pictures of us in the plane.

Thursday, August 5—Our first day, the only one, really, in London, was a dilly. The minute we stepped off the plane, on which we had slept not a wink, there were about six photographers all snapping away. Interviews by reporters with those heavenly British accents, and then a drive to the Whitehall Hotel on Bloomsbury Square. Bloomsbury Square sounds so storybook-ish.

Eric Piper, a *Daily Mirror* photographer, told Robin all about her beloved Beatles. He had even taken pictures of them!

London is busy and exciting. I'd love to see it when we have all the time in the world. Everything we saw was through the windows of a taxi or the bus on the way from the airport.

Friday, August 6—We were supposed to meet Russ and Bill in the lobby at 8 a.m., eat and leave from Paddington Station for Falmouth.

I slept as one drugged and when Russ knocked on the door I awoke as though I'd been raised from the dead. We tore around washing, dressing, packing. Then we found that with the new clothes we had bought on Oxford Street there wasn't enough room in our suitcase. Russ waved his magic wand and there were cardboard cartons for us.

Russ and Bill bought us a huge bag of fruits and candy bars to eat on the train because it was a five-hour ride. After some confusion arising from uncertainty as to which track our train was on, we got in the compartment and slid through Paddington on our way to the Cornish Riviera, pulled by an engine called the Western Trooper.

We felt as though we were playing parts in an English movie. As Robin said, we hardly dared to speak for fear of breaking the spell.

When the train pulled into Truro, George [Barmann, who had flown to England earlier] appeared. Seems he and Vic Roberts, a transplanted Londoner, had come from Falmouth to take us the rest of the way by car.

I'll always remember our first glimpse of the Greenbank Hotel in Falmouth. We came into a conservatory-like entry way leading off a lovely flower garden in front of the hotel. From it we could look straight through the lobby on to a blue, blue harbour with sailing boats anchored peacefully and sea gulls wheeling about, the sun streaming into the glassed-in lounge.

The manager, Avon Tregenna, has arranged for Robert and me to have a lovely room at the top of the hotel overlooking the harbour. He said it is so quiet Robert will be able to get a good rest.

Tom Reedy, the AP man from London, an American from Pennsylvania, by the way, told me over our tea: "This will be another Dunkirk."

Saturday, August 7—Frank Goldsworthy of the *Daily Express*, London, has converted his hotel quarters into a chart room. We call him admiral and keep track of Robert on his charts.

CBS television news and United Press called. The reporters say this is nothing to what it will be when Robert gets here. I do wish he'd come soon. It's so hard to wait now that we are actually here and it'll be more fun to explore Cornwall with him.

Sunday, August 8—A Belgian ship [the *Belgulf Glory*] saw him today. The best guess now is a week from today, just as he said, on August 15.

I guess his beard isn't too long. There seems to be some dispute about it. Some captains say he has one and others don't mention it. Just so he has a moustache.

The crowd seems to be gathering; the dining room is more crowded. After dinner we took a taxi and visited Pendennis Castle where Bill [Ashbolt] took some pictures of us hanging on to the battlements. Shades of King Arthur!

Monday, August 9—Things are moving right along. Today some sailors [and Bill Jorgensen and Walter Glendenning] from Penzance saw Robert. Soon he will be meeting ships every day.

Tinkerbelle

Russ had Bill and Eddie Worth [an AP photographer] drop a letter from me to Robert today. [Actually, it was dropped by the R.A.F.]

A man from the BBC named Robert Forbes came over from Plymouth to interview me. He also drove Robin and me [Douglas was shopping in town] over to Plymouth to be on TV.'

17

TOWARDS evening on August 9th *Tinkerbelle* and I were alone again on the ocean, the trawler *Roseland*, the R.A.F. Shackletons and the smaller civilian plane (which, I found out later, had brought out Bill Ashbolt and Eddie Worth) having departed to return to their bases. The wind died to a mere whisper, making it difficult to maintain steerageway. We rolled about in the swells for two or three hours before another breeze sprang up, this one from the south, enabling us to roll along right on course. We kept going in fine style until about 3 a.m. when we hove to. I had to have sleep.

The next day (Tuesday, August 10th) I awoke at 7 a.m. (G.M.T.) and we resumed our pace. The noon sight put us at 50° 19' N. For the last two days we had moved steadily northward toward Ireland, which meant we were in the clutches of another current. According to the *Sailing Directions*, it was probably Rennell's Current, which flows at one to one and a half knots northward across the western approach and entrance to the English Channel. Our bumping into it indicated, at least, that we were getting close to the channel.

We struggled all afternoon and part of the night to get back down below 50° N, but a sextant shot at Polaris during the night put us even farther north, at 50° 25'.

On Wednesday, August 11th, clouds covered the sky, making it impossible to shoot the sun, so I couldn't be sure where we were exactly. I just had to do the best I could with dead reckoning and hope the sun would come out again before we got into deep trouble.

That night, when I was putting out the sea anchor and taking down the sails, I lost the mains'l halyard up the mast. Fortunately the end of the halyard didn't run through the masthead sheave; the shackle that serves to attach the halyard to the head of the sail was too big to go through it. But how to get it down again, that was the problem. And I had to get it down or I wouldn't be able to raise the sail.

It was too dark then to see what I was doing, so I decided to wait until morning. I had a hard time getting to sleep because of worrying about how to go about retrieving the halyard end. I knew I couldn't climb up the mast since my weight would certainly capsize the boat. I wasn't panicky, for I knew that if worst came to worst I could unfasten the forestay and lower the mast in its tabernacle, which would make it simple to recover the halyard and shackle. But lowering the mast at sea would be a tricky operation and I didn't want to do it unless it was unavoidable. I hoped there was another way.

After some cogitation in the morning (August 12th) I decided the topping lift might be it. This consisted of a light Dacron line that ran through a small block at the masthead and had both its ends attached to the end of the boom. With wire and a pair of pliers I improvised a little grappling hook, lashed it to the topping-lift line and ran it aloft.

It took about thirty minutes of flipping the line about to accomplish it, but finally I snagged the shackle with the grappling hook and, much to my relief, was able to pull the halyard end back down, shackle it to the head of the mains'l and then, joy of joys, hoist the sail. We were ready to get cracking again. It was a great pleasure to have escaped so easily from what might have been a rather sloppy situation.

We had to spend part of the morning riding to the sea anchor because the wind blew too hard for us to sail safely, but even so, sometime during the day we crossed the meridian of 10° W, completing the last full stride in the oceanic countdown to Falmouth, England. There were less than five degrees of longitude left to cover. We should reach our harbour haven (and possibly it would seem like heaven, too) in less than a week, maybe in as little as five days. The voyage was advanced in age now; it was old, full of 'years'. The end, with its mingled joys and sorrows, was near.

It was still quite cloudy. At midday, however, the sun came out long enough for me to get a good latitude shot. It showed we were farther north than ever, at 50° 33' N, and that meant we were within sixty-five miles of the coast of Ireland. Something had to be done or we'd make an unintentional landfall on Cape Clear.

The trouble was that besides the current we had a southeast wind to fight, and that meant tacking. And that, in turn, meant slower progress; and I wasn't in the mood for dawdling. I did everything I could think of to propitiate Aeolus and induce him to shift the breeze around to the south or southwest, but nothing worked. It came down to making a choice between tacking and landing in Ireland. I chose tacking.

I had nothing whatever against Ireland or the Irish; it was just that I had started out to sail to England and my family and newspaper colleagues were waiting for me there. So the only decent course of action was to do my level best to get there. We went over on to the port tack, heading southwestward on a course of 220°. This took us southward against the current all right, but it also took us *away* from England. It was only on the starboard tacks, if the wind held in the southeast, that we'd be able to head *towards* England.

Early in the afternoon, while still on the port tack, I heard a plane to the south; in fact, I continued hearing it for half an hour or more. I thought that probably it was the R.A.F. back, trying to find me, and later I learned the R.A.F. *had* been out looking for me and that its failure to find me had aroused considerable concern on shore. (I hoped Virginia wasn't worried. I had told her that small-boat voyagers were reported lost rather frequently, erroneously, and not to be unduly alarmed if I was so reported. As I had feared, it was widely reported that I was lost, but of course I wasn't. It was simply that nobody knew where I was except me.

About the time the sun dipped below the western horizon, the wind moved into the southwest, enabling *Tinkerbelle* to sail southeastward on a broad reach. We were on the home stretch, sprinting for the finish line.

The breeze was so good I decided to keep going all night and sometime after midnight we passed down the aisle between two long rows of trawlers, so brilliantly lighted they gave the ocean a festive look. We seemed to be rolling along the surface of a mammoth liquid birthday cake between two ranks of flickering candles. The experience put me into a happy, partyish frame of mind.

When daylight returned, I suddenly realized it was Friday the thirteenth and I wrote in the log: 'I hope this isn't an unlucky day.' It wasn't.

All that day and the following night we continued sailing southeastward, battling the Rennell Current, working our way to a lower latitude so that we could pass to the south of the Scilly Isles and into the English Channel. I believed that would be much safer than trying to go to the north of the Scillys because along the northern route lay the dangers of the Seven Stones, a mile-long group of exposed rocks, and Wolf Rock, a lighthouse-topped hazard some eight miles southwest of Land's End.

We continued moving southeastward throughout the next day (Saturday, August 14th) and through about half the night. Shortly before midnight we approached a particularly brightly lit trawler and I thought I had better go up and check our position. As we drew near, I saw what seemed to my unsophisticated eyes to be some sort of pagan rite, perhaps a ritual of initiation. Persons clad in yellow oilskins (and I'm almost positive some of them were women) were kneeling on the deck and then rising and kneeling again. Then they would disappear into the hold for a while, only to reappear and go through the whole rigmarole again. I simply couldn't understand what it was all about.

I hated to disturb whatever was taking place, but I hated even more to go without a check on our position. So when we got to within ten or fifteen yards of the trawler I yelled with all my might, 'Which way to Bishop Rock?'

Tinkerbelle

It was a silly question; I'll admit that freely because I knew the way perfectly well. (Bishop Rock was a navigation hazard near the southwestern edge of the Scilly Isles and on it stood Bishop Rock Light, a hundred-and-sixty-seven-foot-high granite lighthouse. It was used as a point of departure or arrival by most of the ships entering or leaving the English Channel, and it was about forty-five miles away on a heading of 20° from where we were at that moment.) So, O.K., it was a silly question, but surely it was good enough to serve as the opening gambit in a conversation. But do you think I got a reply, or so much as an acknowledgement that I had been heard? No, sir! Those yellow-coated figures kept right on with their ritual without so much as blinking an eye.

'Ahoy! Hey, there!' I yelled. 'Can you tell an alien where to go to register?'

Still no reply.

I pulled myself together, filled my lungs and let go with a torrent of sound of sufficient volume to rattle *Tinkerbelle*'s sails: '*Sprechen Sie Deutsch? Parlez-vous français?* How's the fishing? Catching any sea monsters?'

Nothing. No one on the deck of the trawler, if that's what it was, even looked in my direction. Everyone just kept on kneeling, rising and disappearing into the hold for a time. It was queer. It was the strangest thing I'd ever seen in my life, and I had seen some pretty strange things in my time. And I still don't have the faintest idea what it was all about.

By then *Tinkerbelle* was past the ship and moving out of voice range and, anyway, it was obvious that no one was going to pay any attention to us, so we kept on going. I had a lot of fun mulling the whole thing over in my mind, though, and I wondered what sort of headline I would have written if a story about the experience had come over the *P.D.* copy desk while I was working there. Probably I would have written something like:

SAILOR SLIPS;
GOES SILLY
AT SCILLYS

A couple of hours later, at about 1 a.m., I put out the bucket and got some rest even though we were very close to the shipping lanes. I reasoned that the dangers arising from exhaustion were greater than the danger of being run down. I was so tired that I had no trouble at all falling asleep. Knockout drops couldn't have accomplished it any faster.

In the morning (Sunday, August 15th) I woke up just in time to see a trawler (it looked exactly like the one of the strange ritual) moving off, apparently after having examined *Tinkerbelle* at close range. I popped out of the cabin and shouted after it. The response was the same: zero.

Listening to the BBC during breakfast, I heard that Virginia was aboard a trawler searching for me; in fact, she had been out on the sea for several days. I wished that I had some way to let her know where I was. How I looked forward to seeing her again! No more solo voyages for me; that was for sure. Any future sailing trips would be in a larger boat and with Virginia and the children.

The noon sun shot showed we were down to about 49° 40′ N, about twelve miles south of the latitude of Bishop Rock Light, so it was safe to turn eastward, or even a little north of due east, to head into the channel toward the famous Lizard Point that I had heard so much about in the accounts of other voyages. The Lizard was now about sixty miles away and Falmouth, our journey's end, was only twelve miles beyond that. It would all be over in a couple of days, three at the most.

It was a nice day, mostly sunny, with only a few small clouds in the sky. During the afternoon I saw lots of ships and at one point experienced another, brief hallucination. There was a trawler behind us and I imagined that Virginia was on it, trying to reach us. But *Tinkerbelle* and I had been caught in a whirling maelstrom and were in danger of being sucked under. The water was very confused and rough and, as I looked astern, I hoped and prayed that Virginia's trawler wouldn't be caught, as *Tinkerbelle* and I were, and dispatched into the depths. I even went so far as to yell at the trawler, 'Stay out! Stay out! It's too dangerous here!' (I'm sure if they had been able to hear me they would have thought I had blown my top.)

The trawler skirted the terrible area where we were and finally went out of sight over the horizon. That seemed to snap me back to reality.

We kept on moving all afternoon on a course of about 75°. The sea seemed to be crowded with ships. There were lots of freighters and trawlers and once I even saw a big passenger liner. In the evening I had dinner and afterward, about the time the sun dropped out of sight, resumed sailing. There were some clouds close to the horizon in the northwest and others scattered about to the south, all tinged with red from the afterglow of the sunset. Then, all of a sudden, I saw a light flashing (seemingly from the clouds) in the northwest, off *Tinkerbelle*'s port quarter. It went: Flash, interval, flash, long interval, flash, interval, flash, long interval, flash, interval, flash, long interval. . . . Could it be true? Was that *really* it?

With trembling hands I got out my light list and turned to the proper place. In the column on 'Characteristic and Power' were listed these facts: 'Gp. Fl. W. (2); period 15s; fl. 0.7s, ec. 1.6s; fl. 0.7s, ec. 12.0s; Cp. 720,000.' Translated into normal English this meant: Group, flashing, white (2 flashes); duration of total cycle, 15 seconds; first flash, 0.7 second; eclipse, 1.6 seconds; second flash, 0.7 second; eclipse, 12 seconds; candlepower, 720,000.

I timed the flashes and the intervals of darkness between them. There could be no doubt now; it was Bishop Rock Light. And it was exactly where it should have been, according to my navigation. That was the most amazing thing of all. If I hadn't been afraid of falling overboard, I would have jumped up and danced all round *Tinkerbelle*'s little deck! It was great to see something, at last, that I knew was on land, even though I couldn't see the land itself.

In high spirits I sailed on through the night on a course for the Lizard. It was a wonderful brisk sail in the moonlight, but as the first hints of dawn appeared in the east I grew so drowsy I periodically fell asleep at the tiller and, several times, almost put

Tinkerbelle into a jibe. I decided I simply had to stop for some rest, so I hove to under sail, without the sea anchor, and dropped into unconsciousness in the cabin.

The next thing I knew, I heard voices shouting, 'Matey, wake up, wake up! Yank, are you there? Mr. Manry, wake up!' I jumped out of the cabin and saw an English trawler with four or five men at the rail calling out between cupped hands.

I was surprised that they knew my name, but glad they had awakened me, for I knew I shouldn't be sleeping in those heavily travelled waters. And then, as I drew alongside I got another, bigger shock; they asked for my autograph! They must be daft, I thought. Why in the world would they, or anyone, want *my* autograph. But I obliged, happily.

It turned out that the skipper of the trawler, the *Trewarvenneth*, was a fine-looking Cornishman named Harry Small, and he was the brother-in-law of Captain Hunter of the *Excellent*, the *Trewarvenneth*'s sister ship, which was scouring the ocean for me with Virginia aboard. Captain Small soon had Captain Hunter on the radio-telephone, told him he had found me and gave him our position. And Captain Hunter replied that he was already headed for the *Tinkerbelle* and would arrive in about four hours. I was delighted to know that in just that length of time I would see my lovely wife again.

I thanked the captain and crew of the *Trewarvenneth*, which then went on about its own business, and pushed on for the Lizard. Soon things really began to pop.

An R.A.F. Shackleton flew over and dropped another canister, this one with a message saying, 'Sorry we have not been with you since Monday. You have done well. Position now: 49° 32' N, 06° 05' W. Mrs. Manry aboard trawler PZ513. Will home her to you now. Comdr. R. A. Carson, Royal Air Force.' The big plane started circling about, sending out that signal for the *Excellent*.

Then a handsome Royal Navy frigate, H.M.S. *Brereton*, hove into sight and, after it got close enough, its captain and two sailors came over to *Tinkerbelle* in an inflated rubber boat powered with an outboard motor. We had a wonderfully pleasant little visit as we moved along side by side. The captain, Lieutenant Commander Nick Barker, gave me a bottle of fresh milk, the first I'd had in more than two and a half months. I'll never forget how delicious it was. He also gave me a sailor's hat ribbon with H.M.S. *Brereton* printed on it in letters of gold, as well as the pleasure and honour of signing my name in the *Brereton*'s guest book. Then he putt-putted back to his own ship, which also was emitting a homing signal for the *Excellent* and which began circling round *Tinkerbelle* like a mother hen watching over a chick.

'Wonderful welcome,' I had written in the guest book, and it certainly was. It was so marvellous, so totally different from what I had expected, that it took on a sort of Alice in Wonderland quality, an out-of-this-worldness that left me numb.

Virginia's diary for the previous seven days tells vividly her side of the story.

'*Tuesday, August 10*—Poor Robert, the winds are practically gale force, and we heard tonight on TV that he had been swept overboard several times. Luckily, he has a lifeline around his waist. He must be exhausted. I do wish we could do something to help him.

Bill Jorgensen hired a trawler and went out and interviewed him. Everyone in Cleveland knew it, but we didn't. Our boys are kind of put out. I told them if they ever go to look for Robert to take me along, too.

Wednesday, August 11—We have chartered a trawler and Russ and Bill and Eric Piper, and Paul Hughes, a *Daily Mirror* reporter, and I are going out to look for Robert. It's all very hush, hush. I have to be up at 5 a.m.

Thursday, August 12—We left the hotel at 6.30 and raced in Paul Hughes's car to Newlyn. I'll never get used to English driving. It's terrifying. Paul says all it takes is "a bit of dash and verve".

Our trawler is the *Excellent*, and this is my first time on the sea. It's a lovely day and I'm enjoying it.

The captain is Ernie Hunter and the crew are Jock Skinner, Bob Sowden and Bert Morris. Bert is also the cook, and he gives us meals fit for any first-class hotel. He's really a whiz in the galley. I don't know how he does it.

They all treat me like visiting royalty. Jock told me about Scotland and Bob drew me a sketch of the *Excellent*.

Friday, August 13 to Sunday, August 15—Our trawler trip was more like a pleasure cruise than anything else. Sometimes I felt guilty for enjoying the cruise so much when poor Robert was alone in his little cockleshell in the vast ocean. I did acquire a sense of oneness with him, though, which was impossible to feel ashore.

We searched the horizon so diligently I began to see red sails everywhere I looked. Looking out over the waves I could understand how it would be nearly impossible to find him without *Tinkerbelle*'s red sail.

Paul and I had a tendency towards seasickness and we took all our meals at the stern of the boat. Luckily, as long as I stayed out of the galley I was able to keep my meals down. Bert told me to keep on eating, no matter whether I lost a meal or not. The seasick pills made me groggy, so I did a lot of sleeping.

Paul, probably because of *his* pills, was always flopping down somewhere to sleep. One time he curled up in one of the fish nets and went to sleep, and Bob sewed him up in it.

The *Excellent* has a terrific roll to it. It rolls so far over the sea comes in through the scuppers on one side and gets halfway across the deck. Then, when it rolls to the other side, the sea goes back out on the first side and in on the other.

The boys are in constant touch with land by radio. And now and then Russ and Bill communicate with the *Plain Dealer* by radio and transatlantic cable. The fellows back at the newspaper can't seem to understand why we can't find Robert.

We passed several trawlers. One of them we took to be French and among us we figured out enough French to ask if they had seen "*un petit bateau avec rouge* sail". They stared at us in bewilderment and then gave us that peculiar sign, chopping the palm of one hand with the side of the other. It turned out they were Dutch!

Tinkerbelle

No sign or word of Robert and we have had to put back to Newlyn for more supplies and fuel. I still feel he's all right.

Monday, August 16—I couldn't get to sleep last night. The bed wasn't rocking and it was too quiet. Guess I missed the sea. Anyhow, we got up early and made off to Newlyn once again. This time, hopefully, we'll find Robert.

It was a sparkling, bright blue day and it felt good to have a deck under our feet again. We were all filled with high hopes.

Bert gave us some old bread, which we crumbled and tossed to the scores of gulls following us. I couldn't help remembering the last time I had thrown bread to the sea gulls was when Robert was loading his supplies aboard *Tinkerbelle* in Falmouth, Massachusetts.

Russ and I had a conversation about my feelings concerning Robert's safety. I told him I felt that when Robert left Falmouth, Massachusetts, he became one of the sea creatures and, since God watches over them, I felt sure He had Robert in His care, too. Maybe it was childish, but I felt I just had to have faith. And what is life itself but many acts of faith? I have believed from the beginning that worry would avail me nothing. It couldn't possibly help Robert and it could drive me mad.

While we were talking Bert came out and said, 'The captain wants you in the wheelhouse.'

I ran along the deck and climbed the little ladder into the wheelhouse. Captain Hunter said he had just heard by radio that his brother-in-law, the commander of another trawler, had found the *Tinkerbelle* a few miles southeast of the Scilly Isles. Robert had been curled up in the cabin, asleep.

From that moment on a carnival air prevailed aboard the *Excellent* with dancing on the deck and slapping of backs. Soon an R.A.F. plane flew over so close we all ducked and Captain Hunter, who had piloted a boat to help evacuate the British forces trapped at Dunkirk during World War II, thought for a moment that he was back there.

Bert fixed us some sandwiches because there wouldn't be time for a proper meal, and we were too excited to eat anyhow. The *Excellent* moved at top speed to meet Robert and *Tinkerbelle*.

I remember Eric came up to me, took my chin in his hand and said, "Are you happy, luv?"

I felt tears of joy springing into my eyes as I answered, "Oh, yes," and said a little prayer of thanks.

Dolphins, that had previously kept their distance, then began ducking underneath the trawler and diving from one side of it to the other. Then, as suddenly as they had appeared they vanished.

Russ, up on the observation deck, shouted for us to come up there. We all climbed up the ladder and saw what had become of the dolphins. There were two on each side of the bow, escorting us to Robert. What better sign of luck did we need?

Captain Hunter kept scanning the horizon with his eagle eyes (no binoculars for him) and finally announced that he had spotted *Tinkerbelle*. I don't know about the others, but as for me, even using binoculars, it was a good long time before I made out that little red dot that was *Tinkerbelle*'s mainsail.

But what a moment that was!'

In three hours the *Excellent* was in sight and in less than another hour it was alongside and I got my first glimpse of Virginia. She looked great; tanned and fit, as though life at sea were agreeing with her. And she had on slacks and a pretty blue jacket and hat that seemed just right. I don't remember what I said first or what she said. Everything was so exciting and happening so fast. My mind reeled.

I'm sure I must have said it was good to see her, and no doubt she said she was happy to see me, but I can't remember. I was too dazed. I must also have said 'hellos' to Bill and Russ of the *P.D.*, and Paul Hughes and Eric Piper of the *Daily Mirror*, to whom I was quickly introduced, and to Captain Hunter and his good crew. We were like a happy family having a wonderful time at a picnic.

'Well, *Tinkerbelle* got you to England after all,' I called over to Virginia.

'Yes,' she said. 'Even got me here before you.'

When *Tinkerbelle* was securely moored beside the *Excellent*

Virginia jumped down beside me and we hugged and kissed. It was marvellous to have her in my arms again, to be together. The photographers kept asking us to kiss and hug some more so they could get pictures, and of course we didn't mind. We could have gone on for hours. Virginia said she liked the looks of my moustache and didn't mind its tickling. I was glad to hear that. She was also delighted with my slimmed-down looks. (We discovered later that I had lost forty pounds.)

We sat down in *Tinkerbelle*'s little cockpit with our arms around each other, but there was hardly any opportunity for a private conversation. The two photographers kept asking us to pose and the two reporters kept firing questions at us. All of us were spinning like tops in a scene of wild, happy confusion.

I found out later that Bill had told the Englishmen on the *Excellent*, 'Wait'll you hear his laugh.' And I guess they weren't disappointed, for I did considerable laughing and with as much gusto as ever. It seems to me that moments of happiness are times for laughing, and I have seldom if ever been happier than I was at that reunion with Virginia. Even the apprehension I had felt over Russ's being the *P.D.* promotion director disappeared, for I learned that there would be no brazen attempt to capitalize on my voyage. I deeply appreciated the *P.D.*'s forbearance. That made everything absolutely perfect. Maybe old Dr. Pangloss was right after all; maybe this *was* the best of all possible worlds.

Bert, the *Excellent*'s chef, handed me a nice big mug of oxtail soup, but I was kept so busy answering questions I only had time to take a few sips of it before someone shouted, 'We gotta get going,' and there was a mad scramble on the trawler to get Virginia back on board and return to Newlyn. Virginia, it seemed, had become the *Plain Dealer* team's 'secret weapon'. By getting exclusive stories and pictures of her high-seas reunion with me the *P.D.* men hoped to ease the pain of the 'Atlantic scoop' perpetrated by Jorgensen and Glendenning. So, at the first sign of an approaching boatload of rival newsmen, they whisked the soup out of my hands and leaped to pull Virginia up on to the *Excellent*. They had to start moving, anyway, to get the story filed in time for the *P.D.*'s deadline.

Tinkerbelle

Well, getting Virginia back up on the *Excellent* wasn't nearly so simple as it had been to get her down on to the *Tinkerbelle*; but Bill and Russ were willing to try. They grabbed Virginia's arms and pulled, thinking she would be able to help by getting a toe hold on the side of the ship. But there was no place for a toe hold; the hull was too smooth. So there she dangled, suspended two or three feet above the water.

Virginia said later she had visions of having to hang there all the way back to Newlyn, if Russ's and Bill's arms held out. Frankly, I didn't have that much confidence in their arms. I thought she'd drop into the water any second. And there I was, unable to help because *Tinkerbelle* had drifted too far away.

Suddenly Paul Hughes thought of a way to avert catastrophe and rushed forward. He reached down to grab my darling wife by what he later referred to as her 'haunches', but then, at the last second, he saw the horrified look on my face and decided he'd better not go through with it. He explained afterward that he wasn't going to offend, knowingly, a man who had just sailed the Atlantic singlehanded.

The situation was becoming truly desperate when Bert, one of the crew (good old Bert, Virginia called him ever after), lunged low enough to grab her ankles, raised them, and then rolled her inboard over the railing like a sack of flour. Luckily neither of the photographers recorded the humiliating event.

There was no time to observe the proprieties. We all waved quickly and then the *Excellent* sped away, Newlyn bound, just as the first boatload of rival newsmen arrived. This new batch of reporters shouted over questions and I shouted back answers for thirty minutes or so as *Tinkerbelle* continued on towards the Lizard. Then the boat headed back to harbour, to be replaced by another boatful of curious interviewers. It went on like that until darkness began to fall. There were five or six boats altogether, I think, and believe me, some of those English journalists were go-getters. Karl Dyer, a reporter for United Press International, wasn't satisfied with shouting back and forth. He stripped to his shorts, put on a pair of water wings and swam over to get a

Tinkerbelle

better look at *Tinkerbelle* and me. And there was another chap—
I didn't get his name, I'm sorry to say—who tried to row over in
his boat's dinghy but got dumped into the sea instead.

Finally it was night and *Tinkerbelle* and I were alone together
once more. It was our last night alone together; our last night
on the sea.

18

SOON after night cloaked the sea, and before the moon arose, I noticed the loom of a bright light brushing the sky to the northeast. I was pretty sure it couldn't be anything but the Lizard Light, but I got out the light list to make certain. The book said the Lizard Light was white, flashing, and had a period of three seconds, of which 0.1 second was flash and 2.9 seconds was eclipse. Its strength was 4,000,000 candle power. I hadn't known there were lights that bright.

I timed the sweeps of the loom. It was the Lizard Light all right.

A table in the front of the book indicated that the light, which stood on a cliff and was two hundred and thirty feet above the water, could be seen from a distance of about twenty miles. However, what I saw was not the light itself but its beam in the sky, so we were undoubtedly a good deal farther from it than that; probably closer to twenty-five miles away. It would be dawn before we got to it.

Tinkerbelle skipped joyfully over the waves, headed straight for the light like a horse galloping towards the barn. There was an extra little jauntiness in the spread of her sails, an extra snap in her step, an extra sauciness in the wiggle of her stern. I was proud of her. And happy.

She had guarded me well. Although being knocked overboard had been frightening, especially the first time, we had come through unscathed, thanks to *Tinkerbelle*. She simply wasn't the sort of boat to leave one behind (unless she was rigged for self-steering) because she had the admirable habit of facing the wind and stopping whenever the tiller and mainsheet were released.

Tinkerbelle

Yes, *Tinkerbelle* had protected me. She had never allowed herself to be turned bottom up (as I had feared might happen) and even on those few occasions when one of the bigger breaking waves had flipped her over on her beam ends she had righted herself at once. If she had been able to steer herself all the way, I'm sure she could have crossed the ocean entirely on her own, without any help whatever from me.

Besides righting herself after each knockdown, she had steadfastly kept herself watertight and buoyant. I had expected that at some time along the way she might be filled with water, which I would then have had laboriously to pump out of her; but that calamity never even came close. Nor had there been any significant breakage of her gear, aside from what happened to her rudders.

Tinkerbelle never allowed me to get into a really serious predicament and, consequently, I never became panic-stricken or fearful that we might not reach England safely. I was confident of her seaworthiness before I started the voyage (I wouldn't have started otherwise) and grew more and more pleased with her capability as she demonstrated again and again that my faith in her was not misplaced. In my opinion she was, and is, a nautical gem.

There were some scary moments, some moments of sharp loneliness and some other moments of depression, but for the most part the voyage was a great, glorious, happy adventure. I wouldn't have missed it for the world. And as the fulfilment of a long-time dream, it had a special, deep significance for me that only those persons who have long desired and then achieved can fully appreciate.

It had been an eventful voyage, too. The log revealed that I had sighted about sixty ships in the vast expanse of ocean between Vineyard Sound and the Scilly Isles; and, of these, two had looked *Tinkerbelle* and me over to make sure we were all right, four others had exchanged words with me 'on the run' and five more had actually stopped to converse. One of these last five had also picked up letters to mail when it reached port and another had given me a complete hot meal, the equivalent of a banquet. I had seen one or more vessels on thirty-three days of the voyage (which now was approaching the end of its seventy-seventh day) despite my efforts to stay away from the shipping lanes. The longest I had gone without sighting a ship was nine days, between June 21st and 30th.

All this, it seemed to me, pointed to the fact that the Atlantic was an exceptionally sociable ocean, and a crowded one. Apparently I was never more than a few days away from help if I had needed it and had used the Victory Girl emergency transmitter to summon it. The tradition of helping those in distress that exists on the sea was heart-warming to behold in action, and I hoped all those captains who had taken the time to rush over to rescue me, only to find that I didn't need rescuing, would forgive me for causing them concern and delay. I saluted them with sincere thanks and respect.

I also owed a debt of gratitude to the U.S. Weather Bureau and the U.S. Naval Oceanographic Office, as their reports on winds and waves to be expected on the voyage had proved astonishingly accurate. The largest waves had been twenty-footers, but we hadn't met many of them, fortunately. Most of the time the waves were under twelve feet high and the wind blew at less than twenty-five knots. We were forced to ride to the sea anchor thirteen times (not counting the times when I was sleeping) and were becalmed thirteen times for varying periods, the longest being about a day.

The moon had risen at about 9.30 p.m. and had now, just before midnight, added its magical touch to the channel scene as we continued slapping, sliding, sloshing toward the Lizard Light. The light itself was visible at last. It had a strangely hypnotic effect. A few minutes of staring at it made it seem very close, although the length of time required to reach it proved it was still many miles away.

As *Tinkerbelle* jogged along gaily at about four knots, I was enchanted by the sparkling moonglow in the water and the warm lights of far-off freighters. I had felt we were sailing through historic waters when we left Falmouth, Massachusetts, but now as we approached Falmouth, England, that feeling was intensified a hundredfold. What an utterly fascinating land this was.

Falmouth, up ahead, only a dozen miles beyond the flashing Lizard Light, was noted for many things. Long ago Phoenician, Roman and Greek traders had visited the site of the city seeking tin, corn and hides. Then came Danes and Vikings, seeking conquests and, after them, Frenchmen seeking revenge. It was from Falmouth that Bartholomew Gosnold had sailed in 1602 on his voyage of discovery to Cape Cod. It was not certain that he landed at the site of Falmouth, Massachusetts, but at any rate he had sailed by, and when Cape Cod's Falmouth was incorporated in 1686 it took the name of the town from which he had begun his voyage. So the two Falmouths definitely were linked in history.

It was to England's Falmouth that the schooner *Pickle* brought the official news of Nelson's tragic death in 1805 at the moment of his greatest triumph, the defeat of a combined French and Spanish fleet off Cape Trafalgar on the southern coast of Spain. It was from Falmouth that a British warship sailed to take Napoleon to his exile on the island of St. Helena. And it was into Falmouth that Captain Kurt Carlsen and his first mate, Kenneth Dancy, were brought in January, 1952, after being rescued from the freighter *Flying Enterprise*, which, after their heroic fourteen-day struggle to get it into port, sank off the Lizard. As a matter of fact, the trawlers *Roseland* and *Excellent* had participated in the dramatic *Flying Enterprise* rescue effort.

Falmouth harbour also had been the jumping-off point or terminus of quite a few transatlantic small-boat voyages. The voyage of the 18-foot *City of Bath*, begun in Newfoundland, had ended there in 1881. So had the 1947 voyage of the 22-foot *Adventure*, which had begun at Miami, Florida. The voyage of the 17-foot raft *L'Egaré*, sailed from Halifax in 1956, ended there, too, as did the 1960 voyage of the 26½-foot *Humming Bird*, which had started in Antigua in the West Indies. Headed the other way across the Western Ocean, Humphrey Barton and Kevin O'Riordon sailed the 25-foot *Vertue XXXV* from Falmouth to New York in 1950; Ernst Karulis and Jan Paltins sailed the 25-

foot *Polaris* from there to Panama in 1949–50, and Patrick Ellam and Colin Mudie jumped off from the same place on their voyage in *Sopranino* in 1951. Other voyages begun at Falmouth were those of the 31-foot *Uldra*, 24-foot *Wanderer II*, 29-foot *Moonraker* (Dr. E. A. 'Peter' Pye's famous cutter), 20-foot *Skaffie* and 25½-foot *Valkyr*.

I gazed at the flashing light ahead and wondered what *Tinkerbelle*'s voyage had accomplished. Well, for one thing, it had helped to make an honest man of me. When I had asked Virginia to marry me I had promised her two things: one, that we would travel, and two, that although I might be a headache I would never, never be a bore. Well, in fifteen years of marriage we had had a couple of vacation trips to Canada, but it could hardly be said that I was making good on the promise of travel. And as for the second pledge, after twelve years on a newspaper copy desk I was becoming a crashing bore, without even the relief of being interesting enough to be a headache. So the situation was critical. It was beginning to look as though I had lied and had married Virginia under false pretences. But *Tinkerbelle* saved the day. She banished boredom from our lives and, although she sometimes became a bit of a headache, it only made her that much more interesting. And she made good on my promise of travel for she took me to England and in the process influenced the *Plain Dealer* to send Virginia and the children over to meet me, an exceedingly kind and gracious act on the *P.D.*'s part. Virginia appreciated it immensely, I knew, because for years she had dreamed of visiting England. So, *Tinkerbelle* made a dream of hers come true as well as one of mine.

What had the voyage achieved besides making dreams a reality? I think probably the most important thing it had done for me was to enable me to stand back, away from human society ashore, and look at life for a little while from a new perspective. The Atlantic Ocean had not been a place for trivialities and I think, perhaps, that fact may have done something to make me a better person inside than I had been before. Anyway, I hope it did.

Although I was lonely and discouraged at times, my primary feeling was of contentment and peace. My boat was my dearest companion and though the wind and sea were sometimes my adversaries, they were mostly friendly and even when they were not they behaved with straightforward honesty according to their inherent natures. To know them was to respect them.

I must confess that, seen from the peace and quiet of mid-ocean, many aspects of life on land seemed grim indeed. Well, we might as well face it; in some basic ways life ashore *is* grim, especially for underprivileged or underequipped persons. I couldn't help thinking of the grey flannel suit brigades in the big cities ashore, living in a kind of lock-step frenzy, battling noisy highway or subway traffic to get to work in the morning and to return home in the evening, existing on pure nervous energy in between, having to be ever alert to opportunities to get ahead and on guard against the encroachment of rivals.

Henry Thoreau said, 'The mass of men lead lives of quiet desperation,' and he was probably right. In my life, certainly, ihere had been many periods of quiet desperation, although I was sure my existence had been less harried than that of most men. I shuddered to think what those less fortunate than I were enduring.

One of the implications of these musings was that my voyage in *Tinkerbelle* had been prompted by an itch and was itself a form of scratching. That was true. The voyage was something I simply *had* to do, had wanted to do for a long, long time. In fact, I had wanted to do it so intensely and for such a long time that my natural timidity, the basic Walter Mitty—Caspar Milquetoast cast of my character, had finally been beefed up with a fair-sized dash of Captain Ahab. And that's when planning for the cruise had got under way in earnest.

The story in the Falmouth *Packet* had referred to me as a hero, but that was absurd. As far as I was concerned, I wasn't taking any great risks, and I was doing something I enjoyed intensely. I really couldn't understand why so much excitement was developing in Falmouth. I'd heard on the radio that a tremendous welcome was being planned and that the mayor had even postponed his vacation in order to be there to greet me when I stepped ashore. And there was talk of thousands of people being on hand to watch *Tinkerbelle* arrive. It seemed as though a real ordeal was shaping up for me and I'll have to admit that for a few moments I considered turning off to port and heading for Penzance in order to escape it.

I had thought that since England was a maritime nation and had had her full share of adventurous sailors little attention would be paid to *Tinkerbelle* and me. I had expected to sail into Falmouth Harbour almost unnoticed, moor my boat at a quay and go to a hotel for a nice bath and sleep. Then, in the morning, I would look for the Falmouth representative of the Associated Press, tell him that I had just sailed the Atlantic singlehanded and that I thought my newspaper back in the States might be interested in having a story about it. Now, it appeared, it wasn't going to work out quite like that.

The impulse to duck away from all the hoopla that was being prepared in Falmouth was strong, but then I thought of how wonderful the R.A.F. had been to me and how well I had been treated by the personnel of the *Roseland, Trewarvenneth, Excellent* and *Brereton* and that my family and *P.D.* colleagues were waiting for me in Falmouth, not to mention the mayor and the crowds, and that I was to be a guest in the country, anyway. It would be inexcusable to skip out and dash the hopes and expectations of all those people, so I decided to go on in as I had planned and face the music.

Dawn was approaching now. The stars disappeared as the inky blackness of the sky gradually changed to grey and then grew lighter and lighter with each passing minute. Up ahead the Lizard Light was still flashing faithfully with its regular three-second rhythm. It was not yet possible to tell how near or far it was, for judging distances over water was extremely difficult, especially when there was nothing of a known size to gauge by.

We kept going as we had all night before the southwest breeze, *Tinkerbelle* taking it over the port quarter, heeling pleasantly to starboard. More light filled the heavens. Finally, in another thirty minutes or so, the outline of a steep headland could be distinguished from the sea and sky. Land! At last! Land! Solid, firm, immovable land! It was the Lizard rising steeply from the ocean;

and rolling northeastward from it was the pleasant, green, undulating shoreline leading to Falmouth!

It was a breath-taking view, and it grew even more striking
as the daylight increased in intensity and revealed the details of
rocky cliffs, lovely green trees and even greener fields, attractively
landscaped houses and interestingly winding roads. I consumed it
with my eyes, spellbound, transported, enraptured. What a
sublime sight.

'Only twelve miles to go,' I told *Tinkerbelle*.

The thought brought on a faint stabbing of pain. The voyage
was almost over. It was in its hoary old age, moving swiftly
toward its end, its death.

19

THIS day, our seventy-eighth since leaving Cape Cod, promised to be momentous. There seemed to be a portentous tingle in the air, as if it were charged with electricity. I could feel goose bumps rising on my skin and spasmodic shivers running up and down my back. I hoped I could live through what was coming.

We were about four miles off the Lizard, as close as I cared to get because of what I'd heard about the dangerous rip tides that swept around its base. I didn't want *Tinkerbelle*'s bones to be added to those of other vessels that littered the ocean floor in that area. So we stayed a comfortable distance offshore.

I backed *Tinkerbelle*'s genny and lashed down her tiller to heave to for some breakfast. It seemed prudent to eat at once, while I had the chance, to build up strength for what might lie ahead. I also bathed as well as I could, shaved, got my moustache into the best shape possible and put on the cleanest clothes I had. And then I spruced up *Tinkerbelle* with Old Glory flying from a staff at her stern and the Union Jack fluttering from her starboard shroud. I must say she looked a gallant little lady with those flags snapping merrily in the breeze.

When all these preparations were completed, I looked shoreward again and found that the Lizard Light had stopped blinking. About the same time the sun rose above the edge of the sea and, soon after surrounded us with pleasant warmth. It heightened the colours and rolling configuration of the countryside: that beautiful, beautiful land. It revealed, too, that the sky today, August 17th, would be blue. It was going to be a wonderful day.

We started moving again, northeastward towards the fearsome

Manacles, jagged rocks that reached out from the shore like the lower jaw and teeth of a gigantic monster. The wind had shifted into the west and had become several knots lighter, but we were still able to travel at a good clip. There were no other vessels in sight; we had this section of the channel all to ourselves.

I looked back over the stern towards the sea we were leaving behind and again I don't mind admitting I felt a few sharp pangs of regret. There was peace out there of a sort one could never find on land; there was quiet, too, and even more important, a challenge that brought out the best in one and focused it on basic, consequential things. I felt the experience had enriched my life; and I hoped that, through me, it might touch the lives of others.

I had become well acquainted with loneliness and I believe that gave me a greater comprehension of the value of human companionship. The sea had its drawbacks, though; there was no doubt about that. It couldn't give you a formal education (or even a well-balanced informal one), or love, or a helping hand when you needed it. The sea was cold, disinterested, impartial. There was no real warmth to it, no sharing of knowledge or feelings. And yet there was one hugely wonderful thing to be said for the sea: it was always the sea—constantly, perpetually, invariably, uniformly, eternally the sea. It was the sea and nothing else. It couldn't dissimulate. It couldn't say one thing while thinking another. It couldn't flatter you and turn your head. There wasn't a treacherous or dishonest wave in its whole massive body.

Another thing I liked about the sea was that I could pit myself against it without fear of injuring another human being. Nothing I did mattered at all to the sea; nothing I did could hurt it in the least. But in the hurly-burly of life ashore, where people were pitted against one another in a furious scramble for success, it was almost impossible to avoid hurting others or being hurt by them. I wasn't much of a scrambler and that's why I liked that nice cosy seat on the *P.D.* copy desk. It was a relatively peaceful spot, like the eye of a hurricane.

We were approaching Black Head now, about halfway between

the Lizard and the Manacles, and as I looked towards the west I saw a sailing boat disengage itself from the shore and head towards us. Then other craft, sailing boats and motorboats, came into sight to the north, all moving in our direction.

The first sailing boat, the one in the west, closed in fast and as it passed those on board waved in a most friendly way and called out, 'Well done! Well done!' And I shouted back, 'Thank you! Thanks for coming out to see me!' It was the first of hundreds of similar exchanges that took place that day.

As we approached the Manacles, I thought that we were probably sailing over the very same channel floor that the Invincible Armada had sailed over more than three hundred and seventy-seven years earlier while on its way to meet the British fleet off Plymouth. And no sooner had the possibility popped into my mind than another armada appeared on the scene, this one English and headed south, straight for *Tinkerbelle* and me. It came towards us fast, turned and then swept us up into its bosom to escort us the remaining few miles to Falmouth; and as it moved along it continued to grow. It was a fantastic sight.

One of the first boats to reach us was an R.A.F. launch carrying a few of the pilots who had so kindly watched over us as we neared the coast. Someone on the launch thrust a marvellous big sandwich and a nice cup of hot coffee into my hands. How good each tasted! It was about noon and I was getting hungry.

Shortly after that some Royal Navy helicopters arrived to form an umbrella over us as we sailed in. It was wonderful of them to come and I appreciated the honour immensely; the only trouble was that the backwash from the rotors whipped *Tinkerbelle*'s mains'l back and forth in an alarming way that prevented it from functioning properly. It behaved like a whirligig. I guess the choppers saw what was happening, for in a very short time they considerately moved off and things slipped back more or less to routine.

I think it was about one o'clock when we passed by the menacing Manacles, keeping well offshore for safety's sake. And then the boats really began to swarm around us. They were just like bees around a hive. It was absolutely astounding. I heard a newsman estimate that there were three hundred craft surrounding *Tinkerbelle*, which made this armada more than twice the size of the Spanish one, in numbers of vessels if not in total tonnage. I think perhaps the man may have put the figure a little high in the enthusiasm of the moment, but, anyway, there were an awful lot of boats out there. I doubt if anyone had seen anything like it since Dunkirk.

Many of Falmouth's commercial craft had gone to work ferrying people out to see *Tinkerbelle* and me as we neared the harbour. They were jammed to the gunwales and whenever one went by a chorus of 'Well dones' would fill the air. And then I'd call out 'Thank yous' and we'd all wave happily to each other. Americans often think of the English as being a little stiff and standoffish, but let me say at once that isn't true. I have never met more friendly, more warmhearted people than I met that day. They couldn't have been nicer.

And I must say those Englishmen were no slouches when it came to business. You can believe this or not, but postcard pictures of *Tinkerbelle* sailing along in the midst of that armada were being sold even before we reached the harbour entrance. How it was accomplished, I don't know. But I do know it was being done, because I got one of the cards while we were still miles from our goal.

Radio newsman Robert Forbes got in some pretty fast licks, too. He came aboard *Tinkerbelle* and tape-recorded an interview with me as we sailed along, then said 'Thank you', got back on his own boat and churned off. A few minutes later, while we were still sailing towards Black Rock, at the mouth of the harbour, I heard the interview over a portable radio on an adjacent boat. It was a novel experience for me to be interviewed in the first place (as a former reporter, I was accustomed to asking questions instead of answering them), but to be interviewed and then to hear the interview within a very few minutes, that was really something!

Before we had progressed very far past the Manacles, the fishing boat *Girl Christian* came alongside and on it were Virginia and Robin and Douglas. It was wonderful to see the children at last, and to see Virginia again. I could hardly wait until we were all together ashore. What a marvellous reunion it would be. The *Plain Dealer* and *Daily Mirror* newsmen were also on the boat and it was good to see them again, too. We all chatted like magpies for a few minutes and then the *Girl Christian* hurried back to shore. Those aboard her were to meet me when I docked at Custom House Quay.

By this time it was after 6 p.m. and although we were only about two miles from the harbour entrance it began to look as though *Tinkerbelle* wasn't going to make it in before nightfall. The wind had fallen off to almost nothing. We were held to an agonizingly slow pace. But then the harbourmaster, Captain Francis H. Edwards, came along and offered me a tow. I had hoped the *Tinkerbelle* would sail in by herself so I was reluctant to accept the offer, but then I thought of all the people waiting on shore to see us (including the mayor) and how disappointed they might be and, in fact, how disappointed I would be, too, if we didn't make it before dark, so I finally agreed.

We were soon moving again at a lively pace and the increased tempo seemed to accentuate the holiday mood of the escorting armada. Boats circled, crisscrossed and flocked all about us. Several times I thought we were going to be crushed. People cheered and shook my hand and gave me the thumbs-up victory sign and passed me things to eat. One young fellow in a small runabout stayed alongside for quite a while and gave me a couple of Cornish pasties. A few persons simply wanted to touch me, as if I had some magical power to impart. Others just shouted, 'Well done!' 'Good show!' or 'Glad you made it, mate!'

I patted *Tinkerbelle* on the stern and said, 'Well done!'

It was nearly seven when we approached Black Rock. Off to port the shore was a solid mass of people and behind them, at the top of a small hill, were the ruins of Pendennis Castle, ancient guardian of Falmouth, its ramparts crowded with more spectators. If I half closed my eyes, it was easy to imagine the spectators were Romans defending the castle against attacking Saxons. It was a spectacular sight.

We turned to port, moved past Falmouth's famous docks and

shipyards and on to the Custom House Quay. People were everywhere: standing along the shore, perched on window ledges, leaning out of doorways, crowded on to jetties, thronging the streets, clinging to trees and cramming the inner harbour in boats of every size and description. The whole place was teeming with humanity. I heard later that fifty thousand people were there to see *Tinkerbelle* and me complete our voyage.

I was simply dumbfounded, numbed by the enormity of it all and not a little bewildered. It was just too much to take in all at once.

I put down a couple of fenders to protect *Tinkerbelle* from the stone quayside and then, after seventy-eight days of living on a pitching, rolling, swaying boat, I stepped ashore. And almost fell flat on my face!

The quay seemed to be shaking, as if an earthquake were in progress. I wobbled about and staggered like a man who had had too much grog; and with all those people watching, it was embarrassing. I could see it was going to take a few days to get back my land legs.

Most of what happened after that is blurred in my mind. I was too stunned to comprehend fully, or remember. I do recall, though, that every boat and ship in the harbour let go with its horn or whistle and shook the whole waterfront with reverberating sound as the crowd yelled, R.A.F. Shackletons flew overhead in wigwagging salutes and a band on the quay (I heard later it was the St. Stythians Silver Band) played 'The Star-Spangled Banner' and 'The Stars and Stripes Forever'.

I hugged and kissed Virginia, Robin and Douglas and then met Samuel A. Hooper, mayor of Falmouth, who looked most impressive in his scarlet robes and golden chain of office. He welcomed me to the city and I apologized for delaying his vacation. Then I knelt and kissed the stones of the quay in thanksgiving for a safe passage across the ocean and in gratitude for the warm welcome I was receiving.

The pier was a mass of faces. People waved flags, pointed cameras, fired flashbulbs, cheered. I waved and shouted back, 'Hi, everybody!' When a newsman asked me what I thought of the welcome, all I could say was 'I'm flabbergasted!' But I felt as if I'd been elected President.

Then it was time to go. We were led through the crowd toward some cars on the quay and Virginia and I were asked to get into the back of one of them. Before I got into the car, I felt pricks of conscience at the thought of leaving *Tinkerbelle*. I looked back to where I knew Russ Kane and the Falmouth police were looking after her, but she was hidden by the high side of the quay and by the crowd. I couldn't even see the tip of her mast.

It was all over now, all behind us. The voyage was dead. I felt a lump rising in my throat. I looked around at the thousands of people on the quay and on the shore, and I heard the 'Well dones' and felt the handshakes of those nearest to me. And then I knew that, for *Tinkerbelle* and me, our voyage over, what Tinker Bell's friend Peter Pan had once said was true: To die *was* an awfully big adventure.

Comments for Sailors

Tinkerbelle's voyage, I believe, supports the theory that a boat's size has little or no bearing on seaworthiness (only on comfort) and tends to prove that very small boats, reasonably well designed and handled, are capable of crossing oceans. (However, I hope no one reading these pages will assume that *any* small boat is able to cross an ocean, because in that direction lies potential tragedy.) The principal factors that made *Tinkerbelle* capable of the voyage, were I think, her watertightness with hatches closed, her unsinkableness and her self-righting ability. Of course, many other factors also were involved, but these three were probably the most important, and the absence of any one of them might have resulted in insuperable difficulties.

My general advice to anyone contemplating an ocean cruise in a small boat is to get all the sailing experience you can, especially in the boat you expect to use, read all you can about the voyages of others, and, most important of all, profit to the fullest possible extent from your experience and reading. Don't gloss over hazards that should be faced squarely. And don't take chances unnecessarily. By this I mean don't reason thus: Yes, I know the mains'l halyard is badly worn in one spot, but it's probably strong enough to last through this voyage. Or: The bilge pump seems to be working all right, so I don't see why I should have to check its insides or take along spare parts. It is folly to leave a potential source of trouble uncorrected.

It is important to assume, I think, that at one time or another your boat will be completely submerged and/or capsized and, to be extra safe, that it will be filled with water. So you need a boat capable of coping with each of these possibilities. If you don't have such a boat, the risks you face will be correspondingly greater.

The cockpit or foot well should be small so that, if filled by the sea, it will not add a dangerous amount of weight to the boat, making it sluggish and lacking in buoyancy. *Tinkerbelle*'s foot well was reduced in size through the temporary installation of a box-like contrivance containing flotation material at its aft end and a storage compartment at its forward end. It was a worth-while alteration because the remaining part of the foot well *was* filled with water several times.

If a conventional keel sailing boat weighing a ton or more is rolled over or pitchpoled (that is, somersaulted stern over bow) by an enormous wave, it will almost certainly be dismasted and suffer other serious damage. However, I think *Tinkerbelle* could be rolled over and possibly even pitchpoled without suffering grave injuries because she weighs only six hundred and fifty pounds, and her hundred-pound daggerboard-keel is not heavy enough to cause sufficient strain to break her mast while righting her. I can't prove this. It is simply a feeling I have acquired, partly through reasoning and partly through familiarity with *Tinkerbelle*'s usual behaviour.

If I were to repeat the voyage, the only change I would make in *Tinkerbelle* herself would be to equip her with roller reefing or with an extra set of reefing points. I would also add a hacksaw, a pair of tinsnips, a small can of machine oil, a spare radar reflector and a second Dacron genoa to my stores. I could have used the hacksaw and tinsnips in repairing the broken rudder. The machine oil would have helped to keep my tools from rusting, although I improvised machine oil by melting Vaseline on the stove. The radar reflector would have replaced the one lost overboard and the second Dacron genoa would have allowed me to make *Tinkerbelle* steer herself more often. If I had been able to do that, I might have done more reading.

On a repeat voyage I would not take any cotton clothing whatever except possibly shoregoing clothes sealed in plastic bags. Everything else would be of wool, for wool retains body warmth even when it is wet. Wet cotton, on the other hand, becomes chilly and then, when it dries, the salt in it makes it stiff so that it chafes against your skin.

Incidentally, the plastic bags in which I packed my cans of food and many other items were sealed by folding a piece of Teflon tape over the open end of each bag in turn and going over it with a hot iron. I found the iron worked best when it was set for woollens, although some experimentation was necessary to get the proper combination of heat and time to secure an air-tight bond. Of course, the same piece of Teflon served to seal all the bags.

I had very few health problems. During the first month the prolonged contact with salt water made my fingers and toes swell rather painfully, but twice-daily applications of skin lotion and Vaseline cleared up this condition. Similar treatment, plus a course of acromycin antibiotic capsules, kept the salt-water sores on my buttocks from developing into anything serious. I found that the sores began to heal as soon as I switched to wearing wool next to my skin. Salt-saturated cotton underclothing tended to irritate them, causing me considerable distress.

When I began the voyage, I was somewhat overweight at two hundred pounds. All the way across the ocean I dined very well indeed, from the point of view of quantity if not quality, and so I expected to arrive in England weighing as much as I had at the start, if not more. But, very much to my surprise, I found I had lost forty pounds. (Possibly this means that a good way of losing weight is to go on a canned-food diet.) I suffered no ill effects, however, and at the end of the voyage I still had thirteen gallons of water and a month's supply of food.

Despite the periods of depression and the hallucinations, my mental health apparently remained good (unless you believe I was insane to make the voyage in the first place). I have been interviewed by three psychiatrists, two of whom specialize in the study of human reactions to monotony and loneliness, and have learned from them that my responses were predictably normal. It seems that sagging morale and hallucinations are experienced by practically all singlehanded voyagers, although not all of them admit it publicly in their books.

Tinkerbelle

The lack of sleep and the drug I took to keep myself alert no doubt accelerated the appearance of the hallucinations, but the visions themselves were largely the result of my mind's efforts to cope with the solitude and danger. My mind invented people, both friends and enemies, so that I wouldn't be alone or without help in facing the hazards of the vast, empty ocean.

I wish now that I had done more with photography. It is not especially easy to sail a boat and take pictures, either stills or movies, at the same time, so I found that the high points of the voyage, periods of very rough weather or the moments when I was conversing with the captains of ships that stopped to see if everything was all right, went unphotographed. I was simply too busy doing other things at those times. Which makes this a good argument against singlehanded voyaging, because, if a second person had been present, he could have taken the pictures while I handled the boat, or vice versa.

The picture I most regret having missed is the one of the giant 'sea worm' I saw. I wish I had taken the time to get out my cameras and go back to photograph it. Who knows? It might have proved to be some as yet uncatalogued creature of the sea.

Moisture and heat are the worst enemies of photographic film, especially colour film, but the film aboard *Tinkerbelle* was not damaged to any great extent. Heat was no problem at all since the cabin temperature, out at sea, never got above seventy degrees; but moisture was another matter. Still, the only film that suffered moisture damage was 16-mm. movie film that had been left in the camera for several days. When the camera was not in use, I kept it sealed in a plastic bag, but apparently this did not prevent some moisture from reaching about twenty-five feet of film and altering the colours slightly.

The still camera, being designed for underwater as well as above-water use, protected the film from moisture very well; and as soon as a roll was exposed I popped it back into its sealed container. But the movie film wasn't as easily protected. It was all right as long as it was in its original package and, after exposure, when I resealed it in the package with cellulose tape. But while *in the camera* it was vulnerable.

In addition to being sealed in its original packages after exposure, all the film (both before and after exposure) was kept sealed in large plastic bags, which also contained silica-gel moisture-absorbing tablets.

Another minor disappointment of the voyage was that I never got to take any underwater pictures, even though I had an underwater camera. The homemade device I had for thrusting the camera below the surface and operating it from above contained a heavy brass plate and when the second rudder broke I had to use this plate as part of the material for making repairs. And that put the underwater picture device out of action before I got around to using it.

Now, about expenses. The total cost of the one-way passage to England, not including the cost of the boat and the expense of repairing and remodelling it, was roughly $1,000. Since it would have been possible to fly to England in June for approximately $400 (first class) or $270 (tourist), the voyage was actually a rather expensive way to cross the Atlantic Ocean. But the experiences of the voyage, both the pleasant ones and the unpleasant ones, more than compensated for the difference in cost. In fact, to me, they were priceless; I wouldn't have traded them for anything.

One more comment should be made. The $750 in travellers' cheques I had among my miscellaneous supplies was to pay for getting *Tinkerbelle* and me back to Cleveland from England. I didn't use it, however, because the *Plain Dealer* very kindly took care of this expense.

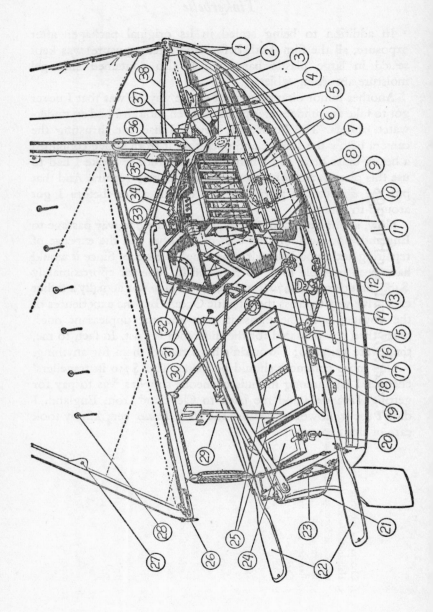

Tinkerbelle and her Fittings

1. Chocks for mooring lines
2. Half-inch Dacron line wrapped around mast, with swivel shackle at forward end for attaching sea-anchor line
3. Mooring cleat
4. Red and green combination running light
5. Case for six-volt battery powering all lights
6. Fixture to facilitate tying down supplies securely
7. Switches to control running light, stern light and masthead light
8. Porthole with ⅜-inch plastic cover to prevent breakage by waves
9. Barometer
10. Fire extinguisher
11. Lowered daggerboard-keel
12. Jam cleat for sheet used with small jib
13. Bilge pump
14. Handhold
15. Bridge-deck compass
16. Bronze strap for attaching lifeline
17. Self-bailing cockpit foot well
18. Oarlock
19. Second part of oarlock
20. Stern light
21. Safety line attaching rudder to boat
22. Oars used for rowing or to wing out twin genoas for self-steering with following wind
23. Oarlock fixture at stern
24. Storage compartment hatch
25. Removable 'box' designed to reduce size of cockpit foot well; flotation material in aft portion and storage space under hinged lid in forward portion
26. Swivel at end of boom to which topping lift is attached
27. Reefing cringle
28. Reef point
29. Boom and mast crutch
30. Waterproof electrical socket for attaching cord of spot-light
31. Fixtures for securing cabin hatch cover
32. Cabin dome light
33. Winch and line for raising daggerboard-keel
34. Fixture on which rod that holds daggerboard-keel in raised position rests
35. Cleats for jib and mainsh'l halyards
36. Slot through which daggerboard-keel is raised or lowered
37. Rack for charts and other papers
38. Raised rub rail providing handhold for anyone in water

Equipment and Supplies Taken on Voyage

NAVIGATION BOOKS AND EQUIPMENT—*Radio Navigation Aids, Atlantic and Mediterranean Area*; *Rules of the Road*; *The Nautical Almanac, 1965*; *H.O. 214, Tables of Computed Altitude and Azimuth*, three volumes covering latitudes 30° to 59°; *Sailing Directions, South Coast of England*; *United States Coast Pilot No. 2*, covering Cape Cod area; *Piloting, Seamanship and Small Boat Handling*, by Charles F. Chapman; pamphlet on *Sea and Swell Observations*; book of *Tidal Current Charts* for Cape Cod area; *Primer of Navigation*, by George W. Mixter; *Navigation the Easy Way*, by Carl D. Lane and John Montgomery; light lists; universal plotting sheets; all necessary charts (protected in waterproof plastic chart cases); surplus U.S. Air Force sextant; Hallicrafters WR-3000 transistor radio receiver with earphones; 2 Danforth course protractors; 1 wind-speed meter; 1 alarm clock; 2 wristwatches; 1 stop watch; 2 dividers; 2 Army-type hand-bearing compasses; 1 mounted, bridge-deck compass; 1 sounding lead and line; 1 log-book; 3 notebooks; indelible-ink ballpoint pens; pencils.

GENERAL BOOKS—*Gone With the Wind*, by Margaret Mitchell; *The Spy Who Came In from the Cold*, by John Le Carré; *The Elements of Style*, by William Strunk, Jr., and E. B. White; *Birds of the Ocean*, by W. B. Alexander; *How to Exercise Without Moving a Muscle*, by Victor Obeck; *The Stars*, by H. A. Rey; *20 Years and 20 Hits for the Harmonica*; *World Almanac* for 1965. (*Birds of the Ocean* was the only book I found time to read.)

TOOLS—1 saw, 3 screwdrivers, 1 adjustable-grip pliers, 1 non-adjustable pliers, 1 hand drill with assortment of bits, 1 hammer,

4 C clamps, 2 files, 1 small wood plane, 1 adjustable wrench, 1 metal measuring tape, 1 pocket emery stone, 2 pocketknives, 1 sail repair kit (containing sailor's palm, needles, twine, marlinespike, beeswax and marline), 1 cold patch kit for repairing inflatable raft or life jacket, 1 chisel, 1 hard rubber mallet, 1 wire cutter, 1 sheath knife, and marlinespike, 1 scissors.

SPARE PARTS, MATERIALS AND EQUIPMENT—1 rudder; 1 set of gudgeons and pintles; 1 tiller; 1 stem plate; 1 chain plate; 1 mast tang, 1 stainless-steel stay (to replace either a shroud or the forestay); brass bolts and screws of all sizes; sandpaper; copper tacks; copper boat nails; liquid rubber caulking material; waterproof glue; fibreglass cloth, resin and hardener; 3 sets of D batteries (8 batteries to a set) for radio; 4 sets of D batteries (2 to a set) for flashlight; 3 batteries for anchor light; 3 Hot Shot 6-volt batteries for running lights and spotlight; bulbs for flashlight, running lights and spotlight; 8 blocks (pulleys) of various sizes; 100 feet of $\frac{3}{8}$-inch nylon line; 100 yards of light nylon cord; 2 sea-anchor buckets; 6 shackles of different sizes; assortment of pine, plywood and oak planks; various lengths of brass, copper and stainless-steel wire; pieces of sheet brass; 6 cans of gas for foghorn; 1 cylinder of gas to inflate life raft; 1 $2\frac{1}{2}$-pound Danforth anchor, 12 sail slides and 12 clips; 12 jib slides; caulking cotton; hose for cockpit drain; wood putty; assortment of rope thimbles; 1 turnbuckle; 6 clevis pins; 1 pint of grey paint; 1 pint of spar varnish; 2 yards of sailcloth; 6 wire rope clamps; 2 rolls of chafing tape.

SAFETY EQUIPMENT—1 Mae West life jacket; 1 inflatable life raft with cylinder of gas; 1 fire extinguisher; 1 anchor light; 1 spotlight; 1 gas-operated foghorn; 6 night flares; 6 day flares; 1 deck-mounted bilge pump; 2 portable pumps; 1 signalling mirror; 1 barometer; 1 Victory Girl SOS signal transmitter; 2 dye markers; 1 life-preserver cushion; medical kit (contents listed below); 1 bucket sea anchor; 1 solar still for making freshwater from seawater; 1 white tropical helmet; 10 packets of silica-gel to help keep film, sextant and radio dry; 2 pairs of sunglasses; 1 lifeline; 1 compass corrector and pelorus; 1 set of oars; 3

waterproof rubberized canvas bags for storing equipment; 1 radar reflector; 1 extra survival fishing kit; 2 rubber sleeve chafe preventers; 1 flashlight; 1 plastic emergency sextant; 5 emergency food packs (each one containing a 5-day supply of vitamin tablets, malted milk tablets, chocolate bars and biscuits); sufficient poly-ethylene foam flotation material to make boat unsinkable; survival kit (contents listed below).

MEDICAL KIT—(Packed in moistureproof case) 1 haemostat, 1 scalpel with spare blades, 1 tweezers, 20 disposable syringes, 12 disposable sutures, 2 tubes of bacitracin ointment, 100 3 x 3 gauze pads, 2 Ace bandages, 3 rolls of adhesive tape, 3 rolls of gauze, 24 safety pins, 8 small splints, 200 aspirin tablets, 1 package of powdered alum, 1 bottle of nose drops, 1 inhaler, 200 salt tablets, 2 pounds of Vaseline, 1 can of talcum powder, 6 small packets of toilet tissue, 1 tube of zinc ointment, 1 bottle of sun lotion, 1 bottle of Kaopectate, 1 oral thermometer, large bottle of liquid antiseptic, 1 bottle of laxative, 1 tube of anaesthetic eye ointment, 1 tube of antibiotic eye ointment, large bottle of acro-mycin antibiotic capsules, dexedrine, nembutal, benadryl, tincture of belladonna, phenobarbital, morphine, codeine, paregoric, 4 tubes of anaesthetic skin ointment, skin lotion, pills to combat motion sickness or allergy, *First Aid*, published by the American Red Cross, *The Ship's Medicine Chest and First Aid at Sea,* a U.S. Public Health Service publication.

SURVIVAL KIT—1 pound of malted milk tablets, 16 bars of tropical chocolate, 4 cans of pemmican, 30 high-energy dextrose wafers, 8 cans of vacuum-packed water, 6 night flares, 2 day flares, 1 dye marker, 1 signalling mirror, 1 fishing kit, 1 tube of suntan lotion, 2 packages of hygienic tissue, 1 bottle of insect repellent, 1 flash-light, 1 waterproof container of matches, 1 distress whistle, 1 distress flag, 1 can opener, a first-aid kit with instructions for use, 1 sheathed hunting and fishing knife, 1 compass.

SAILS AND GEAR—1 red nylon mains'l, 68 square feet; 1 white cotton mains'l, 68 square feet; 2 white cotton jibs, 22 square feet each; 1 white Dacron genoa, 38 square feet; 1 white cotton genoa, 38 square feet; 1 green cotton storm jib, 9 square feet; 1 green cotton trysail, 25 square feet; 150-foot $\frac{1}{2}$-inch nylon anchor line; all running rigging of $\frac{3}{8}$-inch Dacron line; 10 feet of $\frac{1}{8}$-inch shock cord; 10 feet of $\frac{1}{4}$-inch shock cord; 8 sail stops made of shock cord; 2 whisker poles for winging out cotton jibs; 1 8-pound Danforth anchor; 2 plastic-foam fenders (one of which served as float for sea-anchor bucket).

GALLEY EQUIPMENT—1 canned-heat stove in gimbals, 27 large cans of canned heat, 1 frying pan, 1 saucepan, 1 knife, 1 fork, 1 spoon, 100 matchbooks in waterproof plastic container, 3 bottles of liquid salt-water soap, scouring pads and dishcloths for cleaning pans and silverware, 2 plastic nonsinkable cups, 1 seaman's knife with can opener on it, 4 folding army-type can openers.

PROVISIONS—28 gallons of water carried in 40 half-gallon, 3 one-gallon and 1 five-gallon plastic containers; 40 cans beef slices and potatoes; 30 cans turkey loaf; 24 cans peas; 23 cans peas and carrots, 23 cans corn; 6 cans chili; 6 cans Vienna sausage; 4 cans boned chicken; 5 cans beef stew; 6 cans stuffed peppers; 4 cans stuffed cabbage; 8 cans beans and wieners; 8 cans corned-beef hash; 5 cans shrimp; 5 cans tuna and noodles; 8 cans spaghetti and meat balls; 2 cans ham loaf; 3 cans chicken and noodles; 10 cans diced beets; 10 cans succotash; 10 cans sweet potatoes; 10 cans diced carrots; 30 cans assorted fruit juices; 30 cans carbonated soft drinks; 40 cans Bartlett pears; 20 cans fruit cocktail; 20 cans sliced peaches; 10 cans condensed milk; 2 cans plum pudding; 1 jar hard sauce; 8 cans oleomargarine; 5 cans cherries; 40 small packets raisins; 140 assorted candy bars; 20 dehydrated meat bars; 10 dehydrated bacon bars; 10 cans pemmican; 10 cans egg salad; 8 cans fruitcake; 20 cans white bread; 100 cereal bars; 40 starch jelly bars; 8 dehydrated Spanish omelettes; 8 servings dehydrated scrambled eggs; 200 individually packaged servings of coffee, dehydrated cream and sugar; 20 portions grape jelly; 20 portions strawberry jelly; 20 portions marmalade; 1 bottle brandy; 20 servings orange drink; 20 servings cocoa; 60 packets biscuits; 90 multivitamin capsules; 90 ascorbic acid tablets; ketchup; mustard; Tabasco sauce; curry powder; salt; pepper; turkey stuffing; bouillon cubes.

CLOTHING AND PERSONAL GEAR—1 waterproof anti-exposure suit, 1 set of oilskins, 1 pilot cap, 1 knitted watch cap, 4 cotton undershirts, 4 cotton undershorts, 2 turtle-neck sports shirts, 2 V-neck sport shirts, 2 pairs of cotton thermal underwear, 4 pairs of woollen socks, 2 pairs of cotton trousers, 1 pair of woollen trousers, 1 woollen shirt, 3 sweaters, 2 pairs of rubber-soled deck shoes, 1 pair of leather shore shoes, 2 shoregoing shirts, 1 shore-going jacket, 2 pairs of shoregoing trousers, 2 neckties, 1 visored yachting hat, 1 red nylon windbreaker, 1 safety razor and spare blades, 2 cakes of salt-water soap, 2 washcloths, 2 face towels, 2 bath towels, 1 toothbrush, 1 tube of toothpaste.

PHOTOGRAPHY EQUIPMENT—1 Nikonos 35-mm. still camera, 1 Revere 16-mm. magazine movie camera, skylight filters for both cameras, 52 50-foot magazines of 16-mm. Kodachrome II, 12 rolls of 36-exposure 35-mm. Kodachrome II, flashgun for Nikonos, 10 dozen blue flashbulbs, Weston exposure meter, closeup lenses for Nikonos, neutral-grey test cards for determining exposure, lens shades, home-made device on a pole for thrusting Nikonos camera into the sea and operating it remotely for taking pictures underwater.

MISCELLANEOUS—Writing paper and envelopes, $750 in travel-lers' cheques, 10 one-dollar bills (to cover postage of letters picked up at sea), 6 ballpoint-pen refills, 3 sponges, 3 rolls of cellulose tape, 1 American flag, 1 American ensign, 1 British flag, 1 yellow 'Q' flag, plastic bags of various sizes, spring clips to hold plastic bags shut, 1 ink marker, 1 chromatic harmonica, 1 hand warmer and fuel, 2 woollen blankets, passport, health certificate, boat ownership papers.

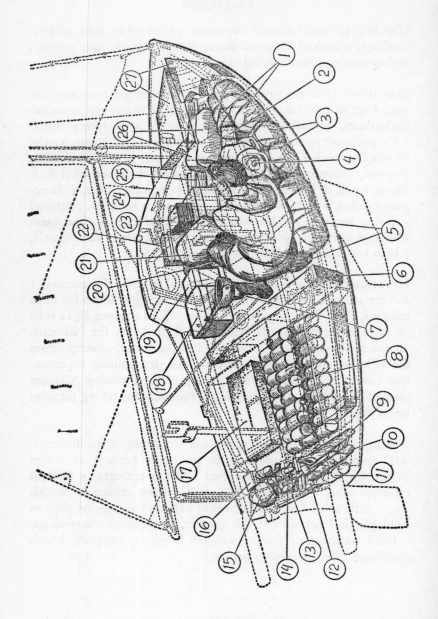

Stowage of Supplies

1. Two bags of food, one week's supply in each bag
2. Watertight, rubberized canvas bag containing navigation books, cameras and log
3. Two more bags of food
4. Blanket used as pillow while sleeping. Several positions were tested for sleeping and the one shown proved most satisfactory.
5. Bags of clothing and photographic film
6. Flotation material
7. Canned-heat stove in gimbals
8. Forty half-gallon plastic bottles of drinking water (not all shown)
9. Saw
10. Other tools
11. Survival fishing kit
12. Packages of spare parts, screws, bolts and batteries

13. Anchor light
14. Compressed-gas horn
15. Extra sails
16. Solar still for converting salt water into fresh water
17. Plank of flotation material (similar plank on starboard side)
18. Victory Girl emergency SOS transmitter
19. Survival kit
20. Five-gallon plastic container of water
21. Bag of food with another underneath
22. Radio receiver
23. Sextant
24. Medical kit in airtight case
25. Assortment of lumber for making repairs
26. Two more bags of food
27. Two more flotation planks

Unbroken

by
ALASTAIR MARS

To the undying memory
of

LIEUTENANT JOHN RENWICK HAIG HADDOW
D.S.C., ROYAL NAVY

and all those Sub-mariners who did not return

A Ship is Born

November, 1941. Kharkov had fallen and the German army
advanced through the snows towards Moscow. In Africa
the New Zealanders captured Bardia and General Auchinleck
launched the offensive that was to result in the relief of Tobruk.
In the Mediterranean, the disasters of Greece and Crete still
fresh in our minds, we were doing no more than hold our
own. The *Ark Royal* had been sunk, and Mr. Churchill told
Parliament that we were losing a monthly average of 180,000
tons of merchant shipping. While Chiang Kai-shek called
upon the Western Powers to join in the war against Japan,
America remained uneasily neutral. In Yugoslavia the
Tcheckniks under Mihailovitch harried the German occupa-
tion forces. Nuremberg had been bombed and Marshal
Pétain led the government of occupied France. The conquest of Abyssinia and the defiance of Malta were two bright
stars in a black, uncertain night.

At home the people of Britain went about their business
with that quiet confidence other nations call arrogance.
There was rationing, the Windmill Theatre and jokes about
Woolton Pie and the Home Guard . . . Nightly raids on
Merseyside and London . . . Walt Disney's *Fantasia* and
the Polish Army choir . . . A million women employed in
munition factories . . . As they hammered rivets, forged
steel, and dug at bomb débris, sports fans discussed the recent

soccer international in which England had beaten Scotland by two goals to nil. . . .

Farmers tended their fields, fishermen cast their trawls, miners sweated in the ugly darkness of the pits. Aircraft, tanks, bombs and shells rolled from the production lines. Housewives worked miracles with the rations—and found time to drive ambulances and man Wardens' Posts. Children were educated and grandparents came from retirement to "do their bit." Parks became allotments, taxis hauled fire pumps. As scientists evolved new and more terrible weapons of destruction, a lunatic fringe demanded "peace at any price." In the drive for scrap, park railings became Bren-carriers, dustbins destroyers and aluminium saucepans Spitfires.

And at Barrow-in-Furness in this gloomy, mournful November, as just one tiny part of the great wartime scene, a ship was being born. . . .

It was a grey, depressing afternoon, and as the taxi rattled from the station to the Victoria Park Hotel, my wife huddled closer to my side. Occasionally she shivered, not from cold, but at the bleak melancholy of Barrow. For my part, I was too excited to be affected by the ugliness of industrial Lancashire. At last, after months of nail-biting impatience as captain of a training submarine, I was on my way to take command of the *Unbroken*. She had been launched some months earlier by the wife of "Tubby" Linton, one of the greatest of all submarine commanders, and was near completion. Only God and the Sea Lords knew what the future held for me, but it could be no worse than the soul-destroying repetition of training duties. Understandably, Ting, my wife, did not see things that way; apart from other considerations, no woman likes to have her husband leave her when she is expecting a baby.

6

I was twenty-six years old and bubbling with enthusiasm. To use the expression of the day, I was "mad keen." Perhaps a little apprehensive, too. For it was no small responsibility to have the lives of thirty-two officers and men dependent, to a very large degree, upon the efficiency of my leadership. In a submarine, fifty fathoms deep, there is no second chance, no opportunity for apologies. With the crew as the fingers, and the captain as the brain, you can compare it to an engineer removing the fuse from an unexploded bomb. When the fingers are supple and responsive the fuse will be removed safely—if the brain transmits the right messages.

It was then my turn to shiver, but with the self-assurance of youth I quickly brushed aside such thoughts and speculated, instead, on how soon I would take the *Unbroken* to sea.

At the hotel we quickly checked our bags and made for the bar. We were greeted by a host of old friends. There was "Tubby" Linton, waiting to take the submarine *Turbulent* to the Mediterranean; Paul Skelton, standing by to deliver a newly built submarine to the Turks; Lieut.-Commander Maitland-Makgill-Crichton (oddly, he did not boast a nickname, and was always called Maitland-Makgill-Crichton) then captain of the destroyer *Ithurial*. There were others, too, but seeing Paul Skelton affected me most.

We have all our own particular memory of the September afternoon when Mr. Chamberlain announced the declaration of war. On that Sunday, I was navigator of the submarine *Regulus*, and was drinking with a group of friends at the United Services Club, Hong Kong. Apologetically, a Chinese steward told me I was wanted on the telephone. It was Signalman Cheale calling from the *Regulus*. "Sorry to bother you, sir," he began, "but the balloon's gone up. . . ."

7

I returned to my table, ordered another round of drinks, and broke the news.

A few exclamations, then a long pause. Although there was little we could say, there was another, deeper reason for our silence. We were thinking of the other sub-mariners throughout the Navy, each known to the other, each a friend. Already the boats at home would be patrolling the shallow familiar waters of the North Sea and the Channel. . . .

Exactly six years later, the war over, I sipped a whisky and soda in the ward-room of the submarine *Tudor* as she sailed home from the Far East. Sam Porter, her captain, was one of the few who, like myself, had been a sub-mariner before the war. Inevitably, perhaps, we started to work out, with the aid of the Navy List, those who were left. The result was depressingly sad.

Only one in ten remained in the submarine Service. A few had reached the age limit for submarines; strain and sickness had claimed their share. But the majority were dead. We had lost a lot of friends.

Of the three submarine commanders knocking back doubles in the bar of the Victoria Park Hotel, I was to be the lucky one. On that November evening in 1941, however, we knew better than to talk of the future. Instead we hid ourselves in the security of the past, and laughed and cracked jokes and raised our glasses. It was not until the early hours that I floated happily to my bed.

Vickers' yard at Barrow is a private city of noise and steel; a fevered fantasy in a surrealist nightmare. On the vast slipways the grinning near-skeletons of every type of war vessel, from 8,000-ton cruisers to pathetic, rat-like submarines. Around them, curiously menacing, giant cranes, derricks and monstrous sheer-legs. Then, dwarfing even the cranes, the heavy and light machine shops, the gun-mounting, electrical and battery shops. Armaments stores, engineers' stores, lay-apart stores. Rigging lofts and mould lofts.

With Paul Skelton at my side, I picked my way along the uneven roads of the shipyard to the *Unbroken*, known for signal purposes as P.42. I looked at her—and gasped. Speckled with rust, she was far from completion. The conning-tower and its surrounding structures were in place, but no gun had been fitted, the deck casing was only half completed, there were no periscopes, and a huge rectangular hole in the pressure hull revealed the absence of the motors. Instead of looking a sleek, new submarine, she made me think of a sorely battered hulk salvaged from the ocean depths. Only the barnacles and seaweed were missing.

I turned to Paul Skelton and shouted above the noise: "I suppose I'm responsible for keeping this sieve afloat."

He laughed, cupped his hands and bellowed in my ear: "Lord, no. The firm looks after all that. You don't accept any responsibility until you take her to sea." He broke off as a short, sour-faced man in overalls passed by. "Hey, Jock!" he yelled.

The man in overalls walked over. He looked at me speculatively, and with the experience of years, roared effortlessly above the din: "Och, I know. You dinna have to tell me." He jerked a thumb as dark and as hard as teak against my chest. "This gentleman's belonging to yon submarine, an' he's worried."

I grinned and nodded. The Scot spat expertly into the mud. "We've been bringing submarines into the worrld for the past forty years. Dinna fret yourself."

I looked at him with respect, realising, as though for the first time, that the shipyard was made up of more than just steel and noise. Every ship that left Barrow took a part

9

of Jock with her, whether in the sound security of a rivet, the strength of a steel plate, or in the expert adjustment of an electrical lead. His uniform was his dungarees, his medals the scars and callouses on his hands. Tell him so and he would laugh in your face, yet in his heart was the secret pride and knowledge that there would be no battle honours or naval victories without him and his mates toiling in blitz-threatened Barrow.

Meekly I followed Paul Skelton to the office block, feeling strangely confident that order would emerge from the chaos, and that it would not be long before the gloom of November gave way to a sunny, victorious spring.

I sent the Admiralty a signal to the effect that I had assumed command of the P.42, and on the following day drafted a further signal inquiring about the arrival of my crew. By return I received a detailed message giving me the names and times of arrival of the key members. Names on a sheet of paper. Only one meant anything to me: Sub-Lieutenant John Haddow, who had served with me aboard my training submarine H.44. It was comforting to know he was joining the *Unbroken*, for while the others were as yet no more than ciphers, Haddow was a good, proven officer on whom I knew I could rely.

At last the officers and men of my crew arrived, and when they had been given their billets ashore life became serious. The *Unbroken* was no longer *my* ship, but *our* ship, and since success and survival depended so greatly upon the efficient running of the boat, and since every man-Jack of us would be responsible for some part of that efficiency, we checked, and re-checked and counter-checked every rivet and split-pin from the top of the periscopes to the base of the keel.

December—the month of Pearl Harbour. The American

Navy suffered a vicious, crippling blow, and the events that followed brought blackness to the grey clouds hanging over the civilised world. The Japs invaded Malaya. The *Repulse* and *Prince of Wales* were sunk. Hong Kong fell, Burma was threatened, and half of Malaya was in enemy hands. To help balance these disasters we pushed Rommel from Benghazi, while the Russians held the Germans at the gates of Moscow and Leningrad.

Meanwhile, the *Unbroken* neared completion. The periscopes were lowered into position, the motors fitted. In floating dock the rusty hull was burnished and coated with preservative. The vitally important Asdic set was fitted. (Asdic sets are carried by both surface vessels and submarines. In, for example, destroyers, they reveal, by sending out supersonic waves and measuring the echo, the presence, proximity, course and speed of underwater craft. In submarines they serve the same purpose and also work in reverse—they can reveal the presence, speed, et cetera, of surface craft.) The Asdic set installed and tested, a thousand petty details had to be settled, from the fitting of floor-boards to the ordering of tablecloths and toilet paper. Our "teeth" were fitted: eight torpedoes, sleek and blue, each with a warhead containing 1,000 lb. of explosive.

A task I did not relish was giving a pep-talk to the ship's company. I knew what I wanted to say, and my words were sincere enough, but in wartime, when speech-making is a disease, and everyone utters the same exhortations, promises and sentiments as the man before, sincerity is reduced to trite clichés and worn-out platitudes. To say something new you needed to be a Winston Churchill. None the less, a pep-talk was expected of me, and I mustered the ship's company in the office block, and addressed them something like this:

"I shall be an exacting captain. I know what I want down

to the smallest detail, and I'm going to get it. You can promise your wives and families that you will return to Britain the crew of a successful submarine." (This was no small promise at a time when half our submarines entering the Mediterranean were being sunk.) "I have, however, another, more important duty—to destroy the enemy wherever he may be found. And we shan't shirk the job of finding him. Therefore we have two jobs—to be successful and to survive. To achieve these I need every ounce of loyalty and strength you can give. Remember that I am the sole arbiter of what is good for you, and my orders are to be obeyed implicitly. You may expect work, work, and more work. If any of you joined submarines to get away from discipline you are in for shocks. You will learn more discipline with me than you dreamed of—the proper sort of discipline: self-discipline.

"I don't give a damn what you do ashore, so long as you are ready for your duties at the appointed time. This doesn't mean you can run foul of the shore authorities, and when you do, don't forget that *I* shall have to punish your misbehaviour. Your officers are young, but they have the weight of my experience and training behind them. Obey them without question, for even a bad order well executed leads to a better result than a good order ruined by indecision. A bad order can be countermanded, a slackly obeyed order leads to confusion. In a submarine confusion means disaster.

"One final thing. What was good enough in other submarines will not be good enough here. Nothing is 'good enough' for me. I'm going to have the best, and only the best—and you're going to give it to me."

I dismissed them, hoping I hadn't sounded too pompous.

All in all, I think it went down quite well, although later, when walking through the ship, I noticed that in every mess had been pinned up copies of a newspaper advertisement for Mars Bars. It said, as I remember: "Nothing but the best is good enough for Mars."

On a grey, snow-flecked morning, the *Unbroken* was wound out across the dockyard basin for a final test. For the first time, the ship's company went to diving stations —the equivalent of action stations in a surface ship. As "passengers" we carried dockyard and Admiralty officials and observers. All hatches except those in the conning-tower were shut and clipped, and I stood alone on the bridge, excited, exhilarated and very proud. No nervousness now. A mere six hundred tons, we might be, and our armament no more than a 3-inch gun and four torpedo-tubes, but I felt, with reckless self-assurance, that we were more than a match for the Italian, German and Japanese navies combined!

I leaned over the voice-pipe. "Open One and Six main vents."

As the vents were opened, the air in numbers One and Six main ballast tanks was replaced by an inrushing flood of water, and we settled a little in the basin. I ordered the other main vents to be opened until we rode on just the air contained in number Four tank. I shut the voice-pipe cock on the bridge, stepped backwards down the ladder inside the conning-tower, pulled the upper hatch down above my head, pushed home the clips and inserted the locking pins. I slid down the ladder into the control-room and the signalman secured the lower conning-tower hatch after me. "Up for'ard periscope." With a hiss it slid from its well.

"All right, Number One?"

"Yes, sir," replied Taylor, the first lieutenant.

I lowered the handles at the side of the periscope and gazed at the surrounding dockyard. "Open number Four main vent."

Engine-Room Artificer Lewis flicked a lever. The air rushed from number Four tank. Slowly we sank beneath the level of the water in the basin. As the needles on the depth gauges crept past ten feet I ordered: "Shut Four main vent."

The vent of number Four tank was shut, and the air still trapped inside it provided a cushion upon which we remained suspended in the water. The entire submarine was now submerged, with the exception of ten feet of periscope protruding incongruously from the centre of the basin. We were down.

"From for'ard, sir. Fore hatch leaking badly."

What exaggeration! If the leak is a bad one, we'd be down by the bows—and we aren't.

"Tell 'em to clip it tighter." *They'll have to get used to piddling little leaks—and to bigger ones!* But dark, weather-beaten Archie Baxter, the foreman from Vickers', leapt forward to give his advice.

While half the ship's company checked and counter-checked for signs of leaks, the remainder performed the tedious business of an inclining experiment to test stability. The sailors' part was to shift ten tons of pig iron from one part of the boat to another. After an hour and a half the job was done. We could go back up. "Stand by to surface," I ordered.

"Check main vents," ordered Taylor.

"All main vents checked shut, sir," came the report. I nodded, satisfied. "Surface."

"Blow One and Six main ballast tanks," Taylor called.

14

E.R.A. Lewis opened two of the direct blow valves. Air, at four thousand pounds per square inch, screamed through narrow steel pipes to the tanks at bow and stern, forcing out and replacing the water. We rose to the surface. Signalman Osborne opened the upper conning-tower hatch and I climbed out to the wet bridge.

Our first dive was behind us. If only every future dive would be as simple!

On 28th January, we received our sailing orders from the Naval Officer in Charge, Barrow-in-Furness: "Proceed to Holy Loch under the escort of H.M.S. *Cutty Sark*."

Lieutenant Taylor and I arranged to see our families in Scotland, but for the rest of the crew the sailing orders meant all the embarrassing false gaiety of last good-byes. No one knew, or dared to speculate, when they would come back, how they would come back—or if they would come back at all. But there were brave smiles, gallant assurances and confident promises.

The morning was bleak and grey, and the wind played a merry game with our commissioning pennant and White Ensign. The lock gates opened and we saw the escort vessel, *Cutty Sark*, standing out to sea. The wires securing us to the dock were let go, and as we gathered way the bows were buffeted by saucy, dancing waves. We raised our hands to the men who built her, and they replied with a lusty cheer.

"Give 'em hell, Skipper!"

"You bet we will!"

In Morecambe Bay we dipped to the swell. White-flecked sea surged angrily over the casing, splashing spray on to the bridge. The first voyage of the *Unbroken* was going to be a rough one.

As we passed the north of the Isle of Man the full force of the gale struck us on the port beam, and the *Unbroken* rolled considerably in the short, heavy swell. There were only three of us on the bridge—myself and the two look-outs —and with good reason. In a crash-dive you start to go down immediately the klaxon sounds, and you permit yourself only fifteen seconds in which to submerge. These fifteen seconds allow just enough time for three men on the bridge to get below and close the hatches above them before the boat goes under. If there were more than three men trying to get below, the conning-tower hatches would still be open as the submarine went down, the control-room would be half-flooded, and it would be the devil of a job to secure the hatches against the inrush of water. (There were to be times when the *Unbroken* completed the operation in twelve seconds!)

It was dark by the time we sailed into the Clyde estuary, guided by the shaded blue stern light of the *Cutty Sark*. We spent the night alongside the depot ship, *Forth*, in Holy Loch, and in the reluctant, cinereous Greenock dawn, moved round to the famous submarine testing waters of the Gareloch.

Diving trials followed, first at comparatively slow speeds, then at full speed—in our case eight-and-a-half knots. At that speed, when the hydroplanes give the submarine a stomach-turning tilt, it takes but a few seconds to dive from periscope depth to ninety feet—and, if you are not on your toes, only a few seconds more to dive from ninety feet to hull-splitting disaster on the bottom. Throughout the day the trials continued. We dived to periscope depth and worked up to full speed. I gave the order: "Hard-a-dive on both hydroplanes," and the submarine tilted to an angle of fifteen degrees, bows down. This might not sound a very acute angle, but in a submarine heading for the bottom at speed,

16

it is. Down ... down ... down, until the hydroplanes were reversed and we hoped to God she would pull out of the dive. She did, every time—and we sent our silent thanks to the men of Barrow.

Trials, trials and more trials until, in mid-February, we went to Arrochar at the top of Loch Long for the final trial, testing our torpedo-tubes. Here Lieut. Taylor and I were to spend the last four days with our families. It was a happy interlude.

On the afternoon before sailing, Sub-Lieutenant John Haddow, the armament officer, accompanied Ting and me on a picnic tea by the shores of Loch Lomond. Before we returned to Arrochar we lay on the sands and sipped Loch Lomond water, observing the local superstition that it would bring us luck. At eight o'clock next morning Ting walked to the pier with me. The *Unbroken* lay only a hundred yards off shore, a low, grey shape against the snow-covered mountains. There was little we could say that was not better left unsaid. Wartime farewells—as so many of us know—are profoundly upsetting moments over which it is better not to linger. Ting was obviously distressed, while I felt a pang of regret that I would not see my child, due to be born any day.

"I won't think much of you if you don't come back," she said.

I gave an easy salute, turned, and boarded the motor boat that was to take me to the *Unbroken*. As we cast off, Ting's "Cheerio" echoed across the water.

On 20th February, as we sailed into the calm waters of Holy Loch, I received the signal: "Daughter born yesterday. Both doing well." Forty-eight hours later the *Unbroken*, a minute fragment of Britain at war, sailed south to "seek out and destroy the enemy wherever he may be found."

Chapter One

Cape St. Vincent disappeared into the sea astern, and we set course past Cadiz for Cape Trafalgar. Within forty-eight hours we would be at Gibraltar.

Ten-thirty. The ward-room was dark and silent. I unbuttoned the collar of my jacket and stretched out on the settee that served as my bed. Sleep was elusive, and as I lay there, restless and ill-tempered, I became strangely conscious of the sounds around me; noises that were normally so much an essential background to submarine life they were never heard nor noticed—the dominant clatter of the engines, an occasional voice, the scrape of a boot against an iron ladder, the apologetic shuffle of slippers through the ward-room. Percolating through them all the angry moan of the sea as it swished past our sides. For the first time in many years I became aware, too, of the strange smell peculiar to submarines: the curious combination of oil and damp and gas that dries the mouth and lines the throat.

I twisted on the hard, unyielding cushions and wished we were at Gibraltar where there would be mail from home— news of my wife and the daughter I had not seen. June. We had agreed to call her that. I wondered whom she resembled, and hoped Ting had left hospital to join her aunt at Aldeburgh. I wondered what was happening back in England, and how Paul Skelton and "Tubby" Linton were getting on—and then there was no time to wonder about anything. . . .

"Night alarm!" The voice of Taylor boomed down the voice-pipe into the control-room.

What the devil's this? As the order was relayed through the boat by alarm buzzer, I leapt from the settee, grabbed my glasses from the table, slithered across the control-room and climbed to the bridge. I heard Taylor order a change of course. The moon was high and to the south, the sea was glass-smooth, there was hardly any wind. Taylor was leaning over the voice-pipe. He turned towards me. "Darkened ship on port bow, sir. I'm altering course to intercept." To the voice-pipe: "Midships . . . Steady!"

From the helmsman below: "Course, sir, oh-seven-oh."

Taylor raised his glasses. "There she is now, sir, bearing green three-oh."

I levelled my glasses parallel to his. In the bottom half of the lenses the blackness of the sea; in the top half the dark grey of the cloud-filled night. Between, on the sharply defined line of the horizon, the smudge of a small ship without lights. I thought at once of the warning we had received that "Q" ships—armed trawlers masquerading as innocent fishermen—were lurking in the area. According to the law of things they should not have been able to operate so far from home, but it appeared that Vichy France or the Spanish were permitting the Germans secret use of their ports. A serious menace to Allied shipping, a "Q" trawler was quite a handful for a small submarine to tackle. Equipped with both Asdic and depth charges, she carried a gun that outranged our own, while her defence against submarines was the knowledge that her short length made her a difficult torpedo target. Since we did not expect to meet friendly forces until the next day, the ship on the horizon might well be such a vessel. The odds were not altogether against us, however. With naval radar little more than a good idea on a drawing-board, we might be able to creep to within a thousand yards, pump ten quick shells into her, or try our luck with a torpedo. . . .

Taylor "trimmed down"—ordered the flooding of numbers Two, Three, Four and Five main ballast tanks so that we rode on the air contained in numbers One and Six only. This caused us to settle in the water, reducing our silhouette, and also kept us ready for a quick dive.

"Gun action stations," I ordered.

The five men of the gun's crew, who had mustered at the foot of the conning-tower when "Night Alarm" was sounded, clattered to the bridge and climbed over to the gun platform. Smoothly, quickly, silently, they unlocked the gun and unclipped the watertight ready-use lockers with their ten rounds of ammunition. Haddow, the armament officer, who would direct the fire of the gun, had already joined me on the bridge with Signalman Osborne. The ammunition party closed up to form a human chain from the magazine to the gun. Haddow leaned over to the gun platform. "Bearing green three-oh. . . . A ship . . . Range oh-three-oh . . . Deflection twelve left . . . With H.E., *load*!" The gun swung on its mounting. "Gun ready!" Haddow reported. "Ready to open fire, sir."

"Very good."

Silence. We waited, tense. I felt certain the others could hear my heart thumping against my ribs. The seconds dragged by. As we neared each other, there was no mistaking that the unknown vessel was a trawler. *Well, you so and so, can you see us or not?*

From the control-room: "All tubes ready."

20

From the Asdic operator: "H.E. green two-five ... Single screw ship ... Reciprocating engine ... Ninety revs." This confirmed she was a trawler, and told me additionally that she was approaching us at nine knots.

"Osborne, make the single letter challenge."

The Aldis lamp stabbed a thick beam in the direction of the trawler. "Challenge made, sir."

No reply. Again we challenged—and again. Still no reply. Was she trying to lure us closer? By rights we should open fire.

"In international code, tell her to stop."

We were near enough now for the flashing of the Aldis lamp to illuminate the trawler like a miniature searchlight.

She looked British.

If it's one of ours what the hell are they up to? Or is it really an enemy ship playing clever? We're only a thousand yards off her, and she could massacre us with machine guns. . . . "Haddow!"

"Sir?"

"Fire one round across her bows."

With a flash and a roar, a 3-inch shell screamed through the air, pitched some two hundred yards ahead of the trawler's bows and ricocheted into space.

It served its purpose: an immediate reply came to our challenge. To confirm, we again challenged and again received the correct reply. So she *was* British, but I was in no mood to extend a big hallo. For one thing, I was furious with the operational staff at Gibraltar who had not bothered to inform me of the trawler's presence in the area; for another I was anything but impressed by the trawler's look-outs and her delay in answering my signal. My immediate feeling was that she had deserved to be sunk.

We altered course to pass under her stern. As we did so,

a great cloud of smoke billowed from the trawler's funnel. She, too, was altering course—straight towards us!

She's going to ram us! "Stand by to dive . . . Full ahead together . . . Fire a night grenade."

In the light of the recognition firework the gun's crew, signalman and look-outs scampered below followed by Haddow. I was alone on the bridge with Taylor. "She'll depth-charge us if we dive," he said.

"My God, I believe she would."

Then, without warning, the trawler's gun flashed and a shell screamed over our heads. Again she fired.

We were in a real mess. If we stayed on top she'd blow us out of the water. If we dived she would depth-charge us. Yet she was British—unless the enemy had got hold of our recognition signals. I thought quickly. "Signalman on the bridge," I yelled.

Osborne climbed through the conning-tower hatch, Aldis in hand, lead trailing behind.

"Make the rudest two-word signal you can think of."

The Aldis beamed across the water. "Done, sir."

Yes, the trawler was British for, as though obeying Osborne's impolite signal, she altered course away from us. As she did so there burst forth one, then two great flares which slowly parachuted down to the sea. The trawler had fired star shells. This was the most extraordinary piece of stupidity I had come across in many a long day. We had been quite visible to the trawler, and the star shells served no purpose save to attract every U-boat within a radius of thirty miles. I relieved my feeling by giving the trawler's captain a severe bottle before sending him about his business. (On arrival at Gibraltar I discovered he was senior to me, but he apologised for the incident, none the less. I learned also that he shot down a Focke Wulf during his patrol, and I could not resist asking: "What with? Star shells?")

Order restored, I returned to the ward-room. Haddow was there already. "Well," I said, "you've fired your first round in anger."

Ever the good armament officer, he shook his head. "Waste of a damn' good round, sir," he complained.

As I sat on the edge of the settee, I was overcome with an unaccountable weariness. It was not so much the excitement of the past forty-five minutes—for it was only that short period since Taylor had ordered "Night Alarm"—as a tremendous sense of anticlimax. I felt vaguely cheated, and made to look silly. I muttered a curse that embraced the whole world, lay back, and was soon asleep.

I had yet to realise that commanding a submarine was one long series of frustrations and anticlimax, punctuated only occasionally by the thrill of positive achievement.

If it served no other purpose, the encounter with the trawler provided the crew with a fresh topic of conversation, and gave new animation to the interminable games of solo, cribbage and ukkers in the messes. Routine life aboard a submarine is a dull, monotonous business. You eat, sleep, test and exercise; read, argue and write letters home; speculate and reminisce—and all the time the air becomes heavier and more sour, tempers grow short and nerves are frayed, and you curse the day you ever volunteered to serve in these caricatures of sardine tins. Yet, with human perversity, you know deep down in your heart you would not be elsewhere . . .

It may seem strange, but although it was not three months since they had joined the *Unbroken*, and although we were living in the closest proximity, I knew very little about my officers. There was a certain reticence, as though we realised that the time would come when we would share

23

one communal soul in which nothing was secret. Aware of this in some indefinable way, we held ourselves back, as though to delay that final moment of truth.

John Haig Haddow I knew better than the others, of course, for he had served in my training submarine—a hazel-eyed Scot, barely twenty-one years old, very tall and willowy, with an undemonstrative toughness that was often mistaken for softness, and a great sense of humour. Taylor, plump and jolly, was some three years older than myself, a reservist from the Merchant Navy. Paul Thirsk, the navigator, was also a reservist: tall, blond, handsome and twenty-three years old. Later, Peter Churchill summed him up admirably when he said: "Thirsk is the type of man you would like your sister to marry." Women did, indeed, fall for him by the score, but he spurned them all and devoted his passion to the care and maintenance of an ancient check golfing jacket which he always wore when on watch. He claimed it brought him luck.

We were still comparative strangers, even though we lived, ate and slept together in a ward-room that measured no more than seven feet by nine—including two feet of passageway for people passing from for'ard to aft. Our beds consisted of two settees and two bunks, while lockers beneath the settees completed our austere furnishings. Not that the sailors were better off, of course. Some were lucky enough to have settees on which to sleep, others slung hammocks, while the remainder had to bed down as best they could in the for'ard torpedo-room.

The discipline of routine dominated our topsy-turvy lives —the routine of a day which scheduled breakfast at 10 a.m. and the midday meal at eight in the evening, and which did not permit us to see daylight and sunshine save through the end of a periscope. We dived at dawn and surfaced

24

at dusk, and it was only during the hours of darkness, when the submarine was illuminated by the dull glow of dim red lighting that we were able to smoke, stretch our legs over a tot of rum and pause to reflect upon the unhappy life of those who served in surface vessels. Even so, despite the feeling of well-being that followed the heavy dinner cooked by Able Seaman Bramhall in his cubbyhole of a galley, there was no real slacking of pace. The ship was divided into three watches—red, white and blue—each doing two hours on and four off. While those off watch were able to sleep and sigh over their pin-ups, there was plenty of work for those on duty. Propelled on the surface by our diesels, an E.R.A. and two stokers stood guard over a thousand moving parts in the steel jungle of our engine-room. The main electric batteries had to be recharged, while cylinders were refilled with the compressed air that enabled us to surface. Men were on watch by the pumps, torpedo-tubes and cooling machinery. The wireless office received and decoded signals. An electrical rating toured the boat checking and testing battery readings. On the bridge, an officer and two ratings scanned sea and sky, while a helmsman, Asdic operator, Petty Officer of the Watch, duty E.R.A., messenger and "spare hand" were crowded into a control-room hardly bigger than a garden shed.

None the less, for a submarine at sea in wartime we were as relaxed as ever we could be.

It was a fine, calm day when the *Unbroken* approached the Pillars of Hercules, slipped into Algeciras Bay and glimpsed Gibraltar town nestling at the foot of the fortress. In the foreground the familiar long grey moles of the artificial harbour. Alongside the moles the ships of Force H: the old battle-cruiser *Renown*, the battleship *Rodney*, the aircraft carrier *Eagle*, and a handful of destroyers. In the southern corner of the basin, by the dry docks, the submarine depot ship *Maidstone*, our temporary home. This small force was all we had with which to defend the Western Mediterranean and a large slice of the Atlantic against all comers—German, Italian, and, if need be, Vichy French.

I felt we made a brave sight as we entered harbour. Our grey paint had held, and a brand new ensign, many sizes too large, flew from our tiny masthead. The sailors shared my pride in the occasion, and stood as stiff as Marines as they lined the casing in their bell-bottoms and white, roll-neck jerseys. We passed the towering sides of the *Renown*, *Rodney* and *Eagle*, bos'ns' pipes shrilling in salute, smug in the knowledge that despite their comparative enormity we could destroy any one of them with a minimum of effort. They, on the other hand, might never find, far less sink, us. Without their escorting destroyers they were powerless against a submarine—even against the undersized *Unbroken*, half the displacement of the average. For a young lieutenant it was a satisfying thought!

The *Maidstone*, to which we secured, was a floating dock-yard equipped with torpedoes, ammunition, water, oil, food, spare parts and all the essentials for repair work. Aboard her were engineers, electricians, artificers, shipwrights, doctors and even a dentist; all with magnificently equipped work-shops, foundries and surgeries. Little praise was ever given to the depot ships, but our submarines—and thus the Mediterranean war—depended upon them to no small degree.

Business was slack aboard the *Maidstone* when we arrived. She had no flotilla of her own to mother, but acted as a sort of Clapham Junction for submarines entering and leaving the Med., travelling from England to Africa, and from Africa to England. She was responsible, also, for a couple of transport submarines running supplies to beleaguered Malta.

As I climbed the ladder up her side, I hoped we would be allowed one "working up" patrol from Gib. before being sent into the Med., but Captain G. A. W. Voelcker, her Commanding Officer, had some shocks for me. As he paced his cabin, hands clasped behind his back, this lean, versatile captain, who was later to go down with the *Charybdis* in the Channel, looked serious and worried. What he told me amounted to this:

British submarines in the Mediterranean had, in some months, destroyed fifty per cent of the men, munitions and armour sent from Italy to the enemy forces in North Africa. The lion's share of this destruction was the work of the 10th flotilla based at Malta; a group of boats that boasted, among others, such commanders as Wanklyn, Tompkinson and Cayley. Their leader was that superb submarine strategist Captain (now Rear-Admiral) G. W. G. Simpson—"Shrimp" Simpson as he was called with affectionate disrespect. No army could stand the losses that Rommel had suffered at the hands of the 10th flotilla. Consequently the submarine base at Malta had received the unremitting attention of the Italian and German air forces, and the point came when bombing caused so many casualties that the remnants of the flotilla had to flee to Alexandria. Our submarines out of the way, Rommel was building up the strength to launch what was to be his last great offensive.

(Later, he was to push the Desert Rats back to Egypt, capture Tobruk and Mersa Matruh and move close enough to threaten Alex. Once again the remnants of the 10th had to move, this time to Beirut. With them went the reduced 1st flotilla whose permanent home was at Alex. On the way to Beirut our largest depot ship, the *Medway*, was sunk.

27

Fortunately, half her store of torpedoes was sent ahead by land, otherwise submarine operations in the Eastern Med. would have come to a complete standstill.)

Even by April things were grim. The two submarines entering the Med. immediately before the *Unbroken*'s arrival at Gib. had both been sunk. Wanklyn and Tompkinson had been lost, and the sea-bed was littered with our wrecks. The *Una*, commanded by Pat Norman, Harrison's "P.34", and the *Umbra*, commanded by Lynch Maydon, were the only submarines of the old 10th flotilla left—and they were at the far end. When the *Unbroken* arrived at Malta she would be the only submarine afloat in a heart-breaking scrap-yard of bomb- and mine-shattered hulks.

My immediate reaction to the news was to say: "Well, let's sail for Malta right away and get cracking," but Captain Voelcker shook his head.

"No," he said, "you can't even get into the Grand Harbour at Valletta. Apart from his tremendous bombing effort on the island itself, the enemy has carried out a complete blockade by mining. The 'searched channels' are absolutely blocked with every variety of mine that German and Italian ingenuity can devise. We don't even know how to sweep some of the more complicated ones. Even if we did, all our sweepers have been sunk! By an all-out effort of his Mediterranean air forces the enemy has managed to deny us the effective use of Malta. But as soon as he lets up, or as soon as we can get a few fighters in and operate them, your chance will come."

With a long face and a heavy heart I left him.

Two of the veterans of Malta, long overdue for home, had managed to stagger to Gib. where they were receiving temporary repairs before limping back to England. There was the Polish *Sokol*, commanded by Boris Karnicki. She

28

had suffered terrible poundings, both at sea and at Malta, and it was a miracle that she made Gib. Teddy Woodward, commanding the *Unbeaten*, also crawled into Algeciras Bay on one battery, the other smashed by bombing.

Understandably, they were not anxious to discuss their experiences. The slaughter and the havoc were too vivid in their minds to be the subjects of chatty conversations. In any case there are some things it is better not to know.

March at Gibraltar is a dreary month, but we enjoyed it after the chill of a northern winter. A great attraction were the shops, piled high with all the ingredients of feminine allure—cosmetics, silk stockings, chocolates, dress lengths, scents, and dainty underwear. They had been exported from England, and while they would have satisfied only a minute portion of the home market, at Gibraltar they served to impress the Spanish that England was still a wealthy land of luxuries, and that "starvation" stories to the contrary were nothing but enemy propaganda. We bought as much of it as we could afford, and sent it to England with pals on homeward-bound ships. The Customs at the other end did not seem to mind—unless some idiot started selling the stuff in the Black Market—and I had pleasing visions of a silk-gowned Ting, the envy of utility-frocked Aldeburgh.

I could only assume she was now at Aldeburgh. To our annoyance and disgust there was no mail awaiting us aboard the *Maidstone*. Something had gone wrong somewhere—one of those irritating mix-ups which every Serviceman experiences at some time or another, and which, although small in themselves, are vastly upsetting to the individual.

There was an eleven o'clock curfew at Gib., but when the crew of the *Unbroken* decided to throw a party at a local

29

"boiled-oil shop" they were certain the Provost-Marshal had not intended that they should be included in the regulation. Consequently they were to be seen returning to the dockyard in the early hours of the morning along a zigzag course any U-boat conscious skipper would have envied. The sudden personal appearance of the Provost-Marshal had a steadying and sobering effect, however. The songs died on their lips and they dispersed as fast as their legs could carry them. A few, who shall be nameless, climbed a tree and waited for the Provost-Marshal to pass. As he walked beneath the branches there was a breathless moment until one rating, discovering that wine-drinking and tree-climbing do not mix, was violently ill. Furious—and rightly so—the Provost-Marshal blew his whistle, and what seemed like an entire regiment of soldiers appeared from the neighbouring rocket sites. A merry game of hide-and-seek ensued before the sailors made their escape. We were then living in the spacious and comfortable quarters of the *Maidstone*, and with great ingenuity the celebrants managed to sneak aboard without falling foul of the officer of the watch. As none of them were caught, the Provost-Marshal did not discover from which ship the wrongdoers came, and I did not hear of the matter officially. I learned of it in dribs and drabs around the *Maidstone*, but thought it as well to turn the aural equivalent of a blind eye. Such things often happen, for Jack ashore is an uninhibited soul. Indeed, it will be a bad day when he is not.

The *Maidstone* was a tribute to the ingenuity of her designers, for despite her bulk, it seemed impossible for so many amenities to be crammed between her sides. From our point of view the most agreeable of these amenities was the living space provided for the officers and men of the submarines attached to her. While the sailors had large mess-decks in which to shake off their claustrophobia, the officers were given individual cabins, each a small "bed-sitter." There were film shows and recreational facilities, too, but our life was hardly a giddy round of pleasure. No ship can be too efficient, and we spent our days, backed by technicians from the *Maidstone*, testing, checking, adjusting and oiling against the happy moment when I would order: "Fire one!" and a "kipper"* would tear through the sea towards an enemy vessel.

The ward-room of the *Maidstone* was almost empty, and I sipped a lonely horse's neck at the bar. I was depressed, and as I stared moodily at my glass I mourned the fact that I was having an awful war. No adventure, excitement, amusement or feeling of usefulness. I reckoned I might just as well be at home with Ting as wasting the weeks in Gib. waiting for something to happen.

My thoughts were interrupted by the appearance of a messenger. "Excuse me, sir, but the captain would like to see you in his cabin."

What's this? Another apologetic explanation for us not going to Malta? "I'll be right along." With a complete absence of enthusiasm I made my way aft.

Captain Voelcker was alone in his day cabin. He invited me to sit down.

"Well, Mars, you know you're the only submarine around these parts, don't you?" The question was purely rhetorical and I did not feel it needed an answer. He smiled. "Know anything about folboats?"

"No, sir, except that they're canvas folding boats, like canoes."

Voelcker nodded. "There's a special operation for you

*Torpedo. ("Tin fish" is no longer used by sub-mariners.)

31

in a week's time." My heart raced. "Utmost secrecy is essential. I am telling you, and you alone, that it will involve landing people on the coast of France. You'll be away about a month and you'll land a party of four. Your job is to get them there and see they paddle ashore safely in their folboats. They've probably never seen a submarine before and will be a damned nuisance. That's too bad. Their leader is a bloke called Churchill." He saw my expression and laughed. "No, not that one! This is a Captain Peter Churchill. You'll meet him and his desperadoes later. In the meantime we've got some folboats and you can amuse yourself finding out how they work." He smiled. "That's all for the present."

Cloak and dagger, eh? What a turn up for the book! I hurried back to my cabin and summoned Taylor.

"Number One, we must be ready for a patrol five days from now. It'll be a long one. Allow for a month, then add another fortnight for emergencies. You can count on having five passengers with us for at least half the time. We'll be carrying two folboats. There will be extra equipment, too. You'll have to find room for it all for'ard. This is no ordinary patrol. I don't know the details yet, but all measures must be taken to keep secret that it's spy stuff until the folboats come aboard. When that cat is out of the bag I'll have a word with the ship's company. In the meantime it's just between ourselves. Even Thirsk and Haddow aren't to know. O.K.?"

The gleam in Taylor's eyes told me that this was the sort of thing he'd been waiting for. "Aye, aye, sir. Will be done."

"Just one thing, Number One."

"Yes, sir?"

"As this is our first real patrol, come and see me if any doubtful points crop up."

"Certainly, sir. Where is it going to be, or shouldn't I ask?"

"Don't know myself yet."

He strode off with great élan, anxious to get cracking.

I returned to the ward-room. There was little I could do now. The submarine was as "worked up" as I could make her and I was reasonably satisfied. Except for planning the details of the job I could not assist in the boat's preparations. That was the responsibility of each department, with the first lieutenant answerable for the overall results.

I sent for Thirsk and Haddow. "Like to go boating this afternoon?"

"Bit chilly for sailing, isn't it, sir?" said Haddow, doubtfully.

"Not really the weather at all," added Thirsk.

"Ah, but this is a different sort of sailing," I assured them. "Folboats. Jolly interesting."

Thirsk and Haddow looked at each other, unconvinced. The former screwed up his face. "Be a bit blowy, sir," he ventured.

"Nonsense. This afternoon we'll collect a folboat from the depot ship and try it out. I'm told it's quite fun." They still appeared unimpressed. "Consider it an order," I added.

That afternoon we took a three-seater folboat, in a dubious state of repair, round to Rosia Bay—a reminder of the balmier days of 1932 when I had swum there with the angel fish and trod in terror of the sea egg. We were the only bathers. Maybe everyone was busy, although I could not guess what at, or perhaps the bathing season had not officially opened.

Half a gale blew in from the Atlantic, which produced "I told you so" expressions from Thirsk and Haddow, but I egged them on with a story to the effect that I'd often shot the rapids in Canada and that this was kid's stuff in comparison. As we rigged the folboat on a small mole, I thought the frame rather fragile for the boat's size, but we launched it, climbed in and paddled around in the sheltered water until we had mastered the thing. By this time Haig Haddow was shivering like a willowy babe in the wood, and I allowed him to retire. I thought a good way of testing the seaworthiness of the boat would be to go out to the rolling waters beyond the mole, and a reluctant Paul Thirsk came as my one-man crew.

We had travelled about a hundred yards beyond the protection of the mole when the contraption began to hog and sag as though its back was broken. When we finally turned towards shore I discovered that it did, indeed, suffer from this distressing defect, but I could not prevent it from rolling over and ditching us. Thirsk's blasphemy over the loss of a brand-new Ronson lighter, which had been lying at the bottom of the boat, was not softened by the certain knowledge that Haig Haddow was laughing his head off on the safe, dry mole. The sea was rougher and the current stronger than we thought, and it took us half an hour to manœuvre the folboat back to safety. Politely Haig Haddow helped to haul the wreck to the beach, and refrained from comment. Paul Thirsk, however, could not resist remarking: "Great stuff this boating, sir. How did you enjoy it?"

I have only been in one folboat since, and that was a different sort of skylark.

Joe Cowell, the *Maidstone*'s Staff Officer (Operations), introduced me to Peter Churchill. If I had expected him to be a blond, titanic Viking in the best traditions of the heroes of the twopenny bloods, I would have been disappointed. Of medium build, dark, and with deep, intelligent eyes, he would only be distinguishable in a crowd by his charm and a certain sense of authority. Here was a strong character, I felt, unassuming and quiet, yet capable of decisive violence should the occasion arise.

In the cabin of Captain "S"—Captain commanding the submarine flotilla—the plot was unfolded. We were to land four agents on the south coast of Vichy France, two at Antibes, and two at a suitable spot to be chosen by me. Churchill was to land with them but would return aboard. When this mission was completed, and not before, we were to have a few days' free-lance operations in the Gulf of Genoa—a little titbit for being good boys.

I was somewhat concerned about Antibes Bay. I recalled school holidays there when plenty of fishing boats had been about. Perhaps all that had been changed by the war, but it was going to be a tricky problem getting in and out of the tiny bay none the less. There was little doubt that we would have to enter the bay, for my folboat experience had shown me that those canvas craft were suitable only for the shortest and calmest of journeys. But I held my peace, for these were problems that would have to be solved on the spot.

The need for secrecy was obvious. Everyone knew that we carried out clandestine ops against the enemy coast, but it would be suicide to have the Germans know in advance where the next one was going to be. I decided that without mentioning the matter to "S" I would do a little scattering of red herrings.

The patrol orders with our destination cryptically labelled "W.M.P. 13" in my pocket, I sent for Paul Thirsk. "Tell me, old boy, have we the charts of the north-west African coast from here down to Sierra Leone?"

"No, sir. We've all the Med. charts, and our passage

35

charts from Gib. to the U.K., and from Suez to Colombo and Mombasa."

"Then arrange to draw these others from the dockyard. Have them delivered direct to the boat. Then check and correct them in the control-room."

"Aye, aye, sir. But is it all right to be seen doing it?"

"I want you to be seen—but be as furtive as you can. Get it?"

Thirsk smiled. "Aye, aye, sir."

I could see that Number One was becoming anxious about our destination. "Can you tell me where it's to be, sir?"

"I'm sorry, Taylor, but I'd better keep it under my hat."

"Yes, sir . . . Two folboats are being embarked this afternoon. Would you like to see the ship's company in the dinner-hour before the folboats arrive?"

"A good idea. Make it eleven-forty-five."

"Yes, sir. There's one thing, sir, that worries me a little."

"What's that, old boy?"

"There's a buzz going around that we're doing a patrol down the West African coast, Dakar way."

"Is there now? Thanks for letting me know. I'll have a word to say about buzzes when I see the ship's company."

Just before lunch the crew crowded into the control-room and overflowed into the passageways beyond. I reminded them how their lives depended in no small degree on secrecy. I told them about the folboats, and added: "But don't start making wild speculations. They mean nothing. Folboats are a part of a submarine's equipment in the Med. Just the same, I don't want any mention made outside the boat of any special equipment we take aboard. It is not to be

36

spoken of even in the depot ship." I concluded by warning them that rumour was a fickle jade liable to play them false.

After tea on 11th April, Peter Churchill and his party came aboard. As they were considered part of the boat's armament, Haddow attended to their needs. Churchill was allotted the fourth sleeping-place in the ward-room. This was practical, for although we numbered three officers apart from myself, one was always on watch at sea and came down to occupy the bunk of the chap who had relieved him. Thus one billet was always unoccupied. Churchill's four desperadoes were distributed among the petty officers' and seamen's messes, which meant even more overcrowding in the for'ard torpedo-room. The party's baggage, including certain weapons of sabotage, were taken aboard, and Haddow examined these latter items with the professional interest of an armament officer. It was as well that he did so, for included among them were pencil-bombs filled with plastic explosives and designed to be attached to aircraft. Operated on a barometer principle, they would explode when the aircraft reached a certain altitude and the air pressure decreased. The desperadoes did not realise it, but such drops in pressure occur in submarines, too, and the pencil-bombs might well have exploded during the voyage and made a very nasty mess. They were sent ashore far more quickly than they were brought aboard!

We were due to sail at five o'clock. I changed into my seagoing dress—old trousers, kapok jacket, towel-scarf, old cap and binoculars—and went to say *au revoir* to Captain Voelcker. As we chatted, Joe Cowell burst in.

"I'm sorry, sir, but Mars will have to wait. The 'Pay' has gone ashore with the keys of the safe and we can't get the money. I've sent a car to bring him back."

This was the first I'd heard of any money, and shortly afterwards an apologetic Supply Officer arrived with four black silk body-belts. Each contained a million francs. And so, with four million francs tucked beneath my arm, I crossed the plank to the *Unbroken* and climbed to the bridge.

"Ready for sea," Taylor reported.

"All right. We're off."

I handed the loot to Thirsk. "Nip down and lock this in the ward-room safe, will you?"

I looked for'ard and aft. The plank had been withdrawn and we were secured to the *Maidstone* by single wires at bow and stern.

"Group up . . . Let go."

The wires splashed into the oily water of the harbour.

"Main motors ready grouped up, sir," said a voice from below.

"Half astern together."

We slid away from the *Maidstone*. A wave from Captain Voelcker . . . More waves . . . "*Bon voyage*" from Joe Cowell. Through Algeciras Bay into the centre of the Strait. Curious watchers on the Spanish shore saw us sail south-west in the gathering dusk. Out of sight of their prying eyes we swung around to east-north-east.

We entered the Mediterranean.

Chapter Two

It was quite dark now, and we remained surfaced. I told Paul Thirsk to set a zigzag course to pass west of Majorca and into the Gulf of Lions, and stayed a while on the bridge before handing over to Taylor who was officer of the watch. The night was cool and quiet, its flat nigrescence broken only by the dull glow of a small forest fire on the Spanish mainland. We might have been on a routine exercise in peacetime, for in the tranquil darkness it was difficult to realise that ahead of us at Malta the skies were torn with the scream of bombs and the furious bark of anti-aircraft guns; that beyond Malta towards Alex. the seas were being churned into foaming fury by the death agonies of our shattered convoys; that the sands of Africa to the south-east were crimson with the blood of the Eighth Army. It all seemed very remote and a little unreal. It was difficult to grasp, too, that in a week's time we would be nosing into the hostile waters of Antibes Bay to land saboteurs and spies. I did not envy our passengers their task, for while success might mean some transient glory, failure meant the rubber truncheon and a firing squad. For us, death would be relatively clean. Why, I wondered, do people volunteer for such jobs? Was it some fiery patriotism? Sense of duty? Fatalistic indifference? Desire for adventure or gain? A glorious madness? Perhaps, I reasoned, it was a little of all those things, or maybe it was none of them—that it was con-

sidered a job of work that had to be done; no more, no less.
I went below to take a closer look at them.

Defying all known laws, the five had squeezed themselves
into the ward-room together with Haddow and Thirsk.
Peter Churchill greeted me with a winning smile. "The
gallant gentlemen are rather nervous," he said.

"I don't blame 'em," I replied. "If I was going to paddle
ashore at Antibes I'd be nervous too."

Churchill laughed. "It isn't that that's worrying them.
It's this submarine of yours. They don't like the idea of
diving and surfacing. I've assured them there's hardly any
sense of movement, but they don't seem very comforted.
However, let me introduce you."

I shook hands first with Jean, a silent Breton of doleful
countenance who spoke no English and whose French seemed
confined to the phrases: "*Veux manger . . . Veux dormir . . .
Veux fumer . . . Soif.*" During the voyage we were able
to satisfy his needs so far as eating and sleeping were concerned—he did little else, in fact—but he was most upset
when we told him he simply could not smoke every time
the fancy took him. "Self-control!" Haddow would cry,
but the Breton merely curled his lips and looked more woe-
begone than ever. On such occasions, however, a tot of
rum worked wonders.

The second desperado was Léon, a tall, sharp-eyed Englishman who looked Spanish and spoke perfect French. The
third was Bill, also English, and also bi-lingual. The fourth
member of the party must have been a very good agent
indeed, for I cannot remember a single thing about him!

Not that there was much to be remembered of the others,
either, for they disclosed little about themselves—a tribute,
no doubt, to their excellent training—and we considered
it wiser not to ask questions. Consequently our chatter

was confined to amiable small talk, punctuated by anecdotes from Peter Churchill. He was a great raconteur and spent most of the voyage taking our minds from our duties with an endless flow of stories.

The days passed, and domestic life aboard the *Unbroken* kept to its routine pattern. To help break the dull sameness of the days, and to keep the crew up to scratch, I gave them plenty of exercises—dummy attacks, gun-drill, rehearsals in damage control, and change-round positions in which everyone learned to do everyone else's job. Our passengers thought it all highly amusing—until I exercised emergency increases in depth without warning them to hold on to their stomachs.

One morning I spotted Bill banging the sides of his hands furiously against the control-room ladder. "What on earth is that for?" I asked.

He held out both hands. "Feel," he invited.

I did so. From the outsides of his little fingers to the wrists the skin was as hard and horny as tough leather. "Banging them helps to harden them," said Bill. With one hand he cut the air in a short, sharp arc. "The Judo chop," he explained. "You can kill a man that way." He grinned and returned to his banging.

Slowly we made our way north-west. Cartagena . . . Cape Palos . . . Alicante . . . Cape San Antonio . . . the Gulf of Valencia. Here we were greeted by half a gale, our passengers took to their bunks. Apart from the mess and their personal discomfort, they caused Churchill and myself no little worry for they needed to be at the peak of condition when they were landed. To make matters worse the heavy seas were slowing us down, and we were in danger of being late for the rendezvous with the agents ashore. Our orders allowed for one postponement of twenty-four hours.

I stood on the hail-battered bridge with Taylor, cursing and blasting the weather, while the crackling electric flashes of St. Elmo's Fire danced a lively jig on our periscope standard and aerials, lighting us up like a Christmas tree from bow to stern. It was as well the weather prevented enemy aircraft from patrolling the area.

"We must press on," I yelled to Taylor. "We've got to make up this lost time."

"She's bumping badly, sir," he shouted back. "Rolling a lot, too." The words entered my ear mixed up with a gallon of spray.

"Yes," I replied. "Can't be helped, though."

"Very uncomfortable for'ard. Torpedoes may break loose."

"Shouldn't do. Not if they're properly secured. Pass the word for the T.G.M.* to inspect them. It's not really rough. We're just pitching into it a bit. That's all."

As I uttered the words we came out of the lee of the Balearic Islands and a violent, savage sea crashed against our side. A huge wall of water poured over the bridge.

"You'll have to slow down, sir," Taylor bawled. "You're breaking her up."

I was certain the thunderous noise of the sea was playing tricks with my hearing. "*What?*"

To my astonishment, he repeated his opinion. *He must be out of his mind. What blasted impertinence!* "Don't worry about the boat. I can do that. I've been through a Pacific typhoon in a submarine and know something of their strength. We continued at the same speed."

At that moment the last of St. Elmo's Fire was swept away, and in its final sparkle I glimpsed a doubtful expression on Number One's face. I nodded to him. "Good night,

*Torpedo Gunner's Mate.

and don't forget we'll need star sights in the morning if there's any break in the cloud."

Taylor nodded back. "The Pilot knows about it, sir. Good night."

I went below with mixed feelings. On the one hand I felt guilty at leaving Taylor on the bridge in introspective solitude during a gale, while on the other hand I was furious at what I considered his confounded cheek. *Has he forgotten I'm the Captain? How dare he accuse me of breaking-up the boat?* I was particularly upset because this was not the first difference we had had, and even the suggestion of bad feeling is fatal among a small group of men living in such proximity as we were. Stretched out on my settee, I tried to persuade myself that it was a storm in a teacup, a fraying of tempers that had been aggravated by the thunder of the night and which would blow over with the coming of the dawn. None the less I did not sleep easily.

At noon on 19th April I peered through the attack periscope into the semicircle of Antibes Bay. It is a little bay, for the rocks flanking it lie only half a mile apart, and the town of Antibes hiding in the northern corner gives the overall scene the effect of having been constructed solely for the picture-postcard trade. A light breeze stirred the gentlest of ripples on the placid blue water, and there was not even a rowing boat in sight to cause me alarm. It appeared that Peter Churchill had been right when he promised no fishing boats. Satisfied, I ordered courses that took us in a large, slow circle, and summoned Haddow, Taylor and Thirsk to join Churchill and myself in the ward-room. Briefly I outlined my plan.

"To-night we'll approach the bay from eastward and creep in to within seven hundred yards of the spot where Churchill wants to land. This cuts to the minimum the distance he has to travel. His job is a tricky one, and since his pals know nothing about folboats they'll be a dead weight on his hands.

"For our part, we have no navigational aids, such as small lighthouses, to guide us. We'll choose some handy rocks on the chart, and guide ourselves in by getting Asdic ranges and bearings from them. All right so far?" I scanned their eager faces. They nodded. "Good. Thirsk. You will steer her in from below, acting on Cryer's Asdic bearings. I'll keep a visual look-out on the bridge. Haddow will be with me as officer of the watch. Taylor, you will be on the casing to supervise the embarkation. Lee, the T.G.M., will be responsible for getting the folboats in and out of the for'ard hatch, and he'll also be responsible for shutting the hatch in a hurry if the need arises.

"In the position I've chosen, we'll be only four hundred yards from the nearest rocks, but I'm taking the chance that no one will be standing there with binoculars at one in the morning! Since we'll be end-on to the shore and trimmed down, I don't think we can be seen without binoculars. Any questions?"

There were none. "The plan is," I continued, "that Churchill will go ashore in one of the folboats and make contact with his pals there. By the time he returns we'll have his two desperadoes waiting in the second folboat. Off they go together, Churchill will guide his friends to the agents ashore, then return to the submarine towing the second folboat behind him. Churchill will then make one more trip to take ashore the remainder of the equipment. That's all there is to it."

The conference broke up. I was glad the planning part of our operation was over, and looked forward to a little excitement and action. But "the best-laid schemes of mice and men gang aft a-gley" when the elements become capri-

44

cious, and with the setting of the sun the mistral swept down the valley of the Var from the Alps, the sky lowered, and rain squalls lashed the sea. This was not going to help the launching of the folboats. None the less, we would have to take a chance, and with a melodramatic accompaniment of thunder claps and the flashing of vivid blue lightning, we surfaced.

As we closed Antibes I stood on the bridge with Haddow and Churchill. The rain poured down. It was eleven o'clock. The operation was due to start at midnight. As the minutes crawled past we stood in gloomy silence, until Haddow remarked: "I think it's easing up, sir."

"I doubt it," I said, and tried to stamp the water from my shoes.

But Haddow was right. As suddenly as it had started the squall died away, the wind dropped and the night was clear again.

"Thank goodness for that," said Churchill.

"Yes," I replied dully.

"You don't seem very enthusiastic," he complained.

"I'm not. Look." I pointed into the darkness. On the port beam was the unmistakable silhouette of a darkened boat. *A damn' nuisance!* "I don't want anyone reporting our presence here, and I can't make a noise with the gun . . . I think I'll ram the bastard. Haddow. Alter course to intercept."

As Haddow crossed to the voice-pipe and ordered the alteration of course, and as I continued to curse and blast the presence of the boat—which had no right to be darkened if a neutral—Churchill grabbed my arm. "I've just remembered something," he said. "That boat looks like a Spanish felucca, doesn't it? When we were at Gibraltar I was told a felucca would be landing some of our chaps somewhere

45

on this part of the coast. It's a wild possibility, but supposing that's them? We can't sink them, can we? Nor can we take a chance."

"Damn them at Gibraltar! Why the hell didn't they tell me?"

As Churchill muttered something about "Security" I leaned over the voice-pipe and ordered a return to our original course towards the bay. But the damage had been done, for as we swung round another squall overtook us and Thirsk's voice came up from the control-room.

"Something wrong somewhere, sir. The echo-sounding machine is giving depths which don't check with those of the chart. We're somewhere off course. I'm a bit lost."

"Either that or the echo-sounder's gone haywire."

"Yes, sir."

"Send up a party to take soundings with a hand lead and line from the casing."

"Aye, aye, sir."

Within a matter of seconds the sounding party appeared through the conning-tower and made their way for'ard. Impatiently I drummed my fingers on the steel framework of the bridge.

"Seven fathoms, sir,"

"*Eh?* Check it." *Seven fathoms? I'm trying to discover whether its seventy or seventeen! Now everything's gone haywire.* . . . "Well?"

"Seven fathoms, sir."

I crossed to the voice-pipe. "Thirsk! They report seven fathoms."

"*Seven?*"

"Yes."

"We *are* lost!"

Indeed we were. It was an incredible situation. Despite

all our learning, contraptions and gadgets, despite our technical knowledge, charts and machines, the sea had tricked us.

I made a quick decision.

"Listen, Churchill, we've twenty-four hours in hand, and the weather's against us, anyway. I'm going to call it off for to-night. Haddow! Alter course away, and we'll stooge around until to-morrow night."

"Aye, aye, sir."

Feeling a complete idiot I went below. My only consolation, for what it was worth, was the knowledge that I had been proved right in pressing ahead despite the weather on the journey up.

We spent the next day dived some miles south of Nice. At last the sun sank below the horizon and the darkness of night crept over the water. Fortunately the weather held and the sky was clear when we surfaced. Three miles from Antibes I stopped the engines lest their noise should betray us to those on shore, and switched to the motors. We slid towards the bay in deep and utter silence.

Haddow was with me on the bridge, tin-hatted, a revolver at his side. He surveyed my own helmet and revolver and glanced at the two look-outs armed in a similar manner. "Proper warlike, aren't we?" he whispered.

"Yes," I replied, "but with this particular job to do, the last things we want to hear are the guns of war."

"Too true, sir."

Slowly we approached the rocks into the open entrance of the bay. To my horror I saw that the entire foreshore was ablaze with twinkling lights!

"Stop both!"

The main motor switches were broken and the propellers stilled.

What the hell's this? Were they expecting us? . . . But they can't have been . . . I swung my glasses. "I've got it!"

"What is it, sir?" asked Haddow.

"Fishing boats, that's what they are."

"Why the lights?" he asked.

"It's a trick of fishermen the world over. They're using acetylene flares to attract the fish. It's not as bad as it looks." I crossed to the voice-pipe. "My compliments to Captain Churchill and ask him to come to the bridge."

He was with me in no time at all.

"Well, old boy, that's Intelligence, that is. Take an eyeful. Your blasted bay is littered with fishing boats and the whole place is lit up like a Brock's benefit."

He gazed thoughtfully through my glasses, then turned towards me. He seemed nervous. "Well?" he asked.

"Oh, you'll be able to get in all right." I hoped I sounded as casual as I intended.

"Quite," he replied. "However, I want to get out as well as in."

"Ever come across these illuminated boats before?"

"No."

I swallowed and when I spoke I did so with a tremendous effort at calmness. "In that case you'll have to take my word for it that they can't see a damn' thing. They're as blind as bats except for a radius of a yard or so from their flares. In shipping routes these fellows are literally a flaming menace. They can't even see a fully lighted ship approaching them. You'll be able to slip between them in your canoe without being spotted. As you go by there'll be enough light by which to thread a needle or read a book. But for God's sake trust me and take my word that *they'll be too blinded by light to see you*."

"Are you quite sure?"

"Absolutely."

A pause.

"All right, I'll try it."

"Good show." I relaxed and realised I was sweating like a pig. I must have put all I had into convincing Churchill that I was not sending him into the gaping jaws of death! "We'll get the folboats up, shut the hatch, trim down to reduce silhouette and sneak in as per plan."

I was beginning to enjoy myself again. "Diving stations," I ordered. "Stand-by gun action!" The ship's company flew to their posts; the gun's crew closed-up at the foot of the conning-tower.

"Control-room."

"Sir."

"Tell the T.G.M. to let the bridge know when he's ready to open the fore hatch and get the boats up."

"Message passed for'ard, sir."

"Very good. Ask the navigator to speak on the voice-pipe."

"Navigator speaking."

"Pilot, give me the course to close our position. Come up here and get a land fix first. There's plenty in sight at present."

Thirsk's tall figure blocked my view of the shore as he took his bearings with methodical precision. Typically, he did not waste time inquiring about the lights blazing off shore. Such chit-chat could come later.

Number One's voice floated up the voice-pipe. "All ready for'ard, sir."

"Thank you. Man the gun!"

The gun's crew rattled up the conning-tower ladder and hustled through to the gun platform. At the same time ratings manned the two Vickers' guns on the bridge.

"Number One. Come up now with the folboat party."
As his head rose through the conning-tower I ordered: "Open
fore hatch. Up folboats."

While the folboats were coaxed through to the casing we
were as exposed as ever a submarine could be, for it was
impossible to dive with the fore hatch open. If surprised,
we could do no more than defend ourselves with the gun or
try an almost hopeless attack with torpedoes. We were
no longer a submarine, in fact, but a cumbersome torpedo-
boat with her engines stopped. No sub-mariner cares for
such moments.

After what seemed an eternity, but what was timed by
the stop-watch as three minutes flat, the report came through:
"Fore hatch shut and clipped."

Thank God for that.

Then Paul Thirsk's voice: "Course for position, two-
seven-oh. May I start the echo-sounder, sir?"

"Yes, please, but don't transmit on the Asdic until I give
the word. Group down, slow ahead together. Steer two-
seven-oh." Almost imperceptibly we gathered way.

We trimmed down, causing the entire pressure hull to
sink below the water, and left only the bridge, gun platform
and a foot of casing showing above the sea. Consequently
we were invisible to the naked eye save at a range of well
under a quarter of a mile.

Soon we were in position and I stopped the motors. After
a final look round, the first folboat was launched, and Churchill
climbed over the side of the bridge. "Remember," I said,
as his face drew level with my own, "*you can see them, but
they can't see you.*"

He muttered: "Keep an eye on me," sat in the boat and
started to paddle swiftly and silently towards the shore.
He disappeared between two lights.

So far, so good. The night was still quiet save for the fishermen, and as I followed Churchill's progress through my glasses I was struck by the dreamlike atmosphere of it all. Surely this was far too peaceful and simple? There should be a dramatic appearance by the enemy, a pistol-firing chase, and a last-minute rescue. . . . My whimsey was cut short by the sight of Churchill paddling furiously back towards the *Unbroken*.

"What do you think it is, sir?" asked Haddow.

"Damned if I know," I replied.

Apprehensive and a little irritable, I waited until Churchill drew close, then climbed down to the casing to meet him. He was breathless from his exertions.

"What's up?"

"Naval patrols. There are several men in rowing boats. I'm sure they're naval. They hail each other."

"Listen," I said, as evenly as I could manage. "I've come nearly a thousand miles to do this job, and I'm not going to have the thing ruined by a few inoffensive fishermen. That's all they are. They only hail one another to help keep station and to let one another know of the catch. . . . Look." I pointed. "They're moving away slightly from your line of approach. You've a better chance now."

"What will you do if they chase me?"

"I'll come and rescue you."

"Would you use force?"

"They have no right to use force on you. If they try, we'll retaliate. We must smack it about. There's only just enough time to get through before dawn."

I breathed a sigh of relief as he streaked back towards the shore. We saw him pass through a gap between the lights and he was then lost from sight.

"Tell our two braves their canoe will be at the door in

half an hour's time, and tell the navigator to give them the money."

"Aye, aye, sir," acknowledged the control-room.

We waited, restless. The strain was beginning to be felt now, for despite the apparent calm, we did not dare relax. The current had pulled us nearer the rocks that formed the crescent horns of the bay, and the acetylene lamps had thinned out, suggesting that the fishermen were going to pack up for the night. So long as Churchill did not bump into them . . . The gun's crew fidgeted. Still we waited. I sent Bill and "the Ghost"—the fourth spy whom I cannot remember—down into the folboat.

"Here he comes," said Haddow.

Paddling furiously, Churchill drew alongside. "All's well," he greeted me.

"Your two lads are already in the folboat with their suit-cases and money . . . . I'm going to turn the Unbroken round while you're ashore, so expect us to be facing seawards. Cheerio."

With a quick wave the two folboats made for shore. This time we would have to wait at least an hour.

"H.E.* bearing green nine-oh!"

God, what's this? A patrol?

"Probably a small diesel boat."

It still might be a patrol. If it was we could only try to bluff them. "Ask Jean to come to the bridge—and quickly."

By this time the starboard look-out had also reported the ship. "Now approaching from starboard beam," he added.

"Haddow! Get the gun on her."

Through my glasses I could see that she was a motor

*Hydrophone effect from revolving propellers.

52

fishing vessel showing no lights. She could be anything: smugglers, a naval auxiliary, or fishermen off for a black-market catch. Her course indicated that she had left Antibes harbour, north of the bay, and was heading for the open sea. She would pass fairly close under our stern. I heard from the casing the whispered reports: "Trainer on!"; "Gun-layer on!"; "Gun ready."

I said to Jean in French: "Hail him and tell him to keep clear of us and the bay. Tell him we're on special patrol."

Jean shouted across the water. His broad Breton accents added an authentic touch, for half the French Navy is re-cruited in Brittany. It was a knee-shaking moment, and it flashed through my mind that if she did not acknowledge our hail within a very few seconds it would mean she was a naval craft and had not fallen for our bluff. I would have to open fire. But an answering shout quickly echoed across the water, and the trawler altered course away from us.

"Before this night's out one of us is going to have a heart attack," Haddow whispered.

As the trawler was lost to sight we went astern, turned round, and slid back into the bay stern first. When it was time to leave we could make a quick exit.

More agonised waiting. Cocoa was sent up for those on the bridge. The gun's crew were unlucky. Below, the air must have been thick and sour, for only those in the control-room were able to appreciate the freshness of the open conning-tower hatches. It needed the diesels to be running to suck fresh air through the boat.

"Do you think he's made it, sir?" asked Haddow.

I shrugged. "God knows."

It was quiet enough ashore, but that signified nothing.

If Churchill had been apprehended, his captors would make no unnecessary sounds to put us on our guard. Instead they would notify Toulon and have fast patrol vessels sent in search of us. *For how long can I leave the* Unbroken *exposed like this? How much time is Churchill worth balanced against the boat and its crew?* Questions without answers. I chewed my lip and wished to heaven we were far away to sea.

Finally Churchill loomed out of the dark, towing empty folboat behind him.

"For God's sake snap into it, chum," said Haddow. "Dawn's just around the corner."

Churchill wasted no time, but took the remaining gear aboard his own folboat and was soon on his way back to the shore. While he was away the other folboat was hauled on to the casing and lashed down. Churchill returned within thirty minutes, and as he hove into sight, Taylor called from the casing: "There are two men."

For a fearful moment I thought he said: "There's a woman," and envisaged terrible complications. But it was another man, right enough. There was no time to ask questions, however. Churchill's folboat was lashed to the other, the gun was secured, and everyone was sent below except the officer of the watch, the look-outs and myself. We moved out of the bay. As we gained distance from the shore the submarine was brought to full buoyancy. Again the gun was manned, the fore hatch was opened and the folboats disappeared below.

"Fore hatch shut and clipped."

"Clear the casing. Fall out diving stations. Patrol routine."

The operation was over.

South of Cap d'Antibes a lighted ship hove in sight. She was moving fast to the north-east and passed about two miles away from us—a Vichy destroyer. She was a little late.

In the ward-room Churchill introduced me to his "guest" —a French ex-naval officer named Baron d'Astier de la Vigerie, but who went by the name of Bernard. He was one of the leading lights of the resistance movement. After we had shaken hands I told Churchill of the destroyer.

"One of the fishermen must have seen us and reported to the police. They, no doubt, telephoned Toulon. We were lucky, eh? A few minutes earlier . . ."

"Well, it was fun while it lasted," I said. "Now I want some sleep. It's nearly light."

Churchill smiled. Then, gravely: "Thank you very much."

"Don't mention it," I replied.

The next afternoon took us to the Bay of Agay where we were to land Jean and Léon. There was no precise spot where they had to be put ashore, and I chose a small beach between clusters of rocks. Up on the cliffs stood the Agay signalling station, but they could not see us, although the submarine was just visible from the shore at the point where Churchill landed his charges. The landing was a simpler duplication of the other. I closed to within two hundred and fifty yards of the shore, and the two spies paddled away with their wireless sets in one folboat, escorted by Churchill in the other. It was all over in twenty-five minutes.

The game of cops and robbers ended, I had three days left in which to settle down to the business of sinking ships before we started towards Gib.

I sent for Thirsk and we pored over the charts. For'ard, Leading Telegraphist Johnny Crutch lost no time in sewing two daggers—symbols of two "special" landings—on our otherwise virgin Jolly Roger.

Chapter Three

Twenty-third April.

At 11 a.m. we reached a position dominating the approaches to Genoa. It was a dramatic moment. At last we were in the "free for all" area—that section of sea in which any vessel could be sunk on sight. For the first time since her launching, the *Unbroken* was patrolling the Mediterranean hungry for a kill. The order: "Diving stations," and the report: "All tubes ready," were no longer the parrot cries of just another exercise. This time we meant business.

The boat buzzed with excited chatter and wild speculation. Routine tasks were performed with revived zest and vigour, and even the motors seemed to purr with new-found sweetness. Naturally, I was pleased to see the crew in such good spirits, yet their enthusiasm afforded me a certain anxiety. For if an attack did come our way, it *had* to be successful. After all the months of waiting and training and anticipation, there would be a morale-shattering anticlimax if I failed them now. There was also the knowledge that as we were the only operational submarine in the Western Mediterranean, everyone at Malta and Gib. was hoping and praying for our safety and success. They were willing us their strength and their hearts, their prayers and their sinews, and I knew how much they hoped and expected of us. Such was our meagre shoe-string of resources, even the tiny *Unbroken* was a considerable weight in the balance of Mediterranean power.

It added up to a heavy and frightening burden of responsibility.

At eleven-fifteen we planed towards the surface, and as the water drained from the periscope glass I saw in the far distance the masts of numerous yachts and schooners. They made a charming sight against the green background of the Italian mainland—until one realised they were anti-submarine vessels. For a moment I was tempted to tackle one, but I knew we must concentrate on bigger game. Perhaps, if nothing else turned up, we would sink a schooner before making off. Such an action would undoubtedly close the port for a few days, for the Italians were more than a little sensitive of our submarines, and it would demonstrate that despite many misfortunes the Royal Navy still packed a punch.

So we bided our time and waited, slowly patrolling back and forth, with a constant and hopeful watch through the periscope. We ate hurriedly, and grabbed short spells of sleep, but the day and the night passed without incident. Disappointment stilled the chatter of the crew. Worried, I debated with myself whether or not to push off and hope for better luck on the way home.

And then, on the following day, towards the end of the afternoon watch, we drew a horse. An outsider, but a horse.

I was in the ward-room writing up the patrol report when Taylor's voice roared out: "Captain in the control-room! Diving stations!"

Within three seconds I was at his side, and as I took the periscope from his hands he informed me: "Smoke to the nor'-west." There was a sudden prickling at the back of my neck. . . . Yes, there was smoke right enough. I altered course to intercept, and swung the periscope to sweep the rest of the sea and the sky. Both were empty. "Group up!" I ordered. "Full ahead together. Eighty feet."

The hydroplanes tilted the boat to an acute angle and the illuminated depth-gauge needles swung slowly round their dials. We shuddered as the propellers lashed us into greater speed. Down, down, down, in a rattling, rolling dive. . . . At eighty feet we straightened out. We were running blind towards our quarry—but were safe from prying aircraft. *Speed! Oh, for more speed!* I gripped hard the rungs of the control-room ladder and tapped my foot with impotent fury.

At our maximum underwater speed of about nine knots, it took us fifteen minutes to travel two miles, a distance a torpedo could cover in a fifth of the time. I ordered a return to periscope depth. "Up periscope." First the sky. Still empty. Then on to my target. A quick calculation told me she would pass across our bows in about twenty minutes—but at the impossible range of 12,000 yards. The chance of a hit at anything over 8,000 yards was infinitesimal. *We must get nearer.* "Group up. Eighty feet. Full ahead together."

Again we plunged downwards and forward. Fifteen minutes, each an eternity of waiting, ticked past. Thirsk, meanwhile, identified our target in Talbot Booth's book of silhouettes: a merchantman of 4,000 tons and some three hundred and fifty feet in length. Oh well, 4,000 tons were better than nothing. . . .

We crept up for a final look. The sea and sky remained empty save for our quarry wallowing along her unsuspecting way. I felt a moment of pity for her crew, doubtless sleeping off their *vino* and garlic lunch.

"Range now?"

"Seven thousand yards, sir."

"Bearing?"

"Green one-five."

The figures were fed into the "fruit machine" operated by Haddow and Thirsk—an extraordinary contraption which, when given such information as the speed, bearing and range of the target, revealed just where and when a torpedo should be fired in order to score a hit. It was not infallible, depending as it did upon human estimations and calculations, but it was a help. On this occasion it told me we had two minutes to spare before she crossed our sights. I decided to creep nearer and reduce the range.

My heart raced and my mouth was dry.

From for'ard: "Number One tube ready" . . . "Number Two tube ready" . . . "Number Three tube ready."

From Cryer: "Still a steady one-two-oh revs., sir." Normally this would mean she was doing twelve knots, but I was certain that this cargo walloper had never done more than ten in her life, and was now crawling along at eight.

The D.A.—director angle—was set on the periscope by Chief E.R.A. Manuel, his arms around me holding the handles steady on the bearing as I watched the target creep into our narrow circle of view.

With infuriating slowness she approached the centre sight line.

Her range was so great that we would have to fire a dispersed salvo at forty-five second intervals—an unconscionable time to wait.

She was almost touching the sight line.

I swallowed.

"Stand by. . . . *Fire One!*"

59

The boat recoiled and bounced to the shock of the discharge, and a pressure on the ears indicated that the compressed air which fired the torpedo had been vented back into the boat. (The air had to come back into the submarine, for if it followed the torpedo into the sea, it would make an enormous white bubble.)

From for'ard: "Number One tube fired."

From Cryer: "Torpedo running."

Through the periscope I followed its track as it closed the distance between us and the merchantman. Despite its forty-five knots, the torpedo seemed to creep through the water like an aquatic snail. On . . . on . . . on, until Haddow, holding the stop-watch, ordered: "Fire Two!"

Lord, was that forty-five seconds? It seemed as many minutes.

"Number Two tube fired."

"Torpedo running."

A quick glance at the cloudless and still empty blue sky, then on to the track of the second torpedo.

At last: "Number Three tube fired."

"Torpedo running."

Now we could only hope. Savagely I gripped the periscope handles. "We've *got* to hit her," I whispered. "We've got to." I straightened, gestured with a finger, and the periscope was lowered back into its well. "Eighty feet. Group up. Full ahead together. Starboard twenty-five. Steer north."

It was essential to get away from the tell-tale spot where the torpedo track started.

I stood at Haddow's side and watched the seconds tick past on the stop-watch. Everyone's ears were strained to catch the sound of a hit.

One minute.

60

Someone spoke but was immediately silenced. I raised my eyes and saw Churchill peering round the door of the ward-room. He winked. I winked back.

Two minutes.

We were a fair distance now from the torpedo tracks, so I ordered: "Group down. Slow ahead together." As speed was reduced the clattering vibrations diminished, and we would be able to hear more clearly the sounds of any explosions.

Six minutes.

I was soaked with perspiration and the air inside the submarine was a heavy foul blanket. To its natural staleness were added the odours of three dozen people who had neither bathed nor washed their clothes for a fortnight.

Seven minutes.

Still we waited. A heavy despair seized my heart. By this time the torpedoes had run 8,000 yards. Either we had missed the merchantman, or she was out of range. . . . Then we heard it—the unmistakable sound of a torpedo striking home, a noise Churchill described admirably as an outsize monkey-wrench falling on a corrugated iron roof. There was a great, spontaneous cheer from the sailors. Two minutes later we heard two deeper explosions as the other torpedoes hit the bottom.

Slowly we returned to periscope depth. The merchantman was stopped and down by the stern. A plume of white steam trailed upwards from her funnel. She listed badly to port. "We've got her," I announced. "Want a look, Number One?"

Quickly Taylor fixed his eye to the periscope. "She seems to be sinking stern first," he said—and another cheer filled the boat.

There was no longer any point in loafing around at periscope depth. The water was clear and calm and a patrolling aircraft might well sweep across from the Italian mainland. We dived to eighty feet, "fell out" diving stations, and headed seawards.

I felt I could claim the ship as "hit, probably sunk." She had a long way to go to the beach, and with Cryer's report that her propellers were stopped, a severe list to port and a hit in the stern, it did not seem a wild claim. My only fear was that no one would believe we had managed such a sinking at a range of over 8,000 yards. (There were, indeed, a few doubts about it among the sub-mariners at Gib., but they were quickly silenced when confirmation came through that the merchantman had gone down. Crutch, meanwhile, needed no confirmation before sewing a white bar on our Jolly Roger to signify the achievement.)

Steering southwards at eighty feet, we waited anxiously for retribution. Receiving a signal from the sinking merchantman, it was quite possible for a team of destroyers or patrol craft to be sent in search of us, backed up by low-flying aircraft. But none came, and I blessed our good fortune, and allowed myself to relax. I had forgotten the old Spanish proverb: "Take what you want, says God, and pay for it."

We had taken what we wanted, and were to pay for it with the ugliest incident I had yet experienced in the submarine service.

We spent a further thirty-six hours in the Gulf of Genoa anxious to stalk fresh prey, but the enemy kept his distance and the time came to start back towards Gibraltar. Although disappointed, I reckoned that even if we had a clear run home our patrol had been justified. We were "blooded" and I had proved myself to the crew.

In a way I was not sorry to pause for breath, for the intense concentration needed for the attack on the merchantman, coming after a long, debilitating period at sea, had left me tired and temporarily washed-out. But I was back on top of my form and impatient for further action when, at dawn on 26th April, soon after we dived, Thirsk called out: "Diving stations! Captain in the control-room!"

Through the periscope I saw to starboard a schooner of some 200 tons. We were twelve miles off Bordighera, and still in the "free for all" area. Hospital ships, boats carrying comforts to prisoners of war, and neutral vessels, would be some thirty miles to the south in the "safe" area. Consequently I did not need to examine any books before deciding to attack her.

"Stand-by gun action," I ordered—and again experienced a heart-thumping, throat-drying thrill of anticipation.

The gun's crew hurried into the control-room from for'ard and waited, curious, at the foot of the conning-tower.

"Open the lower lid, sir?" inquired Signalman Osborne.

"Yes, open up."

He unclipped the lower hatch and the gun's crew, led by "Pedro" Fenton, the gunlayer, climbed the conning-tower. As we surfaced he would open the upper hatch and lead the gun's crew to their action stations. It would be one of the rare occasions when a rating was first out of the conning-tower, and the reason was to save valuable seconds manning the gun. Haddow would follow them, timing his arrival to coincide with the firing of the first round so that he could start correcting the fall of shot immediately. Then it would be my turn.

"Bearing green three-oh, a schooner," I informed Haddow. "Range oh-one-five. Open fire with H.E. on surfacing."

As Haddow passed this information to Fenton I turned to Taylor. "Take her down to forty feet." I lowered the periscope.

We started blowing the main ballast tanks at thirty-eight feet, held the boat down with the hydroplanes, reversed them and shot towards the surface like a cork.

"Up periscope."

The schooner was steaming slowly on the same course. "Deflection six left," I told Haddow, "and remember the range is closing."

"Aye, aye, sir."

At twelve feet Taylor blew his whistle. As we made the last few feet to the surface the hatch flew open, the gun's crew scrambled out, and a flood of water poured down the conning-tower. I followed Haddow to the bridge just as the first shot was fired. The schooner was now some 1,500 yards away.

The first shell went to the left of her, the second over, the third I did not see, the fourth scored a hit—then the gun was silent.

"What's the matter?" I yelled.

"Breech jammed against round in the gun, sir."

How the devil did they manage that? "Open fire with Vickers."

One of the two machine-guns on the bridge refused to fire at all. The other gave a feeble burst, coughed and was silent.

At that moment the schooner ran up a large new Italian flag. I caught my breath and tensed myself for unseen artillery to open fire on us. I had to act quickly. "Stand by numbers Three and Four tubes," I roared down the voice-pipe.

Powerless to do anything but wait for an Italian shell to

64

scream past my ears, I muttered a brief, heartfelt prayer. Then, from the voice-pipe: "Numbers Three and Four tubes ready, sir."

Thank God something's still working! The range was now no more than 800 yards. "Starboard ten," I ordered. Our bows, two torpedoes ready in the nose, swung towards the schooner. As she was only crawling along I aimed my first "kipper" just a fraction ahead of her bows. "Fire Three."

The boat rebounded, there was a burst of spray and the two-ton monster crashed into the water. To my disgust and horror its bubbling wake passed ahead of the schooner. She must have stopped just as we fired.

Incredibly, there was still no retaliation.

From the casing: "Still can't clear the jam, sir."

"Then clear the casing."

The gun was trained fore and aft and locked in position, and the gun's crew returned below. I leaned over the voice-pipe. "Fire Four!"

There could be no mistake this time. The torpedo was aimed at the centre of a sitting target. I cleared the bridge, and waited alone for the macabre, but fascinating, sight of a 200-ton schooner being blown to smithereens.

To my dismay, however, I saw no track racing through the water. The torpedo had disappeared! It was a nightmarish moment, and as I wondered whether I had gone mad there came the ear-rending roar of a thunderous explosion —beneath our own bows. Accompanied by a scorching blue flash that momentarily blinded me, it threw me against the side of the bridge and literally bounced the *Unbroken* out of the water. With a crash we slapped back into the sea, and as we righted ourselves there was a third plangent

65

uproar below as equipment, crockery and machinery were hurled across the boat.

I climbed to my feet, still in one piece, but badly shaken. No serious damage could have been suffered below, either, or I would have been informed by now. Although dazed I could guess what had happened. The torpedo had refused to function after leaving the tube and had nose-dived towards the bottom until, at perhaps a hundred feet, the pressure of the water had actuated the firing mechanism.

I licked my lips and felt a chill run down my spine. *What the devil's the matter today? It's the 26th, not the 1st of April.* . . .

Back on an even keel we were again closing the schooner. There was still no sign of any retaliation and I reflected bitterly that they were saving their ammunition, content to watch us conveniently destroy ourselves. "Enough is enough," I muttered, and crossed to the voice-pipe. There was little left for us to do, but I was damned if I was going to be seen off by a scruffy schooner. "Stand by to ram!" I called. "Stand by to board."

At this point Haddow approached me carrying, not the Bible—as well he might—but a book listing vessels on the protected run. As we neared the schooner, the boarding-party ready in the conning-tower, I waited for at least a machine-gun to open fire in my direction. But we advanced in tense, uneasy silence. And then, as we drew close, we were able to discern the crew lining the deck—their hands above their heads!

"They've surrendered!" I cried. A moment later I could distinguish two minute flags flying from the schooner's masthead.

They were about the size of ladies' handkerchiefs—ladies'

66

dirty handkerchiefs. "Lord," I murmured, "I think she's a P.O.W. comfort ship."

By this time I could see her name, and as I read it out Haddow exclaimed: "You're right, sir, she *is* a comfort ship."

I felt a great wave of relief that I had not sunk a mercy vessel, but this emotion was soon replaced by black fury. I had wasted two torpedoes, had jammed my gun, had smashed a mass of equipment, had almost sunk myself, and had been made to look a blithering idiot—all because some cretin of a schooner captain could neither keep to a proper course nor fly a clean, decent-sized flag. I seethed.

"Stop both," I called down the voice-pipe. "Fall out boarding-party."

It was then another thought struck me—that it would never do for the schooner to report she had been fired upon by a British submarine. I remembered Peter Churchill was proud of his linguistic ability. Here, then, was a chance for him to air his Italian.

"Captain Churchill on the bridge!"

A minute later he scrambled through the conning-tower hatch. I handed him my megaphone. "Ask them, in Italian, what the hell they think they're doing in this area. Then tell them to get to the south where they ought to be. Put it over as though you're the captain of this boat."

As he bawled at them in Italian it struck me that Churchill made a convincing Wop U-boat skipper with his grey siren-suit, tanned skin and black curly beard, and I was reminded of the night in Antibes Bay when we had pretended to be Frenchmen. This bluff worked, too, and the schooner turned away to the south after making some pathetic excuse about being blown from their course by the wind.

In a better mood now, I ordered: "Clear the bridge," adding to Haddow: "Press the tit as you go down." He did so, and the klaxon's stridence filled the submarine. I took a last look at the schooner, glanced round the sky to see if any aircraft were creeping in on us, saw the gun disappear beneath a white swirl of foam, and stepped into the conning-tower as the water gurgled up outside.

Down below I discovered that the damage we had suffered was quite superficial and had made more mess than mischief. None the less it was necessary to go through the tedious and unpleasant task of holding an inquest. Why had the gun jammed? Some fool had rammed home a shell without removing the base clip. Why had the Vickers misfired? They, too, had been loaded incorrectly. Why had the torpedo failed? It had not been checked to see that its propeller was in the "starting" position before it was hauled into the tube.

I decided against issuing individual punishments. Instead the entire ship's company would learn I had not been joking when I warned them at Barrow that only the best would satisfy me. They spent the entire dog-watches that day doing the severest exercises since the trials back in Scotland.

Later, in the ward-room, desperately tired and ready for sleep, I was greeted by a jittery Bernard and a slightly damaged Peter Churchill. It appeared the latter had been asleep when we tackled the schooner, and the first he knew of our encounter was when the wayward torpedo blew us out of the water. It also blew Churchill out of his bunk. For a moment the poor chap didn't know whether we were still afloat or plunging to our deaths. To add to his confusion he was struck on the head by a flying electric toaster and a pair of dividers stabbed him in the knee. Badly shaken, he sheltered beneath the ward-room table with

Bernard wondering what the dickens it was all about, until I summoned him to the bridge. Hearing of this, my admiration for Churchill increased tenfold, for he had given no indication of the nerve-destroying shock he had suffered when he gallantly hectored the skipper of the schooner.

Next morning yet another incident was added to our chapter of accidents. We dived at dawn, as was our custom, but it took us over ten minutes to get down. The reason, without becoming too technical, was that the water kept in the submarine to help us dive had been pumped out during the night. Fortunately, during the period our tail was stuck in the air no enemy aircraft paid a visit, but I was not in the mood to let the matter pass lightly. Taylor, as first lieutenant, was responsible for our diving trim and irrespective of who actually made the error, it was Taylor who got it in the neck. I was reluctant to give him a bottle —it in no way improved our relationship—but the slip-up might well have cost us our lives.

During the final leg of the journey to Gib., I finished my last letter to Ting. I had written several on patrol and would post them in a batch on return to harbour. Needless to say, my thoughts were always with Ting in her Aldeburgh cottage. I would visualise her dancing with the pongos on Saturday nights at the Brudenell Hotel, or walking along the front in her green slacks and brightly coloured jerseys. Aldeburgh was such a small, quiet, quaint old town it never crossed my mind it was a target for bombing and machine-gun attacks; that it was in a perpetual state of alarm as the point where enemy bombers crossed the coast for their raids on London; that it was "windy corner" for night actions in the North Sea against German E-boats.

I am glad I did not know these things at the time. It was better to think of Ting and our child safe in a charming and isolated seaside resort—and never once did she write a word to disillusion me.

I wondered what June looked like, whether she would be beautiful, whether she would be jealous when I came home—if I came home. I wondered what the little cottage was like inside, and would picture myself there with them.

On 2nd May, exactly three weeks after leaving Gibraltar, we sailed back into Algeciras Bay, the crew lining the casing and the Jolly Roger fluttering above our heads. Entering harbour after a patrol is a moving experience, for mingled with the pride of the occasion comes the shock of realising you might never have come back at all; might never again have seen these well-remembered landmarks and heard the familiar voices of friends. One patrol or a dozen, this feeling of surprise would still be there.

We secured alongside the *Maidstone* and I went aboard her to report to Captain Voelcker. My legs were stiff and unresponsive as I climbed the depot ship's ladder, the result of lack of exercise and cramped living, and my thighs and shins were aching by the time I entered the "cuddy"—the Captain's cabin. Thinking of the misfortunes listed in my patrol report I presented myself to "S" with mixed feelings, but he soon put me at my ease with a cheery: "Glad to see you back. Have a sherry."

I did.

"We've had early information about the spies you landed," Voelcker continued. "All four of them are doing well. More than that Intelligence won't say, but it's enough to show that you did your part of the job satisfactorily."

As Voelcker was congratulating me on our kill in the

Gulf of Genoa we were joined by Peter Churchill and Bernard. The news of Bernard's presence had already been grape-vined round Gib., however, and in no time at all a couple of Army Intelligence officers came to whisk him away for interrogation. The party broke up and I made for my cabin and a much-needed bath. An hour later, resplendent in monkey jacket, bow tie and crisp linen, I took up a strategic position by the ward-room bar. I was able to relax with a free mind. The crew had been fixed with leave at the local rest camp, our list of defects had been handed in, and the patrol report was written. Our misfortunes were best forgotten. For a couple of days, at least, I could take it easy.

Our stay at Gib. was beset by numerous petty irritations. During our patrol Laval's pro-German government had taken over in France, and there was a strong likelihood that French capital ships and cruisers stationed at Casablanca would attempt to break through the Straits to join the rest of their fleet at Toulon. If they did it would be our duty to sink them. The watch on leave had to be recalled from the rest camp, and we spent a tense week ready for sea at a moment's notice. Fortunately, the scare died down, but was immediately replaced by a different one—the threat of saboteurs.

The danger of sabotage by frogmen based in hostile Spain had become very real, and our nights were constantly disturbed by motor launches chugging round the harbour dropping miniature depth charges on suspected intruders. Our own sentry was warned to "fire first and ask questions later"—an order that nearly led to the deaths of certain members of the Gib. army garrison.

A group of them decided to "capture" the *Maidstone*

71

via the submarines tied alongside, and our sentry's dreams of home were interrupted one night by the appearance of two swimmers clambering over our bows. He drew his revolver, but some sixth sense stayed his hand. Instead of firing he challenged them, and they promptly "surrendered." In no time at all they found themselves under guard aboard the *Maidstone*, very lucky to be alive.

When the frogman scare had died down it was found that one of our main batteries had become contaminated with oil from a leaky fuel tank and needed to be replaced. This was a major job of work and entailed removing part of the casing, lifting a cover plate from the pressure hull, and then hoisting out one hundred and twelve cells, each weighing a quarter of a ton. Then, new cells fitted, and the heavy connections strapped down, everything had to be replaced. It was a laborious lengthy job which kept the crew hard at work just when they needed—and deserved—a rest.

At this time a personal problem came to a head. I could not get away from the fact that Taylor and myself had certain incompatibilities of temperament. Such differences might pass unnoticed in a big ship, but they are exaggerated and distorted in the emotional confinement of a small submarine. Taylor, I decided, must be replaced. It was no reflection on him as a man or as a sailor. It was simply that our temperaments did not allow us to serve together. As there were no spare first lieutenants aboard the *Maidstone*, I asked Haig Haddow to take the job. It was an embarrassing moment for both of us, but he said, simply: "Yes, sir. Can do." Next came the unpleasant business of going to "S" and asking that Taylor be relieved. Captain Voelcker did his best to dissuade me, but I was firm and insisted that it would be him or me. I took a risk there, for "S" might well have said: "Very well, it'll be you." After all, Edward Stanley was aboard the *Maidstone* spending his time trying to break a C.O.'s leg so that he could take his place at sea! In the end, however, "S" gave way and John Haig Haddow took over. (It is only proper to add that Taylor went to another submarine, won his own command, and served with distinction.)

Lieutenant "Ted" Archdale, R.N., a very fair, very precise twenty-year-old from Northern Ireland, came as armament officer, and we were also given the luxury of a "spare" officer—"Tiger" Fenton, R.N., a dark, thin and wiry lieutenant from Oxford, also just twenty years old.

This time a great wad of mail had been awaiting us at Gib., and I spent a nostalgic hour catching up with news of Ting. She had taken a cottage at Aldeburgh, and both she and June were fighting fit. Excitement entered her life when Vickers invited her to Barrow to launch a new submarine, the P.48. She was delighted to accept, of course. Not only did they pay her fare and hotel bill, but rolled out a red plush carpet from the station to a waiting Rolls-Royce, and treated her as if she were visiting Royalty. Escorted to the launching by the commander of the cruiser, *Jamaica*, she smacked a bottle of empire wine across the bows of the P.48, then put a further, moderate supply of the stuff to an even more exhilarating use! It appeared that a good time was had by all.

Our troubles and breakdowns put in order, we were able to enjoy ourselves once more. There was plenty of bathing, picnicking and swimming, and the officers could go sailing at the Yacht Club—remembering to keep clear of the Wrens, most of whom still examined the number of rings on your arm before examining the regularity of your profile. The boat's hockey and soccer teams did their stuff, and sustained more casualties on the murderous gravel grounds than the enemy were to inflict. It was all very jolly and amiable, until a month had passed and boredom crept in. None of us were sorry when the news came through that we were off to sea again.

By this time we had been joined by two "S" class submarines, including the *Safari* commanded by the legendary Ben Bryant and the *Unison* commanded by Lieutenant K. C. Halliday. When the *Unbroken*, *Unison*, *United* and *Unbending* went to Malta to rebuild the 10th flotilla, the "S" boats were to help form a new 8th flotilla based on Gib.

Four of us were to take part in this next operation; the protection of a Malta convoy from Italian surface forces. An enemy cruiser squadron was known to be based in the Tyrrhenian Sea, and the four submarines were to take up a patrol line between Cagliari, the Italian naval base in southern Sardinia, and Palermo in Sicily. *Unbroken* was given the billet nearest the Sicilian coast, but as the four of us had to cover a line one hundred and eighty miles long, the chances of intercepting an enemy force were not great.

How we cried out for more submarines! But there were none. Rumour had it that the Americans had been asked to send boats to the Med., but had declined saying their submarines were too large to operate in those clear, restricted waters. True or false, it made us feel extremely proud.

Chapter Four

Twelfth June.

At 5 a.m. we dived near Marittimo Island off the north-west coast of Sicily and proceeded to our station north of Cape St. Vito between Trapani and Palermo.

All that day and most of the next passed without incident, and while the crew were conscious now of the folly of reckless speculation, they were soberly aware of the desperate need for our mission to succeed. This was not merely a case of trying to sink an enemy ship for the sake of an extra bar on our Jolly Roger: the fate of Malta and the Med.—and thus, perhaps, the war—might well depend upon the arrival or non-arrival of the convoy from England. Hungry now for both guns and bread, Malta could not survive for ever on mere fist-shaking gestures of defiance.

At this point the convoy would be nearing the Skerki Channel before passing between Cape Bon and Marittimo. As we had not been informed of its precise movements, or of the size and deployment of its escorting force, we did not know exactly when they would enter the Sicilian Channel. My calculations told me that for a period on 15th June, between leaving their Gibraltar escorts and linking up with aircraft from Malta, the merchantmen would be nakedly alone, presenting the Italian cruisers with a perfect target. I could only guess where this gap would occur, as

V.A.C.N.A.'s* staff at Gib., for reasons best known to themselves, had kept us in ignorance of the overall plans for the operation. All the *Unbroken* could do was remain in position off Cape St. Vito until the enemy cruisers were sighted or reported.

Soon after we surfaced on the night of the 13th we received a signal from *Safari*. She had sighted the cruiser force which had left Cagliari and was steaming in our direction. I read the signal and climbed to the bridge, grinning happily. A cruiser force—and all ours! I altered course to intercept.

Just before midnight *Unison* sent me another enemy report, and by plotting the two I reckoned the cruisers were heading for Marittimo. I adjusted my own course towards the island.

Hopes ran high when the darkened lighthouses on the Sicilian coast started to flash, suggesting the enemy was about to pass our way and needed the lights to aid navigation.

At one-thirty we saw searchlights and bursting ack-ack fire over distant Trapani. Our aircraft from Malta were doing their stuff.

As we peered into the moonless and starless night, hardly daring to breathe, straining to catch the slightest hint of throbbing engines or crashing bow-waves, the thrill of the situation captured our imaginations. At two o'clock however, the wind was taken from our sails. In the wireless office Petty Officer Willey intercepted a reconnaissance aircraft's report to Malta—the cruisers were over a hundred miles to the north-east of us and steaming east. Since leaving Cagliari they had made considerable alterations of course at speeds which put us right out of the picture with our surface maximum of less than twelve knots. It transpired they had passed near enough to *Unison* for her to fire a salvo

*Vice-Admiral Commanding North Atlantic Station.

76

—a following long shot that had little chance and did, alas, miss.

We dived at dawn as a fresh outbreak of ack-ack fire punctured the Trapani sky. Too weary now to be aware of our frustration and disappointment, we slept while we could and kept a permanent watch at periscope depth. But the day passed uneventfully, and we surfaced at dusk wishing we had something more practical than prayers to offer for the convoy's safety.

Soon after midnight we received a signal from V.A.C.N.A. at Gib. The ever-alert aircraft from Malta had spotted the cruisers leaving Palermo three hours previously. Our hearts leapt at the news, for we were only seventy miles from the port and good fortune might bring the enemy our way. We closed Marittimo again, assuming the warships must pass there if they were making for the convoy.

An hour later Cryer reported: "Heavy H.E. bearing oh-seven-oh; distant; moving right." The cruisers, right enough. But they were ten miles off and legging it away from us. Once again we had been cheated of a target.

Bitter at our inability to do more than limp slowly after the rapidly disappearing cruisers, we pressed forward as best we were able. We dived at dawn, and at eleven o'clock we heard it—the crashing of bombs and the bursting of shells as the cruisers, backed by aircraft, commenced their attack upon the convoy. We did not realise it then, but four merchantmen were sent to the bottom. For seven hours our ears were tortured by the sounds of the convoy's anguish, and through the periscope we saw the black smoke of death hanging over the horizon some fifty miles to the south. Malta's hopes, and the hopes of the Allies, were fading fast beneath that brilliant sky. In the morning a convoy had been sailing to relieve beleaguered Malta. As dusk gathered only a pathetic handful of wreckage floated on the oil- and blood-stained sea.

That evening we sighted the foretops and mainmasts of two of the cruisers as they returned from their victory, but they were ten miles off and inside Marittimo. Again they had dodged us, and two months were to pass before we finally caught up with them. . . .

I was upset at my inability to plot the enemy's movements which caused me to lose a fine target. As I commented in my patrol report: "It is to be noted that in my attempt to appreciate the course of action of this enemy cruiser force, I was seriously handicapped by my complete lack of information regarding the positions and movements of our own convoy and naval forces. I submit such information should be supplied in future as it is disheartening to feel the enemy probably has more knowledge of this subject than oneself."

The Admiral at Gibraltar agreed with this sentiment.

On the morning of 17th June, awaiting further orders from V.A.C.N.A., we dived at 4.30 and I decided to grab a few hours' sleep. I had not been long turned in when I was awakened by the familiar: "Captain in the control-room!"

I found myself there half-asleep. I noticed we were below periscope depth and still diving. Thirsk, the officer of the watch, explained. "A Cant seaplane, sir, searching the area. Dawn patrol, perhaps. I'm going down to seventy feet. She's some way to starboard at the moment, but she's been milling around all over the place."

The mention of the Cant soon woke me up. Designed for anti-submarine work, and with such a low speed they could almost hover like helicopters, they were a flaming nuisance. I gave this one a quarter of an hour in which

78

to clear off, then crept back to periscope depth. (The art of such a manœuvre is to glide gently upwards using no extra speed, in order to avoid disturbing the even pattern of the smooth sea. Then, if your tormentor is still around, you can slip down again before he spots you.) At forty feet I raised the attack periscope. There is always a fascination about peering through a periscope, even for the thousandth time. At first you see nothing but the clear blue water thirty feet above your head. As you rise the light broadens until, with a crystal flash, the periscope bursts through the surface and you are gazing at the world above the sea.

On this occasion, however, the romance was shattered, for as the periscope broke surface I found myself looking straight at a very large, very horny and very rusty mine! It floated high on the surface only fifty yards from my eye—and we were heading straight for it. No, not quite straight. The thing would pass down our port side—but only just.

I swallowed, but said nothing. There was, indeed, nothing to say or do. The mine was so close to us that any disturbance might detonate it. I hoped it was a simple contact mine and not acoustic or magnetic as well. It was not barnacled and had therefore been laid fairly recently, and although its top was wet, the sea was not splashing over it, suggesting it had only just broken from its mooring. I thanked God it had not freed itself a minute later. . . .

As though hypnotised, I watched the brute as it receded past the port beam. I switched the periscope to the sky. The Cant had gone. I sighted back on to the mine and beckoned to Thirsk. "If you want a whiff of reality," I said, "take a peek at that."

He did so and gave me an odd smile.

With a wave of my hand I returned to the ward-room.

Three hours later V.A.C.N.A. came through by wireless and ordered our immediate return to Gib.

. . . . . .

There were few smiling faces awaiting us at Gib. God knows they had little about which to smile. Four of our best and fastest supply ships and tankers had been wiped out, and although a handful of fighters had got through —flown from the escort carrier before she turned back to Gib.—they were useless without fuel. Four minesweepers and six M.L.s got in but could do little without fighters.

Malta was really in a bad way. The ships of Force K —the destroyers and cruisers based on Malta which had inflicted such magnificent damage on the enemy in late 1941 —had been sunk or disbanded. Its last cruiser, *Penelope*— "The Pepper Pot"—had struggled into Gib. badly damaged long since. None the less, Malta fought on. Apart from anything else, she had diverted a thousand German bombers from the Russian front at a time when the *Luftwaffe* needed them at Stalingrad. But now, at the end of June, 1942, it looked as though the George Cross Island had shot her last bolt. Rommel was romping towards Alex. with the most highly mechanised army in the world. While his supply lines were measured in hundreds of miles, those of the Eighth Army stretched for thirteen thousand.

This, and more, was explained by "S" at a conference aboard the *Maidstone*. Present were the C.O.'s of the other submarines at Gib.

"We *must* get to Malta," Captain Voelcker said. "The only way to save the Eighth Army and give them time to build for a counter-attack is to cut off Rommel's supplies. There is no way of achieving this save by operating from Malta. There are two obstacles: getting there through the minefields and the sound chance of being bombed to hell on arrival. Overcoming the first obstacle depends upon good fortune. The second can be overcome by spending the days submerged on the bottom of Valetta harbour and surfacing only at night. Unpleasant, but expedient." He broke off and surveyed the gathering. "Mars."

I jumped. "Sir?"

"I've decided that you will have the privilege of leading the new 10th flotilla back to Malta. It won't be easy getting there and it won't be a picnic when you arrive. But I feel you can cope. Later you will be followed by the *Unison*, *Unbending* and *United*."

There was nothing to say but: "Thank you."

The *Unbroken* was docked for a quick scrape and paint. It was impossible to guess when the next opportunity for an overhaul would occur, for all the dry docks at Malta had been bombed out of existence. Coat after coat of anti-fouling composition was applied, our cracked and worn paint was sand-papered down, the rusty patches were burnished and covered with preservative, and we finished the job with four coats of deep blue paint. I could imagine what the crew were thinking by the time they started on the fourth coat—*Fighting's supposed to be our line, not pansying-up for some inspection*—but there was method in my thoroughness. Blue was the colour of the sea, and blue would be the colour of the *Unbroken*. I intended that we would stay blue, for in the clear waters of the Med. red rust patches were easily spotted from the air.

While the sailors painted and the *Maidstone's* technicians gave us a thorough overhaul, I spent a great deal of time with David Ingram who had made many trips to Malta through the minefields with the *Clyde*. There was no such thing as following her route, for her track varied with each journey. Underwater navigation is a tricky business. You cannot keep to a set, marked course as though you were driving a car along Piccadilly. To keep only to within a mile of your prescribed route while submerged and blind is not as irresponsible as it sounds, for your slow cigar of a submarine is greatly at the mercy of unknown underwater currents and tides. In any case, even if one could keep to a few yards of a former route, a deviation of inches might involve hitting a mine. So despite Ingram's experience and and valuable advice I was going to be very much on my own.

There was no doubt concerning the density of the minefields, for the Germans and Italians had used E-boats, aircraft and U-boats to mine every possible approach to Malta. The island was a night's jaunt from Augusta in Sicily, and as the enemy believed you could not mine a section of sea too heavily, hardly a night passed without new ones being laid. In certain waters it is possible to sail beneath a minefield, but the approaches to Malta, and Valetta in particular, were too shallow to permit such a simple way out of the problem. *Clyde* had run her supplies to a point on the island's south coast, and the particular hazards of Valetta were unknown. The last submarine to sail from there was the *Olympus*, commanded by Lieut.-Commander H. G. Dymott. She was bringing from Malta the commanders and crews of the P.36 and P.39, both of which had been sunk by bombing, and she struck a mine outside the harbour. Although surfaced at the time, only five of the hundred-and-twenty men aboard the *Olympus* managed to swim back to harbour. The rest were lost.

In the interests of security, the crew were told they were

preparing for an ordinary patrol, but the cat was out of the bag when our kit was brought aboard from the *Maidstone*, and we stocked up with engineering and electrical spares. I lectured the crew on the need for secrecy, and I'm glad to say my lecture was heeded. Secrecy was kept—until two cases of Scotch were sent from Government House boldly inscribed, for all the world to see: "LORD GORT, MALTA"!

For the officers at Malta we loaded gin and sherry, while the sailors at the base there—H.M.S. *Talbot*—were remembered by the inclusion of three tons of dehydrated vegetables.

Stuffed with extra gear and food, some had to be stowed in the ward-room. Our tiny living-space, already overcrowded by the presence of "Tiger" Fenton, was a shambles, much to the chagrin of our "flunkey," Able Seaman Butterworth. The war had cruelly interrupted this young man's career as a student of economics, and when he arrived at Barrow he was detailed off as "ward-room hand" to the annoyance of both himself and the numerous volunteers who saw in the job an opportunity to nobble the ward-room gin. Young Butterworth—he was barely twenty—brightened our lives considerably, although not always intentionally. Tall and slender, with aristocratic features, I sent him to our digs at Barrow to give Ting a hand with the housework during her pregnancy. He proved himself most cheerful and kind, and his farewell to Ting is firm in her memory: "You know, Mrs. Mars, I'd much rather stay here with you than go to sea with your husband."

For all his innocence, and the inevitable raggings it produced, he was a hard worker and one of the few sailors who never missed a patrol.

Seeing the chaotic state of the ward-room, Haig Haddow

sent for Butterworth. "Look at this bunch of bananas," he fumed. "What the devil do you think the Captain's going to say when he comes down? Butterworth? Did you say your name was Butterworth? Butterworthless is more like it."

"Sir! You can't speak to me like that," came the indignant reply. "I am a gentleman with two banking accounts."

"Good God," said Haddow, "I never knew!"

Before leaving Gib. I had a final look on the charts at QBB 255—the name given to the main enemy minefield. It lay, a vast, rectangular threat blocking the Sicilian Straits, bounded by a line drawn from Marittimo across to Cape Bon, from there down the Tunisian coast to Ras Mahmur near Hammamet, then across to Pantellaria and up to Cape St. Marco on the south coast of Sicily. Since enemy convoys used it, the area was not entirely mined, but it was a tough enough spot just the same.

I spent our last night at Gib. sitting on a balcony of the Rock Hotel watching, perhaps for the last time, the setting of the sun over the distant Atlantic. I felt very relaxed and calm, and strangely confident of success—despite the pessimistic implication of the letter in my pocket. When we had first arrived at Gib. I considered the possibility of getting killed and decided I ought to make some provision for Ting and June. The answer seemed to be an insurance policy. Not a large one—just a thousand pounds for Ting in the event of my non-return. In my pocket was the insurance company's reply. Yes, they would willingly insure me, but the premium for a thousand pounds was five hundred smackers a year! Since my pay was less than five hundred a year I decided I could not afford to get killed even if a convenient opportunity presented itself!

The following afternoon we waved farewell to the *Maidstone* and sailed eastwards to pour a tiny drop of lubricating oil on Mr. Churchill's rather rusty "Hinge of Fate."

. . . . .

Our journey passed quietly until 4 a.m. on 18th July when we dived to eighty feet south of Marittimo for the passage through QBB 255. I decided on a direct, bold route, suspended half-way between bottom and surface, that would take us straight through the minefield via Cape Granitola. The distance of the run was sixty miles—fifteen hours of it at four knots.

The thought of QBB 255 gave us all the jitters. The sense of helplessness. . . . The fact that you cannot hit back but are permanently on the defensive, listening, waiting, magnifying every jolt and movement. . . . You speak in whispers as though loudness of voice will, in some indeterminable way, add to the hazards, and you are reluctant to make any but the most necessary gestures or movements. It is a nerve-racking business.

Inside the minefield I had the mine-detecting unit—a refinement of the Asdic—switched on in an effort to plot the pattern of the mines and sail between them. A regrettable action. We plotted mines, right enough—ahead, to starboard, to port, above, below—everywhere. Cryer's eyes popped from his head as he reported each new echo, and a few wild expressions and quivering lips were to be seen in the control-room. I found it difficult to overcome a tremendous temptation to alter course as the mines were reported, but common sense prevailed and we continued dead ahead. A submarine going through a minefield can be compared to a man walking through line upon line of soldiers with a ladder on his shoulder and his eyes shut. As he passes through one line he *may* hit a man in the line in front, but if he swings round he is *certain* to hit, not one, but half a dozen. So we kept to the straight and narrow.

Slowly, blindly, we crept forward, while the air thickened and our sweat-soaked clothes clung to our bodies, until, unable to bear any longer Cryer's maddening and demoralising reports, I ordered: "Switch that damn' thing off and never switch it on again!"

The hours dragged past in uneasy, clock-ticking silence. We lapsed into a half-sleeping state of stiff-jointed, head-throbbing weariness, and it came as a shock to realise that it was nine o'clock—we were through the minefield, and could surface.

Surface we did, and fresh air never smelled sweeter. I altered course to starboard for the sixty-mile run that would take us to our final hazard—the mine-blocked channel into Valetta.

We dived at the entrance of the channel as the new day opened a reluctant, bloodshot eye over the eastern horizon. The channel was sixteen miles long, shaped, roughly, in a semicircle, only half a mile wide at its broadest point, and beset by strong currents and tidal streams. To add to our difficulties, the big periscope was jammed in low power, and we could not obtain long-range fixes of position from the Malta coastline. As our orders were to surface at sunset one mile from the Castile Signal Station, we pressed on and hoped God was still with us.

After the exhausting fifteen hours in QBB 255 I was devoid of emotion towards this second minefield, and my mind was assailed with other, sadder, thoughts—memories of friends and messmates of yesterday whose shattered bodies lay but a few fathoms below our hull. It is said that mourning is selfish—that you weep, not for the dead, but for your own loss. That may well be true, and my memories were a shroud of grief, for I had lost many good friends and noble companions among those tortured waters. . . .

It was the end of a beautifully calm summer's day as we turned ninety degrees to port towards Grand Harbour. The periscope revealed a sky untroubled by cloud and waters unrippled by breeze.

"Diving stations! Stand by to surface," I ordered.

"Check main vents," said Haddow.

"All main vents checked shut, sir."

Haddow turned to me with a smile. "Ready to surface, sir."

"Very good. . . . Thirsk. Time of sunset, please."

"Seven-forty-six, sir. Two minutes to go."

"What's the private signal?"

"T-A-G, sir."

I nodded my thanks. *Unser Tag.* How appropriate.

I told Osborne to take a look through the periscope at the Castile Signal Station. "Got it?"

"Yes, sir."

"Right. Follow me up and give the private signal without delay."

"Aye, aye, sir."

Once again the boat was alive with movement and chatter. It was more than a reaction to the minefields—it was an awareness of the fact that we were starting on the greatest of our adventures together.

"We're in position, sir," Thirsk reported. "I make it sunset."

"Surface!"

Osborne opened the lower lid, allowed me to climb to the top of the conning-tower, then followed armed with the six-inch Aldis lamp. As we broke surface I opened the upper hatch, was soaked with water and was greeted by the sound of a bugle call from the fort. I stood aside as Osborne beamed the Aldis towards the signal station. At once they replied.

"Recognition acknowledged, sir."

"Group up. Half ahead together. Start the engines."

Fifteen minutes later we nosed towards the Lazaretto on the shore of Manoel Island. A voice called across the water. "Here you are! Number two billet, between these buoys!" I recognised Lieut.-Commander Hubert Marsham waving from the foreshore. I waved back.

We were soon moored bow and stern to the buoys and a pontoon was run out to connect us with the shore.

A minute later I was saluting Marsham and shaking hands with Lieut.-Commander Giddings, the First Lieutenant of the base. He was second in command to Marsham who had taken charge in the absence of "Shrimp" Simpson.

Marsham led me to the ward-room. "I expect you'd like a gin."

"You bet," I replied.

"I feel I owe you one," he continued. "You've no idea how glad I am to see you."

I smiled. "You may rest assured of this, my dear sir. You're not nearly as glad to see me as I am to see you!"

Understandably, the sailors lost no time making their presence felt in and around Valetta. Although beer was rationed to one bottle per man per week, many ratings had "bottled their tots" during the voyage from Gib., and were well stocked with good, strong naval rum. The practice of bottling one's tot was quite illegal, and officially it did not happen, but I would be interested to hear of an alternative explanation for the uncertain footsteps of the watch ashore as they staggered across the pontoon to the island. My own attitude towards the matter was quite simple: with all the uncertainty of to-morrow at sea, let them enjoy themselves to-day on shore so long as they do not get into any serious trouble.

After the first novelty of Valetta, however, very few of the crew bothered to cross to the town from Manoel Island. Apart from one or two doubtful cafés, Valetta had little to offer save rubble and air raids.

The inevitable nightly raid, now accepted as an essential part of the islanders' lives, shattered the peace of our arrival. It followed a pattern familiar to most people in Britain— bombs, shells and tracers filling the night and the ears with monstrous noise and fire, then the unreality of the quiet that followed the All Clear. The raids on Malta differed from those at home in two respects: their greater frequency, and the fact that they left few fires burning, for there was little to burn on the island's rugged sandstone.

It was arranged that while one watch and an officer stayed aboard at night to deal with possible emergencies, the remainder would sleep in the comparative safety of the air-raid shelters of the Lazaretto, an old hospital-cum-storeroom dating back to the Knights of Malta. The officers were permitted to sleep "upstairs," but were instructed to make for the shelters if the raids were "Sixty Plus"—if sixty or more aircraft were in the attack. The men ashore in Valetta were told to take cover if things became really nasty.

After twenty-four hours at Malta we were joined by the *United* commanded by Tom Barlow. We got together to congratulate one another on coming through in one piece and to share a general hate against QBB 255. Later that night Captain Simpson flew in with a skeleton staff of three officers, and at dawn next day four minesweepers started a sweep which blew seventy mines from our inward route!

I was anxious to get to sea on patrol before enemy bombers sank us in harbour, as they had sunk other submarines before us, but there was nothing doing. I kept pestering the Staff Officer, Bob Tanner, until he said, rather pompously I thought: "Don't chase the war, young Mars. The war will catch you up."

How right he was!

Finally I learned the cause of the delay. We were to take part in OPERATION PEDESTAL, the defence of the now famous August convoy to Malta.

On 30th July we sailed, our orders scribbled by Captain Simpson on a signal-pad, but comprehensive for all their brevity. We edged down the channel escorted by fighters, and preceded by the minesweeper *Rye*—a pleasing change to our method of arrival.

Our patrol was to start off Naples and then to work down the Calabrian coast until we found a suitable spot to gun the main railway to the south. Thoroughly to wreck the railway would be as good as sinking a large merchantman, for it was so heavily used it was estimated that for every twenty-four hours it was out of action Rommel lost 14,000 tons of supplies. After the bombardment we were to take up station near Messina with at least four torpedoes remaining to protect the convoy against any cruiser force that might loom up. The whole operation would take about eighteen days.

. . . . . .

The minesweeper turned for home, and we experienced again the nerve-fraying miseries of QBB 255. We survived it and surfaced at dusk, and I took up my position in my newly designed "bedroom"—the bridge. To save time in the event of action I'd had a specially constructed steel deck-chair lashed to the bridge. The two ends of the canvas seat and back were made with pockets that fitted over the chair's framework. Thus, if there was some flap I would leap to my feet, grab the canvas and throw it down the conning-tower, all in one movement. Its "smack" against the deck of the control-room would serve as the first indication that something was afoot. Unfortunately there were to be occasions when I rushed below forgetting the canvas, and Morgan, the second coxswain, was kept occupied manufacturing new ones.

Two incidents marked the next seven days—both unsuccessful attacks on enemy merchantmen. They cost me four torpedoes and I experienced the same nagging uncertainty I had known in the Gulf of Genoa—the fear of the effect of these failures upon the crew. They were working hard and risking their lives, and when it came to the great moment it appeared as though I let them down. The situation was such that one of three things had to follow—success and a new lease of life, a watery grave, or my being relieved by a new C.O. As far as I was concerned, only one of those three alternatives was at all satisfactory.

Chapter Five

The *Unbroken* was the first of the "U"-class submarines to be fitted with a 3-inch gun. Former boats had been equipped with 12-pounders, toys of little use against anything bigger than a rowing boat. Because of this, train-wrecking had been a hazardous, cloak-and-dagger affair carried out by intrepid gentlemen operating from folboats. Outstanding among them was the army's Captain "Tug" Wilson who did magnificently courageous work paddling ashore from submarines and laying explosive charges along the lines.

Ours, however, was to be a more elaborate and snappier job.

During the afternoon of 8th August we examined the shore between Paola and Longobardi through the high-power periscope; a short stretch of coast high on Italy's instep along which the electric track was in full view. After a conference in the ward-room I decided to do my strafing at a point a mile north of Longobardi. It held many advantages, including the useful landmark of Mount Cocuzzo, an absence of civilian houses, and deep water inshore.

After sunset, as the dusk melted into night, we steered to within three-and-a-half miles of the coast. At 9 p.m. we surfaced and crept towards land at four knots, propelled by our near-silent motors. Fifteen hundred yards from shore we stopped—and waited.

The next hour passed in dark gentle silence. The night was black and starless, relieved only by the red and green railway signals and tiny pin-points of light sneaking through the curtains of the Longobardi cottages. With luck we would soon be giving the inhabitants a new item of conversation with which to enliven their small-town gossip. . . . I stretched my arms and turned my face into the soft, off-shore breeze. There was only the slightest of swells to give any feeling of movement, and the look-outs saw nothing around them but dark, empty sea. Below, the crew were at diving stations. It would be a hot, sticky night for them, for there was little ventilation without the engines running, and the boat was already an oven after a day submerged. In the control-room Thirsk studied his charts and checked them against the echo-soundings. The area was well mapped and we were able to determine our gun range to within fifty yards. The gun's crew were huddled on the casing, their feet but a few inches from the water, the first round of flashless night ammunition ready in the breech.

One grave fear was uppermost in our minds—that our target might be blacked-out and we would have to fire blind at the distant sound of its electric motors. If that were the case, our charts giving us the range only to within the nearest fifty yards, we could fire a hundred rounds without doing an iota of damage. I could, of course, fire a star shell, but that would reveal our presence to every sentry, aircraft and ship within a radius of thirty miles. The problem caused me a great deal of concern until, at ten-ten, a train came into view heralded—to our joy—by a large headlamp. Its seemingly disembodied beam moved mysteriously through the night, and we were able to obtain an accurate, last-inch, range from it. A few minutes later an up-train passed—assuming they did travel "up" to Rome—and at ten-forty our own bundle of fun came into sight. She, too, was adorned with a great lamp.

We had moved to within 900 yards of the shore, and at a whispered order the gun's crew closed up. Archdale leaned across the bridge, "Range a thousand yards, deflection twenty right. Independent firing. Open fire when she reaches the datum point."

"Aye, aye, sir."

There was a long pause as the gun held the train in its sights until it reached the datum point.

Ten forty-six.

With a roar the gun opened fire, its tiny spurt of crimson swallowed quickly in the darkness. The shell screamed through the air and exploded with a tremendous crash.

A hit, by God!

Indeed it was. There was a vivid blue flash as the overhead wires were brought down and in its brilliance I saw the engine detach itself from the coaches and idle on down the track. Again the gun roared, and again. After five rounds, all of them hits, the carriages and trucks were crackling merrily with dancing yellow fires. The signal lights were out—the power was off. Archdale transferred his attention to the engine and methodically blew it to pieces.

By 10.48 it was all over. With cold-blooded ease we had deprived Rommel of at least twenty-four hours of supplies —14,000 tons' worth. It had been achieved in precisely two minutes at a cost to ourselves of ten rounds of 3-inch ammunition. I was elated with the brilliant shooting of Fenton and Co., for it was an extraordinary feat, performed with the smooth, effortless ease of a not too difficult gunnery exercise. But congratulations would have to come later, for it was essential to get out of the area and start south towards our rendezvous near Stromboli.

Half an hour later I saw the train still ablaze in the distance. It was a reassurance that I had not dreamed it all.

Our daylight patrol position for PEDESTAL was two miles north of Cape Milazzo lighthouse which lay eighteen miles west of the Messina naval base. It was not a comfortable spot, for the enemy were certain to have the area bristling with every anti-submarine device they could muster. I had said as much at Malta, but it was pointed out that the Admiralty at Whitehall were organising the convoy operation, and it was they who had chosen my position. I felt the Admiralty should have confined themselves to giving the route of the convoy, and should have left the business of choosing covering positions for the submarines to on-the-spot authorities at Malta, but I thought it as well to say no more than: "It's a bit close."

At 12.15 on the morning of 10th August, at about the same time as the convoy was passing through the Straits of Gibraltar a thousand miles to westward, we reached a point four miles from our position, and took a look round. Visibility was good, the sea was calm, only a slight breeze blew from the north-east. Owing to a combination of minor faults and bad sea conditions, the Asdic was out of action. But the hydrophones, which picked up audible sounds as distinct from the supersonic noises picked up on the Asdic, were working, and we had not long been there when the report came up the voice-pipe: "Mushy H.E. bearing one-eight-five."

Puzzled, I went below and listened. Through the earphones I could hear a soft tapping; a sound quite unlike any I knew. It seemed to come straight from Cape Milazzo. It was constant, its bearing did not change, and the disturbing thought struck me that we had been picked up by some new-fangled detection device. I said nothing, however, but waited until dawn, when we dived and closed towards our patrol position.

Still the soft, monotonous tapping.

At 9 a.m., four miles north-west of Milazzo lighthouse Thirsk summoned me to the control-room. "Ship coming towards us from the direction of the Cape, sir."

I grasped the handles of the periscope and looked. An enemy patrol tug coming straight towards us. As there was no harbour or anchorage under the lighthouse it suggested she was being "beamed" on to us. I thought at once of the mysterious tappings and did not like the situation one bit.

"Eighty feet. Starboard twenty-five."

Down we plunged, and the next fifteen minutes passed in uneasy silence. And then, just as I was deciding it had been a false alarm, there was a *krrrump*, and the boat shuddered to the explosion of a depth charge. From experience I assessed it at being some four hundred yards off—as were the four others that followed. We promptly went into "silent routine" which meant that in order not to transmit noises for the enemy to pick up, all machinery, such as ventilation, refrigeration and water circulation systems were shut off, leaving only the motors and gyro-compass running.

I glanced around the control-room. Apart from the licking of lips and the wrinkling of foreheads, the others gave no indication of the tense anxiety they must certainly have been feeling. I experienced the same combination of nerves, claustrophobia and fury that I had suffered when sneaking through the minefield for, as on that occasion, we were essentially on the defensive, powerless to hit back unable to run away—simply wallowing there waiting for the enemy's accuracy of fire to improve.

But no more depth charges followed the first pattern of five and after a while we crept back to periscope depth. The patrol tug was about a mile away—steering back towards the Cape. All very peculiar.

We returned to our patrol position, and for an hour nothing happened. At 11.15, however, smoke was sighted —a *Cretone*-class minelayer steaming towards us from the Straits of Messina, escorted by a Cant flying-boat. The hydrophones were still picking up that extraordinary tapping, which seemed to confirm that the enemy was beamed on to us.

We went deep to a hundred and twenty feet, and half an hour later depth-charging commenced.

For an hour it went on: patterns of four or five, with an interval of perhaps ten minutes between each pattern. Oddly —and fortunately—they were seldom closer than within three hundred yards of the *Unbroken*—far outside their lethal range. As a result, we were disturbed by nothing more than heart-jumping *krrrumps* and occasional shudders—but all the time there was the nerve-fraying fear that the next one might hit the bull's-eye, and the *Unbroken* would be the subject of another solemn "Admiralty regrets" announcement. At 1.15 our tormentor was joined by a pal, and the two of them continued the bombardment. We kept to our irregular zigzag, and while I cursed the infernal device that had beamed the tugs on to us, I blessed its lack of absolute accuracy.

My clothes were soaked in sweat, the air in the boat was thick and oily, and my nerves were in a wretched state. If only we had been able to hit back! If only there had been some movement or action to take our minds from the agony of the situation! But no. We could only wait and hope and pray, brooding and exaggerating, picturing a torn, smashed hull and a bubbling, choking, lung-bursting death. . . .

Then, at three o'clock, they moved away. The tension eased. I "fell out" diving stations and told Leading Stoker Fall that he could pass round tea and sandwiches. I was tempted to sneak back to periscope depth for a look round, but reason prevailed and we lumbered along as before— course oh-three-oh, speed one-seven-five revs., depth a hundred and twenty feet.

It was getting on for 6.30 before the enemy made the next move.

That was when Cryer reported "H.E. to starboard!" and before the words were fully out of his mouth a pattern of charges dropped close enough to shake the rivets from our plates.

I felt sick in the stomach. It was approaching dusk, and we simply had to surface before midnight in order to recharge our batteries and replenish our air. If we failed to do this we would be able to survive for no more than a further twelve hours. . . .

We've got to get out of here!

After the first teeth-rattling pattern the enemy reverted to his curious behaviour of bombarding the sea a quarter of a mile away from us, and I took advantage of the fact to slip into the ward-room and to study the charts and plot my next move. We were half-way between Cape Milazzo and Stromboli, having steered roughly north in our attempt to dodge the depth charges. Apart from the fact that the position ordered by the Admiralty was a "natural" for under-water suicide, it was obvious that the enemy, knowing of our presence, would not send his cruisers into the Cape Milazzo area. I decided to choose another position, although it would be impossible to inform "Shrimp" Simpson at Malta of the change. One pip on the W/T and the ever-watchful enemy would be able to fix our position to within the nearest hundred yards. For an hour, to the disturbing background music of distant *krrrumps*, I made a careful appreciation of the inland sea between Malta and Gibraltar. In the end I decided on a position half-way between the islands of Stromboli and Salina, reasoning that it was the best point of interception if the cruisers were using the port of Messina. It put us thirty miles from our ordered position and if it turned out to be a miscalculation, I was well aware of the fact that I'd be hung from the highest yard-arm in Whitehall "as a mystery and a sign"—probably with a cowardice charge thrown in for good measure.

At 7.15 the enemy pushed off, and I assumed that as good Italians they were more concerned with going home to embrace their mistresses than with sinking a British sub-marine. On the strength of this assumption I told Joe Sizer, the cox'n, to issue tins of tongue for a cold supper.

Paul Thirsk did a little simple arithmetic and informed me that exactly seventy depth charges had been hurled in the general direction of the *Unbroken* that day.

At 10.30, fifteen miles from Milazzo, I decided to surface. It was a tricky, yet necessary, decision, for the enemy might well have returned to the area and could be waiting with stopped engines for the *Unbroken* to refill her lungs.

Quietly we went to diving stations and crept up to eighty feet.

We listened. All was silent.

Sixty feet. Still silence.

Periscope depth. I stared intently into the big periscope.

The night was so dark that only a solitary star confirmed that the periscope was actually out of the water. The horizon was indistinct, and a careful sweep did not reveal even the suggestion of a shadow to mar the evenness of the night.

I handed the periscope to Thirsk and told Haddow to plane the boat to the surface and blow number Four main ballast tank with low-pressure air when we reached twelve feet. In this way we would surface slowly and in silence. As the conning-tower broke from the water I leapt to the bridge followed by Archdale and Osborne. Quickly we swept sky and sea through binoculars. Nothing in sight. I reckoned that if we were unable to see the enemy—if he was there—then he couldn't see us, either.

With the faint glow of Stromboli's volcano to port, I ordered: "Half buoyancy. Group up. Half ahead together. Start the engines."

Let's get out of here!

Shortly before dawn we dived fifteen miles north-west of Stromboli, and looked forward to a quiet, lazy day catching up on lost sleep. Having made certain a thorough periscope watch was being kept, I turned in and managed to grab four hours' rest. This was double the stretch I usually enjoyed, and gives some indication of my exhaustion after the strain of the depth-chargings. I had trained myself to sleep with my ears open, as it were, and any sounds, such as alterations to course, immediately wakened me. Apart from these interruptions, it was a standing order that I should be given a shake by the officer coming off watch every two hours in order to know exactly what had been happening —if anything. But on this occasion I slept for an undisturbed four hours—until 12.30 p.m. when we reached the "Mars

Patrol Position" twelve-and-a-half miles west-south-west of Stromboli peak.

The rest of that and the following day were quiet for us—but not for the convoy. As I was to learn later, it had been cruelly savaged.

All fourteen merchant ships were modern and fast, capable of at least fourteen knots. All were of desperate importance to Malta. Accompanying them was one of the most powerful escorts in history. There were the battleships, *Rodney* and *Nelson*, the aircraft carriers *Illustrious*, *Victorious*, *Furious*, *Eagle* and *Indomitable*, the cruisers *Manchester*, *Nigeria*, *Cairo* and *Kenya*, no less than twenty-five destroyers, while six submarines patrolled off enemy ports.

On Sunday, 9th August, the convoy sailed through the Straits of Gibraltar fully aware that casualties were going to be heavy, but quietly confident that the convoy would get through. It did—at a price.

On Tuesday the *Eagle* was hit by four U-boat torpedoes, rolled over and sank. After flying-off thirty-eight Spitfires which reached Malta and gave cover to the convoy later on, the *Furious* returned to Gib. escorted by five of the destroyers. Luckily, a salvo of torpedoes aimed at the *Nelson* missed, but the *Indomitable* was hit by three bombs, the destroyer *Foresight* was torpedoed and sunk, the *Nigeria* was torpedoed and had to return to Gib., the *Cairo* was torpedoed and had to be sunk. The grim slaughter went on. On Wednesday, the heavy covering forces returned to Gib. as per plan, for the enemy control of the air was too powerful even for the remaining three carriers. Two merchantmen blew up on Wednesday evening, and the *Kenya* limped along as best she could after being struck by a torpedo. Wave after wave of bombers, E-boats and U-boats tore into the convoy. Four more merchantmen were sent to the bottom, and the

Manchester was torpedoed—or struck a mine—and had to be scuttled.

The Royal and Merchant Navies suffered terrible punishment in those forty-eight hours, but they won their fight. On the evening of Thursday, 13th August, 1942, three ships sailed into Valetta, and Malta was saved. The following morning two more limped in, including the tanker *Ohio*.

But we knew nothing of this as we watched and waited off Stromboli, and spent Wednesday night baking in a midnight temperature of eighty-eight degrees. I was asleep in my deck-chair when "Tiger" Fenton tapped my shoulder. "Captain, sir! The P.O.Tel. has a signal in the control-room. It's emergency."

Automatically, as I crossed the bridge, I noted the absence of moon, the dull glow of Stromboli, the flat calm of the sea and the part-clouded sky.

Below, Petty Officer John Willey handed me the pink slip. From Vice-Admiral Commanding at Malta, it read: "Enemy cruisers coming your way."

My heart sank and I could have groaned aloud, for "your way" referred to Cape Milazzo, thirty miles to the south. As I wondered what on earth I should do, an explanatory signal came from "Shrimp." At 3 a.m. an aircraft had reported enemy cruisers off Sicily's Cape de Gallo steering east at twenty knots. This meant that they would pass my original position off Cape Milazzo at 7.30 a.m.—in two-and-a-half hours' time.

My immediate reaction was to order a full-speed return towards Cape Milazzo. I could get half-way there by dawn. And the enemy, making a detour around the area of the depth-charging in case we were still there, might well fall into our hands.

I lighted a cigarette and had another look at the charts. As I did so I was struck by a second possibility. The enemy Admiral would know he had been reported because the aircraft which spotted him would have been bound to have dropped a flare. That being so I reckoned he would have the good sense to alter course at least twenty degrees. Since he could not alter to starboard because of land, he would have to alter to port—and into our welcoming arms!

I could see no other alternatives and made a decision which, as far as Lieutenant Mars was concerned, was momentous. We would stay where we were.

We dived early and I altered the breakfast-hour to seven o'clock on the time-honoured principle of food before battle. In the middle of my bacon and eggs, assailed by doubts as to the wisdom of my decision, I heard Cryer report to the officer of the watch: "H.E. ahead, sir."

That was all I needed. With a bound that sent my breakfast crashing to the deck I was in the control-room and holding the big periscope in my hands.

"Diving stations!"

The crew knew what was afoot and hurried eagerly to their positions.

"H.E. bearing two-three-oh . . . Heavy units . . . Fast."

I swung the periscope. The morning was fine but for a distant haze hanging over the surface of the sea. I could see nothing from the direction from which the H.E. was coming. I took the earphones and could hear a confused jumble of noise. It certainly came from heavy ships, but they were a long way off. I went back to the periscope.

My heart thumped like a trip-hammer, but I noticed with satisfaction that my hands were steady and my eyes were clear.

Then I saw them as their masts broke through the haze on the horizon. In my joy I could have danced a jig.

"Bearing now?"

"Green one."

They were now well over the horizon. "Two . . . Three . . . *Four!* Yes, four cruisers in line ahead, coming straight towards . . . Range?"

Chief E.R.A. Manuel read off from the range scale above my head. "Range, twelve thousand, sir."

"Down periscope. Port twenty-five. Group up . . . Up after periscope."

As the smaller periscope cut the surface I had a quick look round for aircraft close to. There were none; but two anti-submarine Cants hovered over the cruisers.

"Down after periscope. Fifty feet."

Fifty feet would have to do. I wanted to keep my eye on this magnificent array of ships, and it would take too long to get down to eighty feet and back.

As the needles passed thirty-five feet I ordered: "Full ahead together." I turned to Haddow. "Two 8-inch cruisers, and, I think, two 6-inch. Anyhow, four cruisers for certain."

Haddow raised an eyebrow. I nodded. He passed the glad tidings over the broadcaster in a commendably calm quiet voice.

Archdale was manipulating the fruit machine, knowing it was my intention to get into a position whereby, as the cruisers passed, I would have the entire lengths of their sides at which to aim. "Course for a ninety-degree track, sir, one-four-oh."

"Steer one-four-oh."

The helmsman eased his wheel. The planesman levelled up.

"Course, sir, one-four-oh."

From Sizer: "Depth, sir, fifty feet."

We shuddered as the propellers lashed the water and the submarine leapt across the enemy's bows at her top speed. Assuming the cruisers kept to their course we would have to get some eight hundred yards off their path, turn around and fire. I had fifteen minutes in which to do this—just time enough.

I then announced an item of information I had kept to myself. "There are eight modern destroyers and two seaplanes escorting. Shut off for depth-charging."

As Haddow relayed the information to the rest of the boat, I felt a moment of queasiness. It was a feeling I knew of old—a boyhood memory of a twelve-stone brute flashing down the touchline of a rugger field, the full back at the other side of the field, and only myself to bring him down. . . .

This time, however, I was not alone. I looked at the faces around me.

Haddow, an enigmatic smile on his lips, watched the depth gauges like a lynx. On him depended whether I would be able to see or not when the moment of firing came. Thirsk was crouched low over his chart, oblivious to everything save the job in hand. Archdale gazed oddly at the fruit machine as though it was about to give birth. On him depended the director angle. Cryer, humped over the now repaired Asdic, had a grin on his face I can only describe as fiendish. E.R.A. Lewis hovered by the telemotor and blowing panels watching the pressure indicators with deep concentration. Manuel stood behind me ready to read off the periscope and keep me clamped to the director angle at the time of firing. The planesmen, communicating numbers and helmsmen sat with their backs to me, working their controls with practised ease.

Throughout the boat it was the same. Men going about their duties calmly, intelligently and efficiently, well aware that this was a "now or never" opportunity—a torpedo attack against heavily escorted units travelling at high speed. There would be no second chance. We had to deliver a single, swift knock-out punch.

"Bring all tubes to the ready," I ordered. "Torpedo depth settings fourteen and sixteen feet."

After a run of three minutes we crept it back to periscope depth. I lifted my finger and the attack periscope was raised until the eyepiece was just clear of the deck. I curled into a squatting position and looked. Still under water. Lewis raised the periscope, slowly dragging my body up with it. As soon as the top glass cut the surface I whisked around to see if anything was too close to us. Then on to the target.

"Down after, up for'ard periscope."

The line of cruisers had altered course to starboard— away from the direction in which we were heading—and had taken up a form of quarter-line. This meant the nearest would be one of the 8-inch cruisers. She would be my target. Although the range was rather more than one could wish, the disadvantage was cancelled by the fact that the new formation presented an excellent multiple target—one of the more distant 6-inch cruisers might be hit by a torpedo that missed the 8-inch job. I congratulated myself on this stroke of luck, and turned to study the eight evil-looking destroyers and their accompanying aircraft—the boys who could well wreck my chances.

Fortunately five of the destroyers were well out of it on the far side of the cruisers. Obligingly, the aircraft had gone that way, too. The aircraft might come back, but I reckoned I was safe at periscope depth for the time being. The other three destroyers were still in line ahead, and if they did not alter course I would be able to sneak across their bows and fire from inside the "screen"—from between them and the cruisers.

"Down periscope."

Archdale looked round. "New enemy course, oh-seven-oh. What speed shall I allow, sir?"

Thirsk said: "Speed from plot twenty-two knots."

Cryer reported: "Two hundred revs.; sir. That gives twenty-five knots according to the table for Italian 8-inch cruisers."

"Give them twenty-five knots," I said. Archdale manipulated the fruit machine.

"Director angle, green three-six-and-a-half."

Thirty-six-and-a-half degrees. That was the amount I would have to "lay off" from the direction in which our bows were pointing. A big angle. It would need care.

"All tubes ready, sir. Torpedoes set at fourteen and sixteen feet."

"Very good." Torpedoes set at that depth, hitting a ship doing twenty-five knots, would make as big a mess as anyone could wish for. I glanced at my watch. Eight o'clock.

I felt good. In my pint-sized submarine I was going to tackle twelve enemy warships all at one time. A story for my grandchildren—if the destroyers and aircraft let me live to tell it!

"Slow together . . . Stop starboard. Up periscope."

The tip of the attack periscope nosed out of the water. I grasped hard the handles as though to stop it protruding too far, and raised my little finger when six inches were exposed. Lewis stopped it dead. I swept round quickly to fix the covering aircraft. They were still over on the other side of the "screen."

From Archdale: "Target bearing green five-oh."

"How much longer to go?"

"Three-and-a-half minutes, sir."

The three destroyers in line ahead were still tearing towards me, although I was just a fraction inside them. With luck I would have a clear view of my target. They could not have picked us up on their Asdics or they would be circling ready to drop depth charges, but they were going to pass us too damn' near for comfort. I could go deep and fire by Asdic, but I was reluctant to do this as firing at a noise is obviously less accurate than firing at a seen object. None the less, we set the Asdic firing angle, just in case.

All this flashed through my mind in less than a second, and a moment later I uttered a loud curse as I saw the nearest destroyer alter course straight towards us. She was no more than fifteen hundred yards off.

"How much do *Navigatori*-class destroyers draw?"

"Fifteen to eighteen feet, sir."

It meant she would pass over our hull but not over the conning-tower. Unless she missed us by the narrowest of margins, her keel would snap off the periscope and sliver our conning-tower with the ease of a tin-opener. It was a risk we would have to take.

Our target.... I swung the periscope. There she was, still on the same course. To my joy I saw that overlapping her was one of the 6-inch cruisers. I had a double length at which to aim.

I winced as I swung back to the destroyers. The crashing bow-wave of the nearest was less than a thousand yards off.

Archdale said: "Just under a minute now, sir."

"Stand by all tubes.... Lewis, if my periscope is knocked off as the destroyer passes over, put up the for'ard periscope without further orders. Understand?"

"Very good, sir."

"Director angle green three-six-and-a-half," Archdale reported.

"Asdic bearing of target green four-two."

"Up periscope. Bearing now? Range now?"

"Green three-nine. Range three thousand."

I swung the periscope. Two destroyers had passed fairly close. The third towered above me. I felt very calm. I could see the stem cutting the water like a monster scythe. . . . The for'ard gun . . . A part of the bridge. She was too close for me to see more, but I was a hair's breadth off her port bow and unless she altered course she would not ram us. With a deafening roar she rushed past, and I caught a momentary glimpse of a scruffy-looking sailor smoking a 'bine as he leaned against a depth-charge thrower.

Manuel's breath was hot on my neck as he strained to keep me clamped to the director angle. As the destroyer's stern flicked past my nose, the target came on my sights.

"Fire One!"

The boat jumped with the percussion.

"Half ahead together. Down periscope."

"Fire Two!" Archdale gave the order from his stop-watch. The fast target allowed for an interval of only eight seconds between torpedoes.

"Fire Three!"

From Cryer: "One . . . Two . . . Three torpedoes running."

"Eighty feet! Group up!"

"Fire Four!"

"Hard a-starboard. Full ahead together."

"Fourth torpedo running, sir."

We spiralled downwards. . . .

Chapter Six

On a south-westerly course eighty feet deep we hurried from the firing position at a rattling nine knots.

I was very aware that the passing destroyer had caused me to fire late and I hoped the speed of my target had been over-estimated.

The seconds crawled past.

The scene in the control-room might have been transplanted from a militant Madame Tussaud's—the tense, still figures, some standing, some sitting, others crouching, all rigidly silent, unblinking and tight-lipped, straining to catch the sound of a torpedo striking home. For two minutes and fifteen seconds we were like that, until a great clattering explosion brought a back-slapping roar of triumph to shatter the illusion.

We've done it! We've hit the cruiser!

Then, fifteen seconds later, a second explosion.

"Tell the boys it's two hits for certain!"

What a moment that was! Fused into one mighty brain and body, the 600-ton *Unbroken* had tackled four cruisers, a couple of aircraft, and eight submarine-killing destroyers. Had tackled them and beaten them. Were we capable of lyric poetry we'd have composed a Psalm of Thanks, for we felt as boastful and as proud as David must have felt that afternoon in the valley of Elah.

We did not have long to glory in our success, however. Four minutes after firing there were other, more sinister explosions—the familiar *krrrumps* of distant depth charges. In a flurry and a panic the destroyers were hurling "ashcans"—depth charges—in a somewhat belated defence of the cruisers.

Then Cryer reported: "Asdic transmissions bearing green one-four-oh, sir." The enemy had pulled himself together and was after us. This was soon confirmed by a pattern not far beyond our stern.

"One-hundred-and-twenty feet. Group down. Slow ahead together."

A minute later we were at a hundred-and-twenty feet, sliding along at less than three knots.

"Silent routine."

The ventilation and cooling systems were stopped, as was every piece of machinery in the boat save the compass and the slowly revolving main motors. Orders were passed in whispers, all unnecessary lighting was doused. The Italians were not as efficient as our own side in the use of Asdics, but they were hot stuff picking up things on their hydrophones.

There were at least three destroyers after us, sweeping in to drop depth charges at the rate of one a minute. The patterns were closer than anything we had experienced before, their nearness judged by two sounds apart from the violence of the vibrations.

One was the sound of "rain." This occurred after an explosion and was caused by gushes of water—often many tons in weight—falling back into the sea. You have seen pictures taken from the surface of depth charges exploding —how the water is forced into the air like the blowing of a gargantuan whale. This water crashes back into the sea like heavy rain, and when you can hear it in a submarine it's pretty close to you. The second noise was a sharp, metallic *click* which preceded the explosions by perhaps half a second. It came from the firing mechanism and to be able to hear it meant, again, that it must be too close for comfort.

In the next forty-five minutes each of our tormentors performed eight or nine runs culminating in patterns of five or seven charges. Many were close enough to bring down the insulating cork from the hull, but I soon came to the conclusion that the enemy had no idea of our depth. The firing was accurate, but the charges were set to explode shallow, and we were out of real danger so long as we kept at a hundred-and-twenty feet.

By nine o'clock, after 105 depth charges had been dropped, it appeared the enemy had either lost us or had gone off for further supplies of depth charges. Had we possessed any more torpedoes it would have been our duty—and pleasure!—to return to the scene of the attack to finish off a lame duck or kipper one of the destroyers. But with our 3-inch gun we would have had as much chance against an 8-inch cruiser as a puppy with a pea-shooter against a rogue elephant. A cruiser is a different proposition from a railway train!

We had no means of knowing whether the enemy had left a destroyer behind to track us at dead-slow speed while the others returned for more depth charges, and after our experience off Cape Milazzo we did not under-estimate the Italian's ability to stick to us once he'd truly found us. Therefore, although all was quiet above us, and no more ashcans came our way, we kept to silent routine until dusk, grabbing a snack meal of cold meat and tea towards noon.

In a way, the *thought* of a depth-charge attack is worse than the attack itself. Once an attack has started there is little to do but wait, sweat and pray, a process less of a strain on the nerves than the fear that there *might* be a ship stalking you, there *might* be an aircraft circling overhead, there *might* be a sudden fury of explosives about your ears. So it was, from nine in the morning until seven at night, we endured ten unbroken hours of silent misery, hardly daring to breathe, talk, or move our cramped limbs.

At seven o'clock we planed to periscope depth.

Nothing in sight. Two hours later we surfaced and sent a report to Malta of the morning's encounter. "Shrimp" Simpson ordered our return.

Next day we received a heart-stirring message from Malta. Air reconnaissance reported that we had hit two cruisers with our one salvo—an all-time record which, so far as I know, stands to this day. I did not think it improper to order an extra tot of rum all round. I felt we deserved it.

Years later I was able to piece together the story of this cruiser squadron. In August, 1942, Italy was badly short of fighter aircraft, and the Germans had promised to provide the air cover for the cruisers' attack on the Malta convoy. The Italians set out but the aircraft did not arrive, and their Admiral, on Mussolini's orders, promptly turned tail for home. On the way we caught him—and serve him right!

The 8-inch cruiser we torpedoed was the *Bolzano*, and although there was only one casualty, the torpedo hit deep in an oil fuel tank and set it on fire. The fire gutted the ship and she had to be beached. Towed to Naples and then to Spezia, she was finally attacked by frog-men and scuttled.

The 6-inch cruiser, *Muzio Attendolo*, had sixty feet of her bows shot off and limped into Messina. Patched up, she was taken to Naples for more thorough repair work. There she was bombed by the Americans and became a total loss.

It is therefore a fair claim to say that we destroyed two

cruisers with our one salvo of torpedoes. As it turned out, severely damaging them was more effective than sinking them, for they tied up a mass of skilled dockyard labour before they were finally written off.

I suppose I should have been wildly excited at the news from Malta, but I was completely exhausted after eighteen days of constant strain. I decided on an unusual experiment. I had wondered on occasion how the boat would manage if I got myself killed at sea. This does not mean I considered myself indispensable, but it did mean that Haddow, as first lieutenant, was lacking in command experience. I decided that my state of extreme fatigue would provide the opportunity of giving Haddow some of this experience.

I gathered the officers in the ward-room. "I'm going to be Admiral for the rest of this trip," I said. "Haig will be skipper, Paul Thirsk Number One, and 'Tiger' will navigate."

I handed Haddow the recall signal and said: "Carry on, Captain. I'm going to be a very lazy Admiral and won't want to know anything. If we meet the enemy it will be up to you to take what action you consider necessary—even though we haven't any torpedoes left!—and inform me when convenient."

All went smoothly, even when we ran into a convoy south-west of Marsala and sailed unpleasantly near an escorting destroyer. We dived swiftly to eighty feet, listened to their Asdics for a few minutes, and wished them damnation as they drew away. We entered QBB 255, and at noon on Tuesday, 18th August, we slid into Number One billet at Lazaretto, Haig Haddow still doing his stuff.

They gave us a royal welcome. The Malts lined the

wharf, cheering, waving and shouting. They were happy. The convoy had got through, they had food to eat, and here was a submarine returning from a successful patrol. Our hearts went out to these valiant little islanders.

The outstanding personality was "Shrimp" Simpson. He is one of the few men I have met of whom it is impossible to say an unkind word. Short, stocky, with gingerish hair and a dazzling smile, he had a wonderful sense of humour that was but seldom hidden beneath short bursts of irascible temper. He was a human dynamo with an endless source of energy who seemed to live without sleep in the Operations-room at Lascaris, his Lazaretto office, or walking around the island with a joke and a smile on his lips. He never inconvenienced anyone without good cause, although he was capable of tearing a miscreant to shreds in no time at all if the occasion warranted it. Above all, he was essentially approachable, a man without side. His C.O.s tried to live up to his example—although few could play hockey with this thirty-nine-year-old's gusto.

As soon as we secured, "Shrimp" whisked me off for a verbal account of the patrol. As we talked, a flow of congratulatory signals poured in. They came from the C.-in-C., from the Vice-Admiral, Malta, from the Flag Officer (Submarines) London, and from Captain "S" of the First flotilla. It was all very satisfying and head-swelling.

All in all, then, we enjoyed ourselves at Malta, the annoying persistence of the air raids balanced by a regular flow of mail from home. Ting and June were still fine, and that was all I wanted to know. The future uncertain, I often cast my mind back over the happy times we spent together in the past, from our first meeting in October, 1940, aboard the *Britannic* returning from Suez to England round the Cape . . .

Our lightning courtship . . . Our marriage in the Cathedral at Mombasa by special licence telegraphed from Nairobi . . . Our honeymoon in the half-empty ship . . . Our wonderful months together despite the gloom of the war . . . Her parting words to me: "I won't think much of you if you don't come back. . . ."

But all good things come to an end, and our fun and games at Malta were brought to a halt with the arrival of Captain R. Wilson, D.S.O.—"Tug" Wilson, the train wrecker. He had flown in via Alex., and we were to take him on his next escapade. Practising in a pond back home, using the motor of a windscreen-wiper, he had invented a new weapon—a mobile limpet. Actually it was a slow-speed miniature torpedo fitted with a special explosive of great power, which could be launched from a folboat and directed at its target. It avoided the danger of ordinary limpet-sticking which involved having to swim beneath the target to fix the explosive, but it suffered the disadvantage of having no time mechanism. This gave the operator a very short period in which to paddle away in his folboat. Our orders were to try out the gadget in the small artificial harbour of Cretone on the ball of Italy's foot.

Before we sailed, "Tiger" Fenton was taken from us. It was pointed out that he had been "extra" to our complement, and there were plenty of demands for him from other, undermanned, submarines. By way of compensation we were given a fully qualified cook. This not only guaranteed a higher standard of meals, but meant that we'd have a trained baker to provide us with bread when stocks ran out.

Wilson was accompanied on OPERATION FOLBOAT by Bombardier Brittlebank, a huge, solid, powerful man of the type you want to have on your own side in a rough house. It was obvious that he would follow Wilson to hell and back.

"Tug" had none of Brittlebank's muscular bulk, being a slim and wiry fellow, radiating confidence. The two of them spent most of their time testing their weapons, of which they had a miniature armoury—three mobile limpets, Sten guns, grenades, knives and pistols.

For our part we carried only one item of gear apart from two folboats—a batch of dummy periscopes which we were to drop overboard in the southern approaches to Messina. Realistic-looking jobs, they would float around and create a jolly little panic when spotted.

In a way "Tug" Wilson and Brittlebank were disturbing passengers, for both were possessed of an all-consuming and morbid passion for their weapons of destruction. They crooned over them with the possessive love of unhappy mothers; oiling, testing, polishing, sharpening and adjusting. They seemed to regard sleeping and eating as no more than unfortunate necessities—cruel periods of parting from their adored ones. It was all very queer.

The plan for Wilson's operation was quite straightforward on paper, but was going to bristle with dangers in the execution.

R.A.F. photographs I had been given showed a 2,500-ton merchant vessel lying alongside the inner wall of the larger artificial harbour of Cretone. This was to be the target for Wilson's mobile limpet. We were to examine Cretone from periscope depth by day, measure the current, and then, when dark, launch Wilson and Brittlebank on their adventure. The two soldiers would be exposed to the greater hazards, of course, but it was not going to be too comfortable for the *Unbroken*. For, unlike "neutral" Antibes, Cretone was an actively hostile port, and I did not relish the thought of loitering there. However, it had to be done, and that was that.

The activity around Cretone was confirmed as soon as

we crept towards the port early in the morning of 5th September. Through the periscope I could see that the town was dominated by a large chemical factory which belched heavy, bilious, yellow smoke over the harbour. Beyond the top of the mole it was possible to see, some two miles off, the masts of two ships. This was better than we'd hoped, for either would make an excellent target for Wilson and Brittlebank, and the fact that they were probably in the process of being loaded with chemicals would add considerably to the explosive destruction of a successful attack. I felt a pang of envy, for I'd have liked a crack at the factory myself. A few 3-inch bricks in the right spot might have blown the whole place to kingdom come.

During that day we kept watch on the town, observing the heavy rail and road traffic. Wilson scribbled cryptic notes on a writing-pad.

Finally he had everything worked out. He indicated the spot where we were to launch him, and made yet another check of the gear to be crammed into the folboat. It would be a heavy load, for apart from two men and three mobile limpets, the canvas craft would be weighed down with pistols, light automatic weapons, grenades, torches, and eight days' supply of food and water. It may sound crazy, but Wilson's plan, if he failed to keep his return rendezvous with the *Unbroken* was to paddle back to Malta—all two hundred and forty miles!

"If driven to it," he told me, "I'll take a coastwise course along Italy's sole, down the east coast of Sicily to Cape Passero, then hop the fifty miles across to Malta overnight."

The day passed quietly until 7 p.m. Then, to my disgust, I saw one of the ships leaving harbour escorted by E-boats. I summoned Wilson to the control-room and beckoned him to the periscope.

"Our blasted targets look as though they're on the move. If they both come out your little caper will be off. I'll have a go instead with torpedoes."

Wilson grunted. It was obvious he wanted the job of sinking the merchantmen all to himself.

I took the periscope from him. I watched carefully, and was able to announce: "It's all right, the other one's staying in."

"This game's too full of climax and anticlimax," murmured Archdale. "I'm sure it's playing havoc with my health and strength."

We laughed, and the tension eased. For the next two hours we stooged around, and at 9 p.m. surfaced in calm water seven miles from the harbour's breakwater.

A special Asdic and hydrophone watch was set for enemy patrol craft; extra look-outs were placed on the bridge. We gave the batteries the biggest charge the generators could produce, and shortly before eleven I ordered:

"Open fore hatch. Up folboat."

Again that agony of waiting as we wallowed helpless and exposed. I peered into the still, moonless night while the folboat party hauled the clumsy canvas to the casing. All was quiet and dark, save for an occasional dull red glow from a factory chimney.

As we approached the breakwater, Wilson joined me on the bridge. "I've decided to negotiate the passage through the main boom, not the breakwater," he told me. "They may have blocked the breakwater. If you can get to a mile off the end of the breakwater, I should say the job will take us no more than an hour and twenty minutes."

I muttered my assent. We both knew the snags, and it was pointless to repeat them. Once his limpets struck home the alarm would be given. It would take him twenty minutes to get back to us, and all that while he would be hunted with every device at the enemy's disposal, including searchlights and E-boats. The Italians had often been attacked by impudent folboatmen, and their thoughts would immediately fly to a submarine lurking beyond the breakwater.

By now we could smell the acrid smoke from the factory chimneys.

The night had cleared a little. Stars could be seen high in the heavens, and a few dim lights stared from the darkness. It was still very quiet. The casing party moved quickly and silently in gym. shoes. Brittlebank went below to collect the gear and provisions.

"Five cables."

The end of the breakwater loomed up dead ahead, bearing due west.

"Stop both."

As we came to a standstill the folboat was launched. After I wished Brittlebank *au revoir* he climbed down to the casing.

I turned to Wilson. "We're close enough now. You've a mile to go due west for the end of the breakwater. When you've left I'm going to turn round and take a position three thousand yards from the end of the breakwater. This will give us a better chance in the event of being hemmed in by patrol craft. If you fail to make this rendezvous because we've been chased away, steer due east to the dawn rendezvous five miles off the breakwater. If we do not meet there, continue due east and we'll be on that line."

"That's fine."

"Well, so long and good luck."

A quick handshake and he was over the bridge and on to the casing. Silently the two men manned their boat and disappeared into the night.

The *Unbroken* gathered sternway.

Chapter Seven

After we turned and took up our amended position, Archdale, Osborne, the two look-outs and myself commenced our vigil. Apart from the gentle lapping of the sea against our side, the Mediterranean night was quiet and still. Thinking of cool English beer and the rustle of summer dresses, I sighed as I peered into the darkness. Our eyes were glued to our glasses, while our ears strained to catch any unusual noise, although there was no guarantee we would hear the limpets strike home. Wilson had argued that the breakwater, plus the special construction of the limpets would muffle the explosion.

The minutes ticked by. Wilson and Brittlebank had left at eleven-forty. We expected them back at one.

To our annoyance the chemical factory started to lay down a heavy screen of acrid smoke. I cursed, for if it became too thick we would not be able to see the flash of Wilson's torch when he signalled his return.

Midnight. Restless, one of the look-outs started to hum softly the opening bars of "Rule Britannia," broke into the "Toreador's Song" from *Carmen*, then lapsed into unhappy silence. I lowered my glasses to rest my aching eyes and wished I could light a cigarette.

The night remained unhappily quiet. A thousand doubts and fears nagged at my brain. Had their overladen folboat been sunk? Were they prisoners of the Italians? Perhaps E-boats were preparing for a sudden dash from the harbour, with searchlight crews ready to bathe the sea in light . . . I rubbed a hand across my eyes. *I'll be cracking up if I go on thinking like this.*

Twelve-thirty. Still no sign or sound of Wilson and Brittlebank. To keep to their schedule, the explosion must come now, for it would take them half an hour of fast paddling to cross the mile and a half of sea that separated us. . . .

I whispered down the voice-pipe: "Control-room time?"

"Quarter to one, sir."

Perhaps his infernal machines have gone off without us knowing. But surely there would have been a flash, even though the breakwater muffled the sound? . . . *Curse this bloody smoke!* I turned to Archdale. "Maybe they had some trouble with the boom."

"It's possible, sir. He was going to take things very carefully because the place was so lively to-day."

"We've stacks of time before the moon comes up," I said, "but I wish to God I knew what was happening across there. It must be——"

"Flash from harbour, sir! Looked like an explosion!"

I swung my glasses. As I did so there was a second eruption of red fire. But no noise. It appeared that Wilson had been right when he said the sound of the explosion would be muffled.

"Thank Heaven for that." But even as I spoke a searchlight beamed across the water. The instinctive desire was to duck as it swung towards us, but it was switched off as suddenly as it had come on.

"What now, sir?" asked Archdale.

"I wish I knew," I replied. "We've just got to hang on and hope."

The next thirty minutes passed in an agony of silent terror. There was no torch signal from Wilson, no dull shape loomed from the darkness. He could not have missed us if he had kept to instructions and steered due east. I leaned over the bridge and whispered into the night: "For God's sake hurry," but the only reply was the monotonous lapping of the sea, as patient and remorseless as time. . . .

"What's that?"

A vague, indefinite noise to starboard. A moment later it cleared to become the throb of a high-speed engine.

"Fast H.E. to starboard."

The game's up! But I said nothing, determined to hang on until the last possible second. I was conscious of Archdale's eyes on the back of my neck, but I refused to turn. I held hard to the side of the bridge, bit my lip and stared towards the shore.

"Vessel on starboard quarter," yelled the look-out.

"Approaching fast."

It was no good. We had to think of ourselves. I crossed to the voice-pipe. "Klaxon! Klaxon!" The helmsman swore and pressed twice the button of the klaxon. As its harsh, ear-piercing stridence roared through the submarine, the two look-outs swung themselves through the conning-tower hatch and slithered down the ladder into the control-room. As Osborne followed the vents opened, and the bridge shuddered with the whip of the propellers. I shut the voice-pipe cock and took a last look at my enemy. An E-boat, doing good speed. Within a minute she would pass directly over us.

As Archdale's head disappeared down the hatch I ordered: "Sixty feet. Shut off for depth-charging."

"Sixty feet. Shut off for depth-charging," he repeated. I hurried after him and prayed that in the darkness some clot aboard the E-boat had mucked up the depth-charge firing mechanism.

At forty-five feet Haddow ordered: "Blow 'Q'."

The noise of the air as it screamed to the quick-diving tank almost drowned Osborne's: "Lower lid shut and clipped, sir."

"Sixty feet, sir," reported the cox'n.

"Boat shut off for depth-charging," reported Manuel. I nodded.

I mopped my forehead, swallowed, and waited for "the heat." But nothing happened. Maybe I had been right, and some numbskull had forgotten to remove the safety-pins of the depth-charges.

I beckoned to Telegraphist Morris. "Let me know when we've been down five minutes."

"Aye, aye, sir."

The five minutes dragged past.

"Port twenty. Steer oh-eight-five. Group down. Slow together."

Then, from Cryer: "I can hear pinging, sir."

Hell and damnation! I had not expected modern anti-submarine craft with Asdics at a piddling little port like Cretone. If they chased me all over the ocean, no rendezvous would be kept with Wilson and Brittlebank—assuming they'd got away. I took a pair of earphones. Cryer was right. There was no mistaking the sound of Asdic impulses. We were in for a hunt.

"Silent routine."

Cryer moved his automatic Asdic control-knob slowly around the compass. There were two enemy craft. Both had Asdics. I crossed to Paul Thirsk and examined the chart over his shoulder. The water was not very deep, restricting our movements, for we did not want to run aground. There was nothing for it but to sweat and endure.

The enemy started hunting us in earnest, but we remained slow and silent and it took them twenty minutes to establish contact. When they did, both ships were to port, and I had just the sea room for a bold alteration of course to starboard. This put the enemy astern and ourselves heading back towards Cretone. They did not guess what we were up to.

By 3 a.m. things were quieter, but still disturbing. For the enemy was combing the sea to eastwards—where we wanted to be to meet Wilson. I decided to describe a wide circle which would bring me to the saboteur's escape route at dawn. By then the anti-submarine vessels should have cleared off.

At 7.30 a.m. we were at periscope depth and ten miles from Cretone. The day was bright and visibility good. We used both periscopes—one to keep watch on sea and sky, the other searching for the folboat. But the sea remained despairingly empty—until 8.20 when a couple of anti-submarine schooners sailed from the harbour.

We kept to our course for another ten minutes, until we were seven-and-a-half miles due east of the breakwater. If Wilson and Brittlebank had escaped along the planned route they would certainly have got that far by now.

The schooners began dropping depth charges, and it seemed they were going to comb the entire area in this manner. Reluctantly I decided to call it a day. There was no more I could do for our gallant friends. I ordered a withdrawal towards the south-east.

In the ward-room, while the events were still fresh in my mind I wrote it all down. My hand was tired and my heart heavy by the time I reached the words: "The loss of this brave officer and his companion is very much regretted, and it is hoped the submarine did all possible for their recovery." Then came the saddest duty a captain knows: writing a letter to the next of kin. I begged Mrs. Wilson to believe me when I said that I was certain her husband would get through, either by escaping, or as a prisoner-of-war.

As it turned out, my optimism was justified. A long time afterwards I discovered that the saboteurs had penetrated the boom after their limpets had exploded—although not, alas, against the ship—but the subsequent chase had been too hot for them. When they realised they would not be able to contact the *Unbroken* they put into operation their plan for paddling back to Malta, but were captured *en route*. This, however, was not to be revealed until many months later, and we sailed south-east from Cretone mourning the loss of two outstandingly brave gentlemen.

Next evening we crept towards the shore where the River Amendolea meets the sea near Cape Spartivento, and where we were to bombard the railway sidings. Subdued after the loss of Wilson and Brittlebank, my spirits were in no way improved at the sight of the sidings completely bare of trains and trucks. It appeared that this patrol was to be a long succession of disappointments. To add to my ill temper a torpedo-boat appeared some miles off, apparently bound for Reggio. But as we moved away from her we spied a handsome-looking railway bridge, and I decided to have a go at that even though the torpedo-boat might turn around and investigate the gunfire.

After the gunlayer and trainer had been given a peep at the target through the periscope we surfaced, and without wasting time opened fire.

In six minutes we pumped thirty-seven rounds at the bridge, a third of them hits. Others exploded on the railway lines, while a few overshot the target and made useful holes in the motor road beyond. It is difficult to destroy a bridge with a 3-inch gun, but it is possible to weaken it. This, I felt, we had done, and if we put the line out of action for twenty-four hours it was as good as sinking a 5,000-ton merchant ship.

As the bombardment compromised our position in no uncertain manner, I thought the time ripe to dispose of our dummy periscopes. They would not be seen that night, but enemy forces searching for us next day would waste a mountain of depth charges attacking them. We dropped them about twelve miles apart. The product of Sam MacGregor's ingenuity, they resembled exactly the British bifocal jobs.

The bombardment of the bridge did much to vent our pent-up feelings, and having acquired the taste for short, sharp gunnery, I set sail eastwards towards the Gulf of Squillace where another railway line was to be found.

We reached the gulf next afternoon, and admired its beauty through the big periscope. We also found a quiet stretch of line between two tunnels. The track was set low down but ran for most of its length over culverts and viaducts. Our plan was simple: to knock a train from one of these viaducts. There was an unfortunate drawback—all afternoon we saw only one train pass. We could but hope, so we surfaced at eight o'clock, closed to within half a mile of the shore and waited.

High in the hills above the railway ran a winding, rolling road, and to our delight and surprise we saw many cars pass along it with their headlights full on. The thought struck me that if the worst came to the worst we could put in some gunnery practice on a Fiat, but I dismissed it as somewhat barbaric.

127

Two-and-a-half hours passed without even the distant whistle of a train and I was biting my nails and cursing the irregular services of the Italian railways. It was pitch dark, and I did not fancy loitering much longer. It was quite possible that some smart Alec in a nearby defence position had sighted us through night-glasses and was madly phoning the whole Italian Navy. To be caught by patrols and flattened against the shore might provide an experience I would be unable to retail to "Soft Joe" over a glass of ward-room gin. I decided, therefore, to bombard the empty line and tear up some tracks.

It was going to be a difficult shoot, for the gunlayer could not see what he was aiming at. To help balance this, we had taken aboard a stock of flashless star shells to go with our flashless high explosive, which meant we would not blind ourselves with muzzle flash. It meant, too, that the enemy would be unable to see from where we were firing.

The gun's crew closed up and I stood with Archdale on the bridge. "Can you identify anything at all?" I asked.

"Absolutely nothing, sir, except the skyline."

That was of no help for the skyline topped the wooded hills high above our heads.

"Well, we'll have to open up with star shells, then seize on the best target they reveal."

"Aye, aye, sir."

"Control-room! Broadcast that we're going to open fire at the track in the absence of a train." To Archdale: "All right, open fire."

The gun roared and a star shell screamed into the air. A second followed. The echo and reverberations were tremendous. It seemed the entire mountain range was cracking open.

The shells burst in dazzling golden light and parachuted slowly to earth. But the scene they illuminated was vastly different from the one we'd expected.

"I can't see any railway line, sir," shouted Archdale.

Neither could I. "Can anybody see it?" I asked.

Out of the corner of my eye I saw the port look-out switch over to see the fun. "Not you! Back to your sector!"

"The line's not in sight," said Archdale. "Of that I'm certain. It must have gone into a tunnel."

That was it. We had drifted a little northwards and were opposite the side of a tunnel. Archdale pointed. "How about that road culvert high on the right, there?" he asked excitedly. "There's a car crossing it now."

I gave my assent and we managed to fire two rounds at it before the star shells burned themselves out. Much to our joy the car came to a halt and the driver, in his panic, forgot to switch off his headlamps, giving us a useful point over which to aim our star shells. For all this the shoot was more spectacular than accurate for the culvert was high up and its range uncertain. It was impossible to make spotting corrections as we were unable to see the shells burst, and those that missed fell like thunder-claps into the ravine. In all, eight star and fourteen high-explosive shells were fired. We may or may not have scored a couple of hits on the culvert, but the star shells certainly started a very promising forest fire. After five minutes I decided to discontinue our Crystal Palace display, and withdrew. As the burning countryside receded in the distance, we felt as gleeful as naughty schoolboys on Guy Fawkes night.

Next day, soon after we received orders to return to Malta, Joe Sizer the coxswain came to see me. Compared to the rest of us, he was positively elderly, for he was not far off his fortieth birthday. Bald and short, he was the most impassive of men, possessed of a reassuring north-country calm. On this occasion, however, his sharp-featured face was wrinkled and disturbed.

"Sorry to bother you, sir, but a great chunk of the frozen meat's been stolen from the 'fridge. I reckon someone doesn't approve of good meat being returned to the base. . . . What I was wondering, sir, was whether you'd authorise an issue of tinned meat to replace the stolen stuff."

My reply was immediate. "Certainly not. The stolen meat has probably been eaten by more than one man. The ship's company will go without meat until the amount's made up."

It was, I knew, an unpopular decision, but it produced a surprise result—the meat mysteriously reappeared and was eaten for supper.

The incident upset me, for it showed a surprising lack of any sense of responsibility on the part of the wrongdoers. Food was pitifully scarce at Malta, and every ounce had to be measured in the blood and suffering of the Royal and Merchant Navies. This may sound pompous now, but the grimness of the situation was very real at the time. I remember Chief E.R.A. Manuel telling me bread was so short in his mess at the base, the president ordered a ration of one slice per man per meal. A thin slice, too, and he illustrated his point by pinning a sample to the notice-board.

In the main, however, stealing was rare aboard the *Unbroken*. A favourite prize was the ward-room silver. Piece by piece it disappeared into the engine-room where the stokers and E.R.A.s whiled away the hours filing it down into natty submarine brooches. The point came when we were almost reduced to eating with our fingers, and Joe Sizer had to make good the loss by bribing a Malt in the dockyard with a pound note and a bag of sugar to supply us with silverware salvaged from the sunken *Pandora*.

Our next patrol was to be off the African coast in search of shipping plying between Tripoli and Benghazi, and we set to sea at 3 p.m. on 25th September after eleven days in harbour. We were escorted down the swept channel by the minesweeper *Rye* in the company of the *Una* and the unchristened P.34.

We surfaced after sunset and battled towards Misurata in a south-easterly gale. The sea was angry, and a high swell brought blankets of water crashing over the bridge. Soaked and miserable, I left Archdale to suffer in solitude and repaired below for my tot of rum with its complementary halibut-oil pills for night vision.

I peeled off my wet clothes, slithering across the ward-room as the boat rolled and pitched. I cursed, and yelled for Butterworth.

His lanky form staggered into the ward-room. I struggled into a pair of old flannels and white submarine jersey. "See if you can get these wet things dried behind the engines—and try, just for once, to bring them back without being either smothered in grease or burned to cinders."

"Yes, sir." He took them with the resigned dispassion of a Jeeves in reduced circumstances. I noticed he had a napkin across his arm, waiter fashion.

"What's for supper?"

"Corned beef, sir." As an afterthought: "*Fricassée.*"

I raised my eyebrows. "All right. We'll have this gastronomic masterpiece in twenty minutes."

He lurched out.

I felt unusually relaxed for a first night at sea. This was invariably the time for doubts and qualms, a moment to worry about the unknown future, a period in which to yearn for the comparative safety of Malta.

"What do you think we'll find down in the desert, sir?" asked Haddow. "Not much traffic down that way."

"No, but what there is is important."

"The trouble there is lack of water," piped up Thirsk. "Too shallow."

"Anyway," said Haddow with feeling. "I'd rather be in the shallow water off the desert than in the deep sands on it."

"By the way," I said, "you can start a little eager speculation among the crew by letting it be known that certain of us have been recommended for decorations."

"Really?" said Haddow. "Any idea who's going to be lucky?"

"None at all."

At that moment half a sea crashed into the control-room and Butterworth skidded into the ward-room, a cup of soup grasped in each hand.

"Twenty minutes was what I said, Butterworth."

"I know, sir. I'm sorry, sir. I thought I'd better bring it while there was some left."

"I suppose," said Haddow acidly, "every rating has already had two helpings."

"Oh, no, sir," came the innocent reply. "Not two. It didn't run to more than one-and-a-kick each. Everybody's very hungry. Nothing to eat in harbour. This sea puts an edge on appetites." Pointedly, he added: "*Some* people's appetites." He marched out, ever the suffering martyr.

As he left, Ordinary Seaman "Trampy" Mullet, the control-room messenger entered. Automatically I rose to my feet and wondered what had happened.

"Any of you gents got a match?" he asked. "All ours is wet."

We looked at him, then at one another, dumbfounded. Haddow was the first to recover. "Here you are, Mullet," he said, handing over a box. "Next time, please ask someone else."

Mullet took the box, nodded and disappeared.

"This place is becoming a mad house," said Thirsk.

Mullet's main duty was assisting Cryer. Both he and A.B. John Jones kept a listening watch on the Asdic and acted as control-room messengers when such a watch was unnecessary. A Hostilities Only rating, Mullet had been working on a farm only six weeks before joining the *Unbroken* at Barrow, and when given his first spell at the wheel his comment was: "I'm a cowhand, not a navigator." Transferred to the Asdic, he was very useful, for he had extremely acute hearing. As Manuel put it, "he could hear the green grass grow."

We ate the corned beef, euphemistically labelled *fricassée*, and washed it down with coffee.

To my annoyance we were recalled on 2nd October before we'd had a chance of a crack at the enemy. But our patrol was enlivened by an ugly little incident in the Gulf of Sirte.

I had closed to within four miles of the port in search of shipping, but the cupboard was bare. As I turned the boat around to let it seawards, the stern started to drop. Such behaviour was not unusual when turning, but on this occasion the damn' thing went on dropping!

Something was caught round the port screw. Something very strong. A wire, in fact. There are only three sorts of wire that catch a submarine's propeller—net wires, buoy wires and mine wires. There were no nets or buoys around.

"Diving stations!" I called. "Midships. Steady as you go!"

A glance at the control-room gauges showed we had been dragged stern-first from periscope depth to forty feet. In a moment we would be bumping the bottom. "Group up! Half ahead together!"

I was in a sweat. Our only chance was to speed the propellers and hope to God they severed the wire. If that didn't work we'd be held in a vice-like grip on the sea-bed—if the screws didn't get smashed up by a tougher-than-usual wire. For an absurd moment I remembered an item of cold comfort I had once been given: "Death on the sea-bed is quiet and gentle. The air grows worse and worse until you finally feel drowsy and fall asleep. . . ."

With a jolt that almost shook my teeth from my head, the *Unbroken* broke free. The boat shuddered and planed upwards. . . . I felt sick in my stomach.

Chapter Eight

I know it is considered bad taste to refer to medals in any terms save those of self-depreciation—*Frankly, old boy, I don't know why they gave it to me*—but the honest fact remains that once a chap knows he's due for a "gong" he's impatient to get it. He wants to pin it up before he bites the dust. Vanity? Arrogance? Conceit? Perhaps. But no worse than mock modesty and hypocritical humility. I remember discussing all this with Lynch Maydon, skipper of the *Umbra*, on our return to Malta, and we consoled ourselves with the thought that the Powers that Be had more important matters to occupy their minds.

After leaving Lynch, I sipped a gin in the Lazaretto ward-room and ran through the "U"-class Captains between his boat and mine—P.35 and P.42. Seven boats had slid from the Vickers launching stage—there being no P.40—and Lynch and myself were the only two left. Of the others, four had been killed and one relieved. God had been good to me, and that, I reflected, was more than compensation for the late arrival of a couple of ounces of ribboned enamel.

Tension mounted as the Eighth Army stiffened its sinews for El Alamein, and Intelligence reported that Rommel was frantically scraping every pint of petrol and ton of armour he could from the Axis High Command. The duties of the submarines at Malta were plain; to prevent convoys from crossing to North Africa and to stop enemy sea traffic between Tripoli and Benghazi. Rommel saved some six hundred miles' worth of petrol for every lorry shipped in this manner, and the economy was worth more to him than blood.

The rebuilt 10th flotilla was now quite strong, comprising the *Umbra, Una, Unbroken, Unison, United, Unrivalled, Utmost, Unruffled* and *Unbending*. In addition we were aided by several submarines, such as the *Safari*, which rightly belonged to the 8th flotilla.

United and *Unbroken* were ordered down the African coast east of Tripoli to have a crack at coastal traffic. Co-operating with us were R.A.F. Wellingtons and Swordfish of the Fleet Air Arm.

At about tea-time on 11th October we parted company with the minesweeper *Speedy* at the outer end of the swept channel and dived on a southerly course. The days were drawing in, and we were able to surface before seven. The sky over the northern horizon was its familiar red, and I looked across Paul Thirsk's shoulder as he wrote in his notebook: "Air raid visible at thirty or forty miles. Feeling well out of it except for £40 left in my upstairs drawer." These wealthy bachelors!

Two days later his entry read: "Entered patrol area north of Khoms. Made landfall and closed land. Expecting fairly quiet time." He may have been a Vasco da Gama when it came to plotting stars, but he should have left forecasting their astrological significance to Lyndoe, for his "quiet time" turned out to be the closest shoulder-rubbing with Death we had known.

The following day we sighted a 4,000-ton ship escorted

by torpedo-boats and shagbats,* well to seaward. For an hour we chased them, but they drew away. Later we heard thirty-seven distant explosions in groups of three to ten. Depth charges. It seemed as though *United* was getting the heat.

We surfaced as soon as we dared in order to break wireless silence and inform Malta of the merchantman's course. Later we saw distant flares as our aircraft combed the sea in search of her. Then came a signal from "Shrimp" saying she had been damaged by an aerial torpedo and that *United* and ourselves were to go in and finish her off.

We altered course towards the position of the crippled ship as reported by our aircraft. I hoped the Fleet Air Arm boys were accurate, although it would be understandable if they were not, for they were operating in the dark, two hundred and fifty miles from base, with nothing on which to fix their positions save unidentifiable desert and sea.

We dived early and at six-five I was called to the control-room to see a *Partenope*-class torpedo-boat coming out of the sunrise straight towards us. My instinctive desire was to dive deeper, out of her way. Then, remembering there was a shortage of likely targets in the area, I decided to attack her. As we started the attack I was nagged by a little voice in my brain that warned me I was behaving foolishly. De-stroyers and torpedo-boats were not targets for a submarine. They were the cats to our mouse when it came to assuming combat roles. In any case, a British submarine was worth ten of them in terms of war potential. If I missed and the come-back was fatal I would let the side down with a bang. . . However, as this particular boat was not zigzagging she provided too tempting a target to miss—even though she had her Asdic switched on and might pick us up. On the

*Aircraft.

137

other hand, of course, she could pick us up whether we attacked or not.

My worries were resolved for me, for when still two miles off the torpedo-boat turned about and returned from whence she came.

At 10 a.m. Malta came through to inform us the merchant vessel was stopped and floundering ninety miles to eastward. As I'd feared, the position given the previous night had been inaccurate. We swung round to eastwards and hurried on, only to suffer another spasm of enraged helplessness. For in the afternoon, four small vessels, including a tug and a decrepit gunboat, waddled past. They were clearly going to the assistance of the damaged supply ship off Ras Khara. They were too small for torpedo targets, but as I prepared to surface to demolish the tug by gunfire, an aircraft wheeled into view. I stomped about the ward-room cursing heartily, until a further signal from Malta directed us to a new position off Khoms. It was estimated that dawn would bring the tug, merchantman in tow, sailing past us.

But dawn brought neither tug nor merchantman. Signal followed signal, and we spent the entire day chasing backwards and forwards across the ocean, tempers deteriorating with each new alteration of course. Frustrated and angry, we swore and fumed, until "Shrimp" came through with positive information that our quarry was beached off the Khoms anchorage. We were to torpedo her there, using just one kipper.

In the ward-room I examined the charts in company with Thirsk and Haddow.

"The place should be free of mines," I said, "although that's pure guesswork on my part. The main trouble is that we'll have to operate in water less than fifteen fathoms deep. Not only will our line of escape be restricted in depth, but in direction as well." I ran my finger along the chart. "Look. After firing there's only one course we can take—turn about and aim for the sea along the path we used coming in. The enemy won't need to be very good with his Asdic to pick us up. They'll know we must be hopping it along a nice straight line at ninety degrees to the coast. It's the only place we could be."

"The trouble with this coast," said Thirsk, repeating his theme song, "is that the water's too damn' shallow."

"How about currents?" asked Haddow.

A good point. In a normal attack, the target, torpedoes and submarine are equally affected by tidal streams and currents. Thus the problem cancels itself out. But when a ship is aground and therefore fixed to the shore, the current can make all the difference.

"As no one here has any local knowledge of Khoms," I said, "that problem is in the lap of the gods." I thought a moment. "The general set is south-east, isn't it?"

"Yes, sir," replied Thirsk.

"That doesn't mean a thing as there are usually countercurrents in these coastal indentations and bays. I'm inclined to allow nothing. Then the error will be only half what it would be if we allowed, say, a knot in the wrong direction."

A tortuous piece of reasoning, but it was the best I could do.

Our spirits were bucked at having a positive destination after buzzing around like drunken bluebottles. But the sight of Khoms through the big periscope had a sobering influence. For one thing the sky was alive with shagbats, indicating that the enemy put a high value on the crippled merchantman's cargo. Tanks, probably, or motor vehicles. Then a torpedo-boat hove in sight and started to patrol between ourselves and our target. Her Asdic transmissions were reported by Cryer with disturbing frequency.

The merchantman was beached a few cables off Khoms main lighthouse. She had a list of ten degrees to port, and her bows pointed east. A schooner lay alongside, while a tug and a second schooner stood by some yards off. It appeared the enemy were investigating the situation to decide whether to attempt to refloat the crippled vessel or remove her cargo and leave her there.

The shoaling waters made a close approach impossible, and the inaccurate charting of the surrounding coast made it extremely difficult to fix our position with the precision the situation demanded. As we crept in I glanced round the control-room, and could see that no one liked the set-up. Nothing was said, there were no signs of panic—simply an almost imperceptible stiffness of bodies and tightness of lips. I thanked my lucky stars I had not yet encountered the moment of panic beloved by film producers when a man rushes to the conning-tower, screaming: "Let me out! Let me out!"

Joe Sizer and "Rattler" Morgan, his second, were as steady as granite as they rotated the planes and kept us at the ordered twenty-seven feet. There was no cheeky grin on Cryer's face as he struggled to maintain contact with the torpedo-boat. His forehead was furrowed and he was plainly worried. I could guess the cause: the water noises along the sea-bed, only a few feet beneath us. Haddow's face was solemn as he leaned over the backs of the planesmen, grasping the conning-tower ladder for support. Occasionally he twisted round to transmit a trimming order on the telegraphs to the pump operators huddled in the bilges.

Archdale was bent over the chart table, feverishly active. Somewhere behind me, Manuel hovered, while Telegraphist Morris was squeezed against the steering-wheel clutching the control-room log with one hand, a pencil at the end of a piece of string in the other. As orders were given he recorded them in the log with the furtive haste of a bookie's runner.

Nervously, ginger-haired Osborne rubbed a piece of brass-work in no need of a polish.

In the ward-room passage Butterworth, his face white and serious, stood ready to check vents and pass messages for'ard.

Aft, beyond the dead and silent engine-room, Scutt leaned with deceptive nonchalance against the wooden guard rails between the main motor switchboards, his eyes glued to the telegraphs.

I saw all this in one hurried moment, and transferred my attention back to the periscope. I shared the common uneasiness, but hoped I did not show it.

We nosed slowly into the shallow water. The trim was perfect: depth twenty-seven feet and not an inch either way. I turned to Haddow. "What's the sounding?"

"Fourteen fathoms, sir." That was the overall depth of the water—twenty feet of it above the casing, fifty-odd feet of it below the keel.

"Cryer! Watch carefully for the torpedo running. It may easily hit the bottom. . . . Stand by Number Three tube. . . Starboard ten . . . Steer two hundred."

We swung sluggishly, and I became too engrossed in the job on hand to experience further doubts or qualms. The torpedo-boat was still patrolling without suspicion. We were within range of her Asdic now, but as we were nearly bows-on to her, we made a small target for its beam.

"Number Three tube ready, sir."

"Very good."

"Course, sir, two hundred."

I took careful aim at the merchantman's funnel.

141

The steering was steady. I was dead on. A sitting shot.

"Range?"

"Five thousand, sir."

"Fire Three! Down periscope!"

"Torpedo running, sir."

At that second, as I clipped up the periscope handles, I saw the torpedo-boat steaming away to eastwards, one aircraft over the target, another coming towards, a third circling Khoms. I was thankful the muddy water would conceal the torpedo track.

We waited, creeping farther into the unfriendly shallows. . . .

"Up after periscope. What is the running time?"

"Running time, three minutes twenty seconds."

The seconds seemed minutes, the minutes hours. I wiped my damp forehead with the towel round my neck.

"Four minutes, sir."

Not a sound. I'll try just one more. "Stand by Number Four tube. Down after, up foremost, periscope."

Crossing from one to the other I looked at the depth gauges. They were as steady as if they had been welded to the dials. "Nice work, Number One. Keep it up."

"Number Four tube ready."

I gazed at the scene ahead. The periscope's magnification was such that my field was almost restricted to the target, the lighthouse behind, the schooner alongside and the tug. No sign of alarm. Once again I fixed my sights on the wretched ship's funnel.

"Fire Four."

The discharge raised our bows.

"Down periscope."

The bubbles on the inclinometer's gauges leapt for'ard. We were coming up.

"Speed her up if you have to," I told Haddow. "We can't afford to break surface here."

A moment's anxious pause, then: "It's all right, sir. We've got her." The bubbles stopped their forward movement and crept back to a central position.

From Cryer: "I can't hear that one."

Blast and hell! She's hit the bottom. She's stuck in the mud there. . . . That's why the other didn't explode. . . . Oh damnation! . . . I was told to fire one kipper into this wreck. I've fired two and they've both missed. What now? Shall I come back to-night? If I do I can creep in to within a thousand yards for a certain hit. On the other hand a hit from a thousand yards would bring a torpedo-boat on to us at a spot where we wouldn't be able to dive. Not worth the risk. In any case I probably won't be able to get into such a favourable position again. . . . All right, one more, and one more only.

"Stand by Number One tube."

I crossed to the after periscope and waved it upwards with my hand. "Sounding?"

"Twelve fathoms, sir."

God's teeth, we'll be aground in a moment! "Hurry up the tube."

"Number One tube ready, sir."

"Clamp me on zero."

Manuel gave the periscope a slight twist. "On now, sir."

"Fire One."

The boat bounced.

"Down periscope. Half ahead together. . . . Hard a-port."

"Torpedo running, sir."

"Up after periscope."

The range had been four thousand yards. Running

143

time: two minutes, forty seconds. We sank slowly as we turned.

"Forty feet, sir."

"All right ... Slow together. Bring her up to twenty-eight. I want to see."

Mullet screwed round on his stool at the wheel. "What course, sir?"

I looked at the chart. "Where's the pencil?"

Osborne rummaged in the bilges under the chart table.

"Hasn't anyone got a pencil?" I roared.

Morris, sensing my rising anger, quickly jerked his from the control-room log and passed it over.

I fiddled with the chart and parallel rulers. As I'd anticipated, there was only one course to steer: back along the road that brought us in. "Bring her round to oh-two-oh."

"Two minutes thirty ... Forty ... Fifty ... Three minutes, sir."

I swore aloud. "Haig, tell the boys we've missed and we're getting out of here."

Twenty-eight feet. Through the after periscope I could see a flap around the merchantman. The schooner had cast off and the tug was flying some sort of signal. As we had not scored a hit, they must have seen the torpedo track pass close. I took a look at the torpedo-boat. She was still going away.

We slipped off without trouble.

That evening in the ward-room we held an inquest. "Maybe I should have taken your advice, Haig," I said. "The current must have foxed us."

"Half a knot of current or half a degree's error in the torpedo course would make all the difference," said Archdale.

"Spilt milk," I muttered. "Perhaps we should have fired a fourth. . . . How are the boys taking it for'ard?"

"I think they're too relieved to be out of the shallow waters of Khoms to care much about us missing," said Haddow.

"I don't blame 'em."

P.O. Willey came in. "Excuse me, sir. Immediate from S.10." With his customary impassiveness he handed me the pink signal slip.

It told us to proceed to a position off Lampedusa. There had been considerable activity around the north coast of Sicily and an important convoy was expected to move southwards across to Africa that night. All available submarines were to close in on it.

I handed the missive to Archdale. "Plot it and give Thirsk the new course and speed." He nodded and went out.

A few minutes later I heard him call up the voice-pipe to the bridge: "Officer of the Watch, please."

"Thirsk here."

"From the Captain. Alter course to three-one-seven. Zigzag 'B.' Three-three-oh revs."

I turned to Haddow. "Spread the buzz, Haig. It'll cheer the chaps up a bit."

That night there was a constant hustle between the wireless office and the ward-room as signals from Malta detailed the convoy's strength and course. There was one large tanker, brimming over with petrol, and four supply ships swollen with tanks and motor vehicles. Escorting them were seven of Italy's most modern destroyers, and more aircraft than our observers could count. Their course appeared to be taking them from Sicily across to Pantellaria, then past Lampedusa and Lampion to Tripoli.

Further signals gave the position of our own forces. While *Unbroken* and *United* were closing in from the African coast, *Safari* had sailed hurriedly from Malta to join the attack. *Utmost*, commanded by "Basher" Combe, and *Unbending*, skippered by Edward Stanley, both returning to Malta after successful patrols, had been diverted to give us a hand.

"Shrimp's" final signal pointed out that the destruction of the convoy could make "all the difference" to the war in North Africa.

We dived at dawn and by ten o'clock were in position between Lampion and Lampedusa. After a hurried meal I sat in the ward-room impatient for some sign of the convoy. But all was quiet until 2 p.m. when *Utmost*, taking a suicidal risk, surfaced to signal that the convoy was just beyond our horizon. Although we did not know it at the time, *Unbending* had sunk one of the escorting destroyers at eleven that morning.

As soon as the signal came through from *Utmost*, I hurried to the control-room, took over the periscope and had the boat shut-off for depth-charging. Five minutes later I saw a smudge of smoke on the western horizon. My heart leapt. Quickly I ordered a change of course towards the enemy.

Twenty-five minutes later we started the attack, our target the oil tanker. Near her were a supply ship of some 7,000 tons, and two smaller vessels, while four of the destroyers circled round throwing up huge white bow-waves. I could see but three of the escorting aircraft. Hindering our attack was the elaborate, irregular zigzag course of the convoy. Twice as the time of firing approached they turned away from us. Then, as I feared they would continue their second turn-away, they swung back.

"Down periscope. What track* am I on?"

*Track angle: the angle at which a torpedo approaches the target.

"A hundred-and-ten degrees, sir."

Tricky. "Stand by all tubes. Up after periscope."

In the small attack periscope the target, four miles away, was invisible, but I could see one of the aircraft flying uncomfortably close.

The convoy was slightly off our starboard bow now with one destroyer sweeping round between ourselves and the target. Another destroyer raced along astern of the first, while a third suddenly swung round and approached us bows-on. If she kept to this course she would almost certainly scrape our stern.

The sea was too choppy for us to keep depth at any speed less than four knots, while waves splashed the periscope obscuring my vision. There was only one way of continuing the attack—stick about five feet of the big periscope out of the water and hope to God the aircraft did not spot it.

"Down after periscope, up foremost periscope. . . . Director angle?"

"D.A. green eleven," said Archdale.

"Down for'ard periscope."

The enemy's speed was only eight knots which would necessitate a long interval between each torpedo. To reduce this I decided to fire as the submarine swung to starboard. It meant that each torpedo would have to be fired by eye —I could not fire the first by eye, then go deep and fire the rest of the salvo on a calculated time interval—but the result would be more accurate.

Time was growing short. To add to my worries the nearest destroyer was no more than a thousand yards off. She would be on top of me in sixty seconds, and a good look-out should already be able to see my "big stick" when it shot out of the water. None the less, up it had to go.

"Up for'ard periscope. Starboard ten."

I saw nothing but water splashing the periscope glass. I cursed roundly. "What's the depth now, Number One?"

"Twenty-six feet, sir."

"Bring her up to twenty-four. I can't see a thing."

"Coming up . . . Twenty-four feet."

"Half ahead together." Time was vital. The enemy were right on top of us. But I soon forgot these things as my sights came on the tanker. There was only one motto for a successful attack: Fire first and worry later.

The periscope was fixed between the tanker's mast and funnel.

"Stand by. . . . Fire One!"

The *Unbroken* bounced as the torpedo shot into the water.

"Fire Two! . . . Fire Three!"

My sights swung on to one of the supply ships. "Fire Four!" I swallowed. My salvo was fired. I swung the periscope, very aware that I was viewing the situation from the top of a long pole sticking high above the surface of the sea.

To my horror I found myself looking straight into the cockpit of a seaplane in a steep bank. "Down periscope! Group up! Seventy feet!" As I clipped home the periscope handles I saw a vague shape drop from the aircraft. I shot out my hand and pressed the klaxon for an emergency increase in depth.

A bomb? I waited, stiffened. . . . No, not a bomb: a marker—and we were now only three hundred yards from the leading destroyer.

"Hard a-port," I called. "Steer one-five-one. Full ahead together."

The air screamed from "Q" tank.

"All torpedoes running, sir."

Down, down, down.

In the torpedo compartment Petty Officer Lee chalked on the tally board the four torpedoes fired—making our total twenty-five—and waited expectantly for the sound of an explosion. But he did not stand idle. He checked that one of the doors to the tube space was properly clipped, saw all was ready for closing the other door in a hurry, and moved his torpedo-firing party to their depth-charge posts in the torpedo compartment where the last kipper of the patrol lay in its rack. Here they would work the fore planes if "local control" was ordered. Above them were the two hatches which might well be the first places to crack open if a depth charge fell too close—the fore hatch through which the torpedoes were brought aboard, and the for'ard escape hatch. On my orders this was always kept firmly clipped from the outside. No one would ever escape through it. We would sink or surface together.

Abaft and below the torpedo party, the for'ard pump worker squatted in his damp, stinking steel dungeon in the bilges, mechanically stopping and starting the ballast pump at the dictates of the electric telegraphs.

Butterworth crouched between the crew space and ward-room, ready to pass messages from the control-room.

In the W/T office, between the control-room and the engine-room, John Willey tried to take his mind from the grimness of the situation by concentrating on a new set of codes and ciphers shortly to come into force. Beside him, signal-pad and stop-watch ready, Johnny Crutch waited to record the bangs.

E.R.A. Leech was in charge of the engine-room where he kept a watchful eye on the rating working the after ballast pump. There was little else for Leech to do save share the general discomfort and fear. The engines were well shut off. He draped himself across an engine casing and hoped for the best.

Farther aft, Scutt and his "winger" stood fiercely concentrating on a mass of ammeters, voltmeters, repeaters and thermometers, as well as telegraphs. The motors whirled beneath their feet.

Right after in the tail, unseen and alone, squatted a stoker. Doubled up in the narrow stern space, his teeth rattled with the vibration of the propellers. He watched the steering and after plane motors, with an occasional unhappy glance at the quivering hull above his head.

Scutt and his assistant were the lucky ones. They were too busy to fear for the sound of depth charges.

"What's the depth round here, Archdale?"

"Something between twenty-three and thirty-four fathoms."

"What's the bottom?"

"That's a bit vague, too. Might be sand or shingle. Possibly even coral."

There was no time to reflect on the shortcomings of the hydrographers for Cryer roared across the control-room: "Enemy in contact. Starboard beam. . . . Another destroyer red one-five-oh. Seems to be in contact, too."

I licked my lips and gnawed at a thumb-nail. *The bastards are certainly close enough.* The supposed supersonic transmissions of their Asdics were clearly audible in the boat.

From Cryer: "Revs. increasing. Destroyer on port quarter coming in to attack."

One destroyer was holding us in contact, directing the other to the attack.

From the volume of the noise of our screws the enemy knew we were doing top speed and would make suitable allowances for his depth charges. We must dodge.

"Group down. Slow together. Silent routine."

A distant, tinny explosion made us all jump.

"A torpedo hit," reported Cryer. For a moment I relaxed and smiled. Then came the sound of a second kipper striking home. Five minutes had passed since the moment of firing.

Whatever happens to us, we've left our mark.

From Cryer: "They're slowing down, sir. One destroyer on each quarter. Both in contact."

The first depth charge was too close for comfort, and the next three were even closer. The destroyer on the starboard quarter had crossed our stern to join the other on the port side, dropping her eggs in our wake as she did so.

"H.E. all round," said Cryer, and as he spoke we heard the familiar noise of an express train tearing from a tunnel as a third destroyer rushed over us to join the attack.

There was a half-minute of silent apprehension, then a great *clang* on the casing. A depth charge had scored a direct hit but, by a miracle, had failed to explode. A moment later it went off below the ward-room, together with three others in the salvo.

An inferno of ear-splitting, bone-rattling chaos was let loose: a lunatic confusion of crashing glass and cursing men as the submarine was turned into a monstrous cocktail-shaker. In the middle of it all, darkness, as every electric-light bulb in the boat was smashed in its socket. A shower of cork from the deckhead rained down. The shock would have thrown me from my feet had I not grabbed at the control-room ladder. The luminous depth-gauge needles jumped from their frames and hung drunkenly useless. Gauges throughout the boat were shattered. I started to lose balance, and was temporarily paralysed with fear as I realised the bows were dipping *We're sinking. This time we've had it. My God, Ting, I've let you down. . . .*

Chapter Nine

Torches were switched on. I pulled myself together and looked across at the barometer glass. It did not look broken. I tapped it. It moved. A slight increase of pressure; no more. The hole could not be a large one. We had a chance.

Manuel stumbled through the gloom. "It's all right, sir. These boats can take it."

The spell was broken. "Thanks, Chief. Check up quickly all round, will you?"

He nodded and went aft. The indicator of "Q" tank flickered. Somehow it had flooded. A moment later an explanation came when the engine-room reported: "After pump hull valve shut."

"*What?* Who the hell *opened* it?"

"They say it jumped open two turns. It's all right now, sir."

The shock of the explosion had opened hull valves—had worked the wormwheel against the worm, supposedly a mechanical impossibility—and water had poured in to lower the bows.

Haddow brushed against me. "Shall I blow 'Q' now, sir?" He was as calm as if we'd experienced no more than a jaunt on a roller-coaster.

"No," I replied. "Mustn't blow. They'll hear it. Put

the after pump on the midship tank, and pump like hell from for'ard with the for'ard pump. It'll need some pumping. We must have shipped a good few extra tons of water. . . . We've got to pump like fury to stop our bows from going down any more. I wonder how far we've dived? Try and get a depth from for'ard. . . . Half ahead together."

From Sizer: "After planes out of action, sir. I can't get any response from them."

There was a second rattling convulsion as fresh depth charges crashed down.

"From aft, sir. Defect on port main motor. Will you stop it, please?"

"Stop port, full ahead starboard. After planes in local control."

"Depth gauges for'ard and aft all smashed, sir," reported Haddow.

"Leech!" He came running from the engine-room. "Open up a pressure gauge on the engine circulating system and get me a depth."

Someone stuck a bulb into a socket and we had some light. At least the fuses hadn't been smashed. But we still had enough trouble on our hands.

From the engine-room: "Depth, sir, one hundred and sixty feet." Were we scraping the bottom? No one could tell.

The light in the electric bulb began to dim. "From the motor-room, sir, large drop in voltage."

The batteries! We had forgotten them in the stress of the moment. Before I could pull my wits together, Sizer reported: "After planes are now in local control but they still aren't responding."

"Tell Leech to go aft and try to find out the trouble."

"Report from the motor-room, sir. Port main motor field regulator gearing smashed. Trying to clear it."

153

Butterworth poked his head into the control-room. "Batteries gassing, sir."

"Thirsk, take a hand and examine the main battery bilges."

I sniffed. An acrid smell of gas. Slowly it became stronger as the choking fumes seeped eerily through the boat.

At that moment another pattern of depth charges crashed into the sea. They were a little way off. Another pattern exploded—even farther away.

"I think they've lost contact," said Cryer.

So we'll choke to death instead of drowning.

The voltage continued to drop. The life in our batteries was ebbing fast.

Jones moved over from the Asdics. In silence he handed me a slip of paper. I screwed up my eyes to read it in the fading light.

> JONES, John. Able Seaman. D/JX 254129.
> Request to go back to General Service.

I grinned and passed it round the control-room. If we'd had our chips, there was no harm dying with a smile.

By this time, despite the uselessness of the after hydroplanes, we were managing to stagger along. Their absence, however, caused us to curve up and down like a switchback at between a hundred-and-twenty and a hundred-and-seventy feet.

The gas was tickling my nose and scratching my throat.

Two more charges exploded to port. "Only two," I murmured. "Perhaps they're running out."

Manuel arrived from aft. "The starboard shaft is revolving quite sweetly," he reported, "and there are no leaks aft.

154

They'll not be long with the port motor, but you won't be able to vary its speed much."

Archdale came to report there were no leaks for'ard, either.

Cryer could still hear Asdic transmissions, but it appeared the tornado was over. We described a large circle to starboard then drew away to the north-west.

A single ashcan went off in the distance. I glanced at the control-room clock. It had stopped at 3.26 p.m. I looked at my own watch: 3.40. It seemed impossible that only fourteen minutes had elapsed since we stood on the threshold of eternity.

The poisonous smoke from the batteries continued to seep through the boat, lying heavily just above the level of the deck. I reckoned that if it did not increase its speed of discharge we would surface before it had a chance to choke us. On the strength of this assumption I allowed myself to relax a little.

We were still alive, and the boat had suffered no serious injury. It was, in its minor way, a miracle, and I thanked God for his mercy. We had been as near to death as was possible without actually kicking the bucket, and I remembered with a wry smile Paul Thirsk's expectations of "a fairly quiet time." And as I thought of Paul I felt very proud of all the boys aboard the *Unbroken*. Their behaviour had been magnificent. There could be no praise high enough.

At 4.20 p.m. I was given a verbal report of the conditions of the batteries. There was a considerable amount of acid in the two sumps, showing that cells in both batteries were broken. There were—praise Heaven!—no signs of salt water to produce chlorine gas. Number Two battery, however, was on fire, and had started giving off heavy smoke. The poisonous fumes, the smoke, and the heat of the fire tainted the thick, heavy air with choking foulness. Again worried, I ordered that distilled water should be hosed over the burning battery to keep the temperature down. The men doing the job were issued with respirators, and I wondered how long it would be before we all wore them.

An hour later we bumped and jolted to periscope depth. Nothing in sight. The light was fading. We surfaced, and I climbed through the conning-tower in the cool calm of the Mediterranean evening as though I were struggling back to sane reality after a bout of nightmare delirium.

As I stood gulping the clear, fresh air, the T.G.M. reported that our remaining torpedo appeared to be in good order. After the pounding I doubted whether its delicate mechanism was still working, but as it was impossible to strip the brute right down I ordered him to have it loaded into a tube.

No one at Malta knew yet of our pasting, and they brightly sent a signal ordering us to patrol off Kuriat the following day. I read it and shrugged. *Why not? We can just manage to dive. There's a torpedo of sorts left, and we've got a gun and plenty of ammo.*

Signals told me the convoy had reformed after "dispersing in confusion," and aircraft from Malta reported that one damaged vessel was being escorted back to Lampedusa by one of the destroyers. She was the second of my torpedo targets. (Next day she was found by Ben Bryant in the *Safari*. Dodging her escort he sent her to the bottom with a well-placed kipper, and as she sank it was seen that her upper deck was crammed with motor transport.) The Malta aircraft could find only five destroyers. There having been seven when the convoy set out, and allowing for the one sunk by the *Unbending*, it was thought a fair probability that one of my torpedoes sank the other as she swept around the convoy. But we never really knew, and claimed only to have damaged the merchant-man.

I ordered a course westward towards Kuriat, and went below for a fuller examination of our wounds. I found we weren't out of trouble by a long chalk.

As I made my way below I hoped we would be able to disconnect Number Two battery and complete the patrol on Number One, but when I reached the motor-room I discovered Number One also on fire. This did not mean that flames were licking our feet. The battery fires were electrical, a red hot mass of metal cell plates, and boiling acid setting alight the vulcanised wood of the cell containers. Lack of air in the batteries prevented the smouldering mass from bursting into active flames, but the temperatures of the batteries were rising fast and the poisonous, blinding smoke poured out with increasing density. It was clear we could not dive again without terrible risk.

"Tell the officer of the watch to alter course to one-eight-oh. We're going home."

I left the electricians to deal with the batteries as best they could and made for the ward-room to draft a signal to White-hall for onward transmission to Malta. Outlining our troubles, I said that the damage was greater than was at first supposed, and that it was unlikely we would be able to dive at dawn. Because of this I requested fighter cover from the first light of day. I added that we could not expect to make Valetta until the middle of the afternoon.

Soon after the signal was sent all hopes of diving next day were completely shattered: the fire in Number Two battery became so fierce we would certainly suffocate if we did not keep to the surface. In any case, gas masks or no gas masks, it was no use diving if there would be no electricity to turn the motors.

With the ventilation running flat out we managed to grab

a cup of soup and a bite of tinned meat for supper. We ate as best we could, sharing the few plates that had not been smashed in the uproar. The decks were scorching beneath our feet, and Scutt spent his time spraying the boat with distilled water. When this gave out he switched to fresh water, of which we still had a good supply.

Examination showed there was not even the smallest of leaks in the hull. I had fully expected that hundreds of rivets would have been sprung, even forced out. But no. Once again I thanked the men of Barrow.

None of us slept that night, despite our extreme weariness, for no one wanted to take a chance on being gassed in bed. Instead, the men off watch crowded into the control-room and found some little relief from the lung-poisoning smoke in the draught that blew down the conning-tower.

After I had eaten I climbed to my deck-chair on the bridge. The night was moonlit with a gentle northerly breeze. The danger of E-boats forced us to zigzag while the moon was up, and we kept a look-out for a U-boat which had been reported in the area. To confuse matters, we expected *Safari* to cross our path while legging it after the remnants of the convoy.

Nor could we forget the trouble below. The battery ventilation outlet was at the after end of the boat's super-structure, and the light following wind wafted the sulphurous yellowy-green smoke over the bridge.

Shortly after midnight we received a signal from "Shrimp" saying we would be met at dawn by a motor launch and that fighter protection would be provided.

Six hours to go.

The look-outs were doubled, and we limped on.

Then, as I sat huddled in my chair, thinking over the events of the past day and wishing I could close my eyes and sleep, a voice called out: "Object bearing red seven-oh."

I jumped up and grabbed my glasses. As I did so the "object" sailed into the moonlight and I recognised the silhouette of the *Safari*. She recognised us, too, and turned away. With a sigh of relief I slumped back into my chair.

Never was a friendly face so welcome as that of Lieutenant John Peel when he drew alongside in M.L. 121. A moment after his arrival an aircraft swept across the sky from the grey dawn over distant Malta.

By nine o'clock everyone below had to wear gas masks. Number Two battery was disconnected, for it was now a bubbling cauldron of molten metal, gas and steam. For the sake of those whose jobs kept them below, the fore hatch was opened, and the remainder of the crew came up top and squatted on the casing. By the time we reached Lazaretto at two in the afternoon, smoke was billowing from the conning-tower as though from a factory chimney.

As the *Unbroken* was nudged into dry dock the seams amidships opened and Number Two battery was flooded with salt water. Chlorine gas filled the boat. Once again we had escaped disaster by the skin of our teeth.

It used to be said among experienced skippers that a submarine could withstand an attack in which a third of her battery cells were broken, but none had been known to withstand the loss of more than half. That was understandable when you consider the amount of force needed to destroy battery cells. Each of the *Unbroken*'s weighed a quarter of a ton, and we carried 224 of them. By this reckoning half weighed twenty-eight tons. If there was enough force to destroy twenty-eight tons' weight of cells, there was enough force to sink the boat.

I had this in mind as I watched the workmen remove the shattered cells from our batteries. The 112 cells of Number

Two battery were an unrecognisable mass of molten junk, and it took the men three days to shovel it out. From Number One battery a dozen cells were removed. A total of 124 cells—thirty-one tons' weight.

Yet we had survived.

Back at Lazaretto I collected my mail. In it was a telegram saying my younger brother, a fighter pilot, had been killed on active service the previous afternoon.

The previous afternoon . . .

It took them four weeks to knock the *Unbroken* back into shape. Every day I visited the dry dock and gazed sadly at her plates, buckled by the force of the depth charges. As Scutt remarked: "They should change her name from *Unbroken* to *Badly Bent*." Paul Thirsk had the task of keeping a watchful eye on the repair work, and when we finally prepared for sea again I decided to give him and some of the ratings a rest from the next patrol. For myself I thought it best to carry on. The boys, I felt, trusted me, and a new skipper takes some getting used to. In any case, since they had to go to sea next patrol, why shouldn't I?

On 23rd October General Montgomery launched the mighty battle of El Alamein, and in the weeks that followed our submarines were busy tearing holes in the enemy's convoys to North Africa. Only the crippled *Unbroken* was left at Malta, and I felt miserably out of it. Then, on 8th November, the invasion of North Africa, and the Germans poured supplies into Tunisia with every ship at their disposal. Fighting was in full swing by the time we set sail on 15th November, fully repaired and almost as good as new.

This patrol lasted twenty-one days, and from the point of view of strain was the worst we had endured. We were only depth-charged once, but were chased backwards and forwards

160

across the ocean with maddening constancy, and without an iota of success.

We all felt pretty shaky when we sailed. The memories of that last patrol were unpleasantly fresh in our minds, and we knew the enemy had intensified his anti-submarine efforts. To add to the normal hazards coastal radar stations had been established to pick up submarines on the surface at night. The enemy did his job well, for we were unable to do anything on that patrol without being made to dive, made to dive deeper, hunted by Asdics or bombed by aircraft.

Towards the end of the patrol, we intercepted one of those signals we dreaded: "*Utmost*, report position." She did not report her position. She could not. She had been sunk by an E-boat off Marittimo. Another fine bunch of sub-mariners had been lost, and I mourned for a personal friend in "Basher" Coombe, her captain.

Joe Martin was at sea in the *Una* while Pat Norman took a rest. He followed *Utmost* into the trap. A suspicious type, Joe never under-estimated the enemy. One night, while sitting in the ward-room, he had "a sort of feeling" and hurried to the bridge. He saw a white streak in the water. "Hard a starboard!" he roared. "Get down!" *Una* dived on the turn—and the torpedo just missed them.

This put an end to the well-worn route back to Malta past Cape Granitola. When we were due to return we were told to take a new course. It started by the Skerki Bank and struck, in deep water, through the Sicilian Channel to Pantellaria, skirted that island and ended up towards Linosa. Unable to take sights, with soundings of no help, and with our log broken down, we had to make a blind rush through the new lane. Our luck held, and on 5th December we were escorted back into harbour.

With feeling I wrote at the end of my report: "This has been *Unbroken's* most arduous and disappointing patrol."

The only person to profit from it was Lieutenant Crawford, Paul Thirsk's relief, who added a little grist to the mill of his experience.

Back at Malta I discovered we had developed a "singing" propeller. This was a serious business, for although the propeller was still quite efficient, it hummed a tune which would delight enemy Asdic and hydrophone operators. We were docked for a quick change, but none of the spares at Base fitted properly. The old one had to go back on. It was asking for trouble, but what else could we do? In any case, having learned that we had been sunk three times by the German radio, we were now feeling rather cocky.

We were stuck with our singing propeller until the end of the commission. It was the port one, and when hunted by enemy Asdics it became necessary to stop the port motor and proceed on the starboard. A nuisance, but it saved our skins.

Christmas was to be spent at sea, and we sailed from Malta on 20th December under a dark, threatening sky. Before we left we were asked if we would rather take our festive luxuries with us, or wait and have a slap-up feed on our return. We decided on the latter, knowing Joe Sizer had scrounged a plum pudding and suckling pig, while a few bottles of beer had been wheedled from a reluctant Naafi. All being well, therefore, we would have two lots of "big eats" for Christmas. There was great speculation as to how Sizer got the pig, but we thought it best not to probe the question too deeply.

We set course past Pantellaria, and after skirting Marittimo proceeded across the Tyrrhenian Sea towards the Bay of

Naples. On the night of 22nd December, soon after surfacing, enemy ships were reported. We dived and I commenced a periscope attack on the nearest one. In the moonlight it seemed a fair-sized supply ship. As we closed, however, I realised I had run into yet another anti-submarine sweep of destroyers. I tossed up in my mind whether to take a risk and attempt to sink one of these pests when a signal was rushed to me in the control-room. Received the moment before we dived, it had just been decoded. It said: "All submarines clear out of an area within fifty miles of Marittimo." Things were getting hot. I consoled myself with the thought that supply ships, not destroyers, were top priority on our list.

We described a wide circle, and when we surfaced on the night of 23rd December after dodging an E-boat patrol, we were back again on a course towards the Bay of Naples.

On Christmas Eve our feeling of peace and goodwill was destroyed by the hordes of enemy aircraft that continually swept over the horizon to plague our lives. When this air activity continued into Christmas Day I felt I was justified in seeking a little peace twelve fathoms down. Asdic conditions were good, and if a target did pass close enough to warrant an attack we could soon come up to periscope depth and wham home a kipper.

Until evening there was little to distinguish Christmas Day from any other on patrol. Then the roast pork and plum duff were passed round, washed down with a bottle of warm Malta beer. Joe Sizer was less meticulous than usual when measuring the rum ration, and we were all mellow and nostalgic by nightfall. I sat in the ward-room feeling sentimental and a little sad, and for the dozenth time I re-read the last letter I had received from Ting before leaving Malta. I stretched out on my bunk and shut my eyes. For a moment I felt sick and unhappy.

163

Chapter Ten

Boxing Day saw us moving across the Gulf of Naples between Capri and the island of Ischia. The forenoon was cold and clouded, and shortly before midday smoke was reported on the horizon. We closed towards it, and I saw an enemy force consisting of two merchantmen escorted by an armed merchant cruiser. The larger merchant vessel was of some 6,000 tons, and I thought I'd make the boys a Christmas present of it.

The convoy was sailing out of the gulf with the obvious intention of creeping round Ischia's Imperatore Point as close inshore as possible. It took us an hour to reach a firing position, and I dispatched four kippers from a range of thirteen hundred yards. The A.M.C. interfered with my aim, for she was weaving ahead of her charges on a wide, sweeping zigzag. I fired just as she changed from a zig to a zag and was only three hundred yards away from us. We went deep and heard the satisfactory sound of a steel-tearing explosion. Then, the cheering over, we waited with the tension of dreadful memory for the *krrrump* of depth charges, but the cruiser failed to pick us up. Nine minutes after firing she dropped a pattern of four, but they were well away from us.

Thirty minutes later we nosed up to periscope depth. Our victim was bows down in the water, fifty feet of her sharp end missing. She was going down. There was no need to waste another kipper. The second merchantman was wallowing back to Naples, escorted by the A.M.C.

We spent the next three days at the entrance to the Gulf of Naples, but the only activity was in the air as transports flew Hun reinforcements to Africa.

Then, on 1st January, by way of a New Year's greeting, and to celebrate my twenty-eighth birthday, I decided to attack a viaduct in the Gulf of Policasro. But the weather was against us and I had to call it off. As we battled seawards through a rolling, crashing storm, P.O. Willey came into the ward-room with a signal. A smile wreathed his usually impassive face. "Congratulations, sir."

My birthday present from His Majesty the King was the award of the D.S.O.

Haddow had been given the D.S.C., Manuel a bar to his D.S.M. Sizer, Willey and Lee, the T.G.M., were also awarded D.S.M.s. Sharp, Lewis and "Pedro" Fenton received "Mentions." Naturally there were disappointments. We all took the same risks, and did the same amount of work. But it was impossible that we should all be given awards, and I hoped the others would regard the decorations as gestures towards the boat as a whole. I think they did, and it was a happy, if uncomfortable, submarine that pitched and tossed on a corkscrew course back towards Malta. In the end the movements became so violent it was impossible to control the boat at a depth of less than seventy feet. Even then she rolled fifteen degrees each way, and there was a great deal of lusty cursing as men were thrown from their feet by the violence of the storm. To add to our annoyance every single item of crockery was smashed—rarer-than-gold cups and plates that Sizer had replaced after the depth-charging only by bribing the Maltese storeman with a jar of rum. We ate off the tables until 6th January when *Speedy* escorted us back into harbour, Jolly Roger flying to indicate our successes.

The high spirits of our welcome were dashed by the news that P.48, commanded by my good and old friend, Michael Faber, had been lost. It was a sad blow for Ting, too: P.48 was the boat she had launched at Barrow. The luckiest man in Malta when the news came through was the Asdic operator of the P.48. Cryer had been given a rest, and P.48 had loaned us one of their chaps to replace him.

Irritating news at Malta was that I'd missed seeing "Tubby" Linton. While we were operating from Gib. and Malta, he had been based at Beirut with the 1st flotilla. Transferred to the George Cross Island to increase our strength in the Central Mediterranean, he had arrived during my previous patrol and was now away on a patrol of his own. I cursed missing him, looked forward to a grand reunion when he returned to harbour, and was tickled pink at the "bottle" he inadvertently caused the C.-in-C. to give "Shrimp" Simpson.

Apart from food, the ward-room at Lazaretto was often short of booze, and when "Shrimp" heard that "Tubby" was coming from Beirut, he signalled Captain "S" of the 1st flotilla: "Please send gin and matches in *Turbulent* for a Happy Christmas." Unfortunately the signal was intercepted by the C.-in-C.'s monitoring staff and taken to Sir Andrew Cunningham. Sir Andrew apparently disapproved of the signal channels being used in such a frivolous manner, and told "Shrimp" so. None the less the gin and matches arrived as part of "Tubby" Linton's armament.

As it turned out, I never did see "Tubby" Linton again. Every time I was in harbour he was at sea and *vice versa*. Finally the tragic news came through that the *Turbulent* had been lost during a valiant attempt to penetrate the defences of Maddalena harbour and sink a cruiser there. With more than 90,000 tons of enemy shipping to his credit, "Tubby" was the most outstanding of all Mediterranean submarine commanders. His V.C., awarded posthumously, had been earned a dozen times over. His was a bitter, irreplaceable loss.

Two other submarines had arrived at Malta while we were away: the *Thunderbolt*—formerly the ill-fated *Thetis*—commanded by Lieut.-Commander "Lucky" Crouch, and the unnamed P.311, skippered by Commander Dick Cayley.

It was as well we had taken the suckling pig, beer and plum duff to sea with us, for when we went in search of our delayed Christmas dinner, we were met with innocent eyebrow raising, expressions of shamefaced guilt, or vague apologies. However, there was an ironic twist to the gluttony. For a long time unused to large quantities of rich fare, the hogs had spent many days in bed with tortured stomachs.

As always, my first visit after handing in my patrol report was to collect mail from Ting. The usual pile awaited me. Malta had offered little opportunity for Christmas shopping, but I had managed to buy a gay tablecloth and some napkins and send them home with an England-bound submarine. Ting reported their safe arrival.

June, now ten months old, was demanding her full share of attention, and Ting, while keeping an eye on her, helped balance the family budget by knitting bed-jackets for the more elegant of Aldeburgh's pin-ups. It appeared, too, that when Ting's aunt was presented with a pheasant shot by the local soldiery, she would pay Ting two bob for the unpleasant business of plucking it! The radio provided an unusual source of revenue, for whenever my name was mentioned over it, certain of the old dears in the town insisted on presenting Ting with stamps for June's National Savings book.

I did not know it at the time—thank God!—but ten minutes after Ting wheeled June out of the post office after posting her Christmas mail to me, the building received a direct hit. The nearest she came to mentioning air raids was a light-hearted reference to the Morrison shelter installed in the back room, and I continued to thank my lucky stars that she and the child were well away from trouble.

Sad news at Malta was that "Shrimp" Simpson was returning to England. His relief was Captain G. C. Phillips, D.S.O., who had a distinguished North Sea record in submarines. Before we made our good-byes, however, there was time for another patrol, off the North African coast.

The situation there had undergone a great change since Paul Thirsk complained the water was "too damn' shallow." The depth was unaltered, and the minefields were still greedy for British ships, but the Eighth Army, advancing as fast as their transport could carry them, had already reached Burat-el-Sun, a thousand miles from Alamein, and were re-grouping for a final thrust towards Tripoli.

The success of their advance was reflected at Malta. Air raids had died to mere token gestures, and the majority of such intruders were soon blasted from the sky by the R.A.F. The enemy could not even carry out a good reconnaissance. Food was in fairly plentiful supply, and M.T.B.s. had arrived to pay back a little E-boat harrying.

There was only one shadow on this excellent state of affairs. Haig Haddow fell sick, and had to be taken to hospital. Paul Thirsk was appointed Number One, and

Sub-Lieutenant J. D. Lanning, a tall, fair, vague-looking young man, came as navigator.

On 16th January we sailed. By the 19th the Eighth Army, again on the move, had captured Misurata and were closing the remaining hundred miles to Tripoli. The Germans were attempting to gather their forces for a last desperate stand behind the Mareth Line on Tunisia's southern borders. Their fleeing land transport harried with ever-increasing fury by the R.A.F., they made an all-out effort to utilise the shipping at Tripoli to hasten their retreat. This shipping was what we were after.

The *Unbroken*'s patrol position was off Ras Turgeuness, and at 4.50 on the evening of the 19th we sighted masts six miles to southwards sailing towards us. As our quarry approached, we identified the 6,000-ton troopship, *Edda*. A torpedo attack was almost unnecessary. She was so laden with troops that her gunwales were awash, and it seemed as though a heavy sea would swamp her. A magnificent target.

She was escorted by two torpedo-boats, and Cryer reported that both had Asdics switched on. Beyond the torpedo-boats, as an added escort, were three schooners. Still vividly haunted by memories of the past, we quickly shut off for depth-charging, for we did not want to join the masses of oily flotsam that littered the area.

Silently we waited as the convoy drew nearer. We adjusted our own position for the attack. The trooper was doing eight knots, and I let her have a salvo of four kippers from a range of fifteen hundred yards.

Then we went down, but not too far down, for the water was only a hundred feet deep. We stopped at seventy—and waited. To our delight there was a shattering detonation as one torpedo struck home.

Then, to my dismay, I heard the familiar noise of a propeller —but without the accompanying express train! It zinged right over the top of the control-room.

What in God's name is this?

Manuel, still the most experienced of us, whispered in my ear: "It's a torpedo, sir, It's circling."

I felt the sweat jump from my forehead. *Hell and damnation, we're going to kipper ourselves! The damned thing's gone wrong somewhere....* I felt a moment of rage towards Lee and his torpedo-men. Then I rebuked myself for being unfair. This was only the second defect in nearly forty torpedoes fired, and in any case some of the torpedoes weren't so hot on arrival from the makers. A second *zzzzing* brought me back to the immediate urgency of the moment.

Instinctively we all ducked. The top of the bridge structure was only fifty feet below the surface and the lunatic torpedo might well be running at that depth by now. It sounded close enough.

Again it came circling round. There was no doubt about it: one more crazy sweep and the damn' thing would blow us to shattering destruction. The sound of its propeller faded into the distance, then came rushing back. Louder . . . louder . . . louder . . . until, by a miracle—and what else could it have been?—the wretched brute shot down past us to bury its nose in the mud of the ocean floor.

Before a shivering reaction set in the first depth charges came down. But they came singly, and a long way off. There were only seven of them. The runaway torpedo had also struck the fear of God into the enemy. Ten minutes after the last ashcan exploded in the distance I ordered a return to periscope depth.

One of the torpedo-boats was still hunting us, but was a good way off. The second was standing by the *Edda*, taking

170

survivors aboard. The schooners were well out of the picture. The *Edda* was sinking stern first. An ant swarm of men slithered over her side into the unfriendly sea. Satisfied, we slipped down again, and returned to periscope depth six minutes later for a final look. The *Edda* had sunk. Despite the lunatic torpedo it had been an easy kill.

Soon it was sunset, and when we surfaced we observed flares and flak from the position of our attack. The R.A.F. were on the job, finishing off the torpedo-boats. I learned later that they claimed the *Edda*, too, but I convinced them that Mussolini's daughter was ours for ever.

The remainder of the patrol was uneventful save for the sighting of "F" boats—enemy landing-craft heavily armed with anti-aircraft guns. As many as a dozen of these guns were of a type similar to the British Bofors, making an "F" boat a serious menace to a surfaced submarine. A submarine could not use torpedoes against them because of their shallow draught, and in a gun battle one 3-inch gun was useless against a massed salvo of Bofors.

As most of the enemy's larger vessels had been sunk, or had fled the scene, our continued presence in the area was considered unnecessary. After seven days at sea we were recalled to Malta to take part in another special operation.

We were met by the minesweeper *Hebe* at the entrance to the searched channel, and as we moved into harbour the cruisers *Euryalus* and *Cleopatra*, escorted by four destroyers, swept past into Grand Harbour. Our Jolly Roger, signifying the success of the patrol, fluttered saucily from the mast, and as the towering monsters crashed by me I felt a resurgence of all the old pride of being a sub-mariner.

On arrival I made a verbal report to "Shrimp" of the

Edda sinking, then brought up the question of the *Unbroken*'s return to England. We had been away eleven months, and I reminded "Shrimp" of the danger of growing stale. I pointed out that more than one submarine had been lost because of staleness—or because success had developed into reckless cockiness—and I assured "Shrimp" that I wanted neither of these things to happen to the *Unbroken*. I added that I was good for perhaps four more patrols, but could not guarantee my nerves and strength beyond that. I concluded by saying that the Admiralty seemed to make no move to recall submarines from the Med. until after they had done a year there, and that our year was nearly completed.

"No one laid down that a year was the maximum time for a submarine to be away," said "Shrimp."

"I know, sir," I replied, "but I give a year as the maximum for the simple reason that a submarine that doesn't get out after a year *never* gets out."

"Shrimp" nodded and said he would do his best.

Then came the business of preparing for our next operation. A visit to Lascaris put me in the picture.

The Eighth Army had reached Tripoli and was advancing towards the Mareth Line. The bulk of the enemy's supplies were coming through the northern ports of Bizerta and Tunis, and the main railway line from these ports ran across the Cape Bon peninsula, down to Hammamet by the sea, then south along the Gulf of Hammamet keeping two or three miles inland. Near Bou Ficha the line crossed a high, vulnerable viaduct. Its destruction would cut Rommel's main supply line in half.

The Germans were well aware of this, and had surrounded the viaduct with so many ack-ack guns the valley bristled like a porcupine.

A new scheme had been evolved: eight commandos would

land from the sea and attempt to blow up the viaduct. The *Unbroken* would take them there and, it was hoped, bring them back.

In general charge was thin, aquiline Commander D. H. Fyffe, D.S.C., R.N.R., a submarine veteran of the First World War. Having trained the commandos for the job he proposed to come with us to see everything went according to plan. In charge of the landing-party was short, wiry Captain J. Eyre of the Royal Engineers, with Lieutenant P. M. Thomas of the Buffs as his second in command: a tough-looking young man who seemed a typical "regular army" type. The remaining six in the party were Fighting Frenchmen.

They brought aboard four folboats and enormous quantities of arms and explosives which, after being landed on the beach, they would have to haul over two-and-a-half miles of rough, heavily defended country. While Thirsk visited the hospital to see Haddow—alas, he was still too sick to rejoin us—I kept a watchful eye on the explosives, for I wanted to be certain they did not embark any of Peter Churchill's "pressurised pencils."

At tea-time on 25th January we cast off and proceeded from the harbour. I asked the two army officers to go below, but they stayed put on the bridge, anxious to miss nothing of the novelty of being aboard a submarine. I didn't press the point: they had enough troubles ahead of them without my spoiling their fun "rubbernecking."

Commander Fyffe, full of nostalgia for the old days, was soon at home, billeted in the spare bunk, in the ward-room. The two army officers were squeezed into the petty officers' mess, while the Frenchmen were bundled for'ard. They seemed very lost and unhappy in their new surroundings, but our boys did their best to make them feel at home, large gulps of rum and sign language compensating for their inability to speak French.

On the morning of 27th January we dived into the Gulf of Hammamet to test the currents, for it was most important the commandos should be landed at the nearest point on the beach to the objective. Through the periscope the town of Hammamet looked tired, sunbaked, empty and lazy; a cluster of white, low-roofed buildings dried up by the desert sun. As I swept the shore towards Bou Ficha where the commandos were to be disembarked, however, the scene changed. The road was alive with heavy traffic moving south. The beach was filled with patrols, marching singly with bayonets fixed, or driving backwards and forwards in lorries and open trucks. The chances against our mission succeeding seemed heavy. I ordered a withdrawal from the gulf, handed the periscope to Archdale who was officer of the watch, and crossed unhappily to the ward-room.

I had not been there ten minutes when an embarrassed Archdale entered and said: "Bit awkward, sir. Commander Fyffe says he's taken over. Told me to carry on."

"The devil he has," I muttered, and hurried to the control-room. Fyffe was studying the shore through the high-power periscope, seemingly oblivious to any danger that might sweep in from the sky. Quickly I crossed to the after periscope, ordered it to be raised and scanned the blue, cloudless heavens. Fortunately they were empty.

Fyffe looked across at me quizzically. "Everything's in hand," he assured me.

I was reluctant to hurt his feelings by telling him that submarine warfare had altered considerably in the past quarter of a century, but I told him, quite firmly, that my watchkeeping officers were capable of doing their jobs.

He looked crestfallen. "I only wanted to give the boys a rest," he assured me.

I smiled, and there were apologies all round. Things returned to normal—Ted Archdale in charge.

Captain Eyre and Lieutenant Thomas had a long look at the shore through the periscope and joined me in the wardroom. They said nothing, but I could tell they were as unhappy about the situation as I was. Rather than brood over it, however, we went over the details of the landing.

"We'll run out now," I said, "and surface after dusk. Then we'll turn around and come back towards your landing-point. On the way in the folboats will be taken on deck ready for launching. I'll take you to within a mile of the beach, stop, and launch all four boats together. We'll give you a course to steer that will take you exactly to the chosen spot. Then it's up to you."

Captain Eyre nodded. "Good. We'll keep all four boats together. After striking the beach they'll be hauled up near the water's edge and turned round ready for a quick rush to the water. Then we'll make inland with the explosives."

"If any alarm is given," I said, "and we have to clear out, I'll let you know what's happening by firing two star shells in the direction of Hammamet. If you don't see a star shell we'll still be waiting for you."

Thomas grinned. "If we see a star shell, that's when we start becoming Frenchmen, eh?"

I grinned back, hoping I concealed the heaviness that lay over my heart.

At 5.30 p.m. we ran out, waited until darkness before surfacing. We turned about and crept towards land on our

175

almost inaudible motors. A light off-shore breeze set tiny waves lapping against the bows, the gun's crew closed up, a double set of look-outs peered anxiously into the night. At full buoyancy the folboats were dragged through the fore hatch. We trimmed down to reduce silhouette and closed the beach along the prepared line of soundings. Not a word was spoken save for the whispered passing of orders, but I could hear, more expressive than speech, the sharp, nervous breathing of all those crowded on the bridge. A mile from shore the motors were stopped.

The black-out ashore was broken with sickening regularity by the headlights of motor convoys racing down the road to the south. The commandos would have to cross this road with their explosives.

The *Unbroken* drifted to a standstill, her bows pointing towards the still and silent beach of Hammamet. I leaned over the bridge and whispered to Archdale: "Launch the boats quietly, keep them secured alongside and get the men embarked."

"Aye, aye, sir."

Commander Fyffe went for'ard to the casing to help the Frenchmen into their boats. "So long, and good luck," he said.

My God, if anyone needs luck, they do.

From Archdale: "All ready now, sir."

"All right." The two army officers moved for'ard. Silently they shook hands with me, then clambered down to the casing. "God speed," I murmured. To Archdale: "Tell Commander Fyffe to send them in."

"Aye, aye, sir."

A minute later they disappeared into the night.

"Half astern together."

Chapter Eleven

We withdrew a few cables, then turned slowly round. Our bows pointed seawards. Fyffe rejoined me on the bridge. We kept our glasses trained towards land, saying nothing, but sharing a common agony of fear for the men paddling towards the shore.

Seven-forty-five. By now they would be on the beach. The minutes dragged by.

At eight o'clock I jumped with alarm as three single tracer shots were fired in the air over Hammamet.

Silence again.

A file of lorries rumbled through the night towards the battlefront.

Restless, one of the look-outs shifted on his feet and muttered to himself. I lowered my glasses and rubbed a hand across my eyes. "Reckon they must be well on their way."

"They've been ashore nearly an hour," Fyffe replied. "Must be a good way inland by now."

"I suppose we'll hear the bang."

"Quite a time to go, yet."

At that moment there were three small explosions and a flash from just beyond the beach.

"Damnation, I don't like that. What do you think they were? Grenades?"

Fyffe sighed. "Might be. That or small mines."

The party were armed with grenades, and if they had used them or had set off mines, the game was up.

And then, as though by a prearranged signal, a row of flares suddenly illuminated the entire beach. No men were in sight, but in the centre of the brilliant, dazzling light were four folboats, neatly lined up a few feet from the water.

The bridge of the submarine was illuminated so plainly I could see every detail of Fyffe's drawn face as he gazed intently at the shore, his brow furrowed, his eyes wrinkled. I remembered my words to Peter Churchill: *You can see them, but they can't see you*, but I knew that it was but a matter of minutes before flares were fired over the sea.

In any case the folboats were exposed and the commandos could never return to the *Unbroken*.

I turned to Fyffe, sick at heart. "What else can we do?"

"Nothing." His voice was flat and empty. "I think it's all over. Have they seen the submarine?"

"Not yet.... Do you agree we should go?"

"Yes. No point sticking our necks out further."

I took a last look at the shore. The scene was unchanged as flare after flare blazed in the sky revealing the four folboats on the bare African beach. I turned to the voice-pipe. "Full ahead together . . . Starboard twenty. Steer one-five-six. Start the engines." The boat leapt to life. I leaned over to the gun's crew. "With star shell, *load!* On bearing red one-five-oh, at maximum elevation, fire two rounds independently." Back to the voice-pipe. "Control-room. Broadcast that we are firing star shell to indicate to the commandos our withdrawal. The alarm has been raised."

The flares from our shells hung like candelabras in the sky before they drifted slowly to earth, dimming as they floated down, sharing our sadness.

"Clear the casing."

The words were hardly out of my mouth when the starboard look-out roared: "Object bearing green five-oh!"

"Klaxon! Klaxon!"

The alarm signal screamed through the boat.

Fyffe bundled through the hatch like an expert, once again feeling the old thrill. I followed, and we rattled down to seventy feet.

An hour later we surfaced to see that flares continued to turn the night over Bou Ficha into day.

Reluctantly we headed for Malta. The commandos were never heard of again.

Our return was sad and silent. Often on the bridge I would find myself involuntarily looking over my shoulder as though expecting folboats from the direction of Bou Ficha. Although I knew there was nothing we could have done but leave when we did, I was glad the responsibility for withdrawing had not been mine. This is no reflection on Commander Fyffe; an admission, rather, of my own relief at not having had to make the heart-breaking decision. Consequently, when Fyffe asked if he might join our "watchkeepers' union," I readily consented, for there is little opportunity for self-searching and recrimination when you are engaged in a periscope sweep of hostile sky and ocean.

Our arrival at Lazaretto was brightened by the reappearance of Haddow, but he came only to say good-bye. He was off home to take his Command course. I was pleased he was in line for his own boat, yet I was sorry to see him go, for his departure meant the loss of a good, trusted friend as well as a fine officer.

Thirsk stayed on as first lieutenant, while Sub-Lieutenant Evatt, son of the Australian statesman, came aboard to relieve Lanning as navigator. He was an extremely efficient young man: tough-looking and dark, very certain of himself, surprisingly undemonstrative for an Aussie. He was only temporary, however, and after two patrols was replaced by B. S. Richards, M.B.E., R.N.V.R., a short, dark sub-lieutenant aged about twenty-four.

Sizer, Willey, Bramhall and a few of the others were given a rest from the next two patrols—dull, uneventful affairs—and on one of them we took with us the *Unbroken*'s next captain: Bevis Andrew, D.S.C., a slim, tall, dark lieutenant addicted to wing collars. It had been decided that although the *Unbroken* was not to return to England until September, I was to fly back in April.

I was beset with conflicting emotions at the news. On the one hand I was glad to be going home. Apart from the physical strain, my nerves were beginning to fray after a year of submarine warfare in the Med. Naturally, I was overjoyed at the thought of returning to Ting and the daughter I had never seen. On the other hand, though, I felt guilty at having to leave behind the officers and men of my crew. They, too, had suffered their share of physical strain and mental stress. They, too, had wives and sweethearts awaiting them. We had come out as one tight-knit unit and I felt we should stay that way until the end. If I went back, we should all go back. It had not been just for myself that I'd raised with "Shrimp" the matter of our recall. But My Lords at the Admiralty had made a decision, and there was nothing I could do save lament it.

We set sail from Malta on 26th March, 1943; my twelfth and last patrol as Captain of the *Unbroken*. Our orders were to make for the Cape Spartivento-Cretone area to harass enemy shipping *en route* for Tunis.

We reached Cretone on 31st March and through the periscope I recognised the landmarks of the ill-fated "Tug"

Wilson operation: the chemical factory belching heavy smoke; the surrounding countryside, fresh and green; the sharp whiteness of the anti-submarine schooners. The night was clear with a cool off-shore breeze. At ten o'clock I huddled into my deck-chair, wished Archdale a quiet watch and closed my eyes.

Perhaps five minutes later I was awakened by Ted's urgent whisper: "Captain, sir."

I jumped up. Archdale pointed. "Bow-wave, sir."

I levelled my glasses. A lean, low phosphorescence not far away. *A U-boat coming from Taranto.* I leaned over the voice-pipe. "Night alarm!" Our bows leapt forward as the motors automatically went to half-ahead.

The enemy was moving fast from port to starboard. It would be thirty seconds before the tubes were reported ready.

"Ship's head?"

From the voice-pipe: "Oh-seven-oh, sir."

"Starboard twenty. Steer one-one-oh."

As the bows swung to starboard I set the torpedo night sight for an enemy speed of fifteen knots. I was about to pass a firing interval below when Archdale grasped my arm. "It's not a U-boat," he cried. "It's an E-boat or a submarine-chaser."

He was right. The lean shape had resolved itself into a fast surface vessel with a wicked-looking gun in her bows.

"Klaxon! Klaxon! ... Eighty feet!" I shut the voice-pipe cock. The spray from the vents shot upwards. I turned towards the conning-tower hatch. Archdale was crouched over it.

"Why the hell aren't you below?"

"Some hold-up in the conning-tower, sir."

"What the blazes is going on down there?" I roared.

"Can't get down, sir," shouted a look-out.

We were diving fast. The water was swirling round the gun.

I gave Archdale a push. "Stand on his stupid head."

He did so, and the cursing chain of men in the conning-tower collapsed into the control-room. Archdale climbed into the conning-tower. Another jam.

The sea rushed through the clearing ports at the sides of the bridge. I jumped on Archdale's shoulders and pushed. With a crash and a clatter he tumbled into the control-room and I found myself hanging with one hand to the ladder, the upper hatch open above my head. I hauled myself up, grabbed the lid, pulled it down and rammed home a clip.

"One clip on!" I yelled. If the men in the control-room thought the upper hatch still open they would have shut the lower one and left me trapped in the conning-tower. I put on the other clip, inserted the locking-pins and slithered down the ladder. My head and neck were dripping with water. The sea had caught up with me as I pulled the hatch down.

Osborne shut the lower lid. In the dull red light of the control-room I could see the depth gauges already showed forty feet. I turned to Thirsk. "Blow 'Q' at sixty-five, then flatten-out at eighty. There's a sub.-chaser on top. May have seen us or heard the klaxon."

I looked down and saw our Bren gun—a recent addition to the armament—lying on the control-room deck. "Manuel! What's this doing here, and what happened in the conning-tower?"

Self-consciously he explained.

I had approved that Cryer should be Bren operator at gun action stations. Consequently, when "Night Alarm" was sounded he handed the Asdic to Jones, grabbed the Bren and his home-made canvas bandolier containing spare clips and closed-up at the foot of the conning-tower with the gun's crew.

Suddenly an imp of the perverse crept into him and he decided he ought to be by my side.

"Permission to go on the bridge, sir?" he asked Thirsk.

"No," said Paul, "you might not be needed."

"I'm going up anyway," he announced.

"You're not."

"Oh yes I am." And with that he started to climb the conning-tower. It was then the klaxon sounded—hence the conning-tower blockage. Paul Thirsk grabbed Cryer's ankles and that, plus the pressure from above, sent the burly six-footer crashing back into the control-room. . . .

I listened to Manuel's story and scratched my chin.

"Where's Cryer now?"

"By the time you got down, sir, the first lieutenant had put him under arrest. He's for'ard in the torpedo compartment."

I grunted. "Tell Petty Officer Lee to keep him there until I decide what's to be done."

"Aye, aye, sir."

At this point Micky Jones picked up our enemy. By some freak of good fortune she had not seen us and was continuing on her course as though nothing had happened.

When the panic died down we surfaced and set course for Cap del Armi, Cryer locked up for'ard.

On the afternoon of 3rd April an unescorted warship hove in sight making for the Straits of Messina at speed. As we started an attack we found it difficult to identify her. I thought she might be a cruiser of the new, small *Regolo* class, but that was pure guesswork since we knew no more about these ships than the fact that they displaced some 5,000 tons. Then, as I swept the sky, I saw she had considerable air protection. I was puzzled that a ship of her size should have aircraft cover yet no surface escort, but decided to postpone further speculation until after we had sunk her.

The attack was a long-range affair, and we fired a salvo of four torpedoes from a position far on her starboard quarter. We went deep to avoid the aircraft, and at the right time heard two explosions. Somehow they did not sound very convincing, but when we crept back to periscope depth we saw only the aircraft, and thought she might indeed have been sunk. Later, however, we discovered our target—the enemy's crack anti-submarine vessel: a converted warship captured from the Greeks—was still in one piece. She had already sunk one British submarine and had nearly finished off another. I was pleased to have had a shot at her, sorry to have missed, and more than grateful not to have known at the time what I was tackling!

The next day we were haunted by aircraft patrols. Their attentions became so persistent I wondered whether the enemy had evolved a method of detecting submerged submarines from the air. In the early part of the afternoon we went down to ninety feet out of their way.

I was in the ward-room when Petty Officer Lee arrived to say: "Cryer says he can hear Asdic impulses."

I frowned. "I though he was for'ard in the torpedo compartment?"

"He is, sir."

"Do you mean to tell me he can hear supersonic Asdic waves without a set?"

"He says he can hear them, sir."

I hurried to the control-room. "Hear anything on the Asdic?"

"No, sir."

I turned to Lee. "Cryer. Do you think he's mad?"

184

"Looks all right, sir."

"No wild eyes or waving arms?"

"No, sir."

Richards was officer of the watch. "Bring her up," I said. "Twenty-six feet. . . ."

As we tilted upwards there was a shout from Jones on the Asdic: "H.E. red one-two-oh."

Cryer was right!

"Diving stations!"

I trained the periscope on the bearing of the H.E., and as the glass broke the surface I gasped. "It's the biggest tanker you've ever seen!" She was a mile away and as I swung the periscope I saw she was escorted by three destroyers and a number of aircraft.

"Bearing now?"

"Red one-three-oh."

"Range now?"

"Two thousand five hundred."

"Start the attack. Bring all tubes to the ready. Hard a-starboard. Group up. . . . Full ahead together."

As the periscope slid back into its well I had a last look before firing—if there would be time to fire at all. "We've got three minutes," I announced. "Go down to forty feet on the turn, but I must be back at twenty-six feet in two minutes." I was seventy degrees on her port bow. "Give me a course for a track angle of a hundred-and-twenty degrees."

The boat shuddered as the propellers lashed the water at their top speed. The *Unbroken* spun like a top to starboard. Excited at the thought of a 10,000-ton tanker, I forgot her escorting destroyers.

"Two minutes at full group up, sir."

"Group down." I turned to Thirsk. "Go to half group

down when you can. Remember that I've got to see what I'm doing." He nodded.

"All tubes ready."

"Stand by. . . . Up after periscope."

As the periscope slid up I whispered to Manuel: "Fix me on the D.A. as soon as I can see. . . . Are you steady on your course?"

"Not quite, sir. Ten degrees to go."

I could see now. I twisted the periscope against Manuel's chest. "Re-set."

"On now." His breath was hot against the back of my neck.

"Leave ten degrees of starboard wheel on. Let her swing."

"Aye, aye, sir."

The cross-wire of the periscope was a quarter of a length ahead of the tanker.

"Fire One."

The boat rebounded.

"Torpedo running."

The tanker's bows touched the cross-wire. "Fire Two."

Again the rebound and pressure on the ears as the air was vented back into the boat from the empty tube. "Fire Three."

The tanker's stern crept to the cross-wire. "Fire Four."

"All torpedoes running."

I pressed the klaxon. "Q" flooded with a rush of air and we went deep. Five minutes had passed since "Diving stations."

There was a shattering explosion.

"We've hit her!" A delighted cheer filled the boat.

"Eighty feet. Shut-off for depth-charging. . . . Group down. Starboard fifteen, steer east. . . . Silent routine."

I relaxed—and remembered. "Tell Cryer to come and man the Asdic." A moment later he bounded aft, grinning all over his face.

The enemy were soon on to us. They dropped thirty-five charges, but none sounded dangerously close. Then they turned back to the crippled tanker and surrounded her against a second attack. We returned to periscope depth for a look. The weather had closed in, but I could see a great cloud of smoke towards the shore. We returned to the depths and a little later heard a long rumbling explosion.

"I hope she's blown up," said Thirsk.

His hopes were justified. It was later confirmed she had gone down. A delightful farewell gesture to the Med. To save face the enemy claimed for the fourth time that the *Unbroken* had also been sunk.

When we surfaced that night we were astounded to see that the bridge had suffered considerable damage during the depth-charge attack. The night sights had been smashed, the framework of the bridge was buckled and crumpled, and the glass of the navigation lights, designed to withstand pressure six hundred feet down, was shattered. Yet none of us in the control-room had been aware of the nearness of the depth charges. The Powers that Be could say what they liked, but the fact remained that we were getting stale. Yet I was the only one going home. To sharpen the boys up a little I gave them a full quota of exercises on the journey back to Malta: practice attacks, emergency increases in depth, gun action stations and change-round exercises.

Dawn of 7th April would see us at the entrance to the searched channel. After we surfaced on the evening of the 6th I began packing my gear. It is strange, but from the moment of starting on that patrol, right until the moment I embarked upon an aircraft for Gib., I was quite unexcited at the thought of going home. Instead I was oppressed by unhappiness at leaving the *Unbroken*, for it is not easy to tear yourself away from a bunch of good, decent men with whom you have lived for seventeen months, and with whom you might well have died.

Before climbing to my deck-chair on the bridge I listened for a moment to all the old familiar sounds and found it difficult to believe I was hearing them for the last time. I would doubtless command other submarines, but every boat has its own peculiar individuality, indefinable but very real, and the *Unbroken*, despite her cold steel bulk, had her own special voice and personality.

Andrew came aboard at Malta and I introduced him to the crew as they stood gathered on the casing. I scanned their familiar faces and a lump came to my throat. Thirsk, Archdale; Sizer, imperturbable as granite; Manuel, wise and confident. "Pedro" Fenton, the gunlayer, and his pal, the irrepressible Jan Cryer. Butterworth, looking as hard-done-by as ever; "Trampy" Mullet badly in need of a hair-cut. Lee, Scutt, Jones, McTeare and the rest—fine, good men every one; as hand-picked a crew as any submarine commander could wish for.

I don't think what I said to them made very much sense. I cannot remember it now, nor could I five minutes after the speech was made. I know I thanked them for all they had done, and made one or two not very funny jokes. But it was all very misty and unreal and sad. There were handshakes and cheers and cries of: "Good luck, sir," and when I walked ashore the slow drag of my feet was due to more than a cramped fortnight on patrol.

Epilogue

I had to wait at Gib. for eleven exasperating days before I sailed home aboard the *Stirling Castle*, a troopship that formed part of a fast, England-bound convoy. It was an odd sensation, travelling on the surface both by day and by night, and as a passenger.

From Liverpool I sent Ting a telegram announcing my safe arrival, and the journey from that grey, ugly seaport to Saxmundham seemed longer than any I had known. I was out of the train before it stopped, and there on the platform, bathed in the sunlight of a fine May afternoon, stood Ting—a glass of whisky held aloft in each hand. To the amusement of the other travellers, we drank each other's health there and then before a rattling, ancient taxi took us the bumping, jolting eight miles to Aldeburgh. There were a thousand things to talk about, and ten thousand others impossible to express. Perhaps the greatest delight of all was to open the cottage door and see my fifteen-months-old daughter lurching about the sitting-room. I was somewhat disconcerted, however, when she took one look at me and started to bawl her head off. After a while she came to accept me, dissolving into tears only when she felt she was not receiving her fair share of attention.

Dusk set the sirens a-wailing, and I realised for the first time that Aldeburgh was not the quiet fishing and residential town of my imagination. It had been badly bombed, had been shot-up by German fighters, and was along the route taken by the enemy when he blitzed London.

My six weeks' leave passed far too quickly, and when it was over I travelled to Northways, the headquarters of the Flag Officer (Submarines) in London, to discover what was to become of me. They told me to go out to grass for a couple of months and they would give me a tinkle when I was needed. That suited me down to the ground, and back I went to Aldeburgh to laze in the sun of the war's fourth summer.

The *Unbroken* was never far from my thoughts. For a long time I was reluctant to open a newspaper or listen to the B.B.C.'s news bulletins, but although the *Saracen* and *Parthian* were included among the smooth, professionally sympathetic announcements of regret, there was no mention of the *Unbroken*.

In August I felt I ought to be getting back into the war again. A second visit to Northways resulted in a Staff job with the Admiral (Submarines) in London. A desk job did not appeal to me at all, and I told them so. I was assured the post was purely temporary, and that soon I would be given another submarine. I had not been wielding my pen for many days when good news arrived: the *Unbroken* was on her way home, and would I like to meet her at H.M.S. *Dolphin*, the submarine base at Gosport? Would I like to? I was thrilled beyond words!

As I was preparing for the journey a message was handed to me. Puzzled and a little worried, I tore it open. It was a note of congratulations from the Flag Officer (Submarines) on my being awarded the D.S.C. Thirsk and Archdale had also been awarded D.S.C.s, while the D.S.M. went to Stoker P.O. Sharp, E.R.A. Lewis, Leading Stoker Fall, the ebullient "Jan Cryer," and A.B. Bramhall. Mentioned in Dispatches were Lieutenant Andrew, Sub-Lieutenant Richards, Scutt—now an acting P.O.—E.R.A. Leech and P.O. Willey. Again names had been omitted—but that's the way these things happen.

I stood among wives, sweethearts and parents on the jetty as the *Unbroken* sailed into view: tired-looking and a little rusty now; not so slick as on the day when she had sailed from England; but as cocky and proud as ever—White Ensign taut in the wind, ratings correctly stiff, the skull of the Jolly Roger grinning its message of triumphant success. I glanced at the womenfolk around me: some smiling, others cheering, a few wiping tears of joyful relief from their eyes. I remembered how worried and uncertain they had been at Barrow, and I wanted to grasp their arms and say: "I told you they'd be all right, didn't I?"

The *Unbroken* was secured, and the ratings poured ashore. The day's tot had been saved, including an extra one for me, and as Sizer poured them out, I heard of the *Unbroken's* adventures since I had left her. On his first patrol Andrew had bad luck with an Italian U-boat. After a good attack they thought they saw a torpedo hit, but the U-boat sailed right through the smoke and splash. The kipper had probably exploded prematurely. They then went close inshore on the north coast of Sicily to sink a schooner, and the highlight of subsequent patrols was a possible hit on a medium-sized supply ship. Selfishly, perhaps, I was less excited about these exploits than I was to see the *Unbroken* back home without damage or casualties, and I felt genuinely miserable when the yarning and reminiscing were over and it was time to return to London.

I tried, as well as I was able, to keep in touch with the

officers and crew of the *Unbroken*, but it was not an easy task. You cannot live for ever in the past, and time dims the sincerity of solemn sworn promises. You develop new friends, new interest, new passions. The fervid reality of to-day becomes to-morrow's nostalgia.

The *Unbroken* was handed to the Russians in 1944, together with her sister ships, *Ursula* and *Unison*, and the battleship, *Royal Sovereign*. They returned in February, 1949, and although the *Unbroken* had survived the heat of the Med. and the cold of the Arctic, had defied depth-charging, bombs and mines, she could not withstand the hammers and acetylene torches of the Newcastle scrap-yard. In 1950 she was towed there and broken up. Perhaps it was better that way. As Tennyson said of the aged Ulysses:

> How dull it is to pause, to make an end,
> To rust unburnish'd, not to shine in use!
> As though to breathe were life.

It was thus fitting that the *Unbroken*, rather than gather slime and barnacles while rotting aged and forgotten alongside some cheerless depot ship, should have given her hard, unyielding steel back into her mother's womb to be reforged and revitalised into a new shining strength. I like to think that the *Unbroken*, in some new shape and form, continues to sail beneath the Mediterranean's blue waters, still of service to her country and the White Ensign.

London, 1952